PE:

University of Hertfordshire

College Lane, Hatfield, Herts. AL10 9AB

Learning and Information Services

For renewal of Standard and One Week Loans,
please visit the web site **http://www.voyager.herts.ac.uk**

This item must be returned or the loan renewed by the due date.
The University reserves the right to recall items from loan at any time.
A fine will be charged for the late return of items.

LAW AND COMPETITION IN TWENTIETH CENTURY EUROPE

Protecting Prometheus

DAVID J. GERBER

OXFORD

UNIVERSITY PRESS

This book has been printed digitally and produced in a standard specification
in order to ensure its continuing availability

OXFORD
UNIVERSITY PRESS

Great Clarendon Street, Oxford OX2 6DP

Oxford University Press is a department of the University of Oxford.
It furthers the University's objective of excellence in research, scholarship,
and education by publishing worldwide in

Oxford New York

Auckland Bangkok Buenos Aires Cape Town Chennai
Dar es Salaam Delhi Hong Kong Istanbul Karachi Kolkata
Kuala Lumpur Madrid Melbourne Mexico City Mumbai Nairobi
São Paulo Shanghai Taipei Tokyo Toronto

Oxford is a registered trade mark of Oxford University Press
in the UK and in certain other countries

Published in the United States
by Oxford University Press Inc., New York

© David J. Gerber 1998

The moral rights of the author have been asserted
Database right Oxford University Press (maker)

Reprinted 2003

ISBN 0-19-924401-4

THIS BOOK IS DEDICATED TO

ULLA-BRITT

ERIC AND MARCUS

Preface to the Paperback Edition

Although this book was published less than three years ago, impending changes in the landscape of competition law in Europe call for a special preface to this paperback edition. The European Commission has proposed the 'modernization' of the European competition law system, and thus the future shape of competition law in Europe will be debated intensely over the next several years. When changes are enacted, as virtually all agree they will be, an expanded number of officials, judges, lawyers, and business decision-makers will be involved in the implementation of the modified system and/or need to understand the factors that will influence its operations. My primary objective in this new preface is to highlight some of the ways in which this book can be of value in both these contexts—in evaluating and structuring change as well as in implementing and living with it.

I cautioned in the book's conclusion that the future of competition law in Europe was anything but certain. Since that writing, concerns about the system have increased in intensity in some circles, and in 1999 these concerns led the European Commission to propose major changes. In some ways, the timing of these criticisms and proposals is curious. Even as some competition law 'experts' and lawyers have criticized the system's operations in recent years, EU competition law has been achieving impressive results. Most prominent has been the increasingly aggressive enforcement of the merger control provisions, which have laid to rest doubts that the Commission would have both the will and the political support to oppose major mergers. The Commission's confident and firm stand in merger cases has been widely acclaimed as a sign of its independence and strength. In addition, revision of the substantive law on vertical restraints in 1998–9 has attested to its flexibility and willingness to change. The Commission's decision to pursue major changes is not driven, therefore, by widespread public dissatisfaction with its accomplishments, but by other factors.

A. THE MODERNIZATION PROPOSALS

The modernization proposals center on two basic changes in the way competition law is enforced. One is elimination of the notification system that has formed the institutional framework of European competition law almost since its inception. This system requires that when firms enter into an agreement that may be prohibited under Article 81(1) of the Rome Treaty because it restricts competition, they must notify the agreement to the Commission if they wish to obtain an exemption from that prohibition.[1] An agreement that has not been notified is effectively precluded from receiving an exemption. The other core change is elimination of the Commission's monopoly on granting such exemptions (Art. 81(3)). According to current law, only the Commission can issue such exemptions. Since the European courts have interpreted Article 81(1) very broadly, the issue of who is authorized to grant exemptions takes on great importance.

These two changes would significantly alter the way competition law operates in Europe.[2] They would change the basic posture of the system from *ex ante* to *ex post* enforcement—i.e. the law would now be enforced primarily in relation to past conduct rather than in the context of screening future conduct. In practice the change may not always be as sharply etched as it appears, because *ex post* enforcement is already a significant part of the Commission's enforcement efforts, but it none the less represents a major change in the way the system operates.

More fundamentally, the proposed changes would greatly expand the roles that national competition authorities and national courts play in the operation of the system. National authorities would become the primary enforcement officials, subject only to guidance from and, in some cases, ultimate control by the Commission. National courts would become far more involved in the system, because if they acquire the capacity to exempt firms from the prohibition of Art. 81(1), the number of private suits in those courts is likely to increase substantially.

The Commission supports these proposals with three interrelated claims. The first relates to efficiency. According to the Commission, the notification procedure wastes scarce resources because officials have to review notifications, and (in addition to being rather drab) this process seldom produces valuable information. The second factor is the anticipated expansion of the EU during the next few years. Even if the situation may be manageable today, the Commission argues, the current structure could not operate effectively if six or twelve additional states were to become members of the EU, as is currently planned. Third, the principle of subsidiarity requires efforts to decentralize decision making, wherever possible moving decisions from Brussels to the member states.

---

[1] Since this book was written, Articles 85 and 86 in the Rome Treaty have been renumbered as Articles 81 and 82, respectively. In this preface, I will use the new numbers.

[2] Both changes are contained in a proposed revision of Reg. 17, the regulation adopted in 1962 to structure the procedural system of EU competition law. They do not require revision of the treaty.

After extensive public discussion of its initial program for reform, the Commission added a proposal that would provide for exclusive application of EU competition law where agreements have an effect on trade between member states. This would further intensify the impact of the proposed systemic changes, but it would not otherwise change them. The proposal has met with significant resistance, and its future seems less certain than the basic proposals mentioned above.

Note that this proposal leaves large parts of the system unchanged or little changed. For example, the changes do not affect substantive law; they are entirely institutional and procedural. In addition, they have little direct impact in several important areas of conduct. They do not, for example, change the way mergers are treated.

B. EVALUATING CHANGE

These proposals call for careful evaluation, not only because of the importance of competition law in European integration, but also because they are widely seen as a test for future changes in other areas of European law. In this evaluation, the story of the system's development provides a critically valuable perspective and tool of analysis. It is especially valuable because the central challenges of competition law in Europe today are in many ways similar to those it has faced throughout its development. It has always had to serve the cause of European integration, for example, and the expansion of the EU to eastern Europe will assure that this integration goal remains paramount far into the future.

The book's main value here is to reveal structures and forces operating on and within the system. That system is the product of intellectual and institutional responses over time to particular problems and issues, and thus the narrative of its development reveals patterns, influences, and expectations that will continue to shape decisions within the system. Moreover, the proposed reforms are rooted in past experience and structured by reference to that experience.

We can now examine several of these forces. Note that in this context I use the term 'European competition law system' to refer to both EU and member state laws, because they are closely interrelated. Changes in one part of the system tend to have impacts on other components and on the relationships among them. Often we can perceive these 'system-effects' only by examining the operation of the system over time.

1. Structures of Thought

Patterns and structures of thought shape and condition the decisions of actors within the system. These include, *inter alia*, concepts, values, preferences, and the patterns of relationship among them. Often they exercise their influence as unspoken assumptions that are revealed only in the context of their use. The book identifies many of them and reveals the ways in which they exercise influence.

Economic constitutionalist thought (especially the German ordoliberal school) has, for example, been an important influence on the development of competition law in both Germany and the EU. It is a well-organized, highly developed idea-system with its own vocabulary, values, and conceptual structures. Once one knows what that body of thought contains and sees how it has exercised influence, much that is otherwise opaque becomes perceptible. As one reviewer of this book suggested, for example, it explains a great deal about the resistance of important individuals and groups within Germany to the modernization proposals.

Similarly, basic conceptions of competition law are fundamental to understanding how those within the system make decisions. Two basic conceptions have been in tension throughout the development of the system, and they are likely to remain in tension indefinitely. In one, competition law tends to be viewed as a device for framing and protecting private rights. In the other, it is understood primarily as part of public, administrative law—and associated with the regulatory goals of the state. These conceptions clash in fundamental ways, and they influence choices about what to do in specific situations.

2. Competition Law's Roles

Conceptions of the role of competition law are particularly crucial. They have shaped the proposals for reform; they are shaping responses to those proposals; and they will shape their implementation. Recognizing these roles and how they have changed over time enables us to analyze how the proposed changes are likely to affect the system's operations. Expectations regarding competition law's roles are central to all decision-making within the system, and they are often difficult, if not impossible, to perceive other than in the context in which they have developed.

The basic role of competition law is, of course, to protect competition from restraints. Even in unitary systems such as United States antitrust law there is often uncertainty about what that means. The uncertainty increases, however, in the multi-layered system of European competition law, where there are at least four basic conceptions of what it means to protect competition.

One centers on economic efficiency—the idea that competition law should be governed primarily by principles of optimum resource allocation and wealth-maximization. As the book demonstrates, such goals have always been part of the system, but they have sometimes been expressed in language that obscures their content. Understanding the forces at work in the system requires knowing how these efficiency goals are understood and expressed as well as the social and political factors that shape the language used. Since the early 1990s, the language used in expressing efficiency concerns has become more theoretical and direct, and they have been given increasing attention, but this often conceals the social and political factors that are operating and thus enhances the importance of revealing them.

A second conception of competition protection centers on economic freedom. Here the issue is the extent to which restraints on competition restrict the decisional opportunities of economic actors. This concept is part of the heritage of classical liberalism that has been such a powerful force for European integration, and it continues to exercise a strong, if sometimes overlooked, influence on competition law decisions in many parts of the system.

A third view addresses the issue of economic power. In this conception, the function of competition law is to prevent firms from using their economic power to undermine competitive (and sometimes political or social) structures. This goal is often associated with German neo-liberalism, in particular, and economic constitutionalist thought, in general, but its influence is much broader, and it has become part of the perceptual and evaluative tools of the system.

Finally, protecting competition is often understood as a means of reducing or eliminating obstacles to economic change and development. In many countries (e.g. Sweden) this goal has often been prominent, and the current and future emphasis in Europe on reducing barriers to economic development is likely to reinforce its prominence.

But in Europe competition law must also serve the goal of integration, a goal whose importance is likely to increase in coming years. This goal is related to the protection of competition, but not coterminous with it, and it often leads to different outcomes. For example, it has led to a relatively restrictive approach to vertical restraints, because such restraints are often used to partition markets along national boundaries. Recent relaxations of those restrictions assume that these boundaries have become less economically significant, but the planned expansion of the EU calls that assumption into question.

Competition law systems in Europe sometimes also pursue a third type of goal. I call it 'regulatory', because it seeks to shape the characteristics of economic activity or to acquire information for policy purposes. Notification requirements are often, for example, designed to provide both general and specific information about economic developments, and many systems specifically allow decision-makers to take economic policy goals other than the protection of competition into account in applying competition laws. The role of these regulatory and political goals has been diminishing in recent years, but it cannot be ignored, and the eastward expansion may combine with changing economic circumstances to re-emphasize it.

This amalgam of objectives has contributed to both economic and political integration and extraordinary economic development during the last four decades. In expanding the role of national officials and judges in the system, however, the proposed changes will increase uncertainty regarding these goals and the relations among them. 'How will decision-makers conceive the role of competition law?' will be a major question, and the answer to it will largely determine the direction of competition law development. The quality and utility of the answers will depend on understanding how these goals have developed.

3. Agendas

The agendas of the various participants in the system are as important as the goals associated with the system as a whole. Gaining insight into who is trying to do what and how the respective agendas relate to each other is a key to analyzing the operations of the system and evaluating how particular changes are likely to affect them. Often these agendas are not announced, but become perceptible only by looking at the decisions that are actually taken.

The agenda of the Competition Directorate of the European Commission is central to this analysis, because it has developed the current proposals and is leading the drive to enact them. Its decisions in this regard are a response to particular circumstances, and thus examining those circumstances and the claims and conflicts relating to them provides insight into the problems the Commission perceives and its responses to them.

The objectives of other actors within the system will, however, largely determine the future of the modernization proposals as well as the ways in which they are implemented and the impact they have. For example, the European Court of Justice will have to determine whether the proposals are consistent with the EU treaties, and both European courts will have to fashion legal doctrine relating to a host of new issues generated by the proposals. Understanding the roles the courts have played thus becomes a way not only of predicting the contours of its responses to these situations, but also of aiding its members in developing those responses. The European Parliament will also play a more central role in the system, and that role will also be shaped by expectations and conflicts imbedded in the system's recent past.

The greater involvement of the member states in the modified system will make their agendas increasingly important. Competition law often affects important national economic and political interests, and efforts to advance those interests will be pursued at many levels. As members of the Council, member states will decide whether the proposals are enacted and in what form, and later they will be in a position to influence the Commission's implementation decisions. Potentially more important will be their roles in relation to their own institutions. As these institutions become principal players in the system, incentives to influence their decisions and opportunities to do so will increase correspondingly.

The story also throws light on the agendas of those directly affected by competition law. For business enterprises, the primary goal is to reduce costs, uncertainty and governmental controls on their activities, but in the context of European integration this goal takes on often unexpected dimensions. In some cases, for example, firms have supported EU-level competition law as a way of 'escaping' from existing or anticipated national regulatory regimes, whereas in others they have preferred national competition law systems over EU law, sometimes even where the national system is at least arguably more restrictive than EU law.

Consumers also have much at stake in these proposals. They have not been organized in ways that have allowed them to exert significant direct influence on competition law, in part because Brussels has not been perceived as easily accessible to such groups. Consumer interests have become better organized and more powerful in many member states in recent years, however, and under the modified system the costs of reaching and influencing decision-makers will be significantly reduced. Moreover, their interests in relation to competition law are often represented by political parties, and the book reveals the often complex dynamics of that relationship, whose importance may dramatically increase as the opportunities for consumers to influence competition law decision-makers grows and the costs of doing so diminish.

4. Sources of Power and Influence

As important as the agendas are, the sources of power to achieve them are equally critical in assessing the operations of the system and plans to change it. The power relationships within the system are complex and frequently opaque, and often they can be perceived only against the backdrop of their evolution.

The value of competition law as a source of power for EU institutions illustrates the point. For both the Commission and the European Court of Justice, competition law has provided status and power. For the Commission, competition law's direct impact on economic activity gives it visibility, attention, and influence. In most other areas of its activity, the Commission must work through other EU institutions or member state governments to influence conduct, but in the competition law area it directly shapes the norms applicable to businesses and takes direct enforcement action. Competition law has also been an important tool for advancing the agenda of the ECJ. As the book details, that court has often asserted its leadership role in the process of European integration through decisions in competition law cases.

For both, however, the value of competition law has been associated with its role in the integration process. The Commission has often enjoyed political support for its competition law initiatives because they have been perceived as necessary to break down economic barriers among states, an overriding goal of all institutions within the EU. Similarly, the ECJ has often used competition law as a 'motor of integration', employing the logic and discourse of integration in developing it. The Commission's proposals would change this delicate interplay between the power of institutions and the roles of competition law in ways that are difficult to predict, but whose importance demands analysis.

The modernization proposals would also change the power position of
member states. Not only will they have a greater stake in the operations of the
competition law system, but they will also have enhanced opportunities to
influence the decision-making process. As long as the Commission has a
monopoly on 81(3) exemptions, member states can influence outcomes in
most cases only by influencing the Commission, and given the institutional
structure of the EU, their opportunities to do so are limited. Under the proposals, however, their own courts and administrators will become principal
players in the system, and thus the relative power of member states and the
importance of their domestic political landscapes will grow.

Public opinion has not been a major source of power in the European competition law system, largely because the Commission has been relatively distant (the so-called 'democracy deficit'), and because domestic competition
authorities have seldom been seen as important enough to warrant their
mobilization. Again, however, the proposals will change that situation. In the
EU, the growing power of the European Parliament will be brought to bear
on competition law issues, and the force of public opinion in relation to
national institutions will grow significantly.

Finally, in a system of complex power relationships and diffused decisional
structures, a small group of 'experts' can often influence decisions in ways
that are important and concealed, and this has been true in the development
of European competition law. In the early years, German economists and
lawyers associated with economic constitutionalist thought provided this
type of leadership. Although the position of that group is not as strong as it
was, it remains important in many contexts. In addition, other more international and less well-defined expert groups have formed, and they often have
significant influence. Commission officials acknowledge that such groups
have been an important impetus for the modernization proposals.

5. Capabilities

The effects of changes in the system will also depend on the knowledge and
capabilities of those who are assigned particular roles under them. During the
development of the current system, the Commission has sought to locate
knowledge relating to EU law in Brussels, creating few incentives for member
state decision-makers to acquire such knowledge. As a consequence, both the
details of competition law and the basic values and objectives behind it have
often been little known and understood not only by those who are supposed
to obey them, but sometimes even by those administering them.

The modernization proposals represent a radical change of direction,
which rests on the rather daring assumption that the necessary knowledge
and capabilities have either been developed in the context of national competition law systems or can be readily enough acquired without that experience.

The story of the system's development provides valuable insights into the effects of both deficits in knowledge and conflicts over its distribution.

C. IMPLEMENTING CHANGE: SOME GUIDELINES

Modernization will give member state judges and administrators far larger roles in the European competition law system. For them, the factors just discussed will become of great immediate importance, because they will need to understand the forces at work within the system. But the book also has another potential role in the implementing context: it points to important lessons that can help to guide that process. Many believe that the greatest risk in the proposals is that judges and administrators, especially in the new and future member states, will apply competition law in ways that are ineffective in achieving the goals of the system and that may even hamper the process of European integration. The history of the system may be the most important source of guidance in avoiding that result. I here suggest some lessons that might be useful in that context, recognizing that many other lessons can be drawn from a narrative as rich as the one presented here.

(1) The speed of change is likely to be an important factor in the process. European integration has proceeded incrementally (if often fitfully), gradually overcoming political, epistemological, and other barriers. It could hardly be otherwise, because the process requires decision-makers to make compromises regarding their own status, power, and resources. The same applies to competition law. Decision-makers have proceeded cautiously in strengthening and expanding competition law, primarily because they have had to create and maintain political support and because they have had to educate both decision-makers within the system and those affected by it. Competition law represents a unique combination of juridical, economic, and political issues that require time to understand, assimilate, and apply effectively. History suggests that changes in the system should not, therefore, require too much too fast of those who will acquire new or heightened decisional responsibilities.

(2) How national decision-makers conceive the implementation process and their respective roles in it is likely to condition the future they shape for it. Two views of this process have been in conflict throughout the development of competition law in Europe. In one, that development is seen as an essentially juridical process in which decisions represent the elaboration, clarification, and implementation of a stable, normative framework for the relationship between government and private economic actors (a kind of economic constitution). In this image, those applying competition law are engaged in the patient process of giving durable meaning to the texts created by political decisions, and thus it entails developing effective methods and practices for interpreting and applying the laws.

Another conception of the process views competition law as primarily a policy instrument. For many, its rules and procedures represent merely a tool for achieving political objectives, either domestic or emanating from Brussels. They are an exercise of political authority for ends that may be short-term or long-term, but that have no claim to 'constitutional' status. In this view, there tends to be less concern with the durability, internal consistency, and stability of the normative regime and with developing methods and practices for informing consistent decision-making.

These two conceptions often lead to fundamentally different ways of making competition law decisions, and experience suggests that the effectiveness of the modified system may depend on which of them has the most influence on member state judges and administrators. In the evolution of competition law in Europe, increases in the effectiveness and importance of competition laws have generally been associated with increased prominence for juridical characteristics. In general, therefore, we can expect that the more force such characteristics have, the more likely it is that the modernization proposals will achieve their aims. This does not refer, as some have suggested, to a US-style conception of antitrust, but to the *specifically European conceptions of competition law* whose development is a central theme of this book.

This suggests that the modernization proposals should be complemented with measures designed to advance and anchor this juridical conception of the process of implementation. This may include, for example, providing an enhanced role for one or more EU courts in reviewing and guiding the decisions of member state judges and administrators' officials. Such measures are likely to be particularly valuable in states in which competition law has had little previous development.

(3) A third issue is related: training the decision-makers. Knowledge will be a critical factor in the operations of the modified system. What member state decision-makers know and how they value and apply what they know will to a large extent determine what they decide.

Perhaps the starkest fact facing the modified system is the relative lack of competition law knowledge and experience among those who will have responsibility for making competition law decisions. Member state judges, in particular, will generally have neither knowledge nor experience in the area, particularly during the formative early years of the modified system. The success of that system will thus depend in no small measure on what they learn and how fast they learn it. The need to inculcate competition law knowledge has been a frequent theme in the development of the European competition law system, and that experience teaches much about how to achieve the desired results.

The question of 'what' to learn should not be viewed too narrowly. Technical legal knowledge is obviously necessary and fundamental. Judges and administrators need to know the applicable texts and how they have been interpreted. This in itself is a major undertaking. But there is more. Competition law presents special epistemic problems, because it involves a variety of interrelated goals, values, and perspectives, and because the economic causation issues that are central to its application are often complex and uncertain. The interplay of these factors can lead to coherent, shared, and predictable decisions only through an understanding of the extent to which practices, assumptions, and methods are shared among EU and member state institutions. These are imbedded in and conditioned by experience, and thus examination of that experience becomes especially important.

The Commission recognizes that such learning is critical to the success of its modernization proposals, and it has accordingly urged the creation of a 'network' among the system's decision-makers, a set of personal and institutional relationships that will facilitate the transfer of information and views. As the book shows, such networks can be of great importance in the development of competition law (as, for example, in Germany), but they should be conceived broadly. Transferring technical information may not by itself lead to the desired results. The network should be designed also to foster analysis of factors that influence decision-making in the various parts of the system and to recognize and reduce differences among them.

Another lesson from European experience regarding knowledge issues is that they fall into two quite distinct categories. One relates to the effectiveness of the decision-making process, as just discussed. Do the decision-makers know enough to make decisions in ways that are both justifiable in terms of the system's goals and methods and generally consistent with the decisions being made in other parts of the system? But knowledge is also an element of power in the system, and thus distributional issues are important. Throughout the development of competition law in Europe, the Commission has been the repository of knowledge of Community competition law, leaving knowledge of member state competition laws to national administrators. Its proposals for change represent a radical, complex, and uncharted revamping of this power relationship, and their effectiveness may depend on the development of strategies for dealing with its implications.

(4) Regardless of their knowledge and training, national authorities and judges will be subject to external pressures from public and private persons and institutions. The economic interests at stake in this area are often substantial and sometimes enormous, and they thus create powerful incentives to influence those decisions. To the extent that efforts to influence competition law decisions are successful, or perceived to be successful, they will reduce the effectiveness of competition law institutions and undermine their role in promoting integration. The problem is greatest with respect to administrators, who are typically less protected from such influences than are judges. Moreover, for reasons explored in the book administrators have played, and will continue to play, the central roles in the application of competition law

in Europe, making the task of protecting them from outside influence particularly critical.

This issue has been a frequent theme in the development of European competition law. It has also been particularly difficult and sensitive. Sometimes conflicts over it have been bitterly fought. At other times, they have been carefully concealed. Looking at the forms these conflicts have taken, the methods used in dealing with them, and the factors that have played a role in shaping them provides important lessons for dealing with them under the modified system.

(5) Incentives will be important in shaping the ways that judges and administrators operate this system, and the history of competition law in Europe has repeatedly demonstrated the importance of structuring those incentives. Outside pressures can never be completely eliminated, nor can the lure of current or future economic benefits from those affected by competition law decisions. Experience tells us that competition law systems must, therefore, provide rewards designed to induce decisions that foster the goals of the system. These may be financial, perhaps in the form of economic support from EU coffers for salaries for competition officials. They may also be less direct. For example, job security and social and intellectual status have been factors in the success of competition law in some countries, as has dependable political and institutional support for difficult decisions. The Commission should seek to build these types of incentives into the system. Note that incentives are important not only in counteracting outside influences, but also in inducing choices among legitimate options within the system, as, for example, in choosing which conceptions of competition law to pursue or which methods of interpretation to apply.

(6) Finally, in Europe competition law requires political support. It is not like areas of law such as private law, which are widely accepted as natural and necessary. In much of Europe, competition law is not deeply anchored in institutional structures or in legal culture or in personal and group value systems, and thus political support is indispensable for its effective development. Support for competition law has been drawn from a frequently changing interplay of political impulses. For example, at different times different institutions—sometimes the ECJ, sometimes the Commission, sometimes particular political parties or intellectual groups in a given member state—have had the power and the willingness to use it to develop competition law. In the highly complex interrelationships of an integrating Europe, recognizing these sources of power and the factors that condition them is often difficult, but immensely important. This book shows just how important that political support has been, which forms it has taken, and what kinds of factors have shaped it.

***

The impending changes in the landscape of competition law will not change the basic themes of European competition law development. The patterns of five or thirty years ago are to a large extent those of today, and they will remain tomorrow, because the fundamental problems will remain basically the same. What will change is the decision-making process. A large group of national officials and judges will be drawn into the process, and they will be asked to perform important and sometimes unfamiliar functions within the system. The story told here will become critically important for them as well as for those who seek to influence or predict their decisions.

One of the book's central themes is that competition law in Europe has been developed by Europeans to meet European needs, and it is important that the changes be understood as modifications of an evolving European 'model' of competition law. Competition law in Europe is not, contrary to popular myth, an import from the United States or the mere extension of administrative controls to a new area, and the current proposals do not represent the adoption of a US-model of competition law. To assume otherwise misreads (or disregards) the history of European competition law and risks not only misinterpreting European decisions, but distorting them as well.

My hope is that this book will be an important part of the debate over the modernization of competition law in Europe and a valuable source of guidance for those who operate within it or seek to understand it. I am convinced that the extraordinarily rich and complex tapestry that is European competition law today can only be understood by looking at how it has been woven, and there has never been a greater need for such understanding. An evolving sense of community, shared values and knowledge, and common goals establish the prerequisites for an effective competition law system, but shared experience provides the cement that can hold those elements together, and it can perform that function only if those involved have a rich understanding of that experience.

Preface

Competition is popular—or so it seems. At least politicians and pundits in most places in the world tend to sing its praises and/or acknowledge its necessity. But what kind of competition and what is and should be the relationship between the process of 'competition' and other components of societal life? Despite their importance, these questions have been relatively little explored. Economic interests and ideologies of left and right have often blocked inquiry into the issues and obscured answers to the questions. This book pursues the inquiry by looking at one component of European experience with competition: the ways in which Europeans have conceived and used law to protect and, sometimes, to shape competition.

The book's perspective is new. In it, competition law is seen as part of the relationship between polity, society, and economy in twentieth century Europe—imbedded in its conflicts, reflecting its key ideas and tensions and shaping its development. Moreover, the perspective is 'European'—it treats the development of competition law as a European phenomenon and probes the relationships among national competition laws and between those systems and the competition law of the European Union. Europe's future is likely to depend in no small measure on how it understands and is influenced by its past relationships with the market, and in this book I seek to shed light on part of that experience.

The idea of writing this kind of book has been my constant (if often neglected) companion for some fifteen years. The project initially seemed daunting and sometimes Sisyphean. How could I (or anyone else for that matter) learn enough about the various European experiences and their relationships to one another to do the project justice? I began to collect and study materials and to discuss aspects of European experience with scholars, government officials, and practitioners in various countries, but I continued to doubt that the project I envisioned could be done as I thought it should be done.

Yet the more I talked with those involved in competition law in Europe and the more I read about twentieth century Europe, the more I was convinced that the result might be worth the effort—the story needed to be told, distorted images needed to be corrected, the dynamics of European competition law systems had to be better understood, and the disparate experiences of European states had to be examined from a 'European' perspective. This conviction was strengthened by the many Europeans who urged me to undertake and then to continue the project, even while warning me about its many risks and difficulties. 'We need such a book', they said. As the process of European integration began a new phase of intensification after 1986, I knew they were right.

A project of this scope can only be carried out with much support from many sources, and I have been extraordinarily fortunate in receiving such support. One result of the plethora of sources of support is, however, that my expressions of gratitude here are necessarily incomplete. For those whom I do not mention here by name, I have tried to express my gratitude at other times and in other ways, and I thank you once again.

A list of the scholars, officials, judges, and practicing attorneys who have shared their knowledge and insights with me would be inordinately long, but I want to mention at least a few. Ulf Bernitz of the University of Stockholm, Wolfgang Fikentscher in Munich and Fritz Rittner in Freiburg have supported the project over many years. Each has shared unselfishly his extensive knowledge and expertise, but each has also gone beyond that, encouraging me to pursue a project that at times must have seemed 'too big', and providing me with materials, contacts, and opportunities for research. To them my debt is great.

Other scholars whose contributions along the way have been particularly valuable include Guido Alpa, Harold Berman, Jean-Jacques Burst, Meinrad Dreher, Louis Favoreu, Richard Helmholz, Ulrich Immenga, Valentine Korah, Wernhard Möschel, Knut Nörr, Stefan Riesenfeld, Eric Stein, Ernst Steindorff, Dan Tarlock, Andreas Thier, and Joseph Weiler. Most of them have commented on drafts of the manuscript or on earlier works that I have used in preparing it or on presentations of the ideas. Their comments have provided insights and corrected at least some of my errors.

Judges, former judges, and advocates general of the European Court of Justice have provided invaluable insights into the workings of that Court. Ulrich Everling, Francis Jacobs, the late René Joliet, Tim Koopmans, and Giuseppe Mancini—each also an eminent scholar—have been of greater help than they might imagine.

David Kennedy and Joseph Weiler at Harvard were kind enough to invite me to present portions of the book at workshops and programs sponsored by the Center for European Legal Research of which they are co-directors. I am very grateful to them for inviting me and to those participating in the programs for their comments. I have also presented portions of the book at conferences at the University of Rome (La Sapienza), the University of Stockholm, and the College of Europe in Bruges, and I am grateful to the respective organizers of these conferences for providing such valuable opportunities.

Numerous officials and former officials of the European Commission and of competition authorities in France, Germany, Italy, and Sweden have graciously shared information about and insights into their thoughts, activities, and methods. Among these Claus-Dieter Ehlermann, Wolfgang Kartte, Kurt Ritter, Eric Sahlin, and Franco Romani deserve special thanks.

Special thanks is also due to three friends who have done much to enrich the project. Hartmut Lübbert in Freiburg has been a source of inspiration, support, and insight into European law and the process of comparison for more than a quarter of a century. Kurt Riechenberg in Luxembourg has been of great value in helping me to understand the workings of the European Union and its courts and putting me in contact with others who could be of assistance in that task. And David Braun in Chicago has not only shared his deep knowledge of the operation of competition law in both Brussels and Berlin, but also facilitated contacts with decision-makers in both places.

I cannot fail to express here my gratitude to some of those who long ago contributed to developing the perspectives employed here. Albert Rabil at Trinity College taught me much about ties between institutional and intellectual traditions. During my graduate study at Yale, seminars in history with Jonathan Spence, Arthur Wright, and John Hall deepened my understanding of comparative history. And at the University of Chicago Law School, Ken Dam and Ronald Coase provided support as well as many valuable insights into the multi-faceted relationships between law and economics that play such an important part in studying competition law.

I wish to thank Deans Lewis Collens and Richard Matasar of Chicago-Kent College of Law for supporting this project over the years. I have also received valuable funding from the Marshall Ewell Faculty Scholarship Fund at Chicago-Kent College of Law and the Deutsche Akademische Austauschdienst. My term as a Norman and Edna Freehling Scholar and the research leave made possible by that status facilitated my research. Peter Schlechtriem was most generous in providing me with the opportunity to teach and pursue my research at the University of Freiburg, and Deans Peter Landau and Bruno Simma of the Faculty of Law at Ludwig Maximilians University in Munich welcomed me and provided support during my teaching and research stays there. I am also grateful to Dean David Van Sandt of Northwestern University School of Law for appointing me a Visiting Scholar there during the final months of preparation of the manuscript.

Librarians at Chicago-Kent College of Law, Northwestern University College of Law, The University of Chicago and at the university libraries in Freiburg, Munich, and Stockholm have been indispensable. In particular, I want to thank Amy Pavlik, John Strzynski, and Mickie Voges of the Information Center of the Chicago-Kent College of Law—Amy for her endless hours of work locating and securing often obscure materials, John for sharing his extensive knowledge of sources and always being ready to help, and Mickie for putting together such a marvelous professional staff.

Many research assistants have participated in the project, both in Chicago and in Europe. I cannot mention all of them, but two of them have been of such special value that I must express my gratitude here. André Fiebig began helping me with the research on this project when he was a first-year law student at Chicago-Kent College of Law, and ever since then (as a masters and then a doctoral student in Germany and while engaged in the practice of law in Washington, Brussels, and later Chicago) he has continued to supply me with valuable information and to contribute his own expertise to the project. Kevin O'Brien has been my research assistant during the final year and a half of the project. He has devoted himself to it in ways that have often gone far beyond what could reasonably be expected of a research assistant. Both have contributed greatly, and I know how fortunate I am to have had them working with me.

I am also fortunate in having had a superb secretary to help in finishing the manuscript. Sharon Smith caught errors, foresaw problems, solved problems and deployed her exceptional powers of concentration and organization on behalf of the project (even under sometimes very trying conditions).

At Oxford University Press, my gratitude goes to Richard Hart for initially encouraging me to publish at Oxford, to Chris Rycroft and Myf Milton for seeing it through with efficiency, understanding and the highest professional standards, and to Margaret Wilkerson for excellent copy-editing.

In writing this book, I have drawn on several works I have previously published elsewhere. In particular, I have adapted and incorporated portions of articles of mine in the *American Journal of Comparative Law* (ch.7), *Harvard Journal of International Law* (ch.9), *The American Journal of Legal History* (ch.3) and the *Hastings International and Comparative Law Review* (ch.6), and I am indebted to the editors of each for their comments and co-operation.

Finally, and most importantly, I want to thank my family. This book is dedicated to Ulla-Britt and our sons, Eric and Marcus. My gratitude for their support of this project—for what they have done and, sometimes, for what they have not done—goes far beyond words. I think they know how much it has meant to me.

Contents

Table of Abbreviations

BDI	Bundersverband der deutschen Industrie (Germany)
BGB	Civil Code (Germany)
BGBl.	Bundesgesetzblatt (Germany)
BGH	Federal Supreme Court (Germany)
BKA	Bundeskartellamt (FCO)
CDU	Christian Democratic Party (Germany)
CFI	Court of First Instance (EU)
CSU	Christian Social Union (Germany)
DG IV	General Directorate IV (EU)
DGCCRF	Directorate General of Competition, Consumer Policy, and the Repression of Fraud (France)
ECJ	European Court of Justice
ECR	European Court Reports
ECSC	European Coal and Steel Community
EEC	European Economic Community
ENA	Ecole Nationale d'Administration (France)
EU	European Union
FCO	Federal Cartel Office (Germany)
FDP	Free Democratic Party (Germany)
FRG	Federal Republic of Germany
GWB	Law Against Restraints on Competition (Germany)
HA	High Authority (ECSC)
IPU	Inter. Parliamentary Union
IRC	Industrial Reorganisation Corporation (UK)
ITO	International Trade Organisation
LRC	Law Against Restraints of Competition (Sweden)
MMC	Monopolies and Mergers Commission (UK)
NO	Office of the Competition Ombudsman (Sweden)
OECD	Organisation for Economic Co-operation and Development
OFT	Office of Fair Trading (UK)
OPEC	Organisation of Petroleum Exporting Countries
RGZ	Entscheidungen des Reichsgerichts in Zivilsachen (Germany)
RTPA	Restrictive Trade Practices Act (UK)
SEA	Single European Act
SFS	Svensk Författnings-Samling (Swedish Collected Statutes) (Sweden)
SME	Social Market Economy Group (Germany)
SPD	Social Democratic Party (Germany)

TEU	Treaty on European Union (Maastricht Agreement)
UK	United Kingdom
US	United States of America
UWG	Statute Against Unfair Competition (Germany)
WuW/E	Wirtschaft und Wettbewerb Entscheidungssamlung
ZHR	Zeitschrift für das gesamte Handelsrecht
ZPO	Code of Civil Procedure (Germany)

I

Introduction

Competition has been both God and devil in Western civilization. It has promised and provided wealth and economic progress; it has also altered the distribution of wealth, undermined communities and challenged moral codes. Over the course of European history laws have frequently been used to control the enormous potential power of this process, but near the end of the last century the idea of establishing a general law to *protect* the process of competition from restraint and distortion developed and gained force, gradually becoming a central part of the legal and economic order in much of Europe and the United States. This book examines European experience in using law for that purpose.

This use of law raises issues central to any society. What role does the market play in the community? How important is economic competition? To what extent is economic power perceived as a problem? How much confidence does the community have in law as a means of achieving collective goals? We will soon look more carefully at such questions, but here it is important to underscore their centrality for political, social and economic life. It is equally important to recognize that a community's responses (or failures to respond) to them can reveal much about its concerns, values and perceptions. Located at the confluence of economic and political power, these issues often act as a prism to reveal forces that otherwise might remain imperceptible.

In Europe, competition law has achieved practical importance far greater than virtually anywhere else (except the United States). Policy-makers have turned to it in order to achieve goals as diverse as economic growth, political stability and economic integration, and thus it has become a central tool for structuring economic and political relationships and a major influence on many types of private economic decisions.

Competition law's importance in Europe extends, however, beyond the domains of government policy and private economic decision-making. It has reflected—and sometimes helped to shape—conceptions of what European society should be. Competition law grew out of the tradition of liberalism that has provided many of the central structures of modern European thought, experience and identity. In that tradition, law and economic freedom are the central means of organizing society and giving it meaning, and competition law, like perhaps no other social institution, marries these two core elements of European life. Yet competition law also reflects the concerns of European societies in this century for social equity, freedom from exploitation and consumer welfare. The goal of protecting competition has often been interwoven with the idea of achieving social justice.

The process of European integration has further enhanced competition law's importance. The core of that process has been the creation of a unified market in Europe, and its success has depended on establishing norms and institutions that make that market both economically effective and politically desirable. Competition law has been a major factor in achieving this success, serving as a 'motor' of integration and generating confidence in 'European' institutions.

But European competition law experience is not only important for Europeans. As post-socialist and other states struggle to develop economies based on the market and polities based on political freedom, for example, one of their main tasks is to structure the relationship between law and economic conduct, and competition law is at the heart of this relationship. Much will depend, therefore, on how decision-makers in these states perceive and assess competition law. What stories do they know about how it has worked? What options and insights can these stories provide? Only in Europe and the United States has there been extensive experience in using law for this purpose, and thus images of European competition law experience are likely to play important roles in shaping decisions about the relationship between law and economic conduct in many parts of the world.

A. IMAGES OF EUROPEAN COMPETITION LAW EXPERIENCE

Given the importance of European competition law experience, one might expect that experience to have been thoroughly studied and its story to have been well told. Yet the opposite is true: the experience has been little studied, and only small segments and limited aspects of the story have been told at all. As a result, both scholarly and public images of this experience are often fundamentally and dangerously flawed. Ideologies, national and linguistic boundaries and sheer ignorance have combined to generate images that are filled with half-truths, non-truths and distortions.

Three forms of distortion are particularly pernicious. One involves the story itself. Few, including competition law 'specialists', are aware of how European competition law systems have developed. Little is known about factors such as why and how competition law systems were created, which ideas, objectives and values have influenced decision-making within them, and the extent to which they have achieved the objectives set for them. In short, competition law's 'identity' remains veiled.

This lack of knowledge leads to images based on speculation and ill-founded assumptions. For example, it is common to hear even generally well-informed lawyers and economists claim that European competition laws are imitations of United States antitrust laws that were created by US occupation authorities after the Second World War. As we shall see, this assumption is fundamentally wrong. Competition law in Europe is based primarily on ideas developed by European thinkers and decision-makers in response to European conditions, and it has spread through Europe along indigenous channels rather than through emulation of US antitrust law.

Similar distortions infect images of how competition law systems currently operate—that is, their institutional and intellectual dynamics. Many believe that competition laws were created and have been maintained by bureaucrats seeking murky objectives in often suspect ways and that they have had little, if anything, to do with central issues of political and economic development. This image obscures the roles that competition law has played in the making of contemporary European societies as well as the extent to which the social, political, and economic concerns and conflicts of those societies have shaped competition laws.

Finally, there is little awareness of the specifically 'European' dimension of this experience. Until recently, competition law has been viewed almost exclusively from the perspective of individual legal systems (either EU or national). This optic has obscured relationships among national competition law systems as well as relationships between national systems and the competition law regime of the European Union. As a consequence, few are aware of shared experiences, common problems and similar solutions. Lawyers, economists, and policy-makers—not to mention the public—in one country typically have little knowledge of the roles that competition law has played in other European countries or in the process of European integration. Not surprisingly, they seldom appreciate its potential importance for Europe's future.

B. PERSPECTIVES AND SCOPE

In this book I examine European competition law experience through lenses designed to provide a more accurate and valuable account of that experience. I identify and explain the forces that have shaped competition law in Europe and illuminate its dynamics today. It is a fascinating story shaped by the interplay of economic, legal and political forces, and it is a powerful tool for understanding not only the possibilities and pitfalls of competition law, but modern Europe as well.

The central perspective is narrative. It captures connections over time among ideas, decisions and their consequences, focusing on the forces that have shaped competition law ideas and the systems based on them. My aim is not to be encyclopedic, but to understand a process of development.

Accordingly, the story includes only those aspects of European competition law experience that have played significant roles in that process.

Within this narrative, I use the concept of 'tradition' to refer to the transmission of elements of that experience over time and across borders. This generates analytical power by focusing attention on the ideas, values and practices that are being transmitted as well as on the process of transmission itself, and this, in turn, provides insights into the factors that influence the 'success' or 'failure' of such transmissions.

A key feature of this lens is that it is 'European'. It asks how experiences from diverse European systems relate to each other and how national developments relate to the process of European integration. While much of our story takes place within particular legal systems, much of it also transcends such boundaries, and the context of European integration gives this part of the story a special poignancy.

We will also look at competition law experience through a systemic lens— one that captures the dynamics of such systems.[1] My concern is with the ways in which societies use legal institutions to protect competition, and I use the term 'system' to refer to the interplay of institutions, ways of thinking, language (texts) and communities relating to that goal. I look at how decision-makers perceive problems relating to restraints on this process and respond to those perceptions. Texts are important in this analysis and so are institutions, but only insofar as texts define and configure decisions and strategies and, in turn, institutions manipulate texts and their interpretation in order to achieve institutional and other political and even private goals.

Finally, my use of the term 'competition law' deserves comment. I use it here to refer to general legal regimes that impose sanctions on conduct *because such conduct restrains competition*—that is, it is the perceived restraint on competition that 'triggers' the system's response.[2] This definition includes legal regimes whose *objective function* is to deter restraints on the competitive process, regardless of the subjective aims of those enacting the law and regardless of the terms used to describe the regime.[3]

---

[1] The concept of 'system' is commonly used to refer broadly and loosely to a nation's legal institutions—hence, e.g., the 'US legal system'. I use it here, however, to analyze how norms and institutions interact in relation to a particular set of objectives – here, the protection of competition. The concept thus becomes more specific, more functional, and, I submit, more analytically valuable, because it focuses attention on the characteristics and consequences of those interactions.

[2] The term 'competition law' causes few problems in English, where it encounters little prior usage. Literal translation of the term into other languages sometimes can, however, create confusion. In German, for example, *'Wettbewerbsrecht'* (competition law) often also includes the law of unfair competition, while the term *'Kartellrecht'* (cartel law) refers to the law relating to restraints on competition.

[3] This definition is not concerned with the ultimate 'purposes' served by competition law regimes or with the effects created by them. Such regimes often serve more than one objective, and they typically affect many types of interests. These factors play important roles in the story, but I do not use them in defining 'competition law'.

Our story will not include regimes that protect competition only incidentally or indirectly. Principles of contract law may, for example, invalidate a contract on the ground that it harms one of the parties. Although this may incidentally eliminate a competitive restraint, it is not our concern, because the function of these principles is to protect a contracting party from unfairness, not to protect the process of competition from restraint. Similarly, unfair competition laws impose sanctions on conduct by one competitor that harms another. Here again the referent is harm to the competitor rather than to the process of competition, and, accordingly, such laws generally fall outside the scope of this study.

We will also pay only passing attention to isolated norms that are directed to particular types of competitive restraints or to particular markets. Laws prohibiting the cornering of specific markets (such as grain) can be found at least as long ago as ancient Rome, for example, and are common wherever organized markets exist, but such isolated enactments are not our concern. Our focus is on *general* legal regimes established and implemented for the purpose of protecting the process of economic competition from restraint.

This book is 'about' the experience of using law for a particular purpose (combating restraints on competition) in a particular place (Europe), but it is also about that use of law and that place. It should be of particular value and interest to those interested in competition law and economic regulation in Europe, but my aim is also to provide insights into the phenomenon of competition law and into the history of Europe in this century.

What happens when law is used to protect competition? Europeans have debated, applied and enforced competition law in an extraordinary variety of contexts during the past century, and this experience provides an exceptionally rich source of information and insight about the political and legal dynamics and economic ramifications of using law for this purpose.

I offer no policy proposals, but I expect the book to be of value to many who make economic policy decisions. Its value for this purpose may be greatest for European decision-makers, for whom the story reveals much about the factors that have shaped and continue to influence the traditions and institutions within which they operate, and it is particularly critical to the process of European integration.

European competition law experience is also, however, a valuable source of knowledge and guidance for policy-makers in states that are today trying to develop market economies and forge appropriate legal frameworks for them. Most such countries have competition law systems, but they generally play marginal roles, at least in part because there is little understanding of the dynamics, costs and consequences of such systems. Policy-makers often face situations that are similar to those faced by Europeans in the recent past, and thus European experience may aid them in identifying and perhaps achieving competition law objectives.

Even policy-makers in the United States should find much of value here. While many European scholars, judges, and administrators have paid close attention to United States antitrust law experience, their US counterparts generally have assumed that they have little to learn from European experience. As a result, there have been few efforts by American scholars to analyze this experience and its potential relevance for the US. Yet to answer fundamental questions about competition law without attempting to relate them to the ways in which other comparable countries have dealt with those problems is foolhardy or arrogant or both. This lack of comparative perspective limits the conceptual tools of antitrust analysis and artificially narrows its experiential base. US antitrust law and European competition law developed out of the same basic cultural and legal traditions; they took shape at approximately the same time in response to the challenges of industrialization and democratization; and each has recognized both the value of competition and the potential harm of unrestrained economic freedom. Yet they are fundamentally different in many ways, and thus comparative analysis can be a useful tool for both.

The book should also be of value to those interested in Europe rather than in law, because I have attempted throughout to see competition law experience as part of the broader fabric of European life. The story reveals much about social, political, and intellectual dynamics during this century, and thus historians and social scientists will find it a source of insights into these domains of European experience. Economists interested in the evolution of economic thought will, for example, discover much about how economic and legal thinking have influenced each other in Europe and about the roles that competition law has played in Europe's economic experience.

Finally, the book is addressed to a central issue of contemporary economic and political life—the relationship between law and economic conduct. When, why and how have public institutions intervened to protect markets and with what results? I suspect that the story will interest general readers concerned about fundamental (and perennial) issues of the role of government in the economy and the relationship between law and economic conduct.

C. THE COMPETITION LAW STORY

Europeans began to develop the idea of such a general law to protect competition almost a century ago. The idea took shape in the 1890s in Austria, where it was a product of Vienna's extraordinarily creative intellectual life. Competition law proposals emerged in order to protect the competitive process from political and ideological onslaughts, and they relied heavily on bureaucratic application of a 'public interest' standard in doing so. One of these proposals gained significant political support, and a competition law was almost enacted—only to be barred by the disintegration of the Austrian legislative process.

Although political events blocked further development of competition law ideas in Austria, such ideas were intensely debated in both intellectual and political arenas in Germany during the decade that bracketed the turn of the century. These conflicts shaped a discourse from which Europe's early competition legislation drew much of its substance and without which its enactment is barely conceivable. Moreover, many elements of this discourse were to become fixtures of European competition law thought.

The first European 'competition law' was enacted in Germany in 1923 in response to the postwar inflation crisis. The system created to implement this legislation became an important factor of economic and legal life in Germany during the 1920s and established competition law as an operational reality rather than merely an idea. It was, however, too weak to withstand the pressures ranged against it, and it was eliminated during the 1930s.

German experience with this system was nevertheless influential in the spread of competition law ideas, and during the late 1920s competition law ideas were widely discussed throughout Europe. By the early 1930s, additional statutes along the lines of the German legislation had been enacted in several smaller European states. More importantly, these discussions and enactments generated a framework for thinking about the roles and characteristics of competition law that was to be used after the Second World War as the basis for competition legislation and that remains influential.

After the end of the war, many European governments turned to competition law as a means of encouraging economic revival, undergirding recently re-won and still fragile freedoms and achieving political acceptance of postwar hardships. Virtually all of these competition law systems were based on the thought and experience of the interwar period. In most of them, however, competition law was imbedded in economic regulatory frameworks that impeded its effectiveness, and it was seldom supported by significant economic, political or intellectual resources. As a result, these systems remained a rather marginal component of general economic policy, and in this respect some have not fundamentally changed even today.

In postwar Germany, competition law took a different turn—one that was to play a key role in the process of European integration and to have extraordinary consequences for the course of postwar European history. This change of direction was prepared during the Nazi period by a group of neo-liberal thinkers who secretly and often at great personal risk developed ideas of how Germany should be reconstituted after the war. In their so-called 'ordoliberal' vision of society, economic freedom and competition were the sources not only of prosperity but also of political freedom. They represented the 'economic constitution' of society, and law, the ordoliberals said, had to protect and implement this constitution. In this view, therefore, competition law acquired a new importance because it was made a basic structure of the political system. It also acquired new characteristics: it was now to operate increasingly according to juridical principles and procedures rather than on the basis of administrative discretion.

These ideas eventually fell on fertile soil in the years after the Second World War. Nourished by the desire for new social ideals and supported by the occupation authorities, neo-liberal reformers enacted a competition law in 1957 that achieved new prominence and a vastly greater economic and political role. Despite often intense opposition from 'big industry', competition law has become a 'pillar' of the 'social market economy', and as such it has played a key role in some of postwar Europe's most impressive economic and political successes.

The creation of the European Economic Community in 1957 created additional roles for competition law and placed it at the center of postwar European history. Competition law was charged with the task of eliminating obstacles to trade across national borders and creating the conditions for an effective and attractive 'European' market, and in this it has been highly successful. The European Commission and the European Court of Justice have overcome powerful opposition to fashion an effective instrument of integration. Yet recent changes in its goals and methods make the future of this instrument anything but clear.

The central place that competition law has assumed in the European Union has created pressure for Member States to align their competition law regimes with that of the Community. Consequently, since the mid-1980s many Member States have either introduced competition laws for the first time (for example, Italy) or revised and strengthened existing laws to make them more like Community competition law (for example, France). Combined with the principle of subsidiarity introduced by the Maastricht treaty, this has created a complex dynamic in which Member States face issues of the roles which their national competition laws should play and how they should operate, and the EU must decide how to modify its own competition law system in order to take into account these changing circumstances.

D. THE EMERGENCE OF A EUROPEAN COMPETITION LAW TRADITION

The story of competition law in Europe has been one of growth and of expanding influence—in this sense, a success story. In it, a vague new idea about the use of law took shape, gradually acquired enough support to be enacted into legislation, and spawned legal regimes that have spread throughout Europe and that have grown (often dramatically) in economic and political importance.

But the 'successes' of this story have been hard won, and they are far from secure. Competition law has struggled for influence against powerful enemies and major obstacles. Foremost among its enemies have been the representatives of 'big' industry. From their perspective, competition laws are generally seen as unwanted constraints on their decision-making prerogatives, and thus they have typically opposed, often vigorously, the enactment, development and enforcement of competition laws. Competition law's 'progress' has typically been greatest during periods when the political influence of these industrial interests has been temporarily weakened.

There have also been many 'natural' hindrances to competition law development. For example, fear of the consequences of this new and 'special' form of law has been and, in some cases, remains a major obstacle to the spread and effectiveness of such laws. The competition law idea is sufficiently different from other forms of law that it often encounters intellectual skepticism and political resistance on this account alone. Questions such as 'Why adopt (or expand or tighten) competition legislation when we don't know what the consequences will be?' have often been heard in the history of European competition law.

There is also a fundamental tension imbedded in the concept of competition law itself. Competition assumes the freedom of economic actors; freedom from constraint is the source of its strength. But laws constrain conduct and reduce freedom, and thus they appear inconsistent with the dynamics of competition. This apparent inconsistency resolves into a tension between two perspectives and the interests associated with them. One perspective focuses attention on the short-term and on law's impact on those constrained by the law; the other looks to the longer term and to the consequences for others of not providing such constraints. The conflict between these two perspectives provides unending drama.

Related to this conflict is the issue of competition law's identity. As the idea of competition law has spread and gained force, it has adapted to changing intellectual influences and economic, political and legal circumstances, and this process has continually raised issues of how to view competition law. Does it represent economic 'regulation'? Or is it a matter of protecting those injured by abuses of power? How does one understand a legal regime that is designed to protect a process? Does competition law serve the interests of consumers or surreptitiously protect producers? Does it even make sense to talk about competition law in such general terms or should the questions always be more specific—which consumers and which producers?

At the core of our story is the emergence of such an identity—a European competition law 'tradition' that contains answers to at least some of these fundamental questions. Concealed by political and economic interests and ideologies, national borders, intellectual blinders, and the opaqueness of the process, such a 'tradition' has been taking shape in Europe for more than a

century. Virtually all European countries have participated in this process in
some way, although some have played far more significant roles than others.
This tradition has transmitted ideas and perceptions over time and across
borders, and it has played a central role in both the integration of Europe and
the economic and social progress of the last four decades.

The substantive content of this tradition has become increasingly well-
defined since the mid-1970s. A set of conceptions about the roles and basic
characteristics of competition law allows us now to talk (cautiously) about a
European 'model' of competition law towards which European competition
law systems have been moving. In this model, for example, competition law
is seen as a *sui generis* form of law for which special institutions and procedures are appropriate. It represents a hybrid of administrative and juridical
elements in which the administrative elements have been dominant, but the
juridical elements have become increasingly important. We will look more
carefully at such elements, but for now I merely introduce the process of
tradition formation as a key element of the story.

E. SHAPING COMPETITION LAW—SOME THEMES

Several sets of factors have played key roles in shaping the European competition law tradition and continue to mold thought and practice within it. Like
actors in a play, they change stage positions and importance as scenes change,
but they remain central figures, and understanding their roles reveals much
about the story itself. I introduce them here as an aid to understanding our
story, but they may also be part of a more generally applicable framework for
analyzing the development and operation of competition law systems.

1. Perceiving competition

Whether and how law is used to protect competition often depends on how
competition is perceived. Competition is an abstract concept. It represents
neither a concrete 'thing out there' nor a 'natural' category, but a cultural
construct. One can 'see' something called 'competition' only where one's
language, training and experience give that concept meaning. Increasing
recognition of the process of competition, particularly among political decision-makers, has been a critical factor in the development, implementation,
and success of competition law ideas.

Perceptions of competition are interwoven with images of its consequences.
A community's experiences with competition combine with its images of such
experiences elsewhere to shape its expectations of the consequences of
increased or diminished competition in the future. Where, for example,
decision-makers associate increased competition with a period of economic

progress, they are likely to perceive it quite differently than if they see it as a cause of social conflict and upheaval. Similarly, images of competition's success—or failure—in one country are likely to affect perceptions of it by decision-makers in other countries who consider this experience relevant to their own circumstances.

What decision-makers 'see' when they look at the process of competition also shapes competition laws. How they design and apply competition law norms may depend, for example, on which part of the competitive process they are looking at. Are they looking at competition among large firms or small ones? Is their concern with local markets or international ones? Are they looking at competition among groups of enterprises (for example, cartels) or among the members of such groups? These issues of perception inevitably shape decisional outcomes and system dynamics.

2. Evaluating competition: of benefits and harms

A second set of factors involves evaluating competition and its effects. Where the competitive process is perceived, it is also evaluated; values and standards are applied to it. Competition is not likely to be protected unless it is considered beneficial—at least by influential persons or groups, and the more beneficial it is seen to be, the more likely it is that laws protecting it will be enacted and effectively enforced. The potential economic benefits of competition have been widely recognized in Europe since at least the middle of the nineteenth century, but the evaluation of competition has changed dramatically. In some situations the focus has been on the material benefits of competition; in others it has been on perceived negative concomitants of unrestrained competition such as the concentration of economic and political power, harm to small and medium-sized firms or harm to specific communities or social groups.

Analysis of competition law experience thus requires awareness of the values being used in assessing competition. Decisions as to which types of norms are included in competition statutes, how they are interpreted by administrators and judges, and the extent to which they are enforced often depend on how specific types or forms of competition are evaluated. If, for example, decision-makers view the competitive activities of large firms *vis-à-vis* smaller firms as exploitative and unfair, they are likely to introduce and enforce norms designed to restrain the conduct of the 'exploiting' firms. If, on the other hand, they see such conduct as a necessary means of competing with large rivals from other countries, they are less likely to introduce and stringently enforce such norms.

It is important, therefore, to ask who is evaluating competition, in what contexts and for what reasons, and to uncover the values that are being applied. The political ideologies, social visions and even religious sensibilities of legislators, bureaucrats and judges have played important roles in the development and operation of competition law regimes.

3. Competition law's aims: what, if anything, needs protection?

Assuming that competition (or a particular conception or form of competition) is valued, a further question is whether law can and should be used to protect that process from restraints. Many have argued, as the Chicago School of Law and Economics currently does, that the competitive process will protect itself better than governmental intervention can and that, in general, the best way to protect competition is to leave it alone. Where this image prevails, competition laws are likely to be of marginal importance. Where, in contrast, decision-makers believe that competition is inherently vulnerable— that the very freedom on which its success rests is likely to be used to restrict it—competition laws tend to prosper.

Attitudes, experience and assumptions about specific forms of competition, the appropriate roles of law in responding to them, and the effectiveness of legal institutions in performing particular tasks, also influence the uses to which competition law is put. What exactly is it that needs protection? Should law be used to deter agreements among competitors? To control mergers and acquisitions? Can judges (or administrators) be expected to understand complicated and ever-changing economic arrangements? Such questions and responses to them are at the heart of competition law dynamics.

4. Means and ends: how to protect competition

A final set of factors relates to the means used to protect competition. If law is to be used to protect competition, what types of laws, procedures and sanctions should be employed and for which purposes? For example, should competition law be seen as part of 'private law'—the legal framework for resolving disputes between private actors—or 'public law', a form of state regulation. Or should it be a hybrid, and, if so, composed of which elements? We examine how such questions have been posed—and answered.

a. Specialness

A central feature of the European competition law tradition has been the idea that competition law is special and that using law to protect competition moves outside of law's 'normal' domain. In this view, competition law is a new type of law which deals with problems for which traditional legal mechanisms are inappropriate, and thus it requires correspondingly non-traditional methods and procedures. It is a view that contrasts sharply with the approach of US antitrust law, which relies primarily on traditional legal forms and institutions in protecting competition.

b. 'Spirit'

This image of competition law's specialness has led to a large measure of caution in European competition law regimes. Lack of experience with these issues, difficulties in predicting the consequences of legal intervention, and political pressures relating to such intervention have led legislators, administrators, and judges toward restraint in fashioning and applying competition law norms.

The inherent uncertainty of trying to protect a process reinforces this cautious stance. Laws generally protect rights: the legal system determines whether and to what extent rights have been invaded and then seeks to prevent such invasions and/or to compensate the victims. To protect a process is a far vaguer objective. What constitutes harm to the process? What can the legal system do to eliminate or reduce such harms?

This sense of specialness and the perceived need to prevent competition law from harming economic development has also led to an emphasis on competition law as a constructive social force rather than a constraint on conduct. The discourse of European competition law systems has tended to emphasize their roles in creating and maintaining the conditions necessary for effective competition rather than merely eliminating objectionable conduct. The focus generally has been on pragmatic thinking and constructive results rather than on the strict application of abstract norms, although this may be changing.

c. The 'economic power' focus

This conception of competition law favors making economic power a central element in its substantive norms. It suggests that law should intervene only where restraints on competition result from the use of such power. The underlying notion is that there is little value in applying norms without regard to the power of those engaged in the conduct, because only economic power-holders can harm the competitive process. In US antitrust, in contrast, more abstract and formalistic conceptions of competition law norms have often prevailed.

d. Identity and methods

Whether competition law should be understood as a part of economic policy or a 'legal' regime has been a constant (though seldom clearly articulated) theme in the development of European competition law. Viewed as an element of economic policy, such laws are likely to be seen primarily as a matter for the discretion of administrators charged with applying a relatively vague standard such as 'the public interest'. In Europe this perspective has been and continues to be prominent. If, however, one understands competition law as a means of protecting a valued social good, it is likely to be treated as a matter more of legal rights, juridical analysis, and judicial decision-making than of administrative discretion. Articulated principles move toward center stage.

This perspective has been gaining in influence in Europe, but its 'victories' remain fragile.

e. Locus of power within the system

As with any legal regime, competition law dynamics revolve around questions such as 'Who has power within the system?', 'Who makes the various types of decisions that drive the system?', 'What are the types and sources of influence on these decision-makers?', 'Should "scientific" analysis predominate or political and economic expediency?' In European competition law systems, bureaucrats play a central role, but other players also often have significant influence, and (often disguised) conflicts over power within the system are endemic.

f. External influences on the system

Competition law involves 'big stakes', often impinging on the decisional pre-rogatives of business firms that have significant political influence. This creates pressures on decision-makers within competition law systems, and often the issue of inducing their commitment to a system's objectives is a major factor in how the system operates. The wide variety of disparate and potentially conflicting values and goals associated with competition law regimes complicates the problem. For example, are the interests of consumers most important? What about small and medium-size firms? And political goals such as the protection of economic freedom or the dispersion of economic power? It is seldom easy to reconcile these goals or to choose among them.

g. Flexibility and dependability

A final category of factors involves stability and change within competition law systems. Pragmatically-oriented and in some countries still somewhat untested, such systems are supposed to remain flexible and open to change. On the other hand, they are expected to be effective in deterring harmful conduct. Those making competition law decisions are, therefore, often caught between the desire for flexibility and the need to provide legal security and reliable information to economic decision-makers. In a world of globalization and rapidly changing forms of competition, this is treacherous terrain.

* * *

This study of European competition law experience begins by looking at the nineteenth century. This was the century in which competition became a creed, economics a science, and the market a dominant force in society, and thus the ideas and experiences of that century shaped the competition law ideas that began to develop during its closing years. A sense of that century's main themes provides a necessary background for understanding the development of competition law ideas in the twentieth century.

The book concludes by looking back over the almost completed twentieth century and asking what European experience with competition law during this century might suggest about competition law's roles and prospects during the next. Even as creeds, sciences, and societal ideals evolve during the coming century, economic competition is likely to remain central to social life. Moreover, global technological integration, environmental concerns, and conflicts between rich and poor nations may make political and legal decisions regarding that process more central than ever.

II

Freedom, Law, and Competition: The Nineteenth Century as Prelude

The idea of creating a new type of law to protect the process of competition began to emerge at the end of the nineteenth century, and thus the experiences and perspectives of that century were its progenitors as well as its sculptors. This chapter paints with broad strokes (and concomitant overgeneralizations) the nineteenth century forces that were to shape the development of competition law in the twentieth century.[1]

A marginal idea as the century began, the concept of competition had become enormously important by its end. It had been hailed as the remaker of man, a new Prometheus that would create wealth, diminish poverty, reduce class distinctions and secure freedoms. Yet in the last decades of the century it was more frequently assailed as humankind's betrayer. Europeans thus developed a profound ambivalence toward economic competition, and the European conception of competition law that began to develop at the end of the century reflects this ambivalence.

The fortunes of the competition idea were tied to the rise and fall of liberalism. From the French Revolution until the mid-1870s, the promise that reducing governmental restraints on economic actors would produce wealth, progress, and happiness was exceptionally powerful, stirring imaginations and shaping political developments. But during the last quarter of the century that promise turned sour. The ideas that would structure modern European competition laws were a product of European liberalism, but they were conceived in a context of uncertainty and doubt about liberalism's promise.

We will concentrate on three aspects of nineteenth century experience. The first is the development of ideas, attitudes and values relating to economic conduct, in general, and competition, in particular, because these forces shaped perceptions of the need to protect competition. A second focus is on the process of economic development itself, for events controlled the success of ideas even as they were being formed by them. Finally, we examine some of the legal ideas and institutions that near the end of the century began to shape thought and action concerning the possible use of law to protect competition.

[1] Because much of this chapter relates to broad themes about which there is extensive literature, I have kept footnote references here to a minimum, including material only where necessary and referring primarily to English language general works and works with good and/or recent bibliographical information wherever possible.

A. LIBERALISM AND POLITICAL FREEDOM

The genesis of the idea of protecting competition was imbedded in the idea of protecting freedom, and thus it is important to review briefly the role and substance of the concept of freedom in the nineteenth century. The French Revolution ushered in a European century in which this concept acquired for many an almost religious dimension. It became a powerful talisman that spawned reverence and provided justifications for a wide range of claims.[2] Law basked in its semi-sacred glow, for it was seen as the indispensable tool for achieving 'freedom'.

Liberalism was the political, social, and intellectual 'movement' that surrounded this talisman and made freedom and law the core of its credo.[3] The institutions and traditions of liberalism not only scripted thinking about economic competition, but also carried its political fortunes. In the conceptual and institutional matrix of liberalism, therefore, political and economic elements were often tightly interwoven, and their relationship plays an important role in our story.

The political component of the liberal agenda focused on changing the existing political system in which kings and princes wielded power according to their own discretion. It sought to redefine political power, and, above all, to restrict and redistribute existing concentrations of such power. Its principal tool and driving force was the idea that political freedom was a *right* and that government had to be organized so as to protect that right.

Political freedom had both negative and positive dimensions, and law was necessary to achieve *both*. Liberals sought freedom *from* discretionary political power by subjecting such power to the constraints of laws, especially constitutions. Law was at the center of this process: it *created* freedom by constraining power. The transfer of this basic idea from political thought to the economic sphere was a key conceptual move in the development of European competition law.

The positive component of political freedom centered on participatory rights—that is, increased participation in the political process by those who previously had been excluded from it. Power should be subject to the expressed will of the governed. Here again, law was necessary to create the conditions of freedom: laws, particularly constitutions, had to create, recognize, and enforce participatory rights. This conception of the role of law

---

[2] For a useful account of the freedom ideal during the nineteenth century, see Herbert J. Muller, *Freedom in the Modern World: The 19th and 20th Centuries* (New York, 1966).

[3] The literature on European liberalism in the nineteenth century is vast. For an historical survey centered on the nineteenth century, see Guido de Ruggiero, *The History of European Liberalism* (R. G. Collingwood, tr., Oxford, 1927; reprinted Boston, 1959). *Liberalismus* (Lothar Gall, ed., Cologne, 1976) contains extensive bibliographical material.

would also be transferred to the economic sphere in creating the European concept of competition law.

These two freedom-generating functions of law were intertwined, for the process of constraining power could seldom be divorced from the process of creating participatory rights. This idea was perhaps most clearly developed in the idea of the *Rechtstaat* or 'law-based state', which was developed in the nineteenth century, primarily by German liberals.[4] Here law's function was to provide a constitutive framework for political power that anchored *both* the freedom from discretionary power *and* the freedom to participate in making political choices. Law as a 'framework for freedom' was the key image. This idea of a constitutional framework would be applied in the twentieth century to economic conduct and emerge as a shaping force within European competition law.

The drive for political freedom was rooted in the growing size and strength of the bourgeoisie. Merchants, bankers, and bureaucrats as well as doctors and lawyers sought to increase their control over their own destinies and to reduce the discretionary power of hereditary elites. In short, they wanted more power, and liberalism justified their claims and aspirations.

By the end of the century, liberalism had begun to achieve many of its political goals. Constitutions—written, or, as in Britain, unwritten—were in place in the major European countries. The middle classes had achieved a measure of political power in most countries, albeit sharing control with kings and nobles in a variety of arrangements. Elections increasingly played a role in distributing political power, and voting rights increasingly were extended to (male) members of the middle classes. Most European countries were moving, if hesitantly, in the direction that liberals had mapped out for them.

B. THE BATTLE FOR ECONOMIC FREEDOM

Just as liberals sought to free political conduct from the discretion of absolutist rulers, they also sought to free economic conduct from the constraints imposed under those regimes. At the turn of the nineteenth century, economic conduct was often subject to extensive regulation—either by governments or by mediating organizations such as guilds. In most countries, absolutist governments regulated economic conduct in order to increase and conserve the wealth of the state and to protect the economic prerogatives of the ruling elites, and they protected—or at least tolerated—guilds because, *inter alia*, they often provided support as well as economic and social stability.[5]

---

[4] See, e.g., Friedrich Darmstaedter, *Die Grenzen der Wirksamkeit des Rechtsstaats* (Heidelberg, 1930).
[5] See generally Antony Black, *Guilds and Civil Society in European Political Thought from the Twelfth Century to the Present* (Ithaca, N.Y., 1984).

Liberals sought to free economic actors from these governmental and guild restrictions, and it was in this context that they developed the idea that economic freedom was also a right. Their agenda was to enact laws that would establish these rights, thus removing obstacles to economic liberty and increasing the scope of private choice in economic decision-making.

The political and economic components of liberalism were, therefore, closely related, each benefiting from the attractions of the other. The individual should not only have the political freedom to be ruled by laws in whose creation he participated, but the economic freedom to make choices such as where to work, what to produce, and what to do with the profits. In both cases there was a right to be free from control and a right to participate in a process.

This battle for economic freedom generated a new way of looking at economic activity, and competition was at the center of this image. Adam Smith's 'invisible hand' gave both shape and value to the idea of competition.[6] Although Smith was not the first to articulate the concept of competition as a distinct process—the physiocrats had already done that—his work developed and popularized it. As the nineteenth century progressed, individual economic transactions were increasingly perceived as part of a process called competition, and the capacity to perceive it as such was a precondition to the development of competition law.

But the idea of the invisible hand did more—it made competition immensely important. Competition produced benefits. According to Smith, the competitive interaction of free individuals seeking personal gain produced wealth.[7] If economic actors were free, their interaction would lead to higher standards of living for the nation as well as for the actors themselves. In contrast, he said, governmental and guild controls on private economic decisions actually made states poorer and weaker by interfering with this process.

This new image required a fundamental restructuring of perceptions of economic activity. It had long been assumed that government controls were necessary to 'the wealth of nations' because they co-ordinated economic activity and assured that it would be directed to useful purposes. But Smith recast this control function as an *obstacle* to community well-being rather than a means of achieving it. Competition and regulation came to be seen as opposites, and for many this symbolic dichotomy still retains visceral force.

Smith saw other benefits in competition that were at least as important as its economic ones, and that also required fundamental restructuring of thought patterns. He argued, for example, that competition was not a threat to the social fabric of the community. Traditional conceptions of economic

---

[6] For a recent discussion of Smith's role and influence that reviews the literature and challenges some of the traditional views, see Jerry Z. Muller, *Adam Smith in his Time and Ours: Designing the Decent Society* (New York, 1993).

[7] This was a central thesis of his famous *Wealth of Nations*. Adam Smith, *An Inquiry into the Nature and Causes of the Wealth of Nations* (R. H. Campbell & A. S. Skinner, eds., Glasgow, 1976; orig. pub. 1776).

conduct had portrayed the search for private profits as a threat to community stability because it led individuals to attempt to benefit at each other's expense and thus caused conflicts and disharmony. This image provided a powerful rationale for government regulation of the economy: it was necessary to prevent disharmony. From Smith's perspective, however, competition could produce its own form of harmony. The market could regulate itself, and everyone would gain in the process, thereby increasing rather than diminishing the stability of communities. This transformed the idea of community, basing it on dynamic processes rather than on static conditions.

For Smith and his followers a 'competitive' order had the additional benefit of being more just. Competition would distribute economic benefits, not according to the discretion of rulers but through the impartial and objective 'laws' of the market. Moreover, participants would receive rewards that were 'fair' in the sense that they were tied to success in the competitive struggle. For those who stood to gain from it this was an attractive concept of fairness.

Finally, this image of society provided a new concept of order. The patterns of human interaction that had structured life for so long were being rent during the nineteenth century by industrialization and urbanization, but for the liberals, competition could explain and justify what often appeared to be terrifying changes. Smith's message was that there really was order beneath the chaos, but one had to look at events from a different perspective in order to see it.

This new conception of the economic process was the seedbed for both the modern science of economics and the ideology of economic liberalism. As a consequence, economic 'knowledge' was intertwined and identified with liberal ideology for most of the century. From its inception, economic science was imbedded in the discourse of liberalism, and liberalism, in turn, fertilized the growth of economics as a science and relied on its conceptual apparatus.

This image of economic activity and of the value of competition was appealing, particularly to members of the bourgeoisie who saw themselves as its primary beneficiaries. It represented a tool for eliminating constraints and institutions that were designed to benefit someone else, be it the ruler, the nobility, or guild masters.

Yet the economic component of liberalism sometimes also found support among members of ruling elites who opposed many of liberalism's political goals. For them, economic freedom was instrumental—a means of achieving economic progress and enhancing personal and national wealth. In Prussia, for example, a politically conservative government introduced reforms in 1810 that called for a radical turn toward economic freedom. The motivation was not ideological, but rather an effort to strengthen Prussia's economy.[8]

[8] See generally Barbara Vogel, *Allgemeine Gewerbefreiheit, Die Reformpolitik des Preussischen Staatskanzlers Hardenburg 1810–1820* (Göttingen, 1983). There is also a good brief description in James J. Sheehan, *German History 1770–1866* at 303–10 (Oxford, 1989).

The allures of economic freedom eventually led to many of the legal and institutional changes called for by the liberals. During the first two-thirds of the century, governmental restraints on economic activity were reduced or eliminated. Guilds lost much, if not all, of their legal protection. Laws were passed guaranteeing business freedom and thus assuring that individuals could pursue economic objectives without regard to guild membership or government regulations. Restrictions such as the requirement of governmental approval to incorporate a business were eliminated. By the mid-1870s many of the objectives of economic liberalism were being achieved.

During the third quarter of the century, economic events seemed to confirm liberal beliefs. From 1848 through 1875 (what Eric Hobsbawm calls the 'age of capital') few could doubt that eliminating governmental fetters on the economy would lead to economic progress.[9] A 'boom' rolled across Europe. Fueled by technological, organizational and, above all, transportation advances,[10] European economies generated dizzying increases in industrial production and immense improvements in living standards, at least for the middle and upper classes. This surge was most impressive in central Europe, but the pattern was common throughout Europe and led to a rush of confidence in the liberal image of the economy.

C. INDUSTRIALIZATION: EXPERIENCE AND LEGACY

As liberalism contained the central tradition of thought about economic conduct during the nineteenth century in Europe, industrialization represented the central economic experience.[11] At first the two fit together nicely. Liberalism encouraged and accelerated industrialization, and industrialization produced the economic boom that seemed to confirm the validity of liberal ideas. It represented 'proof' of the value of competition. But during the latter part of the century, industrialization also generated political, social, and economic forces that undermined the liberal image of society.

The experience of industrialization poured across Europe throughout the nineteenth century, providing a common experiential base for economic and

---

[9] This boom period is well described in Eric Hobsbawm, *The Age of Capital 1848–1875* at 29–47 (New York, 1975).

[10] For an insightful description of the technological aspects of this process, see Joel Mokyr, *The Lever of Riches: Technological Creativity and Economic Progress* 113–48 (New York, 1990).

[11] For a leading recent treatment, see Sidney Pollard, *Peaceful Conquest: The Industrialization of Europe 1760–1970* (Oxford, 1981). The now standard account of industrialization's technological aspects is David S. Landes, *The Unbound Prometheus: Technological Change and Industrial Development in Western Europe from 1750 to the Present* (Cambridge, 1972). For a valuable survey of European economic development during this period, see Alan S. Milward & S. B. Saul, *The Development of the Economies of Continental Europe 1850–1914* (Cambridge, Mass., 1977).

social thought. Beginning during the eighteenth century in England,[12] the process jumped the English channel to Belgium and spread outward, losing some of its force as it progressed and only brushing the eastern and southern extremities of the continent. As it progressed, it transformed society and created the structures of a new form of competition.

The core of the industrialization process was the ascendance of the factory system. At the turn of the nineteenth century, factories either did not exist or were of marginal importance in most areas of Europe outside of England.[13] Goods were produced primarily in the shops of artisans or in the homes of farmers or peasants (the 'putting-out' system). But by the end of the century, the factory system had become the dominant form of production for many goods in most places.

On one level, industrialization was a technological process. Where once an individual artisan produced individual goods with his own skill and energy, the factory assembled raw materials, provided machines and power and hired workers to run the machines. More important for our purposes was the organizational revolution that accompanied it. The factory system changed the characteristics of competition, creating the structures that competition law would be invented to regulate and that remain familiar today, structures that little resembled the image on which Adam Smith and other early liberal writers had based their theories.

Industrialization changed the unit of competition, replacing the individual artisan or group of artisans with the organized unit of machine-based production. Hierarchies of managers increasingly made competitive decisions, as owners began their long journey toward the peripheries of economic decision-making. And artisans were replaced by salaried laborers—factors of production to be purchased at the lowest possible cost. Laborers had few decision-making rights and were heavily dependent on the will of the managers. Subjected to new forms of organizational discipline, they operated as cogs in the larger wheel of the enterprise.

Industrialization also changed the process of competition. The rationalization of production—maximizing production and minimizing costs—began to replace quality and dependability as keys to competitive success. Decisions increasingly were made according to a cost-benefit analysis that has since become standard in Western societies, but which was alien or at least secondary before industrialization.

Those who made competitive decisions had correspondingly fewer incentives to concern themselves with either individual employees or the

[12] One can discern forms of industrialization during earlier periods, but the process gained cohesion and definition during the eighteenth century. See Paul Mantoux, *The Industrial Revolution in the Eighteenth Century: An Outline of the Beginnings of the Modern Factory System in England* (London, 1961).
[13] The main exception is the northeastern section of the European continent that is now included in Belgium and the Netherlands.

community in which they operated. The increasing separation of management functions from ownership functions further encouraged concentration on the calculus of profit at the expense of other considerations. Managers were paid to make money for owners, and they could ill afford to consider other values. Competition increasingly was carried out by a new group of men according to new rules, and the moral and community values that once constrained the search for profits were losing their force.[14]

Size became an increasingly important factor in competition, as the factory system demanded ever larger organizations. The image of competition as a contest among individuals based on talent, effort, and resourcefulness seemed to have little to do with battles among corporate units with hundreds and soon thousands and tens of thousands of employees.

Competition also became increasingly international. Around mid-century the revolution in transportation technology that included steamships and railroads expanded the geographical scope of competition, as increasing numbers of companies began to compete on ever broader geographical fronts. European firms increasingly competed not only in other European countries, but also in distant markets such as the Americas, and they increasingly also secured their raw materials from distant sources.

This type of competition entailed a new emphasis on technology—and, eventually, science—as forms of competition. The technical ability to improve production, lower costs and create new products became more central to the competitive process, and this, in turn, created further incentives to increase firm size in order to be in a position to finance greater investment in technological competition.

In the transition from small-scale to large-scale and from family-owned to publicly-owned enterprise, the ability to borrow funds became increasingly important. Access to financing took on new importance as banks became necessary partners of business at all levels, from the local bank to international banking houses such as that of the Rothschilds that financed not only industries, but governments as well.

Finally, the growing size and geographical scope of competition made government an ever more important factor in private economic competition. Size gave firms the power to influence government for their own ends. An effective and attractive way of increasing domestic sales, for example, was to raise tariffs on competing imports. The use of government to achieve competitive advantages increased dramatically during the 'Great Depression' of the latter part of the century.

This new face of competition appeared more ominous and less human than it had seemed in its earlier community-based setting. Competition did not take place between small producers, but between large organizations.

---

[14] For discussion, see Karl Polanyi, *The Great Transformation* (Boston, 1957).

Decisions were made not by individuals with personal relationships and human dimensions, but by enterprises operating according to a rigid profit principle and in response to often distant stimuli. And success depended less on human skills and more on various forms of institutional power.

The advance of this new form of competition also had powerful social consequences. Industrialization extirpated workers and their families from their (typically rural) communities and the customs and supports that were central to life in such communities. Individuals and nuclear families typically faced uncertain and often harsh situations in which they had few rights, little power and less support. In addition, the increased population density generated by factories was associated with unhealthy, overcrowded living conditions. Industrialization thus created a new social class—the urban proletariat, and its members frequently perceived little reason to laud the benefits of competition.

Factories also displaced. Artisans were typically losers in the industrialization process, because factories could almost always produce goods more cheaply than they could. As a social group, therefore, artisans became bitter opponents of industrialization and all it stood for, and they did all they could to secure protection from its march.

Industrialization thus created not only the characteristics of the modern competitive process, but also many of the forces that would demand that the process be regulated. By the end of the century, industrialization was viewed by many as a frightening, life-degrading monster, and liberalism was blamed for its creation. Before the 'old interference' of mercantilist stripe could be totally eliminated, the social consequences of industrialization led to calls for new forms of governmental regulation to curb the harms of industrialization.

D. THE GREAT DEPRESSION AND THE FRAGILITY OF CAPITALISM

But liberal dreams were not only clouded by the social consequences of industrialization, they were dashed by the apparent failure of competition to accomplish its stated goals. The 'Great Depression' formed a third strand in the story of liberalism during the nineteenth century.[15] Triumphant in most areas in the 1860s, liberalism was discredited by the economic crises that

---

[15] See Hans Rosenberg, *Grosse Depression und Bismarckzeit* (Berlin, 1967) and his 'Political and Social Consequences of the Great Depression of 1873–1896 in Central Europe', 13 *Econ. Hist. Rev.* 58 (1943). Although it has become customary to refer to the entire period from 1873 to the mid-1890s as the 'Great Depression', it was not a depression in the modern sense of the word, because most, if not all, countries registered production gains over the period as a whole. See generally S. B. Saul, *The Myth of the Great Depression, 1873–1896* (2d. ed., London, 1985). There has been much recent controversy among historians about the economic characteristics of the period, but our concern here is with contemporary perceptions of the depression rather than with assessing the accuracy of those perceptions.

began in 1873 and lasted until the mid-1890s. During this period, economic freedom was transformed from a cherished objective to an often bitter disappointment, and this disillusionment was to shape the interpretation of competition in the first half of the twentieth century.

Economic troubles struck suddenly in 1873. The crash of the Vienna stock market in that year triggered similar debacles throughout Europe as well as in the United States. The speculative bubble of the 1860s burst, leading to major bankruptcies, ruin for important families, and a sharp downturn in production, profits, and prices. Disastrous European harvests in the mid-1870s combined with increases in North American wheat sales in Europe to deepen the crisis. The first full-scale depression of the new global economic system led to shock and outrage at this new and sinister aspect of capitalism.

The sense of anger and disillusionment grew deeper as the crisis of the 1870s was followed by a prolonged period of general economic malaise that lasted until the mid-1890s.[16] During this period, prices and profitability remained low, and instability and uncertainty remained high. Sharp downturns of as much as two to four years were common, and, although there were periods of growth, the uncertainty of profits and jobs and the apparent intractability of the problem created a widespread sense of disappointment and frustration throughout much of Europe.

E. MANAGED COMPETITION

The tandem forces of industrialization and depression brought about new forms of economic organization and altered the relationships between economic and political institutions. Businesses increasingly sought co-operation and government support, and governments were increasingly willing and able to provide such support.

Businesses responded to the depression by turning away from competition and toward co-operative arrangements, and political leaders who often had been weaned on the idea that governmental 'interference' stood in the way of economic progress began intervening more vigorously on behalf of business interests. 'Freedom' and 'autonomy' were replaced as watchwords by 'collective action', 'organization', and 'stability'.[17] For many, competition soon seemed more an enemy than a friend: it was held responsible for the rapid and

---

[16] The profitability problem rested on fundamental cyclical and structural problems that were but dimly recognized by contemporaries. Excess industrial capacity throughout Europe was a major culprit. The boom of the 1860s had generated heavy capital investment, particularly in new labor-saving technology, and production growth thus quickly outstripped demand and led to falling prices and low business profits.

[17] For a good short overview, see Eric Hobsbawm, *The Age of Empire 1875–1914*, ch. 2 (New York, 1987).

unpredictable economic swings that were ruining firms and destroying individuals.

Initially, businesses turned toward 'co-operation' in self-defense. The crises of the 1870s had capsized many firms, and continuing pressure on prices and profits kept this threat very much alive. This induced many firms to co-operate for the purpose of maintaining prices. As a result, cartels expanded rapidly from about 1880, flourishing most prominently in Germany and Austria. By the 1890s, cartels were considered 'natural' parts of the economic landscape in many parts of the continent.

Cartel arrangements took many forms, but their common objective was to eliminate or regulate competition among cartel members. They were a mechanism for avoiding the harms of 'excessive' competition, and in countries such as Germany and Austria where they were most successful they fundamentally changed views of competition. Competition that was not 'managed' came to be seen as 'excessive' and thus a justification for competitors to join together to regulate it.

Increases in business co-operation were accompanied by new alliances between government and business that were to play major roles in the development of competition law in Europe. The liberal credo had called for government to 'go away and let business alone,' but with the onset of the Depression, business welcomed government back.[18] The state was increasingly expected to provide aid to troubled firms, to limit access to the domestic market by foreign competitors and generally to 'influence' the market. Britain provided an important exception to this trend, and it went further in some countries (for example, Germany) than others, but it was common throughout Europe.

Co-operation among competitors frequently focused on influencing government, and the growth of government, in turn, provided an incentive for increased business co-operation. Particularly on the continent, businesses increasingly joined together in trade associations and interest organizations whose main goals were often to influence legislators and bureaucrats. They wanted, above all, higher tariffs to protect them against foreign competitors, but they also sought government subsidies, loan guarantees and the like.

But if business increasingly needed government, those in government also increasingly needed business. Governments that were still largely controlled by traditional elites or alliances between elites and bourgeois elements found themselves unable to ignore the previously little heeded demands of weaker social groups that were either created by industrialization (the proletariat) or suffering its effects (artisans). In most of Europe elected legislatures were introduced in the course of the nineteenth century, and by the end of the century these institutions were becoming both stronger and more democratic,

---

[18] For an overview of this 'transformation', see Norman Stone, *Europe Transformed* 42–73 (Glasgow, 1983).

though they often had little real power.[19] This gave rise to political parties that increasingly needed funds for use in influencing voters, and the modern scramble for corporate funds began.

Nationalism helped to cement this alliance. As international competition came increasingly to be perceived as a battle among nations played out on the field of profits, governments, and private firms began to develop a nationalistic rhetoric in which they were expected to work together for the sake of the national welfare. A prominent form of this co-operation was, for example, the manipulation of tariff barriers in order to exclude foreign competition.

What we now refer to as 'imperialism' was an important part of this alliance. Governments saw the acquisition of foreign territories as a means of securing outlets for the products of domestic companies as well as a source of raw materials for domestic production.[20] Foreign territories were portrayed and understood as an antidote against economic hard times at home, and, above all, a source of competitive advantage over other European rivals.

These alliances between business and government did not, of course, go unnoticed by those who were either excluded from them or felt harmed by them. By the end of the century, workers were being mobilized in socialist parties of various kinds whose ultimate goal was to wrest power from the ruling elites. Moreover, the artisans and small shopkeepers who felt squeezed between the proletariat and the bourgeoisie organized powerful movements that were directed against both.

Although these groups typically did not acquire enough votes in legislative assemblies to achieve their demands directly until after the turn of the century, they did influence governments. Liberal and conservative politicians increasingly adopted policies in order to appease the working classes and the *petite bourgeoisie* and thus to avoid the social disruption they threatened. The clearest example of such tactics is the social legislation of Bismarck in Germany, but it was a common enough pattern.[21]

---

[19] Despite advances, legislatures frequently were also not very democratic. Nowhere was there universal suffrage until after the turn of the century. Often the right to vote in parliamentary elections was conditioned on property ownership, tax payments and other requirements that excluded large segments of the population. Moreover, even where suffrage had been extended, governments often erected hurdles to participation in the legislature so as to restrict membership to the upper and middle classes. Sometimes these were overt, such as laws preventing socialists from being members of national legislatures. In other cases, they were more subtle, such as lack of compensation for serving in the legislature. See Eugene N. & Pauline R. Anderson, *Political Institutions and Social Change in Continental Europe in the Nineteenth Century* 377–93 (Berkeley, 1967).

[20] See, e.g., A. P. Thornton, *Doctrines of Imperialism*, ch.3 (New York, 1965).

[21] See Gerhard A. Ritter, *Social Welfare in Germany and Britain* (Leamington Spa, 1986).

F. RE-EVALUATING COMPETITION AND ECONOMIC FREEDOM

The combination of prolonged economic malaise and increasing awareness of the social consequences of industrialization brought about changes not only in institutions, but also in ways of thinking about competition and economic freedom. Whereas the first seven decades of the century witnessed growing confidence in the market and in the wealth-generating powers of competition, the last three focused on its failures. Greater economic freedom had not provided economic stability and ever-increasing wealth, and its social costs had proven far higher than anticipated. Moreover, its economic promise seemed to explode just as its social consequences clamored for attention. Competition law was part of the response to the 'failures' of liberalism, and it was shaped by these new concerns, attitudes, and interpretations.

1. Darwin: competition as nature's God

The late nineteenth century was in some ways a halcyon period for the general idea of competition. The Darwinian image of human history that was restructuring social thought gave the process of competition *the* central role in the story. Competition became the key to explaining how individuals, communities and nations operated, how they had come to be what they were, and what they were likely to become.[22] In short, it became a central device for interpreting human actions.

The concept of competition was closely associated with another powerful idea—progress, which many in the late nineteenth century came to see as the very engine of social and even moral experience. According to Eric Hobsbawm,

In material terms, in terms of knowledge and the capacity to transform nature it seemed so patent that change meant advance that history—at all events modern history—seemed to equal progress. Progress was measured by the ever rising curve of whatever could be measured, or what men chose to measure. Continuous improvement, even of those things which clearly still required it, was guaranteed by historical experience.[23]

The idea of progress became an integral part of the view Europeans held of their present and a principal means of explaining their relationship to both their past and their future, and competition was often seen as a necessary adjunct to it.

---

[22] See Jacques Barzun, *Darwin, Marx and Wagner: Critique of a Heritage* 38–55 (2d. ed., New York, 1958).

[23] Hobsbawm, *The Age of Empire*, 26. For the classic work on the idea of progress, see J. B. Bury, *The Idea of Progress* (New York, 1932). A provocative and insightful recent study is Christopher Lasch, *The True and Only Heaven: Progress and Its Critics* (New York, 1991).

But competition also had a darker side: for many, its power was a curse. Its very prominence led them to see it as a cause of contemporary problems and the enemy of all that had been good in the world—communities, morality, and religion, to name a few examples. In particular, the less fortunate saw competition as the source of their pain, and many turned to socialism to save them from it.

Competition became even more odious to these groups when voices from the upper and middle classes assigned competition a new and still broader function—to justify the plight of poor workers and displaced artisans. Their sacrifices were to be understood as necessary to the progress of the community as a whole. True, the industrial proletariat did not have an easy time of it, but, according to this view, they were performing a service to their neighbors. This may have alleviated the guilt of some, but it did little to inspire respect for the idea of competition among those were destined to make the required sacrifices, and it was this latter group whose political power was increasing.

2. Rethinking economics: broken image, broken ties

Those who in the late nineteenth century sought to understand the specifically economic aspects of competition were thus caught between two conflicting general images of competition. On the one hand, it was a motor of progress and a central component of social thought; on the other, it was an often vilified idea that economic actors themselves were increasingly rejecting in favor of co-operative arrangements and governmental alliances.

The crises of the 1870s and 1880s had also exploded their image of the economic process. The idea that the 'invisible hand' of competition would regulate economic conduct and provide wealth and stability no longer seemed tenable. Economic facts seemed to belie competition's promises, and this led many in the fledgling economics profession to reject classical economic doctrines as flawed, naive and of little value in practice.[24] At the very least, economists had to admit the inadequacy of the intellectual tools they had been using to interpret economic facts and predict economic consequences. As Joseph Schumpeter wrote, this was a time in which 'there occurred breaks with tradition as distinct as we can ever expect to observe in what must always be fundamentally a continuous process'.[25] The turn away from liberal doctrine was perhaps most pronounced in Germany and Austria, where 'Manchesterism' became an epithet.

The crisis went to the very nature of economic knowledge. For some economists, the depression had not invalidated the basic methods of economics.

---

[24] For an overview, see Joseph A. Schumpeter, *History of Economic Analysis* 761–66 (New York, 1954).
[25] Ibid., 753.

The natural-science model remained valid, as did the deductive-theoretical process through which it generated knowledge, and the economists' task was still to discern universally-valid rules of economic conduct. The vast changes in economic life merely required further refinement and elaboration of the existing theoretical principles. This basic response had its most notable adherents in England, where Alfred Marshall was establishing a neoclassical orthodoxy, and in Austria, where marginal utility theory was providing new avenues of analysis.[26]

Other economists, however, interpreted this new data as proof of the fallacy of searching for universal principles of economic conduct. In particular, the German historical school argued that each '*Volk*' had its own behavioral characteristics, as did each era, and that these should be the focus of economic thought and research rather than the search for universally-valid principles. In this view, the economist's primary task was to understand the history and evolution of economic conduct for a specific group at a particular time. The perspective was radically empiricist, rejecting the deductive methods of classical economics as irrelevant to real life.

The most dramatic confrontation between these two positions was the so-called *Methodenstreit* (methods controversy) between the Austrian Carl Menger, who emphasized the need for theoretical improvement, and Gustav Schmoller, leader of the German historical school.[27] This conflict was accompanied by high levels of personal animosity between the two schools, and neither side shied away from vituperation. As a result, it supplied drama for economists throughout Europe for several decades.

This split among European economists had important consequences for thinking about competition and its regulation. The historical school came to dominate the economics profession in Germany and to reject compromise with other schools, and its dominance there lasted until at least the First World War. Elsewhere its influence remained secondary, albeit sometimes significant. The result was a 'nationalizing' of the economics profession and the virtual isolation of German economists.

In addition to neo-classicism and historicism, a third response to the apparent inadequacies of conventional economic thought centered on the work of Karl Marx.[28] Marx argued that both historicist and neo-classical forms of

[26] See *The Marginal Revolution in Economics* (R. D. Collison Black et al eds., Durham, N.C., 1973).

[27] For discussion of the conflict, see, e.g., Gerhard Ritzel, *Schmoller versus Menger: Eine Analyse des Methodenstreits im Hinblick auf den Historismus in der Nationalökonomie* (Diss. Basel, 1951), and Reginald Hansen, 'Der Methodenstreit in den Sozialwissenschaften zwischen Gustav Schmoller und Karl Menger—seine wissenschaftshistorische und wissenschaftstheoretische Bedeutung', in *Beiträge zur Entwicklung der Wissenschaftstheorie im 19. Jahrhundert* 137 (Alwin Diemer, ed., Meisenheim am Glahn, 1968).

[28] For a recent, broad-gauge review of Marxian doctrine and its relations with 'mainstream' economics, see Ernesto Scrapanti & Stefano Zamagni, *An Outline of the History of Economic Thought*, ch.4 (Oxford, 1993).

analysis were fundamentally flawed because they failed to appreciate the class factors in economic development. For Marxists, depressions were endemic to capitalism, and thus the only means of avoiding them was to change the economic system. According to Marx, the means of production had to be controlled by the political process, and economic planning should replace competition as the economy's steering mechanism. Although few academic economists were Marxists during this period, all economists were confronted with Marxist thought, and by the 1890s many were wrestling with the issues it raised and accepting at least some of its claims.

The effects of this dissatisfaction and disarray among economists were not limited to the profession itself, but altered the roles of economic thought. For example, it destroyed the symbiotic relationship between liberalism and economics that for much of the century had played such an important role in strengthening each. Economics and liberalism had developed together, sharing the same basic conceptual apparatus and making the same claims regarding its utility. In the 1880s and 1890s, however, neither liberalism nor economics seemed to benefit from the relationship, and the 'alliance between liberalism and economics was broken'.[29] In the following decades this split would weaken both.

Loss of confidence in the liberal image of the economy also left popular opinion without a framework for understanding the depression, and the result was a search for scapegoats. Liberals were a particularly popular target. Liberal economic doctrine had always had opponents who emphasized the potential harms of an unregulated economy, but liberalism's triumphant mid-century march had muffled their shouts. When liberalism faltered, however, its opponents attacked with new fury.

Such attacks focused on banks, 'mobile capital', 'big industry', and Jews.[30] The basic theme in this search for scapegoats was that the power and ruthlessness of one or another of these groups was causing economic suffering. Their members were accused of controlling economic developments for their own benefit and thereby exploiting the rest of the population. The theme would echo tragically a few decades later.

3. The emergence of social issues

The desire to assign blame was fanned by the growing awareness of the harms associated with 'unbridled competition'. As the image of the invisible hand lost its magical hold during the 1870s, the social consequences of capitalism acquired a new poignancy. Although not unknown earlier, they had been

---

[29] Schumpeter, *History of Economic Analysis*, 765–66.

[30] Fritz Stern discusses these themes in detail in the context of a biography of Bismarck's personal banker, Gerson Bleichröder. Fritz Stern, *Gold and Iron: Bismarck, Bleichröder, and the Building of the German Empire* (New York, 1984).

more easily ignored (at least in the middle and upper classes) because competition was expected to solve the problem—eventually. But if, as had now become clear, competition was not a magical potion that would eventually produce economic well-being for all, its social harms became more difficult to accept.

Because liberals believed that competition and economic growth would cure social ills, they generally paid little attention to 'social' issues. Liberalism's long dominance of progressive thought in Europe thus left a kind of intellectual vacuum regarding these issues, leaving it to 'socialists' of various stripes to structure thought about the social consequences of industrialization and liberalism and create the political movements to remedy them. It also meant that social reformers were forced to define themselves by their opposition to liberalism, and this oppositional definition became a *leitmotif* of European thought for more than a century.

Early in the century utopian socialists such as the Scottish industrialist Robert Owen and the French Saint-Simonians brought the potential social consequences of the factory system to public attention. They recognized the harms of dislocation, family disruption and poor living conditions that often accompanied a 'liberal' society, and they offered solutions designed primarily to maintain community structures and human values in the face of industrialization. The utopians seldom achieved significant political power, but their moral vision and their goal of a communitarian response to industrialization influenced their successors.

By the 1860s a new and more aggressive brand of socialism had emerged. The lack of social concern among political leaders convinced Karl Marx and others that the only way to improve social conditions was for the masses to acquire the political power necessary for them to protect their own interests. They began, therefore, to organize workers and to preach the need for class solidarity and political action.

Toward the end of the century a third category of 'socialists' emerged, seeking social improvement within existing institutions. Groups such as the Fabian socialists in England and the *Kathedersozialisten* (socialists of the lectern) in Germany and Austria retained some degree of confidence in the market and in parliamentary democracy, but they believed that government had to do much more to protect and provide for the poor and to counteract the social consequences of industrialization. Each of these groups sought to limit the harms associated with 'too much competition'.

4. Community: a new context for competition

This increased concern with the social consequences of economic progress reflected—and contributed to—an increasing emphasis on 'society as community'. The liberal image of society as an amalgam of individuals seeking their own interests became less attractive as societal images based on community and on social solidarity gained favor. Frequently associated with nationalist tendencies, these images were more influential in central Europe than in the traditional strongholds of liberalism in England and France, but they grew in power throughout Europe.

The German sociologist Ferdinand Tönnies captured the change most vividly in his distinction between *Gemeinschaft* and *Gesellschaft*.[31] In a *Gesellschaft*, he said, people were held together by formal bonds of law and interdependence in the face of external threats. The social unit was a means to individual ends. A *Gemeinschaft*, in contrast, was organic; individuals belonged together and functioned as parts of an integrated whole. For Tönnies, the social and economic changes of the nineteenth century had led away from *Gemeinschaft* and toward *Gesellschaft*, and socialism was the only available means of moving back in the other direction.

These emerging communitarian ideals confronted liberalism's image of competition. For liberals, competition was a means of improving social and individual well-being, but from a *Gemeinschaft* perspective, competition loomed as an enemy. *Gemeinschaft* required co-operation and the accommodation of individual interests to the commonweal, but competition, in contrast, demanded that individuals be concerned first and foremost with their own self-interest. Moreover, while a *Gemeinschaft* protected its weaker members, a *Gesellschaft* told them to work harder.

From this communitarian perspective, competition looked suspiciously like exploitation. The combined effect of competition and of political and economic inequality was that the strong would get stronger, the weak would get weaker, and the strong would use their strength to take from the weak.

5. Competition as culprit

By the turn of the twentieth century competition looked far different than it had a quarter of a century before. Its potential benefits had been too well demonstrated to be called into question, but now images and consequences other than purely economic ones were in the forefront of many minds. Competition had become associated with large, powerful firms rather than with personal liberties. Giant factories and proletarian squalor were more prominent on its historical palimpsest than were romantic images of the individual entrepreneur. Competition was implicated in creating the social divisions that were so troublesome, and, at the same time, it was divorced from other conceptions and images that previously had justified and made it more attractive. Competition had grown too prominent in too many ways; it had carried too much of a burden; and it had too obviously and painfully failed to satisfy the expectations that had been placed in it.

---

[31] Ferdinand Tönnies, *Gemeinschaft und Gesellschaft* (Leipzig, 1887).

G. THE LEGAL DIMENSION

Toward the end of the nineteenth century these political, economic and social forces combined to urge the idea that competition should no longer be left to itself. Competition's benefits were recognized, but so were its fragility and its dangers, and calls increased for governments to both protect it and control it. But could laws be used to protect it? And, if so, how? Responses to those questions were shaped by existing legal traditions and institutions, some of which were European in scope, others national. I here identify some of the more important trans-European factors involved, leaving examination of specific national factors for later chapters.

1. Contributions of the *Ius Commune*

The tradition of the *Ius Commune* played an important role in this shaping process. Developed from the study of Roman law during the late medieval period, this tradition continued as a central feature of continental legal systems until the advent of the modern codes during the nineteenth century.[32] It carried legal principles and associated values and patterns of thought without which competition law is likely to have developed, if at all, along quite different lines. Three norms, in particular, were at the center of this influence.[33]

One was the just price norm, which provided that for any transaction there was a 'just' price and that significant deviation from that price could invalidate the transaction.[34] This norm has played a key role in the relationship between law and economic conduct since the late medieval period, and in some legal systems it remains significant today.

Its importance in setting the stage for our story rests primarily on three factors. First, it firmly imprinted on European legal consciousness the idea that market transactions were subject to concepts of justice. From as early as the twelfth century and into the modern period it required that virtually *all* market transactions be evaluated from that perspective. As a result, whether participating in the market or concerned with regulating it, Europeans became accustomed to looking at market transactions through normative lenses.

---

[32] It is perhaps more than coincidental that the dominant influence in the development of the European competition law tradition has also been the country in which the *Ius Commune* retained its direct force longest. The *Ius Commune* was authoritative in many of the German states until German unification in 1871, and it remained so for many purposes in the German empire until the German Civil Code (the BGB) became effective on January 1, 1900.

[33] I have elsewhere explored the evolution of these norms during the High Middle Ages. See David J. Gerber, 'Prometheus Born: The High Middle Ages and the Relationship between Law and Economic Conduct', 38 *St. Louis U.L. Rev.* 673 (1994).

[34] See Reinhard Zimmermann, *The Law of Obligations: Roman Foundations of the Civil Law Tradition* 255–70 (Capetown, 1990). James Gordley pursues the evolution of thought in this area throughout *The Philosophical Origins of Modern Contract Doctrine* (Oxford, 1991).

Second, this concept focused attention on price in assessing whether transactions were 'just', and thus price became the central 'signal' or 'indicator' of economic justice. In general, a transaction was just if the price was just. As a consequence, the process of determining whether a price was just became a fixture of thought about the market. Moreover, the need to apply this just price norm ingrained the assumption that there always was such a price; it became an established societal expectation.

And, finally, the just price norm was legally enforceable. It was not merely a moral principle discussed mainly by philosophers, nor was it just an issue of ethics. The intertwining of morality and law in relation to economic justice that became such an important part of the European legal tradition in the High Middle Ages imbued it with *both legal and moral force*.[35] The just price norm was enforced in courts of law, and it was widely used as the basis for legislation at many levels of government.

The concept of usury (German, *Wucher*) played a similar role. In continental legal systems, this concept generally has had a far broader meaning than it does in contemporary English usage, where it refers to the charging of excessive interest. Its basic message has been that a transaction in which one party knowingly exploits the weakness or inability of the other is invalid.[36] Drawing from the same mixture of religion and law that informed the just price norm, this broad concept of usury was of much practical significance wherever the *Ius Commune* was applied, and in countries such as Germany it remains important even today.[37]

Its primary significance for the development of competition law was its legacy of sensitivity to inequalities in bargaining position. It made the issue of whether one party was 'exploiting' another a basic category of thought about economic transactions. This was, for example, a common theme in late nineteenth century controversies over the inequalities resulting from industrialization—the same controversies that in countries such as Austria and Germany spawned discussion of competition legislation.

A third norm of the *Ius Commune* that was important in preparing the way for competition law was the prohibition of monopoly. The *Ius Commune* tradition carried several provisions of Roman law that prohibited monopolizing trade.[38] These provisions typically imposed penalties for manipulating markets in certain goods, particularly necessities, and they frequently were used as the basis for local statutes.

---

[35] See Gerber, 'Prometheus Born', 714–20.

[36] See Zimmermann, *Law of Obligations*, 153–77. The evolution of thought about usury is treated in Benjamin Nelson, *The Idea of Usury* (2d. ed., Chicago, 1969).

[37] See, e.g., German Civil Code (BGB) §138.

[38] These provisions and their subsequent influence are discussed in detail in Roman Piotrowski, *Cartels and Trusts: Their Origin and Historical Development From the Economic and Legal Aspects* (London, 1933). See also Gerber, 'Prometheus Born', 720–33.

Conceptually, this monopoly norm is related to the idea of competition law. Although it treated only specific forms of market manipulation, it was directed at the use of market power to distort market processes, and it helped to imbed in European legal consciousness the perception that such conduct was illegal. The influence of the monopoly norm on the evolution of competition law in Europe should not, however, be overestimated, because for several centuries preceding the nineteenth century most important markets were heavily regulated by governments and intermediary organizations such as guilds, and thus little attention was paid to the monopolization issue.

Taken together, these three *Ius Commune* norms transmitted and anchored concepts and values that would help to shape the European competition law tradition. They were studied, albeit with varying degrees of intensity, wherever Roman law was studied, and even into the nineteenth century that included much of Europe. Moreover, they were incorporated into statutes and other regulatory measures throughout Europe.

2. Price manipulation statutes

During the nineteenth century the *Ius Commune* tradition lost its status as a formal 'source of law' in much of Europe, to be replaced by legislation which, in turn, frequently incorporated its basic norms. Statutes prohibiting certain forms of price manipulation by merchants were part of this process. Often modelled on the Roman law monopoly provisions we have just discussed, these enactments were forerunners of modern competition laws. The most prominent example was Article 419 of the French Penal Code of 1810, which was introduced in an effort to prevent the manipulation of shortages after the Napoleonic wars, particularly the hoarding of necessities. Although originally enacted in a pre-industrial setting and aimed at market manipulation by merchants, these statutes were often expanded later in the century to apply to the new phenomena generated by industrialization.

These statutes played various roles in the development of competition law in Europe. In some countries, they reinforced the perceptions and values that condemned exploitation and other forms of competitive distortion, and in so doing they encouraged more comprehensive attempts to deal with these problems. In other contexts, however, such statutes may have reduced incentives to enact more comprehensive legislation to protect competition. The French provision referred to above seems, for example, to have had such an effect. Opponents of comprehensive competition legislation frequently argued that its existence precluded the need for such legislation, and the old provisions were not repealed until such a competition statute was finally enacted—in 1986!

3. Law and economic freedom

A third strand of nineteenth century legal experience that was to inform the development of competition law was legislation to create and protect economic freedom. As we have noted, legislation eliminating or reducing governmental and guild restrictions on economic activity was enacted in many parts of Europe during the early and middle parts of the century, and it often acquired major practical and political significance. Such statutes were the central means by which the middle classes achieved economic opportunity, and as such they were a focus of concern not only of lawyers and bureaucrats, but of virtually all important political and economic actors. As one historian puts it, 'The battle for economic freedom (*Gewerbefreiheit*) is *the theme* of the first two-thirds of the nineteenth century [emphasis in original]'.[39]

This type of legislation represented a step toward modern conceptions of competition law. It established economic freedom as a right, and it carried the 'constitutional' message that governments had a responsibility to protect the *right to participate in the economic process.* The conceptual step from protecting the right to participate in the economic process to protecting the process itself was not a long one.

Moreover, the discourse in which such laws were imbedded supported such a step. The campaigns for laws protecting economic freedom emphasized that such freedoms had very practical benefits—they were to increase material prosperity *by increasing competition.* Competition came to be seen as *the mechanism* by which economic freedoms were to generate the economic progress that they promised! Enhancement of competition came to be accepted as a justification for such laws, and that justification could readily be applied to the idea of protecting the process of competition directly.

4. Protecting competitors—unfair competition laws

Laws relating to 'unfair competition' played a similar role in preparing the way for competition law. While liberals opposed government intervention in the economy, they supported the use of law to protect individual competitors from unfairness.[40] On one level, this was a postulate of fairness. The liberal program was premised on the claim that the economic process had to be open to all on the basis of at least formal equality. Competition was a game that had to be played according to the rules, and, consequently, unfair competition had to be combated.

---

[39] Harald Steindl, 'Die Einführung der Gewerbefreiheit', in 3/III *Handbuch der Quellen und Literatur der neueren Europäischen Privatrechtsgeschichte: Das 19. Jahrhundert/Gesetzgebung zu den privatrechtlichen Sondergebieten* 3527, 3540 (Helmut Coing, ed., Munich, 1986).

[40] Economic liberalism emphasized the need to protect the 'purity' of competition. See, e.g., Franz Wieacker, *Privatrechtsgeschichte der Neuzeit* 544 (Göttingen, 1967).

On a more immediate and practical level, unfair competition laws were necessary to fill a regulatory void left by the elimination of guilds and similar organizations. Guilds typically had well-developed procedures for minimizing conflicts among their members and penalizing conduct that would give one member an undue or unearned advantage over another. Moreover, since guilds depended on political support, they sought to assure that their activities were perceived as furthering the public interest, and they often strictly enforced rules to prohibit their members from engaging in deceptive or other practices that might undermine this perception.

With the demise of guilds in many areas during the nineteenth century, unfair competition law regimes took over these functions, seeking to protect competitors against fraud, misrepresentation and other forms of unfair conduct.[41] The French courts took the lead, beginning as early as the 1820s. Although French legal theory denied that courts could 'make law,' French courts used the scanty tort provisions of the *Code Civil* to develop a broad framework of legal principles relating to unfair competition,[42] and these ideas spread throughout much of continental Europe during the course of the century.

Consistent with liberal ideology, unfair competition law was—and continues to be—understood as private law. Such regimes provide enterprises with a right to sue their competitors for impairment of their capacity to compete. These norms are not enforced by government agencies, and they do not claim to protect society or consumers other than indirectly.

Nevertheless, unfair competition laws were associated with the idea of 'purifying' the competitive process, thus encouraging the perception that the process required protection, and this, in turn, supported the idea of a generalized legal regime to provide such protection. Unfair competition laws also helped to sculpt the regulatory space for competition laws, because their existence obviated the need for competition laws to be concerned with fairness issues.

5. Administrative law

The rise of administrative law, particularly during the second half of the century, was also critical to the emergence of competition law.[43] As we have seen,

---

[41] The best survey of this on a European scale that I have found is Siegbert Lammel, 'Recht zur Ordnung des Wettbewerbs', in 3/III *Handbuch der Quellen und Literatur der neueren Europäischen Privatrechtsgeschichte: Das 19. Jahrhundert/Gesetzgebung zu den privatrechtlichen Sondergebieten* 3749–3852 (Helmut Coing, ed., Munich, 1986).

[42] For discussion, see Walter J. Derenberg, 'The Influence of the French Code Civil on the Modern Law of Unfair Competition', 4 *Am. J. Comp. L.* 1 (1955).

[43] There is a comprehensive comparative look at administrative law in Europe in Jürgen Schwarze, *European Administrative Law* (London, 1992). This is an abridged version of the same author's *Europäisches Verwaltungsrecht* (Baden-Baden, 1988).

industrialization bred expanded government, and the rapid growth of government during that period spawned a correspondingly rapid development of legal thought and institutions focused on controlling and directing administrative activity.

Administrative law became a distinct component of the legal system in most, if not all, European legal systems. It acquired its own methodology and often its own institutions (such as administrative court systems). In so doing it provided a new tool for dealing with new problems and a means of overcoming the conceptual and attitudinal rigidities associated with more traditional areas of law. The role it sculpted for administrative activity would become central to most European competition law regimes.

6. Conceptions of law and its roles

Finally, the nineteenth century supplied general conceptions of law and attitudes toward its roles that shaped the development of competition law in the twentieth century. At the beginning of the nineteenth century the very idea of general laws to protect the process of competition would have been difficult, if not impossible, to conceive; by the end of the century, that was no longer true. That idea presupposed conceptions of the role of legislation that were not established until the latter part of the century. Prior to that time, legislation typically was used either for narrow, specific goals or to codify existing customs and norms, but seldom, if ever, to create new general laws to regulate a new area of life.

One set of obstacles to a broader view of legislation was located in conservative, traditionalist thought. Through much of the nineteenth century, there was resistance to expansive uses of legislation on the grounds that they would disrupt well-established principles and patterns of life.[44] For many in the ruling elites this was a powerful argument. Others used a weaker form of the argument, accepting that legislative changes might be necessary, but contending that legislators generally had insufficient knowledge of the consequences of legislation to justify intervention. Broad-scale legislation was justified only when the time was ripe, and there was a strong presumption against such ripeness. Powerholders also had political incentives to support such views: new forms of legislation were often disruptive and potentially destabilizing, and the ruling elites had little taste for such disruption.

Liberals also resisted expansive new uses of legislation, but on other grounds. For them, such legislation was suspect because it might interfere with political and economic freedoms, and thus they placed high requirements on legislative projects. Liberal theory required that legislation be

---

[44] This was a basic thrust of Friedrich Carl von Savigny and his 'historical school of law'. For discussion, see Wolfgang Fikentscher, III *Methoden des Rechts: Mitteleuropäischer Rechtskreis* 37–77 (Tübingen, 1975).

justified by well-developed, reasoned arguments that had proven successful in actual cases. As a result, liberals generally rejected legislation outside of the traditional private law area.

There were also conceptual obstacles to the idea of using law to protect competition. As we have seen, the concept of competition led a relatively furtive existence until the middle of the century, and it would have been difficult to conceive legislation to protect that was dimly perceived and little understood. This was particularly true because of contemporary expectations relating to the language of legislation. Under the influence of German 'legal science', European legal thought at the end of the century was accustomed to demanding a high degree of conceptual precision, particularly in general legislation.[45] Concepts were to be not only precise, but also systematically related according to principles of deductive logic. A law to protect competition law could not satisfy such requirements—the idea was too new. Its language could not be conceptually precise, at least not in the same way that private law could, because it could not draw on the decades, even centuries, of analytical attention that private law enjoyed.[46]

Similarly, the sharp cleavage between 'public law' and 'private law' that was a prominent feature of late nineteenth century legal thought was an obstacle to the development of competition law, because competition law does not fit easily into either sphere.[47] It is not easily conceived as private law, because it does not focus on injury by one private party to the private rights of another. Yet it does not fit easily into the category of public law, because it does not protect the rights of private parties against the state.

By the end of the century, some of these obstacles to legislation were breaking down. There was growing familiarity and comfort with the idea of using broad-scale codes or code-like legislation to deal with major areas of societal concern. Moreover, the emphasis on precise conceptualization and careful deductive structuring in legislation was beginning to wane. At the same time, the competitive process became better understood and economists were developing a more sophisticated language for rendering it.

[45] See Mathias Reimann, 'Nineteenth Century German Legal Science', 31 *Boston Coll. L. Rev.* 842 (1990).

[46] See Alan Watson, *The Making of the Civil Law* 99–143 (Cambridge, Mass., 1981).

[47] This cleavage is based on the notion that private law regulates the relationships among private persons, while public law regulates the relationship between persons and the state, and that the two spheres have little in common. As public law developed during the late nineteenth century, it tended to be treated as almost a separate world of thought and practice, with different professors, courses of studies and institutions, and this distance has remained an important feature of continental European law.

H. SETTING THE STAGE FOR COMPETITION LAW

By the closing years of the nineteenth century, the stage had been set for a new type of law that would protect competition. The idea of competition law had become familiar, so there was a recognized 'something' to protect, and competition had demonstrated its potential benefits, so there were reasons to protect it. Yet the harms from 'uncontrolled' competition had become evident, so there were also reasons to control it.

Political decision-makers are not inclined to incur costs and risks in order to protect something with which neither they nor their constituents are familiar. At the beginning of the nineteenth century, competition was not a widely-recognized 'something'. It was, at best, a vague idea in the minds of a few. The nineteenth century gave it form and profile. During the course of the century, Europeans learned what it was and became accustomed to talking and thinking about it as a distinct process. Significant segments of the population came to perceive in the private gain-seeking decisions of individual economic actors a *process* with more or less predictable contours and consequences. This satisfied one requirement for the genesis of a general legal regime to protect competition.

The middle decades of the century fulfilled a second; they demonstrated the enormous potential of the competitive process. 'Competition' had worked; experience had demonstrated its power. It *could* generate extraordinary wealth! That was the lesson of the 1850s and 1860s, and from then on its immense *potential* value was unquestionable. Consequently, when the process was threatened toward the end of the century, a natural response was to defend and protect it.

Yet nineteenth century experience with competition was contradictory. The last decades of the century had revealed how unreliable competition could be and what harms 'excessive' competition could cause. Its wealth-producing effects seemed fickle, appearing to operate only under perplexingly opaque circumstances. Moreover, whatever prosperity was created for the few had to be paid for, it appeared, by the misery of large, and rapidly growing, segments of the population. Not surprisingly, those sensitive to such harms sought ways to control the process that was causing them.

This led to a fundamental ambivalence regarding competition. From some perspectives, it was predominantly good, even godlike in its promise of prosperity. From others it was the incarnation of evil. One set of experiences and values seemed to demand its protection, while another called for its control. How one viewed competition depended on what one was looking at and on the experiential and conceptual lenses one used.

The nineteenth century has had another—and frequently unnoticed—impact on the evolution of competition law: it provided the foundation for a competition law tradition that would become trans-European in scope and content. The process of competition came to be understood in similar ways throughout Western Europe at roughly the same time and in the same economic and social contexts. Industrialization and its concomitants had transformed most of Western and Central Europe by the end of the century, bringing with them the same types of material benefits and similar changes in patterns of life and thought. Moreover, the key economic events that structured the interpretation of economic society paid little heed to national boundaries: the mid-century boom and the Great Depression that followed it were European events far more than they were national events.

Similarly, the same basic conceptual, moral and legal systems structured thought and attitudes about the competitive process throughout Europe. For example, the doctrines of liberalism that gave competition its identity and assured its familiarity knew no national boundaries. Likewise, the values and ideas of social justice that developed in response to industrialization—from Christian concepts to Marxist ideology—were trans-European, varying in detail from one national system to another, but alike in basic structures.

The traditions and perceptions of the nineteenth century thus provided the basic elements necessary for the development of competition law. Moreover, the trans-European texture of these nineteenth century experiences made possible the evolution of a competition law tradition during the twentieth that would be European in scope.

III

Fin-de-Siècle *Austria: Conceiving Competition Law*

During the last decade of the nineteenth century a set of ideas was articulated in Austria that was to become the original core of the European competition law tradition. Representing an uneasy alliance of liberalism and administrative controls, they were the product of new and creative thinking about the uses of law. In this chapter I examine the shaping of this new conception of law, the factors that generated support for it, and the circumstances that (temporarily) defeated it.[1]

That this important step in European legal thought was taken in turn-of-the-century Vienna is hardly surprising. The capital of the Austro-Hungarian empire was then an extraordinarily fertile intellectual milieu that produced powerful impulses in many areas of art and science.[2] Sigmund Freud was reshaping thought about the human psyche; Gustav Mahler and Arnold Schoenberg were creating new forms of music; Carl Menger and Eugen Böhm-Bawerk were developing a fundamentally new approach to economics; and Ludwig Wittgenstein was preparing to chart a new course for philosophy. Conceiving a new form of law was but one creative impulse among many.

The structures and experiences of late nineteenth century Austrian society set the stage for this creative act. That society was suddenly confronted with conflicts that its political institutions were either unwilling or unable (or both) to address effectively, and a liberal elite was caught between awareness of the need to respond to these disintegrative forces and institutional and attitudinal resistance to such a response. Economic experience during the late nineteenth century was interwoven with structural factors in ways that generated profound ambivalence about the roles of economic competition in society.

---

[1] Scholars generally have paid little attention to the Austrian origins of European competition law. For two important exceptions, see Bernhard Grossfeld, 'Zur Kartellrechtsdiskussion vor dem Ersten Weltkrieg', in IV *Wissenschaft und Kodifikation des Privatrechts im 19. Jahrhundert* 255–96 (Helmut Coing & Walter Wilhelm, eds., Frankfurt a.M., 1979) and Helmut Schulte, *Das Österreichische Kartellrecht vor 1938* (Diss. Münster, 1979). I have treated this part of the story in somewhat greater detail in David J. Gerber, 'The Origins of the European Competition Law Tradition in *Fin-de-Siècle* Austria', 36 *Am. J. Leg. Hist.* 405 (1992).

[2] For evocations of the Austrian intellectual milieu during this period, see Carl E. Schorske, *Fin-de-Siècle Vienna* (New York, 1980); Alan Janik & Stephen Toulmin, *Wittgenstein's Vienna* (New York, 1973); and *The Viennese Enlightenment* (Mark Francis, ed., New York, 1985).

A. THE POLITICAL FRAMEWORK

The political situation in which competition law ideas took shape was marked by the emergence of powerful societal conflicts in the midst of institutional rigidity and complexity. Liberal, conservative, bureaucratic and various nationalist elements were all vying for power within an anachronistic and highly complicated institutional framework, and combat between the forces of change and of continuity was nowhere more visible or more intense.

The empire—and, above all, the emperor—represented continuity. At the end of the nineteenth century Austria was a constitutional monarchy and part of the Austro-Hungarian empire.[3] The keystone of this structure was the emperor,[4] Franz Joseph, who had been emperor since 1848 and symbolized centuries of tradition. By the 1890s, his long reign had generated respect and a kind of reverence across the many lands of the empire. He also had enormous power. Although he was occasionally forced to accede to demands for a more constitutional system, there were few real limits on his power even at his death in 1916.

The bureaucracy was the other pillar of continuity.[5] For centuries—and particularly since the administrative reforms of Maria Theresa and Joseph II in the late eighteenth century—the imperial bureaucracy had applied detailed regulations to many areas of societal life. This ingrained an expectation that government officials would make most important decisions within the empire. The growing social, ideological, and political strife during the closing years of the century further highlighted the bureaucracy's role as a source and symbol of stability and dependability; it was generally seen as the only political institution that might be capable of effectively responding to these problems.

The Austrian legislature could offer the prospect of political change and democracy, but it had limited power to move in that direction. It was important enough to be a repository of aspirations and a stage for symbolic political acts, but it was not yet powerful enough to play a role in resolving society's conflicts. Moreover, it was not yet even particularly representative.[6] Deputies to the lower house were elected by estates. Suffrage extended only to males,

[3] Austria and Hungary were separate entities for many purposes, each, for example, having its own legislature and conferring its own nationality, but an intricate set of procedures coordinated the policies and activities in areas such as foreign relations.
[4] The Habsburg monarchy in the 1890s was still an imposing edifice. Although it had lost important territories in the course of the nineteenth century, notably in Italy, the monarchy still included, in addition to present-day Austria and Hungary, much of what are now the Czech and Slovak republics as well as significant territories in the former Soviet Union, Poland, Romania, Italy, and the former Yugoslavia.
[5] For discussion, see William M. Johnston, *The Austrian Mind: An Intellectual and Social History 1848–1938* 45–75 (Berkeley, 1972) and Robert A. Kann, *A Study in Austrian Intellectual History* 12–145 (New York, 1960).
[6] See Robert A. Kann, *A History of the Habsburg Empire: 1526–1918* 329–42 (Berkeley, 1974).

and there was a poll tax that in the 1870s effectively restricted participation in the electoral process to the propertied classes and that was only gradually eliminated during the following decades. Members of the upper house were appointed by the emperor, primarily from the landed nobility.

B. DIVISIONS AND CONFLICTS WITHIN AUSTRIAN SOCIETY

The ethnic, national, and class cleavages that would eventually overwhelm Austrian society were beginning to rend it in the 1890s, although the irreversibility of this process and the imminence of its denouement were not yet obvious. Nationality was the most prominent of these disintegrative forces, and conflicts between nationality groups tended to feed other societal antagonisms. Austria traditionally had been dominated by its German-speaking population, which was concentrated in the territory of modern Austria and in parts of Bohemia.[7] The royal house itself was German, the capital was a German city, and the bureaucracy, the upper classes and the educational, religious and military leadership were culturally and linguistically German.

Other national groups within Austria, such as the Czechs, Poles, Moravians, and Slovenians had long endured second-class status, but by the 1880s they were demanding improvements in this status. Many sought increased political rights and increased recognition of their cultures and their languages. The result was a growing animosity between the non-Germans, who sought power, and the Austro-Germans, who sought to protect the rights, privileges, and benefits they enjoyed.

Nationalism fed on class stratification, which was exceptionally rigid by Western European standards, with lineage virtually the sole determinant of position within the highest levels of society. The great families still lived primarily on landed estates and controlled not only social status, but much of the country's wealth as well. A *haute bourgeoisie* consisting of high-ranking bureaucrats, professors, lawyers, doctors and the upper echelons of industry and finance constituted a second social stratum, which dominated policymaking as well as economic, cultural and intellectual life and which was 'unique in Europe for its aesthetic cultivation, personal refinement and psychological sensitivity'.[8] Liberalism was its credo.[9]

A lower middle class consisting primarily of artisans, shopkeepers, and lower civil servants played a pivotal role in Austrian society during the late nineteenth century.[10] At mid-century relatively passive, its members had by

---

[7] In 1880, 37 per cent of the population of Austria was German-speaking. William A. Jenks, *Austria under the Iron Ring 1879–1893* 4 (Charlottesville, Va., 1965).

[8] Schorske, *Vienna*, 298.

[9] See Georg Franz, *Liberalismus: Die Deutschliberale Bewegung in der Habsburgischen Monarchie* (Munich, 1955).

[10] For discussion, see Schorske, *Vienna*, 65–68.

the 1890s come to distrust and often despise the liberal bourgeoisie that was above them and to fear those below them, and this distrust and fear developed just as the class was being enfranchised. This class provided the electoral substrate for the anti-semitic, anti-big business Christian Socialist party that stormed the Austrian stage in the late 1880s.

At the bottom of the scale were the peasants and the agricultural and industrial laborers. Excluded from the classes above them, they became increasingly aware during the 1880s and 1890s of their disadvantages and of their potential power to force redress of at least some of these disadvantages. In particular, the urban workers came to perceive industrialists and liberals as their exploiters and their natural enemies, and they generally espoused socialist ideologies.

A large Jewish population, particularly in Vienna, added another element to this picture.[11] By the turn of the century Viennese Jews were powerful and sometimes dominant in banking and industry as well as in the professions and in cultural and intellectual life.[12] There were also many Jews among the shopkeepers of the cities.

C. AUSTRIAN LIBERALISM: IDEOLOGY AND SOCIAL CLASS

By the 1890s, the divisions within Austrian society had become often bitter and sometimes violent antagonisms, and the main target of resentment was the Austro-German upper-middle class. The non-German nationalities resented the Austro-Germans because of their dominance of cultural and economic affairs; the lower classes resented them because of their economic and political power; and the upper class cared little for their interference in domains of Austrian life long reserved for the nobility. The large Jewish contingent in this group added a religious component to this resentment and provided a convenient target for all who felt aggrieved. Jewish dominance in banking created rancor among virtually all classes, and among the lower middle classes this combined with fear of competition from and exploitation by Jewish shopkeepers to create the virulent anti-semitism of the 1890s.

This resentment of the Austro-German upper middle class was important in the development of competition law ideas because of the close identification of that class with liberal values. Here liberals constituted a social-political-economic class rather than merely a political orientation, and the term 'liberals' was often used to refer to the entire class. As a consequence, liberalism—and, hence, values such as economic freedom—came to be seen by many as the source of all of society's ills. As Carl Schorske has put it,

[11] See generally, e.g., *The Jews of Austria: Essays on their Life, History and Destruction* (Josef Fraenkel, ed., London, 1967).

[12] See, e.g., Herbert Matis, *Österreichs Wirtschaft 1848 bis 1913: Konjunkturelle Dynamik und Gesellschaftlicher Wandel im Zeitalter Franz Josephs I*. 409–10 (Berlin, 1972).

The liberals had conjured up new forces and new claimants to political participation: Slavic nationalists, Socialists, Pan-German anti-semites, Christian Social anti-semites. They neither integrated these new movements into the legal order nor could they satisfy their demands. The conflicting groups may have had different heavens, but they shared the same hell: the rule of the Austro-German liberal middle class.[13]

Thus social, ethnic, and religious resentments were all projected onto the 'liberal' class.

D. THE RISE AND FALL OF THE LIBERALS

The fortunes of this class were thus intertwined with the fate of competition as both idea and social force, and the generation that created and supported the concept of competition law in Austria had contradictory experiences of competition and economic freedom. Nowhere did competition more triumphantly succeed and then more ignominiously fail than in Austria in the second half of the nineteenth century, and, as a result, the idea of competition was first apotheosized and then vilified.

1. The Austrian economy

In assessing Austrian experience with competition, we need to note several characteristics of the Austrian economy. One was the continuing importance of the agricultural and artisanal sectors of the economy. More than 50 per cent of the population was still engaged in agriculture at the end of the century. Moreover, industrialization lagged well behind countries such as England and Germany, and it was very unevenly diffused throughout the empire, with most industry concentrated in Bohemia and in the area surrounding Vienna.[14] Artisans continued, therefore, to represent an important part of the economic picture, and this group was passionately opposed to the industrialization process and those—the liberals—who were associated with it.

Austrian industrial firms were often still owned at the end of the nineteenth century by families, and many were either foreign or Jewish or both. There was comparatively little public ownership of corporations, partly because Austrian corporate law placed more significant restrictions on the use of the corporate form than were found in many competing countries.[15] This pattern

---

[13] Schorske, *Vienna*, 303.

[14] For discussion, see Ivan T. Berend & Gyorgy Ranki, *Economic Development in East-Central Europe in the 19th and 20th Centuries* 112–19 (New York, 1974).

[15] For example, Austrian law required government approval to form a stock corporation (until 1899) and a high minimum capital investment. See generally Herbert Hofmeister, 'Die rechtlichen Aspekte der Industrialisierung in der Österreichisch-Ungarischen Monarchie 1873–1918', 24 *Österreichische Osthefte* 271, 279–82 (1982).

of ownership meant that the highest social classes had relatively little sympathy for industry (because they owned little of it) and it also provided ample grounds (nationality, social antagonism, antisemitism) for resentment against industry.

Due in part to such ownership restrictions, Austrian industry was also heavily dependent on bank financing to supply its capital needs.[16] Many of the banks operating in Austria were, again, either foreign or Jewish or both, and those that were not were generally owned by other Austro-Germans. Particularly by the end of the century, the influence of banks within Austrian industry was strong,[17] and it was a frequent subject of criticism.

Finally, Austrian firms were protected by tariffs designed to assure that intra-empire consumers would buy Austrian goods rather than the frequently superior manufactured goods emanating from northern and western Europe.[18] As a result, these firms tended to produce consumer products for sale within the empire, and they had little incentive to compete on international markets against their more advanced neighbors.

2. The (apparent) triumph of competition

Prior to 1860, liberals had little influence in Austrian politics; at mid-century the emperor and the aristocracy still ruled Austria. Those espousing the liberal agenda—primarily professionals, bureaucrats, and businessmen—enjoyed respect and at least mild support from most social classes,[19] but, in general, they remained outside the power structure.

Humiliating military defeats at the hands of France (1859) and Prussia (1866) were however to destroy confidence in aristocratic leadership, and, as a consequence, the emperor created Austria's first parliamentary democracy and handed the reigns of power to the liberals. As one observer has commented, '[n]ot their own internal strength, but the defeats of the old order at the hands of foreign enemies brought the liberals to the helm of state'.[20]

On gaining political power the liberals significantly reduced state intervention in the economy, and this move was soon followed by dramatic improvements in economic performance. The success of the Austrian economy from

---

[16] See David F. Good, *The Economic Rise of the Habsburg Empire 1750–1914* 206–18 (Berkeley, 1984); Richard L. Rudolph, *Banking and Industrialization in Austria-Hungary: The Role of Banks in the Industrialization of the Czech Crownlands, 1873–1914* 91–121 (Cambridge, 1976) and Eduard März, *Österreichische Industrie- und Bankpolitik in der Zeit Franz Josephs I.* 221–29 (Vienna, 1968).

[17] Alexander Gerschenkron has convincingly argued that this dependence on bank financing was a central characteristic of Austrian capitalism. See Alexander Gerschenkron, *Economic Backwardness in Historical Perspective* 14 (Cambridge, 1962).

[18] N. T. Gross, 'The Industrial Revolution in the Habsburg Monarchy', in *The Emergence of Industrial Societies* 228, 258–59 (Carlo Cipolla, ed., Brighton, 1976).

[19] Albert Fuchs, *Geistige Strömungen in Österreich 1867–1918* 6 (Vienna, 1949).

[20] Schorske, *Vienna*, 5.

1866 through 1873 seemed to prove to all levels of society the wisdom of allowing competition to reign unfettered, and the liberals took full credit for the Eldorado that their policies seemed to be producing.[21]

3. The Great Depression

But the economic depression that commenced in 1873 soon discredited liberal leadership, and the political power of the liberals continued to dwindle throughout the rest of the century.[22] The economic crisis of the 1870s was particularly dramatic in Austria.[23] Its objective impact was intensified by Austria's dependence on agriculture and on external financing for its industries, and its subjective force was heightened by its contrast with the speculative euphoria of the 1860s. The sharp decreases in production of the 1870s were followed in Austria as elsewhere in Europe by a long period of low prices, low profitability and slow production growth.[24]

As important as were the economic facts in conditioning thought about economic issues, the *interpretation* of those facts may have been more important. What people thought about *why* there was a depression and what it meant profoundly influenced their perceptions of the economic process. Here there was little ambiguity. Virtually everyone saw the economic misery as a failure of liberalism—proof that unrestrained competition was folly.

This interpretation of the economic facts penetrated all areas of society. Economists and other experts generally rejected 'Manchesterism' as a flawed and naive doctrine that might work well in theory, but was of little value in practice,[25] and this perspective became dominant within the educated classes. This view served the political goals of both Marxists and Christian Socialists, who forcefully propagated it among artisans and workers.

4. Reactions

Among the political and economic elites, this perceived failure of liberalism quickly led to calls for 'collective action', 'organization', and 'stability'.[26]

[21] Despite such claims, state intervention in the economic sphere undoubtedly contributed significantly to the economic successes. See Matis, *Österreichs Wirtschaft*, 37–38.

[22] See Schorske, *Vienna*, 5. In 1879, the emperor replaced the liberals with a coalition of their opponents. Count Taaffe, the new prime minister, unified the major enemies of the liberals—including artisans, laborers and conservatives—in a so-called 'Iron Ring' around liberal hopes, and this coalition remained in power until 1893.

[23] See Hans Rosenberg, 'Political and Social Consequences of the Great Depression of 1873–1896 in Central Europe', 13 *Econ. Hist. Rev.* 58 (1943).

[24] There has been a controversy in recent scholarship about the actual rate of production growth. For conflicting interpretations, see Good, *Economic Rise*, 170–76, and John Komlos, 'Is the Depression in Austria after 1873 a "Myth"?', 31 *Econ. Hist. Rev.* 287 (1978). See also generally S. B. Saul, *The Myth of the Great Depression* (2d. ed., London, 1985).

[25] See, e.g., Eugen von Böhm-Bawerk, 'The Austrian Economists', 1 *Annals of Am. Acad. of Pol. and Soc. Sci.* 361, 361–65 (1891).

[26] See Matis, *Österreichs Wirtschaft*, 367–413.

Events had turned competition into an enemy. Businesses reacted to the depression by foregoing independence and seeking help from the government and co-operation from each other. The traditions of Austrian mercantilism were given new impetus, as government involvement seemed to many to be the only way out of the economic doldrums.

Yet these governmental actions often also fanned resentments. There was, for example, a widespread perception among national groups other than the Austro-Germans that economic policy was systematically used by the latter to their own advantage. Such groups frequently cited high tariffs, for example, which favored producers over consumers and thus, since the producers were virtually always Austro-Germans, increased the economic power of that class.

Competition law ideas were developed just as Austria was emerging from this 'Great Depression'. The problems, issues and perceptions of that period thus dominated the experience of those who developed these ideas and supported the legislative proposals that grew out of them.

5. Social Forces

In addition to these economic factors, three powerful social forces combined to undermine the bourgeoisie's power and to create a deep ambivalence toward liberal values that would be reflected in Austrian competition law ideas. One was democratization. In 1882, the government expanded the franchise to include many members of the lower middle classes, hoping to secure the allegiance of the new voters. It had the opposite effect: it accelerated the development of mass parties based on national and class antagonisms.

A second was the nationalism that became virulent in the 1880s and 1890s. Each national group had its own party or faction, whose sole and avowed aim was to obtain better treatment for that group. Since the Austro-Germans held most of the power, the objective of the non-German groups was to force them to share it. Naturally, German nationalists responded by forming their own parties whose chief aim was to protect those interests.

Finally, industrialization created an industrial proletariat, particularly in Vienna, and thus provided the seedbed for Marxist parties. These parties urged workers to view employers, and the middle class in general, as their exploiters and thus their natural enemies. The Marxist-oriented Social Democratic party developed quickly beginning in the mid-1880s, and by the 1890s it had a significant voice in parliamentary politics. Moreover, it was a voice that seemed certain to increase in power.

E. CARTELS: PROMISES AND PROBLEMS

Austrian competition law ideas were generated in this tense situation by a 'liberal' class that was still powerful, but now threatened, and whose confidence in the central liberal tenet of economic competition had been undermined by events. In effect, it compensated for loss of confidence in one component of liberalism by supporting it with another. This effort took concrete form in response to a particular form of competitive restraint—cartels.

Cartels began to form in Austria in the late 1870s and continued to increase in number and in economic power through the first decade of the twentieth century.[27] Initially, they were formed in concentrated major industries such as coal and steel, but they gradually extended their reach throughout most areas of Austrian industry. By the 1890s they had become dominant forces in the economy, controlling production and prices in key industries.

These arrangements provided a co-operative mechanism for counteracting falling prices and excess capacity, and industrial leaders used them to stabilize economic conditions and increase the profitability of individual firms. As cartels grew in power, they also became increasingly aggressive, using their control over markets to induce membership, secure compliance with cartel decisions, raise prices to consumers and secure lower prices from suppliers.

Often closely tied to major corporations and industries such as iron and steel, banks spurred the rapid development of cartels as a means of bolstering their own financial stability.[28] The price-supporting features of cartels tended to protect their weaker members, and thus banks frequently urged the formation of cartels in order to reduce the likelihood of loan defaults by cartel members and enhance their own profitability and influence.

A protective tariff policy also encouraged cartel development.[29] Especially after 1878, tariffs excluded all or most foreign competition on many domestic markets and thus allowed cartels to raise prices higher than otherwise would have been possible. This made cartel membership more attractive and increased the power of cartels *vis-à-vis* their members.

Finally, several characteristics of the Austrian economy were conducive to cartel growth. For example, the purchasing power of most population groups within the empire was relatively low, making it difficult to achieve high margins on consumer goods, and thus Austrian cartels were often intended 'to

---

[27] See generally, Good, *Economic Rise*, 218–26, and Berend & Ranki, *Economic Development*, 156–62.

[28] According to Gerschenkron, cartels were 'stepchildren' of the banks. Gerschenkron, *Economic Backwardness*, 15. See also Rudolph, *Banking and Industrialization*, 104–6 & 165–74.

[29] According to one expert, 'The entire cartel structure . . . was closely tied to the system of tariff protection.' Rudolph, ibid., 166.

achieve the economies of specialization in a low-income market which were otherwise not possible'.[30]

At first the public paid little attention to cartels. In part this was because Austrian cartels tended to be secretive. Under Austrian law, such arrangements did not represent valid and enforceable contracts, and thus Austrian cartels were generally careful to avoid publicity. Even where there was information about cartels, however, they were not viewed as a cause for concern. There was a widespread perception that cartels generally had beneficial effects on the economy. According to a contemporary expert,

[c]artels descended almost like lightning from the no longer so bright heaven of belief in the 'free play of forces', the harmony of competition of liberal economics. They have perhaps more than any other of the new patterns that sprang from economic liberalism contributed to giving a swift blow to the dogma of 'free competition', even by practitioners.[31]

They generally were viewed as children of necessity (*Kinder der Not*) that served to establish order and to avoid the chaos of ruinous competition.

Cartels became a topic of academic discussion in 1883, when Friedrich Kleinwächter, an Austrian economist, published a book describing the sudden emergence of this new form of economic activity.[32] Although this work generated analysis and discussion of the causes and consequences of the cartel movement, there was no cry for government action to deal with cartels. They continued to be viewed as a natural and inevitable stage in the development of capitalism rather than a problem to be combated.[33]

By the 1890s, however, cartels were being viewed more critically.[34] In part this resulted from the growing number of reports of aggressive and harmful cartel conduct by cartels. In addition, the growing size and power of cartels made them appear increasingly ominous.[35] Changing values and a changed political situation also encouraged this shift in perspective. The growing intensity and breadth of resentment against liberals as a class was one factor. By the 1890s cartels had come to be seen by many as tools of the discredited Viennese liberals, and the anti-liberal sentiment that penetrated all levels of society came to include and even focus on cartels. The bitterness and disappointment directed at liberals, in general, and bankers, industrialists, and Jews, in particular, were now also directed at cartels.

---

[30] Alan S. Milward & S. B. Saul, *The Development of the Economies of Continental Europe 1850–1914* 322 (Cambridge, Mass., 1977).

[31] Albert Schäffle, 'Zum Kartellwesen und Zur Kartellpolitik', 54 *Zeitschrift für die gesamte Staatswissenschaft* 467 (1898).

[32] Friedrich Kleinwächter, *Die Kartelle* (Innsbruck, 1883).

[33] See, e.g., Josef Grunzel, *Über Kartelle* 1–20 (Leipzig, 1902).

[34] See generally Bruno Schoenlank, 'Die Kartelle: Beiträge zu einer Morphologie der Unternehmer-Verbände', 3 *Archiv für Soziale Gesetzgebung und Statistik* 489–91 (1890).

[35] See, e.g., Otto Wittelshöfer, 'Der Österreichische Kartellgesetzentwurf', 13 *Archiv für Soziale Gesetzgebung und Statistik* 122, 123 (1899).

New ideologies also cast cartels in a new light. During the late 1880s and 1890s the new mass parties engendered and exploited populist sentiment against 'big business', and cartels were a particularly convenient target of their attacks. The Social Democrats saw big business as responsible for exploitation of the laborers, while the Christian Socialists inveighed against big industry and cartels for harming artisans and shopkeepers. Finally, the pan-Slavs viewed big business, including cartels, as a tool by which the Austro-Germans were exploiting the Slavic peoples.

All of this led to demands for cartel legislation from intellectual as well as political circles. Everyone recognized that cartels sometimes engaged in harmful conduct, but the real issues were whether anything should or could be done about these harms, and if so, how.

F. THE LEGAL STATUS OF CARTELS

The irony of demands for legal sanctions against cartels is that some sanctions already existed; they were just ineffective. In the 1890s Austria was the only European country to have legislation that generally invalidated cartel agreements, and the relevant provision of that legislation had been in effect for almost a century. This legislation served one of the functions of law—to identify unacceptable behavior, but it did not achieve another—to deter the proscribed conduct.

The Austrian provision invalidating cartel agreements was a re-enactment of an 1803 statute intended to prevent merchants from profiting from shortages caused by the Napoleonic wars, particularly in necessities such as food. The original provision designated as a criminal offence agreements among members of a particular trade or business 'for the purpose of increasing the price of a good without work and to the detriment of the public'.[36] It was, therefore, conceived not as a general framework for protecting competition, but as a response to the specific problem of hoarding.

In 1870 this provision was transferred out of the criminal law and into a new statute (the *Koalitionsgesetz* or Coalition Statute) the main objective of which was to allow workers to form associations, but to restrict the activity of such associations by voiding agreements to strike.[37] Section 4 of this

---

[36] 'The agreement of several or all of the business people in a particular business for the purpose of increasing the price of a good without work and to the disadvantage of the public, or to reduce such price for their own purposes, or to create shortages is to be punished as a serious criminal violation according to the degree of participation in same'. Justizgesetzsammlung Nr. 626, quoted in Schulte, *Das Österreichische Kartellrecht*, 32.

[37] Koalitionsgesetz of April 17, 1870, Reichsgezetzblatt 1870, Nr. 3. For relevant portions of the text, see Reichsamt des Innern, *Denkschrift über das Kartellwesen*, pt. IV, 59 (Berlin, 1908).

statute also invalidated 'agreements between business people for the purpose of increasing the price of a good to the disadvantage of the public'.[38]

This statute proved to be of little value in combating industrial cartels, however, because it could be easily circumvented.[39] The only mechanism for enforcing the statute was a civil suit by a cartel member, and, given the purpose of cartel agreements, such suits would always be rare. Moreover, even this possibility could be avoided by inserting an appropriate arbitration clause into the cartel agreement.[40]

G. TOWARDS ADMINISTRATIVE PROTECTION OF COMPETITION

The ineffectiveness of existing private law mechanisms led some to search for an alternative legal basis for combating cartels, and it was in this context that basic features of what would become the European 'model' of competition law were developed.

1. Formulating the solution

The outlines of a new solution were first articulated in 1894 at a conference of the highly influential *Verein für Sozialpolitik*, which viewed itself (with some justification) as the intellectual vanguard of economic and social policy.[41] Although primarily a German organization, it also included leading economists and policy analysts from other German-speaking countries and thus provided an important link between developments in Germany and Austria.

The proposal was presented by Adolf Menzel, a highly-respected Austrian legal scholar.[42] The legal treatment of cartels was a central topic of the conference, and Menzel presented the principal paper on that topic. Thus, the impetus for European competition law development did not originate, as some have assumed, in a mere extension of bureaucratic regulatory claims.

---

[38] This provision seems to have been included in order to promote parallel treatment of employers and employees and thus to contribute to labor peace. See generally, Joseph Weidenholzer, *Der Sorgende Staat* 133–41 (Vienna, 1985). It was apparently something of an afterthought, and it was presented by the government as having little importance. Schulte, *Das Österreichische Kartellrecht*, 40–43.

[39] In cases where the Coalition Statute did not apply, the Austrian Civil Code could also be used by a cartel member to invalidate a cartel, but this provision had little practical importance in relation to cartels. See Schulte, ibid., 75–80.

[40] Austrian courts initially held that arbitrators were not required to apply the provision, but this possibility was removed by a reform of the Code of Civil Procedure (ZPO) in 1895 that required arbitration panels to apply that provision. For discussion, see ibid., 43–45.

[41] See generally, Franz Boese, *Geschichte des Vereins für Sozialpolitik 1872–1932* (Berlin, 1939).

[42] Menzel was a central figure in both private and administrative law, and he was also influential in the development of labor law during this period. See Weidenholzer, *Der Sorgende Staat*, 158.

The ideas were generated by a leading scholar in a superior academic forum and in response to the concerns of intellectual leaders that cartels represented a major policy problem.[43]

For Menzel the problem of cartels, and the justification for regulating them, was that they eliminated competition and could thus be used to increase prices and thereby harm society.[44] His analytical starting point is, therefore, consistent with modern competition law theory, both in Europe and in the US, which focuses on the economic harm caused by interference with the mechanism of competition.

In Menzel's view, however, cartels could be economically justified where they were likely to produce benefits that outweighed their potential harms. This point was not new; it represented the standard view of cartels in contemporary European economic thought.[45] Menzel entered new ground when he argued that legislation was necessary that could prevent the harms caused by some cartels without interfering with the benefits produced by others.

Menzel's central theme was that previous solutions to the problem had not worked and could not be expected to work and, consequently, that a new legal framework for cartels was necessary.[46] The criminal law, he claimed, was clearly inappropriate for use in regulating cartels.

Either the relevant criminal law provisions are very broadly drafted—i.e., directed against every business coalition—in which case they are unfair and practically unusable. Or only those coalitions directed at the exploitation of the public or monopolization of a particular branch will be subjected to penalties; then, however, it is extraordinarily difficult for the criminal judge, who is obviously somewhat further from economic life, to evaluate the economic justification of the organization.[47]

His careful review of attempts to apply criminal law to cartels led him to conclude that their practical impact had been 'extremely limited'.

He also found civil sanctions such as the invalidation of contracts to be of little value. Such provisions could be useful only where a cartel member was willing to go to court against the cartel to avoid a contractual obligation, and this would rarely happen. Moreover, experience in Austria, France and elsewhere had shown that such provisions could almost always be avoided by organizational or contractual maneuvering.

---

[43] It is important to remember that during this period leading bureaucrats and members of parliament often were also intellectuals. For discussion of the roles and status of 'intellectuals' during this period and the lack of compartmentalization among intellectuals, see Janik & Toulmin, *Wittgenstein's Vienna*, 14–19, and Johnston, *The Austrian Mind*, 46–47.

[44] Adolf Menzel, 'Referat über die wirtschaftlichen Kartelle und die Rechtsordnung', 61 *Schriften des Vereins für Socialpolitik* 23 (1895).

[45] See, e.g., Klaus Herrmann, 'Die Haltung der Nationalökonomie zu den Kartellen bis 1914', in *Kartelle und Kartellgesetzgebung in Praxis und Rechtsprechung vom 19. Jahrhundert bis zur Gegenwart* 42–8 (Hans Pohl, ed., Stuttgart, 1985).

[46] Menzel, 'Referat', 43–45.   [47] Ibid., 44.

Finally, he rejected what today might be called a 'Chicago-school' response to the problem. Some people believed that no legislation was needed, he reported, because free competition would itself prevent the cartel from significantly raising prices and would eventually lead to its collapse. 'This view', he said, 'requires no serious refutation; it has the facts against it'.[48] Ironically, his example was the United States. 'In North America, the land of the greatest economic freedom', he said, 'whole branches of industry and commerce have been monopolized'.[49]

He concluded, therefore, that an administrative solution was the only feasible response, because it provided a flexible mechanism for evaluating cartel behavior. His proposal for an administrative law solution did not, however, include details, establishing only two general principles of operation. First, the state had to be able to acquire information about cartels. In his view there was too little information about these powerful new organizations even to evaluate the need for controls on their activities. He proposed, therefore, that all enterprises entering into cartel agreements be required to register their agreements and to provide adequate information to administrators on request.

Menzel's second requirement was that all organized cartels—that is, cartels that had some form of administrative machinery—be classified as public 'associations' (*Vereine*) and be subject to a separate legal regime specifically for cartels—a set of norms and procedures specifically intended to regulate such behavior. Each legal system would provide the substantive content for this legal regime according to its own needs and values. In Menzel's view this might mean that a state agency should have authority to invalidate particular acts of a cartel or even terminate its existence, but he specified neither the norms themselves nor the sanctions to be used in enforcing them.

Menzel's presentation emphasized the key role of legal thought in solving the problems raised by cartels. He argued that legal scholarship was essential to devising an effective response to the cartel problem. Economists and others could identify the problems, but the legal experts had to provide an intellectual framework for solving them. We can also detect here the codification perspective that was so prominent at the time. Menzel was arguing that a broad legislative framework should be created to deal with a domain of societal life.

2. The government's proposal

Menzel's proposals led to intensive debate and controversy within political and intellectual groups, particularly in Vienna, and less than three years later the government proposed a competition law statute which reflected the influ-

---

[48] Menzel, 'Referat', 44.   [49] Ibid.

ence of those proposals, but went beyond them. The government's proposal was important for the development of competition law ideas because it made them a major political issue and prevented their marginalization as a purely academic topic.[50]

As this proposal was being drafted in 1897 the political circumstances in Austria in 1897 were conducive to legislation curtailing the autonomy of cartels. The national government was a weak coalition that could ill-afford to ignore the groundswell of sentiment against big business. Demands by national groups for greater autonomy were increasing in intensity, forcing the government to try to placate the most troublesome groups. Moreover, the government was in financial straits and wanted to increase excise taxes, particularly on goods of cartelized industries, and this could be expected to heighten resentment among the lower classes against industry and to fuel the growing popularity of the Social Democratic and Christian Socialist parties.[51]

In the capital the political situation was even more precarious and dramatic. In the Viennese elections of 1895 the Christian Socialist party had mounted a virulent attack against big business, in general, and cartels, in particular, as exploiters of the people, and they even threatened to municipalize major companies if they won the elections. The rhetoric had been heard before, but its intensity had increased, and now, for the first time, the rhetoric was associated with an electoral victory. In 1895 a Christian Socialist, Karl Lueger, won the mayoral election in Vienna.[52] Vienna had been 'the [liberals'] political bastion, their economic capital, and the radiating center of their intellectual life', and now it too was lost. The first European competition law proposals were much influenced by this anti-big business sentiment and in this regard surprisingly similar in their origins to United States antitrust law.

---

[50] Those proposals were detailed and accompanied by an 'Official Explanation' that analyzed the problem at length and explained how the proposals would solve them. The text of the proposed statute and its 'Official Explanation' are reprinted in *Reichsamt des Innern, Denkschrift über das Kartellwesen*, pt. IV, 80–117 (Berlin, 1908).

The bill and the Official Explanation were obviously prepared with attention to high intellectual standards and thus provided a focus for discussion as well as a resource for later analysts and legislative draftsmen. According to an article in Vienna's leading newspaper on the day following first submission of the proposal to the *Reichsrat*, the Official Explanation was 'prepared with exceptional knowledge of the issues, complete mastery of the relevant legislation and specialized literature' *Neue Freie Presse*, June 2, 1897, at 4, col.3. For a similar comment, see, Julius Landesberger, 'Der österreichische Cartellgesetzentwurf', 24 *Zeitschrift für das Privat- und Öffentliche Recht* 575, 581 (1897).

[51] For discussion, see Wittelshöfer, 'Der Österreichische Kartellgesetzentwurf', 124, who claims that such a proposal was important politically because the government was about to increase consumer taxes and thus had to try to reduce opposition to those tax increases by pressuring cartels in those industries not to further increase prices, or at least giving the appearance of trying to exert such pressure.

[52] Although Lueger won four successive mayoral elections in the years 1895 through 1897, the emperor refused to confirm him as mayor until his fifth such victory in 1897. For discussion, see Schorske, *Vienna*, 144–45.

The government's analysis of the cartel problem followed Menzel's, but was more detailed. According to the Official Explanation that accompanied this proposal, the statute was intended to prevent competitors from agreeing to eliminate competition among themselves. Freedom of competition was its central objective.

The value of free competition was analyzed primarily in resource-allocation terms that have a decidedly modern ring. Focusing on the purchasing power of the consumer, the Official Explanation recognized that price increases attributable to the monopoly power of cartels represented a charge on the goods similar to that of a tax.

[The administration considers it its earnest duty] to take care that the ability of the populace to produce is not burdened above and beyond the necessary weight of taxes through private agreements whose objective is to saddle consumption with enforced restraints similar to indirect taxes.[53]

The essence of the problem was thus the forced transfer of wealth from consumers to cartel members.

This 'tax' on consumers also had a fiscal impact. The government relied heavily on consumption taxes for revenues, and cartels reduced revenues from such taxes by increasing prices for the goods and thus diminishing the ability of consumers to purchase them.[54] In effect, cartels not only transferred wealth from consumers to producers, but they also harmed government finances in the process.

In addition to this economic analysis, the government also saw two other major threats from cartels that related specifically to the Austrian political and social situation. The government claimed that cartels led to concentration of capital in the hands of the few and thus increased social inequality and exacerbated social tensions.[55] Moreover, cartels created an institutional framework for economic planning that could facilitate transition to a planned economy in the event of a socialist legislative victory.

The Official Explanation recognized that all cartels had the potential for harm, but it accepted the proposition that some cartels brought economic benefits such as market stabilization that might justify their existence. The state's obligation was to identify the cartels that were, on balance, harmful and to protect the public against the harms they caused.

The need to distinguish 'good' from 'bad' cartels was at the core of the analysis, and it conditioned the government's response to the cartel problem. The proposed regulatory system was justified primarily on the grounds that it was most appropriate for that task.

The government proposed an essentially administrative solution to the cartel problem. It authorized an office within the finance ministry to secure, evaluate and publicize information about cartels and to regulate their conduct

---

[53] Official Explanation, 67.   [54] Ibid., 66.   [55] Ibid., 69–72.

according to a general statutory standard. A central task of this office was to gain and publicize information about cartels. According to the proposal, cartels would be required to have a detailed charter containing information such as the objectives of the cartel and the activities, characteristics, rights and duties of its members (§2). No cartel agreement would be valid unless such information was in writing, approved by a notary, and reported to the finance ministry within eight days (§4). Particularly important decisions of the cartel, including, for example, those relating to the establishment of prices and production quotas were required to be reported within 24 hours. The material reported to the ministry was to be included in a cartel register that would be open for public inspection (§5). The proposal also provided the finance ministry with broad authority to inspect books and documents of cartels and their members, and it provided powerful enforcement tools for coercing information from firms that were not inclined to provide such information (§7). Information acquired in such inspections was not, however, to be made available to the public.

The Official Explanation emphasized the government's belief that obtaining and publicizing extensive information about cartels would of itself solve many of the problems created by cartels, because it would induce cartels to avoid conduct perceived as harmful to society.[56] The expectation was that the success of this information function would avoid the need for extensive regulatory action.

Where the threat of publicity did not deter harmful conduct, the proposal provided the ministry with authority to prohibit the execution of cartel decisions where they reasonably could be expected to 'increase the price of a good or service to the disadvantage of the purchaser or decrease the price to the disadvantage of the seller, in a way which was not justified by the objective economic situation and obviously harmed designated tax revenues or the purchasing power or revenue-generating power of the population (§8)'. Where there was evidence that the cartel actually intended to achieve one of these prohibited objectives, the ministry could go so far as to terminate the cartel or prohibit any changes in the cartel agreement (§8).

The proposal provided for direct government intervention in economic decision-making, but only where the cartel used its economic power to increase its prices above a competitive level or coerce a reduction below such a level in prices charged to it. In the usual case of price increases, therefore, the ministry would have to determine that such an increase caused significant 'disadvantage' to the buyer and that it was not 'justified by the objective economic situation'. The standard was far from precise, but it is important to note that it was conceived as objectively applicable. The ministry was not authorized to intervene on the basis of its own policy considerations, but only

---

[56] Ibid., 78–79.

where intervention was justified by reference to the application of legal principles. The proposal did not, however, provide for judicial review of administrative decisions.[57]

The ministry was to have authority to impose both civil and criminal law sanctions. Where the ministry prohibited a cartel, for example, it could invalidate the contract in the civil courts. A knowing or grossly negligent violation of the ministry's order could also lead to criminal prosecution.

Not all cartels were to be subject to this administrative authority, but only those that controlled the production of goods (such as sugar, spirits, beer, mineral oil and salt) on which the government imposed excise taxes. This limitation was viewed as a temporary expedient which would allow testing of the regulatory scheme, and the government apparently intended to increase the scope of the regulation if it proved effective.[58] It was also consistent with the proposal's fiscal justification. Finally, reducing the number of affected industries promised to limit the sources of political opposition.

3. Responses to the government's proposal

The government submitted its cartel proposal to the legislature in June of 1897 and again—with minor revisions—in October, 1897, and March, 1898. By then, however, chaotic conditions in the legislature precluded any serious consideration of the proposals. Mounting tensions among nationality groups had broken into open conflict in 1896 when the government sought to allow increased official use of languages other than German. The ensuing battles led to virtually complete disruption of the Austrian parliament, and it remained largely paralyzed by the disruptive tactics of one or another of the national groups or political parties for several years.[59]

Yet the parliamentary chaos did not prevent the government's proposal from becoming a focus of attention and debate. It was frequently discussed in the press, and many of the leading figures in the political and intellectual life of Vienna wrote books and articles responding to it.

Virtually all commentators agreed on some aspects of the proposal. There was general agreement, for example, that the government should take some action with regard to cartels. Moreover, most agreed that the response should be based on administrative rather than criminal or civil law. In addition, while there were occasional arguments that the government should intervene

---

[57] Before forbidding a cartel decision or terminating a cartel, the finance ministry was to secure the formal opinion of a commission chaired by the finance minister. This twelve-member commission was to be appointed by the finance minister and consist of six bureaucrats from outside the relevant tax office and six 'experts'.

[58] Schulte, *Das Österreichische Kartellrecht*, 131.

[59] In November, 1897, the emperor invoked a provision of the Austrian constitution that authorized the bureaucracy to govern in exceptional circumstances, and it did so for the next ten years, thus by-passing the legislature.

only indirectly by reducing tariff protection in industries where cartels were causing harm, commentators generally agreed that the law should contain legally enforceable conduct norms.[60] Finally, virtually everyone supported measures to force cartels to disclose more information about their activities and to make much of this information available to the public.[61] The basic features of the government's response to the cartel problem were, therefore, widely accepted.

Criticism of the proposal generally reflected concern that it might encourage or at least permit government action that could harm or even destroy cartels. Industry was a predictable source of this criticism, but more important for the subsequent development of the ideas were other sources. For example, Social Democrats sought to protect the cartel movement because they saw it as a step on the path to socialism.[62] Cartels increased the 'planned' component of the economy, and the Social Democrats believed that this would smooth the way for the introduction of a socialist planned economy. Moreover, they saw cartels as a basis for justifying increased legal protection of organized labor as a counterweight to the power of cartels. Thus, socialist leaders were willing to tolerate 'temporary' exploitation of the working classes by industry in order to move more rapidly toward the political goals of the socialist movement—and concomitantly increase their own power.

Support for cartels also came from an important group that we will call the 'social liberals'. Many leading bureaucrats and intellectuals respected liberal values, but insisted that capitalism be 'socially responsible'.[63] They tended to see cartels as an inevitable stage in the development of capitalism and valued the role of cartels in social stabilization. For them, interference with cartels would at best be futile, and it could disrupt economic and social development. Perhaps the most important proponent of this view was Franz Klein, a leading figure in Austrian law and politics in the decades around the turn of the century, who would also influence competition law developments outside Austria. Although he agreed that government had to have more information about cartels and that it may well need some coercive power to treat severe cases of exploitation, he believed that any such power should be channeled through private law and be very limited in scope.[64]

---

[60] See generally Emil Steinbach, *Der Staat und die modernen Privatmonopole* 26–29 and 37–38 (Vienna, 1903).

[61] See, e.g., *Neue Freie Presse*, Oct. 13, 1897, at 9, col.4, and 10, col.1.

[62] See generally Max Hitschmann, *Kartelle und Staatsgewalt* 4 (Vienna, 1897).

[63] See Weidenholzer, *Der Sorgende Staat*, 203–10.

[64] Klein is perhaps the best-remembered Austrian scholar and bureaucrat of this period. He was twice minister of justice in the first two decades of the twentieth century and directed the revisions of Austrian civil procedure (1895–1897) that were to have a far-reaching impact on European civil procedure. See Herbert Hofmeister, 'Franz Klein als Sozialpolitiker auf dem Gebiete des Privatrechts', in *Franz Klein: Leben und Wirken* 203–215 (Herbert Hofmeister, ed., Vienna, 1988) and idem, 'Franz Klein (1854–1926), zur 130. Wiederkehr seines Geburtstages', 1984 *Österreichische Richterzeitung* 200 (1984).

Many critics of the proposal believed that its central weakness was that it gave too much discretionary authority to a government ministry.[65] They feared that such discretion could lead to excessive governmental interference with cartels or to corruption of the administrators or both. Some suggested a more precise statutory standard as a means of resolving the problem, arguing that the problem was the vagueness of the proposed administrative authorization.[66]

Others concluded that the problem could only be solved by locating administrative responsibility in an independent agency.[67] A frequent suggestion was that a cartel court be created to apply the law or at least review administrative decisions.[68] The problem, they argued, was not the vagueness of the proposed standard, but the location of power in an agency that was subject to political and economic pressures.

A third group argued that the discretion problem was insoluble under existing circumstances because those that would be affected by the legislation were so powerful that, in practice, the bureaucrats would not be able significantly to influence their conduct.[69] For them, the only solution to the problem was to limit the ministry's authority to intervene. Broad regulatory authority would, they argued, create new problems without having any realistic chance of achieving its stated goals.

4. Interpreting the legislative failure

Despite efforts in the following years to enact some version of the original competition law proposals,[70] no such legislation was enacted. Since, however, the failure to enact such legislation was largely attributable to the disintegration of the legislative process, the proposals were not seen as having been 'defeated'. As one contemporary observer summarized the situation, '[t]heir introduction [that is, the competition law proposals] was followed by the period of severe crises which violently shook our national life and made the legislature unable to work for years. But strong impulses emanated from these proposals'.[71]

[65] Wittelshöfer, 'Der Österreichische Kartellgesetzentwurf', 133.
[66] See, e.g., Schoenlank, 'Die Kartelle', 591–92.
[67] See, generally, Landesberger, 'Der österreichische Cartellgesetzentwurf', 595–96 and Steinbach, *Der Staat,* 41–43.
[68] See, e.g., Steinbach, ibid., 178.
[69] See Wittelshöfer, 'Der Österreichische Kartellgesetzentwurf', 134–35.
[70] In 1899 the Industrial Council, the organization of chambers of commerce, formed a special committee to look into the cartel law issue, and in 1901 it presented a new draft for a cartel statute. This draft was based on the government proposals, but it weakened them significantly. In 1900 the ministry of commerce engaged in extensive review of the possibility of such legislation and published a position paper recommending various measures to combat the 'abuses' of cartels. Neither proposal became law. See generally, Grossfeld, 'Zur Kartellrechtsdiskussion', 266–68.
[71] Julius Landesberger, 'Welche Massregeln empfehlen sich für die rechtliche Behandlung der Industrie-Kartelle?', II *Verhandlungen des 26. Deutschen Juristentages* 366 (Berlin, 1903).

H. WHY *FIN-DE-SIÈCLE* AUSTRIA?

Why then did these new ideas about the use of law emerge in turn-of-the-century Austria? And why did they find support and acceptance there? One reason was simply that many members of the Austrian educated class were looking for new solutions. Throughout Europe the 1890s were, as Eric Hobsbawm has written, an 'era of new strategies'.[72] There was a willingness to search for new answers, and this creative attitude was particularly influential among Viennese liberals.[73]

The idea of using law to protect competition also represented an attempt to protect the values of competition and economic freedom that were symbolically and economically important to the Austro-German upper middle class that still dominated the bureaucracy and intellectual life of Vienna. It was particularly attractive to members of that class, because their social position, economic status and values were increasingly under attack.

Liberal ideals (often supported by Jewish traditions) also contributed a strong belief in the value and efficacy of law. The idea of creating a new kind of law to protect competition reflected a high degree of confidence in the legal process, for it involved using law in a new way to treat a complicated new social phenomenon. Austrian competition law proposals thus offered the hope of a felicitous marriage between two central values of nineteenth century liberalism—competition and law.

These ideas also corresponded to the general intellectual posture of the Austrian liberals. The Austrian intellectual and political atmosphere in the 1890s was charged with tension between the need to change and the fear of fundamental change, and the competition law proposals embodied this tension. They boldly sought to use law in a new way to solve a pressing societal problem, but they proceeded cautiously, seeking to avoid disruption of existing economic and social patterns.

While these factors tended to favor the emergence of competition law ideas, they may not adequately explain the strong political support for those ideas, because another cardinal tenet of the liberal tradition—minimization of governmental interference with the economy—stood in the way. Consequently, without additional sources of impetus it seems unlikely that the liberals would have produced a law that significantly expanded the state's authority to intervene in the economy.

But there were other sources of impetus. One was disenchantment with and distrust of 'unrestrained' competition. The experience of the two decades after the Great Crash of 1873 had convinced virtually everyone that too much economic freedom was likely to harm not only competition, but society as

---

[72] Eric Hobsbawm, *The Age of Empire 1875–1914* 99 (New York, 1987).
[73] Schorske, *Vienna*, xvi–xvii.

well. The depression seemed to have shown free competition to be a false god, and many attributed the suffering that followed to 'excessive' competition. This experience tended to undermine allegiance to the idea that the economy should be kept free of legal controls.

This distrust of the competitive process resonated in other parts of Austrian society with a powerful communitarian tradition. Austria's political and cultural traditions—not least, Roman Catholicism—long had emphasized the commonweal and the value of community. Competition defied those values and was thus perceived by many as suspicious and alien. Moreover, these communitarian values urged that the powerful of society—for example, big business and powerful cartels—be subject to communal concepts of justice and fairness, and the longstanding invalidity of price manipulation agreements under Austrian law symbolized these communitarian claims. While not an effective deterrent to cartel misconduct, the existing legal principles gave weight to the idea that government should restrict economic freedom in order to protect society from its abuse.

The intense antagonisms of class, ideology and nationality that were rending Austrian society in the 1890s heightened the need for at least symbolic assertions of community and provided a further impetus for those in power to regulate cartels. Democratization and the threat of socialism demanded that governing elites at least gesture at the symbols of community in order to demonstrate their concern for all classes and nationalities, and competition law proposals served that purpose. By proposing to subject cartels to legal controls, the government sent a message that powerful industries would not be allowed to exploit other classes, and Austro-German leaders declared that the state would prevent (Austro-German) industrial power from being abused to the disadvantage of Slavs and other nationality groups.

Finally, competition law was a direct response to the anti-business ideologies of the new political parties that were emerging in the 1890s and threatening the established order. Their rhetoric drew on traditional communitarian values, but also appealed to resentment of the liberal class, fear of exploitation, and, often, anti-semitism. Both Social Democrats and Christian Socialists attacked big business because of its power to exploit, and the idea of competition law provided an answer: those in power would restrain attempts at exploitation by big business.

Cartel legislation thus faced little political opposition. The large industrial firms that would have been most affected by the legislation were its natural opponents, but the political power base of business was in the liberal upper-middle class whose representatives in the bureaucracy had lost much of their confidence in the competitive process and, as we have just seen, had other reasons to support the idea of competition law. Moreover, because most Austrian firms sold primarily on the tariff-protected markets of the empire, they could not easily argue—as, for example, German cartels were arguing—

that their freedom was important to the entire society and that cartel legislation should be avoided because it would hurt their international competitiveness.

I. SHAPING AUSTRIAN COMPETITION LAW PROPOSALS

Many of the same factors that spawned support for the government's competition law proposal also influenced its shape. The basic premise was that cartels should not be harmed, but their conduct should be restricted. This acknowledged the benefits of co-ordination among competitors, while also recognizing the potential harms that such co-ordination posed for the competitive process and for the consumer. It thus represented a compromise between the liberal value of economic freedom and the interests supporting it, on one side, and the communal values of solidarity and protection against exploitation and their beneficiaries on the other.

This compromise was conceived as a general normative framework for the economy that would subject cartels to greater societal control by avoiding abuses of power and the exploitation of the weak by the strong.[74] It fused three basic elements. Liberalism provided the core value of maximizing the scope of freedom and competition in economic decision-making. Austrian traditions contributed reliance on 'enlightened' bureaucrats as neutral arbiters of conflicting societal interests and protectors of the public good. And the constitutional ideal of the *Rechtsstaat* subjected the regulatory conduct of these officials to objective legal standards that were to prevent them from acting arbitrarily or seeking extrinsic personal or policy objectives.

The proposal was based on the idea that the objective of protecting competition has little to do with the traditional goals of civil and criminal law and thus requires a legal regime specifically adapted to achieving that objective. This assumption precluded reliance on the procedures of the ordinary courts and compelled reliance on the bureaucracy.

The tradition of bureaucratic centralism in Austria encouraged this casting of competition law in an administrative mold. According to this tradition, state bureaucrats were primarily responsible for the welfare of society; relatively little attention was paid to private initiative as a source of social progress. Willingness to place trust in an educated and enlightened bureaucracy may have increased during the late nineteenth century, because the bureaucracy alone provided a sense of stability and order and thus a basis for

---

[74] This basic idea was also evident in other Austrian legislation of the period such as labor law. See, e.g., Herbert Hofmeister, 'Die Rolle der Sozialpartnerschaft in der Entwicklung der Sozialversicherung', in *Historische Wurzeln der Sozialpartnerschaft* 278, 291–309 (Gerald Stourzh & Margarete Grandner, eds., Vienna, 1986) and Weidenholzer, *Der Sorgende Staat*, 179–218.

believing that there might actually be workable solutions to society's seemingly intractable problems.

Reliance on the bureaucracy was also nurtured by political thought that emphasized the role of the bureaucracy as a neutral arbiter of conflicting interests within society. Professor Lorenz von Stein, professor of political science (*Staatswissenschaft*) in Vienna from 1855–1888, was especially influential in developing and propagating new intellectual support for this view, particularly within the educated middle class. Stein was a dominant intellectual figure in Vienna and inculcated his views in many of the upper echelon bureaucrats of the 1880s and 1890s. The competition law proposal posited a conflict between the economic interests of the cartels and their members, on the one hand, and the welfare of society, particularly consumers, on the other hand. It then provided a broad legal framework within which cartels would have to operate and authorized the bureaucracy to gather and publicize information about cartels and mediate conflicts arising from potentially harmful cartel conduct.

The configuration of power within Austrian society also contributed to this reliance on the bureaucracy. The Austro-German middle class continued to dominate intellectual life as well as the bureaucracy, and its representatives continued to respect liberal values such as economic freedom and competition. This group thus sought a bureaucratic solution which was based on law, but in which its own members had most of the real power.

Above all, they sought to preclude influence from the legislature. The socialist, anti-liberal, and anti-big business attacks that were reaching crescendo proportions in the mid-1890s created concern within the liberal middle class that such groups might soon take over the legislature and initiate fundamental changes in Austrian society that would reduce the power of the liberals. By establishing an administrative system, the liberals could at least forestall the potential harm to their interests that such political changes seemed likely to produce.

This basic conception of competition law as a new type of law based on administrative enforcement of juridical norms shaped other aspects of the system. It meant, for example, that the substantive norms had to be general, providing decision-makers with significant discretion. This also reflected epistemological assumptions, particularly the late nineteenth century emphasis in Austria on the historicity of legal decisions—that is, the perceived need to examine the specifics of any situation in its concrete historical setting before reaching judgment.[75] A legislature could not 'know' in advance whether

---

[75] The historical school of German legal scholarship had a significant impact in Austria during this period. See Werner Ogris, 'Die Historische Schule der Österreichischen Zivilistik', in *Festschrift für Hans Lentze* 449, 494–95 (Nikolaus Grass & Werner Ogris, eds., Innsbruck, 1969).

particular conduct should be prohibited. It may also have reflected increasing skepticism regarding deductive reasoning in law.[76]

The concept of abuse of power also began to take shape in this context. Although the term 'abuse' did not crystallize as a common description for this standard until the 1920s, the central provision of the proposed Austrian legislation sought to limit 'unjustified' uses of power. This concept continues to play a central role in virtually all European competition law systems.

The proposal was also molded by an important negative influence—United States antitrust law. US experience was widely discussed during the Austrian debates, but the Austrians rejected United States law as a model.[77] In particular, the lack of flexibility and cumbersomeness of the US treatment of cartels as well as its reliance on the regular court system were thought to have encouraged the formation of trusts and thus to have increased economic concentration. The Austrians tended to fear such concentration more than they feared cartels.[78]

* * *

The competition law ideas developed in Austria at the turn of the twentieth century provided the seeds for the development of the European competition law tradition. They provided not only a framework for analysis of the problem of economic competition, but also a model for responding to that problem. As we shall see, Austrian ideas, leaders and experience were to play an influential role during the parliamentary and scholarly debates in Germany that would eventually lead to the first European competition legislation.

This model was a response to industrialization, democratization and their concomitant social transformations. In turn-of-the-century Austria these processes were moving forward rapidly, and the rapidity of change intensified awareness of both their benefits and their harms. Steeped in humanistic traditions and classical scholarship but frequently also immersed in the practical problems of industrialization and democratization, the elite that crafted this response was unusually sensitive to both the values that were being lost and those that were replacing them.

As a result, competition law ideas reflected what they sought to preserve from the past as well as their visions of the future. Economic competition was valued, but subject to considerations of community welfare; administrative

---

[76] As Carl Schorske describes so well, there was a pervasive sense of distrust of concepts and of language in the 1890s in Vienna, and this also may have influenced the *ad hoc* character of the legislation. See Schorske, *Vienna*, 19–20. See also Janik & Toulmin, *Wittgenstein's Vienna*, 65–91.

[77] See, e.g., Landesberger, *Der österreichische Cartellgesetzentwurf*, 578.

[78] See, e.g., Steinbach, *Der Staat*, 31–34. For discussion of the role of US antitrust law in the early debates in Germany and Austria, see Fritz Blaich, 'Die Rolle der Amerikanischen Antitrustgesetzgebung in der wirtschaftspolitischen Diskussion Deutschlands Zwischen 1890 und 1914', 22 *ORDO* 229 (1971).

decision-makers were considered competent to deal with the conflicts arising from competing private and public goals; and the respect for law and its mechanisms was sufficiently broad and deep to create confidence that neither businesses nor bureaucrats would lightly flout community norms. European competition laws continue to be based on this constellation of insights and values.

IV

Germany before the First World War:
Fashioning the Discourse

The cataclysmic end to the empire of the Habsburgs consigned Austrian competition law proposals to virtual obscurity. At least in part as a result of Austrian experience, however, competition law ideas had also been planted in Germany, and it was here that they would flourish—eventually. Although a competition statute was not enacted in Germany until after World War I, many of the ideas that informed that legislation took shape during the two decades that preceded the war. During this period, ways of thinking about using law to protect competition were formed that were to channel future developments and influence legislative and judicial decisions far into the future. In this chapter our focus is on understanding those ideas, the forces that impelled them, the roles they played and the obstacles they faced. We look at this early experience in some detail because of the central role of German thought and experience in the subsequent development of competition law in Europe.

We look first at how Germans experienced economic competition during this period, because ideas and attitudes about using law to protect competition grew out of this experience. We then examine the patterns of thought that shaped the way this experience was perceived and remembered and the resulting efforts to protect the competitive process. As always, categories and structures of thought continuously shaped the experience of events even as those events were influencing both the ideas themselves and the roles they played.

A. EXPERIENCING COMPETITION: INDUSTRIALIZATION, DEPRESSION, AND MANAGED COMPETITION

Three strands of late nineteenth century German experience were central to shaping thought about competition—industrialization, depression, and 'managed' or 'organized' competition. The speed and intensity of industrialization in Germany made its concomitant social transformations particularly abrupt and caused competition to appear particularly menacing. At the same time, the 'depression' undermined confidence in competition as a dependable source of prosperity. Finally, the public and private 'organization' of competition suggested that competition worked best when it was regulated.

1. The Depression experience

German experience with competition in the late nineteenth century was colored by profound disappointment and anger. Not unlike the Austrian experience, it is a story of expectations raised and then disappointed and of the resentment caused by dashed hopes. The high expectations for competition were created during the third quarter of the century, as German economic development surged with extraordinary vigor.[1] In particular, the late 1860s and early 1870s witnessed rapid growth in industrial production, profits and investment. Industries of all sizes prospered, much of the middle class revelled, and a wave of materialistic optimism rolled through German Europe. Competition was worshipped as an icon of progress and a source of prosperity.

This adulation of competition was intensified by the confluence of economic and political developments, as the economic boom coincided with the unification of Germany in 1871. For many Germans, the surging economy seemed to provide a unifying identity after decades of turmoil and division, and the prospects of a unified market within a unified German state promised an economic future even brighter than the already dazzling present.

When this heady euphoria was crushed by the sharp economic downturns that began in 1873, the result was a residue of bitter disappointment that colored images of competition for decades. Competition increasingly came to be seen as an unruly and deceptive force that could not be depended on to produce wealth and stability, and few in Germany would experience economic competition as an essentially positive form of social interaction until after the middle of the following century.

This disappointment helps explain why the last quarter of the century was experienced by many as a 'depression' even though the period as a whole demonstrated significant economic growth.[2] The economic crises of the 1870s were serious and frightening, but by the end of the decade economic growth had resumed—albeit on a more restrained scale. Despite the malaise and disgruntlement of businessmen, economic expansion proceeded rapidly, if fitfully, during the following two decades, as the effective mobilization of credit sources and technological and organizational advances increased investment and production. While profits were often difficult to achieve, the signs of economic progress were seldom far from view.

---

[1] See, e.g., Alan S. Milward & S. B. Saul, *The Development of the Economies of Continental Europe 1850–1914* 17–70 (Cambridge, Mass., 1977) and Helmut Böhme, *Deutschlands Weg zur Grossmacht* 320–40 (Cologne, 1967).

[2] For discussion of this so-called 'Depression' see Hans Rosenberg, *Grosse Depression und Bismarckzeit* (Berlin, 1967); Karl Erich Born, *Wirtschafts- und Sozialgeschichte des deutschen Kaiserreichs (1867/71–1914)* 107–19 (Stuttgart, 1985); and Reinhard Spree, *Wachstumstrends und Konjunkturzyklen in der deutschen Wirtschaft von 1820 bis 1913* (Göttingen, 1978).

To refer to the period as a whole as one of 'depression' is, therefore, particularly misleading in the case of Germany. According to modern economic terminology, it clearly was not, because the economy expanded rather than contracted over the period. Subjectively, however, it was a depression. Producers' concerns—overproduction, low profitability and uncertainty— were the central problems, creating the perception within business circles that competition in its unfettered form simply did not work well.

2. Industrialization—German style

The intensity and character of German industrialization made competition seem not only an unreliable means of organizing economic life, but a menacing one as well. The exceptionally rapid growth of industry entailed abrupt economic and social disruptions, giving capitalism, competition and the entire process of economic modernization a somewhat demonic air. By the last decades of the century industrialization was seldom perceived as a 'friendly' process, even by those who supported it, and this tarnished images of 'capitalism' and 'competition', which were seen as its progenitors.[3]

The pace of German industrialization during the second half of the century was, in part, a function of its relatively slow pace during the first half of the century. Beginning comparatively late, and hampered by political disunity, industrialization made relatively slow progress in German Europe during the first half of the century. At mid-century, the German states generally lagged well behind their neighbors (especially those to the north and west) in most measures of economic development.

During the third quarter of the century, however, the integration of markets among the German states (first in the form of the *Zollunion* and then through the unification of the *Reich*), technological advances (particularly the railroads), and the liberalization of economic policies ignited a wave of industrialization. Although slowed by the crises of the mid-70s, rapid industrialization resumed by the end of the decade, and by the end of the century, German industrial production rivaled that of England and had outstripped other European countries.

This speed and intensity made industrialization in Germany objectively more destabilizing and subjectively more ominous than in countries where the process was slower. In England, for example, an urban proletariat was formed over several generations, but its German analogue was created within a few decades. Consequently, the industrialization process displaced artisans more quickly and undermined agricultural communities more abruptly than

---

[3] On German industrialization generally, see Knut Borchardt, *Die Industrielle Revolution in Deutschland* (Munich, 1972) and W. O. Henderson, *The Rise of German Industrial Power 1834–1914* (London, 1975).

had been the case in England. This economic and social disruption led, in turn, to fears and foreboding about the industrialization process.

Other characteristics of German industrialization intensified both its disruptions and the perceptions of its effects. One was the dominance of heavy industry. Whereas industrialization in countries such as France involved a relatively broad mix of large, small and intermediate-sized organizations, German industrialization centered on the rapid development of large factory complexes. Coal and iron, giant smokestacks and huge factories—these became the symbols of German capitalism. They represented proof of national accomplishment and the promise of wealth, but for many they were also symbols of dislocation and misery.

The rapid development of heavy industry required 'big business'—enterprises capable of providing and co-ordinating the extensive financial and managerial resources necessary for the operation of large factories. Size thus became a further defining feature of German industrialization. By the turn of the century, German industrial firms had often become far larger than their rivals in France and even England, and the pace of economic concentration was unprecedented.

These two factors were associated with a third—high levels of vertical integration. The organizations that ran the new heavy industries often did not merely own factories, but also often controlled production from the source of supply to the marketing of the finished products.[4] They had little in common with the small enterprises of the first two thirds of the century and of classical competition theory. They represented power; for some, this power was an escutcheon, for others a source of fear.

These characteristics of Germany's economic development had important implications for the organization of financial resources. Commencing industrialization late and moving quickly, German industrial firms frequently had to rely on banks for financing to a greater degree than their counterparts in Britain and France, where internal equity financing generally played a larger role. Moreover, the predominance of heavy industry and large enterprises generated particularly close alliances between German companies and their banks, and, as a result, banks often acquired not only enormous economic power, but important political influence as well.

Finally, German industrialization tended to be directed more toward international markets than was common elsewhere in Europe (except in Britain). Key sectors of German industry had become dependent on international markets by the end of the century. One of the consequences of this for our story is that it allowed German industry to counter any threat of governmental

---

[4] For discussion of the evolving structures of German industry, see Jürgen Kocka, 'The Rise of the Modern Industrial Enterprise in Germany', in *Managerial Hierarchies: Comparative Perspectives on the Rise of the Modern Industrial Enterprise* 77–116 (Alfred A. Chandler, Jr. & Herman Deams, eds., Cambridge, Mass., 1980).

restraints on its activity with the argument that such restraints would impede its ability to compete on world markets.

The juxtaposition of this rapid and highly concentrated industrialization process with abrupt social and economic transformations and the experience of 'depression' generated highly ambivalent attitudes toward competition around the turn of the century. Within a few decades German Europe had been transformed from an amalgam of generally small, largely agricultural states into a unified state with European leadership in many industries. The speed of this transformation was in many ways remarkable, but it also created powerful political, social, and intellectual tensions. Competition as process and value was at the center of those tensions.

3. Managed competition: the public component

The disappointments and fears created by 'depression' and rapid industrialization also encouraged 'organization' of the economy.[5] Increases in both public and private regulation of competition that occurred throughout Europe during the final quarter of the century were particularly obvious, pervasive and apparently effective in Germany. Consequently, by the end of the century many Germans were disposed to believe that the solution to the harms apparently resulting from unrestricted competition was to manage the process.

Rapid growth in governmental regulation was common in Europe in the late nineteenth century, but in Germany this process had additional historical and political dimensions that shaped the relationship between the economy and the state. Central here was a strong tradition of bureaucratic control of economy and society in most German states. Most notably in Prussia, but elsewhere as well, government bureaucracies had long played major roles in directing and controlling economic activity. The boom decades of the 1850s and 1860s had seen a dismantling of many traditional governmental controls, but this period was too short to break long-standing traditions and well-established attitudes, and thus the crises of the 1870s quickly led decision-makers to revert to greater reliance on governmental controls.

The political imperative of nation-building also encouraged co-operation between the state and the economy. For more than two decades after unification a central concern of Chancellor Bismarck's government was the political integration of the formerly independent states, and bureaucratic control over

---

[5] For discussion of 'organized capitalism' in Germany, see *Organisierter Kapitalismus* (Heinrich A. Winkler, ed., Göttingen, 1974) and Gert Brüggemeier, *Entwicklung des Rechts im Organisierten Kapitalismus: Materialien zum Wirtschaftsrecht, Vol.1: Von der Gründerzeit bis zur Weimarer Republik* (Frankfurt a.M., 1977). The concept of 'organized capitalism' has been criticized, *inter alia*, for its lack of precision. See, e.g., Volker Hentschel, *Wirtschaft und Wirtschaftspolitik im Wilhelminischen Deutschland: Organisierter Kapitalismus und Interventionsstaat* (Stuttgart, 1978).

the economy was seen as an important aspect of this process. The bureaucracy was also a central lever by which Prussia maintained its dominance within the newly-united state.

The international context of industrialization created additional incentives for government control of the economy.[6] Increasing government control of international trade served the purposes of the bureaucracy by augmenting the power of those entrusted with trade policy decisions. Moreover, the nationalism that grew in importance during the latter part of the century created pressure on the government to increase its intervention in the economy and thus secure maximum advantages for Germany in the international arena. By the early years of the twentieth century, the perceived tie between economic performance and German military strength was becoming increasingly strong.[7]

4. Managed competition: the private side (cartels)

As with the public 'organization' of competition, its private organization was not unique to Germany. What distinguished the German situation was the power, permanence and importance of cartels.[8] In Germany, cartels did not remain marginal institutions, but became defining features of the economy. They tended to be larger, more numerous and, above all, more permanent than elsewhere in Europe. As such, they were central to the experience of competition.

The size, power and number of German cartels impressed many observers. By 1900, there were approximately 400 cartels in Germany. Although many of them originally were alliances of smaller firms against industry leaders, by the end of the century they frequently included industry leaders. As a result, they ceased to be primarily 'defensive' institutions designed to protect groups of relatively weak competitors and became powerful economic institutions that often controlled entire industries. They also became more permanent. In neighboring countries such as England and France, 'crisis cartels' that formed during the seventies and eighties typically disbanded with the end of the crisis to which they were a response, but in Germany the cartel movement continued to prosper even after those crises had passed.[9] Moreover, in the 1890s a

---

[6] The role of international trade issues in the process of consolidating power in the new German states is a central theme in Böhme, *Deutschlands Weg*, esp. 474–587.

[7] See, e.g., Bruno Seidel, 'Zeitgeist und Wirtschaftsgesinnung im Deutschland der Jahrhundertwende', 83 *Schmollers Jahrbuch* 131, 143 (1963).

[8] For description of the cartel movement in Germany during this period, see Erich Maschke, *Grundzüge der Deutschen Kartellgeschichte bis 1914* (Dortmund, 1964); an English-language version is Erich Maschke, 'Outline of the History of German Cartels from 1873 to 1914', in *Essays in European Economic History 1789–1914* 227 (F. Crouzet et al eds., London, 1969).

[9] See Hans Pohl, 'Die Entwicklung der Kartelle in Deutschland und die Diskussionen im Verein für Sozialpolitik', in IV *Wissenschaft und Kodifikation des Privatrechts im 19. Jahrhundert* 206–35 (Helmut Coing & Walter Wilhelm, eds., Frankfurt a.M., 1979).

second wave of cartelization swept German industry, and by the turn of the century Germany had become known as the 'Land of the Cartels'.

As they grew larger and more permanent and acquired greater control over the markets in which they operated, effective constraints on their conduct diminished. The more supply they controlled, the more effectively they could control output and thus the greater was their power over price. Their increased control of markets also enhanced their ability to coerce non-members to join cartels and existing members to abide by cartel rules—for example, through boycotts of those who dealt with non-members.

We need not explore in detail the many factors that contributed to the extraordinary success of the cartel movement in Germany, but several deserve note for the light they shed on the dynamics of German cartel development. One was the speed of German industrialization. Fueled by virtually boundless optimism, investment in production facilities during the boom years of the 1850s, 1860s, and early 70s dramatically expanded industrial capacity. This impelled firms in such industries to share markets with each other rather than to compete and risk huge losses.

The characteristics of German industrial development also played a role. Goods that were central to German development were often also well-suited to cartelization. Coal, iron and chemicals, for example, were comparatively easy to standardize and thus to cartelize. In addition, German industry tended to be particularly dependent on bank financing, and banks often fostered cartel arrangements in order to stabilize markets and reduce defaults and bankruptcies.

Also important were political factors. One was indirect—international trade policy. In 1879, Bismarck moved abruptly from a liberal international trade regime to a system of tariffs that was designed to protect German industry from world competition. This artificial restriction of access to the market by foreign competitors made it possible for domestic producers to combine to raise prices above competitive levels.

A second political factor was more direct, if less apparent. The imperial bureaucracy often favored cartels because they served its interests, providing a convenient and low cost means of acquiring information about and influencing economic developments. Moreover, for the *Kaiser* and much of the ruling elite, cartels were not only a means of control, but tools for the attainment of other political and military ends. Cartels predominated in those areas of the economy—heavy industry and chemicals, for example—that were most important for Germany's international influence and for the development of its military potential.

Finally, cartels reflected a strong co-operative ethos in German society.[10]

[10] For discussion of corporatist ideas in Germany, particularly the continuities between public and private forms, see Volker Berghahn, 'Corporatism in Germany in Historical Perspective', in *The Corporate State: Corporatism and the State Tradition in Western Europe* 104–22 (Andrew

The values of co-operation and community had long enjoyed relatively high status in Germany, and during the final decades of the century there was a renewed emphasis on community in response to the threat of class conflict and social disintegration. Social support for the general proposition that co-operation is better than individualism nourished the growth of cartels.

B. THE CLOUDED IMAGE OF COMPETITION

German experience with competition during the second half of the century darkened images of the competitive process, but the tools of interpretation applied to that experience amplified this effect. Powerful strands of both academic and popular thought combined with political factors to obscure the benefits of competition and focus attention on its harms. Strong nationalist and corporatist impulses cast co-operation as the hero of German economic successes and competition as a supporting player that could be harmful if left uncontrolled.

1. The fragility of German liberalism

A key to understanding both the murkiness of German images of competition and its weakness as a value lies in the course and character of nineteenth century German liberalism. As we have seen, competition as both concept and value was an important part of liberalism's 'family of ideas'. It was intertwined with liberal agendas and borne by liberal traditions and institutions. But in nineteenth century Germany these traditions and institutions never acquired the breadth and depth of respect and influence that they enjoyed, for example, in England or France. In Germany, liberalism's roots were weaker, the soil less nourishing and the conditions for growth often hostile.[11]

One reason why the roots of German liberalism did not run particularly deep was that they had little time to develop. While liberal political and economic ideas were being absorbed into the intellectual and experiential fabric of society in England and France during the first half of the nineteenth century, they often remained marginal on German soil. Their 'alienness' was part of the problem. The liberal program was largely seen as an import—its economic component coming primarily from England and its political portions coming from France and England. This meant that liberal ideas bore a stamp of foreignness, and in a country searching for its own identity, this was not

Cox and Noel O'Sullivan, eds., Hants, England, 1988). See also Ralph H. Bowen, *German Theories of the Corporate State: with special reference to the period 1870–1919* (New York, 1947).

[11] For an account of nineteenth century German liberalism, see James J. Sheehan, *German Liberalism in the Nineteenth Century* (Chicago, 1978). For German liberalism generally, see Dieter Langewiesche, *Liberalismus in Deutschland* (Frankfurt a.M., 1988).

likely to be helpful. German opponents of liberalism frequently stressed this alienness until after World War II.

A related obstacle was the political situation, which in most areas remained generally inhospitable toward liberal ideas throughout the first half of the century. German states were typically small, often autocratic and seldom inclined to welcome the changes in political and social structures that liberals sought. In many states, repression made even the expression of such ideas hazardous, and even when such expression was tolerated, it was often confined in practice to very small intellectual elites.

Where liberalism did make progress, it was often weakened by the severing of its economic from its political elements. In Prussia, for example, several governments experimented with liberal economic ideas such as reducing government controls on commerce, but they often rejected political demands such as expanded voting rights.[12] This weakened the institutional basis for permanent economic reforms. Moreover, this bifurcation distorted economic liberalism by instrumentalizing it. It became a tool in the hands of governments that could change it or withdraw support for it as political winds changed, and thus it could not serve as a foundation for new economic and political structures.

The revolutionary movements of 1832 and 1848 extended this divorce between economic and political liberalism to the liberals themselves. Virtually all liberals were people of property, and many had little sympathy for 'the masses'. These revolutions intensified their fears that the lower classes would threaten their own security and interests. For the remainder of the century, their distrust of democratic movements often interfered with efforts to implement the political component of the liberal agenda.[13]

The lack of a unified German 'state' also hindered liberalism's development. As long as Germany was a cultural entity but not a political one, institutions seldom extended beyond the political boundaries that separated the various German states. As Sheehan puts it, 'Liberals may have felt part of a national movement, but almost all of them acted within the confines of their own communities'.[14] This isolated liberal groups and institutions from each other and often prevented them from achieving a critical mass of support for their efforts.

The social base for liberalism also tended to be weaker in Germany than it was in Western Europe. In France and England a middle class developed

[12] For an insightful, if brief, description of the Stein-Hardenberg reforms, see Heinrich Heffter, *Die Deutsche Selbstverwaltung im 19. Jahrhundert: Geschichte der Ideen und Institutionen* 84–136 (2d. ed., Stuttgart, 1969). See also Paul Nolte, *Staatsbildung als Gesellschaftsreform: Politische Reformen in Preussen und den Süddeutschen Staaten 1800–1820* (Frankfurt a.M., 1990) and Barbara Vogel, *Allgemeine Gewerbefreiheit: Die Reformpolitik des Preussischen Staatskanzlers Hardenberg 1810–1820* (Göttingen, 1983).
[13] See, e.g., Leonhard Krieger, *The German Idea of Freedom: History of a Political Tradition* 329–40 (Boston, 1957).
[14] Sheehan, *German Liberalism*, 13.

during the early part of the nineteenth century that acquired significant political power and a high degree of independence from the state. It was this class that championed liberal values, because they had the most to gain from their implementation. In contrast, the German middle class developed more slowly and with less independence from the state, not acquiring the political power of its analogues in Western Europe until much later.

In addition, the politically active middle class in Germany had an especially strong bureaucratic flavor. Government civil servants played prominent roles in German liberal institutions and in the development and proliferation of liberal ideas.[15] As a consequence, these ideas themselves often acquired more bureaucratic hues than in countries where they were primarily propagated by the representatives of a merchant-centered middle class.

The relative backwardness of many German states during the first two-thirds of the century contributed to defining this 'special' path for German liberalism by demanding that German liberals focus on issues such as reducing or eliminating the power of guilds that in France and England had long before been basically resolved. This meant that the intellectual agenda of German liberals during this period differed from that of their colleagues in France and England and tended to isolate them.[16]

Finally, the content of German liberalism clouded images of competition. In Germany, conceptions of freedom were often overlaid with other ideas that focused on the importance of the relationship between the individual and some greater whole such as the community or the state.[17] Particularly in the early part of the century the German idea of freedom was imbued with Hegelian ideas of the importance of the state, and later Otto von Gierke and others emphasized the need to place it within the context of co-operation in the *Gemeinschaft* (roughly, community). These structures of thought blunted the force of liberalism in promoting the value of competition.[18]

In Germany then liberalism led a more furtive and ambivalent existence than it did in much of Western Europe. The liberal tradition did not become the strong force for clarifying, advancing and implementing the values of competition that it was among many of Germany's neighbors. The economic successes of the 1850s and 1860s brought a surge of confidence in the economic component of liberalism, but it did not last long enough to entrench that confidence, and many Germans abandoned liberal principles and values

---

[15] According to Heinrich Heffter, 'The will to reform lived [in Prussia] only in an educational elite, primarily in the liberal officialdom, which practically alone incorporated political progress . . . and political will'. Heffter, *Deutsche Selbstverwaltung*, 6. See also Sheehan, *German Liberalism*, 19–34.

[16] See Marie-Elisabeth Vopelius, *Die altliberalen Ökonomen und die Reformzeit* 100–21 (Stuttgart, 1968).

[17] Krieger, *German Idea of Freedom*, 125–38.

[18] For discussion, see Knut W. Nörr, *Eher Hegel als Kant: Zum Privatrechtsverständnis im 19. Jahrhundert* (Paderborn, 1991).

as soon as they no longer seemed to produce the hoped for economic benefits. As a consequence, liberalism in Germany tended to be imbued with a sense of its own limits and skepticism toward its own principles.

2. Nationalism and the search for community

The fragility of the liberal tradition and its institutions in Germany left competition murky as a concept and suspect as a value and rendered it vulnerable to the forces that ranged against it during the last quarter of the century. The most prominent of these was nationalism, for with the founding of the Second *Reich* in 1871, state-building became the central theme of political and economic thought and action, subsuming and distorting other goals and values to fit its mandate. The national government and its supporters sought to undergird the formal process of unification and give it substance and permanence by inducing acceptance of the symbols, values and institutions of the new state, and this process of identity creation and resocialization shaped the evolution of political patterns.

This integration imperative conflicted sharply with central values and objectives of liberalism. The essence of liberalism was, for example, the value of individual freedom; nationalism urged its opposite—subsuming individual freedom on behalf of the greater (national) good. Liberalism was basically internationalist in outlook, founding its appeal on universally valid principles that were to reduce barriers among peoples; nationalism was diametrically opposed. These and other tensions between the two were fundamental and did not long remain submerged. Nationalist imagery soon overwhelmed liberal political organizations.

During the 1870s, the liberals also lost favor with Chancellor Bismarck. He had befriended liberal organizations during the 1860s and early 1870s when their universalist rhetoric served his political goal of uniting Germany and their economic policies enjoyed broad popular support. When the economic crises of the mid-1870s undermined that support, he quickly turned against the liberals. By the end of the decade he was using protective tariffs as the basis of a new alliance between conservative landowners, big business and the bureaucracy that would largely control the future of the second German Reich (and plant some of the seeds from which the third one developed).

By the 1880s, the drive to integrate was shifting its focus away from the horizontal divisions within Germany (conflicts between regions) and toward vertical conflicts—that is, those between social classes and occupational groups. Locked in what appeared to be an intransigent and largely undemocratic political situation, and subject to the extraordinary tensions of rapid industrialization and its social and economic consequences, Germany seemed to many to be fragmenting along class and other lines. Industrialization swelled the urban proletariat during the 1880s and 1890s, and by the 1890s this emergent class had established a strong and increasingly assertive institutional voice in the form of the Social Democratic Party. Artisans often vehemently opposed the industrialization process, seeking at every turn to halt its progress or at least compensate for its effects.[19] Agricultural communities often also felt isolated, forgotten and threatened. Particularly during the 1890s, thought about what was happening to society tended to be organized as a debate about industrialization: *Agraarstaat oder Industriestaat?*—should Germany be an agrarian state or an industrial state?[20]

These conflicts also generated intellectual and organizational efforts to counteract or at least camouflage them. Leaders in many areas responded to these social tensions by seeking and preaching 'community'—the need for solidarity and co-operation among Germans. As one commentator put it, 'The ideal of a harmonious national community, articulated according to functional groups, has shown a remarkable tendency to cut across lines of party, class, region and religious confession. . .'.[21] Efforts to achieve community on a symbolic level increased as its absence on the objective level become more apparent. On all levels, however, this emphasis on community tended to denigrate competition and individual freedom as values.

Particularly important for our story was the anti-big business attitude that grew out of this communitarian discourse during the 1890s. 'Big business' came to be seen as the enemy of community during this period, being held responsible for the social conflicts and disruptions that were becoming increasingly apparent. There was a growing public demand that large industrial firms not be allowed to exploit others within the community and that they justify their conduct in terms of community welfare.

By the end of the century, therefore, competition as a basis for social organization had few friends and many enemies. Liberalism had become enmeshed in a network of corporatist values and institutions that overshadowed and often distorted its message about competition. Large segments of public sentiment had turned against competition because of its association with big business and capitalism, and even business leaders often did not support it, because they considered co-operation and cartels to represent a superior form of organization. Its period of glory was only vaguely remembered by most. Competition had acknowledged benefits, but most saw it as a potentially dangerous process. It was to be welcomed, if at all, only when it was subject to community controls.

[19] For the attitudes and perspectives of the *Mittelstand* during this period, see, e.g., David Blackbourn, 'The *Mittelstand* in German Society and Politics 1871–1914', 4 *Social History* 409 (1977).

[20] For discussion, see Kenneth D. Barkin, *The Controversy over German Industrialization 1890–1902* (Chicago, 1970).

[21] Bowen, *German Theories*, 218.

C. INTERPRETING CARTELS

The clouded and vaguely ominous image of competition that emerged toward the end of the nineteenth century provided the background against which competition law ideas took shape, but those ideas developed as a response to a specific phenomenon—cartels. We need to examine how this phenomenon was viewed and interpreted in order to understand this response.

1. The economics profession and its perspectives

The German economics profession played a central role in shaping thought about competition, in general, and cartels, in particular, and its intellectual traditions provide keys to the origins of competition law thinking.[22] Reviewing German economic thought in the late nineteenth century is all the more important because it differed significantly from that of its neighbors and because failure to recognize these differences has so often led to misinterpretations of decisions and events in Germany.

One clue to the dynamics of nineteenth century German economic thought is its source in an eighteenth century intellectual tradition called 'cameralism', which viewed economic conduct primarily from the perspective of its value to the state.[23] In the cameralist tradition, economic thought was understood as part of the science of government (*Staatswissenschaft*). Cameralist writers typically were also economic advisors to a local prince who also supported the university where they taught, and they generally focused their attention on questions such as how tax revenues could be increased and whether free trade would benefit the sovereign. This cameralist background imbued economics in Germany with a view of the economic process in which the state played the central role.

During the early decades of the nineteenth century, some German scholars and journalists began to pay attention to the economic ideas flowing principally from England which we now refer to as 'classical economics'. In particular, the influence of Adam Smith's ideas grew significantly throughout the first half of the century. This influence gradually produced a clearer conception of the concept of economic process—that is, identifiable cause and effect relationships that had distinctly 'economic' characteristics and that had no

---

[22] For useful overviews, see Harald Winkel, *Die Deutsche Nationalökonomie im 19. Jahrhundert* (Darmstadt, 1977) and Dieter Krüger, *Nationalökonomen im wilhelminischen Deutschland* (Göttingen, 1983). For general discussion of the development of German thought concerning cartels, see Arnold Wolfers, *Das Kartellproblem im Lichte der deutschen Kartell-Literatur* (Munich, 1931).

[23] For discussion, see Albion W. Small, *The Cameralists: The Pioneers of German Social Polity* (Chicago, 1909). For an insightful recent analysis, see Keith Tribe, *Strategies of Economic Order: German Economic Discourse—1750–1950* 8–31 (Cambridge, 1995).

necessary ties to governmental policies. As these doctrines were assimilated, however, they were also often adapted to German conditions in flexible and creative ways which took account of the economic, political and social circumstances in the German states.[24]

The influence of Smithian and Ricardian ideas grew slowly, only gradually defining an independent sphere of intellectual inquiry. Serious writing about economic issues long continued to be done primarily by those who held university appointments in political science, philosophy or law. Economics (*Nationalökonomie* or *Wirtschaftswissenschaft*) did not emerge as a distinct discipline in Germany until the middle decades of the century, when scholars dealing with economic issues increasingly came to understand their work as a distinct form of scientific endeavor. Institutional arrangements also began to reflect this self-understanding, as academic chairs began to be created that focused on economic issues.

Nevertheless, the cameralist tradition long influenced basic attitudes and perspectives, not least by emphasizing the role of the state in thinking about the economic process. 'Without doubt the influence of the cameralist tradition . . . limited the principle of unrestrained competition and gave the state great importance as guarantor and leader of moral and economic-social progress'.[25]

The influence of these 'new' economic professionals increased in step with the growing importance of economic issues during the second half of the century. The boom years of the 1850s and 1860s turned attention toward understanding the causes of the sudden prosperity, and economists were needed to explain why things were working so well. Then, as the mystery of the Great Depression stretched out over the following decades, economists remained in the limelight, but for different reasons. Now they were needed to explain what had gone wrong and to suggest new directions. By the end of the century they had achieved—albeit temporarily—what one authority has called 'a key position within the social sciences'.[26] The prestige enjoyed by economists at this time helps explain why economic thought seems to many to have 'dominated' legal thought regarding competition legislation.[27]

For our purposes the most important feature of German economic science during the second half of the century was the dominant role played by the historical school of economics.[28] Historicism played roles else-

---

[24] This is the central thesis in Vopelius, *Die altliberalen Ökonomen*.   [25] Ibid., 3.

[26] Otto Brunner, cited in I Dieter Lindenlaub, *Richtungskämpfe im Verein für Sozialpolitik: Wissenschaft und Sozialpolitik im Kaiserreich vornehmlich vom Beginn des 'Neuen Kurses' bis zum Ausbruch des Ersten Weltkrieges* 10 (2 vols., Wiesbaden, 1967).

[27] See, e.g., Fritz Blaich, *Kartell- und Monopolpolitik im kaiserlichen Deutschland: Das Problem der Marktmacht im deutschen Reichstag zwischen 1879 und 1914* 36–37 (Düsseldorf, 1973).

[28] See generally Winkel, *Die Deutsche Nationalökonomie*, 82–121. Keith Tribe suggests that the label 'historical school' is often of little value in analyzing the economic discourse of its

where,[29] but its influence in Germany was exceptionally strong, and by about 1890 it had achieved intellectual and institutional predominance within the German economics profession. As Friedrich Lutz describes the situation,

> Since [Gustav Schmoller, the leader of the historicist school of economics] had the ear of the Prussian minister of culture, he could assure that no theoretician received a chair [in economics] in Prussia or even in Germany. If one wanted to study theory in German-speaking territory between 1880 and 1914, one had to go to Austria.[30]

As a result, historicism played central roles in shaping thought about cartels.

On one level, historicism in economic thought merely reflected history's central role in nineteenth century European thought. The century's rapid and fundamental changes focused attention on history as a means of answering perplexing questions about how societies had become what they were and about where they were going. These issues may have received particular attention in Germany because political change was so long resisted and issues of identity remained so long unresolved, but, whatever the causes, historical methodology became a key component in many, if not all, areas of German social thought during the nineteenth century.

In economics, however, historicism acquired an additional, ideological dimension that reinforced its influence. German historicists defined themselves by their opposition to 'Manchesterism', a reductionist version of classical economics that became influential during the middle decades of the century.[31] 'Manchester' economists insisted that the role of government be reduced to a minimum, rejecting virtually all forms of government intervention in social and economic life, including, for example, protectionist tariffs and regulatory support for the working classes. These doctrines became especially influential during the heady days of the 1860s and early 1870s when events seemed to confirm their validity. According to Lujo Brentano, then a young economist and later one of Germany's leading economic thinkers, 'opinions from neither the left nor the right have a chance against this doctrine [Manchesterism] that is so dominant in the legislature and the press and in which the laws of nature under the influence of restrained egoism have created the best of all worlds'.[32]

---

supposed adherents because there were also very significant differences in their thought. Tribe, *Strategies of Economic Order*, 66–94. While he is undoubtedly correct in asserting that this general label may be misleading in some situations, such a categorization is valuable for our purposes because it is precisely the shared assumptions and perspectives of these economists that illuminates the dynamics of cartel law thinking.

[29] See, e.g., Joseph A. Schumpeter, *History of Economic Analysis* 819–24 (New York, 1954).

[30] Friedrich Lutz, *Verstehen und Verständigung in der Wirtschaftswissenschaft* 18 (Walter Eucken Institut, Tübingen, 1967).

[31] See, e.g., Julius Becker, *Das deutsche Manchestertum* (Karlsruhe, 1907).

[32] Lujo Brentano, *Mein Leben im Kampf um die soziale Entwicklung Deutschlands* 73 (Jena, 1931).

It is common to distinguish between at least two phases in the response to Manchesterism.[33] The first, the so-called 'older historical school', was active during the middle decades of the century. Nourished by Hegelian philosophy, economists such as Bruno Hildebrand and Karl Knies sought to establish the need for historical interpretation of economic data as a counterweight to what they considered the oversimplification and distortions of the Manchesterites. During this period historicism was essentially an academic critique of classical economic doctrines.[34] Historicists did not challenge the basic core of classical economic doctrine. What they rejected was the inflexible and absolutist application of certain ideas of classical economics. They claimed that this 'absolutizing' of economic theory had little to do with reality, and they emphasized the need to see the historical 'imbeddedness' of economic activity.

From about the 1860s, historical school thinking acquired new dimensions among a second generation of economists often referred to as the 'younger historical school'. The 'boom' years had led to a rush of materialism that many of these economists found both socially harmful and personally distasteful. More importantly, the 'pauperism' that had become evident in the 1840s was quickly acquiring menacing proportions among urban proletariats. The economists of the younger historical school argued that the influence of Manchesterism was largely responsible for these and other social and economic problems, and they took it upon themselves to combat its influence. According to James Sheehan, 'The historical tradition's concern for empirical reality and its national orientation seemed far better equipped to solve the problems of German society than laissez-faire liberalism'.[35] Thus in their hands historicism became more than a mere methodological perspective. It became an ideological tool for achieving particular policy objectives.

The historical school's central claim was that economic knowledge was historically conditioned and that, as a result, abstract general principles concerning economic behavior—such as 'the invisible hand'—had limited value. Economic conduct occurred within specific cultural and historical contexts, they argued, and it could not be understood without understanding those contexts. Knowledge about economic reality could be gained, therefore, only through the detailed study of historical circumstances and the inductive search for patterns reflected in them. Economic actors were conditioned by

---

[33] Joseph Schumpeter identified a third stage of development that was represented by what he called the 'youngest historical school'. This group, he argued, was led by Max Weber, Werner Sombart, and Arthus Spiethoff, and it was characterized by an increased focus on responding to Marxist thought. Schumpeter, *History of Economic Analysis*, 815–19.

[34] For a good general description of early historicist economics, see W. J. Fischel, 'Der Historismus in der Wirtschaftswissenschaft dargestellt an der Entwicklung von Adam Müller bis Bruno Hildebrand', 47 *Vierteljahresschrift für Sozial- und Wirtschaftsgeschichte* 1 (1960).

[35] See James J. Sheehan, *The Career of Lujo Brentano: A Study of Liberalism and Social Reform in Imperial Germany* 52 (Chicago, 1966).

ethical, religious and legal factors, and, therefore, the idea of 'economic man' was a theoretical construct with little value for understanding the real world.

As the historical school moved toward control of the German economics profession during the 1870s and 1880s this epistemological assertion increasingly structured the discourse and perspective of economics in Germany. Scholarship in economics centered on in-depth study of the specific circumstances of a particular people at a particular time. 'Pure'—or deductive—theory was generally disparaged, and little was produced in Germany for decades.[36]

For members of the historical school, these epistemological and methodological propositions were interwoven with what they called 'ethical' objectives, which focused on the need to combat the harmful social consequences of industrialization. Their message was that Manchesterism led to a disintegration of society and prevented the state from taking steps that it was ethically bound to take, especially in regard to the plight of the working classes.

The institutional center of the historical school was the *Verein für Sozialpolitik* (social policy association).[37] Founded in 1871, it became within a few years the most important organization of social scientists in Germany, retaining that mantle until the 1930s.[38] Particularly during its early decades, this organization opposed *laissez-faire* doctrines in favor of government intervention to address social issues. As a result, members of the school were dubbed by its opponents as *Kathedersozialisten* ('socialists of the lectern'). They were not Marxists, but they were spurred by a concern for social justice, and they sought a middle way between Marx and revolution, on the one hand, and *laissez-faire* policies, on the other.

The close ties between the methodology of historicism and the agenda of the *Verein* help explain the self-induced isolation of German economists that became such a prominent feature of the European economic landscape between the mid-1880s and the First World War. The *Methodenstreit* between the German historical school and Austrian economists (discussed in Chapter II) was nominally about economic methods, but its virulence can best be attributed to the political implications of using those methods. The German historical school saw itself as a bulwark against the pernicious influence of Manchesterism, and its members saw in Austrian economic thinking a source of support for Manchesterism.

---

[36] Occasionally a leading economist urged the importance of both perspectives, but this was rare. See, e.g., Adolph Wagner, *Grundlegung der Politischen Ökonomie* 166–71 (3d. ed., Leipzig, 1892).

[37] The official name was for many years '*Socialpolitik*', which included an anglicized '*Social*' rather than the German '*Sozial*', but the two spellings were often used interchangeably. I here use the German spelling for the sake of consistency. On the difficulty of translating '*Sozialpolitik*', see Sheehan, *Career of Lujo Brentano*, 46, n.1.

[38] For accounts of the creation of the *Verein* and its early years, see Brentano, *Mein Leben*, 72–82, and Sheehan, *Career of Lujo Brentano*, 46–94.

2. German economists view cartels

The historical school provided the lenses through which the phenomenon of cartels in Europe was first subjected to in-depth analysis, and this gave it extraordinary influence in the evolution of competition law thought. German economists paid more and earlier attention to cartels than did their colleagues elsewhere because cartels achieved greater and earlier importance there (and in Austria) than they did elsewhere. As we have seen, within some two decades cartels became the central form of economic organization of German industry, and this created incentives for economists to study this new phenomenon and to interpret it for others.

The perspective on cartels developed in Germany during these decades was a fusion of three distinct conceptual lenses, which I will label 'classical economic', 'historicist' and 'ethical/political'. These lenses are analytically distinct, although they tended to be used together, and few of those using them would have distinguished among them.

Although German economists generally eschewed the value of deductive economic theorizing, they accepted and utilized many of the basic economic insights of classical economics. They recognized, for example, that agreements among producers to control output restricted competition and thus tended to raise prices and harm consumers. They further recognized that a cartel might acquire sufficient economic power to act like a monopolist, and they understood many of the economic consequences of monopoly.

Despite their awareness of these general principles, they relied little on them in *evaluating* cartels. Here the historicist perspective was controlling. Their historicist lenses emphasized the uniqueness of the context in which cartels were operating and required economists to assess cartels not by the application of abstract criteria but as *responses to specific factual circumstances.* This led them, for example, to the perception that cartels were a product of industrialization and, therefore, something fundamentally new and different. There had been agreements between competitors before, of course, but German economists chose to emphasize the distinctiveness of the phenomenon and to pay little heed to similar arrangements in the past.

From this perspective, cartels appeared as natural—and, therefore, appropriate—institutional responses to the overproduction and instability of the period. The main concern of the German historical school was the *producer* rather than the consumer! They saw *too much* competition rather than too little. The practical problems these economists faced were overproduction and economic instability, and from this perspective cartels seemed useful. Cartels regulated production, which is exactly what the economists of the period wanted, and in doing so they promised to reduce the cyclical fluctuations that were a bane to so many.

A further implication of this perspective was that cartels were inevitable and that, therefore, attempts to eliminate or control them were likely to be ineffective and potentially harmful. The historicists' view of economic development said, in effect, that new forms of economic organization develop in response to the needs of the time, and there is, therefore, little reason to be concerned about them. Moreover, when coupled with Darwinian assumptions about the shape of history, this perspective portrayed cartels as an ineluctable development that represented improvement and should be welcomed.[39]

A third lens employed by the historical school applied a particular set of ethical values in assessing cartels. It evaluated cartels by reference to ideals of co-operation and social harmony that were, in turn, a response to accelerating social conflict. As we have seen, this school was concerned with the need to improve the lot of workers and thus reduce social disruption. Its members saw cartels as serving this end by blunting the often devastating impact of economic crises on the position of workers. German economists were generally convinced that cartels reduced the overproduction that was the cause of these crises, thus providing greater employment stability and reducing pressures on firms to exploit their employees.[40]

This concern for the working class gave ethical issues an important role in interpreting cartels. Most important among these was the high value placed on co-operation, which was seen as ethically superior to competition and 'egoistic individualism'. In this view, firms that were co-operating rather than competing would not be as compelled to focus only on their own short-term profits and therefore would tend to treat their workers better and counteract the threats of social conflict. As Franz Wieacker puts it, '[Before the war] the communitarian ideology that dominated all groups (even including the classical liberals) saw in cartels a form of organization for the entire economy that conformed to their system. Entrepreneurs, economic planners and socialists could integrate it into their economic models for very different reasons. . .'.[41] In short, cartels were more likely to be better for society as a whole than unrestrained competition.

Viewing the economy from this 'ethical' perspective, these economists began also to pay attention to the issue of economic power.[42] They began to portray power as a threat to the operation of both economy and society. There had, of course, been discussion of monopoly before, but the economists

[39] For discussion of the role of Darwinism during this period, see Fritz Bolle, 'Darwinismus und Zeitgeist', in *Das Wilhelminische Zeitalter* 235–87 (Hans-Joachim Schoeps, ed., Stuttgart, 1967).

[40] See also Rainer Schröder, *Die Entwicklung des Kartellrechts und des kollektiven Arbeitsrechts durch die Rechtsprechung des Reichsgerichts vor 1914* 42–45 (Ebelsbach, 1988).

[41] Franz Wieacker, *Privatrechtsgeschichte der Neuzeit* 546 (Göttingen, 1967).

[42] See Hans-Jürgen Scheler, *Kathedersozialismus und Wirtschaftliche Macht* (Diss. Berlin, 1973).

of the *Verein* saw power in situations other than the classical case of monopoly. They examined, for example, the issue of the economic dependency of one firm on another and the role of a firm's economic power on its treatment of workers. These early efforts laid the groundwork for highly durable perspectives on economic conduct.

The 'ethical' advantages of cartels were often contrasted with American trusts. According to the historical school, cartels encouraged positive ethical attributes such as restraint and honesty in economic conduct and concern for weaker competitors. Trusts, on the other hand, were portrayed as naturally rapacious, deceitful and willing to harm not only consumers and competitors but society as a whole.[43]

This, in turn, resonated with the voice of German nationalism. A central theme in discussions of cartels was their positive effect on the 'strength' of the nation. There were two components of this image. The most prevalent and direct one portrayed cartels as promoting Germany's ability to compete internationally, and in Wilhelmine Germany this was a powerful argument. A major focus in virtually all areas of German popular and educated thought was Germany's need to compete effectively in the world—militarily, economically and culturally.[44] A second factor was the supposed contribution of cartels to internal social cohesion. By reducing rapaciousness, moderating cyclical economic variations and generally improving economic welfare, cartels were portrayed as weaving the social fabric more tightly and thus strengthening the nation.

The image of cartels produced by the combination of these lenses was essentially positive. Cartels seemed natural, inevitable and ethically superior, and they provided a solution to the pressing problems of overproduction and instability. True, they imposed costs on society by increasing prices to consumers, but this seemed a small price to pay for their benefits.

By the turn of the twentieth century, however, the conduct of cartels was making some of these claims more difficult to maintain. According to an economist speaking in 1902, 'Cartels and trusts, necessary products of the process of economic development, are janus-faced. They represent powerful weapons in the competition between peoples and peaceful means of increasing the productivity of human toil; they can, however, just as well turn into tools of brutal discretion, shameless profit mania and hateful exploitation'.[45]

[43] See, e.g., Gustav Schmoller, 'Das Verhältnis der Kartelle zum Staate', 116 *Schriften des Vereins für Socialpolitik* 237, 267–68 (1906).
[44] This theme was central during the 1890s. See J. A. Nichols, *Germany after Bismarck: the Caprivi Era 1890–1894* 138–53 (Cambridge, Mass., 1958).
[45] Heinrich Waentig, 'Welche Massregeln empfehlen sich für die rechtliche Behandlung der Industriekartelle?', I *Verhandlungen des 26. deutschen Juristentages* 63, 65 (Berlin, 1902).

D. RESPONSES TO THE CARTEL PROBLEM—THE COURTS

During the 1890s, the harms caused by cartels became an increasingly prominent object of public concern. A new wave of cartelization that began in the early 1890s had shown that the cartel phenomenon was neither temporary nor limited to a few industries, but had become a basic organizational form for economic activity. Cartels were also becoming more powerful, controlling ever larger shares of the markets in which they operated. This, in turn, allowed them to be more aggressive, not only in raising their own prices and forcing down the prices of their suppliers, but also in coercing non-members to join their ranks. The result was increasing alarm among actual and potential victims of cartels as well as those concerned with the public interest.

But what, if anything, should be done about cartels? For many, the answer was clear: nothing. Cartels were a fact of modern capitalism. Prohibiting them was unthinkable, and regulating them might cause more harm than good. Yet as evidence of harm mounted, the perceived need for a public response grew. If there were to be constraints on cartel conduct, however, who should establish them and how should they be enforced? Was it a private law problem—an issue of rights of private entities *vis-à-vis* each other? If so, should it be dealt with by the courts or did it require a legislative response? Or should it be viewed as a regulatory problem? And, if so, what kinds of regulatory steps should be taken? The responses to these questions were to structure the subsequent evolution of competition law, not only in Germany, but throughout Europe.

1. Conceptualizing the cartel problem

As cases involving the legal status of cartels began to appear during the 1880s, the courts provided initial responses to some of these questions in deciding how existing norms should be applied to what was seen as a new phenomenon. Although eventually the legislature was to become the primary force in the development of European competition law, it was in German courts that important issues were given authoritative shape.

When the courts began applying general principles of law to cartel cases, they found little assistance in existing legal literature. In part, this was because of the perception that cartels were fundamentally new, which had given legal scholars little time to analyze and comment on them. In addition, however, legal scholarship during this period was pre-occupied with other kinds of issues, particularly those related to the codification of private law. As a result, the courts were largely 'on their own' in devising responses to the problems created by cartels.

The disputes that came before them typically involved either relationships among cartel members or rights as between cartels and former members.[46] The legal problems of cartels were, therefore, initially presented and understood primarily as issues of contract law! The focus was on private justice among contracting business entities, and other considerations were refracted through that lens.

The courts initially conceptualized the problem by pitting two cardinal principles of nineteenth century legal thought against each other.[47] The first of these was contractual freedom (*Vertragsfreiheit*), the right to decide with whom and about what one made binding agreements. This principle had been prominent for much of the century, because it embodied and symbolized personal freedom and emancipation from governmental and guild controls. It was also central to the private law codification project that preoccupied German lawyers during the last two decades of the century. Applied to cartels, it suggested that firms should be free to join cartels if they wished, and if they agreed to membership in a cartel, they should be bound to their agreement.

In the cartel context, this principle seemed to collide, however, with the principle of business freedom (*Gewerbefreiheit*), which had equally strong credentials and similar symbolic weight. This was the principle forged during the first two-thirds of the century that private firms should have the right to decide freely what kinds of business operations they would engage in and how they would conduct their businesses. Cartel members who sought to terminate membership or otherwise violate cartel agreements often argued that the agreements should not be enforced against them because the cartels interfered with their decision-making and thus violated the principle of business freedom.[48]

While the apparent conflict between these two principles focused attention on the legality of cartels, there was a second level of analysis that was symbolically less powerful, but potentially more important for solving the problem. Here the issue was the degree to which general principles of contract law constrained the activities of cartels. The key legal concept was that of *Sittenwidrigkeit*,[49] which allowed courts to invalidate contractual provisions that violated the 'fundamental moral sense' of the community, and the question was what kinds of cartel provisions or conduct might have that effect. Although German courts began to apply this standard as early as the 1880s,

[46] My discussion of this case law is much indebted to Schröder, *Die Entwicklung des Kartellrechts*, 9–18.

[47] See, e.g., Walter Strauss, 'Gewerbefreiheit und Vertragsfreiheit: Eine Rechtsgeschichtliche Erinnerung', in *Wirtschaftsordnung und Staatsverfassung: Festschrift für Franz Böhm zum 80. Geburtstag* 603–14 (Heinz Sauermann & Ernst-Joachim Mestmäcker, eds., Tübingen, 1975).

[48] See, e.g., Schröder, *Die Entwicklung des Kartellrechts*, 68–74.

[49] See, e.g., Bay. OLG (Bavarian Appeals Court), Dec. of April 7, 1888, 43 *Seufert's Archiv* 16 (1888). For further discussion, see Schröder, *Die Entwicklung des Kartellrechts*, 11–15.

the case-by-case approach was too slow and too amorphous to satisfy many who sought a response to cartel abuses.

2. Legalizing cartels: the *Saxon Wood Pulp* case

As lower court cases proliferated, there was a growing need for authoritative guidance in treating cartels, and in 1897 the country's highest court, the *Reichsgericht*, handed down a decision in the so-called *Saxon Wood Pulp* case that provided answers which would remain authoritative for more than fifty years.[50]

The case involved a cartel agreement entered into in 1893 by a group of wood pulp producers in Saxony. The cartel clearly dominated a small, regional market. The industry had been in serious difficulty, and the cartel's members argued that the arrangement was necessary in order to prevent numerous bankruptcies. The cartel agreement included, *inter alia*, a requirement that members of the cartel sell their wood pulp through an agent designated by the cartel. Violation of this provision justified the cartel in imposing a contractual penalty. When one of the members violated this provision by repeatedly selling its products directly to purchasers, the cartel imposed such a penalty and sued to recover it. The defendant claimed, however, that it was not obligated to pay because the agreement violated the principle of business freedom.

According to the *Reichsgericht*, the substantive issue was whether the agreement violated the principle of business freedom as contained in the *Gewerbeordnung* (Business Code) of 1869, which enshrined the principle that 'every person shall be permitted to engage in any business'.[51] The Court saw the principle of business freedom as serving two distinct purposes—to protect the public welfare and to guarantee individual freedom. It concluded that neither of these invalidated the cartel agreement.

As important as the result was, the Court's framing of the issues was at least as significant. The Court addressed the public interest issue in broad terms, virtually equating the 'public interest' with the general economic consequences of cartels. If cartels as an organizational form were generally harmful to the economy, they harmed the 'public interest'. If their general economic effects were essentially positive, they did not. This formulation viewed the 'public interest' from the perspective of historicist economics and made economists its arbiter. In so doing, it also eliminated traditional legal concerns about individual harm and about 'justice' from this part of the test.

[50] Reichsgericht, Dec. of Feb. 4, 1897, 38 *RGZ* 155 (*Sächsisches Holzstoffkartell*). For discussion, see Franz Böhm, 'Das Reichsgericht und die Kartelle', 1 *ORDO* 197 (1948); Wernhard Möschel, *70 Jahre Deutsche Kartellpolitik* (Tübingen, 1972); and Burckhardt Röper, 'Der wirtschaftliche Hintergrund der Kartell-Legalisierung durch das Reichsgericht', 3 *ORDO* 239 (1950).
[51] §1(1), Gewerbeordnung für den Norddeutschen Bund von 1869 (June 26, 1869) (BGBl. 245).

In posing the issue in this fashion, the Court made resolution of the legal issue turn on its own evaluation of the economic literature on the subject! At a time when conventional legal doctrine assigned to courts a largely passive role, this was anything but judicial restraint, and it exemplifies what Regina Ogorek calls 'the strange mixture of constraint and freedom' that some German courts exhibited during this period.[52]

On the basis of its analysis of the economic literature, the Court declared that cartels not only did not harm the public interest, but were generally beneficial. According to the Court,

> . . . if the firms in a particular branch band together to eliminate or control price reductions among themselves, their co-operation can be seen not only as a justified application of the drive to self-preservation, but also—as a general rule—a service to the public, provided that such prices really are continuously so low that economic ruin threatens the firms.[53]

The Court reasoned that by preserving competitors from ruin and maintaining adequate prices cartels helped to prevent the economic 'catastrophes . . . associated with overproduction'. This policy judgment was the cornerstone of cartel 'legalization'.

Embodied in this conclusion was an assumption about economic knowledge that was to have far-reaching consequences. The Court's conceptualization of the economic situation implicitly accepted the epistemological assumptions of the historical school, according to which the standards for evaluating economic phenomenon should not be fixed and abstract, but flexible and situational. The Court's message was that basic economic issues were to be judged according to the historical school's 'appropriateness' standard.

Repeated references to the 'trade' in which the cartel was operating (for example, '*Gewerbsbranche*' and '*Gewerbsgenossen*'), and the lack of reference to 'markets' indicates the shape of the Court's reasoning. The Court here uses the language not of neo-classical economic analysis, but of contemporary social concerns about the protection of social groups. The difference in perspective is critical. Viewing the problem through historicist lenses led the Court to concentrate on immediate policy problems—that is, protection of a trade—and not to look for solutions in general principles of market operation.

While concluding that cartel agreements did not, in principle, violate the public interest, the Court identified two situations in which a cartel agreement

---

[52] Ogorek has shown that images of the 'automatic' character of judicial decision-making were not as powerful as many have thought. Regina Ogorek, *Richterkönig oder Subsumtionsautomat? Zur Justiztheorie im 19. Jahrhundert* 274 (Frankfurt a.M., 1986). For an analysis of influences on German judges during this period, see Rainer Schröder, 'Die Richterschaft am Ende des Zweiten Kaiserreiches unter dem Druck Polarer Sozialer und Politischer Anforderungen', in *Festschrift für Rudolf Gmür* 201-53 (Arno Buschmann et al eds., Bielefeld, 1983).

[53] Reichsgericht, Dec. of Feb. 4, 1897, 38 *RGZ* 155, 157.

might do so. It stated that a cartel might violate the statute where 'it obviously is intended to establish an actual monopoly and to exploit consumers unfairly (*wucherische Ausbeutung*), or where these results are actually achieved by the agreements reached and arrangements established'.[54] Thus, if the agreement either obviously intended to establish a monopoly or actually did so, it could be invalidated. Without elaborating on these exceptions, the Court declared that there was no indication that either was relevant to the current case.

The Court thus brought fairness concerns back into the analysis, but it marginalized their roles. They were not part of the basic test of the legality of cartels, but relevant only as exceptions to the general principle. The Court's formulation of the issue and application of the test suggest that it expected 'exploitation of the consumer' to be rare. Despite the cartel's clear domination of the relevant market, the Court did not even see an issue of monopolization, indicating that the monopolization exception would apply only where there was total monopolization of a market.

The second component of the Court's business freedom analysis focused on whether the cartel agreement violated the individual cartel member's right freely to choose how and where to conduct its business. Rather than attempting to fashion an analysis that took into account the specific characteristics of the cartel issue, the Court relied on principles developed to assess noncompetition clauses—that is, contractual provisions in which an individual or firm agrees not to operate a particular business at a particular place (most commonly found in contracts involving the transfer of business assets).[55] The decision thus cast the individual freedom issue as one of 'reasonable restraints' on the extent and duration of cartel restrictions, indicating that restrictions would not be considered excessive unless they permanently eliminated the firm itself or an entire component of its business.

This standard was not well-suited to cartels, because, unlike noncompetition agreements, a principal function of cartel agreements is to *maintain* the economic viability of its members rather than to eliminate firms from the market. Moreover, as Knut Nörr puts it, 'The principle of business freedom was reduced to the problem of non-competition clauses'.[56] Nevertheless, without explaining how this test should apply in the cartel context, the Court concluded that the wood pulp producers had not violated it.

---

[54] Reichsgericht, Dec. of Feb. 4, 1897, 38 *RGZ* 155, 158. For discussion of the *Wucher* concept as understood at the time, see Leopold Caro, *Der Wucher* (Leipzig, 1893).

[55] Reichsgericht, Dec. of Feb. 4, 1897, 38 *RGZ* 155, 158–59. For detailed discussion of the case law on noncompetition clauses, see Schröder, *Die Entwicklung des Kartellrechts*, 59–76.

[56] Knut W. Nörr, *Die Leiden des Privatrechts: Kartelle in Deutschland von der Holzstoffkartellentscheidung zum Gesetz gegen Wettbewerbsbeschränkungen* 17 (Tübingen, 1994).

3. The aftermath

Although the *Saxon Wood Pulp* decision settled the basic issue of cartel legality, two other major issues faced German courts in the years that followed. Initially, their primary tool for developing such limits was the monopoly exception contained in the *Wood Pulp* case, and they did develop a body of cases which provided mild, but reasonably clear restrictions.[57]

After the German Civil Code entered into force on January 1, 1900, the courts also began to use its provision on *Sittenwidrigkeit* as a source of conduct limits. Section 138II provided that agreements that violated 'fundamental moral principles' (*Gute Sitten*) were invalid, and this 'general clause' gave the courts more discretion in treating cartel agreements than did the concept of monopoly. Subsequent legal literature has paid little attention to these cases, but recent studies have shown that the courts developed conduct guidelines by applying this provision to prevent cartels from taking unfair advantage of those with whom they contracted. The conceptual apparatus of the case law in this area may, however, have obscured the policy issues involved. According to Knut Nörr, 'In this way the cartel and monopoly problem became caught in the mesh of definitions and distinctions of *Sittenwidrigkeit* such as the relationship between means and ends, the balancing of interests of both parties, the advantages here and disadvantages there. . . .'[58]

4. The judicial contribution

The judicial response to cartels was important on several levels. The main practical consequence of the *Wood Pulp* decision was that it held cartel agreements to be, in principle, valid and enforceable under German law. The *Reichsgericht* was seen as having 'legalized' cartels, giving them a 'letter of immunity' behind which they operated for more than a half century.

At least as important, however, was the judiciary's role in shaping thought about cartels and competition. The *Reichsgericht* helped to establish a framework for interpreting cartels that was to remain highly influential for decades. The *Wood Pulp* decision established as authoritative the proposition that cartels were basically positive institutions. They were portrayed as an effective force for coping with the overriding problem of the day—overproduction. Moreover, the legalization of cartels turned attention away from the general issue of the validity of cartel agreements and focused it on the conduct of cartels in specific situations. The issue of harm was particularized, inhering not in the structure of a specific type of contractual arrangement, but in the consequences of particular conduct. The idea of abuse of power that has become

---

[57] For discussion of the case law, see Schröder, *Entwicklung des Kartellrechts*, 185–242.
[58] Nörr, *Leiden des Privatrechts*, 11.

central to European competition law developed out of this attempt to find conduct limits.

The importance of the *Wood Pulp* decision is reflected in the attention that has been, and continues to be, paid to it in German competition law literature. There was, for example, much discussion of it during the deliberations that led to enactment of the current German competition law in the 1950s,[59] and even in the 1970s the issue of whether the decision was 'correct' was part of discussions of competition law in Germany.[60]

Ironically, perhaps the most important consequence of the *Wood Pulp* decision was that it turned attention away from judicial solutions to the cartel problem. Although the case did not close the judicial path to developing a legal framework for cartels, it was widely perceived to have done so. It had, after all, legalized cartels and provided little apparent control on their activities. For many, this meant that legislation would be necessary to protect society from the harms associated with cartels.

E. THINKING ABOUT CARTEL LEGISLATION

In the wake of the *Saxon Wood Pulp* case, political groups as well as the media soon began calling on the *Reichstag* to investigate cartels. This pressure mounted after 1900, spurred by a recession and by increasing public awareness of the extent to which cartels were using their power to increase price levels and coerce membership. During the ensuing decade, the legal and economics communities wrestled with the issues of whether there should be legislation, and, if so, what it should contain. Their efforts generated a framework for thinking about cartel legislation that was to become and long remain highly influential.

1. Economists and the cartel law debate

How one looks at the issue of whether to enact cartel legislation depends on how one looks at the cartel phenomenon itself. The economists of the historical school took the lead in interpreting cartels, and their image of cartels dominated thought about cartel legislation throughout the prewar period. This dominance reflected the prestige and influence that the economics profession enjoyed during the decades around the turn of the century, and it was underscored by the *Reichsgericht*'s reliance on economic thought in assessing the legality of cartels.

The *Verein für Sozialpolitik* provided the stage on which the economists' views of cartel legislation took shape and the institutional vehicle through

---

[59] Böhm, 'Das Reichsgericht'.
[60] Möschel, 70 *Jahre Deutsche Kartellpolitik* (Tübingen, 1972).

which these views achieved influence. The *Verein* met biennially, and during this period its meetings were a center of attention in the world of German social and economic thought.[61] The papers and proceedings of these meetings often became principal sources of information and analysis regarding the issues involved—for both contemporaries and later scholars. Moreover, the *Verein's* influence was not limited to academic thought; non-academics were often involved in *Verein* meetings, and these meetings often attracted significant media attention. The issue of cartel legislation was a focus of both its 1894 and 1905 meetings.[62]

We have encountered the 1894 meeting before, because it was here that Adolf Menzel made his pathbreaking proposal for a general competition statute. The theme of the discussions there was that cartels were basically positive institutions and that nothing should be done that might harm them. While maintaining this positive image of cartels, however, the *Verein* also sought to raise awareness of the harms cartels could produce. Critics generally focused on specific cases in which cartels maintained or increased prices to the detriment of those purchasing from them or in which cartels used their power to coerce outside firms to join. Importantly, these instances were not yet seen as part of a general problem caused by the organizational form itself. The particularism of historicist thought long hampered this perception.

Nevertheless, there were numerous calls, in addition to Menzel's, for legislative responses to these specific problems. These proposals generally centered either on economic policy measures such as reducing protective tariffs and encouraging the formation of 'counterweight' organizations such as consumer co-operatives or on the creation of an administrative office which would exercise some limited form of information-gathering and perhaps supervisory functions with respect to cartels. The idea of requiring cartels to disclose information to such an office seems to have gained the most support, but even this support remained cautious.

The tone and results of the meeting corresponded to its awareness-creation format. The discussions tended to be general and exploratory. Although a variety of legislative proposals were proffered, there was little general support for any of them. The shape of the discussions suggests that few had thought seriously about the issue and even fewer had formed solid opinions. The basic conclusion from the meeting seems to have been that too little was known about cartels and the harms they might cause to justify creating any significant restrictions on their conduct.

In addition to raising awareness of the cartel problem, the 1894 meeting had another important consequence. It was the occasion on which a rift

---

[61] See Lindenlaub, I *Richtungskämpfe,* 33. For general background on the *Verein*, see Franz Boese, *Geschichte des Vereins für Sozialpolitik 1872–1932* (Berlin, 1939).

[62] For discussion, see Bernhard Grossfeld, 'Zur Kartellrechtsdiskussion vor dem Ersten Weltkrieg', in IV *Wissenschaft und Kodifikation des Privatrechts im 19. Jahrhundert* 255–96 (Helmut Coing & Walter Wilhelm, eds., Frankfurt a.M., 1979).

began to develop in the bond between *Bildung* (education) and *Besitz* (property) that had been so critical to the conservatism of German politics during the Wilhelmine period.[63] Sensing a threat to cartels from the *Verein*'s activities, several leading industrialists began to attack economists—and, implicitly, academic thought in general—for being out of touch with reality and potentially harming the interests of the state.[64] The rift between industry and policy-minded intellectuals would continue to grow.

By the time the *Verein* revisited the cartel law issue in 1905, much had changed.[65] The growing public sentiment in favor of a government response to the increasingly aggressive actions of some cartels centered attention on the question of *what* rather than *whether* action should be taken. Gustav Schmoller reported in opening the cartel law sessions that there had been a turn of opinion against cartels during the preceding year,[66] and this anti-cartel movement put the *Verein*'s discussion in the public spotlight. For many, including Schmoller, it was the most important issue of economic policy in Germany.

Schmoller set the tone of the cartel discussions in presenting the principal paper.[67] Nearing seventy and chair of the *Verein* since 1890, he remained highly influential. He began by reasserting the general historicist view of cartels as essentially positive institutions and certainly preferable to the trusts that he believed would be formed if there were legislation to prohibit or significantly limit cartels. He derided those who proposed such restrictive legislation as 'fanatics of individualism . . . who know very little about the real world and its current economic situation . . . [and] who either don't know or don't want to know anything about the abuses of the old free competition'.[68]

Schmoller no longer concluded from this, however, that the state should refrain from taking action with regard to cartels. While holding to the position that the government should be careful not to harm cartels, he admitted that they sometimes abused their power and that, therefore, the state should establish a cartel office that would supervise their activities. This office should be empowered, he said, to gather information on cartels and to enforce certain general norms for cartel activity, including those relating to treatment by cartels of their members and the use by cartels of exclusive contracts. He even suggested that state representatives be placed on the supervisory boards of some particularly powerful cartels.

---

[63] According to Hans Delbrück, a contemporary political leader, 'Education and property, which until now have joined together to rule Germany, are beginning to move away from each other'. Quoted in Lindenlaub, I *Richtungskämpfe*, 59.

[64] For discussion, see Lindenlaub, I *Richtungskämpfe*, 54–57.

[65] For background, see Georg Weippert, 'Die wirtschaftstheoretische und wirtschaftspolitische Bedeutung der Kartelldebatte auf der Tagung des Vereins für Socialpolitik im Jahre 1905', 11 *Jahrbuch für Sozialwissenschaft* 125 (1960) and Boese, *Geschichte des Vereins*, 109–22.

[66] Schmoller, 'Das Verhältnis der Kartelle zum Staat', 241.   [67] Ibid., 237.

[68] Ibid., 256–57.

The meeting revealed significant support for the idea that the state should do something like that for which Schmoller called, although there was no agreement on the details. Important for the future development of thought about cartel legislation, however, was the rapidly strengthening assumption that any solution should be an administrative one. Despite Max Weber's warning that an administrative solution was not likely to provide the kind of 'objective' supervision of cartels that Schmoller was suggesting, the idea of an administrative solution was well-received, and there was little serious consideration of private law models.

The popularity of administrative, case-by-case responses was associated with a growing tendency to perceive and to conceptualize harmful cartel conduct as 'abuses' of economic power. This conceptualization provided a means of maintaining the positive image of cartels while at the same time criticizing cartel conduct, and it was to become a fixture of European thought relating to cartels and economic power generally.

The degree to which sentiment had turned against cartels is reflected in the legislative measures proposed at the meeting, many of which envisioned extensive measures to curb cartel abuses. There was, for example, discussion of the idea of establishing a state commission that would establish maximum prices for cartels. There were even calls for nationalizing cartels that were taken seriously by some leading economists. The message from the economics profession had changed significantly since the 1894 meeting.

2. The role of the legal community

While economists focused on the harms and benefits of cartels and the possible consequences of regulating them, the legal community turned its attention to the forms any such governmental action might take. Available conceptions of 'how' such legislation might be structured naturally influenced thought about the issue of 'whether' to legislate, but the relationship between the two issues was seldom discussed.

a. The legal community: contours and influence

The contours and social roles of the legal community were key factors in the development of competition law ideas. In Wilhelmine Germany, that community was defined by education rather than by economic interests or professional roles. It consisted of a relatively small number of *Juristen* (that is, those who held legal degrees) and its most prominent members tended to be bureaucrats, professors and, to a lesser extent, judges.

Bureaucrats were more important in this community than they are today.[69]

---

[69] For discussion of the German bureaucracy in the nineteenth century, see, e.g., Hansjoachim Henning, *Die deutsche Beamtenschaft im 19. Jahrhundert: Zwischen Stand und Beruf* (Stuttgart, 1984).

Until the First World War, all higher bureaucrats in the *Reich* were required to have university law degrees.[70] Consequently, all were part of the community of *Juristen*, and, as we have seen, the bureaucracy had enormous power in the Wilhelmine political system. In part this power rested on traditions of bureaucratic leadership and on the weakness of other political institutions (for example, the legislature), but it was reinforced by Bismarck's political strategies.[71] For him, enhancing the power and status of the bureaucracy was a means of centralizing and unifying the new country and increasing the government's control over events and decisions. In addition, by placing Prussians in leading positions in the bureaucracy, Bismarck and his successors sought to avoid any dilution of Prussia's power and influence within the *Reich*.

Many members of the *Reichstag* (some of whom were also bureaucrats) were also part of this community. Although much less powerful than the imperial bureaucracy, the *Reichstag* was important as a political forum. Thus the legal community combined the most powerful political decision-makers (the bureaucrats) and the legislators, giving opinion formation within that community extraordinary influence.

In the years around the turn of the century, strong conservative and nationalist influences pervaded this community. Gone were the years earlier in the century when lawyers led the fight for political rights and societal change. For most purposes, German *Juristen* as a community had become defenders of the status quo.

Social background was one factor in this conservatism. Virtually all *Juristen* were drawn from an 'education bourgeoisie'(*Bildungsbürgertum*) or the lower ranks of the aristocracy.[72] They were 'Mandarins', to use Fritz Ringer's evocative term, and as such they were part of an elite that controlled most institutions within German society. As the social conflicts emanating from industrialization sharpened during the 1880s and 1890s, this elite became increasingly concerned with preserving the structures that afforded its members wealth and power. Their education reinforced 'Mandarin' values by generally emphasizing the importance of the state and the necessity of maintaining existing political and social structures in the face of threats from socialists and workers.

If, despite these social and educational pressures, a law graduate managed to harbor other values, the state applied often intense pressure to suppress them.[73]

[70] For discussion of this '*Juristenprivileg*', see, e.g., Wilhelm Bleek, *Von der Kameralausbildung zum Juristenprivileg*, esp. 286–308 (Berlin, 1972).

[71] For discussion, see Eckart Kehr, 'The Dictatorship of the Bureaucracy', in Eckart Kehr, *Economic Interest, Militarism, and Foreign Policy* 164–73 (Gordon A. Craig, ed., Grete Heinz, tr., Berkeley, 1977).

[72] For discussion of the evolution of this group, see Fritz Ringer, *The Decline of the German Mandarins: the German Academic Community, 1890–1933* 15–25 (Cambridge, Mass., 1969).

[73] See Eckart Kehr, 'The Social System of Reaction in Prussia under the Puttkamer Ministry', in Eckart Kehr, *Economic Interest, Militarism and Foreign Policy* 109–31 (Gordon A. Craig, ed., Grete Heinz, tr., Berkeley, 1977).

Beginning in the 1880s, those who supported significant social or political change were 'purged' from the ranks of the *Reich*'s '*Beamten*' (life-tenured higher civil servants, professors and judges), particularly if they inclined toward socialist ideas. Thus the professional future of law graduates depended on maintaining conservative orthodoxy.

b. *Approaching the cartel law issue*

The *Saxon Wood Pulp* decision, the growing economic importance of cartels, and public interest in restraints on cartel conduct led the legal community to pay increasing attention to the issue of cartel legislation in the early years of the twentieth century. Its members produced a spate of articles and books on the issue, and it was featured at the biennial conventions of the *Deutscher Juristentag* (German Jurists' Association) in 1902 and 1904.[74]

These conventions played a key role in shaping the legal community's views on the issue—far more important than any analogous convention could have today. The *Juristentag* had been *the* convention of the German legal community since its founding in 1860, and in this pre-mass communication era it was the forum where leaders of the community met and sought to influence each other as well as the rest of the community. Its meetings often focused on key legal and policy issues, and the power of the legal community meant that such meetings often had an exceptional influence on public policy thinking.

The formulation of the topic at the conventions is significant: 'Which measures are appropriate (*empfehlen sich*) for the legal treatment of industrial cartels?' The issue posed was not *whether* any measures were appropriate for responding to the cartel problem, but *which ones*? At both conventions there was extensive and often heated debate on the issue both in specialized sections and in the plenum. As one commentator has put it, 'we encounter here an extremely agitated scene'.[75]

At the 1902 meeting the primary issue was whether to adopt conduct standards for cartels or merely require them to provide information about their operations to a government office. Of the four principal speakers on the issue only one, the Austrian law professor Adolf Menzel, called for legislation that would directly affect cartel conduct.[76] A German judge opposed any legislation,[77] while another Austrian law professor and a German economics professor favored a disclosure requirement for cartels.[78] The speakers thus represented a broad range of views, and Austrians were given a prominent

---

[74] For a description of these meetings as related to the cartel legislation issue, see Grossfeld, 'Zur Kartellrechtsdiskussion'.

[75] Ibid., 279.

[76] III *Verhandlungen des 26. Deutschen Juristentages* 277–289 (Berlin, 1902).

[77] III *Verhandlungen des 26. Deutschen Juristentages* 290–298 (Berlin, 1902) (Landesgerichtspräsident Nentwig).

[78] I *Verhandlungen des 26. Deutschen Juristentages* 294–388 (Julius Landesberger) and 63–71 (Heinrich Waentig) (Berlin, 1902).

place, presumably in the expectation that their recent experience with cartel legislation proposals might be useful for Germans seeking to fashion their own thinking on the subject. After intense and ultimately inconclusive debates in which Austrian participants tended to favor cartel legislation more than their German colleagues, it was agreed that the high level of interest in the topic required that it be put on the agenda again for the 1904 meeting.

At the 1904 convention the situation appears even more agitated, and it had also become more politicized.[79] Because of the known proclivities of the Austrians to favor more aggressive steps to curtail cartel abuses, some Germans had sought to bar Austrians from the convention.[80] While this effort was unsuccessful, no Austrians (and no academics) were asked to give prepared papers, which were presented exclusively by Germans (one practicing attorney, one appeals court judge and an in-house corporate lawyer).[81] All strongly supported cartels and opposed any action that might harm them, even including a disclosure duty. The choice of speakers suggests that the leadership of the organization was seeking to turn opinion against the idea of cartel legislation.

The commentator on these papers was, however, Franz Klein, a former Austrian Justice Minister and a highly respected jurist,[82] and his role gave the German-Austrian conflict new dimensions. For Klein, abuses by cartels created serious harm to individual freedoms and could not be ignored, but he argued against legislation to regulate cartels, preferring to place primary responsibility in the hands of bureaucrats who would be charged with molding general economic policy to reduce the ability of cartels to cause harm.[83] He also proposed (as he had in 1902) the creation of a price commission to investigate instances of cartel misconduct and publish its findings. This commission would not have enforcement powers, although Klein suggested that these might be added in the future.

Klein's position reflected the skepticism of a committed liberal toward government intervention in the economy. Yet it also reflected the perception of harm from cartel abuses that had led to Austrian proposals for cartel legislation. In particular, Klein was concerned about monopolistic pricing by cartels. He proposed, therefore, the following resolution:

---

[79] Fritz Blaich, a careful student of the debates, considered this meeting to represent 'a complete change of direction'. Blaich, *Kartell- und Monopolpolitik*, 42–43.

[80] Grossfeld, 'Zur Kartellrechtsdiskussion', 288.

[81] II *Verhandlungen des 27. Juristentages* 28–44 (Berlin, 1904) (Rechtsanwalt Scharlach) and I *Verhandlungen des 27. Juristentages* 45–56 (Oberlandesgerichtsrat Schneider) and 3–56 (Landesgerichtsrat Dove—Syndikus der Handelskammer zu Berlin) (Berlin, 1904).

[82] For biographical information on Klein, see *Forschungsband: Franz Klein (1854–1926)— Leben und Wirken* (Herbert Hofmeister, ed., Vienna, 1988). His major writings and speeches regarding the proposed German cartel legislation are collected at Franz Klein, I *Reden, Vorträge, Aufsätze, Briefe* 229–308 (Vienna, 1927).

[83] He did not, however, want bureaucrats to have regulatory power, because he feared 'corrupting' influences on their decision-making. See Klein, I *Reden*, 234.

The *Juristentag* considers that the issues that have arisen through the cartelization process and the activities of cartels should primarily be regulated by administrative policy and economic legislation. It considers quick and effective protection necessary against exaggerated, economically unjustified price increases, particularly against those through which the economically less advantaged are most seriously affected.[84]

Despite forceful, sometimes personal, attacks from the German participants against Klein,[85] he persuaded the plenum to approve the resolution (as amended by substituting 'recommended' for 'necessary'). Klein's arguments provided a means of resolving the tension within the legal community between the perceived need to combat cartel abuses and the reluctance to proceed to regulation. They also reflected a high degree of confidence in the role of administrators, specifically their capacity to fashion economic policy that would minimize such abuses.

F. THE POLITICAL (MIS)FORTUNES OF THE COMPETITION LAW IDEA

While lawyers and economists struggled to shape thought about cartel legislation, political parties faced the issue on the level of practical politics. During the decade after the *Saxon Wood Pulp* decision, the issue of cartel legislation became a highly-charged focus of political activity. These early efforts to enact cartel legislation played an important role in the evolution of political consciousness among population groups beginning to see in the legislative process a means of achieving ends which they identified as their own. This political 'awakening' resembled the populist pressures that led to antitrust legislation in the US and belies the common assumption that the US was somehow unique in this regard. The transmission of popular pressure into legislation took longer in Germany, but it occurred.

1. The political context

The relative weakness of democratic institutions in Wilhelmine Germany was the primary reason for this delay in transforming political impulses into legislation. Political power remained concentrated in the *Kaiser*, the chancellor, and the bureaucracy, and each of these centers of power combated legislative attempts to impose controls on cartels.

The *Kaiser*'s extraordinary power was the core of this resistance. He could appoint and dismiss the chancellor and government ministers, veto most legislation and, under some circumstances, enact laws without the approval of the *Reichstag*. Consequently, if the *Kaiser* wished to control political out-

---

[84] IV *Verhandlungen des 27. Deutschen Juristentages* 500 (Berlin, 1904).
[85] IV *Verhandlungen des 27. Deutschen Juristentages* 676 (Comments of Rechtsanwalt Scharlach) (Berlin, 1904).

comes, he could, and Wilhelm II often did. Crowned in 1888 at the age of 29, he believed that as a Hohenzollern he had a divine right to rule and that the legislature had no right to interfere with his prerogatives.

Wilhelm was preoccupied throughout his reign with advancing Germany's economic and military might, and thus he was not inclined to accept threats to its industrial base.[86] The heavy industries that supplied ships and military hardware were heavily cartelized, and the desire to protect them was reason enough for him to oppose cartel legislation. There was, therefore, little likelihood that he would allow any significant cartel legislation to become law.

The chancellor and the imperial bureaucracy controlled most governmental decisions, and they also had few incentives to favor cartel legislation. First, they could not risk the displeasure of the *Kaiser*. Second, by the 1890s the bureaucracy was increasingly driven by a conservative ideology in which the preservation of the social status quo was a pre-eminent value, and interference with cartels would threaten that stability. Third, Prussians generally held the highest positions in the imperial bureaucracy, including the departments that might have taken the initiative on cartel legislation, and they were unlikely to interfere with cartels, because Prussia was home to much of the heavy industry and raw material production in which cartels were prominent.[87] And, finally, Germany's economic success had given the country much longed-for international prestige, prosperity, and power, and cartels were widely seen as a factor in that success.

Another institutional obstacle to cartel legislation was the *Bundesrat* (Federal Council), the upper house of the legislature, which would have to approve cartel legislation. Its members were appointed by state governments and answerable directly to them. They were often drawn from the nobility and served the diplomatic function of negotiating compromises between sectional interests. They had no reason to support a proposal that might displease state governments or involve major sectional conflicts, and a cartel law was likely to do both.

2. Support for competition legislation

This situation meant that any effort to achieve cartel legislation had to focus on the lower house of the legislature, the *Reichstag*. The *Reichstag*'s formal power was limited, for its proposals had to be approved by the *Bundesrat* and could generally be vetoed by the *Kaiser*. Nevertheless, *Reichstag* majorities were necessary to enact most forms of legislation, and thus even Bismarck, who hated legislatures, had to seek support there. In addition, the *Reichstag* was an important forum for public debate, and its activities often became a

---

[86] The classic treatment of these issues is still Eckart Kehr, *Schlachtflottenbau und Parteipolitik 1894–1901* (Berlin, 1930).

[87] Blaich, *Kartell- und Monopolpolitik,* 15.

focus of public attention. It was here that the ideas of economists and lawyers regarding competition law were translated into political dynamics.[88]

The *Reichstag* was the only political institution in Wilhelmine Germany that was directly responsible to the populace, but it was not as democratic as it appeared. For example, although deputies were elected by universal manhood suffrage, they received no compensation for their services, thus restricting membership to those of independent means and those paid by the parties they represented. In addition, electoral districts were not adjusted for changes in population, so that they did not reflect the extensive urbanization that occurred after the initial districting in 1867. Nevertheless, the *Reichstag* was directly elected, and by the turn of the century the interests of many groups within German society were represented there.

Prior to 1900, the *Reichstag*'s actions regarding cartels were of little importance for the development of competition law ideas. Although it began to pay attention to problems caused by cartels as early as the late 1870s, these early debates tended to treat cartels as aspects of larger policy decisions.[89] For example, the first debates about cartels occurred in 1879 in the context of proposed tariff increases, because legislators recognized that increased industrial tariffs would encourage cartelization. Similarly, cartel arrangements were investigated and criticized in 1891 because they contributed to the high price of railroad track sold to the newly nationalized railroads, and later in the decade there was much discussion of the monopolistic practices of John D. Rockefeller's Standard Oil Trust.[90] Despite popular pressure, especially regarding Standard Oil, the *Reichstag* took no significant action.

With the turn of the century, however, the *Reichstag* began to focus on the issue of general legislation involving cartels. In part this was a response to changing economic circumstances. The brief economic recession that began in 1900 highlighted the plight of workers and small businesses, and as cartels acquired increasing control of ever more markets, the anti-big business sentiment that had swelled during the 1890s was increasingly directed against cartels. There was growing awareness that cartels could and often did cause significant economic harm to both consumers and other producers. In addition, the initial political successes of cartel legislation in Austria suggested not only that such legislation was important, but also that it might be politically obtainable. Finally, the extensive attention that economists and lawyers paid to the cartel issue forced political parties to confront it.[91]

[88] My treatment of the parliamentary developments is much indebted to the research in Blaich, *Kartell- und Monopolpolitik.*

[89] For fuller discussion, see Schröder, *Die Entwicklung des Kartellrechts,* 5.

[90] See Fritz Blaich, 'Der "Standard-Oil-Fall" vor dem Reichstag. Ein Beitrag zur deutschen Monopolpolitik vor 1914', 126 *Zeitschrift für die gesamte Staatswissenschaft* 663 (1970).

[91] See generally Fritz Blaich, 'Die Anfänge der deutschen Antikartellpolitik zwischen 1897 und 1914', 21 *Jahrbuch für Sozialwissenschaft* 127 (1970).

Pressure for some form of cartel legislation came from three main groups. Those who purchased goods produced by cartels were harmed by the higher prices which the cartels were able to charge. Those who sold to cartels protested the power of cartels to force down prices on their products. And small and medium-sized firms often complained that cartels coerced them into membership. The complaints and concerns of these groups gradually found political expression and generated support.

The articulation and representation of purchaser interests was pivotal. The tendency of cartels to raise the price of goods above competitive levels and thus shift resources from purchasers, particularly consumers, to producers was widely recognized and well-publicized. It thus represented a powerful potential impetus for legislation. This potential was blunted, however, by the weakness of the vehicles for its expression. In turn of the century Germany, 'consumer interests' as such had neither a voice nor significant institutional support. Consumer interests seldom acquire definition and force unless democratic institutions provide opportunities for their development, and in Germany that had not yet occurred.

Consumer interests tended to be subsumed within other interests. Particularly during the early cartel debates, they were typically subsumed within the vague idea of harm to the 'general public'. More importantly, they tended to be subsumed within the category of harm to workers as a class. Here the problem was that the party that primarily represented worker interests, the Social Democratic Party (SPD), showed little concern for the issue. For the social democrats, nascent consumer interests were overshadowed and suppressed by the ideology of class.[92]

The SPD's original lack of support for cartel legislation is important. That party expanded rapidly during the 1890s, and by the turn of the century it had become a powerful institution in the *Reichstag*. Had it forcefully advocated cartel legislation, such legislation is likely to have come earlier and taken a stronger form than it did. Such legislation also seemed to 'fit' one of the main themes of the party's political imagery, which was that workers were exploited by capitalists. This seemed to call for SPD support of cartel legislation to protect against such exploitation, and in the early political debates regarding cartels the SPD appeared to be moving in that direction.[93] Some of its top leaders vigorously protested the effects of price increases on the weaker

---

[92] This submersion of the interests of consumers within the category of workers' class interests was an important factor distinguishing the dynamics of competition law development in Europe from those in the United States.

[93] For discussion of the SPD's positions regarding cartel legislation, see Eduard Reuffurth, *Die Stellung der deutschen Sozialdemokratie zum Problem der staatlichen Kartellpolitik* (Diss. Jena, 1930); Schröder, *Die Entwicklung des Kartellrechts*, 56–59 and 136–40; and Blaich, *Kartell- und Monopolpolitik*, 209–17.

members of society and blamed cartels for these increases.[94] It seemed as if the party might focus on the harms to workers *qua* consumers, but it did not.

Instead, a different component of the SPD's imagery blocked this connection and led the SPD to support cartels.[95] Perhaps encouraged by their rapid political advances to believe that the victory of socialism was not far away, the SPD leadership increasingly viewed cartels in terms of their own plans to achieve political power. Adopting a Marxist version of Hegelian thought, the SPD leadership came to see in cartels a step on the path toward socialism, because they were an inevitable part of the development of capitalism that would lead to the victory of socialism. According to Rainer Schröder, 'The general economic development fit so well into the logic of Marxist economic thought that one paid little attention to the difficulties caused by a price and sales policy that was perceived as unjust'.[96]

From this perspective, cartels served the SPD's purposes by creating a more organized economy. This greater organization of the competitive process would, they thought, facilitate even further organization by the state, which they, the socialists, would complete when they achieved political power. During the critically important debates regarding cartels in the first decade of the twentieth century, therefore, the SPD generally declined to support legislation that might impose significant limits on cartel activity.[97]

With the withdrawal of the SPD from active support for cartel legislation, the representation of consumer interests fell to the Center Party, the only other significant party that sought to represent the interests of workers.[98] This party was supported by the Roman Catholic church and sought to represent the interests not only of Catholic workers, but of the *Mittelstand* (basically, owners of small and medium-sized businesses) as well. For the Center, the

---

[94] In parliamentary debates in 1890, for example, August Bebel, one of the party's most prominent leaders, condemned cartel pricing policies as 'exploitation of consumers'. For discussion, see Blaich, *Kartell- und Monopolpolitik*, 71.

[95] The change of direction seems to have taken place rather quickly around the year 1902. See Blaich, Ibid., 119.

[96] Schröder, *Die Entwicklung des Kartellrechts*, 58. He points out later in the same work that 'The position of the social democrats was influenced by an eschatological perspective, which made the problems of earthly existence seem acceptable in comparison with the expected revolution'. Ibid., 140.

[97] Resistance to cartel legislation was occasionally associated with claims by social democrats that cartels were valuable for the purpose of stabilizing employment for workers and thus should not be harmed. See, e.g., Blaich, *Kartell- und Monopolpolitik*, 88. The cartel issue undoubtedly played important roles in the development of socialism, although this issue does not appear to have been studied carefully. It was perhaps the single most important economic policy issue during the period when socialist leaders such as Eduard Bernstein were developing and promulgating new 'revisionist' images of socialist policy. At the very least, it focused the attention of social democrats on the tension between an eschatological, Marxist perspective and the immediate economic interests of their supporters.

[98] For discussion of the Center Party during this period, see, e.g., David Blackbourn, 'The Problem of Democratization: German Catholics and the Role of the Centre Party', in *Society and Politics in Wilhelmine Germany* 160–85 (Richard J. Evans, ed., London, 1978).

cartel issue had the attraction of serving its two prime constituencies, and thus this party provided the primary political impetus for cartel legislation until the First World War.

Yet this dual constituency also tended to compromise, dilute and often obscure consumer interests in cartel legislation, because the *Mittelstand* provided the leadership of the party, and impetus for cartel legislation was cast in terms of their interests. This effect can be seen in the Center's call in 1900 for an official investigation of cartels,[99] which caused the *Reichstag* for the first time to focus on the issue of general legislation regulating cartels. The request was part of an attack on the coal cartel for high prices that 'oppressed large population groups'. Yet the stated objective in making the request was 'protection of the small and medium-sized firms in trade, particularly in retail trade'.

The Center often also tied demands for a cartel law to Catholic social doctrine. Around the turn of the century this doctrine was influential in many parts of Germany, particularly in formulating political appeals to the working classes. It emphasized the value of social, religious and national communities and the need to protect the weaker members of that community. This line of thought led the Center to advocate controls on 'abusive' cartel conduct, but it militated against any sharper form of interference with cartels, because cartels were assumed to be necessary for the economic welfare of the community and for job stability.[100]

3. The alliance against cartel legislation

The political impetus for cartel legislation was not only hampered by these institutional and conceptual weaknesses, but it was also opposed by the Bismarckian alliance between heavy industry, big agrarian interests and the bureaucracy.[101] The parties representing cartelized industries, that is, particularly heavy industry and 'big' agriculture, were well organized, powerful and committed to preventing cartel legislation, and the bureaucracy furnished them with critical support on the cartel issue.[102]

The impact of this alliance is best illustrated in the so-called Cartel *Enquête*.[103] As we have seen, members of the Center Party requested a major investigation of cartel activities in 1900. They undoubtedly hoped that such

[99] Blaich, *Kartell- und Monopolpolitik*, 103.

[100] For discussion, see Blaich, ibid., 217–21.

[101] For discussion of the creation of this alliance in the struggle over tariff policy, see Böhme, *Deutschlands Weg*, 474–587. See also Dirk Stegmann, *Die Erben Bismarcks: Parteien und Verbände in der Spätphase des wilhelminischen Deutschlands* 131–76 (Cologne, 1970).

[102] For the influence of the bureaucracy and its growing aristocratization after 1879, see Böhme, ibid., 582–84, and Hans-Ulrich Wehler, *Bismarck und der Imperialismus* 112–93 (Cologne, 1969).

[103] For discussion of the *Enquête* and the circumstances surrounding it, see Blaich, *Kartell- und Monopolpolitik*, 237–69.

an investigation would defuse the everpresent argument made by opponents of cartel legislation that too little was known about cartels to justify legislation. The *Reichstag* endorsed the request, but, as was customary during this period, it did not carry out the investigation itself. It asked the imperial bureaucracy to do so.

The bureaucracy did conduct an investigation, but it did so in a way that impeded efforts toward cartel legislation for several years. In response to growing academic and public pressure to investigate cartels, the bureaucracy had begun to consider some form of cartel investigation even before the *Reichstag*'s request. In 1899, the official appointed to make recommendations regarding this issue, presented an internal memorandum calling for the establishment of an office that could demand and disseminate information concerning cartels. Apparently as a result of interest group pressure, however, he was quickly told not to bother the cartels. He was allowed to gather some information until 1904, and in the following year he took a prominent position with one of the leading cartels.

The government's public investigation in the *Enquête* reflected a similar aversion to developing information that might be harmful to cartel interests. In response to the *Reichstag*'s request for an investigation, the minister of the interior assured the *Reichstag* that his ministry would begin a serious investigation of cartels and that, therefore, the *Reichstag* could leave the task to the ministry. This assurance effectively put potential legislative activity 'on hold' for years. Since an investigation seemed imminent, little could be done until it had produced additional information.

The investigation was delayed for almost two years—until 1902, and, once started, it proceeded very slowly until it was terminated in 1905. The bureaucracy's handling of the investigation suggests that its primary objective was to protect cartels rather than to shed light on their activity.[104] The proceedings featured testimony from many high-ranking cartel leaders, although representatives of other groups opposed to the unlimited power of the cartels were also included. The government refused to compel witnesses to provide information, and it did not question those who did or allow them to be questioned by others. They were essentially allowed to bring forth the information they wanted to make known. The minister high-handedly scuttled discussion of issues that might reflect too negatively on cartels. The famous economist Lujo Brentano resigned his role in the investigation because he considered that the procedures were not designed to address the actual problems and provide the necessary information.[105]

---

[104] The conduct of the bureaucracy in relation to cartels lends support to recent critiques of claims of 'neutrality' on the part of the bureaucracy. See, e.g., Jane Caplan, ' "The Imaginary Universality of Particular Interests": the "tradition" of the civil service in German history,' 4 *Social History* 299 (1979).

[105] Brentano, *Mein Leben*, 236.

4. Cracks in the wall: establishing a cartel office

The bureaucracy's dilatory and obstructionist tactics in the *Enquête* effectively prevented progress toward cartel legislation for years, but in 1908 an economic recession and electoral victories for parties demanding action on the cartel issue led an overwhelming majority of the *Reichstag* to support a proposal of the Center Party to establish a cartel office in the imperial bureaucracy that would gather and disseminate information on cartels.[106] As a contemporary commented, these debates provided a bizarre situation in which 'in front of the entire country the *Reichstag* appeared through great numbers of speeches from all parties more or less as the prosecutor of cartels, while the representatives of the government . . . appeared as their defenders'.[107]

Since the *Reichstag* could not itself require the bureaucracy to establish such an office, however, the proposal took the form of a request to the bureaucracy. At first, the bureaucracy merely ignored the request, but, finally, after similar requests from strong *Reichstag* majorities in the succeeding legislative sessions, the bureaucracy finally set up a small office to acquire information about cartels. Before it could be made fully operational, however, 1914 intervened.[108] One of the leaders in this fight to establish a cartel law was Gustav Stresemann, who represented small and medium-sized enterprises and who in 1923 as *Reichskanzler* enacted the first German cartel legislation.[109]

Two events during this period deserve note. The first was the enactment of a statute in 1910 that created a potash cartel and provided administrative supervision of its operations.[110] This was the first time that the Wilhelmine government had required the creation of a cartel, and its supervisory apparatus indicated that one response to problems created by cartels was to establish administrative supervision of their activities.

The second was the publication in 1912 of a monograph that quickly became a center of attention among those interested in cartel law issues and was to have a major influence on Weimar cartel legislation. The book was Fritz Kestner's *Der Organisationszwang* (roughly, coercion to organize).[111] In

[106] For discussion of the crisis year of 1908 and the 'extraordinary' increase in public anger directed at the conduct of cartels, see Schröder, *Die Entwicklung des Kartellrechts*, 140.

[107] Dr Uth, 'Die jüngste Kartelldebatte im Reichstag', 6 *Kartell-Rundschau* 250, 251 (1908).

[108] These events are described in Blaich, 'Die Anfänge der deutschen Antikartellpolitik'.

[109] For discussions of his role, see Blaich, *Kartell- und Monopolpolitik*, 131, 142.

[110] See Knut W. Nörr, 'Das Reichskaligesetz 1910: Ein Musterstatut der organisierten Wirtschaft', 108 *Zeitschrift der Savigny-Stiftung für Rechtsgeschichte* 347 (1991).

[111] Fritz Kestner, *Der Organisationszwang: Eine Untersuchung über die Kämpfe zwischen Kartellen und Aussenseitern* (Berlin, 1912). Oswald Lehnich published a second edition of Kestner's book in 1927—Oswald Lehnich & Fritz Kestner, *Der Organisationszwang. Eine Untersuchung über die Kämpfe zwischen Kartellen und Aussenseitern* (2d. ed., Berlin, 1927). He then included much of the contents of that book in a book he published under his own name in 1956 and that continued to be influential into the 1960s—Oswald Lehnich, *Die Wettbewerbsbeschränkung: Eine Grundlegung* (Cologne, 1956).

it, he demonstrated that cartel coercion, both internal (with respect to its members) and external (with respect to non-members), was a fundamental threat to the entire legal order, because it undermined the assumptions of competitive freedom on which that order was based. At least partly because of his work, this focus became an important feature of the first German cartel legislation and of cartel law thinking in Germany during much of the Weimar period.

G. THE LEGACY OF PREWAR EXPERIENCE

Although pre-war efforts to enact competition legislation in Germany were unsuccessful, they established the conceptual, attitudinal and institutional fundaments on which competition legislation would be built after World War I. They also generated a distinctive view of cartels and of the potential role of law in relation to them that eventually was to channel much European competition law thinking.

Debates in academic and political fora focused public attention on the cartel problem and on the question of how the government should respond to it. A decade of well-publicized attention by economists, lawyers and legislators made it difficult for subsequent decision-makers to ignore these issues. In addition, the widespread support that evolved during the first decade of the twentieth century for some form of governmental response to the cartel problem created expectations that there eventually would be such a response. Prewar thought and experience thus established basic perspectives on both the problem and its solution, and when political circumstances changed after the First World War, this framework served as a ready basis for political action. Many of those who made economic policy and legal decisions in the 1920s had taken part in these controversies and formed their opinions within this framework.

The perception and interpretation of cartels by economists, lawyers and bureaucrats defined the 'problem'. While Austrian proposals had articulated the cartel problem in broad, relatively abstract terms centering on the concept of restraints of competition, the German perspective was narrower, seeing cartels as an independent problem unrelated to broader issues. This difference in perspective reflected differences in economic thought between German historicist thought and the more theoretical and conceptual discourse of Austrian economics.

The role of economists in shaping this perception of the problem deserves emphasis. It was the German *economists'* view that came to dominate thought about cartels and cartel legislation. The legal community basically accepted the image of cartels provided by the economists rather than developing, as it might have, a framework for evaluating the cartel phenomenon based on legal categories such as, for example, contractual fairness.[112]

In this view, the evaluative issue was whether institutions were appropriate for the time and circumstances, and from that perspective cartels were basically positive institutions. They were seen as superior to both excessive competition and alternate forms of organization such as trusts, because they assured and rewarded important social values such as co-operation rather than baser forces such as individualism and egoism, thus reducing conflicts among competitors and protecting rather than exploiting the weak. This basic perception of cartels and the competitive process persisted in many parts of Europe until recently, and its echoes continue to reverberate.

This meant that the problem had to be located not in the contractual arrangement or the organizational form, but in specific conduct. It did not inhere in the nature or characteristics of cartels, but was perceived as *ad hoc* and particularistic. The question was when cartels went too far, and this led to the concept of abuse of power as a central structural idea in responding to the cartel problem.

As perceptions of the problem acquired structure and stability during the early years of the twentieth century, so did conceptions of how to respond to it. One key move was a rapid increase in the 'legal' characteristics of these conceptions. Whereas initial responses to the cartel problem were conceived as *ad hoc* issues of government *policy* applicable only to specific industries and situations, more 'juridical' conceptions of response soon moved to center stage. Reflecting the dominance of legal training and experience among Wilhelmine decision-making elites, legal vocabulary—norms, their interpretation, and their enforcement—became central to this discourse.

Conceptions of response to the cartel problem had to focus on legislation, because the 'legalization' of cartels in the *Saxon Wood Pulp* case blocked the path over general principles of law and the regular courts. The issues were whether to introduce legislation and, if so, what kind of legislation. This distinguished the German situation from that in many other European countries, where it was assumed that responses to the cartel problem would be developed by the judiciary using principles of private and commercial law.

The idea of creating a new type of legislation to deal with cartels generated cautionary and hesitant attitudes. On one level, this stemmed from fear of harming a form of economic organization that seemed to many to be economically and socially valuable, superior to alternate forms of organization, and inevitable as a matter of social evolution. It was also rooted in the conservatism of a ruling elite for whom cartels seemed to serve their own economic, political and social interests.

---

[112] See also Blaich, *Kartell- und Monopolpolitik*, 36–37.

Several characteristics of contemporary legal thought also contributed to this attitude. Historicism, for example, emphasized the organic relationship between legal norms and national experience.[113] Law was supposed to develop slowly from the 'spirit of the people'. This made German *Juristen* suspicious of bold new legislative initiatives that were not rooted in German experience. The powerful influence of 'legal science' had a similar impact. It demanded conceptual precision and deductive systematization, and the lack of experience with norms of cartel conduct precluded even modest levels of conceptual precision.

These perceptions of the problem and attitudes about how to respond to it naturally shaped conceptions of the form of potential legislation. In this context four ideas were central: (1) any legislation should relate exclusively to cartels, (2) gathering information should at least initially be the major focus of legislation, (3) solutions to the problem should focus on 'abusive' conduct, and (4) administrative decisions should be the basic mechanism of response.

The perception that cartels were a distinct problem unrelated to more general issues of economic power or even to other similar arrangements in pre-industrial society narrowed the scope of response, so that German thinking and legislation focused almost exclusively on the cartel problem rather than on the broader issue of restraints of competition. Had Germany adopted the broader Austrian conception of competition legislation, the history of competition law in Europe might have been very different.

The idea that legislation should at least initially center on gathering information about cartels was attractive, because it was a means of 'signalling' society's concerns about cartel 'abuses' without actually interfering with cartel activity. It acknowledged the concerns of those who claimed that there was insufficient information on which to construct conduct norms, but it could be portrayed as a first step in the direction of establishing such norms.

Where discussions of response went beyond information-gathering, they generally focused on identifying and discouraging harmful cartel conduct rather than on cartel arrangements themselves. The central image was that cartels should be prevented from engaging in conduct that was 'abusive' in that it unfairly harmed others in the community—either customers or competitors. This conception has colored European thinking about competition law ever since.

Finally, there was general agreement that any responses to the cartel problem should rely on administrative decision-making. The judicial road seemed closed or at least inadequate, and negative perceptions of US experience discredited legislation modelled on it, particularly any thoughts of criminalizing forms of cartel conduct.[114] This left few alternatives other than an adminis-

---

[113] For discussion of historicism in German legal thought, see, e.g., Wolfgang Fikentscher, III *Methoden des Rechts: Mitteleuropäischer Rechtskreis* 37–77 (Tübingen, 1975).

[114] See Fritz Blaich, 'Die Rolle der Amerikanischen Antitrustgesetzgebung in der wirtschaftswissenschaftlichen Diskussion Deutschlands Zwischen 1890 und 1914', 22 *ORDO* 229 (1971).

trative response. Moreover, the contemporary enchantment with the idea that the bureaucracy provided a 'neutral' arbiter of the conflicting interests in society made this alternative attractive.

On the level of tangible results, prewar efforts to create cartel legislation were hardly impressive—in the end, no significant general legislation was enacted. The institutional obstacles were too great, the perception of harm too indistinct, and the fear of interfering with economic interests and processes too powerful. Yet intellectual developments and perceptual changes created political momentum toward some form of competition law. Despite strong opposition from the *Kaiser*, the imperial bureaucracy and heavy industry—the most powerful political forces in the *Reich*—all parties in the *Reichstag* had agreed by 1908 to demand creation of a cartel office that would at least investigate cartels, and this was widely understood as merely a first step toward more significant regulation. Moreover, they exerted enough pressure on the bureaucracy that it finally agreed to create such an office. Under the circumstances, these were significant accomplishments.

The controversies over cartel legislation and the political momentum that eventually emerged from them had consequences in many areas of German life. Some were political. For example, the issue of cartel legislation sharpened perceptions of consumer interests and increased awareness of them by focusing attention on the harms that cartels could inflict on individuals *qua* consumers. This, in turn, highlighted the conflict between big business interests, on the one hand, and consumer and *Mittelstand* interests, on the other, and thus contributed to anti-big business sentiments and tended to encourage democratic consciousness.

These conflicts also exacerbated conflicts within industry itself—specifically, between 'big business' such as iron and steel, which tended to be heavily cartelized, and the smaller, processing industries which were generally harmed by the cartelization of their suppliers. As Helga Nussbaum has demonstrated, this created tensions within industry and within the 'bourgeoisie' generally that were to have significant political consequences.[115] But these tensions did more—they helped to shape cartel legislation, which served primarily to protect smaller, processing firms from cartel coercion.

The process also had social consequences. The controversy over cartel legislation produced tensions within the ruling elite that had appeared to be virtually monolithic in the 1880s and 1890s. For example, it strained the close ties between the academic/intellectual and ownership components of this elite that had contributed so much to the stability of the Wilhelmine state. As it became increasingly obvious that cartels often caused harm not only to consumers but to small and medium-sized industries, academics and journalistic commentators often found themselves in conflict with the representatives of

---

[115] Helga Nussbaum, *Unternehmer gegen Monopole: Über Struktur und Aktionen antimonopolistischer bürgerlicher Gruppen zu Beginn des 20. Jahrhunderts* (Berlin, 1966).

industry that denied or downplayed such harm and with bureaucrats who used their power to protect cartelized industry.

While ideas about competition law were taking shape and gaining support in Germany and Austria, other European countries were either paying little serious attention to problems posed by cartels or continuing to rely on private law and criminal law in responding to those problems. As a result, when political circumstances aborted further developments in Austria, Germany found itself with a 'headstart' in thinking about competition law and creating the foundations for its enactment and enforcement, and this has allowed German thought and experience to play central roles in the European competition law tradition.

But why did other countries not move in this direction? Part of the answer is that outside of Germany and Austria cartels were less important. The cartel as a form of economic organization did not there become a dominant form of economic organization. Cartels tended to grow less rapidly in size and economic influence, and thus they did not elicit the same concerns and the same level of response. Political factors probably also played a role. As David Landes has observed, in Germany and Austria business interests were subordinated to goals of national unity during this period, whereas in the rest of Europe, and particularly in France and England, economic interests tended to control governmental policy.[116] Finally, there was no analogue in other countries to the abrupt 'closing' of the judicial road that occurred in Germany. Existing remedies in civil or criminal law were assumed to be sufficient to deal with any problems that cartels might present.

---

[116] David S. Landes, *The Unbound Prometheus: Technological Change and Industrial Development in Western Europe from 1750 to the Present* 6 (Cambridge, 1972).

V

The Interwar Period: Competition Law takes Root

The competition law ideas that had been debated in Austria and Germany before the war spread throughout Europe during the interwar period. In Germany, many of these ideas were enacted into law in the aftermath of the First World War, and by the end of the decade there were competition laws in other European countries. Moreover, competition law had become an important theme in discussions of law, business and economic policy on both the national and international levels. Although the depression of the 1930s temporarily submerged these ideas, they would resurface after the Second World War.

In this chapter we focus on Europe's first experiences with competition law and on the spread of these ideas within Europe. We pay less attention to the formation of ideas than we have in the last two chapters, not least because the interwar period generated relatively few new ideas that would exert a lasting influence on competition law developments. The themes of the period were generally drawn from prewar thought, but during this period they took root in European legal and economic experience.

A. TOWARD A GERMAN CARTEL LAW

Germany remains at the center of our story, because it was there that competition law ideas were most extensively discussed and broadly implemented, and because this experience played important roles in the evolution of the European competition law tradition after the Second World War. The cartel law enacted in Germany in 1923 was the first general legislation in Europe specifically intended to protect the process of competition, and thus it attracted attention not only from those in other European countries who sought such legislation, but also from those who opposed it. For both supporters and opponents of competition law, German experience became a point of reference for discussion and analysis.

1. The war economy: regulation and nationalism

The First World War was probably the first major war in which industrial production was recognized as a key element in military success,[1] and thus many European governments greatly expanded their regulation of industry in order to control it and, hopefully, to enhance its contribution to their war efforts. In Germany such controls were more extensive and effective than in many other European countries, and, more importantly, they were widely accepted.[2] The nationalism that was used to legitimize the war interwove economic regulation with positive images of the nation's struggle against its external enemies. As a result, Germans became accustomed to extensive economic regulation, and many came to value it.

Cartels played key roles in this wartime regulatory scheme, thus adding to the complexity of German experience with cartels. The government recognized that it was easier to control the activities of a relatively small number of cartels than those of a large number of independent firms, and thus it required existing cartels to enforce its program and compelled the cartelization of many areas of the economy that were not already cartelized. As a result, cartels became even more pervasive than they had been before the war. The war effort not only legitimized cartels by making them a tool of government, but also glorified them by bathing them in the symbols of nationalism. They became part of the nation's collective effort and closely identified with its national purpose. The war thus reinforced the generally positive images of cartels that had been common in the early decades of the cartel movement, but that had begun to darken after the turn of the century.

2. Postwar themes

The wrenching impact of the war's denouement and immediate aftermath established two themes that would dominate political, social and intellectual developments in Germany until the Nazi takeover in 1933—uncertainty and conflict.[3] The end of the war ushered in a decade and a half filled with disintegrative pressures and with often desperate efforts to counteract them. The first European competition legislation was enacted and implemented in the midst of, and in response to, this instability.

[1] For discussion of the relationship between economic and military power during the First World War that places it in a broader historical context, see Paul Kennedy, *The Rise and Fall of the Great Powers* 256–74 (New York, 1987).

[2] See generally Gerald D. Feldman, *Army, Industry and Labor in Germany: 1914–18* (Princeton, 1966).

[3] For a recent, in-depth discussion of the postwar period, see Richard Bessel, *Germany After the First World War* (Oxford, 1993). Covering a somewhat larger time-frame in great depth is Gerald D. Feldman, *The Great Disorder: Politics, Economics and Society in the German Inflation, 1914–1924* (New York, 1993).

The war ended with a revolt of soldiers and workers that forced the abdication of the *Kaiser* and an end to the empire. On many levels it signaled a sharp break with the past, and it left a continuing conflict between social groups with allegiance to pre-1918 societal ideals and those attached to the values and political ideals associated with the revolution. For years the ideas and experiences of the war and its aftermath coexisted uncomfortably with the images and ideals of the prewar period.

For several years after the end of the war supporters of socialist ideals controlled the government and enjoyed much popular support. Their avowed objective was to move toward a socialist society in which the values of equality and community would guide political decision-making and in which effective representation of the interests of workers would be assured. Under their aegis the so-called 'Weimar' constitution was promulgated in 1919 as the basis for such a society.

This Weimar Republic was far more democratic than the prewar political system. With the institution of the emperor eliminated and the role of the former *Bundesrat*, now rebaptized as the *Reichsrat*, significantly reduced, the *Reichstag* became the central source of political legitimacy. In addition, the constitution contained numerous social democratic ideas that were intended to bolster and secure the rights of workers.

Political leaders of this period formulated and sought to implement plans for Germany's economic future that combined socialist and nationalist imagery and values. A central theme in these plans was that the economy should serve the interests of the society, and here the key idea was that of *Gemeinwirtschaft* (roughly, community economy).[4] These plans began to be drawn even before the war ended, principally by Walter Rathenau and Wichard von Moellendorf. Both viewed the economy as an object to be structured; von Moellendorf went even further, portraying it as a machine that had to be constructed and maintained. Although there was some talk of nationalizing industries, the primary emphasis was on enlisting private industry in the service of the 'national will'.

These ideas were popular and influential. For many—mainly industrial and agricultural workers—they represented a means of securing what they considered a fairer portion of the fruits of their labor. For those in the middle classes who feared the effects of socialism and 'worker dominance', they represented an attractive alternative to state ownership. For bureaucrats, they

[4] See generally Friedrich Zunkel, *Industrie und Staatssozialismus: Der Kampf um die Wirtschaftsordnung 1914–18* (Düsseldorf, 1974). Ralph Bowen discusses these plans and puts them in context. See Ralph Bowen, *German Theories of the Corporate State: with special reference to the period 1870–1919* 160–207 (New York, 1947). See also Charles S. Maier, 'Society as Factory', in Charles S. Maier, *In Search of Stability: Explorations in Historical Political Economy* 19–70 (Cambridge, 1987).

had the additional allure of promising them prominence and power.[5] These basic images of the economy as the servant of society were to remain influential long after the specific idea of *Gemeinwirtschaft* had lost its lustre.

No sooner had the Weimar Republic been established, however, than a majority of German voters turned away from socialist leadership and returned to coalitions drawn largely from prewar elites. Short-lived coalitions featuring centrist or right-leaning majorities (that is, bourgeois parties) governed the republic for much of the remainder of the decade, and they often looked to prewar ideas for guidance.[6] The SPD continued to enjoy loyal and often powerful support, primarily among working groups, but it generally played the role of an opposition party.[7]

The tension between these two conceptions of society fostered conflict and instability throughout the Weimar period. Workers and others who supported socialist ideals resented the Weimar political system because it failed to fulfil the expectations of social justice that had been raised during the postwar period, while members of the middle and upper classes often resented that system because it did not go far enough in eliminating the socialist elements from government and returning to prewar institutions and goals. Parties of the right and center squabbled over power positions in rapidly changing coalitions, while always aware that the Social Democrats had a fundamentally different agenda for the future of Germany and a solid base of support among workers that might soon sweep away anything that the ruling parties created.

These conflicts contributed to—and were nourished by—a general sense of political instability based on lack of confidence in Weimar's political leaders and institutions. There was widespread dissatisfaction with the institutions of 'democracy'. The constantly shifting coalitions of the *Reichstag* inspired little confidence that they could deal effectively with the class conflicts at home or the demands and threats from the outside world. Combined with this lack of confidence in Weimar's institutions was widespread mistrust of the political class itself. For many, the legitimacy of the entire class of leaders was undermined by the *Dolchstosslegende* (knife-in-the-back legend) in which Weimar's leaders were portrayed as having engaged in a selfish act of treachery in ending the war. The use of such narrative symbols to explain defeat in war and disorder at home was prevalent, and it undermined the legitimacy of Weimar's political leaders.

[5] According to one source, virtually all the members of the economics ministry in 1920 were still fully plan-economy oriented. Eckhard Wandel, *Hans Schäffer: Steuermann in wirtschaftlichen und politischen Krisen* 55 (Stuttgart, 1974).

[6] For discussion, see Michael Stürmer, 'Koalitionen und Oppositionen: Bedingungen parlamentarischer Instabilität', in *Die Weimarer Republik* 237–53 (Michael Stürmer, ed., 3d. ed., Frankfurt a.M., 1993).

[7] See Hagen Schulze, 'Die SPD und der Staat von Weimar', in *Die Weimarer Republik* 272–86 (Michael Stürmer, ed., 3d. ed., Frankfurt a.M., 1993).

Until about 1925 extreme economic uncertainty accompanied this political instability and exacerbated the lack of confidence in political institutions. Inflation was the dominant factor in creating this uncertainty, and it had many causes. One was the government's policy of financing the war primarily by loans rather than taxes. This required postwar governments to use the printing presses to pay off wartime loans, thus rapidly increasing the money supply. In addition, demand exceeded supply in many industries (especially the heavy industries) for years after the end of the war, and this exerted continual upward pressure on prices. Finally, the Versailles treaty imposed high reparations obligations on Germany, hampering its efforts at economic recovery. The combination of these factors led to the legendary inflation of 1923 that aggravated class conflicts and threatened new revolutions.

For our purposes the conflicts and uncertainties of the postwar period are primarily important because of the responses they engendered. Political discourse—and sometimes political action—was dominated by the search for societal integration and political and economic stability. The threats of social disintegration and political upheaval were seldom far from the minds of German politicians and policymakers.

The integration theme operated on two interconnected levels. One was woven around the nation as symbol. In a society riven by class conflicts, this was the one symbol of cohesion, and its role in mobilizing German society for war demonstrated its potential. A second level emphasized ideals of co-operation and commonality of interest among Germans as neutral legitimating principles. Both favored institutions and arrangements that tended to foster co-operation and avoid conflict. The search for stability and order was closely tied to the pursuit of societal integration, because social and political conflicts posed the major threat to order. In a society that had so recently undergone such extraordinary change and instability, the desire to keep some control on change was profound.

But the contrast between these ideals and Weimar's political reality was jarring. Few expected political institutions and leaders to respond effectively to society's problems (which probably intensified the need to pursue them at the symbolic and discursive levels). The elected political institutions—that is, after 1919, the new *Reichstag*—instilled little confidence. Short-term coalitions came and went, and there was little sense that the political process was likely to produce either greater order or more societal integration.

The one institution that both symbolized stability and order and held out the promise of actually contributing to their realization was the bureaucracy—largely because it was viewed as 'neutral'. The bureaucracy had long played the role of political stabilizer, and the circumstances of Weimar intensified the need for it to continue to play that role. It is not surprising, therefore, that the bureaucracy was given responsibility to deal with the problem of cartels.

These patterns of response also affected the way people thought about the economy and the state's relationship to it. Images of *Gemeinwirtschaft* left a residue of assumptions, values and attitudes, many of which long remained influential. The basic idea that the economy should operate in the service of the society as a whole resonated strongly with calls for stability and societal integration, and its appeal forced political leaders of all stripes to take heed— at least on the level of political rhetoric.

The search for symbols of stability and societal integration also generated a continuing emphasis on organization and co-operation among economic actors. It lent appeal to the image of German firms co-operating to find solutions to the extraordinary problems faced by the economy during the postwar years—for example, demobilization, economic disruption and inflation.

3. Roles and images of cartels

In these volatile circumstances, cartels came to play new roles, and images of cartels changed accordingly. For several years after the end of the war, the importance and influence of cartels seemed to be waning. The destruction of industrial capacity during the war combined with the need to pay reparations in kind to France and other victorious countries kept supply on many markets significantly below demand. This reduced the capacity of cartels to maximize the revenues of their members by controlling output, and it reduced incentives for firms to participate in cartels and weakened their economic leverage.

Many cartels were, therefore, either disbanded or on the path toward dissolution when accelerating inflation in 1921 provided cartels with a new *raison d'être*.[8] In the context of high inflation, cartels were increasingly used not to control output, but to protect their members from the impact of inflation. They provided a mechanism by which the prices charged by cartel members could almost automatically be increased in response to increases in the price of the goods and services they purchased. As a result, producers were able to shift the primary burden of the inflation to their purchasers and, ultimately, to consumers.[9]

Political events and the shifting deposits of ideas that accompanied them joined with these changes to alter images of cartels. During the immediate postwar period, cartels continued to be seen primarily as positive contributors to the national well-being, fitting nicely into the then popular categories and assumptions of *Gemeinwirtschaft*. They represented co-operation and organization rather than individualism and conflict. The thrust of postwar

---

[8] According to one observer, it meant 'a complete change in the meaning of cartels'. Oswald Lehnich, *Die Wettbewerbsbeschränkung: Eine Grundlegung* 320 (Cologne, 1956).

[9] See Georg Rotthege, *Die Beurteilung von Kartellen und Genossenschaften durch die Rechtswissenschaft* 126–27 (Tübingen, 1982).

political and economic thought emphasized the need for planning toward a socially desirable goal and eschewed *laissez-faire* individual striving, and cartels seemed to correspond to those needs. Cartels were also politically useful, because they represented a kind of compromise between state ownership as called for by socialist doctrine and the private ownership that practical politicians of all political persuasions agreed was necessary for the economy to recover.

As traditional elites regained political power after 1920 and the ideas of *Gemeinwirtschaft* began to lose force, images of cartels began to darken. For many Germans, cartels increasingly became associated with the potentially harmful power of big business rather than with service on behalf of the nation. Moreover, the perception that cartels were contributing to inflation led to a powerful public reaction against them. As inflation reached epidemic proportions in 1922 and 1923, expanding poverty among the economically weak and fear of economic ruin among the middle class led to the spread of what some called 'cartel hatred (*Kartelhass*)'.[10]

B. CARTEL LEGISLATION BECOMES A REALITY

1. Pressure for cartel legislation

The public outcry against cartel practices soon led to calls for a government response. While some critics clamored to eliminate cartels, their calls garnered little support. Cartels had been basic organizational structures of the economy for decades, and it would have been difficult for most contemporaries to imagine their elimination. Moreover, cartels had only recently been glorified as servants of the national will, first during the war and then in the context of ideas of *Gemeinwirtschaft*, and a complete reversal of assessment within such a short period of time was unlikely. Finally, most serious observers realized that the German economy could ill afford the disruptions that a prohibition of cartels would certainly bring.

Most calls for a government response to cartel activities focused, therefore, on the conduct of cartels rather than on their existence. Political pressure for legislation to control cartel conduct began to take shape in the *Reichstag* in 1920, when the state of Bavaria requested that the government investigate cartels and make proposals 'to avoid the harms to the economy resulting from abuse of monopoly positions, particularly the dictatorial imposition of unfair prices and purchase conditions on processors, merchants and consumers'.[11]

---

[10] Ibid., 127.

[11] Cited in Lehnich, *Die Wettbewerbsbeschränkung,* 323. Bavaria had relatively little heavy industry, and thus its generally smaller firms often had to buy from cartels. Rotthege, *Die Beurteilung von Kartellen,* 130.

The *Reichstag* approved this request, but the ministry of economics rejected it on the grounds that it was not the time for new statutes that would restrict economic freedom.[12] This act of defiance recalls the patterns of government-industry 'co-operation' established during the Wilhelmine period: as in the decade after 1900, the *Reichstag* sought legislation to control cartels only to have the bureaucracy block their efforts.

As inflation accelerated, however, the pressure for legislation increased. In March, 1923, the *Reichstag* approved a report of its economic committee calling on the government to present 'as soon as possible' a cartel statute 'through which the excesses of cartel activities would be eliminated'.[13] This report called, *inter alia*, for the creation of a cartel register, the formation of a consumer advisory board for cartels, and a right of the government to veto decisions of cartels at the request of this consumer advisory board.

Support for these efforts came from two primary sources. One consisted of firms that had to purchase from cartelized industries. These were mainly in processing industries, and they tended to be small or medium-sized. The political influence of institutions representing this *Mittelstand* had increased because of the increased role of parliament in the Weimar political system. Consumers were the other main source of pressure, and here again the increased power of the *Reichstag* in the new republic gave them a stronger voice than they had before the war. Inflation was increasingly directing this voice against cartels.

But institutional vehicles for carrying the consumers' messages were not yet well-developed. The best organized were the consumer co-operatives that developed in the postwar period and took the lead on many consumer issues, including the cartel issue.[14] This issue was particularly important for co-operatives, because it implicated their own institutional interests. Many cartels sought to protect themselves against the impact of inflation by binding wholesalers to particular manufacturers and thus reducing or eliminating competition at the wholesale level. This tended to increase the prices that co-operatives had to pay, and often it even became difficult for co-operatives to purchase goods produced by cartelized industries.

The role of co-operatives in representing consumer interests restricted options available for cartel legislation. Cartels and co-operatives are structurally similar: both eliminate or reduce competition among their members, albeit for different reasons and in different ways. This similarity meant that in promoting consumer interests, co-operatives had to be careful not to employ principles that might be used against their own organizational form, and attacking cartel agreements in the abstract would have entailed that risk.

[12] Lehnich, *Die Wettbewerbsbeschränkung*, 325–26.
[13] Ibid., 333.
[14] The Cooperative movement is discussed in some detail in Rotthege, *Die Beurteilung von Kartellen*, 273–327.

Despite these pressures, however, the bureaucracy initially refused to take action. It tried to deal with the cartel problem as it had before the war—through 'co-operation' with cartel leaders. Officials of the economics ministry sought to persuade the cartels to avoid egregious conduct that might lead to interference by the *Reichstag*. They also established informal organizations such as mediation boards in which the economics ministry and cartel leaders jointly endeavored to control cartel excesses.[15] While these efforts may often have restrained cartel conduct, they also tightened the 'alliance' between the bureaucracy and cartel leadership, one of whose principle objectives was to keep the legislature and the courts out of 'their territory'.

2. The strange birth of cartel legislation

But by mid-1923 inflation had become rampant, and the public pressure for governmental action threatened to undermine the still fragile governmental system.[16] Rapid erosion of the purchasing power of the *Reichsmark* caused severe hardships among many groups within German society and rekindled fears of revolution.

In hopes of stabilizing the situation, Friedrich Ebert, the German President, appointed Gustav Stresemann to be the new chancellor in October of 1923. In an increasingly polarized political situation, Stresemann was one of the few politicians who seemed to be in a position successfully to lead a centrist coalition government.[17] Stresemann's political fortunes depended on his ability to mobilize public support for such a coalition, and thus in his inaugural address he announced an economic program that was designed to bring inflation under control. It included domestic measures designed to restore confidence in the economy as well as international negotiations to reduce the effects of reparations payments. Responding to the perception that cartels contributed significantly to inflation, he also announced his intent to include a cartel law in his program.[18]

Within a month of his inaugural address, Stresemann invoked what were, in essence, emergency powers in issuing the 'Regulation Against Abuse of Economic Power Positions (hereinafter, the 'Cartel Regulation' or the 'Regulation').[19] It was the first legislation in Europe to create a general

[15] See, e.g., Lehnich, *Die Wettbewerbsbeschränkung*, 325–30.
[16] For the economic situation, see Fritz K. Ringer, ed., *The German Inflation of 1923* (New York, 1969).
[17] For biographical background, see Henry Ashby Turner, Jr, *Stresemann and the Politics of the Weimar Republic* (Princeton, 1963) and Felix Hirsch, *Stresemann: Ein Lebensbild* (Göttingen, 1978).
[18] See Rudolf Isay & Siegfried Tschierschky, *Kartellverordnung* 31–34 (2d. ed., Mannheim, 1930).
[19] Verordnung gegen Missbrauch wirtschaftlicher Machtstellungen, 1923 *Reichsgesetzblatt* [RGBl.] I, 1067 (Nov. 2, 1923). An English translation appears in Robert Liefmann, *Cartels, Concerns and Trusts* 351–57 (D. H. MacGregor, tr., New York, 1932).

normative framework—albeit a loose one—directed at reducing restraints on competition.

The Regulation was 'emergency' legislation in both a formal and a practical sense, and this was to undermine its force. Formally, it was enacted pursuant to special constitutional authority available to the chancellor only because of the crisis situation (that is, the runaway inflation). Thus it was neither debated nor approved by the *Reichstag*. This lack of democratic legitimation was a frequent theme of later critics and undoubtedly impaired the Regulation's effectiveness. It was also 'emergency' legislation in the practical sense that it was generally understood as a specific response to a specific crisis situation (the inflation). It tended to be viewed, therefore, as a provisorium, a foreign element in the legal system, rather than a permanent and integral component of that system.

The proposal was an important part of the government's efforts to stabilize the political situation—a symbolic statement that the government would demand solidarity from all segments of society, including big business, and that it would seek a fairer distribution of the burdens of the inflation. Although there was a certain incongruity between the stated goals and the emergency nature of the Regulation, it was intended to counteract the perception of unfairness that was threatening the entire political system.[20]

In conjunction with the enactment of the Regulation, the government issued a well-publicized explanation of its objectives.[21] This statement began by asserting that the Regulation was to be understood as part of the government's overall plan to 'increase production and free the economy from unproductive restraints' and thus reduce inflation. The government emphasized that the Regulation sought to combat inflation by 're-establishing real market freedom'.

This affirmation of the idea that 'free competition' was a key to economic policy and served the public interest came at a time when most voices either paid little attention to the idea or rejected it. The Regulation provided an anchor for this liberal idea in the discourse of the Weimar period, but it was not weighty enough to secure it against the attacks that would soon submerge virtually all liberal ideas.

The Official Explanation also emphasized, however, that the government did not wish to eliminate or even harm cartels. The problem, it insisted, was not cartels as an organizational form. It ascribed to cartels 'an economically significant function', and claimed that their elimination would not contribute

---

[20] 'The real significance of the Regulation in its short-term context was that it became an element of trust and integration for a governmental system that was again just beginning to achieve stability'. Carsten Scharnweber, *Deutsche Kartellpolitik 1926–1929* 22 (Diss. Tübingen, 1970).

[21] This official explanation continued to be included in most commentaries on the statute and remained an important element of the discourse surrounding the statute. See, e.g., Isay & Tschierschky, *Kartellverordnung*, 414.

to market freedom, but would harm the *Mittelstand* by creating even larger business units against which small and medium-sized businesses would have to compete. Instead, it claimed that the problem was the conduct of cartels—the 'serious abuses' they created. The purpose of the Regulation was to combat these abuses by 'forc[ing those involved] back to the consciousness of [social] responsibility that had often been lost'.

3. The cartel regulation

The Regulation was drafted by a small group of bureaucrats in the economics ministry operating under exceptional time pressure, and thus we have little direct information about influences on the drafting process. The *Reichstag* proposals that had been made the preceding year clearly had little influence. These had centered on establishing a consumer council that would have the authority to combat cartel 'abuses', but such ideas were absent from the Regulation. The drafters may have avoided the consumer council idea because it was too politically controversial or because proposals based on something as untried as a consumer council were too uncertain and potentially too disruptive. They may also have found it congenial to maintain the power created by such a system in their own (that is, the bureaucracy's) hands rather than place it in the hands of a new quasi-governmental body that might interfere with their own individual and collective objectives.

Instead, the Regulation's drafters drew heavily on prewar thinking.[22] The basic concept of the Regulation—that is, to rely on *administrative* measures to combat the *abuses* of power—corresponds, as we have seen, to the conception of cartel law that was at the center of prewar discussions. Moreover, most of the important ideas in the Regulation can be found in those earlier debates.

The Regulation's principal drafter was Hans Schäffer, a leading bureaucrat in the economics ministry, and it reflected his commitment to the idea of 'regulated and peaceful co-operation between the government and the economy'.[23] According to his biographer, Schäffer was always trying to find a 'balance between social groups'.[24] Schäffer and his colleagues in the ministry had also been strongly influenced by the *Planwirtschaft* ideas of Rathenau

---

[22] Knut Nörr's claim that 'the Cartel Regulation did not stand at the end of a continuous development of Cartel law thinking' is correct in one sense, but potentially misleading. Knut W. Nörr, *Die Leiden des Privatrechts: Kartelle in Deutschland von der Holzstoffkartellentscheidung zum Gesetz gegen Wettbewerbsbeschränkungen* 49 (Tübingen, 1994). It is true that the specific provisions of the Regulation were based neither on existing precedents nor on the proposals that had been made during years immediately before its enactment. Yet the basic ideas clearly stemmed from the turn-of-the-century proposals and debates concerning cartel law.

[23] Eckhard Wandel, *Hans Schäffer*, 56. Socialists and those favoring government economic planning apparently wanted sharper controls. Ibid., 68.

[24] Ibid., 35.

and von Moellendorf, although by 1923 Schäffer himself was apparently moving toward more reliance on market mechanisms.[25]

Given the popular agitation over cartels, it is not surprising that the government recommended some type of legislation against cartels, but Stresemann's personal sensitivity to this issue was probably responsible for the high priority attached to it. As a long-time advocate of cartel legislation, Stresemann is likely to have seen this emergency situation as an opportunity to enact legislation that he had been hoping for years to see enacted.[26] Moreover, his experience is likely to have influenced the form and direction of the legislation. In the prewar conflicts over legislation he had represented firms in processing industries that had to purchase from cartels, and this undoubtedly colored his thinking about how to respond to the problem.

The emergency circumstances under which the Regulation was drafted made it unlikely that the Regulation would be a masterpiece of statutory draftsmanship, and it was not. Lacking a clear conceptual structure, its provisions often fit together poorly, and this lack of consistency and clarity was to be an object of repeated criticism within the legal community for as long as the Regulation was in effect. In issuing the Regulation, the government declared its intention to provide a more carefully worked out version when circumstances allowed. It never did.

The Regulation contained two basic approaches to the cartel problem.[27] One was a broad general provision that gave the government authority to take action against cartel conduct that harmed the public interest. It represented the basic form of competition legislation that would proliferate throughout Europe after the Second World War. A second approach provided specific measures designed to weaken the coercive power of cartels.

The government apparently expected the first of these approaches to be the most significant in practice.[28] The central provision here (§4) authorized the Minister of Economics to take enforcement measures where cartel or other similar agreements were deemed to 'endanger the economy as a whole (*Gesamtwirtschaft*) or the general welfare (*Gemeinwohl*)'. 'Endangerment' was presumed where 'in a manner not justified by the economic situation, production or sale is restricted, prices increased or maintained . . . or when economic freedom is unfairly impeded through boycotts . . . or through the establishment of differing prices or conditions'. The Regulation used the

[25] For discussion of these activities and the influence of Moellendorf and Rathenau on Schäffer, see ibid., 26, 40–42, and 53. Schäffer had also been second in charge of drafting the 1918 *Gesetz zur Gemeinwirtschaft*.

[26] Stresemann began calling for cartel legislation in 1907 and led the National Liberal Party's support for cartel legislation in 1908. See Fritz Blaich, *Kartell- und Monopolpolitik im kaiserlichen Deutschland: Das Problem der Marktmacht im deutschen Reichstag zwischen 1879 und 1914* 138–48 (Düsseldorf, 1973).

[27] It also provided (§1) that cartel contracts were not valid unless in writing.

[28] According to one expert, §§ 4 and 10 were to be the 'core' of the Regulation. Lehnich, *Die Wettbewerbsbeschränkung*, 338.

concept of 'abuse' to refer to the use of economic power in a way that harmed the public interest, and this concept became central to the discourse of competition law in Europe.

In enforcing this provision, the Minister of Economics had three basic choices. He could (1) ask the newly-created Cartel Court to invalidate the agreement, (2) order that any cartel member be permitted to withdraw from the agreement immediately, or (3) order that copies of the relevant agreements be submitted to him, in which case they would become valid only when he received them. This reporting requirement could also be made applicable to future agreements involving the same parties.

This basic abuse concept was then extended beyond cartels and made applicable to any firm or group of firms possessing monopoly power. Section 10 provided that where a firm or group of firms used a position of economic power in setting contract terms or prices that were likely to endanger the economy or the general welfare, the Minister of Economics could ask the Cartel Court to authorize rescission of the contract. This provision made the Regulation not just 'cartel' legislation, but 'competition' legislation.

The second basic approach of the Regulation also focused on economic power, but it was aimed at reducing such power rather than controlling it. Specifically, these provisions sought to combat the capacity of cartels to coerce conduct by their members and by others. They reflected the concern with 'organizational coercion' that Kestner's book had made the center of discussions of cartel legislation in the years immediately before the war.

Section 8 was intended to reduce the power of cartels over their members by allowing a cartel member to withdraw from the cartel for 'good cause', regardless of the provisions of the cartel agreement. 'Good cause' was presumed to exist where 'the economic freedom of action of the terminating party is unfairly restrained, particularly in regard to production, marketing or the establishment of prices'. If a cartel opposed such a withdrawal, it could bring the case to the Cartel Court, which would decide whether 'good cause' existed. The idea here was that by making it easier for member firms to withdraw from cartels, the Regulation reduced the coercive power of cartels over their members and thus reduced the capacity of cartels to cause harm.

The following section (§9) then sought to reduce the power of cartels over non-members. Here the mechanism was to impede the ability of cartels to use certain devices commonly used for such coercive purposes. It prohibited the use of boycotts and 'disadvantages of similar importance' without the prior approval of the president of the Cartel Court. Such approval was to be denied if the measure 'represented a threat to the economy as a whole or would unfairly limit the economic freedom of activity of the party involved'.

The Regulation created an enforcement system that was fundamentally administrative and relied heavily on discretionary policy judgments. With few exceptions, decisions relating to enforcement were placed in the hands of administrators who were subject to few text-based constraints on their decisions. This was particularly true for the general abuse provisions, which could only be activated by the economics ministry. Private initiative played a significant role only in the context of §8. Thus the economics ministry was the key actor in the competition law system.

The new Cartel Court was a special 'court' within the administrative system rather than part of the regular judiciary. It primarily exercised judicial functions such as hearing appeals from some administrative actions under the Regulation, but some of its functions were essentially administrative. The presiding judge and his deputy were appointed by the president of the *Reich* and had to be qualified to be judges in the regular courts. For each case handled by the Court, the president of the Imperial Economic Court (*Reichswirtschaftsgericht*) had to appoint four additional members: one from the Imperial Economic Court, one independent expert who was expected to represent the 'general welfare' and one representative for each side of the dispute. This court was the first of the many 'special courts' for competition law matters that are common in Europe today.

The system created by Stresemann's legislation thus represented an early form of what I call an administrative control system of competition law. The two main elements were a substantive focus on 'abusive' conduct and a procedural reliance on discretionary administrative measures to control such abuses. Both elements were consistent with prewar thinking, and this basic model would come to dominate much of European competition law thought and practice until quite recently.

C. THE CARTEL REGULATION IN PRACTICE

The institutional system created by the Regulation was quickly put into operation. The Stresemann government had made it a political symbol, and successor governments could ill afford the likely political consequences of not enforcing it. The Cartel Court was soon making and publishing opinions, and enforcement activities under the Regulation became a central concern of many of the country's leading legal professionals. Books, articles and commentaries on the Regulation abounded throughout the Weimar period, and the system it created remained an important part of German legal experience until the onset of the Great Depression in 1929.[29]

[29] For descriptions of the Regulation and its operations, see Lehnich, *Die Wettbewerbsbeschränkung* 335–464; Nörr, *Die Leiden des Privatrechts* 49–76; Scharnweber, *Deutsche Kartellpolitik*; and Georg Rotthege, *Die Beurteilung von Kartellen*, 167–216. A leading commentary on the Regulation is Isay & Tschierschky, *Kartellverordnung*. There is relatively little in English on this experience. See Liefmann, *Cartels, Concerns and Trusts*, 165–204; Heinrich Kronstein & Gertrude Leighton, 'Cartel Control: A Record of Failure', 55 *Yale L.J.* 297 (1946); and William C. Kessler, 'German Cartel Regulation under the Decree of 1923', 50 *Quart. J. of Econ.* 680 (1936).

The Regulation was important for the legal profession because it played an important role in the decisions of many German businesses. Operation of the system created by the Regulation demanded close attention from cartels and their member firms, and this assured widespread dissemination of competition law ideas. Moreover, as cartelization became increasingly international, especially after 1925, this process helped to spread such ideas beyond Germany's borders, because foreign lawyers, businesses and bureaucrats also had to take the Regulation into account.

1. The formal enforcement mechanism

In analyzing the operation and impact of this system, it is important to distinguish between its formal and its informal dimensions. The two often operated quite independently of each other, leaving separate records and having distinct impacts on the subsequent development of competition law.

The 'formal' dimension of the system refers primarily to the official activities of the economics ministry and the Cartel Court—that is, those activities that were authorized by statute and had formal legal consequences. Included here, above all, are decisions that affected the legal status or rights of cartels or their members. The primary record of these activities is the published body of decisions of the Cartel Court, and most observers have based their conclusions about the operations of the Regulation on this record.

This component of the system did not develop as many had expected it would. The general abuse provisions of §§4 and 10, which had been expected to be of prime importance, played little role in the published opinions of the Cartel Court. Decisions were rare and of little importance, primarily because these provisions could only be used by the economics minister, and he seldom chose to use it! To do so would have been inconsistent with the 'co-operative' arrangements between the ministry and the cartels that constituted the informal system for achieving compliance with the statute.

The refusal of the economics ministry to activate the general abuse sections had one particularly salient effect on the development of the system: it precluded the Cartel Court from giving content to key concepts such as 'abuse' and 'harm to the public welfare'. As a result, the court was effectively prevented from developing the Regulation as a source of conduct norms for cartels. Moreover, since there were few cases dealing with these issues, the legal and business communities had little incentive to pay attention to them and seldom did.[30]

Denied the opportunity to develop this component of the system, the court focused almost exclusively on two sets of issues—the definition of cartels and the coercion provisions (§§8 and 9). The issue of cartel definition was central

[30] The government was often criticized for its failure to implement these provisions. See, e.g., Lehnich, *Die Wettbewerbsbeschränkung*, 405.

to the operation of the Regulation because for most purposes it determined the Regulation's scope; the Cartel Court's treatment of the issue was also important for the development of competition law after the Second World War because it influenced the drafting of the new German competition law statute.

The scope of the Regulation was defined in §1 by reference to 'contracts and decisions which contained obligations regarding the treatment of production or distribution, the use of standard contract terms, the means of setting prices or the charging of prices'. This provision then specified that 'syndicates, cartels, combinations and other similar arrangements' were included. On its face, this appeared to mean that any agreement which included obligations of the type specified was subject to the Regulation. Writers on the subject were quick, however, to insist that the provision was only intended to apply to cartels.[31] Moreover, since the Regulation did not define cartels, these same writers were in a position to supply their own definitions, and these definitions severely restricted the Regulation's scope.

The leading definition of cartels was that of Robert Liefmann, who defined cartels as 'contractual combinations between enterprises that are of the same type and that remain independent—for the purpose of monopolistic domination of the market'.[32] This definition was interpreted to contain two principal limitations on the scope of the Regulation. It required both a monopolistic intent and a 'corporate' structure.

Constrained to begin with the highly restrictive cartel definition established in the literature, the Cartel Court only partially succeeded in broadening it in the direction that the language of the text seemed to require. It largely eliminated one major restriction, but maintained the other. It held that the definition of cartel did not require monopolistic intent, but required only that the agreement be suitable (*geeignet*) for monopolization.[33] The court accepted, however, the requirement that a cartel have a corporate or corporate-type structure, and this effectively eliminated vertical agreements from the Regulation's scope.[34]

These restrictions on the development of the Regulation were a significant benefit to cartels, and it is likely that cartels 'contributed' to establishing them, at least indirectly. The roles and connections of the writers who were the impetus for these restrictions suggest one mechanism through which cartels exercised this influence. Writers in this new and academically still rather marginal area were seldom full-time legal scholars. Practicing lawyers—many

---

[31] See generally Rudolf Lukes, *Der Kartellvertrag: Das Kartell als Vertrag mit Auswirkungen* 66 (Munich, 1959).

[32] Robert Liefmann, *Kartelle, Konzerne und Trusts* 9 (6th ed., Stuttgart, 1924).

[33] See, e.g., Cartel Court, Dec. of March 15, 1927, 25 *Kartell-Rundschau* 395, 398 (1927) (No. 88).

[34] Cartel Court, Dec. of Jan. 8, 1932, 30 *Kartell-Rundschau* 176, 180–81 (1932) (No. 177).

of whom had close ties to cartels—were thus able to dominate the legal literature. These ties created incentives for such writers to narrow the scope of application of the Regulation and thereby benefit the cartels that were or might become their clients. The court eventually resolved these definitional issues, but the process took time, and in the interim the scope of application of the Regulation was highly uncertain.

The overwhelming majority of cases decided by the Cartel Court involved §8, which permitted a cartel member unilaterally to terminate its membership in certain cases where the cartel sought to coerce that member's conduct.[35] One expert estimated that more than four-fifths of the court's decisions were issued in cases under this provision.[36] The primary reason for its prominence in the experience of the Cartel Court and thus in the legal literature was its procedural 'accessibility'. Whereas the general abuse provisions could only be used by the economics minister, private parties could initiate cases under §8; it was the only provision of the Regulation in which private parties had this right.

Although these cases were primarily concerned with the unfair use of power *within* a cartel organization and thus of little direct relevance to the development of competition law, two aspects of this experience are important for our story. First, that experience indicates the extent to which the Cartel Court was inclined to protect cartel interests. For example, the court interpreted the scope of §8 very narrowly, allowing firms to withdraw from cartels only where the cartel's coercive conduct threatened the *existence* of the withdrawing firm.[37] Similarly, it required that the withdrawing firm exhaust all remedies available within the cartel organization before withdrawing.[38] Since most cartels had mediation boards, this requirement created a significant financial obstacle to termination and correspondingly increased the coercive position of cartels *vis-à-vis* their members.

The second factor of importance for our purposes was the way the Cartel Court portrayed cartels—that is, the images of cartels which its language and practice disseminated and to which it gave authoritative weight. The court tended to emphasize the value of cartels, developing concepts and doctrines that reinforced positive images of them. It established, for example, the idea that a cartel should be seen as a 'protective community' (*Schutzgemeinschaft*) in which the members were obligated to take care not to harm each other.[39] This image

---

[35] For discussion of the case law under §8, see Lehnich, *Die Wettbewerbsbeschränkung*, 349–69 and Kessler, 'German Cartel Regulation', 683–91.

[36] Lehnich, *Die Wettbewerbsbeschränkung*, 349–50.

[37] See, e.g., Cartel Court, Dec. of December 15, 30 *Kartell-Rundschau* 106, 114 (1932) (No. 172). See also the influential article by Hans Carl Nipperdey, 'Wettbewerb und Existenzvernichtung', 28 *Kartell-Rundschau* 127 (1930).

[38] See generally Scharnweber, *Deutsche Kartellpolitik*, 71–72, and Cartel Court, Dec. of March 7, 1929, 27 *Kartell-Rundschau* 217 (1929) (No. 112).

[39] Cartel Court, Dec. of May 15, 23 *Kartell-Rundschau* 348 (1925) (Nr. 54). See generally Scharnweber, *Deutsche Kartellpolitik*, 64.

emphasized the ethically positive character of cartels, and it was used after the Second World War initially to combat legislative efforts to prohibit cartels and then to attack enforcement of the legislation that had been enacted.

Virtually all of the other cases decided by the Cartel Court arose under §9, which required prior approval by the president of the Cartel Court where cartels engaged in boycotts or similar coercive activity.[40] Here also the court's decisions demonstrated a high degree of support for cartel interests. Although its early decisions tended to interpret the provision broadly so as to protect the business freedom of victims of cartel coercion, it later sharply reduced such protection.[41] As in the decisions under §8, it generally withdrew protection unless coercive measures threatened the 'economic existence' of the firm against which they were taken.[42]

2. Informal regulatory patterns

To view only this formal record would, however, be misleading, because the system also had an informal dimension which was at least as important and which is necessary for explaining later developments. This 'informal' dimension included activities of government officials in which authority derived from the Regulation was used to achieve conduct modification without official proceedings.[43] 'According to the principle of *do-ut-des* [roughly, if you give to me, I'll give to you] information was exchanged, compromises developed and bigger conflicts avoided'.[44] It is a use of competition law authority which remains prominent in many countries.

In the Weimar period, this informal dimension of the system was grafted onto the 'co-operative arrangements' that already existed between organized industry (particularly the Association of German Industry—*Reichsverband der deutschen Industrie* or RDI) and the economics ministry. Here decisions about potentially objectionable conduct could be discussed and evaluated in private and in the context of long-term relationships that were valuable to both sides. The Regulation became a new negotiating factor within a system of relationships that had operated since the late nineteenth century.[45]

[40] Although the Ministry of Economics was not involved in the enforcement of this provision, the president of the court in this context was acting in an administrative capacity. For description of the case law, see Lehnich, *Die Wettbewerbsbeschränkung*, 371–402.

[41] For discussion, see Knut W. Nörr, *Zwischen den Mühlsteinen: Eine Privatrechtsgeschichte der Weimarer Republik* 151 (Tübingen, 1988).

[42] See, e.g., Cartel Court, Dec. of Feb. 13, 1929, 27 *Kartell-Rundschau* 220, 223–24 (1929) (No. 111).

[43] The most detailed discussion of this dimension of experience under the Regulation is Scharnweber, *Deutsche Kartellpolitik*.

[44] Ibid., 58.

[45] As Henry Ashby Turner has commented, 'Throughout most of the republican period, Germany's capitalists could also count upon support from the Economics Ministry'. Henry Ashby Turner, Jr., *German Big Business and the Rise of Hitler* 34 (New York, 1985). For insightful remarks on the factors that led to this support, see ibid., 35–36.

The need for compromise was the central dynamic of this system. Industrial leaders and government officials both profited from the relationship, and thus both were prepared to compromise to maintain it. The two groups shared a common goal—to avoid cartel conduct that might lead to potentially harmful political or popular reactions against either cartels or the administrators responsible for regulating them, and they needed to work out mutually acceptable guidelines for such conduct.

Cartel leaders and administrators also profited from this co-operation in other ways. Administrators needed this informal system in order to have any significant impact on cartel conduct. The cartel office was very small and had few resources.[46] As a result, it was not in a position to achieve effective enforcement through formal, confrontational methods. In addition, central provisions of the Regulation were so vague as to provide little guidance for business conduct, and, as we have noted, the Cartel Court often had little opportunity to give them meaning. Moreover, in those areas where the Cartel Court did have such opportunities, its decisions could hardly have given administrators confidence that it would support their interpretations.

This informal system was also attractive to officials on the personal level because it integrated them into the process of economic decision-making and gave them a degree of influence within it. This supplied many officials with power and prestige to which they otherwise would not have had access, and some subsequently turned this influence and the contacts associated with it into attractive positions in industry.

For the cartel leaders, these informal arrangements were preferable to the formal enforcement of rules that might not only restrict and encumber their activities, but draw attention to them as well. A more confrontational situation would have increased compliance costs and generated additional conflicts among cartel members. Finally, this co-operative system gave cartel officials a large measure of influence within the 'enforcement' process and presumably improved their access to and influence with other bureaucrats in the economics ministry.

Such a co-operative arrangement was consistent with the overarching objective of many of Germany's leading firms during this period: stability. As Peter Hayes put it in describing the situation of IG Farben, Germany's huge chemical company, 'IG's leaders saw their major extramural task as securing an orderly, predictable context in which to operate . . . . [They sought] to promote calm and co-operation among chemical producers around the world, the governments that presided over them, and the factions that contended within Germany'.[47]

---

[46] For discussion, see Scharnweber, *Deutsche Kartellpolitik*, 19.

[47] Peter Hayes, *Industry and Ideology: IG Farben in the Nazi Era* 4 (Cambridge, 1987). For further discussion of Farben's search for stability during this period, see ibid., 32–68.

In creating benefits for both sides, this informal mechanism necessarily also strengthened the co-operative relationships themselves. According to one commentator, it 'juridically fixed and stabilized' these relationships,[48] thereby further perforating the lines between economic and political power and undermining public confidence in the institutions of the republic.

Some officials saw the dangers of this system and sought to move away from it. In the mid-1920s, for example, the then economics minister, Robert Curtius, attempted to break or at least weaken some of these arrangements between ministry officials and cartel leaders, but it was too late.[49] The system had become too valuable to its participants, and they had sufficient power to maintain it.

3. Effectiveness

Commentators have generally claimed that the Regulation had little influence on the structure and conduct of cartels.[50] Although the effectiveness of this dual enforcement system in modifying conduct is difficult to assess, its effects may have been greater than is often assumed. As Hans Schäffer remarked in 1929,

> The desire to avoid a direct intervention by the cartel authorities has led in several hundred cases to changes in cartel provisions. Not to be forgotten are also the many ... organizations whose business activities have been influenced to moderation. Those involved in these things know that this influence is not small.[51]

The Regulation provided government officials with broad discretionary authority that became part of the compromise process, and, as mentioned above, it was in the interests of both bureaucrats and cartel officials to avoid cartel conduct that might increase hostility to cartels. Because perceptions of the Regulation's effectiveness were significant in the development of European competition law, we need to explore some of the claims of ineffectiveness.

Critics of the Regulation point, for example, to increased cartelization in the years after enactment of the Regulation as evidence of its ineffectiveness.[52] Cartelization did increase,[53] but, as Knut Nörr has pointed out, the

---

[48] Scharnweber, *Deutsche Kartellpolitik*, 28.   [49] For discussion, see ibid., 47–50.

[50] See, e.g., Kronstein & Leighton, 'Cartel Control'. The post-World War II literature on the Regulation is often suspect, because much of it was produced in the context of the controversy over a new competition law, and each side in those debates sought to use Weimar experience for its own purposes.

[51] Quoted in Nörr, *Die Leiden des Privatrechts*, 63.

[52] See, e.g., Comments of Franz Neumann, II *Verhandlungen des 35. Deutschen Juristentages* 786 (Berlin, 1928).

[53] 'According to rough estimates, the number of cartels increased from the end of the world war to the beginning of the Great Depression from 1,000 to 3,000'. Scharnweber, *Deutsche Kartellpolitik*, 2.

Regulation was not intended to reduce cartelization but to control cartel conduct, and thus this increase is not an appropriate criticism of the system's effectiveness.[54] Nevertheless, a main thrust of the Regulation was to reduce the ability of cartels to coerce conduct, and if it had done so, this should have reduced the profitability and thus the attractiveness of cartels. The increase in cartelization at least suggests, therefore, that the Regulation did not significantly reduce coercive conduct by cartels.

Others claim that the Regulation was a failure because neither the Regulation nor the system it created established clear conduct rules whose enforcement could have curtailed harmful cartel activity.[55] This is only partially true. The Cartel Court did not develop such rules in the context of those provisions that were specifically intended to protect the process of competition—that is, the abuse provisions, but this was because the economics ministry did not give it the opportunity to do so. The court did, however, develop conduct guidelines in those areas of the law in which it had opportunities to do so (§§8 & 9). The experience of the Cartel Court demonstrated, therefore, that this type of 'special' court could deal effectively with such issues, and this experience may have encouraged other European countries to include such courts in the competition law systems they subsequently created.

A third set of criticisms focused on the unevenness in the system's impact. It is claimed, for example, that despite broad language that made the Regulation applicable to dominant firms as well as cartels, it was enforced only against cartels, thus indirectly encouraging firms to merge and increasing the level of concentration in German industry. There is no dispute that the Regulation was enforced almost exclusively against cartels. According to one contemporary commentator, 'It [the Cartel Regulation] seems to be directed at all monopolists, whether they are cartels or not; in practice it affects only the cartels; single companies, concerns and trusts with monopolistic market positions are mentioned, but not affected'.[56] Yet application to other entities could hardly have been expected, given the economic, political and legal contexts of the system's operation. The Regulation was addressed to one problem—cartels, and there had been very little thought given to applying such legislation to single-firm monopolies. Moreover, political support for the Regulation related specifically and exclusively to cartel conduct, and any attempt to expand its scope would have been politically very hazardous for Weimar's generally shaky government coalitions. Finally, the ministry's limited resources for cartel enforcement made any such expansion all but impossible.

---

[54] Nörr, *Die Leiden des Privatrechts*, 62.

[55] See, e.g., Kessler, 'German Cartel Regulation', and Kronstein & Leighton, 'Cartel Control'.

[56] Arnold Wolfers, *Das Kartellproblem im Lichte der deutschen Kartell-Literatur* 131 (Munich, 1931).

It has also been claimed that the Regulation had a disproportionately greater impact on weaker cartels, but this claim requires scrutiny. In its strong form, the claim is that economically powerful cartels were little affected by the Regulation, either because they had the resources necessary to avoid violating the law or because they had sufficient political influence within the economics ministry to avoid its impact.[57] The main evidence for this claim is that most cases before the Cartel Court apparently involved smaller cartels.[58]

This criticism of the system is based, however, on the assumption that the only enforcement mechanism was the formal one, and thus it may distort our picture of the system and the roles it played. As we have seen, the informal component of the system is likely to have been more effective in modifying cartel conduct than the formal compliance mechanism, and there is little basis for assuming that its restraining influence was greater with respect to small cartels than to larger ones. The ability of ministry officials to influence cartel conduct in specific cases depended on a wide variety of factors, including the political situation, the power of the cartel involved, its sensitivity to negative publicity, its interest in maintaining the integrity of the informal enforcement system, and the importance of the issues to the cartel members and the economics ministry. Such factors are likely to have yielded compliance pressures in many cases that were at least as effective with respect to large cartels as to smaller ones.

D. RESPONSES TO THE CARTEL REGULATION

As with the Weimar Republic itself, the Cartel Regulation found few enthusiastic supporters. The emergency procedures and circumstances under which it was enacted weakened its claims to legitimacy and made it vulnerable to attack. Moreover, the government's comment at the time the Regulation was enacted that it might soon be replaced by more permanent legislation encouraged its opponents to try to weaken it. As a result, there was virtually constant controversy about the Regulation for the remainder of the decade, and this controversy shaped the way both contemporaries and later commentators saw the Weimar experience with competition law.

---

[57] Oswald Lehnich, a bureaucrat in the ministry of economics who was involved in applying the Regulation during the Weimar period, remarked many years later that the ministry was faced with 'an insoluble problem' because the statute was insufficiently precise to apply consistently, and thus the big cartels were able to avoid violating it. Lehnich, *Die Wettbewerbsbeschränkung*, 342.

[58] Scharnweber, *Deutsche Kartellpolitik*, 71.

1. Contexts of response

The operation of the Regulation that we have just discussed relates to the period from 1924 until shortly after the onset of the Great Depression in 1929, when the Regulation was significantly changed and the system it had created lost most of its importance. This was the comparatively 'normal' period in the brief history of Weimar Germany. The prospects for social integration and political stability seemed to be improving, at least in comparison with the preceding decade. Class and other societal conflicts remained intense, but they appeared more manageable, and the political situation, although still labile, seemed less likely to end in catastrophe. This normalization was most obvious in the economic sphere. The German economy grew significantly, producing jobs and in some parts of society even a sense of impending prosperity, and this reduced economic pressures on political institutions.[59]

After 1924, the German economy began to be rapidly reintegrated into the international economy. Largely severed from world markets by economic and political circumstances after the war, many German businesses now focused attention on regaining foreign markets. This sudden increase in the perceived importance of international markets combined with existing patterns of domestic economic organization (that is, the high level of cartelization) and nationalist values to urge German firms to co-operate with each other when operating in the international arena. The nationalism that was so important as a symbol of cohesion at home thus also helped to shape the reaction of German firms to international competition.

Internationalization also contributed to a new emphasis on economic rationalization. Faced anew with international competition and particularly concerned about the economic power of the United States, German industry recognized the need to rationalize its operations. The idea of rationalization thus acquired great force during the second half of the decade, demanding— and justifying—new management techniques and new technologies.[60] This rationalization movement also played an important socio-political role. As Charles Maier has put it, 'Albeit for very different reasons, all the enthusiasts of scientific management and technological overhaul were seeking to deny the necessary existence of the prewar model of ideological conflict and to validate a new image of class relationships'.[61]

---

[59] See generally Harald James, *The German Slump: Politics and Economics 1924–1936* (Oxford, 1986).

[60] See, e.g., Maier, 'Society as Factory', 19; Robert A. Brady, *The Rationalization in German Industry. A Study in the Evolution of Planning* (2d. ed., New York, 1974); Mary Nolan, *Visions of Modernity: American Business and the Modernization of Germany* (New York, 1994); and Werner Sombart, *Rationalisierung in der Wirtschaft* (Düsseldorf, 1927).

[61] Maier, ibid., 23–24.

2. Thinking about competition and cartels

In this setting, two basic sets of images combined to shape thought about the Regulation. One was of the economy and the role of cartels in it. Cartels were here seen as necessary institutions whose development the state should protect rather than hinder. The other was a view of the role of law and legal institutions in which the Regulation appeared as a poor tool for the wrong job. We will examine some of the factors that shaped these images in order better to understand responses to the Regulation.

Although economic historicism as a conscious methodological and philosophical position had lost the dominant position that it had enjoyed during much of the Wilhelmine period, its assumptions continued to shape the way economists and political decision-makers understood the economic process and the role of government in it. History, particularly in its evolutionary garb, remained a central tool for interpreting economic activity and responding to economic issues. What people saw when they looked at the economy was largely shaped by the historicists' question of how its structures corresponded to the needs of the time. This perspective implied that society—that is, the state—could and should take an active role in modifying those structures in response to its perceptions of current needs. The economy was something to be 'organized' and 'managed'. From this perspective, issues such as the extent of economic freedom and the intensity of competition held little attraction. They were not seen as tools with which the society could actively respond to the challenges of the day, and hence they found little resonance in Weimar thought.

The importance attached to the idea of economic 'organization' was not new, but during the Weimar period new elements reinforced and modified it.[62] During the war and immediate postwar years, the idea was closely associated with the concept and discourse of *Gemeinwirtschaft*. In this context, it focused on public controls on economic decision-making. It had a clear political role: it provided a middle ground between socialism and capitalism.

Later in the Weimar period the focus shifted away from the dominant role of the state. Sensing less need for governmental 'protection', the business community increasingly sought to eliminate regulations. At the same time, economic policy writers built on and/or incorporated existing corporatist ideas in ways that emphasized the role of organization, but made it an increasingly private concept in which the government's role was one of support for industry rather than planning.

The economist Werner Sombart was perhaps the most influential of these writers. Sombart claimed that the Western economies were entering the phase

---

[62] See generally Nörr, *Zwischen den Mühlsteinen*, 3–7.

of economic development that he called 'late capitalism'.[63] It was a higher, more developed stage of development in which the key to a nation's economic success was the effectiveness of its organization. Firms needed to co-operate with each other, and governments needed to support these efforts. Sombart built in some respects on Rudolf Hilferding's prewar ideas about 'organized capitalism', which probably enjoyed their greatest influence during the Weimar period.[64]

A view of the economy that pointed in the same direction, but derived from very different sources was the idea of the 'bound economy' (*Gebundene Wirtschaft*). Here the discourse and rationale of organization related primarily to the private sphere. Its primary spokesman was the economist Eugen Schmalenbach, who observed that in industrial production fixed costs were rapidly increasing as a percentage of total costs and concluded that this increase required an organizational mechanism for spreading the risks of overproduction.[65] These costs meant, in effect, that firms had to be bound together in some way. Cartels and trusts were the two available mechanisms, and the cartel solution represented a politically and socially more acceptable form of spreading these costs than did trusts. This conception became popular, especially during the second half of the decade, and it cast rationalization and cartelization as related and complementary responses to the problems of German industry.

The organization idea also appealed to other values of the Weimar period. In the unstable, conflict-ridden social situation of the period, political and economic discourse emphasized community and the need for ethical controls on conduct, while chastising institutions that were likely to create additional conflict. The society's fragility made ideas that seemed to encourage conflict highly suspect, leaving little room for values such as competition and economic freedom. Higher levels of organization were attractive because they promised to reduce economic conflict.

Such values also found little nourishment in the economic thought of the period. The economics profession no longer enjoyed the prestige that it had enjoyed in the Wilhelmine period, and it was splintered.[66] Some economists

---

[63] See, e.g., Werner Sombart, *Der Moderne Kapitalismus*, esp. Vol. III: *Das Wirtschaftsleben im Zeitalter des Hochkapitalismus* (Munich, 1927) and *Die Ordnung des Wirtschaftslebens* (2d. ed., Berlin, 1927).

[64] These were made the basis of the official party line at the SPD Convention in 1927. Claus-Dieter Krohn, *Wirtschaftstheorien als Politische Interessen: Die akademische Nationalökonomie in Deutschland 1918–1933* 79 (Frankfurt a.M., 1981).

[65] See Eugen Schmalenbach, 'Theorie der Produktionskosten-Ermittlung', *Zeitschrift für Handelswissenschaftliche Forschung* 41 (1908). For discussion, see Krohn, *Wirtschaftstheorien*, 87–92. This perspective on cartels was generated primarily within the new discipline of *Betriebswirtschaftslehre* (Business Economics) that was rapidly gaining importance during this period. For discussion of its development, see Keith Tribe, *Strategies of Economic Order: German Economic Discourse—1750–1950* 95–139 (Cambridge, 1995).

[66] For discussion of German economic science during the Weimar period, see Karl Hauser, 'Das Ende der historischen Schule und die Ambiguität der deutschen Nationalökonomie in den

remained avowedly historicist; others adopted neo-classical perspectives
from Austria and England; while still others favored a kind of synthesis that
drew heavily on the ethical and social objectives of the prewar *Kathedersozialisten*. As a result, the voices of those economists who did place a high
value on competition were often lost in the cacophony that surrounded
economic discourse.

Although many economists in Germany began during the Weimar period
to look at the economy through more theoretical lenses, these perspectives
were not well-established. The long dominance of historicism in German economic thinking had been broken, but its structures had not been eliminated,
and thus they remained an obstacle to viewing economic freedom and competition as values deserving of protection. Moreover, the more theoretical
economic perspectives were often imported, and in an age of both conscious
and unconscious nationalist predilections their foreign origins may have
made them suspect in the eyes of many German economists.

From this perspective so colored by historicism and the ideal of 'organization', cartels continued to appear valuable and necessary.[67] The idea that they
represented a 'higher' form of organization and thus a more appropriate
response to the historical situation had been a powerful influence on views of
cartels before the war, but the refinement, development and popularization of
this evolutionary perspective on economic organization by Sombart and
others further strengthened that influence.

Internationalization and rationalization also strengthened support for cartels. The magnitude of these tasks seemed to require a higher degree of organization for industry—in the form of either cartels or trusts. Colored by the
afterglow of historicism and 'ethical' economic thinking and propelled by the
need to operate within a discourse of societal responsibility, German thought
overwhelmingly favored cartels. The uncertainty and risk of societal cleavage
intensified the diabolical image of trusts that had been prominent since the
late 1890s. For most German economists and officials, there could be no
doubt that cartels were the superior choice.[68] They reduced conflict, protected
the existence of smaller firms and thus were more consistent with social justice and the welfare of society as a whole.

The discourse of nationalism added its own flavor to this support. As
German firms after 1924 increasingly focused on international competition,

Zwanziger Jahren', in *Geisteswissenschaften zwischen Kaiserreich und Republik* 47–74 (Knut W.
Nörr et al eds., Stuttgart, 1994); Ernst Heuss, 'Die Wirtschaftstheorie in Deutschland während
der 20er Jahre', in ibid., 137–58; Jürgen G. Backhaus, 'Wirtschaftsverfassung und ordnungspoli-
tische Grundvorstellungen im nationalökonomischen Denken der Zwanziger Jahre', in ibid.,
403–21; and Krohn, *Wirtschaftstheorien*.

[67] On the development of economic thought about cartels, see Krohn, *Wirtschaftstheorien*,
79–86.
[68] Siegfried Tschierschky, 'Der 35. Deutsche Juristentag zur Kartellfrage', 26 *Kartell-
Rundschau* 487, 488 (1928).

cartels seemed to represent the appropriate vehicle for facing that competition. Business leaders had success with the argument that by co-ordinating their efforts through cartel arrangements, German firms could share risks and pool resources and thus be in a better position to defeat their 'alien adversaries'.[69]

There was little room in these discussions for the idea that the cartel as a form of organization might, *in principle*, be harmful. Some economists were paying increasing attention to the price-increasing consequences of cartel arrangements, and there was some talk about the probability that cartels would engage in harmful conduct, but the perception that they represented a restraint of competition that was *intrinsically* harmful found no place in the discourse of the period. This development would require fundamental changes in the imagery used in thinking about cartels.

3. Attacks on the regulation

Given these views of competition and cartels, the Regulation was not likely to be popular. True, controls on certain types of cartel conduct were not necessarily inconsistent with this positive image of cartels. Cartel supporters might even have welcomed them on the grounds that they might tend to defuse political pressure that otherwise could lead to more drastic measures against cartels. But this move was not made, perhaps because cartel supporters found it unnecessarily risky in the uncertain political currents of Weimar. Instead, the Regulation was subjected to a barrage of criticism from many quarters.

Foremost among the critics of the Regulation were—not surprisingly—representatives of those German industries in which cartels were common. For them, the Regulation was at best a nuisance and at worst a significant interference with business operations. Thus their attacks began almost as soon as the Regulation was enacted.[70] Firms complained that it harmed their efficiency and thus their international competitiveness, and these were powerful arguments during a period of economic weakness in which there was a pressing need to regain world markets.

Increases during the Weimar period in the number and size of cartels swelled the voices of opposition from this camp. By 1929 the number of cartels in Germany was estimated at 3,000, and few who were associated with those cartels supported the Regulation. Moreover, the diminishing likelihood of either a socialist revolution or a socialist political victory may have encouraged industry's representatives to be bolder in their criticism of the Regulation because they had less reason to fear political 'backlash'.

[69] For discussion of the campaign to establish this perspective, see Scharnweber, *Deutsche Kartellpolitik*, 105–8.

[70] For discussion of the literature, see Wolfers, *Das Kartellproblem*, 139–52.

But representatives of industry were not alone in their demands for a weakening of the Regulation. Their criticism was predictable and self-interested, and by itself it probably would have had little impact on the way Germans or others viewed German experience with the Regulation. Far more important in this respect were the economists, lawyers and bureaucrats who shaped images of the economy and of the role of the Regulation in it, and most of them also sought to weaken the Regulation.

The value that many economists associated with cartels naturally led them to oppose a law that might harm cartels. This was especially true because the perception of value derived largely from an evolutionary perspective. If cartels were inevitable responses to the historical situation, any government action that 'interfered' with that mission was not only 'dangerous', but futile.

The Regulation was also caught in a basic conflict of economic perspectives that would become a theme of European competition law experience. Some economists—primarily those influenced by the neo-classical economic thinking flowing from England—supported the aim of protecting competition, but opposed the Regulation because it represented 'governmental interference' in the economy. Others who were more influenced by social concerns or Schmoller's tradition of 'ethical' economics did not necessarily oppose governmental regulation of business, but they often saw competition more as a potential harm than a positive good and thus rejected the idea of protecting it. One part of the profession thus supported the means of the Regulation, but opposed its ends; the other supported the ends, but opposed the means. The result was that neither supported the Regulation.

The Regulation also found little support in the legal community. Its members generally joined the chorus of voices lauding the value of cartels and opposing the Regulation's interference with them. This position appears to be contrary to the self-interest of that community, because the existence of the Regulation represented a source of revenue and power for many members of the profession, particularly practicing attorneys, but bureaucrats as well. It thus deserves particular attention.

The criticisms of the Regulation by legal professionals often closely resembled those proffered by economists and industry. The now familiar litany of claims about the evolutionary necessity of cartels, their value in reducing societal conflicts and so on was a major part of the legal community's criticism of the Regulation, indicating the extent to which these assumptions and perspectives were ingrained in the thinking of Weimar's political elite. The perceived need to protect cartels outweighed more parochial considerations of the self-interest of the legal community.

But that community also lodged a number of specifically juridical complaints against the Regulation. Its members portrayed the Regulation as a poorly-drafted mixture of essentially incompatible elements from public and private law that made it incoherent and unworkable. Its language was decried as unacceptably vague. Key concepts such as 'general welfare' were, for example, seen as too indefinite to be usable.[71] Moreover, this vagueness provided administrators with extensive discretion that violated principles of 'legal security'.[72] Some of the harshest criticism was directed against the Cartel Court, which was seen as a fundamentally flawed institution that operated as a court without meeting the minimum procedural, organizational, and personnel requirements expected of a court.

These criticisms reflected the application of traditional legal standards and expectations to the Regulation and the system it created.[73] The problem was that the Regulation did not fit comfortably into existing legal categories. The system was neither public law nor private law, but a mixture of elements from both. For legal commentators, this contradicted basic axioms of legal thought and created a fundamentally incoherent system.

The legal community took an 'official' position regarding the Regulation at the 1928 meeting of the *Deutscher Juristentag* (German Jurists' Association),[74] where one of the principal topics was 'Whether German and Austrian cartel law should be changed or unified'. This meeting became the object of much popular as well as political and scholarly attention. According to one observer, 'the public paid exceptionally intense attention to the proceedings, so that the discussion was on an extraordinarily broad basis. To this extent, the meeting was far more than the discussions of an association of jurists'.[75]

After airing many of the above criticisms against the Regulation, the speakers and the 'overwhelming majority' of participants nevertheless agreed that some supervision of cartels and market-dominating enterprises was necessary. The *Juristentag* thus recommended replacing the Regulation with a fundamentally different kind of supervisory mechanism that would have been considerably weaker than the existing system.[76]

According to the proposal, cartels would be subject to two types of 'controls'—one administrative and based on policy considerations, the other

---

[71] Ibid., 151, n.86.   [72] Scharnweber, *Deutsche Kartellpolitik*, 102–03.

[73] The legal literature on cartels was overwhelmingly concerned with trying to fit cartels into existing juridical categories. The leading works such as Julius Flechtheim's *Die Rechtliche Organisation der Kartelle* wrestled primarily with issues of corporation law: how should the relationship between the various corporations combined through the cartel agreement be understood? See Julius Flechtheim, *Die Rechtliche Organisation der Kartelle* (Mannheim, 1912). For discussion, see Annegret Heymann, *Der Jurist Julius Flechtheim: Leben und Werk* 37–47 (Cologne, 1990). For a penetrating analysis of Weimar legal thought generally, see Oliver Lepsius, *Die gegensatzaufhebende Begriffsbildung: Methodenentwicklungen in der Weimarer Republik und ihr Verhältnis zur Ideologisierung der Rechtswissenschaft im Nationalsozialismus* (Munich, 1994).

[74] *Verhandlungen des 35. Deutschen Juristentages* (Berlin, 1928). For discussion of this conference, see Tschierschky, 'Der 35. Deutsche Juristentag'. Organized industry apparently played an important role in 'structuring' these discussions. See Scharnweber, *Deutsche Kartellpolitik*, 120–31.

[75] Lehnich, *Die Wettbewerbsbeschränkung*, 409.

[76] These proposals can be found in II *Verhandlungen des 35. Juristentages*, 850–52.

juridical and operating on traditional legal principles. This structure was designed to provide a more rational and coherent system by separating administrative and juridical elements.

The administrative component authorized the economics minister to demand information from cartels and market-dominating firms and to impose administrative sanctions in cases where they abused their power. He could not, however, impose sanctions without first consulting a committee of experts from industry about possible solutions to the problems raised by such conduct, and cases where these consultations did not solve the problem were expected to be rare. Administrative decisions could be appealed to the administrative courts, which could determine issues such as abuse of administrative discretion. The juridical component of the proposed system was narrow, subjecting the issue of internal cartel coercion to private law principles to be applied by the regular courts. The controversial preventive control provision of the Regulation (§9) was to be abolished. Despite the strong support for these proposals at the 1928 *Juristentag*, political circumstances and economic events precluded serious consideration of them at the political level.

There was also little support for the Regulation within the bureaucracy, which demonstrated its dislike of the Regulation in the so-called *Wirtschafts-enquête*, a large and well-publicized project in which commissions established by the government examined in detail many aspects of the economy.[77] The issue of cartel policy comprised an important segment of this investigation, and, as in the similar exercises almost thirty years earlier, the bureaucracy 'staged' what was supposed to be a neutral investigation of cartels. It was staged in the sense that industry apparently had a great deal to say about who would speak and how the dialogue would be shaped, and, presumably as a result, speakers favoring the industry position were numerically dominant.[78]

Speakers repeatedly attacked the Regulation's interference with business and the risks this interference presented for the German economy, although they avoided calling for the abolition of cartel controls. The picture presented to the public emphasized the value of cartels to the German economy and the need to relieve them of regulations and institutions (that is, primarily, the Cartel Court) that created uncertainty and impediments to industry's effectiveness and its ability to compete internationally.

How do we explain this widespread support among lawyers, bureaucrats and economists for industry's position? One answer may lie in the social situation. As Fritz Ringer has shown, the Weimar period was uncertain and threatening for these German 'mandarins' as a group. The turmoil within

---

[77] For sections treating cartel issues, see 'Ausschuss zur Untersuchung der Erzeugungs-und Absatzbedingungen der Deutschen Wirtschaft', *Verhandlungen und Berichte des Unterauschusses für allgemeine Wirtschaftsstruktur*, pt. IV (Berlin, 1930).

[78] Those listed as 'practitioners' were, for example, without exception affiliated with the *Reichsverband der Deutschen Industrie*. Scharnweber, *Deutsche Kartellpolitik*, 85, n.2.

German society threatened their social status; their financial ‘position was undermined by inflation; and their intellectual position was threatened by growing challenges from both the left and the right.[79] This tended to make them dependent on those segments of the 'old order' that had a stable power base—that is, big industry and the central bureaucracy. These groups formed a kind of loose alliance to protect their common interests, and within it, lawyers and economists acquired opportunities for influence that had become rarer in society at large. This alliance had the additional benefit of providing resources to bolster the shaky economic position into which many Mandarins had fallen. Lawyers were particularly dependent on industry. Many were paid by big business, directly or indirectly, and, given the enormous economic concentration represented by cartelized industry, it must have been very difficult to take an opposing position.

The political situation tended further to strengthen this dependency, especially toward the end of the period. As confidence waned in the capacity of the Republic to develop 'roots', and hopes for a reasonable 'center' melted, this alliance drifted toward the right. As it did, resentment in the middle classes against parliamentarism and democracy flourished, increasing pressures on its members to support industry and reject the Regulation. Finally, as nationalism increased, the Regulation was increasingly seen as 'Western' and 'foreign' and, therefore, dangerous.

4. Support for stricter controls on cartels

These calls for a weakening of the Regulation emanated from the most powerful groups in society and thus dominated the legal and economic literature of the period, but there were also voices that called for the opposite—a strengthening of such controls. Although these voices had little immediate influence on outcomes and events, they were a significant part of the political debate and influenced thought about competition law not only in Germany, but elsewhere in Europe as well.

Support for stricter controls on cartels came mainly from the left side of the political spectrum, particularly the Social Democratic Party, where changing ideologies and political agendas were altering views of cartel legislation. Recall that the SPD's position during the pre-war debates was based on the assumption that cartels were a higher form of organization that would help to pave the way for a socialist planned economy. This led the party's leadership generally to reject—or at least not to support—legislation that might interfere with the success of cartels and thus impede progress toward the SPD's ultimate goal—political victory. For most, eschatology dictated cartel policy.

[79] See generally Fritz K. Ringer, *The Decline of the German Mandarins: The German Academic Community, 1890–1933* (Cambridge, Mass., 1969).

During the Weimar period, especially its latter half, a different view of history and of the party's path to power changed their views of cartels and cartel policy.[80] The party was moving somewhat uncertainly toward a more short-term and pragmatic view of economic policy in which it increasingly focused on the immediate welfare of its supporters rather than on evolutionary assumptions about what the perhaps distant future might bring. Spurred in this direction by competition with the communists and the Center Party for working class votes, SPD leaders increasingly saw economic policy as a matter of immediate political battles rather than of an evolutionary process.

From this 'revisionist' perspective, cartels looked much different than they had from an eschatological perspective. The social democrats now sought to 'capture' the popular resentment against cartel excesses by demanding more stringent cartel controls. Their focus was on the perception that cartels often charged unjustifiably high prices, and they argued that such controls were necessary in order to protect workers *qua* consumers as well as small businesses and their employees from this predation.

These demands were given prominence and new emphasis during the second half of the decade, as leaders of both the SPD and the 'independent unions' (*Freie Gewerkschaften*) moved to revitalize flagging enthusiasm in their ranks by calling for government to do more to protect the interests of workers. The issue of cartel legislation became a central factor in these efforts. The catchword attached to this rather vague revitalization movement was 'economic democracy' (*Wirtschaftsdemokratie*),[81] but the ideas associated with it were a combination of socialist theories, images from the *Gemeinwirtschaft* days, and pragmatic political themes.

By 1927, the SPD was calling for competition legislation that was significantly stronger than the Regulation.[82] It proposed, for example, the creation of an independent cartel office that would have wide-ranging authority to gather information from cartels, order them to reduce prices, or even to dissolve them where they were found to have abused their power. The proposal also included a call for an international cartel authority that would have similar, although weaker, authority to combat international cartels. These proposals drew from a body of ideas that was being widely discussed not only in Germany, but also in other European countries and particularly in

---

[80] For discussion of the evolution of social democratic revisionism, see Carl E. Schorske, *German Social Democracy 1905–1917: The Development of the Great Schism* (Cambridge, Mass., 1955) and David Abraham, *The Collapse of the Weimar Republic: Political Economy and Crisis* (2d. ed., New York, 1986).

[81] The writer who was most closely associated with this 'economic democracy movement' was Fritz Naphthali. See Fritz Naphthali, *Wirtschaftsdemokratie, Ihr Wesen, Weg und Ziel* (Berlin, 1928).

[82] For details, see Eduard Reuffurth, *Die Stellung der deutschen Sozialdemokratie zum Problem der staatlichen Kartellpolitik* (Diss. Jena, 1930). For a contemporary account of the SPD position, see Franz Neumann, 'Gesellschaftliche und staatliche Verwaltung der monopolistischen Unternehmungen', *Die Arbeit* 393–406 (1928).

Scandinavian countries, where social democratic parties had close ties to the German Social Democrats.

While demands for tighter controls on cartels came primarily from socialist quarters, a few representatives of what we can call a 'social liberal' perspective argued along similar lines. What linked these isolated voices to each other and to social democratic efforts was the claim that consumers should be protected from exploitation—for both economic and political reasons. Economists such as Franz Oppenheimer, for example, operated from a largely liberal theoretical base, but emphasized values such as economic equality and the importance of the 'social question'.[83] One of his students was Ludwig Erhard—the principal architect of the postwar German economic 'miracle' and perhaps the most important figure in the creation and early success of competition law in Germany after the Second World War.

5. Status quo as compromise

Despite the often highly-publicized controversy over the Regulation, it was not significantly changed until after the Depression of the 1930s had begun. As with so much in Weimar, talk failed to produce constructive action. The weak and transitory coalitions of the Republic were unwilling to risk the political repercussions of a change in either direction. Although the leading parties and leadership groups (other than the SPD) generally favored a weakening of the Regulation, it served as a symbol of political control over the economic power of cartels and of big business in general, and thus politicians did not dare to weaken it. Moreover, since the system generally did not seriously interfere with cartel operations and may have provided political 'insurance' against harsher responses, the status quo was a convenient compromise.

6. Depression and Nazi period

The onset of the Great Depression in 1929 began to change the roles and form of cartel legislation. In 1930 the Regulation was amended by emergency legislation that significantly reduced the juridical component of the system, transferring most authority for abuse issues to the economics ministry and all but eliminating the role of the Cartel Court in such issues. When the National Socialists took power in 1933 the Regulation ceased to serve the purposes for which it had been created. Hitler's government began to construct a regulatory scheme that turned the Regulation on its head by requiring cartelization and integrating cartels into the state apparatus. Nazi economic policy was not concerned with protecting the process of competition, but with eliminating or at least marginalizing it. We will not look further at this experience because it

---

[83] See, e.g., Christoph Heusgen, *Ludwig Erhards Lehre von der Sozialen Marktwirtschaft* 68–78 (Bern, 1981).

played little, if any, role in the subsequent evolution of the European competition law tradition.

Weimar experience represented an important step in the development of European competition law. For the first time in Europe, competition law ideas were not merely discussed; they were enacted as legislation and made part of an operating legal regime. Many German officials, lawyers, and businesspeople became accustomed to the existence and operation of a law whose basic objective was to combat uses of economic power that harmed the competitive process. In short, competition law ideas and practice became an important part of legal and economic experience.

1. Images of the problem

At the center of this experience was a growing perception that cartels often acted in ways that were harmful to society. According to Franz Wieacker,

The cartel regulation of 1923 that was pushed through in the uproar over inflation took into account for the first time the insight that was characteristic of the later phases of the competitive economy, that contractual freedom without control over the power concentrations that it itself makes possible leads to conditions in which the freedom of the stronger leads to the lack of freedom of the weaker.[84]

Two elements of this image are central—cartels and conduct.

From today's perspective the focus on cartels often seems oddly narrow, but in Weimar Germany cartels were, as we have seen, the dominant form of industrial organization, virtually equated by many with 'big business' and 'big capitalism'. Cartels wielded—or at least seemed to many to wield— immense economic and political power, and thus to constrain their uses of economic power was to control the use of such power generally.

The second component of this perception—that the problem was one of conduct rather than of organizational form or contractual arrangement (as, for example, in the US)—was of capital importance for the development of competition law in Europe. As we have seen, the overwhelmingly positive images of cartels as institutions that pervaded both educated thought and public opinion required that the harms they caused be perceived as issues of conduct. This perception had begun to take shape before the war, but during the Weimar period it became an established image.

There was also a sharper image of who was being harmed by such conduct. The voice of consumers (a category still primarily associated with 'workers')

---

[84] Franz Wieacker, *Privatrechtsgeschichte der Neuzeit* 546 (Göttingen, 1967).

as victims became stronger and more distinct. There were still references to harms to small and medium-sized enterprises, and in practice the Regulation operated primarily to protect against these harms, but the focus of popular and policy concern was shifting to the harms that cartels could inflict on consumers. When cartels raised prices, consumers were harmed, and politicians and journalists increasingly emphasized this cause-effect relationship. As in the Wilhelmine period, the discourse of cartel law fostered the evolution of a distinct consumer identity.

Emerging conceptions of the organic nature of economic activity gave further definition to perceptions of harm. In particular, the idea of an economic constitution (*Wirtschaftsverfassung*) was gaining currency in economic and political circles. It depicted the economy as an organic whole in which all parts were structurally related to each other, and it focused attention on how conduct by some could harm these structures and the operation of the whole.[85] During the Weimar period this idea was not yet used normatively, but after the war it would be—and to great effect.

2. Images of response

Weimar experience also gave form and substance to images of how to respond to the problem, and some of these ideas were to become standard components of European competition law systems. Whether one viewed Weimar experience positively or negatively, the Regulation provided an experiential reference point for thinking about competition law issues that had not previously existed in Europe. The perceptual landscape of this experience provides clues to the dynamics of many subsequent developments.

The perception that the Regulation was a response to legitimate popular demands was an important feature of this landscape. Experience with the Regulation was part of the democratization process in Germany—an expression of the interests of the less powerful *vis-à-vis* elite powerholders. Popular outcries against cartel conduct were a main impetus for the legislation, and the system operated against a backdrop of continuing popular sentiment against cartel abuses. From its inception virtually no one in a position of power or responsibility dared to deny the need for some such controls on the abuse of economic power.

Moreover, this was widely perceived as legislation to protect consumers—whether it did so effectively or not. This consumer perspective grew in influence as it generated information that justified its use: the more it revealed harms to consumer interests, the more those who identified with those

[85] See Knut W. Nörr, 'Auf dem Wege zur Kategorie der Wirtschaftsverfassung: Wirtschaftliche Ordnungsvorstellungen im Juristischen Denken vor und nach dem Ersten Weltkrieg', in *Geisteswissenschaften zwischen Kaiserreich und Republik* 423–52 (Knut W. Nörr et al eds., Stuttgart, 1994).

interests found the perspective useful. The idea that 'consumers/workers' deserved protection from the machinations of powerful business enterprises was nourished by the growing political voice of consumer interests and by ideas of national solidarity and community. The relatively vague images of the objectives of cartel legislation that had characterized prewar thought now took on sharper contours.

During the Weimar period, images of competition law also became increasingly juridical. Pre-war discussions of how to respond to the problem were often cast in terms of economic policy rather than law, but by the late 1920s, few denied the need for some form of cartel law. The issue now was 'What kind of cartel law?' Establishing the idea that the problem could not be dealt with merely through economic policy tools and that a juridical response was necessary was a critical step in the development of European competition law thought.

The system's operations gave additional substance to this juridical image. Formal procedures, judicial decisions, volumes of commentaries on the statute—the legal vocabulary became ever denser. This juridical texture became part of experience with competition law for many lawyers, administrators and business decision-makers.

This juridical image was specifically administrative. It was public law in the continental sense, structuring the relationship between the state and its nationals. Decisions were made primarily by administrators, subject to control by a 'special' court that was outside the regular system. Private suits were permitted only to a limited extent and then only in the context of relations between cartels and their members, not in the context of protecting the public against harms caused by cartels. Competition law was here 'cast' in an administrative mold within which it in many ways still operates.

Consistent with prevailing images of the nature of the cartel problem, images of response were focused almost exclusively on the effects of specific conduct rather than on characterizing conduct from a theoretical perspective. Where the effects of such conduct were harmful to society, the Regulation labelled the conduct as 'abuse' of economic power, and, although the abuse provisions were little used, the concept became a powerful symbol of the need to protect society against the harmful conduct of powerful firms. As such it was to become a permanent fixture of European competition law.

The Regulation also expanded the scope of response: its abuse provisions were applicable not only to cartels, but to any dominant firms. In practice the Regulation was applied almost exclusively to cartels, but its language also applied to other enterprises possessing economic power. This was a significant conceptual move from prewar discussions of response to the cartel problem, because it acknowledged that the cartel problem was part of the larger problem of combating the harmful conduct of economically powerful firms.

Even as competition law became a reality rather than merely a matter of speculation, the system's operations remained opaque. Its closed-door negotiations among bureaucrats and industry leaders seldom led to headlines about cases won or conduct changed, and thus there were few instances in which the public could see results from the operations of the system. Some knew that the system had a measure of effectiveness in constraining cartel conduct, but the general public and many politicians suspected that it accomplished little.

Both a cause and a result of the system's opacity was the lack of structure in its language. Although there was a general sense that the Regulation was to protect against abuses of economic power, there were few conceptual structures to guide decision-making. Most importantly, the central idea of protecting competition law did not become a major part of the discourse of competition law. Stresemann had affirmed the importance of protecting competition when he enacted the legislation, but the dominant political and economic imagery marginalized that mechanism. The generally negative reputation of liberalism virtually barred the touting of such goals, particularly among the two political groupings that represented the cause of the 'little man' and the consumer and provided important political support for the system—the Social Democrats and the Center Party. Both were guided by corporatist models—albeit very different ones—that precluded attaching value to competition as such!

Not surprisingly, the system was widely seen as a failure, particularly during the latter part of the decade. Few were satisfied with this particular way of addressing the cartel problem, and that dissatisfaction played a role in the postwar creation of a different type of cartel legislation. Those who in the early 1950s favored stricter controls on cartels and a more energetic effort to control abuses of economic power frequently referred back to this dissatisfaction with Weimar experience. Their message often was that such legislation did not and could not work effectively to protect competition.

This disappointment with the Regulation did not, however, lead to rejection of the competition law project itself. One reason it did not was that the system had been seen from its inception as an unfinished product, a temporary expedient that had been hastily constructed and would be replaced by a better version. One could have a negative view of the Regulation and yet still be confident that a 'better' competition law would be effective.

3. The Regulation's economic and political roles

The subjective components of Weimar experience—attitudes, perceptions, and images—occupy center stage in our story, because they transmitted experience over time and among national communities. Yet the objective components of that experience—what happened—also play an important role in this process.

We have noted the difficulties involved in assessing the economic impact of the Regulation. It undoubtedly tended to constrain the conduct of many cartels in many situations, but there is no way of measuring the extent of that impact. We encounter similar difficulties in discerning the impact of the Regulation on the structure of German industry—that is, whether firms merged in order to avoid the impact of the Regulation. This is especially difficult because the Weimar period was sandwiched between two anomalous periods—war and revolution on one side and depression and war on the other. This makes interpreting data on economic concentration highly speculative. There is, however, anecdotal evidence that firms often merged in order to avoid the impact of the Regulation, particularly during the latter part of the period.[86]

The Regulation's political roles were more obvious and perhaps more important. The Regulation was enacted in response to political pressure, and there was often intense public interest in its operations and its reform. This was not 'forgotten' legislation that was only the concern of a few administrators and business leaders. Its most significant role may well have been as a political symbol that the government was doing something to restrain cartel conduct. In this sense the Regulation probably served a stabilizing function, because it provided a mechanism that was designed to protect those who felt aggrieved by specific cartel practices and by big business in general. This 'democratizing' role was important in defining the policy directions of the political parties that represented 'the common person'—that is, the Social Democratic Party and the Center Party.

On yet another level, the Regulation also reinforced patterns of government-industry co-operation in Germany. In effect, the system required government bureaucrats to negotiate with cartel leaders about their operations in a context in which both shared the basic objective of avoiding undue public criticism of their decisions. The result was increased interpenetration of economic and political power and a perceived commonality of interests between government representatives and industry leaders.

One consequence of these arrangements between government officials and 'big business' may have been to undermine public confidence in Weimar's governmental system. They at least contributed to the perception that the system was being subverted from its intended objectives and that those whose expectations of protection had been raised were not, after all, receiving such protection. It was a dangerous perception.

As we look at the spread of competition law ideas through Europe, it will be valuable to remember that for most observers Germany provided the only

---

[86] According to Professor Stefan Riesenfeld, who was a lawyer in a major German firm in Breslau during this period, mergers and acquisitions were often motivated by a desire to avoid having to deal with the issues created by the Regulation. Professor Riesenfeld mentioned this to me in private discussions in Chicago on October 7, 1995.

example of an operating competition law system. German experience with the Regulation during the 1920s was the common reference point. This gave German thought and experience a foundational role, and made them highly influential in setting the basic structures of European thought and practice.

F. THE DIFFUSION OF COMPETITION LAW IDEAS

Although German experience with competition law during the interwar period was far more extensive than elsewhere in Europe, competition law ideas were discussed and debated in many other countries, particularly during the second half of the 1920s, and several other European countries enacted competition laws. This largely forgotten diffusion of competition law ideas and experience is necessary for explaining competition law developments after the Second World War, because it created a common pool of 'European' ideas and generated the perception of a 'European' model of competition law.

1. Trans-European commonalities

Commonalities in European experience facilitated the spread of these ideas. Common problems and similar pressures confronted decision-makers throughout Europe, particularly in shaping the relationship between state and economy. These forces shaped perceptions of cartels and conceptions of how to respond to them that took on a degree of uniformity across Europe.

The political and economic exigencies of the war created some of these common features. Virtually all European governments were compelled to engage in extensive economic regulation during the war, and this meant that for the first time in modern economies, government administrators were making many of the key decisions about production, prices and the distribution of goods. This wartime experience demonstrated not only that such controls were possible, but—surprising to many—that they could sometimes be relatively effective. It also demonstrated to political elites some of the potential advantages such regulatory regimes offered for enhancing and exercising their own power.

The war also set in motion economic and political developments that maintained elements of wartime regulation well after war's end. The financial upheavals of the postwar period required increased regulation of banks and other financial institutions; massive disruptions of social and family patterns, not to mention individual lives, seemed to demand—or at least to justify—increased government intervention to restore or maintain basic conditions of social order; and labor movements called for increased government involvement in the employment relationship and increased protection of workers.

The economic circumstances under which governments tried to respond to these increased demands were often troublesome, complicated and chaotic, at least in comparison to the prewar period.[87] For example, the aftermath of war created shortages, particularly in the production of consumer goods, as well as obstacles to the distribution of goods and services. These then fueled sometimes virulent and widespread inflation and made the control of inflation a central political issue in many countries, at least through the middle of the decade.

While creating new burdens on government, the war and its aftermath also often undermined confidence in existing political structures and in the classes that directed public affairs. For many, the war had cast doubt on the legitimacy and capacity of traditional leadership groups. This was particularly true among industrial workers, who increasingly expressed their discontent in the form of socialist movements that achieved growing political power in many countries in the wake of the war. Moreover, the victory of bolshevism in Russia in 1917 provided a constant reminder to European leaders of the potential power of such movements. These developments challenged bourgeois hegemony and authority, placing political elites in an essentially defensive posture for much of the interwar period, as they sought to regain and maintain some form of stability in the face of continuing threats of disorder.[88]

Democratic parliamentary institutions grew in number and in formal authority after the war, but few were satisfied with their effectiveness, including traditional elites, who often sought to circumvent formal political institutions. As we have seen in the case of Germany, these elites often found extra-parliamentary mechanisms for sharing and exercising power. Their strategies usually involved class-based alliances that were centered in bureaucracies, but also included business leaders and lawyers.

Turmoil and uncertainty also engulfed thought about political and economic issues. After World War I, it was no longer possible to assume—as many had before the war—that Europeans basically had 'the right answers'. The intellectual strategies that had sustained development in the long nineteenth century that ended with the war lost much of their force. Liberalism as an intellectual framework for guiding intellectual decisions was, as Friedrich von Hayek once put it, 'all but extinguished' at the end of the war.[89] For some, Marxism offered an alternative basis for organizing thought and ambition; for others, reified forms of nostalgia served that function; while yet others focused their efforts on finding a middle position which could justify

[87] For discussion of the economic situation, see Derek H. Aldcroft, *From Versailles to Wall Street: 1919–1929* (Berkeley, 1977).
[88] For detailed discussion, see generally Charles S. Maier, *Recasting Bourgeois Europe: Stabilization in France, Germany and Italy in the Decade after World War I* (Princeton, 1975).
[89] For discussion, see Eric Hobsbawm, *The Age of Extremes: A History of the World, 1914–1991* 109–41 (New York, 1994).

extensive government regulation in economy and society without reference to the theoretical apparatus of Marxism.

2. The spread of competition law experience in the 1920s: Sweden and Norway

Supported by these commonalities, competition law spread beyond Germany in the mid-1920s. Not surprisingly, this occurred in countries with cultural, intellectual and political ties to Germany, notably Sweden and Norway. Their legislation was not consciously modeled on German legislation, but it was shaped by the discourse that had developed in Austria and Germany.

In both Sweden and Norway, legislative proposals to protect competition had been debated in the years immediately preceding World War I.[90] During this period, German cultural and intellectual influence was strong in both countries, and these prewar debates were conducted in much the same terms that we have encountered in the German debates around the turn of the century.

After the war ended, calls for competition legislation again became a major public policy concern. In Sweden, the *Riksdag* ordered a public investigation and evaluation of the costs and benefits of competition legislation in 1920, apparently in part at the insistence of farmers who were concerned about concentration in the food industry. This investigation led to the creation in 1921 of a Trust Commission (*Trustkommitté*) that was to develop permanent legislation in the area and that in the interim had authority to investigate specific conduct of cartels and market-dominating firms.

In 1925, permanent legislation was enacted, but it was far weaker than some of the proposals that had been discussed.[91] It authorized the government to investigate cartels and monopolistic firms for purposes of determining their influence on prices and competition. This included authority to impose fines on firms that failed to provide properly requested information. The determined opposition of Swedish industry apparently precluded the enactment of more extensive legislation. Key elements of Swedish industry relied on international operations and justified their opposition on the grounds that such legislation might harm their international competitiveness.[92] The limited scope of the legislation was also justified on the theory that in a small and homogenous country like Sweden, publicity would generally suffice to deter abusive conduct. In any event, the legislation was seldom used.

---

[90] For discussion, see Ulf Bernitz, *Marknadsrätt* 411–13 (Stockholm, 1969). Bernitz' work has been of much value for my discussion of Swedish and Norwegian experience.

[91] Lagen om undersökning angående monopolistika företag och sammanslutningar, *Svensk Författningssamling* (SFS) 1925: 223 (Law on Investigations Relating to Monopolistic Enterprises and Mergers). For discussion, see Bernitz, *Marknadsrätt*, 414.

[92] For discussion of the Swedish economy during this period, see Johan Myhrman, *Hur Sverige Blev Rikt* 109–25 (Stockholm, 1994).

In Norway, efforts to enact a competition law went significantly beyond the Swedish legislation. There the postwar price controls that were common in Europe were not eliminated, as was common in most other European countries, but were gradually transformed into a mechanism for combating restraints on competition.[93] A temporary statute of 1920 required registration of restrictive agreements and dominant enterprises and gave general authority to government officials to investigate abuses of economic power, primarily as a means of reducing inflationary pressures.

During the early 1900s there was much political controversy about the prospects for competition legislation, and there were even proposals to prohibit cartels.[94] In 1916 the government appointed a commission to study the issue and, if necessary, propose legislation, and it became the scene of well-publicized clashes that lasted from 1920 until the passage of permanent legislation in 1926. The Price Directorate was particularly prominent in these debates, aggressively calling for a system to combat restraints of competition and thereby combat inflation.

The fight over competition law was part of the often bitter battle between leftist and conservative forces that pervaded Norwegian society and politics throughout much of the interwar period.[95] Norway's leftist parties tended to support the introduction of competition legislation as a means of reducing inflation and increasing the relative political and economic strength of unions and workers. The idea of controlling abuses of economic power fit well into their agenda, which called for reducing inequalities and power differentials at all levels of society. Conservatives generally opposed it on the grounds that it would harm the profitability of Norwegian industries and impair their international competitiveness.

The growing strength of leftist parties during the decade's middle years led to enactment in 1926 of a Law on Control of Restraints of Competition and Price Abuse (generally referred to as the *Trustlov*)[96] which Ulf Bernitz has referred to as Europe's first 'real' competition law.[97] It was broader in scope than the German Abuse Regulation, and it represented a more elaborate and

---

[93] For discussion, see Kristen Andersen, *Rettens Stilling til Konkurranseregulerende sammenslutninger og avtaler: En oversikt over Norsk og Fremmed Rett* 135 (Oslo, 1937).

[94] For detailed discussion of the controversy, see ibid., 137–80.

[95] For discussions of the interwar period in Norway and of these conflicts in particular, see Hans Fredrik Dahl, *Norge mellom Krigene: Det Norske Samfunn i Krise og Konflikt 1918–1940* (Oslo, 1971) and Berge Furre, *Norsk Historie 1905–1940* 124–88 (Oslo, 1972). Useful on the economic history of Norway during this period is Fritz Hodne, *The Norwegian Economy: 1920–1980* 12–69 (London, 1983).

[96] Lov om kontroll med konkurranseinnskrenkninger og om prismisbruk (March 26, 1926). For detailed discussion of this legislation, see Andersen, *Rettens Stilling*, 180–294. See also Ragnar Knoph, *Trustloven av 1926 med Kommentar* (Oslo, 1927). There is very little English-language information on the Norwegian statute. But see Corwin Edwards, *Trade Regulation Overseas: The National Laws* 282–86 (Dobbs Ferry, N.Y., 1966).

[97] Bernitz, *Marknadsrätt*, 394.

intellectually consistent response to the harms associated with cartels and monopolies. Moreover, it closely resembled proposals made during this period by the German SPD and generally supported by other European workers' parties. In Norway, leftist coalitions were in a position to accomplish politically what the German social democrats could only talk about.

The statute established an institutional framework for combating restraints on competition by creating two new institutions. One was an administrative office called a Control Office (*Kontrollkontoret*), which maintained a cartel register, investigated complaints, prepared cases for the Control Council and generally applied the statute's substantive provisions. It was independent of the regular government bureaucracy and thus not subject to control by the ministries. Its director was appointed by the king and had to meet the qualifications to be a judge on the highest court. The Price Directorate that had been in existence since the war was, in effect, restructured as the Control Office—a pattern that would recur in other European countries after the Second World War and then again in the wake of communism's fall. The other new institution was a five-person Control Council (*Kontrollrådet*) which was also independent of the regular bureaucracy and whose members were appointed by the king. This council had final decision-making authority with respect to most violations of the statute, in some cases hearing appeals from decisions of the Control Office.

The system created by the statute centered on a requirement that cartels, dominant enterprises and certain other kinds of enterprises register with the Control Office. Agreements that were not registered as required were unenforceable. Firms with assets or share capital above specified limits also had to file annual financial statements. Information contained in these reporting documents was not, however, generally available to the public. The registration and disclosure requirements were designed to deter harmful conduct by revealing it and by providing a factual foundation for enforcement efforts. To supplement them, the Control Office also received broad authority to investigate the conduct of cartels and dominant firms for violations of the statute.

The statute created two main categories of substantive norms. One prohibited prices that were 'undue' (*utilborlige*) and thus represented a continuation of existing price control provisions. A second category prohibited price discrimination, exclusive dealings and certain boycotts, but only where they were found to be unfair, unduly harmful to those affected or to have a harmful influence on the 'public interest'. The scope of the norms gave the administrative officials a broad range of discretion.

For most offenses the Control Office initiated proceedings and sought an informal termination of the objectionable practices. If these proceedings were unsuccessful, the office could prepare a case for adjudication by the Council, which had authority to make orders regarding prices, terminate cartels and even dissolve corporations (although the last two measures were rarely used).

In addition, violations of the statute were subject to prosecution in the criminal courts as misdemeanors carrying both fines and maximum three-month prison terms, but criminal prosecutions were also rare.

This system remained an important part of the legal environment of business in Norway until the beginning of the Second World War.[98] During that period some 800 cases were decided under the statute.[99] Wilhelm Thagaard, the director of the Control Office throughout its history, was an influential and energetic bureaucrat who made the office an active force (and, as a result, often reaped the displeasure of Norwegian businesses). Thagaard was a moderate socialist who supported government economic planning, but opposed state socialism. He vigorously supported the mission of competition law as a means not only of preventing abuses of economic power, but also of defusing political pressure for more intrusive state involvement in the economy.[100]

Norwegian experience with competition law did not have a major direct influence on the development of competition law in Europe. Its influence outside Norway was limited by that country's small population, its peripheral place in European political and economic affairs and political culture, and its topographical particularities. Moreover, its materials were in a language accessible to few outside of Scandinavia.

Yet neither should its role be overlooked. Europeans interested in competition law issues were likely to be aware of the statute and the main features of the system. In Germany, in particular, information on the statute and its operations was readily available. For example, *Kartell-Rundschau*, the leading German periodical dealing with cartel and competition issues, included numerous articles on Norwegian experience until 1933.[101]

At the very least, Norwegian experience provided an additional example of an operating competition law system. In contrast to the German Regulation, the statute had been widely discussed before enactment and carefully drafted. While operating on some of the basic assumptions of the German legislation, it avoided its more egregious weaknesses. In particular, the Norwegian system operated on a more consistently juridical basis than did its German counterpart. Moreover, the Norwegian legislation was seen as part of a growing

---

[98] The legislation was not repealed until 1953, when it was replaced by legislation that focused more narrowly on controlling prices.

[99] Edwards, *Trade Regulation*, 285.

[100] For discussion of Thagaard and his role, see Furre, *Norsk Historie*, 139, and Fridtjof F. Gundersen & Ulf Bernitz, *Norsk og Internasjonal Markedsrett* 166–67 (Oslo, 1977).

[101] The dissemination of such information in Germany was facilitated by language factors. One was that German tended to be the second language of Norwegian officials, allowing them to publish materials in German and maintain close relations with their German counterparts. A measure of coincidence was also involved. Siegfried Tschierschky, one of the most prolific and influential writers on competition law issues in Germany, apparently knew Norwegian and translated and published materials on Norwegian competition law. See, e.g., Tschierschky's translation of Kristen Andersen, 'Die Aufsicht über Trusts und Kartelle in Norwegen', 31 *Kartell-Rundschau* 163 (1933).

commitment to competition law within some circles, and experience with the Norwegian system showed that such a competition law system could work.

3. The dissemination of competition law ideas: international mechanisms

In the latter half of the 1920s, international organizations also played key roles in disseminating and consolidating competition law ideas in Europe. During that period, the growth and spread of cartels, particularly international cartels, may have been the most prominent economic phenomenon not only in Europe, but in the world. Two high-level international conferences were particularly instrumental in defining perspectives on that phenomenon and responses to it.

The first was the World Economic Conference held in Geneva in 1927, which focused attention on the cartel issue and its potential public policy implications.[102] Organized by the League of Nations and billed as part of the international co-operative process that was to help create prosperity and maintain peace in the world, the conference drew extensive political and popular attention for several years. Preparations for the conference included numerous, often extensive, studies of world economic conditions by leading economists and economic policy specialists. The objective was to bring private experts and government representatives together for the purpose of identifying common problems facing the world economy and developing strategies for responding to them.

International trade issues were the main topic of the conference, and the issue of cartels was one of its centerpieces. These documents and the debates and resolutions of the conference reflected—and perhaps encouraged—much uniformity in views of cartels. The prevailing image of cartels generally followed the contours that had been sketched in Germany under the influence of historicist thinking. According to Karl Pribram, 'It is a striking fact that public opinion, which had in pre-war times in many countries been hostile to the exploitation of monopolistic power by cartels, now became almost all over Europe rather unanimous in acknowledging cartels as unavoidable, or even necessary, outcomes of modern economic development'.[103] In this view, specific cartel conduct might have harmful consequences for consumers, labor or other elements of society, but cartels as an organizational form were assessed positively—as a means of stabilizing economic conditions, promoting the

---

[102] For discussion of the conference, see Carl H. Pegg, *The Evolution of the European Idea, 1914–1932* 76–87 (Chapel Hill, 1983) and Bernhard Harms, *Vom Wirtschaftskrieg zur Weltwirtschaftskonferenz: Weltwirtschaftliche Gestaltungstendenzen im Spiegel gesammelter Vorträge* (Jena, 1927).

[103] Karl Pribram, *Cartel Problems: An Analysis of Collective Monopolies in Europe with American Application* 96 (Washington, D.C., 1935).

rationalization of industry, and enhancing the competitiveness of domestic industries.[104]

There was also a specifically 'international' element in the shaping of this image of cartels. For many, cartels were beneficial because they might contribute to 'economic *rapprochement*'.[105] The idea was that cartels that crossed national boundaries could generate economic co-operation among business leaders (and perhaps unions) across those borders. This potential for co-operation was highly valued, and such co-operation was seen as likely to foster the goals of world peace. Less than a decade after the horrors of the First World War, this idea had considerable force.

While there was little controversy over these basic characteristics of cartels, there were major conflicts over the issue of what, if anything, should be done about the harms associated with them. The organizers of the conference had apparently envisioned that it would recommend some significant government action with regard to cartels, and there were calls for strong competition laws at both the national and international level, most notably from social democrats and other socialists.[106] The German Social Democratic Party, in particular, called for extensive national cartel legislation as well as the introduction of an international system of competition law.[107]

In the end, however, these demands were rejected by the economic experts and government policy-makers who occupied center stage at the conference.[108] Governments were generally wary of national competition laws that might interfere with the competitiveness of their industries, and few took seriously the idea of international controls. The official position of the conference was that at least for the time being national governments should limit themselves to gathering information about the conduct of cartels and monopolistic enterprises and perhaps publicizing such information.[109] The claims were that such publicity would normally provide sufficient deterrence and that any

[104] According to the Official Report, '. . . the Conference has recognized that the phenomenon of such agreements [i.e., cartels] . . . does not constitute a matter upon which any conclusion of principle need be reached, but a development which has to be recognized and which, from this practical point of view, must be considered as good or bad according to the spirit which rules the constitution and the operation of the agreements, and in particular according to the measure in which those directing them are actuated by a sense of the general interest'. League of Nations, *Report and Proceedings of the World Economic Conference Held at Geneva, May 4th to 23rd, 1927*, C.E.I. 44(I); League of Nations Pub. 1927.I.46 at 49(a) (Geneva, 1927).
[105] This concept was the focus of one of the preparatory studies for the conference prepared by a Swiss political economist. See Eugene Grossman, *Methods of Economic Rapprochement* (C.E.C.P. 24(I), League of Nations Pub. 1926.II.29, 1927).
[106] See, e.g., the joint 'Declaration' by leading representatives of European 'workers' organizations', *Proceedings*, 233.
[107] See, e.g., Reuffurth, *Die Stellung der deutschen Sozialdemokratie*, 150–51.
[108] Socialists complained that workers' representatives 'were not represented at the present Conference in the way we would have wished, or as the Preparatory Committee had intended and the Council of the League had indicated'. Remarks of M. Jouhaux to the Conference on May 3, 1927. *Proceedings*, 86.
[109] *Official Report*, 49–51.

additional government interference with cartels might unjustifiably harm the development of a co-operative and effective world economy. The conference report emphasized that national legislation should not 'place an obstacle to the attainment of the benefits which [such cartel] agreements might secure by exhibiting a prejudice against them . . .'.[110]

While the World Economic Conference focused attention on the cartel problem, it did little to articulate a basis for responding to it. Three years later, however, a conference of the Interparliamentary Union took this step, concentrating on how governments should respond to the problems that cartels and other dominant firms created. Its resolutions and recommendations to governments articulated a set of ideas that was to be the core of the European competition law tradition for decades. As commentators pointed out in 1962, the IPU's 'London Resolution . . . states certain basic principles and sketches a system of control and regulation which has, to a great extent, influenced the cartel legislation in most of the Western European countries. . .'.[111]

The Interparliamentary Union has been little noticed since the Second World War, but during the interwar period it was a highly visible institution, particularly in Europe. It had been founded in the late nineteenth century in the belief that bringing together legislators from European and other countries could help solve common social problems and foster international peace.[112] Its main function was to organize and sponsor international conferences on particular topics, and competition legislation was a major topic at its 27th Conference in London in 1930.[113]

The views on cartels and economic concentration represented at this meeting were not markedly different from those that had been aired at the World Economic Conference, but the participants' conclusions about how governments should respond to these phenomena were very different. Whereas the earlier conference had shied away from recommending significant legislative action, the Interparliamentary Union strongly endorsed the enactment of aggressive national competition laws.

Why the differences in outcome? Events during the three years undoubtedly changed some views. The harms caused by cartels and market-dominating enterprises had been much discussed during the intervening years, increasing awareness of the extent of such harms. In addition, the New York stock market crash just a few months prior to the meeting may have created a sense of urgency about responding to the problem. Probably more

---

[110] *Proceedings*, 50.

[111] William Boserup and Uffe Schlichtkrull, 'Alternative Approaches to the Control of Competition: An Outline of European Cartel Legislation and its Administration', in John Perry Miller, ed., *Competition, Cartels and Their Regulation* 60–61 (Amsterdam, 1962).

[112] For general description, see Interparliamentary Union, *The Interparliamentary Union from 1889 to 1939* (Lausanne, 1939).

[113] See Union Interparlamentaire, *Compte Rendu de le XXVI. Conference Interparlementaire* 33–34, 145–71, and 335–73 (Lausanne, 1930).

important, however, were differences in the characteristics of the institutions and the participants. The Interparliamentary Union was a 'peace' organization dedicated to the goal of improving economic and political relations. It is not surprising, therefore, that they advocated a more vigorous response to the problem of economic power than did the government representatives and international economic experts at the World Economic Conference. Although most participants were members of national legislatures, they did not officially 'represent' their governments and were less subject to political influence and business pressure.

The resolution of the London Conference concerning the need for competition legislation passed without opposition (the US, France and Rumania abstained). It took as its basic premise that

.... cartels, trusts and other analogous combines are natural phenomena of economic life towards which it is impossible to adopt an entirely negative attitude. Seeing, however, that those combines may have a harmful effect both as regards public interests and those of the State, it is necessary that they should be controlled. This control should not take the form of an interference in economic life likely to affect its normal development. It should simply seek to establish a supervision over possible abuses and to prevent those abuses.[114]

It called for disclosure requirements and publicity as major factors in combating such abuses, but it also recommended that national governments establish in each country a Committee on Trusts and Cartels that would be independent of the government and that would be primarily responsible for determining whether particular conduct by cartels and dominant firms should be considered harmful and thus an 'abuse' of power. This special governmental organ would also administratively determine which steps should be taken to deter such conduct. These recommendations reflected the influence of German and Norwegian legislation, and they resembled the proposals that social democrats had made—to no immediate avail—at the World Economic Conference.

It is unlikely that anyone present at the London Conference imagined that the basic ideas contained in this resolution would still be guiding competition law thought and decisions more than a half century later, but so it was to be. This is not to suggest that the IPU had sufficient political power to pressure national governments to follow its recommendations, nor that it had sufficient intellectual weight to induce support for them. Its importance rested on its articulation of those ideas as a European 'model' of competition law.

---

[114] Union Interparliamentaire, *Compte Rendu*, 33–34.

G. DEPRESSION, WAR, AND THE ECLIPSE OF COMPETITION LAW

Even as the Interparliamentary Union was debating the need for national and international competition laws, the international economic crisis was deepening, and it soon diverted attention from the idea of using law to protect the process of competition. For the duration of the Great Depression, economic policy energies were concentrated on other issues that were seen as more pressing, such as reducing unemployment and reviving business activity. As in Germany, other European governments saw cartels as convenient tools for seeking economic stability and influencing economic events, and they often encouraged or even required the formation of cartels and subjected them to extensive government regulation, sometimes including the establishment of minimum prices.

Yet even during the 1930s, several European states, including Czechoslovakia (1933), Poland (1933), Yugoslavia (1934), and Denmark (1937), enacted statutes that to a greater or lesser extent bore the mark of the IPU's recommendations.[115] Experience under these statutes played little role in the subsequent development of a European competition law tradition, however, because it was generally limited in both scope and duration and little known outside each state's own borders. Moreover, the Soviet 'reorientation' of Eastern Europe after the Second World War precluded any influence that the experience of countries there might otherwise have had.

As economic depression made way for war at the end of the decade, the reimposition of wartime economic controls further submerged the idea of protecting competition. For many government leaders, competition was anathema, because it interfered with the political solidarity they needed. Wartime controls were inconsistent with competition, and governments usually eliminated or restricted it. As we shall see, however, competition law ideas would re-emerge after 1945 as many of these same decision-makers sought to reconstruct national economies and polities.

H. TOWARDS A EUROPEAN MODEL OF COMPETITION LAW

During the interwar years a basic set of ideas about competition law was gaining currency and support in much of Europe, and it took root in some European legal systems and on the agendas of some important political

---

[115] For Denmark, see I W. E. von Eyben, *Monopoler og Priser* 7–13 (Copenhagen, 1980). According to von Eyben, 'The models for the Statute of May 18, 1937, were the Norwegian *Trustlov* of 1926 and the [IPU's] London Resolutions of 1930' ibid., 8. For Czechoslovakia, see Ervin Hexner, *La Loi Tchecoslovaque sur les Cartels* (Prague, 1935). For a description of the state of cartel legislation in the mid-1930s, see also Heinrich Friedländer, *Die Rechtspraxis der Kartelle und Konzerne in Europa* (Zürich, 1938).

movements. These ideas also began to be perceived as a distinctive 'model' of competition law, a European alternative to US antitrust law. The core conception of this model was that law should protect the process of competition by administratively controlling the harmful conduct of economically powerful firms rather than by prohibiting particular types of conduct. This 'model' came to be referred to throughout Europe as the 'abuse' model of competition law.

Since the 1930s then the perception of two contrasting and often competing models of competition law has been a standard component of European discourse on the subject: the American 'prohibition' model and the European 'abuse' model. In the years after the Second World War, as European politicians and bureaucrats faced the problems of economic reconstruction and the new and sometimes resented hegemony of the United States, this perception both influenced and justified key decisions about whether to enact competition laws and what shape they should take.

The 'Europeanization' of competition law ideas at the levels of both discourse and experience was important for another reason. The ideas and concepts of this model were much influenced by interwar German experience, because Germany was the focal point of competition law development: its experience was the most extensive, and its literature and debates were the most influential. If, however, other European decision-makers after the Second World War had perceived this model of competition law as 'German' rather than 'European', its influence might have been considerably less.

VI

The Postwar Decades: Competition Law and Administrative Policy

In the years immediately following the end of the Second World War the prospects for competition and economic freedom in Europe seemed bleak. Many informed observers saw Europe's future as socialist—a high degree of state control of the economy and a decreasing sphere of operation for personal freedom and economic competition. Yet Western Europe changed direction radically over the next two decades. By the mid-1960s the market economy had regained centerstage, and the process of competition was reacquiring the respect and allegiance that it had lost decades before. Competition law often played central roles in this development.

During these decades competition law moved along two very different paths. Most European countries enacted competition legislation based on the images that had taken shape in the late 1920s and that I call the administrative control model of competition law. In Germany, however, competition law thought and practice followed a different trajectory—one that would eventually change the face of Europe. In this chapter we focus on the first of these paths; in the following two chapters we will look more closely at Germany's deviation from that path.

This chapter treats national competition law experiences (other than in Germany) from the end of the war until the mid-1980s, when the progress of European integration began a new chapter in the story. Our perspective will often be more distant and less detailed than in previous chapters, primarily because we will be seeking to identify patterns in the experience of a number of countries. The details of individual national experiences are less important for our story than the general pattern of these experiences and the attitudes, expectations and patterns of thought associated with them.

After briefly surveying the contexts in which competition law systems emerged and developed, I will describe the general pattern of this experience and then look in greater depth at the experiences of England, France, and Sweden. These countries partook of the general pattern, and yet each was 'special', and thus a more detailed look at their experience fills in the general picture.

Hope framed experience at the end of the Second World War and again in the mid-1980s when European integration once more moved boldly forward. In the years after 1945 the hope was that the many forms of pain so recently inflicted on the people of Europe would give way to stability, prosperity, greater social justice, and more effective mechanisms for preventing the return of war. In the mid-1980s the hope was that the now prosperous nations of Europe had found in the European Union a means of achieving those ends. Competition law was interwoven with both sets of hopes.

1. Reconstruction

A reconstruction imperative dominated the immediate postwar years, and its values, attitudes and experiences conditioned the emergence of competition law.[1] Most European governments were again faced with the need to rebuild shattered economies and stabilize shaky political systems, and for many the pressing immediacy of these needs narrowed horizons. This was not a time of careful and patient thinking about general principles to guide future action, but of *ad hoc* responses to impending crises.

The rapid return to economic well-being in Europe in the decades after the war has tended to obscure the exigencies of the immediate postwar years, but in Europe after 1945 the need for more goods dominated thought. Many people were hungry, and goods, including essentials, were often in catastrophically short supply; in most countries there was rationing even of basic necessities.

Shortages also meant inflation, which was to remain a major economic concern in most countries for a decade or more. This required governments to control prices and combat manipulation of scarce supplies, making price controls a central motif of economic policy. There was little, however, that national governments could do to remedy the underlying problem, at least in the short-run. That would depend primarily on increasing access to goods either through more production or increased imports. National governments were seldom in a position to do either.

The US government was. US aid did what these governments seemed unable to do themselves—it sparked recovery.[2] By infusing billions of dollars in aid into the recipient countries, US loans, and, beginning in 1947, its Marshall Plan aid not only helped to alleviate shortages, but reduced imped-

[1] For discussion of these years, see, e.g., Alan S. Milward, *The Reconstruction of Europe, 1945–1951* (Berkeley, 1984); M. M. Postan, *An Economic History of Western Europe 1945–1964* (London, 1967) and Richard Mayne, *The Recovery of Europe* (New York, 1973).

[2] See, e.g., John Gimbel, *The Origins of the Marshall Plan* (Stanford, 1976) and Charles L. Mee Jr., *The Marshall Plan* (New York, 1984).

iments to economic improvement—such as hard currency shortages. This, in turn, reduced the policy weight that price controls had to bear. Those controls continued to be an important economic policy tool, but US aid at least reduced some of the pressure on prices.

Rapid economic growth did commence in most parts of Europe within a few years after the end of the war. Production levels in most countries exceeded prewar levels by 1949, and by the early 1950s a pattern of expansion had set in that appeared relatively reliable. The Korean War further spurred production gains in many industries, although it also renewed inflationary pressures.

The economic exigencies of recovery from war were tied to political exigencies. One was the perceived need for governments to play a more important regulatory role in their economies. In part, such efforts were driven by economic necessity. Many markets were thin: supplies were limited, and demand was often too great to allow market clearing. This contributed to inflation, encouraged manipulation and, in the eyes of many, demanded government intervention.

Government controls were also driven by demands for 'economic justice' that had been much strengthened by recent privations. Shortages were increasingly viewed in the light of the perceived 'justice' of the economic mechanism that distributed those goods. Europeans had become markedly less willing to acquiesce in distributive arrangements that favored existing social and economic elites, many of whom had recently been discredited by depression and war.

The scope of expectations about what government should do had also significantly widened. The experience of extensive government controls during the war combined with the enormity of the reconstruction tasks to create the expectation that government would play a far larger role than it had typically played in Western European countries before the war. These expectations did not necessarily, however, carry with them very clear ideas about what governments should actually do.

These sensibilities fueled and were fueled by larger political movements. The war had shaken confidence in existing institutions and elites, and, in its wake, political leadership in many countries moved sharply to the left. Socialist and social democratic parties either achieved control of government or greatly increased their influence on national political stages.[3] This leftward turn made possible the enactment and implementation of programs that reflected economic justice concerns, and these, in turn, contributed to the perception and expression of those concerns. The pendulum of politics began to move back to the right within a few years in most of Western Europe, but the concerns had become anchored in the vocabulary of political life.

[3] For general discussion, see Albert S. Lindemann, *A History of European Socialism* 322–61 (New Haven, 1983).

In this cauldron of uncertainty and shifting political currents, the political role of the United States was often as important as its economic aid and not dissociable from it. The war had put the United States in a commanding political and economic position. Like it or not, European governments depended on US economic and military aid for several years, and thus European politicians had to take US reactions into account in a wide range of domestic decisions.

2. Stability and growth (early 1950s–early 1970s)

By the early 1950s, reconstruction had ceased to be the primary lens through which economic and political decisions were viewed. A phase of economic and political stability set in that was to last for some two decades.[4] For Europe as a whole, economic growth remained impressive throughout the period, generating confidence in economic policies and in the political regimes associated with them. There were significant variations in the pace of development of national economies, and there were structural adjustments, but unemployment and business failures remained generally low.

Buoyed by confidence in economic performance, centrist political regimes held the reins of government in most European capitals. With little incentive to change course, they typically pursued economic policies that were focused on maintaining economic growth. At the same time, however, most also expanded the 'welfare net' of social protections and economic benefits for their nationals. The demands that had been laid down as part of the political agenda during the immediate postwar years had to be met. In some cases socialist or social democratic governments rewarded 'their' voters, while in others (for example, France before the election of Mitterand) centrist regimes expanded social support programs in pursuit of those voters.

3. Living with crises (from the mid-1970s through the mid-1980s)

The international economic crises that began with the first oil shock in 1973 changed the scenery dramatically, confronting European economic policymakers with new problems.[5] Inflation returned to center stage as resources were drained from Western economies and transferred to the oil-producing countries of OPEC. Officials were aware that this form of inflation had a new shape. It was not the result of shortages, and it was not pushed by excessive demand. It was largely attributable to increased costs generated by dramati-

[4] Charles Maier has insightfully explored the theme of stability as a political goal in the twentieth century. See, e.g., Charles S. Maier, *In Search of Stability: Explorations in Historical Political Economy* (Cambridge, 1987).
[5] See generally Andrea Boltho, *The European Economy: Growth and Crisis* (Oxford, 1982) and Ralf Dahrendorf, *Europe's Economy in Crisis* (New York, 1982).

cally higher oil prices, and this meant that it was less susceptible to national controls. Nevertheless, some countries responded with direct price controls, while others turned to competition law as a tool for combating the new pressures.

As OPEC-induced price increases coursed through Western economies during the next decade or so, it became clearer that this new form of inflation was also tied to economic stagnation. This was the era of 'stagflation'—inflation in a slow-growth environment. This new phenomenon seemed intractable. Neither traditional price controls nor the Keynesian demand management tools that had stood policy-makers in good stead during the previous decades seemed an effective antidote.

The stagflation of the 1970s and early 1980s was also accompanied by changes in the international competitive situation that created new economic policy problems. One was the emergence of Japanese firms as major competitors—both within Europe and in international markets—and the awareness that there might be more potential low-wage competitors in the East that would soon follow and further undermine European prosperity. Moreover, competition among the major trading countries was beginning to appear more like a zero-sum game. As the economist Lester Thurow has described it, the niche competition of the early postwar decades was beginning to give way to 'head-to-head' competition.[6] Increasingly, Japanese, European, and US firms were producing the same goods for the same purchasers, apparently diminishing the European firms' prospects for profits and expansion. The demise of European steel industries in the face of foreign competition seemed an ominous portent.

The economic turbulence of the period also destabilized centrist politics in many European countries—as voters sought more promising responses to its threats. The French turned to the left, electing the socialist Francois Mitterand president in 1981; the United Kingdom turned in the opposite direction, electing the conservative Margaret Thatcher as prime minister in 1979.

Amidst the swirls of uncertainty surrounding national economic policies, European economic integration offered the prospect of a way out of the dilemma, a basis for renewed confidence in Europe's economic future. Few, however, were confident that the promise could actually be realized and that the political strains associated with trying would not be severe.

4. Themes

Although there were major changes in economic and political conditions over these four decades, several motifs stand out as particularly important for

---

[6] See Lester C. Thurow, *Head-to-Head. The Coming Economic Battle between Japan, Europe, and America* (New York, 1992).

understanding the development of competition law during this period. One was the persistent claim that European businesses were 'backward'. In the years after 1945, for example, Europeans saw their industries as lacking the capital, size, and managerial skills necessary to compete with US firms. By the end of the period, many were claiming that European firms lagged behind their US and Japanese competitors in the technology race. The areas of perceived weakness changed over time, as did the perceived 'leaders', but the theme remained.

One reason it persisted was that it was politically useful. It was used to justify the efforts of national governments to support particular domestic industries as well as the measures they employed to protect them against foreign competitors. If domestic firms were weak, they had to be protected, and in much of Europe such measures were at the core of economic policy. Though there were significant differences in the intensity with which countries pursued these policies, the tacit assumption was that such industries could not compete in the global market without governmental assistance—subsidies and benefits at home and protection at the borders.

This justificatory scheme had roots in domestic politics. In addition to the obvious personal and political benefits to politicians from protecting their own industries, it was tied to economic justice concerns and the internal political forces associated with them. Government assistance to domestic industry can be seen as part of a seldom clearly articulated pact in which European governments promised their nationals that support and protection for domestic industry were necessary to provide the resources necessary for expanding social benefits such as health and retirement insurance, statutory minimum paid vacations, reduced work weeks, and the like. The welfare state ideal that played such an important role in many European countries during this period was thus linked to this protection-based economic policy model.

This pact also implied that government had a responsibility to assure that the firms to which it gave such support acted in a manner consistent with their responsibility to society—that is, that they did not exploit their power to the detriment of others in the community such as consumers, workers, or less powerful competitors. This concept of 'communal' responsibility is critical to understanding the shaping of European competition law.

This set of relationships long provided a stable framework for policy decisions, but the economic crises of the 1970s made this decisional framework less viable. At the same time, the process of European integration was making it less politically acceptable, and thus governments found it increasingly difficult to play those roles. As a result, uncertainty became a central motif of economic policy.

One final motif was the political and economic predominance of the US, which often framed European economic policy decisions, particularly early in the period. Europeans depended to varying degrees and in varying ways on

US co-operation and support, not least because of the bipolar structure of international political relations. The Soviet Union, lest we forget, was not far from Western Europe. European leaders were all too aware of this dependency, and strategies for dealing with it colored many economic and political decisions.

B. TURNING TO COMPETITION LAW

During the decade and a half after 1945 many Western European governments introduced competition laws, most for the first time. In some cases—for example, the United Kingdom—such laws were introduced immediately after war's end, while in other countries such as Belgium efforts to introduce them did not succeed until the late 1950s.[7] Even in those few countries like Italy where such legislation was not enacted, there were often intense efforts to do so.

Why the turn to competition law? The short answer is that political decision-makers perceived it as valuable, but then the question becomes 'Why did this perception have sufficient force to generate enactment of a new type of law at approximately the same time in a large number of European countries?' As we have seen, competition law had been widely discussed earlier, but now competition laws were actually being enacted.

The discussions of competition law in the 1920s and early 1930s prepared the way. From the perspective of the end of the twentieth century, the upheavals of depression and war make the temporal space between 1930 and 1945 seem far greater than it was chronologically. Many Europeans involved in economic policy decisions in the 1940s and 1950s had participated in the discussions of competition law in the late 1920s. In that context they had often heard claims about the benefits of competition law as a tool for responding to economic and political problems, and many had supported such claims. When the reconstruction imperative confronted them with problems such as inflation and the need for rapid economic growth, they were aware of competition law's potential benefits.

Domestic political factors frequently favored such a move. The heightened sensitivity to 'economic justice' issues that was a central theme of postwar European politics made the idea of competition law attractive. Depression and war had intensified demands that economic inequalities be reduced and that national governments combat uses of economic power that tended to exacerbate or reflect such inequalities. Enacting a competition law was a

---

[7] For surveys of this legislation, see Stefan A. Riesenfeld, 'The Protection of Competition', in II *American Enterprise in Europe: A Legal Profile* 197–342 (Eric Stein & Thomas Nicholson, eds., Ann Arbor, 1960) and Hans B. Thorelli, 'Antitrust in Europe: National Policies after 1945', 29 *U. of Chicago L. Rev.* 222 (1959).

means of responding to such demands. Politicians who did so could claim, for example, that they were acting to reduce exploitation of consumers and/or harm to small business, and both were politically attractive claims.

The political locus of earlier discussions also played a role in these dynamics. Socialists and social democrats had urged competition law as a means of controlling exploitation and improving the lot of workers, and they carried this supportive attitude with them as they moved toward political power in the postwar period. Moreover, they had a vocabulary for expressing economic justice demands: the discourse of 'exploitation' moved from the margins to the center of political language.

Transnational factors were no less important in urging the enactment of competition laws. In the immediate postwar period the US exerted considerable pressure on some European countries, most notably the UK, to enact competition laws. US officials often saw competition law as a tool for combating the economic concentration and cartelization that many considered to have fostered fascism in Germany and Italy and economic and political weakness elsewhere. There were also more practical considerations: many were aware that combating cartels was likely to increase access by US business to European markets. There is little evidence that US pressure led directly to the enactment of competition laws (and in some cases it might have led in the opposite direction) but for years after the war US aid was vitally important to many European countries, and with the US paying many of the bills, recipient countries could not blatantly disregard US entreaties.

This US pressure was associated with the international efforts in the late 1940s to create an International Trade Organization (ITO) and to secure acceptance of the Havana Charter, which called upon states to take steps to protect competition, at least insofar as international trade was concerned.[8] The efforts ultimately failed to obtain their objectives because of a lack of political support in the US, but it was a much discussed project that focused attention on the issue of governmental protection of competition. As the economist Corwin Edwards (who was personally involved in this process) reported, several European governments began to prepare legislation on the assumption that the Havana Charter would be enacted, and this preparatory activity was sometimes an important impetus to subsequent legislation.[9] In any event, efforts to enact the Havana Charter further sensitized European decision-makers to the availability of competition laws as an economic policy tool.

Finally, there was a perceptible 'snowball' effect. Relevant decision-makers in one country were aware of at least the basic outlines of what other coun-

---

[8] For discussion, see William A. Brown, *The United States and the Restoration of World Trade* 125–31 (Washington, D.C., 1950) and Claire Wilcox, *A Charter for World Trade* 103–13 (New York, 1949).

[9] Corwin D. Edwards, *Control of Cartels and Monopolies: An International Comparison* 231–32 (Dobbs Ferry, N.Y., 1967).

tries were doing in the economic policy area, particularly after organizations such as the Organization for European Economic Cooperation (later to become the OECD—Organization for Economic Cooperation and Development) began operating in the late 1940s. Each new national competition law tended to increase pressure on those who did not yet have one. Competition law had become fashionable.

C. ADMINISTRATIVE CONTROL AS THE MODEL

Not only was there a wave of new national competition laws during this period, but (except for Germany) they tended to have similar basic characteristics. The central features of the competition laws of Austria, Belgium, Denmark, Finland, France, the Netherlands, Norway, Sweden, and the United Kingdom reflected—to varying degrees—the constellation of ideas from the late 1920s that I call the administrative control model of competition law. These ideas achieved a kind of unspoken orthodoxy among European policymakers that would only gradually lose its force and that at the end of the twentieth century still may have more influence on decision-making than many suppose.

The pervasiveness of this orthodoxy is a key to understanding the competition law dynamics of the period and to interpreting later developments on both the national and regional levels. Yet it is precisely this element of European experience that has been obscured by the failure to employ a Europe-wide lens in considering national competition law systems. This opacity has been self-reinforcing: where national competition laws are not seen as part of a broader picture, there are few incentives to consider their relationships to other systems.

We have already discussed the main features of the model that was developed in the late 1920s. We can now relate it to legislative choices made after the war. Note that in using the term 'model' here I do not suggest that the ideas of the 1920s were consciously chosen as a basis for emulation in postwar Europe. I use it rather to code uniformities in the central features of national competition laws.

The concept of administrative control was the idea that structured these systems: government officials were authorized to take measures against powerful firms whose restrictions on the competitive process were seen as harmful to society. Competition law was thus located in the territory of public law. Typically, it could be located even more precisely—within administrative law. Government administrators played the central roles, and the primary mechanism was the more or less discretionary implementation of economic policy.

1. Norms

In administrative control systems, conduct norms tend to be general and vague, providing little information about the conduct to which they are addressed. The Belgian competition law of 1960 relied, for example, almost exclusively on the concept of 'abuse of economic power'. It provided that

There is an abuse, within the meaning of this Act, when one or more persons possessing economic power shall harm the public interest through practices which distort or restrict the normal play of competition or which interfere either with the economic freedom of producers, distributors or consumers or with the development of production or trade.[10]

Such norms do little to apprise firms of the circumstances under which they can expect officials to take enforcement action. They typically operate as administrative authorizations. In some cases, they authorize officials to initiate particular types of administrative procedures where conduct has designated effects. In others, they appear as general conduct norms, but they are applied and enforced primarily or exclusively by administrators, who typically have extensive discretion in applying them.

The norms generally focus on the effects of conduct rather than on its characteristics, typically authorizing government officials to control conduct where it has specified harmful effects. Sanctions are seldom attached to particular forms of conduct or specific 'arrangements' (such as cartels). This means that the norms generally apply only to economically powerful firms, either by their terms or because only powerful firms (or arrangements among firms) can create the effects specified.

The conduct standard is almost universally associated with the concept of abuse of power, although the term itself is not always used in the legislation. The idea is that uses of economic power that create particular types of societal effects are 'against the public interest'. They are, therefore, considered 'abusive' and subject to control by the government. The term 'abuse' is used to code conduct that has such effects, and for decades it has been common for Europeans to refer to their systems as 'abuse' systems in contradistinction to 'prohibition' systems (of which US antitrust has been the prime example). The abuse concept has often created misunderstandings among foreign observers, particularly from the US, who find it disturbingly vague. That conclusion erroneously assumes, however, that those applying the term expect to derive guidance from interpretation of the term itself. It is important to recognize that in this context the term 'abuse' is being used to 'code' particular kinds of harmful effects.

[10] Act of May 27, 1960, *Moniteur Belge* 4674 (June 22, 1960). For detailed discussion of the legislative history and background of the legislation, see *Pasinomie Année 1960* 554–94 (*VII Série*).

The scope of substantive norms in systems of this type often varies considerably from country to country, but there are some noteworthy patterns. Where specific conduct is identified for close scrutiny or is subjected to especially stringent procedures or sanctions, the focus has tended to be on vertical restraints such as price discrimination and refusals to deal. Where such vertical relationships are not identified for special treatment by the relevant legislation, they have often tended nevertheless to receive the most enforcement attention and thus to have the most significant impact. This reflects the degree to which concerns about the impact of economic power occupied the foreground of competition law thinking during Europe's postwar decades.

Finally, the early legislation generally did not apply to mergers, at least there were seldom specific provisions dealing with them. In the two decades immediately after the war, the idea of controls on mergers was little noticed in Europe, and such controls were not assumed to be part of competition law. In most countries, governments were encouraging the creation of larger corporations, notably through mergers. Many systems did, however, add merger control provisions in the 1970s or later.

2. Institutions and roles

The primary decision-makers in this type of system are administrators. Private suits are seldom permitted, and if permitted, they tend to be available only under very limited circumstances. Usually the legislation establishes a separate administrative office to administer the law. Frequently it also provides for a special 'commission' either to advise administrators on the application of the law or to make decisions, usually subject to administrative or legislative approval.

Administrative decisions are often subject to review, either by administrative tribunals or by a special commission or court specifically created to hear such appeals. These tribunals vary widely in their specifics, but typically they contain a presiding officer who must be qualified to be a judge, plus a group of 'neutral' experts and representatives of business, labor and consumer interests.

Enforcement in such systems tends to be 'soft'. The guiding notion is that administrators should not interfere too much with business conduct. They are supposed to use publicity and pressure as the primary or exclusive means of achieving compliance. Administrative institutions sometimes have authority to declare an agreement invalid, and the authority to levy fines has become more common, but criminal sanctions tend to be either absent or severely circumscribed.

Note that these components fit well together. A basically administrative system comports well, for example, with relatively vague norms and high levels of discretion, not least because vagueness and flexibility tend to increase the maneuvering room— and hence, typically, the negotiating position—of the administrators operating the system. This 'fit' or cohesion of elements has undoubtedly added force and durability to administrative control systems.

D. CHOOSING ADMINISTRATIVE CONTROLS

But why were there such similarities in basic structure among the competition law systems enacted during this period? Given that few have noticed the similarities, the question has seldom been posed—much less answered. In part this is because competition law has been viewed as too peripheral to warrant such studies. In part, however, it has also been due to the lack of an academic 'home' for this type of analysis. Such issues have frequently been seen as too political to be interesting to legal scholars and too legal to interest economists. The consequence has been a paucity of scholarly attention.

In examining the factors that set the mold for European competition law, we need to recall who was making the decisions. The policy-makers and politicians who made the decisions had experienced extraordinary uncertainty and turmoil—two wars, the Great Depression and, often, severe internal strife—for decades, and thus few could have great confidence in any particular economic policy direction. Some believed strongly in the promise of particular solutions, but they could have no experiential base for their beliefs. In addition, they were often under great pressure to achieve rapid improvement in the performance of their economies and thus not to interfere with business decision-making. Where the economy was concerned, caution was the watchword.

Many postwar economic policy-makers had socialist or Christian-communitarian backgrounds, neither of which placed a high value on competition as a value. Each emphasized the importance of subjecting economic decision-making to the interests of the 'commonweal'—that is, to the interests of society or community. In practice, this meant subjecting it to some form of state control. Moreover, this ideological stance colored perceptions of the state, painting governmental activity in friendly, constructive hues. Leaders of these groups typically also derided the negative social impact of what they often referred to as the 'US form of capitalism'.

The pervasiveness of administrative control systems takes on particular poignancy and refractive power when we consider the factors that favored alternative choices. There were many reasons for European countries to follow the US style of competition law—none did. The US was the acknowledged 'father' of antitrust law, having had far more experience with such laws than any other country. It had developed an extensive case law and boasted decades of often high quality writing on the issues involved. This experience alone should have made it an attractive choice. Its rejection becomes even more noteworthy when we recall the enormous political and economic power of the US at this time in relation to Western European governments and note that US officials proselytized in favor of the US antitrust model and put pressure on several governments to enact such a system.

Several factors mentioned above as influences on decisions to enact competition law systems also influenced the shape of the systems created. The interwar discussions of competition law, for example, not only spread awareness of the potential benefits of competition law, but touted a particular form of competition law. The degree of similarity between the model presented at the International Parliamentary Union in 1930 and laws enacted after the Second World War is striking, but almost completely forgotten. In part this is because the influence of the interwar discussions was seldom publicly acknowledged. The interwar period was 'tainted' by depression and war, and this virtually precluded conscious adherence to a 'model' from that period. The influence of these conceptions of competition law operated primarily on the cognitive level—that is, they provided the structures for thinking about competition law. They were 'assumed' to be the form that competition law should take—at least in Europe.

Another factor that has obscured these continuities has been the positivist cast of much European legal scholarship. This perspective focuses attention on 'official' data such as enacted laws or official decisions, but pays little attention to cognitive factors. Since the ideas of the late 1920s were seldom enacted into law before the war, their influence tended to disappear from the positivist field of vision. Failure to perceive these historical continuities helps to explain why the fundamental similarities between European competition law systems have so often been overlooked.

In addition to continuities in ideas from the interwar period, there were continuities of government practice from the war itself. As in the First World War, European governments had imposed extensive regulations on business during the war, and elements of these regulations persisted during the years following the war. To cast the protection of competition in the form of administrative controls fit comfortably into these policy patterns.

Most external influences (except, of course, that of the US) also tended to push in the direction of administrative controls. The Havana Charter was not specific about the form of competition law it called for, but its provisions were more consistent with a cautious, policy-oriented administrative control model than with US-style antitrust. Moreover, as we noted above, adoption of this form of competition law by leading European nations such as England and France undoubtedly encouraged other national legislatures to follow that model. It became the accepted style of European competition law.

Administrative control systems also have advantages for politicians and administrators, and here we need to remember that most European countries are parliamentary democracies in which the political party or parties in control of the legislature also control the executive branch. One obvious advantage for those operating such systems is that they provide administrators (and sometimes politicians) with a means of directly influencing the conduct of powerful economic actors. Rather than merely establishing abstract conduct norms and allowing the courts to enforce them, administrative-political elites can put discretionary authority in their own hands. Administrators can then use such authority as a bargaining tool to negotiate conduct modification or other personal or public benefits from firms subject to those controls.

A second set of advantages is political. Those who enact, maintain and operate administrative control systems can reap political gains from taking action to control 'big business' and abuses of economic power. In effect, administrative control systems helped to fulfil the promise implied in the postwar political pact that justified government protection of industry on the grounds that it would generate resources for social amelioration and conditioned that support on subjecting powerful firms to communal control. Neither the discourse nor the operation of US-style antitrust fit those political needs.

Administrative control systems are also politically attractive because they can be instituted and operated at little cost and with few risks. A government can with minimal expense enact a law authorizing administrative controls to protect competition from 'abusive' conduct. Since the norms and procedures can be left vague, there is no need for extensive legislative preparations and negotiations. An office can then be established and a few bureaucrats assigned to implement the legislative directives. The response can, therefore, be both quick and cheap!

Political risks are limited, at least for a period of time, because it may be difficult for outside observers to determine how much is actually done to implement the legislation. A government can reap the political rewards associated with protecting consumers and small businesses, but whether it actually influences businesses (and thus incurs the policy and personal costs of doing so) is likely to be difficult for journalists and the public to assess. Faced with more pressing economic policy problems, postwar politicians must have found this a congenial prospect. In addition, businesses may find such a system a useful 'cover': it tells the public that economically powerful firms are subject to controls, but it can be operated in such a way that the controls have little bearing on business conduct.

Perceptions and assessments of the competitive process also encouraged an administrative control approach to competition law. As we have seen, economic theorists and political leaders of the interwar period had often praised the potential value of cartels, even though they recognized that cartels and powerful enterprises could use their power to harm society, in general, and competition, in particular. Moreover, particularly in the decades after the

war, governments typically welcomed economic concentration and the creation of large, powerful enterprises as necessary for international competitiveness. Any harms they might cause were outweighed by their necessity,
leaving little space for the idea of preventing the mergers that created them
and providing few structures on which rules regarding harmful conduct could
be built.

The Keynesian ideas that pervaded the thinking of many European economists during the 1950s and 1960s further emphasized the importance of government controls on the economy, particularly in managing demand, and
attached relatively little weight to the role of competition as an economic
steering force.[11] The emphasis was on macro-economic planning and the
adroit use of fiscal measures in fine-tuning economic events. In this intellectual atmosphere it is not surprising that economists seldom focused on the
need to protect the process of competition.

The socialist and social democratic opinion shapers, who played important
roles in many countries during this period, were also unlikely to emphasize
the protection of competition as a goal in and of itself. Their economic policy
discourse favored goals such as the prevention of exploitation and abuse of
power, but it did not valorize competition as such. From this perspective,
administrative control systems and their promise of controlling economic
power were far more congenial.

E. IMPLEMENTING COMPETITION LAWS

The most prominent characteristic in the implementation of European
national competition law systems has been the 'softness' of their efforts to
seek compliance with competition law norms. In general, national competition authorities have received few resources for carrying out the tasks
assigned to them. This has meant small numbers of officials available for
investigation of potentially violative conduct and analysis of economic data
as well as small support staffs. Several years ago US law professor James Rahl
related to me his astonishment when in preparing a book on European
competition law in the 1960s he visited Copenhagen and there learned that
the Danish competition law office consisted, basically, of a director and a
secretary.

The lack of resources has signalled a lack of political will in the application
of competition laws. Regimes have often used competition law systems as little more than a symbolic, hortatory statement that the government has the
power to control potentially harmful uses of economic power. It has been a

[11] For a wide-ranging and perceptive treatment of the various roles played by Keynesian ideas
in Europe and the US, see *The Political Power of Economic Ideas: Keynesianism Across Nations*
(Peter A. Hall, ed., Princeton, 1989).

useful tool for government officials to have, but they have used it sparingly. Often with little or no authority to coerce compliance and with limited political backing or incentives to take vigorous actions, officials have typically been reluctant to risk negative political repercussions from 'interfering' with 'national' industries. Officials have often exercised suasion to modify business conduct, but in general the impact of those efforts has been limited.

In the following sections we look at the experience of France, Sweden and the UK with competition laws. Each of these systems began in a more or less 'pure' administrative control mold, but gradually introduced juridical elements—for different reasons, at times and under different circumstances. I refer to this process as 'juridification'. It has been halting, and the progress has often been limited, but the direction has been clear. This process was an important, but little noticed preparatory step in what appeared to many to be an abrupt reorientation of competition law in Europe in the 1980s and 1990s.

We should note that during this period the competition law system of the European Community had relatively little direct influence on the competition law systems of Member States. National and 'community' competition laws operated within their own sphere, with little interaction between them. We will deal extensively in later chapters with the competition law of the European Union and its relations with Member State competition law systems.

F. FRANCE: COMPETITION LAW AND THE WEIGHT OF *DIRIGISME*

Competition law in France during this period represents in many ways a particularly strong form of the administrative control model, and its operation reveals aspects of European competition law systems that are often less perceptible in other contexts. Competition law long operated in the shadows of dirigistic economic controls, and its gradual and partial emergence from those shadows—its struggle for identity—is an important part of the European story. French competition law experience is also important from another perspective—that of European integration. Since the inception of the European Community, France and French officials have often tended to resist a more vigorous role for competition law in the process of European integration, and French domestic experience with competition law helps explain that opposition.

1. *Dirigisme* as context

The French tradition of '*dirigisme*'—basically, government 'direction' or 'guidance' of economic conduct—has played a key role in the evolution of thought and attitudes toward competition in modern France, and thus we need to look briefly at its outlines. Competition law values and ideas have operated against the background of this tradition, sometimes timidly challenging its premises, more often being forced into a strained accommodation with it.

French *dirigisme* can be seen as a successor form of the mercantilist policies and concepts to which virtually all European countries subscribed at one time or another and to one degree or another in the course of the seventeenth and eighteenth centuries. The basic mercantilist postulate was that a government should direct economic activity in order to achieve its own economic policy goals. Although it has deeper roots,[12] it is frequently associated with Colbert, the famous Finance Minister of Louis XIV, who sought to organize the French economy in the service of the state and established a bureaucratic apparatus for 'controlling' economic conduct.

Patterns of state direction of the economy survived the French Revolution, albeit in attenuated form and within a much narrower sphere.[13] In general, the focus of regulation was on specific aspects of commerce rather than on industry. During the second half of the nineteenth century, the tradition was in some ways interrupted, as the rhetoric of economic liberalism pervaded domestic economic policy. Nevertheless, large-scale business continued to rely heavily on government support even during this period.[14] France industrialized more slowly than its main rivals, England and Germany, however, and thus there was little pressure to control the economic power of industry until after the First World War. The administrative state was in place, but it intervened relatively little in industrial markets.

During the First World War and then again during the depression of the 1930s, the French government greatly increased administrative intervention in the industrial sectors of the economy. Wartime controls did not lead to more permanent regulation, but depression-era policies did. In 1936, for example, the government imposed extensive price controls that provided a vehicle for government control of industry for five decades.[15]

After the Second World War the perceived need to modernize French industry further intensified government controls and gave them a new role. The French recognized that economic weakness had contributed to their recent military defeats, and they placed great emphasis on regaining economic strength.[16] The belief that government leadership was necessary to

[12] See generally Charles W. Cole, *French Mercantilist Doctrines Before Colbert* (New York, 1931).

[13] See, e.g., Francois Caron, *An Economic History of Modern France* 35–44 (Barbara Bray, tr., New York, 1979).

[14] For discussion, see, e.g., Richard F. Kuisel, *Capitalism and the State in Modern France* 1–30 (Cambridge, 1981).

[15] For discussion of French experience with price controls, see Hervé Dumez & Alain Jeunemaitre, *Diriger L'Économie: L'État et les Prix en France: 1936–1986* (Paris, 1989).

[16] For discussion of the restructuring process, see William J. Adams, *Restructuring The French Economy: Government and the Rise of Market Competition since World War II* (Washington, D.C., 1989).

achieve this economic progress led to a program of *planification*, according to which government administrators established economic plans that served as co-ordinating mechanisms for the private sector.[17] These plans did not represent mandatory regulation in the style of state socialism, but mechanisms designed to 'encourage' co-ordination of the efforts of private firms and channel the economy toward goals which government administrators considered appropriate.[18]

Although *planification* as an important part of policy-making dissolved in the 1970s, the basic dirigistic-co-operative relationship between government and industry that it embodied did not. In that relationship the central bureaucracy has authority and responsibility for directing or 'guiding' economic development according to its own visions of France's best interests. Domestically, this means the primacy of industrial policy considerations— that is, policies for fostering particular patterns of economic development, notably through government support of specific industries.[19] Internationally, it means the use of trade policies to protect such industries.

The French tradition of *dirigisme* has been associated with the strength and independence of the central bureaucracy—as both cause and effect. The power of the central administration in Paris has attracted the bright, the well-placed and the ambitious, who have, in turn, augmented and exploited that power. The creation of the famous *École Nationale d'Administration* (ENA) as one of the prestigious *hautes écoles* in 1945 added a further dimension to the prominence of administration in French society.

The vicissitudes of French political development have entrenched the position of the bureaucracy. There have been numerous changes in the constitutional fabric in France during the last two centuries—including five republics—and during the two decades that bracketed the Second World War the average duration of governments was often little more than a year. As political systems, governments and parties have come and gone, the administrative apparatus has remained largely intact, and the perception that the administration is the pillar of the state has become firmly rooted. In the middle of this century, the discrediting of much of the political elite as a result of depression, defeat, and occupation contributed to a quasi-apotheosis of the central administration and its bureaucracy.

Not surprisingly, the legal position of the administration in France both reflects and validates its political power. The central bureaucracy is subject to

---

[17] The inception of *planification* is well described in Francois Duchêne, *Jean Monnet: The First Statesman of Interdependence* 147–75 (New York, 1994) and in Kuisel, *Capitalism and the State*, 219–47.

[18] For detailed discussion of *planification* during this period, see generally John Sheahan, *Promotion and Control of Industry In Postwar France* (Cambridge, 1963) and John H. McArthur & Bruce R. Scott, *Industrial Planning in France* (Boston, 1969).

[19] See *French Industrial Policy* (William J. Adams & Christian Stoffaës, eds., Washington, D.C., 1986).

little interference from outside its own sphere of influence. Under French law, the central bureaucracy is highly autonomous. Its decisions can be reviewed only by administrative courts according to principles and procedures developed by them. These courts, in turn, are officially part of the executive branch. For most purposes, this arrangement insulates administrative actions from the regular courts and the rest of the legal system.

Finally, *dirigisme* has been well anchored socially. As one commentator has succinctly put it, 'In France, strong bonds . . . exist between the public administration and banking interests, industry and commerce. The same men, having similar backgrounds—most beginning their careers in the administration—direct the whole'.[20] This anchoring in the social fabric of power often gives administrators influence well beyond that derived from their formal legal authority.

These structures have left little political or conceptual space for competition law. In the *dirigiste* tradition, decision-making authority is not guided by general legal principles. Its very essence is the assumption that bureaucratic decision-makers can and should control economic events in the public interest.

2. Competition law in France before 1945

With this background in mind, we turn to the complex trajectory of French competition law. In one sense, France can be seen as a progenitor of competition law in Europe. The French revolution introduced—or at least foregrounded—ideas and symbols that were the cornerstone of nineteenth century liberalism, and these, as we know, provided the conceptual foundations for competition law. It was in France that central concepts of economic liberalism such as freedom of contract and freedom of business establishment first acquired political stature on the European continent.

The revolutionary government also gave them legal stature, principally in the so-called *Loi Chapelier* of 1791, which prohibited members of the same branch of business from associating for the purpose of regulating their 'common interest'.[21] This statute embodied the idea that law could be used to protect economic freedom. Its practical importance during the nineteenth century was limited, but it continued to serve as a prominent symbol of the tie between egalitarian ideas and economic freedom.

A provision destined to have more practical importance was enacted in the wake of the Revolution. In 1810, amidst the disruptions caused by the Napoleonic wars, the French parliament enacted Article 419 of the Penal Code, which prohibited, *inter alia*, concerted action to manipulate 'the price

---

[20] René Plaisant, 'French Legislation Against Restrictive Trade Practices', 10 *Texas Intl L.J.* 26, 44 (1975).
[21] Art.II, Law of 14–17 June, 1791, III *Lois et Actes du Gouvernement* 287–89 (1806).

of foodstuffs or other commodities . . . above or below that which natural and free competition would have set'. Violations could be punished by fine or imprisonment. This provision was a response to the manipulation of war-induced shortages, but it remained in effect until 1986.

Article 419 was applied with some frequency in the early decades of the nineteenth century, but only sporadically later in the century.[22] As industrialization proceeded and economic liberalism gained ascendancy, upper middle class business interests acquired political dominance, and during the second half of the century the courts increasingly limited the application of Article 419. Their primary conceptual tool in doing so was to distinguish between 'good' and 'bad' cartels and to apply Article 419 only to the latter. In essence, 'good' cartels were those that regulated competition and thus benefited all, while 'bad' cartels sought to achieve monopoly or harm competitors. The distinction has been common in the early stages of development of many competition law systems, but in France it largely eviscerated in practice what appeared in the statute books to be a powerful tool for combating industrial cartels. It left little more than the illusion of protection.

A second nineteenth century French legal development that was to be important for our story was the evolution of private law claims based on the concept of '*concurrence déloyale*'. Usually translated as 'unfair competition law', *concurrence déloyale* is a set of legal principles that provides a right of compensation to those harmed by the 'unfair' conduct of a competitor or competitors. The success of the French courts in developing these principles is legendary. In an era when they were not entitled, in theory at least, to 'create law', courts in France nevertheless fashioned an entire body of law on the basis of a brief provision of the French civil code that required a party whose wrongful conduct harmed another to pay compensation for the harm.[23]

This evolution drew on two main (and contradictory) sources. One was liberalism's project, which posited that equal opportunity for all actual and potential competitors was a prerequisite for the success of a market economy. Such equality had to be safeguarded in order to develop the confidence necessary to induce participation. The primary concern here was with the 'purity' of the competitive process and incentives to participate in it. A second impetus was rooted in an older image of the market. It focused on standards of fairness as essential to the internal cohesion of communities of artisans and traders and on their relationships with both purchasers of their products and the societies in which they operated. Guilds had often provided these protections, but they had been largely abolished in the wake of the French

[22] For a detailed review, see Francis Deak, 'Contracts and Combinations in Restraint of Trade under French Law: A Comparative Study', 21 *Iowa L. Rev.* 397, 413–449 (1936).

[23] For discussion, see, e.g., Walter J. Derenberg, 'The Influence of the French Code Civil on the Modern Law of Unfair Competition', 4 *Am. J. Comp. L.* 1 (1955).

Revolution, and the principles aimed at combating *concurrence déloyale* could be used to accomplish some of the same objectives.

This area of law became exceptionally important during the nineteenth century, and its development in France seeded similar developments in many other European countries. Moreover, its importance has diminished only gradually in this century, and it remains a highly active and important field of law today. In continuing to signal the importance of undistorted competition in French society and elsewhere, it helped to set the stage for competition law development. But in other respects its impact on the development of competition law may have been less salutary. Although it did not protect the process of competition from restraint, it did seek to protect competition from distortion by protecting competitors from unfair trade practices, and for many the distinction was not (and is not) obvious. It thus occupied some of the regulatory space for which competition law might have been more directly suited, and it absorbed some of the political energy that otherwise might have been directed toward combating restraints on competition.

The First World War and the interwar period further cramped the space available for the development of competition law ideas. As elsewhere in Europe, the war led to increased governmental controls on economic activity, some of which continued in new forms after the war. During the interwar period, corporatist conceptions of the state and of economic activity often encouraged private and public organization of economic activity and denigrated the value of competition.[24] Cartels grew rapidly, and their growth was generally welcomed by French governments as a means of achieving economic stabilization at home and improved competitiveness abroad. In some industries the state even required cartelization in the 1930s.[25]

The early stirrings of interest in the idea of competition law in northern Europe and in the international arena during the interwar period had little resonance in France. French labor leaders such as Léon Jouhaux played key roles in the International Parliamentary Union in the 1920s and at the World Economic Conference in 1927, where the French delegation presented a cartel control plan,[26] but there was no serious effort to protect competition law in France during this period.[27] In 1926, Article 419 was amended—but not necessarily to make it stronger. The changes generally codified the judicial interpretations that had sharply reduced the scope of the provision, assuring

---

[24] For discussion, see, e.g., Kuisel, *Capitalism and the State*, 93–127.

[25] See generally *Direction de la Documentation* (France), *Les Ententes Professionelles Devant la Loi* 95–109 (Paris, 1953). For discussion of the economic context, see Eugen Weber, *The Hollow Years: France in the 1930s* 26–54 (New York, 1996).

[26] II League of Nations, *Report and Proceedings of the World Economic Conference* 168 (Geneva, 1927).

[27] Some statutory proposals regarding cartels included competition law provisions, but their basic thrust was to legitimize and protect cartels. For discussion of the proposals, see *Direction de la Documentation* (France), *Les Ententes Professionelles,* 95–109.

that government prosecutors would have a limited scope of authority for attacking cartels.[28] One commentator has concluded that they were evidently a 'sop to the public which was becoming agitated under the constant rise in the cost of living during and after the war'.[29]

3. War and after: competition law in the service of price control

The evolution of competition law in France during the period treated in this chapter is an often confusing story of *ad hoc* responses to specific problems. Article 419 of the Penal Code remained in force, but its use was severely restricted. The legislature (and the executive) added to it, incrementally, a 'hodge-podge' of specific, and often unrelated and even inconsistent provisions.[30] According to one expert, 'It is essentially during the past forty years that a body of rules has been developed to order, as need be, the phenomenon of competition considered as an instrument of economic policy. But, far from being a planned process, this legislation has been the product of succeeding and sometimes paradoxical acts [of Parliament]'.[31] This welter of provisions can hardly be understood unless it is seen against the backdrop of the dirigistic traditions and controls discussed above. Our first task is to trace the story.

Toward the end of the Second World War and in the immediate postwar period there was much resentment in France against big business and, in particular, cartelized industry. In 1944, De Gaulle expressed the mood when he refused 'to contemplate the re-building of industrial trusts that dominated pre-war France'.[32] Numerous business leaders were implicated in co-operating with the Nazi occupiers, and those involved in transnational cartels were often particularly vulnerable to these charges. There was, therefore, a significant potential impetus for enactment of laws to control abuses of power by cartels and monopolies. Yet the impetus yielded little legislative activity.

The central motif of postwar competition law development in France was set in 1945, when the French government introduced legislation to combat postwar inflationary pressures ('the 1945 *Ordonnance*') and included in the legislation several ancillary provisions aimed at specific restraints on competition.[33] For decades thereafter competition law was basically understood as a handmaiden of price controls, and this perception long colored its development.

[28] For discussion, see ibid., 42–51.

[29] V. G. Venturini, *Monopolies and Restrictive Trade Practices in France* 43 (Leyden, 1971).

[30] For a detailed description of French competition law in the years before the 1986 reforms, see, e.g., Jean-Jacques Burst & Robert Kovar, *Droit de la Concurrence* (Paris, 1982).

[31] Jacques Azema, *Le Droit Francais de La Concurrence* 29 (2d. ed., Paris, 1989).

[32] Quoted in Venturini, *Monopolies*, 67 n.15.

[33] *Ordonnance* No. 45, 1483, of June 30, 1945. For discussion, see Venturini, *Monopolies*, 61–76. An *ordonnance* is legislation authorized by the legislature, but actually drafted and enacted by the executive.

The ancillary provisions contained in the 1945 *Ordonnance* made refusals to deal, price discrimination, and several other forms of conduct unlawful under certain conditions, treating them as 'akin to' or 'assimilated to' unlawful pricing practices. These provisions were designed to protect price-cutting firms from reprisals by manufacturers and distributors, and in some measure they reflected postwar populist resentment of Nazi collaborators and of those who manipulated shortages. They were applied by the administrative authorities as part of the application of price controls, which meant that officials enforcing price controls could investigate potential violations, exert pressure on firms unwilling to discontinue the practices, and, where negotiation failed to result in termination of the practice, submit the case to the public prosecutor for prosecution in the regular courts. This basic system would continue to apply to these specific types of violation, even as new competition law provisions created different procedural arrangements for other types of conduct.

Although this legislation was far from a general competition law statute, it was to be the statutory base for French competition law for the next four decades, as repeated amendments and re-enactments added elements of competition law to it. At least formally, French competition law developed through amendments to price control legislation!

4. 1953–1977: Creating a competition law system

These ancillary price-control provisions were competition law in the sense used here, but their role as such was barely visible, remaining submerged within the price control effort. During the late 1940s, however, pressure to enact a 'true' competition law began to mount, primarily from sources outside France—the international movements associated with the Havana Charter and the efforts of the US government to promote antitrust law. These pressures led to occasional legislative proposals, but none had a serious chance of being enacted until 1952, when inflation resulting from the Korean War again focused attention on the idea.[34]

In response to this inflationary threat, several proposals were made and discussed in the French legislature, and one was even passed by the National Assembly in 1952, only to be defeated in the Senate, apparently as a result of the opposition of French industry.[35] Nevertheless, given the deadlock on the issue, the legislature authorized the executive to enact legislation in *décret* form that, *inter alia*, protected the process of competition, and in 1953 a caretaker government reached a compromise with big business and enacted a decree that added new competition law provisions to the 1945 *Ordonnance*.[36]

---

[34] For discussion of the proposals, see *Direction de la Documentation* (France), *Les Ententes Professionelles*, 109–28.

[35] See Corwin D. Edwards, *Trade Regulation Overseas: The National Laws* 14–18 (Dobbs Ferry, N.Y., 1966).

[36] Decree No. 53–704 of Aug. 9, 1953, *Journal Officiel* [1953] S. IV.1307.

Its central provision (Art. 59*bis*) proscribed 'all concerted actions, agreements, express or implied understandings, or coalitions, in whatever form and for whatever reason, which have as their object or may have as their effect restraint of the free exercise of competition by impeding the reduction of costs or prices or by encouraging an artificial increase in prices'. Two elements of its scope are noteworthy: it dealt solely with 'concerted actions', omitting reference to monopoly or single-firm conduct, and it applied only insofar as the concerted action related directly or indirectly to prices.

There were, however, important exceptions to this general provision. It did not apply (Art. 59*ter*) to conduct that 'result[ed] from the application of a legislative provision or regulation' or which 'the participants [were] able to justify as having the effect of improving or extending the market for their products or of ensuring further economic progress through rationalization or specialization'. The first of these exceptions played a minor role in practice, basically assuring that the *Décret* would not interfere with government-sponsored 'arrangements' among private firms.

More important was the second exception, because it meant that what appeared to be a prohibition operated, in effect, according to the policy-based discretion of administrators. Where participants in collusive activity could establish that their arrangement had the required (but vaguely-defined) positive effects, the system would not interfere with it, and that decision was a matter of administrative discretion. Government economic policy was to foster rationalization, specialization and the expansion of markets, and cartels would be allowed where the bureaucrats in Paris believed that they served those ends.

These new cartel provisions were administered as part of the administrative price control system, but the procedure and the institutional framework had special features. The minister of economics was still the *maître de jeu*, deciding whether to pursue potential violations and determining whether to request criminal prosecutions. The 1953 *Décret* created, however, a *Commission Technique des Ententes* that was responsible for investigating possible violations and advising the ministry on the applicability of the 1945 *Ordonnance*.

This oft-renamed commission played a key role in applying the competition law provisions relating to cartels. Although its opinions were only advisory, the minister generally accepted its factual determinations and policy assessments. This was the principal locus of authoritative consideration of the application of the competition law provisions, and thus it was with reference to this body that competition law arguments were shaped. Since the minister of economics was the ultimate decision-maker, however, firms frequently also sought to influence decisions by direct appeal to that office.

The role of the commission was important, but its importance can easily be overstated. In practice, for example, the commission did not have the resources to engage in extensive investigations and depended heavily on the price directorate to carry out that function. That office usually conducted the initial investigation of matters before the commission, preparing a dossier that then served as the basis for any further investigation by the commission and for its ultimate factual determinations. Moreover, the price directorate played a key role in interpreting the relevant provisions by issuing guidelines (circulars) that became the main source of interpretive guidance.

The commission's proceedings were closed, records were secret, and until 1959 even its opinions were secret.[37] This role for the commission was apparently part of a compromise with business leaders, who feared the creation of a more juridical system. They were familiar with administrative decision-making and willing to accept a competition law apparatus that represented merely an additional component in the network of administrative relationships. They had no incentive to welcome the introduction of a system in which juridical components might reduce their capacity to influence decisions.

The structure and composition of the commission was consistent with this limited, advisory function. Except for its president, all members were 'part-time', meeting only as the occasion demanded. The main criterion for appointments was, in theory at least, expertise in issues faced by the commission. Members typically included business leaders, administrators and an occasional law professor.[38] Until 1977, the commission had only a tiny support staff with little professional competence, and thus it had to depend on the price directorate to perform most aspects of the investigative function.

These three separate sets of provisions and procedures comprised the basic French competition law for almost a quarter of a century. Article 419 continued in force, but it was rarely applied. Some provisions of the 1945 *Ordonnance* prohibited a few specific types of vertical restraints virtually *per se* and provided a procedural mechanism for this determination. And, finally, amendments to that legislation contained special provisions that subjected most potential anticompetitive conduct to what we can call an abuse standard, which had its own procedural regime.

Frequent changes were made in the details of the system. In 1963, for example, the *Ordonnance* was amended to apply also to the abuse of a market-dominating position, although the commission and the enforcement agencies basically ignored this change for more than a decade and only gradually increased their interest thereafter.[39] A 1967 *ordonnance* established a degree of independence for competition law by providing that cartels could be found illegal even where there were no harmful effects on prices.[40] This meant that

[37] Venturini, *Monopolies*, 250. They were thereafter made available to the public, but only some were published in the *Journal Officiel*.
[38] See generally Dominique Brault, *L'État et L'Esprit de Concurrence en France 35–37, 52–54* (Paris, 1987).
[39] Law of July 27, 1963.   [40] *Ordonnance* No. 67.835 (September 20, 1967).

competition law could be said for the first time to have an identity of its own instead of being a mere corollary of price control. Yet it continued to operate within the institutional framework of price control legislation and in a context of widespread governmental influence on business decision-making.

The quarter century in which French competition law was developing in this rather haphazard style is basically coterminous with what a French economist has called the '*années glorieuses*' of the French economy.[41] They were years of sustained economic development in which *planification* and the Keynesian demand-management assumptions that were associated with it were often praised. There seemed to be little reason to alter the relationship between state and economy.

Under these circumstances, it is not surprising that competition law in France operated at the margins of economic and bureaucratic life, little known by the public and generally ignored even within the bureaucracy.[42] Even the relatively modest tools provided by the statute were not vigorously employed. There was little reason to take note of the activities of the commission or of the existence of a competition law: bureaucratic direction of the economy had become well accepted and seemed to be working effectively.

5. 1977–1986: Liberating competition law from price controls

Not until the mid-1970s did the French government turn more resolutely toward protecting competition. This new interest in competition law was part of a gradual reorientation of French economic policy occasioned by the economic crises of the period and by growing awareness of the limits of administrative planning. Opinion had turned against *planification*, and a loosening of price controls came to be seen as necessary to stimulate economic growth. In this context, competition law presented itself as a tool for combating inflation and at the same time improving the efficiency of French firms.

One reason for the changing attitudes toward competition was a change in France's economic situation. The global economic turbulence of the mid-1970s threw into doubt the capacity of the French economy to maintain the strength that it had shown since the end of the Second World War. The shift of resources from industrial countries to oil producers made clear to many that Western economies had entered into a fundamentally new situation, many of whose components were likely to be durable. The most prominent of these was inflation, which had suddenly returned to the center of the economic policy stage. Finally, structural problems demanded attention. A wave

[41] Jean Fourastié, *Les Trentes Glorieuses: Ou La Révolution Invisible de 1946 à 1975* (Paris, 1979).

[42] Frédéric Jenny & André Paul Weber, 'French Antitrust Legislation: An Exercise in Futility', 20 *Antitrust Bull.* 597, 600 (1975).

of mergers in France early in the decade had significantly increased concerns about concentration and its impacts on prices and social structures.

These new economic forces had another striking feature—they were located largely outside the reach of French economic policy. The external causes of this new form of inflation rendered traditional price controls either ineffectual or inequitable in application, and the tools of *planification* had little capacity to constrain concentration or deter its harmful effects. To make matters worse, the French bureaucracy was also now less autonomous than it had been, because the rules and procedures of the European Community limited the scope of its decision-making authority.

One response to these circumstances was to intensify domestic competition, and in the mid-1970s the political configuration in France was favorable to taking steps to strengthen competition law. The French president was a liberal, Valery Giscard d'Estaing, and his premier was Raymond Barre, a former economics professor and author of the leading economics textbook in French universities. Barre was the key figure. He had long been interested in the idea of using law to protect competition,[43] and in 1977 and 1978 he greatly reduced price controls and put in their place a more effective competition law system.[44]

The legislation enacted in 1977 did not radically change the French competition law system, but it prepared the way for more comprehensive changes that would follow in 1986. The effort was avowedly aimed at reorienting French economic '*mentalités*' away from reliance on government controls and toward valuing the process of competition.[45] This was to be done primarily by increasing awareness of competition law, strengthening its sanctions and enhancing the status of its institutions.

New enforcement tools were the center of attention. In particular, the focus was on the commission's expanded authority to impose fines for violation of competition law norms. Equally or more important, however, was the addition of authority to issue injunctions against firms suspected of violating competition law provisions, because this allowed the commission to make immediate and direct enforcement orders. Consumer and other special interest groups were also given the right to bring cases to the commission.

The commission, now renamed the '*Commission de la Concurrence*', was given greater independence and status. It could now, for example, investigate possible violations of most competition law norms on its own and without a ministerial request. In addition, its budget was significantly augmented, so that it now could employ a permanent professional staff.

---

[43] See, e.g., Raymond Barre, 'Quelques Aspects de la Regulation du Pouvoir Économique', 6 *Revue Économique* 912 (1958).

[44] See Hervé Dumez & Alain Jeunemaitre, *La Concurrence en Europe* 76–77 (Paris, 1991).

[45] For discussion of the changes and the circumstances surrounding them, see Brault, *L'État et L'Esprit*, 49–54.

The legislation brought one significant substantive addition to the scope of French competition law by including merger control provisions. On one level, these provisions were a response to the merger wave earlier in the decade. Another impetus for their inclusion had little, however, to do with protecting competition. The European Commission had announced in 1972 its plan to enact merger controls. Leading French officials apparently opposed this idea and considered that having a domestic statute would be a convenient argument against the need for merger controls on the Community level.

The merger provisions had limited scope and force. In essence, they authorized the economics minister to request an opinion from the commission as to whether a merger involving more than a specified share of the market 'by its nature would prevent adequate competition on the market'. If the commission determined that it did, it then had to ask whether the merger 'contributes to economic and social progress to a degree that compensates for its harm to competition'.[46] If the commission found that this 'contribution to progress' standard was not met, the minister could, at his discretion, issue orders, including fines, in order to restore as effectively as possible the competitive conditions that existed before the merger. There was no requirement that mergers be reported in advance, although it was assumed that merging companies would often do so in order to be certain that the merger would not be attacked.

The new rhetoric of competition that had led to these modest improvements in competition law continued to be influential for a time after 1977. Political leaders routinely advocated the virtues of the marketplace, and Prime Minister Barre exhorted the newly-constituted commission to help French business leaders to understand the need for increased competition and to move away from reliance on government for leadership and support.

The rhetoric was, however, soon tested. When the commission did dare in 1979 to take bolder steps in enforcing competition law, more deep-seated attitudes quickly resurfaced. Business and administrative circles did not hesitate to denounce the commission's 'aggressive' conception of its role.[47] The reaction was similar to the French reaction more than a decade later when the European Commission first prohibited a merger under the Community's merger control regulation. The basic message seems to have been 'let us not take this competition law business too seriously'.

When the socialist Francois Mitterrand was elected president in 1981, political support for competition law eroded even further—at least temporarily. Now even the political rhetoric in favor of competition was weaker. During the first years of Mitterrand's presidency, competition law received little political attention. The public perception that competition could benefit the individual worker or consumer had developed little in France, in part

---

[46] For discussion, see Burst & Kovar, *Droit de la Concurrence*, 309–25.
[47] Brault, *L'État et L'Esprit*, 54–63.

because since 1936 the French had relied on government to control prices rather than on competition to reduce them. There appeared, therefore, to be no political incentive for the socialists to promote competition law.

Despite these obstacles, the new commission became more active and effective than its predecessor had been, investigating more cases and using some of the stronger enforcement tools it had received in 1977. Some of the tools were, however, seldom used. Merger enforcement was, for example, minimal. The commission investigated only eight mergers prior to 1986 and recommended that only one be prevented. Nevertheless, as one commentator put it, 'Between 1977 and 1986, public opinion finally became familiar with the existence of controls on restrictive agreements, and economic actors began to take into account in their conduct juridical constraints that had become credible. . .'.[48]

6. In the shadows: competition law experience in France

Competition law barely had an identity in France before 1986. Its contents were scattered and lacked cohesion; its objectives were generally vague; and its institutions had little force. It operated in the shadows of other legal regimes and intellectual and institutional traditions from which it only gradually emerged. It was seldom recognized as an independent subject in universities, where courses and experts on it were rare. It did not even really 'possess' its own name. The term '*droit de la concurrence*' was known, but there was little clarity about its referent. It was frequently used to refer not specifically to what we here call competition law, but to a *mélange* of norms, sanctions and institutions that included competition law, but also elements from unfair competition law (*concurrence déloyale*), and often other areas such as price controls.

The lack of cohesion regarding the contents and procedures of competition law both reflected and contributed to its shadowy existence. Competition law provisions were scattered in various pieces of legislation, each of which represented a response to a specific problem or set of problems. Neither an overarching idea nor the operations of a focused and powerful institution related them to each other.

This terminological uncertainty and lack of focus and structure reflected the murkiness of competition law's objectives. Initially positioned as a minor and ancillary mechanism supporting price control objectives, French competition law long had no independent *raison d'être*. A careful observer could discern specific objectives for specific provisions, but the idea of 'protecting competition' as a general goal had little resonance. There was little room for such objectives in a context of *planification* and predominant industrial

---

[48] Brault, ibid., 50.

policy considerations. The objective of those regimes was to direct growth and resources by political and administrative means rather than through the competitive process. The goal of protecting competition law was thus inconsistent with these regimes and threatened the interests of those who controlled them.

Not only were its objectives unclear, but the methods of achieving them were also indistinct. For most purposes, competition law was overwhelmed by the powerful personality of the French central administration. Competition law provisions were merely one category of statutes administered by a bureaucracy that was at the same time implementing economic plans and controlling prices. There was no basis for giving competition law goals any form of priority.

Above all, competition law in France during this period was marginal. Except with regard to certain specific practices such as refusals to deal and price discrimination, it rarely played important roles in business decisions. During most, perhaps all, of the period under consideration here, French businesses were concerned far more with the impact of price controls and other aspects and vestiges of *dirigisme* than with the occasional and generally minimal risks entailed in violating competition law provisions. Moreover, its role in the legal community was also marginal. Few French legal professionals saw competition law as a field of importance. It maintained a rather tenuous existence in the shadows created by other normative regimes such as price controls and *concurrence déloyale* and by French administrative traditions and by the interests and power positions associated with those traditions.

This domestic experience with competition law helps to explain the frequently observed tendency of French officials in the EU to subordinate competition law to other economic policy objectives. There was little in French experience during this period that valorized an important and independent role for competition law. Competition law was positioned as subordinate and sometimes opposed to industrial policy concerns, and this has often been the position in which French officials have cast it on the European level.

G. EDGING AWAY FROM THE MODEL: SCANDINAVIAN PRAGMATISM

Sweden also introduced an administrative control system a few years after World War II, and it changed little until the eve of Sweden's accession to the EU in 1995, when more significant modifications were introduced. We examine Sweden's experience because it illustrates the operation of such a system in a small, open economy in which international competition has been central to economic policy. It also illustrates a process of 'juridification' that resembles the one we encountered in France, but that is in some ways quite different. In it, a pragmatic view of both economic policy and legal processes gradually imbued an administrative control system with juridical elements. Swedish competition law has seldom been studied outside of Sweden because of the country's relatively small size, narrow language base and the (mistaken) assumption that Sweden is (or was) a 'socialist' country in which competition law could hardly play a serious role. Yet Swedish experience reveals much about the dynamics of European competition law systems during this period and—perhaps—about future avenues of development for competition law in Europe.

Because of widespread misconceptions about Sweden's social and economic situation, it is necessary to emphasize that Sweden is and has been fundamentally 'Western'. Although the Swedish 'welfare state' was more developed than that of many of its neighbors in Western Europe for several decades after the end of the Second World War, Sweden never subscribed to state socialism nor was it subject to significant Soviet influence. Throughout this period Swedish industry has been predominantly in private ownership, and the Swedish government has been careful to avoid excessive interference with market mechanisms, not least because the highly industrialized Swedish economy has long been dependent upon international competitiveness for its prosperity.[49]

1. Postwar circumstances

Sweden enacted competition legislation in response to the economic consequences of the Second World War. Although Sweden was a neutral country, it also suffered major shortages and economic disruptions, inducing the government to maintain extensive economic controls. In many branches of the economy, firms were forced to join government-regulated cartels; goods and services were often rationed; and there were strict price controls.

During the immediate postwar period, Sweden's economic situation was both like and unlike that of its neighbors. It was like theirs in the sense that widespread shortages of materials and goods necessitated a continuation of rationing and price controls. It was different, however, because its production facilities had not been destroyed. Because of the widespread destruction of industrial capacity among its continental competitors, many branches of Swedish industry were not subjected to serious foreign competition for several years after the end of the war.

The Swedish government thus focused on two main economic policy goals.[50] One was to combat inflation. Shortages, especially of consumer

---

[49] For an overview of Swedish economic history from the beginning of the First World War through the end of the period discussed in this chapter, see Mats Larsson, *En Svensk Ekonomisk Historia: 1850–1985* 67–158 (Stockholm, 1991). For a description of Swedish economic policy during this period, see Assar Lindbeck, *Svensk Ekonomisk Politik* (2d. ed., Stockholm, 1976).

[50] See generally Lindbeck, *Svensk Ekonomisk Politik*, 37–62.

goods, induced the government to maintain price controls until 1956. The other focus was on maintaining the efficiency of Swedish industries. Many Swedish cartels were able to sell all they could produce, and thus they were shielded from the market forces that would have tended to weaken them. This, in turn, threatened the potential long-run competitiveness of Swedish industry.[51] If Swedish industries could operate without significant competitive pressure, their capacity to compete internationally was likely to fade as their continental competitors recovered from wartime damage and postwar restrictions. The government sought competition legislation in pursuit of these dual goals.[52]

The Social Democratic Party controlled the government uninterruptedly from the end of the war until the mid-1970s. While foregrounding the interests of 'working people' and greatly expanding social welfare programs, social democratic leaders were well aware that their own success in expanding these programs depended on the strength of the Swedish economy, particularly the international competitiveness of its leading firms. This commonality of interests between government and industry conditioned economic policy decisions and, ultimately, the structure and operations of the competition law system.

2. Development of the legislation

After much debate, the government finally enacted a competition statute—the Law Against Restraints of Competition (LRC)—in 1953,[53] and its basic structure remained unchanged until 1993. The long and careful process of preparing the legislation included detailed review of foreign experience with competition laws,[54] and the LRC reflected comparative influences.[55]

The statute's most immediate goal was to combat inflationary pressures in conjunction with preparing to eliminate price controls. The concept was that promoting competition would reduce costs, rationalize industrial structures and distribution channels and thereby reduce inflation. The longer term goal was to maintain a domestic industrial structure that was sufficiently competitive to assure that Swedish companies would be 'fit' for international competition.[56] Swedish competition law thus began and has remained pre-

---

[51] See Lars Sandberg, 'Antitrust Policy in Sweden', 9 *Antitrust Bull.* 535, 538–40 (1964).

[52] See, e.g., Ulf Bernitz, *Konkurrens och Priser i Norden*, ch. 4 (Stockholm, 1971).

[53] Lag den 25 September 1953 om motverkande i vissa fall av Konkurrensbegränsning inom Näringslivet, *Svensk Författnings Samling* (SFS) 1953:603.

[54] Statens Offentliga Utredningar (SOU) 1951:27, at 483.

[55] See Ulf Af Trolle, *Studier i Konkurrensfilosofi och Konkurrenslagstiftning* 21–37 (Gothenburg, 1963). The United States model was not considered appropriate to Swedish circumstances, largely because it would have involved criminalizing behavior that had always been considered legal and because it was based on the idea of 'prohibiting' conduct rather than restraining abuses of power and the more 'co-operative' form of capitalism that implied. See Stina Holmberg, *Mot Monopolisering? NO's Verksamhet under 25 År* 27–30 (Stockholm, 1981).

[56] Åke Martenius, *Lagstiftning om Konkurrensbegränsning* 26 (Stockholm, 1965).

dominantly a pragmatic, 'constructive' tool of economic policy, with popular politics playing only a minor role. Its primary objective has been to provide the benefits of competition, not to combat injustice or exploitation.[57]

The legislation basically authorized governmental action to eliminate restraints of competition where they had specified effects that were 'contrary to the public interest'. Originally, only cartels and monopolies were subject to this so-called 'general clause', but in 1956—with the elimination of price controls—its scope was expanded to cover most other restraints of competition.[58] The legislation also prohibited on a *per se* basis two specific restraints—collusive bidding and resale price maintenance. It created a new government agency called 'The Office of the Competition Ombudsman' (*Näringsfrihets-ombudsman* or NO) to enforce its norms and a special court (the Market Court) to hear cases under it.

In the early 1970s, rapid increases in the concentration of Swedish industry led the government to establish several commissions to study concentration and its effects.[59] The commission that had been directed to review the effectiveness of the competition statute issued a report in 1978 which recommended, *inter alia*, the inclusion of specific provisions on mergers as well as stronger sanctions to support enforcement efforts.[60] The report created substantial controversy in both government and industry,[61] with the industrial sector strongly opposed to many of the recommended changes, but eventually a new law, the Competition Act of 1982 was enacted,[62] which included many of the recommended provisions on mergers and increased enforcement sanctions.[63] As amended, the basic system remained in place until 1993.

3. The normative scheme

The central mechanism of Swedish competition law was its 'general clause', which provided that:

> If a restraint of competition has a harmful effect within the country, the Market Court may . . . adopt measures to prevent such an effect. . . . A harmful effect shall occur where, in a manner which is contrary to the public interest, the restraint of competition (1) unduly affects the formation of prices,(2) impairs efficiency in business, or (3) hinders or prevents the business activities of another.[64]

---

[57] Bernitz, *Konkurrens och Priser*, 98–101.

[58] Lag angående ändring i lagen av den 25 September 1953 (No. 603) om motverkande i vissa fall av Konkurrensbegränsning inom Näringslivet (SFS 1956:244).

[59] For description, see Holmberg, *Mot Monopolisering*, 46–48.

[60] See Statens Offentliga Utredningar (SOU) 1978:9.

[61] For a summary of the various positions, see Proposition (Prop) 1981/82:165, at 329–554.

[62] Konkurrenslagen (SFS 1982:729).

[63] For a review of these changes, see Staffan Sandström, 'Den Nya Konkurrenslagen', 1 *Pris och Konkurrens* 5 (1983).

[64] SFS 1953:603, §5.

The statute posed three questions: Does the conduct constitute a 'restraint of competition'? Is there a specified effect on society? And is the effect contrary to the public interest? It thus used economic policy considerations to refract the problem of competitive restraints into discrete types of effects and then based the normative scheme on those effects.[65]

The concept of 'restraint of competition' was so broadly interpreted that it played little role other than to establish the jurisdictional ambit of the statute. It was construed to encompass 'every condition which . . . has as its result that competition is not completely free and unrestrained.'[66] It thus included, for example, abuse of a market-dominating position as well as mergers and acquisitions.[67]

Restraints of competition were not, however, seen as necessarily negative; their legal status depended solely on their effects. The statute established three categories of 'harmful' effects. Of these the most important in practice was the price effect, reflecting the fact that the legislature's main concern was to combat inflation. Its purpose was to determine whether in a particular situation the restraint had led to price increases or created a substantial risk of such an effect.[68]

In identifying causal relationships between restraints and price-enhancing effects, the office often used price/cost comparisons,[69] but it also relied on a highly pragmatic use of economic theory for this purpose.[70] According to micro-economic price theory, for example, cartels inherently tend to increase prices, but Swedish competition law officials asked whether a specific cartel in a particular situation had or could be expected to have such a price-increasing effect.

The second effects criterion, 'efficiency', was included in order to emphasize the importance of efficiency and to address situations in which a restraint of competition reduced efficiency without, at least in the short run, affecting prices.[71] The term 'efficiency' did not, however, refer to the neoclassical theoretical model. As stated by the commerce minister in 1956:

[The effort to control competition] does not aim at the free competition of the classical economic model but rather at the competition which is from society's standpoint the most effective competition, i.e., a competition which directs development in that direction which in the long-run can be expected to involve the best utilization of the

---

[65] For detailed discussion in English of the statute and its interpretation, see David J. Gerber, 'Antitrust Law and Economic Analysis: The Swedish Approach', 8 *Hastings Intl & Comp. L. Rev.* 1 (1984).

[66] Martenius, *Lagstiftning*, 43.

[67] On abuse, see Dan Otteryd, 'Missbruk av Marknadsdominerande Ställning enligt Svensk Rätt', 42 *Tidskrift für Sveriges Advokatsamfundet* 242 (1981). For mergers, see Lars Harding, *Kontroll av Företagsförvärv i Sverige* 10–12 (Stockholm, 1983).

[68] Ulf Bernitz, *Svensk Marknadsrätt* 58–59 (Stockholm, 1983).

[69] SOU 1978:9, at 96.   [70] See Ulf Bernitz, *Marknadsrätt* 50 (Stockholm, 1969).

[71] Martenius, *Lagstiftning*, 103.

society's resources. Certain limitations on competition are without question not only acceptable but valuable and actually necessary from the standpoint of society.[72]

The neoclassical model was specifically rejected as being an inadequate measure of the harm resulting from restraints on competition.[73]

Instead, the concept of efficiency was defined by reference to the process of economic development.[74] The objective was to combat obstacles to cost-reduction and rationalization within industry and to encourage improved methods of production and distribution. According to the official explanation of the LRC, a restraint on competition impeded efficiency where it hindered technological or organizational progress or reduced competitive incentives. The establishment of a cartel, for example, could be expected to have this effect because it eliminated incentives for cartel members to compete. Vertical restraints such as resale price maintenance might have this effect by reducing pressures on distributors to develop less costly means of distribution. This concept of efficiency is less theoretically precise than that of micro-economic price theory, but it related the impact of competition law to both consumer price levels and the international competitiveness of the Swedish economy—the two primary economic policy considerations behind the legislation.

'Hindering or preventing' the business activities of another was the third of the effects criteria. On its face, this criterion did not fit easily with the other two, for it appeared to protect the individual competitor rather than the process of competition, but this was not intended. According to the official explanation, 'If a restraint of competition impedes new business from entry or restricts already existing companies in their development, this must in the long run tend to maintain existing business structures and hinder the development of new, more effective forms of enterprise.'[75] The explanation cited examples of restraints likely to have the prohibited effect, including group boycotts, exclusive dealing among a group of buyers and/or sellers and discrimination in prices or other terms by a market-dominating enterprise.[76] Again, economic analysis played a central role in applying the statute, but it was process-oriented analysis. It identified practices that were likely to lead to that rigidity in market structures which the statute was designed to combat.[77]

Assuming conduct was found to cause one of the proscribed effects, the final issue was whether it did so in a manner that was 'contrary to the public interest'.[78] This balancing test specified that intervention was authorized only

---

[72] Prop. 1956:148 at 41, cited with approval in Prop. 1981/82:165, at 43.
[73] SOU 1951:27, at 59.
[74] For discussion and examples, see Gerber, 'Antitrust Law and Economic Analysis', 23–28.
[75] Prop. 1953:103, at 119. [76] Ibid.
[77] See Martenius, *Lagstiftning*, 104–06.
[78] The Swedish term is 'på ett ur allmänn synpunkt otillbörligt sätt'. Translated more literally, it reads 'in a manner which is improper from the standpoint of society in general'. It is, however, clearly intended to represent a public interest standard. See, e.g., SOU 1978:9, at 98.

where the designated harmful effects of a restraint outweighed the economic or social benefits expected to flow from it.[79]

One function of the balancing test was to restrict state interference to cases of 'general interest'.[80] A particular restraint might be of general interest either because of the magnitude of its economic effects or the precedential value of the case in deterring future restraints. Although a variety of factors were considered here, economic factors were given the most weight, particularly the long-run economic effects of competitive restraints.[81] The statute was not, for example, applied to arrangements whereby small producers co-operated with each other in order to compete more effectively with larger producers.

A second function was to take into account public interests other than economic ones. The drafters emphasized that other interests of society might be more important in a particular situation than those economic effects referred to in the statute. Factors found important in this context included, for example, the potential impact of anticompetitive arrangements on the availability of medical equipment[82] and on employment in a regional labor market.[83] The government explained that this balancing test allowed a 'certain amount of room for subjective evaluation', but it argued that in the overwhelming majority of cases application of the concept of societal harm did not present a significant problem.[84]

The small category of *per se* prohibitions was subject to very different treatment from that just described. Apparently borrowed from US antitrust law, the idea was that these two practices—collusive bidding and resale price maintenance—necessarily had the requisite negative effects and could not have redeeming social benefits. They could, therefore, be prohibited outright. The only issue was whether the specified conduct had occurred, and this was determined by the NO in conjunction with the criminal courts. This category of violation was of some practical importance, but we will not examine it further here.[85]

4. Institutions and sanctions

The system created to implement the general clause reflected its pragmatic, constructive premises. Its institutions were to guide the business community toward compliance—gently. They interpreted and applied the norms in order to provide information about what was acceptable conduct, and they relied primarily on informal tools to induce businesses to comply. There were no

---

[79] Bernitz, *Svensk Marknadsrätt*, 58.   [80] Prop. 1956:48, at 39.

[81] See, e.g., Martenius, *Lagstiftning*, 97, and Prop. 1981/82:165, at 31.

[82] *N.O. v. AB Gambro*, Marknadsdomstolens Avgöranden 1976–77, at 89, 112 (No. 1976: 10).

[83] See, e.g., Prop. 1981/82:165, at 51.

[84] Prop. 1956:48, at 39 (in conjunction with the extension of the LRC in 1956).

[85] The Market Court could grant special permission to violate either of these provisions, but very seldom did.

private suits, and until 1982 officials had very limited sanctioning authority. This system reflected the commonality of interests between the government and the business elite. Both recognized the need to safeguard the international competitiveness of Swedish industry, and thus they created a system that discouraged leading businesses from engaging in strategies based on restraining competition, while carefully avoiding 'interference' that might harm industry.

Competition law in Sweden was conceived and has operated as a separate legal subsystem—with its own aims, institutions, and procedures. This conception was encouraged initially by the lack of prior legal sanctions against anticompetitive behavior. The LRC was seen as a sharp break with existing legal practices,[86] and its drafters sought to create a system that was not constrained by existing legal institutions and categories that might interfere with its 'constructive' orientation.[87] It was also nourished by Swedish political and administrative traditions: the concept of an ombudsman was developed in the eighteenth century to 'check' the power of the central bureaucracy, and this notion of separate and distinct centers of administrative power has remained a fundamental part of Swedish constitutional arrangements.

The system was based on the assumption that publicity and negotiation would be the primary means of achieving compliance with competition law norms.[88] The theory was that firms would normally comply voluntarily with the law in order to avoid the negative publicity that would result from legal proceedings and that such a system was more likely to achieve compliance and secure the necessary co-operation of the business community than would a system of prohibitions and penal sanctions.[89] These assumptions presupposed a relatively small, generally homogenous community of business and political leaders with important common objectives.

a. The Competition Ombudsman

The ombudsman's office was the institutional center of the system: legal proceedings started there and generally ended there. Technically, an aggrieved party could bring a case directly to the Market Court if the ombudsman refused to do so, but this was rare.[90] The Swedish ombudsman tradition of establishing independent administrative bodies outside the regular bureaucracy played a significant role in defining the roles of the NO and the

---

[86] Bernitz, *Marknadsrätt*, 421–22.

[87] It was considered politically unacceptable, for example, to impose criminal sanctions on conduct that had long been protected by the principle of freedom of contract. See Holmberg, *Mot Monopolisering*, 27–31.

[88] See, e.g., SOU 1951:27, at 492–97.

[89] See Holmberg, *Mot Monopolisering*, 58–67, and SOU 1951:27, at 17.

[90] The system discouraged such proceedings by permitting them only where the ombudsman had determined that the conduct complained of did not constitute a violation of the statute and by not providing compensation even where the Market Court found a violation and determined that it had caused injury to the complainant.

operation of the competition law system as a whole.[91] Of particular importance in this tradition was the emphasis on the ombudsman's independence from political influence and from the control of the central bureaucracy. This independence was evident in the office's investigatory role. The NO was authorized to investigate and assess possible violations of the statute on its own initiative. It was not dependent on other administrative agencies for referrals as in the UK nor did it have to refer its decisions back to the central administration for action as in France.

If, upon investigation, the ombudsman's office believed that conduct violated the statute, it negotiated with the parties involved in order to persuade them to abandon the practice. With few minor exceptions, the office could not itself order compliance with the statute, nor could it impose sanctions for conduct that had terminated, even if the termination occurred during the proceedings. Nevertheless, in a large proportion of the cases this process apparently led to abandonment or modification of the practice at issue.[92]

Where the ombudsman's informal compliance efforts were unsuccessful, the office could take the case to the Market Court.[93] The office was, however, generally reluctant to take cases to the court, not least because of its limited budget. This reluctance may have been increased by the court's general tendency during the 1970s to establish high proof requirements. As a result, the Market Court heard very few cases per year.[94]

In addition to these official functions, the ombudsman's office emphasized the importance of maintaining close contacts with the business community. Officials from the office frequently spoke to groups of business leaders, explaining the office's position on specific types of practices as well as on general principles of interpretation and enforcement. They also worked informally to encourage the business community to co-operate in enforcing the system's norms. This informal component of the ombudsman's task was widely seen as of great importance to its success.

The size and composition of this office was consistent with the roles assigned to it by law and tradition. It was small (in the early 1980s it had less than 50 full-time employees). The head of the office had to be qualified to be a judge, but the statute established no other qualifications for officials in the office, and it typically had more economists than lawyers in leading positions.

---

[91] The Swedish term is '*Näringsfrihetsombudsman*', which means literally 'ombudsman for business freedom'. The term refers to both the individual who is the ombudsman and the government agency which that individual heads. For detailed discussion of the role of ombudsmen in Sweden, see generally Stig Jägersköld, 'The Swedish Ombudsman', 109 *U. Penn. L. Rev.* 1077 (1961).

[92] See, e.g., *NO—Verksamheten 1982* (Annual Report of the Competition Ombudsman for 1982), 2 *Pris och Konkurrens* 48,66 (1983).

[93] Defendants often agreed to end the practices involved after the case had been submitted to the Market Court. In such cases the ombudsman had to withdraw his complaint.

[94] For statistics, see Annual Report 1982, at 66. In the 1980s the average number of cases handled by the Market Court was about five.

This reflected a belief that the system should not be narrowly legalistic, but should be administered in a practical and constructive manner. Economists were expected to be better at understanding business problems and better at negotiating with business firms than lawyers would be. Moreover, because of their educational and social ties to the small community of important business leaders, officials trained in economics were expected to be well placed to maximize informal compliance pressure.

b. The Market Court

The other central institution in the Swedish competition law system was and continues to be the Market Court (this court has been retained in the 1993 revision of the system, but I will refer to it in the past tense in order to clarify that I am referring to the previous system). Its primary role was to provide an ultimate arbiter of the substantive law. If the NO brought a case before the court, the proceedings there were formal and adversarial, with the ombudsman acting as prosecutor, although the rules of procedure were more flexible than those applicable in the ordinary courts.

If the court determined that there had been a violation, the court or its president alone met with the parties and attempted to negotiate a cessation of the offending conduct. Although this procedure typically secured a significant measure of compliance without compulsory tools, the legislature in 1982 gave the court additional powers to issue injunctions and levy fines. These were seldom used unless negotiations had proven unsuccessful.

The court was specifically charged with creating precedent that would guide business conduct, and thus it issued often lengthy written opinions explaining its decisions. Hesitant to act too much like a regular court,[95] however, the court relied for authority almost exclusively on the legislative history of the statute. Although it referred to fact patterns in prior cases, it seldom cited either prior cases or scholarly commentaries.

The Market Court was a special tribunal created specifically to implement the LRC (it was later given other consumer protection functions); it was not part of the ordinary court system.[96] Its president and vice-president had to be qualified to be judges in the regular court system, but the other members of the court generally were not lawyers. They were appointed on an 'as-needed' basis, and each panel had to include at least three 'experts' (in competition cases two of them had to be professional economists) as well as three consumer and labor representatives and three representatives of industry. This

---

[95] For comments of the former Chief Judge of the Market Court on this function, see Per Westerlind, 'Tio Års Praxis i Marknadsdomstolen—Erfarenheter och Värderingar', *Svensk Jurist Tidning* 401 (1981).

[96] This court was originally responsible only for cases involving the LRC. In 1971 it was reorganized and acquired jurisdiction over cases brought by the then newly created consumer ombudsman. For a general description of the court, see Bernitz, *Svensk Marknadsrätt* 20–23.

composition internalized both the economic competence necessary to analyze
the law's economic issues and the perspectives of the interest groups likely to
be most affected by application of the law. Its composition was consistent
with the 'community-effect' orientation of the Swedish competition law
system—that is, the assumption that the sense of community among business
leaders, competition officials and academics was an effective means of inducing compliance with the statute.

5. Pragmatic juridification

While the Swedish competition law system remained essentially administrative, juridical features became gradually more important in its operations. I
use the term 'pragmatic juridification' to refer to this process because it was
driven by a pragmatic sense of economic policy needs and a pragmatic legal
culture. It is a process that has had analogues in other European competition
law systems.

The core of the process was a steady, unobtrusive increase in the influence
of prior decisions on the system's operation. Changes in the way prior decisions were perceived and used changed the discourse and mode of operation
of the system. Decisions of the Market Court and the NO were increasingly
understood as 'legal' in the sense that they were expected to exert significant
influence over future decisions. In a broad sense, of course, authoritative decisions always tend to influence subsequent decision-making within the same
system. The issue here is the intensity of this influence—the degree to which
prior opinions can be regarded as a reliable basis for predicting future decisions. The Market Court thus gradually created a body of case law that was
treated as authoritative by the NO and by the legal community. Because of
the small number of cases handled by the court, however, this would not by
itself have had a strong 'juridification' effect.

The legislature also added juridical components to the system. For example, while in other countries such as France and England, special competition
law institutions were called 'commissions' and given only advisory responsibilities, the Swedish law called its near analogue a 'court', gave it final
decision-making authority and specified that it should create law for the guidance of the business community. It also created the conditions necessary for
the court to fulfil this function. It minimized the possibility of direct political
influence by placing the court outside of the judicial and administrative hierarchies, and it required the court to publish its opinions.

More significant for the operation of the system was the evolution of the
ombudsman's role. Given the small number of decisions issued by the Market
Court, it was the NO's treatment of *its own decisions* that was critical to the
process of juridification. For most purposes, these decisions represented the
only authoritative interpretations of the statute. Most violations were elimi-

nated at the level of the ombudsman, and thus its mode of operation largely determined the discourse of the system as a whole. The NO could have continued to operate on a largely discretionary basis and to downplay juridical factors, but it chose instead to increase the roles of those elements.

In the early 1980s the ombudsman handled some 400–500 cases per year, publishing written opinions in many of them. Formally, these opinions were not 'binding' on the office in future decisions and thus carried no authoritative weight for the Market Court, but they were 'treated' as authoritative by the decision-makers of the NO, which adopted as an operational principle that it was bound to seek high levels of consistency in decision-making.

As it became clear that the office was operating in an increasingly juridical fashion, the business community increasingly tended to accord the NO's decisions a juridical status rather than treating them merely as instances of the use of discretionary authority. They also seem to have generally welcomed this development. Assuming, as Swedish business leaders could, that the NO's decision-makers were open to the arguments of the business community, and that, in essence, business leaders and competition officials were part of the same 'community of discourse', the business community stood to gain from a juridical mode of operation because it enhanced the predictability of decision-making. Moreover, the discourse of the NO was both economic and pragmatic. This is the language in which business leaders operate and with which they feel comfortable, and thus they had little to fear from the infusion of juridical elements that would merely give structure, perhaps strength, to a perspective that was likely to take due account of their interests.

This analysis may help explain other characteristics of the NO's operations. For example, the NO's decisions were not legalistic in form. They tended to avoid citing prior cases as precedent and to minimize traditional legal analysis, referring for authoritative guidance almost exclusively to the statute's legislative history. The message to the business community was that the language of decision-making was pragmatic and economic, even though juridical elements were influencing its dynamics. This style had other functions as well, signalling, for example, the NO's independence from the Market Court. It also reflected more broadly the influence of the pragmatic Swedish legal tradition, with its strong influences from legal realism.

The role of economics in this process deserves special attention, because it is often overlooked. It is frequently assumed by economists and others that economists contribute little, if anything, to the process that we here call juridification, not least, presumably, because economists often feel ill-at-ease with legal discourse and modes of operation and seldom specifically *intend* to contribute to that process. Economic science and economists can, however, play important conceptual and cognitive roles in legal development, and these have often been neglected. In the Swedish context, at least, economic expertise and analysis contributed to the juridification of Swedish competition law by creating relatively clear conceptual lines that helped to structure decision-making and to give it coherence and predictability. Economic analysis was built into the structure of the legislation, and economists were relied on in applying that legislation. This foregrounding of economics in the competition law system is probably associated with the relatively high status of the economics community in Sweden since the First World War.[97]

Finally, the independence of the NO was a key factor in this process. The ombudsman's office was in a position to operate juridically because it was protected from many of the factors that normally attend bureaucratic decision-making. Whereas bureaucrats in other administrative control systems often try to avoid juridical modes of operation in order to maximize their discretion and, therefore, their negotiating position with regard to the business community or with regard to other bureaucrats, the independence of the NO obviated the need for such tactics. This formal independence was, in turn, given force by Swedish legal and political traditions, which expected independent decision-making from an ombudsman and accorded the office high status.

6. Swedish competition law experience

Swedish experience with competition law prior to the 1993 reforms highlights factors in the dynamics of administrative control systems that often play important roles in our story. In it, the community of discourse and interests between administrative decision-makers and business elites led to a concept of competition law designed to foster the efficiency and international competitiveness of Swedish industry by eliminating the restraints of competition that could impair them. From that perspective, law is seen as a positive, constructive force. This perception of competition law has played significant, if less central, roles in other European countries, and it may become increasingly attractive in the future as Europe's high-wage economies seek to maintain and improve their international competitiveness.

In the Swedish conception of competition law, competition is not understood as a goal in and of itself, but a means for achieving particular economic and social ends. It does not carry the ideological baggage that sometimes has hampered the development of competition law in countries such as France and the UK. In part, this is a reflection of the long control of government by the Social Democratic Party, which shaped the contours of Swedish economic policy during the postwar decades. The social democrats used the market system to provide the economic well-being necessary to support its social welfare

---

[97] For a series of short biographies of Swedish economists that conveys a sense of the evolution of the profession, see Christina Jonung & Ann-Charlotte Ståhlberg, eds., *Ekonomporträtt: Svenska Ekonomer under 300 År* (Stockholm, 1990).

goals, but their ideology did not permit them to laud increased competition as a goal in its own right. They therefore had a strong incentive to avoid infusing competition law discourse with political symbolism. Their opponents from '*borgerliga*' (roughly, bourgeois) parties similarly had little to gain by making competition law a political issue, because the system was already in place and apparently achieving the goals that a competition law system could be expected to achieve.

The Swedish system has operated as a basically closed system in which a small group of administrative officials, business leaders and legal professionals have made decisions against a background of shared interests, and this dynamic has molded Swedish experience. It has, for example, allowed the system to rely largely on persuasive and hortatory rather than coercive enforcement mechanisms and yet achieve relatively high levels of compliance.

This also correlates with the pragmatic style of Swedish competition law. Swedish legal culture has for decades emphasized pragmatism and downplayed the role of formalism. This has facilitated the creation of a constructive style in competition law and the development of a community of interests between business leaders and competition law officials. Factors such as the homogeneity, small size and geographical centralization of the relevant business community have conditioned the creation of that community, and similar factors have influenced other smaller European countries with relatively open economies (such as, for example, the Netherlands).

H. COMPETITION LAW IN BRITAIN: SAME PATTERN, DIFFERENT ACCENTS

One might expect the story of competition law in Britain to differ from that of its neighbors on the continent. Its insularity coupled with important differences between its legal traditions and those of most of the rest of Europe might have led to a fundamentally different conception of competition law. It did not. On the surface at least, competition law experience in Britain resembles the pattern of administrative controls that has dominated other European countries. From the perspective of European integration, these similarities are important because they have provided a common experiential base that has eased mutual understanding and co-operation within EU institutions and forged important links between Member State governments and officials.

Yet British experience has also been different in significant ways. While its competition law system has been based on the administrative control model, English legal culture and its attendant strategies have led to distinctive modifications in that model. In some respects, British competition law has moved further away from that model than have its neighbors.

1. Before the 'Great War': common law as context

Long resistant to the growth of an economic regulatory bureaucracy, British decision-makers in this area have tended to respond to new problems by relying on common law institutions, procedures and modes of thought. In responding to the problem of protecting competition from restraints, therefore, the UK might have followed this pattern and foregrounded these common law forms. That it did not invites explanation, particularly because the common law doctrine regarding 'contracts in restraint of trade' offered a basis for developing a different kind of competition law.

Common law courts were developing this doctrine as a basis for holding certain contracts unenforceable at least as early as the sixteenth century, and the language of those early cases continues to reverberate in common law adjudication.[98] Yet, 'The policy of the civil courts towards agreements in restraint of trade has evolved from one of suppression up to the seventeenth century, through partial recognition in the eighteenth century, to near-abstention in the nineteenth and twentieth centuries'.[99] The doctrines were still being applied, but by the end of the nineteenth century they had been encased in concepts and attitudes that eviscerated their practical importance.

This is not the place to probe the reasons for the virtual 'evaporation' of restraint of trade doctrine, but some of the factors that played a role deserve mention because they shed light on later developments. For one, nineteenth century judges must have been uneasy about applying cases involving restrictions on the activities of a baker who sold his bakery to agreements between powerful industrial enterprises. Prior to the twentieth century, cases to which the restraint of trade doctrine was applied typically involved restraints on an artisan's capacity to practice his trade, either in the context of the sale of a business or as part of the employer-employee (master-servant) relationship. Yet the upper class gentlemen who sat on the Victorian bench tended to perceive the industrial economy of nineteenth century England as fundamentally different from what had gone before, and thus they had little incentive to apply the earlier cases to the 'new' industrial relationships of their time.

A second set of factors relates to the ideology of *laissez-faire*, whose role was so conspicuous in nineteenth century England. As Eric Hobsbawm puts it, 'The history of [British] government economic policy and theory since the Industrial Revolution is essentially that of the rise and fall of *laissez-faire*'.[100] As we have seen, nineteenth century liberalism basically said to government,

---

[98] For discussions of these early developments, see Lord Wilberforce et al., *The Law of Restrictive Trade Practices and Monopolies* 17–44 (2d. ed. London, 1966) and William Letwin, *Law and Economic Policy in America* 18–52 (Chicago, 1965).

[99] C. Grunfeld & B. S. Yamey, 'United Kingdom', in *Anti-Trust Laws: A Comparative Symposium* 346 (Wolfgang Friedmann, ed., Toronto, 1956).

[100] Eric J. Hobsbawm, *Industry and Empire* 225 (Harmondsworth, England, 1969).

'Don't intervene in economic matters unless you absolutely must'. Late nineteenth century English judges tended to take this message to heart, seeing freedom of contract as a pre-eminent value. Although this ideology was challenged by the end of the century, those classes in England from whom judges were recruited were among its last—and often most ardent—defenders.

The international component of nineteenth century economic liberalism also played a role. 'Free trade' was nowhere more vigorously supported than in Britain, not least because it was seen as serving domestic interests. As long as Britain was both the leading industrial power and the dominant colonial power, it stood to gain from a free regime of international trade, because free trade opened foreign markets to the often more competitive British goods and entailed little risk for lost markets at home. The almost religious devotion to free trade among the English ruling classes undergirded reverence for the principle of economic freedom and the general mandate of *laissez-faire*.

The lack of barriers to imports also tended to inhibit the formation and growth of cartels in Britain, and opponents of competition legislation before the First World War frequently argued that this precluded the need for competition legislation.[101] If cartels raised prices above a competitive level, they argued, foreign goods would enter and force prices back down, thus eliminating incentives for cartel formation. There were cartels, and they were not insignificant in numbers and power, but they attained little general importance until after the First World War. A government report issued in 1919 found that 'What is notable among British consolidations and associations is not their rarity or weakness so much as their unobtrusiveness. There is not much display in the window but there is a good selection inside'.[102]

Together, these factors left little room for the idea of using law to protect the process of competition. Not surprisingly, courts throughout the 'long' nineteenth century found reasons for not applying the doctrine of restraint of trade to agreements that might have been seen as restraining trade. Relying on distinctions drawn in the famous 1711 case of *Mitchel v. Reynolds*, for example, they validated such agreements because they involved 'specific' rather than 'general' restraints or because the restraints were reasonably limited in scope.[103]

In the 1894 *Nordenfeldt* case,[104] the House of Lords further eviscerated the doctrine of restraint of trade when it unanimously held that even 'general' restraints could be valid, provided that they were 'reasonable' as between the parties and did not otherwise harm the general welfare. Since prior case law had established that for these purposes the 'general welfare' would almost

[101] For discussion, see Tony Freyer, *Regulating Big Business: Antitrust in Great Britain and America 1880–1990* 90–95 (Cambridge, 1992).

[102] *Secretary's Report to the Committee on Trusts*, 1919, Cmd. 9236, p.17, quoted in Wilberforce, *Restrictive Trade Practices*, 7.

[103] (1711) 1 P.Wms. 181.

[104] *Thorsten Nordenfeldt v. Maxim Nordenfeldt Guns & Ammunition Co.* [1894] AC 535.

always coincide with the interests of the parties, the restraint of trade doctrine had very little remaining utility in protecting the process of competition.

If the common law judges at the turn of the twentieth century saw little need to protect the process of competition, legislators, many of whom were from the same class, were not likely to override that judgment. The courts had given their imprimatur to most types of agreements that might be seen as restraining trade, and legislators had little incentive to enact laws that might alienate business leaders and London's 'City'. In the wake of the turn-of-the-century merger wave, occasional voices from the economics profession began to suggest the need for some form of control of powerful firms, but they found little response in parliament.[105]

2. Between the Wars: protection, regulation, and self-regulation

The First World War exploded many of the ideas and perceptions on which British economic policy had been built. The extensive wartime regulation of the economy demonstrated that such regulations could actually be made to function more or less effectively, even in Britain.[106] It also demonstrated to businessmen the potential benefits of organizing among themselves in order to carry out—or, perhaps, parry—government regulation.

Had the war not fundamentally altered the economic data which had nurtured prewar ideas, these 'lessons' might have been quickly forgotten, but it did. Drained by the financial and human costs of war, Britain in the years following the war was no longer a prosperous nation with a powerful economy that dominated international trade and finance. Throughout much of the interwar period the British economy was beset by depressed business conditions and unemployment that was far higher than anything it had experienced before the war. Despite the advantages that its colonies produced, its enterprises found successes alarmingly elusive.

In the 1920s, Britain's neighbors often did not share its economic plight. In the middle years of the decade, for example, France and Germany were enjoying immediate successes and relatively bright economic prospects, and this contributed to confidence in Britain that its problems were likely to be short-lived—something that revised exchange rates and a healthy dose of rationalization in industry should be able to solve. When depression engulfed much of the rest of the world after 1929, even that confidence disintegrated.

The business community, which still consisted largely of privately-owned businesses, responded to economic hardship by increasingly turning to loose co-operative arrangements such as cartels that were designed to maintain price-levels and avoid 'ruinous competition'. Some also merged to form com-

---

[105] See Freyer, *Regulating Big Business*, 68–75.
[106] For discussion of the British economy and its regulation during the war, see Sidney Pollard, *The Development of the British Economy: 1914–1990* 15–36 (4th ed., London, 1992).

panies (for example, Imperial Chemical Industries) that would represent the United Kingdom in international competition after the Second World War.

Government leaders not only accepted such arrangements, but also generally welcomed and frequently promoted them. They wanted to minimize economic disruption and unemployment and find organizational structures that would allow British industry to regain its international competitiveness. With the advent of the Depression, government sponsorship of industry-wide cartel arrangements increased. With it, the ideal of the independent entrepreneur as the necessary engine of the British economy evaporated, and the hallowed icon of *laissez-faire* was relegated to the realm of rhetoric.

Businesses sought protection not only from the domestic competitive process, but also from foreign competitors. They called for tariff protection to allow them to secure at least their home markets. Again, the British government complied, increasing tariff barriers in the 1920s and even more dramatically in 1931. 'Free trade', the symbolic bedrock of economic policy discourse in Britain for more than a century, was now also eliminated from an increasingly shaky British economic credo.[107]

Despite the growth of cartels and the occasional creation of 'giant' firms through mergers, there was little call for governmental action to control their impact. In the immediate aftermath of the war political leaders and the public became aware of the potential for harm that powerful corporations could inflict, and in 1919 well-publicized laws were enacted against 'profiteering'.[108] These were, however, soon eliminated (1921), and though they probably increased sensitivity to the more general problem of harm from economic power, they seem to have been dismissed as related specifically to the postwar situation.

Throughout the 1920s, however, there was growing concern about the economic power created by mergers and cartels, and several governmental commissions investigated the ramifications of increased economic concentration. They sometimes reported on the potential for harm by economically powerful firms, but no action was taken.[109] Government leaders were not convinced that the problem was weighty enough to warrant action that might interfere with the economic performance of British firms. In short, there was insufficient political, social and intellectual impetus to move in that direction.

In part, this was also because they saw self-regulation as the preferred response. The idea of self-regulation by industry had been developing even before the war, and it was attractive to both government and industry.[110] The

[107] For discussion, see Paul H. Guénault & J. M. Jackson, *The Control of Monopoly in the United Kingdom* 6–24 (2d. ed., London, 1960).

[108] See Freyer, *Regulating Big Business*, 159–64.

[109] For discussion of the various committee reports and their impact, see Charles K. Rowley, *The British Monopolies Commission* 28–34 (London, 1966). See also Guénault & Jackson, *Control of Monopoly*, 15–24.

[110] See Freyer, *Regulating Big Business*, 103–10.

underlying image was that those who controlled powerful businesses were honorable men whose families typically owned the businesses they ran and that they were part of a small and relatively homogenous community whose members considered themselves accountable to each other and responsible for the long-run welfare of British society. They could be trusted not to abuse their power. The self-regulation solution also tapped into vestigial images of *laissez-faire* rhetoric: even if firms were no longer operating independently, and even if government often supported their activities, they were at least regulating themselves rather than being regulated by government.

3. World War II and the administrative response

The second war brought a vastly altered economic situation, new attitudes toward economic power and the distribution of economic resources, new expectations of the role of government, and changes in Britain's political leadership. Together, they led toward the enactment of a competition law in 1948.

a. The postwar context

The economic situation in postwar Britain was complicated.[111] Losses measured in terms of the lives of combatants were fewer than in the First World War, but now there was also the extensive destruction of facilities resulting from German bombing. Production capacities had been strained to—and often beyond—the breaking point, and the physical capacity to produce had been seriously impaired. Added to this were other factors—such as the disruption of international trade and the emergence of the United States as the new centerpiece of the international economy—that darkened Britain's economic prospects. There was also poverty in postwar Britain, much of it dire. With limited natural resources, massive war debts and impaired production facilities, Britain had to import to survive, but it had little capacity to pay for imports.

Nevertheless, most Britons seem to have expected the return of relative economic well-being after a (hopefully) short period of reconstruction.[112] Few countenanced the idea that Britain would never again be the economic power they had known. After all, their main competitors on the continent had suffered as much or more. Germany and France, the two economic archrivals, hardly seemed to have a bright economic future. Many saw no reason why the economic slide that had begun in Britain before World War I and had accel-

---

[111] For detailed discussion of the economic situation, see Alec Cairncross, *Years of Recovery: British Economic Policy 1945–1951* (London, 1985). The general situation, including much attention to its economic policy aspects, is depicted in Peter Hennessy, *Never Again: Britain, 1945–1951* (New York, 1993).

[112] See Hennessy, ibid., 87–118.

erated during the interwar period could not be halted and perhaps even reversed.

The political message of the postwar years featured impatience for change. At the end of the war, British voters gave the reins of government to the Labour Party, which promised major changes in the distribution of Britain's economic resources. Although broader in its social backing and appeal than the socialist and social democratic parties on the continent, Labour's central mandate was to bring about social change in favor of the working classes and to provide greater communal (that is, societal) ownership of economic assets and control of economic conduct.

The swing to Labour was associated with major shifts in the way Britons perceived their society. New 'sensibilities' had begun to form before the war; they acquired status and centrality during the war; and the expectations they created became important factors after the war.[113] A core theme was 'social justice'. It was brought to the foreground in the highly publicized Beveridge Report, which was published in 1942 and came to be seen as a kind of manifesto for social change in England.[114] Among its claims was that postwar Britain should more effectively harness the economic power of large corporations and assure that the nation's economic resources were being used in the best interests of society.

In 1944 another government report focused attention on what was to become the most prominent item on the postwar economic policy agenda—employment. The White Paper on Employment emphasized the need to use economic policy measures to maximize employment possibilities:

Employers, too, must seek in larger output rather than higher prices the reward of enterprise and good management. There has in recent years been a growing tendency towards combines and toward agreements, both national and international, by which manufacturers have sought to control prices and output, to divide markets and to fix conditions of sale. Such agreements or combines do not necessarily operate against the public interest; but the power to do so is there. The Government will therefore seek power to inform themselves of the extent and effect of restrictive agreements, and of the activities of combines; and to take appropriate action to check practices which may bring advantages to sectional producing interests but work to the detriment of the country as a whole.[115]

The linkage of employment issues to prospects for a competition law was a major factor in the support given to competition law by the postwar Labour government.

---

[113] For discussion of the development of thinking about competition policy during the war and immediate postwar periods, see J. D. Gribben, *The Post-War Revival of Competition as Industrial Policy* (Government Economic Service Working Paper, No. 19, London, 1978) and Freyer, *Regulating Big Business*, 233–68.

[114] Sir William Beveridge, *Social Insurance and Allied Services* (1942, Cmd. 6404).

[115] *White Paper on Employment Policy*, Cmd. No. 6527 19 (1944).

b. The impetus for legislation

With the public awakened to the issue of economic power, the Labour Party began to consider some form of competition law soon after taking office in 1945. The idea fit conveniently into Labour's program. It was a means of subjecting economically powerful firms to community needs and of protecting workers, the 'common man' and small businesses from the harms that economically powerful organizations might otherwise inflict. It would thus contribute to the 'social justice' portion of Labour's agenda.

Such a law also promised benefits to the economy as a whole. If it reduced impediments to competition, it might improve the competitiveness of British firms, invigorate the economic process, and combat unemployment. These were goals that were shared by all political parties, and thus there was little opposition to the idea of having some form of law that would at least help to identify the extent of existing restraints on competition, assess their consequences, and perhaps combat them.

The recent work of British and American economists, most notably Joan Robinson and Edward Chamberlin, had helped to heighten the perception that restrictive trade practices might be potentially harmful, and economists influenced by these doctrines had held important positions in economic planning agencies during the war. They made important contributions, respectively, to the theory of monopolistic competition (Robinson) and imperfect competition (Chamberlin), demonstrating, *inter alia*, that incentives for monopolistic practices were common in most markets.[116]

Finally, the United States encouraged enactment of a competition law—through urging and example. US officials urged the UK government to enact a competition law for several years after the end of the war.[117] This urging took place in the context of negotiations over US aid to Britain at a time when British officials were under enormous pressure to secure as much US aid as possible. The enactment of a competition law served as a convenient—and relatively cost-free—means of demonstrating a spirit of co-operation with the Americans.

Example may have been even more important. Numerous British officials, scholars and journalists made more or less officially sponsored trips to the US during the postwar years. Their responses generally included positive impressions of US business practices, and many saw antitrust law as contributing to the successes of the powerful and impressive US economy.

---

[116] See Joan Robinson, *The Economics of Imperfect Competition* (London, 1933) and Edward H. Chamberlin, *Theory of Monopolistic Competition* (Cambridge, Mass., 1933). For discussion of the milieu of economic thought, see G. L. S. Shackle, *The Years of High Theory: Invention and Tradition in Economic Thought, 1926–1939* (Cambridge, 1967).

[117] See, e.g., Freyer, *Regulating Big Business*, 261–67.

c. The Monopolies Act of 1948: the first UK competition law

In the first years after the war the political agenda was filled with matters more urgent than competition law, but in 1948, in conjunction with a loosening of economic controls, the government enacted the Monopolies and Restrictive Practices (Inquiry and Control) Act 1948.[118] The legislation was timid, but it began a long and tortuous process that eventually yielded a formidable and complex competition law system. This timidity was justified by the claim that too little was known about monopolies and restrictive practices and that this scheme would 'create a record' on which further steps might be based.

Declining to follow the US example, the government chose an explicitly administrative form of competition law. The legislation authorized the government minister primarily responsible for commerce and industry (then called the President of the Board of Trade, later changed to the Secretary of State for Trade and Industry) to request investigation of an *industry* where it suspected that there might be competitive restrictions which were harmful to the 'public interest'. Such investigations were permitted only where at least one-third of the total supplies on the market were controlled by one seller (or group of associated sellers) or one buyer (or group of associated buyers). Investigations of individual firms were not allowed, nor were investigations of service industries (although they were later included).

Investigations were carried out by a newly-created Monopolies and Restrictive Practices Commission, which could act only on the basis of such requests.[119] The President of the Board of Trade could specify the tasks of the commission. He could, for example, limit the investigation to facts or include, in addition, assessment of the impact of the restrictions on the 'public interest'. He could even ask for recommendations for governmental action. The legislation provided several non-exclusive criteria that the commission could use in assessing harm to the public interest, including impact on production efficiency, technological progress, and exports.

The commission then reported its findings and decisions to the President of the Board of Trade, who was normally required to publish the report. These reports were intended to expose harmful conduct and to give content to the concept of 'public interest'. He could not, however, take enforcement action himself. That was a matter for Parliament (that is, the government in power) which could seek termination of such practices through negotiation, and, where that proved unsuccessful, it could issue orders relating to the practices, including orders for their termination. Violation of an enforcement order could subject the offending firms to injunction. This arrangement left

[118] 11 & 12 Geo.6, c.66.
[119] For detailed discussion of the Monopolies Commission, see Rowley, *British Monopolies Commission* and A. Sutherland, *The Monopolies Commission in Action* (Cambridge, 1969).

ultimate authority with the politicians and administrators, but placed responsibility for investigation on a separate commission that was given a measure of independence in performing its tasks.

Members of the commission were appointed by the President of the Board of Trade and were to be chosen for their expertise and trustworthiness, and politics were to play no role in appointments. Members were not, however, to be civil servants. The original legislation specified that the commission should contain a maximum of ten members, but this varied in later legislation.[120] The Board of Trade could appoint full-time or part-time members, but generally appointed part-time members.

In the years between its creation and its first major reform in 1956, the competition law system performed little more than an educational function. During that period, the commission completed only twenty-seven investigations,[121] and the government issued only two orders under the statute. This level of activity was not likely to have much impact on business decisions.

The value of the commission's educational function should not, however, be underestimated, because it helped to change attitudes toward competition. As one commentator described reactions to early investigations,

. . . . the businessmen who appeared before the commission, at any rate in the early days, expressed surprise and indignation that their practices should be scrutinized, let alone condemned as pernicious. 'Why', asked typical witnesses before the commission, should a firm or group of firms be adversely criticized for practices which were common to a great part of industry and had been actively encouraged by the Government a short time ago?[122]

In addition, the commission's investigations revealed that restrictive practices were common in many UK industries, and they supported the claim that such restraints were often harmful to the public interest. In its most ambitious statement, the commission in 1955 issued a detailed general report that emphasized the degree to which certain practices such as collective discrimination and group boycotts pervaded British industry.[123] The commission's activity thus prepared the way for creating a more effective competition law system.

---

[120] For example, the Monopolies and Restrictive Trade Practices Commission Act of 1953 raised the number to twenty-five and made top officials permanent and pensionable, but the number was again reduced to ten in 1956.

[121] See Rowley, *British Monopolies Commission*, 330–31.

[122] G. C. Allen, *Monopoly and Restrictive Practices* 84–5 (London, 1968). For discussion, see ibid., 70–88. 'Most firms strongly resented the imputation that what they were doing was contrary to the public interest', ibid., 85.

[123] Monopolies and Restrictive Trade Practices Commission, *Report on Collective Discrimination*, Cmd. 9504 (1955).

4. Creating a dual system: the restrictive practices regime

The commission's general report also put the Conservative government in a difficult position. As a more or less direct result of the publicity surrounding the report, there was significant pressure to respond with new legislation addressing at least some of the problems that the report had identified. Business interests that were major supporters of the Conservative party favored a more 'juridical' system that would reduce the uncertainties and political elements of the current system, but they also feared an increase in 'interference' from competition law.[124]

The government responded by bifurcating the system, leaving monopoly issues under the existing system, but creating a different and significantly more juridical system for 'restrictive practices'. The Restrictive Trade Practices Act (RTPA) that embodied this solution was enacted in 1956, and from then until 1980 (when yet another subsystem was added) the British system was a dual system in which one set of restraints on competition was dealt with by one set of norms, institutions and procedures, while other conduct threatening competition was subject to a different system.[125] The remainder of this section sketches the evolution of the 'restrictive practices' system. I describe it in the past tense in order to emphasize its role in the evolution of the overall British system, although as of this writing it continues to operate.

The RTP system retained some features of administrative control, but its basic characteristics were far more juridical. The legislature here drew on English legal traditions for tools and mechanisms to use in combating certain kinds of restraints on competition. Now, however, it was using those tools in a largely administrative environment.

The basic message of the legislation was that restrictive practices were presumed to be against the public interest and, therefore, unenforceable and illegal. This represented a major shift from the normative starting point of the original legislation, which had maintained a neutral posture toward competitive restraints and merely provided investigative machinery. This neutral approach was maintained in the monopolies system, but in the RTP regime restrictive practices were presumed to be harmful and prohibited, except where they could be justified.

The RTPA refers only to agreements and arrangements, thus excluding monopolies or single-firm conduct, which remained subject only to the provisions and procedures of the monopolies system. The central procedural mechanism was a requirement that agreements containing specified provisions be

---

[124] For discussion of the background to the statute, see R. B. Stevens & B. S. Yamey, *The Restrictive Practices Court: A Study of the Judicial Process and Economic Policy* 10–19 (London, 1965).

[125] Restrictive Trade Practices Act, 1956, 4 & 5 Eliz. 2, c. 68. There have been numerous revisions of the RTPA, each of which made relatively minor changes in the operation of the system.

registered in a newly created Registrar's Office. Such provisions included, for example, the regulation of prices or quantities of goods produced, conditions of sale, persons to whom sales could be made and geographical areas in which goods could be sold. The requirement applied only to firms 'carrying on business in Great Britain in the production or supply of goods' (services would be added in 1973). Failure to register an agreement could lead to a declaration that it was against public policy and void. One objective of the registration requirement was to publicize and thus deter harmful agreements.

Where an agreement was registered, the Registrar had to submit it to a newly created Restrictive Practices Court, unless he concluded that the agreement was not of sufficient economic significance to warrant examination. This court then had to determine whether the agreement met any of the criteria established for exemption from sanctions—the so-called 'gateways'(§ 21). The idea was that under certain circumstances restrictive practices did not harm the 'public interest' and, therefore, should not be subject to sanctions.

The gateway provisions were detailed.[126] Some protected the users of the goods—for example, where 'the restriction is reasonably necessary . . . to protect the public against injury (whether to persons or to premises) in connection with the consumption, installation or use of those goods'(a). Others provided a means by which smaller and medium-sized firms could co-operate to counterbalance the economic power of larger firms (c). Still others related directly to economic policy concerns, as, for example, where 'the removal of the restriction . . . would be likely to have a serious and persistent adverse effect on the general level of unemployment in an area or in areas taken together, in which a substantial proportion of the trade or industry to which the agreement relates is situated' (e).

If the court was not convinced that the agreement 'passed through' a gateway, it could declare the agreement void. Where it considered one or more of the gateway criteria to have been met, however, it proceeded to the next step. It balanced the harm to the public interest against the public benefits the agreement could be expected to produce, invalidating the agreement only if the former exceeded the latter. The legislation did not provide conceptual guidelines for applying this balancing test. If the court invalidated the agreement, firms that continued to operate according to it were subject to contempt of court proceedings, which could include fines.

The Restrictive Practices Court is perhaps the most unique feature of UK competition law.[127] Here English legal culture most clearly set its stamp on the competition law system and differentiated it from patterns common on the continent. The RTP court is in most respects a true court, and it was

---

[126] For discussion, see Wilberforce, *Restrictive Trade Practices*, 379–403.

[127] For a leading and particularly incisive analysis of the court's operation that argues that the court is an inappropriate forum for adjudicating many of the issues before it, see Stevens & Yamey, *The Restrictive Practices Court.*

intended to operate as such. It is generally considered part of the High Court in London (although technically this is not quite accurate) and it follows procedures similar to those of the High Court, including features such as cross-examination of witnesses (although some of the rules of evidence are relaxed). The judges include regular High Court judges, several of whom have been particularly distinguished, as well as lay judges 'qualified by virtue of knowledge of or experience in industry, commerce or public affairs'.

The court enjoys a large measure of independence from external political and economic pressure, and its decisions operate directly rather than depending on approval by administrative or political decision-makers. In constructing a system around this type of court, the RTPA went perhaps further than any other European country in 'juridifying' a segment of its competition law.

During the initial decade of the system's operation, the RTP Court was particularly active because of the need to adjudicate large numbers of newly registered agreements. More than 4,000 agreements had been registered by 1965, including many of national significance. The court seldom concluded that such agreements were justified, and, as a result, the vast majority of them were either terminated or modified to eliminate provisions that fell within the Act. The apparent effectiveness of this system led initially to general approval. According to a 1965 study, 'So far the Court has received an almost exclusively eulogistic reception; and the praise has come from all directions'.[128]

After a decade or so of relatively intense activity, the court settled into a routine in which the agreements it was reviewing became increasingly local, in part because many larger, well-advised firms were in a position to avoid restrictions that had been disapproved in prior cases. The court had created a body of precedent that provided guidance in evaluating many types of agreements, and practitioners generally felt that for those cases they could give reasonably dependable advice concerning the probable outcome of litigation. Another reason that fewer cases of economic significance were appearing before the court may have been that firms were increasingly prepared to take the risks of not registering agreements that fell within the scope of the act.

By the late 1970s, complaints about the efficacy of the system were growing. Critics emphasized frequent difficulties in applying the 'public interest' standard and decried the uncertainty and potential unfairness that attended the use of this relatively vague standard. There was also criticism of the system's formalism, which, it was claimed, invited firms to structure agreements in such a way as to achieve the desired competitive restraints without being 'caught' by the system's formal requirements. Finally, there was growing fear that many restrictive practices were simply not being registered. A detailed interdepartmental review of the system in 1979 concluded, nevertheless, that the potential improvements that might be brought about by an overhaul of the

---

[128] Ibid., 7.

system would not justify the disruptions that such an overhaul would entail, and it recommended against major changes in the system.[129] Despite criticism, the basic characteristics of the RTP system have remained unchanged.

5. The monopolies and mergers regime

With the enactment of the RTPA in 1956 the restrictive trade practices component of the new dual system became the focus of attention and activity for more than a decade. The administrative control system of the 1948 Act, as slightly amended, was maintained, but it was now used only in cases of single-firm conduct. In order to reflect the diminished scope of its responsibilities, the Monopolies and Restrictive Trade Practices Commission was renamed the Monopolies Commission, and the number of its members was significantly reduced. Between 1956 and 1965 it handled few references. Government policy favored the creation of large corporations on the assumption that they would be able to compete more effectively on international markets, and there was little interest in investigating their potential abuses within Britain.

a. The Monopolies and Mergers Act, 1965

Responding to complaints about the lack of control over mergers, the Labour government in 1965 enacted a Monopolies and Mergers Act that for the first time included mergers in the system (renaming the commission the Monopolies and Mergers Commission and increasing its size).[130] The Act's treatment of mergers was, however, 'benign'. Mergers were presumed to be beneficial, but the responsible government minister could refer a merger to the commission if he considered that it might be against the public interest. A merger could only be referred, however, if the resulting firm would purchase or supply at least one-third of a product in the UK or a substantial part of it or if the value of the acquired assets reached a certain level (initially, £5 million). The procedure used was basically the same as used in the case of monopolies, but the requirements for taking action against a merger were higher.

These new provisions were little used for several years, not least because the Labour government of the 1960s actively promoted mergers. In 1966, it created an Industrial Reorganization Corporation (IRC), which actively encouraged mergers until it was disbanded by a Conservative government in 1971.[131]

---

[129] Interdepartmental Group, *A Review of Restrictive Trade Practices Policy*, Cmnd. 7512 (1979).

[130] For discussion of the evolution of merger policy in the UK, see James Fairburn, 'The Evolution of Merger Policy in Britain', in *Mergers and Merger Policy* (James Fairburn & John Kay, eds., Oxford, 1989).

[131] For discussion of the Labour Party's economic policies during this period, see P. Meadows, 'Planning', in *British Economic Policy: 1960–74* at 402–17 (F. T. Blackaby, ed., Cambridge, 1978).

The merger wave of the late 1960s and early 1970s did, however, increase pressures on the government to take firmer action against mergers.

b. The Fair Trading Act, 1973

In the early 1970s, claims that political factors were influencing references to the commission led to the Fair Trading Act, 1973.[132] This legislation created a new Office of Fair Trading (OFT) and gave the Director General (DG) responsibility for administrative decisions in both components of the competition law system. In the restrictive practices system, the DG took over the functions of the Registrar, and in the monopolies and mergers system the DG assumed responsibility for the functions previously exercised by a government minister (usually, the Secretary of State).

The statute was primarily aimed at making the system more effective and its institutions less subject to political and business influences. Unlike the officials who had performed these functions previously, for example, the DG was a non-political appointment, who was to be chosen (by the Secretary of State) on the basis of administrative ability and competence in economic regulatory matters. Similarly, the office was not part of the regular bureaucracy. The Secretary of State could veto references to the commission, but seldom did.

The Act also modified the monopolies and mergers system in several important respects. For example, the OFT now had an affirmative obligation to monitor potential monopoly situations, whereas decisions relating to investigations previously had been left to administrative discretion. It was also given responsibility for advising the responsible government minister as to whether to refer a merger to the commission. Authority to issue compliance orders, including orders to terminate harmful practices, was transferred from Parliament to the Secretary of State, further reducing political influence on decision-making within the system. In addition, the Act reduced the threshold percentage of market control necessary for a monopoly or merger reference from 33 to 25 per cent.

c. Experience with the mergers and monopolies regime

The basic structure of the mergers and monopolies system has not changed significantly since 1973. It remains an administrative system for investigating potential harms from the acquisition (mergers) or use (monopolies) of economic power and exerting compliance pressure on those responsible for such harms. Although the Fair Trade Act of 1973 imposed limited investigatory obligations on the OFT, the system is highly discretionary—to be put in motion when and as administrative decision-makers see fit. With regard to mergers, this discretion is virtually unlimited.

---

[132] Fair Trading Act, 1973, c.41.

The Mergers and Monopolies Commission remains an advisory body whose proceedings are not open to the public and whose only force is informal and derives from the weight accorded its opinions. It does not apply legal norms, but assesses the impact of conduct on 'the public interest'. The commission has often achieved respect for the thoroughness and impartiality of its investigations, but it has not developed conceptual contours for its opinions that might allow them to serve as effective guidelines for business conduct. As a leading commentary notes, '. . . it is difficult to extract a "case-law" from its decisions, although it is possible to identify certain issues that it is likely to take into account'.[133] The public interest standard and the requirement that the commission investigate industries rather than individual firm conduct have thus precluded a more direct impact on conduct.

The system has been used consistently but sparingly. As of the end of the period covered in this chapter, the number of monopoly references that had been issued since the inception of the system (almost four decades) was approximately 80. With respect to mergers, 'From the passage of the 1965 Act to the end of 1985 more than 15,000 mergers are known to have taken place but only just over 3,000 fell within the legislation and of these only eighty-three were referred'.[134] In few cases has the government taken formal action against either mergers or monopolies, either because the commission concluded that the public interest standard had not been violated or because the administrators achieved negotiated settlements.

There have been numerous calls for reform of this system, and it has often been criticized as being ineffective. Administrative decisions (for example, regarding references and the treatment of commission recommendations) have been plagued by inconsistency, subjugation to general economic policy considerations, and, particularly in the early years of the system, political influence. The procedure has been seen as slow and cumbersome, and this has combined with the lack of serious sanctions to limit its effectiveness in deterring restraints on competition.

6. Competition law, 1980: the anticompetitive practices regime

The final major revision of the monopolies and mergers system during the period covered in this chapter came in 1980. As in France and other countries at about the same time, it was the result of a major re-evaluation of competition policy prompted by the growing importance of European Community competition law and by concerns about the international competitiveness of domestic industry. It was also spurred by the high value attached by the

---

[133] Richard Whish & Brenda Sufrin, *Competition Law* 689 (3d. ed., London, 1993).
[134] E. Victor Morgan, *Monopolies, Mergers and Restrictive Trade Practices: UK Competition Policy, 1948–1987* at 41 (Edinburgh, 1987).

Thatcher government to increasing the role of competition in British society.[135]

The immediate impetus for the changes was contained in reports submitted by an interdepartmental committee in 1978 and 1979, respectively, which pointed to inadequacies in the existing competition law system.[136] The central thrust of the studies was that the UK's competition law should more directly and effectively protect the process of competition. They noted that the restrictive trade practices system was hampered in its effectiveness, primarily because its form-based registration requirements could often be avoided and because the system lacked serious sanctions for failure to register agreements that fell within the statute. The monopolies and mergers regime was similarly hindered by the lack of effective sanctions, by the need to investigate industries rather than the conduct of specific firms, and by the long delays involved in carrying out such investigations.

Mrs Thatcher's government was amenable to these recommendations, and in 1980 it enacted a statute (Competition Act, 1980) that contained many of the recommended changes.[137] Characteristically, the new legislation did not replace either of the existing regimes, but created an additional regime which was intended to deter conduct that was likely to harm competition, but which was not being effectively treated under the other two regimes. It specifically did not apply to agreements that were registrable, and it was independent of the procedures of the mergers and monopolies regime.

The central concept of the legislation is 'anticompetitive practice', which is defined as conduct that 'has or is intended to have or is likely to have the effect of restricting, distorting or preventing competition in connection with the production, supply or acquisition of goods . . . or the supply or securing of services in the United Kingdom or any part of it'(§2(1)). In contrast to the concept of a restrictive trade practice, the definition here is effects-based rather than form-based, and this effects orientation was emphasized as one of the Act's major improvements.

Under this new system, the OFT is authorized to investigate the conduct of individual firms rather than entire industries as was necessary under the mergers and monopolies regime. This change was designed to reduce the time needed to carry out investigations, but it also represented a step toward a more juridical system by subjecting conduct to articulated norms rather than assessing their impact on the 'public interest'.

The legislation authorizes the OFT to conduct both informal and formal investigations of the conduct of individual firms where he has reason to

[135] For discussion of Prime Minister Thatcher's economic policy, see Peter Riddell, *The Thatcher Years* 14–42 (Oxford, 1989).

[136] Interdepartmental Group, *A Review of Monopolies and Mergers Policy*, Cmnd. 7198 (1978) and *A Review of Restrictive Trade Practices Policy*, Cmnd. 7512 (1979).

[137] Competition Act, 1980, c.21. For discussion, see Valentine Korah, 'The Competition Act 1980', 1980 *J. Bus. L.* 255 (1980).

believe that a firm has engaged in an anticompetitive practice. The DG can also negotiate with the firms involved and accept an undertaking that the conduct being investigated will be terminated. The assumption of the drafters was that firms identified for investigation would generally prefer to give such undertakings rather than to endure the costs that the investigation or subsequent action by the commission would impose.

Where there is no such undertaking and the OFT finds that the conduct in question is both anticompetitive and appropriate for reference to the commission, the DG must refer it to the commission for final determination. In contrast to the procedures under the monopolies and mergers regime, the OFT does not here consider the issue of 'public interest'. The sole criterion is the economic effects of the conduct. Nevertheless, the issue of whether these are appropriate for reference leaves a great deal of discretion in the hands of the DG.[138] The Secretary of State may also block any reference by the OFT, and thus administrators retain ultimate control over the system's operations.

Where a reference is made to the commission, it must determine whether the conduct is anticompetitive under the terms of the Act and, if so, whether it is also 'against the public interest'. This system does not, therefore, eliminate the 'public interest' standard, but reduces its role by addressing it only at a later stage of the process and by providing inducements for firms to terminate offending conduct before a case reaches that stage.

If the commission finds that conduct is both anticompetitive and against the public interest, it reports this back to the Secretary of State, who can ask the OFT to negotiate a termination of the conduct with the firms involved or make orders directed at the firm, including orders that the conduct be terminated. At this stage, the procedures are similar to those in the mergers and monopolies regime.

This regime is administrative, but its procedures inhibit the 'free' exercise of administrative discretion to a far greater extent than is the case in the monopolies and mergers regime. For example, the legislation regulates this complex procedure in great detail, specifying when and how its many steps are to be taken. It also seeks to make the process transparent by generally requiring publication of findings and references by the OFT, responses by firms under investigation and orders of the commission. This is designed to reduce the discretion of administrative officials and minimize the likelihood of undue influence on the decision-makers. To this extent it represents a form of 'juridification'.

The Act did not have the impact that some had hoped it would have. As a leading economist described the situation in 1987,

---

[138] For comments of a former Director General on this discretion, see Gordon Borrie, 'Competition Policy in Britain: Retrospect and Prospect', 2 *Intl Rev. of L. & Econ.* 139, 145–47 (1982).

The use made of the new procedures so far has not been impressive. Up to the end of 1985 investigations had been made or announced in twenty-one cases. In four of these the companies gave undertakings acceptable to the Director General before the start of a formal inquiry, and in a further seven undertakings were accepted during or at the end of an OFT investigation. In five cases the OFT found no significant anti-competitive effects, and four were referred to the MMC. . . . A few of these cases are quite important in terms of the value of the products or services affected but most of them range from the minor to the trivial.[139]

Investigations generally have resulted from complaints rather than from the initiative of the OFT. Many have come from retailers complaining of their treatment by manufacturers or distributors, but there have been fewer complaints to the OFT than some had expected. Thus, although the system offered the possibility of more direct and vigorous enforcement activity, neither the bureaucrats in charge of the system nor the firms whose interests might have been harmed by anticompetitive practices have been assiduous in pursuing these possibilities.[140]

7. British experience with competition law

When the United Kingdom enacted competition legislation for the first time in 1948, it did so timidly. The legislation epitomized the administrative control model, placing virtually complete discretion in the hands of administrators and politicians and refusing even to presume that restrictive practices were against the public interest. By the mid-1980s, the British competition law system had become a highly complex network of norms and institutions, some of which had acquired important roles in shaping conduct.

Perhaps the most conspicuous characteristic of this system has been its lack of system—its *ad hoc* texture. Similar to the situation in France, but in marked contrast to that in Sweden, for example, competition law in Britain has been marked by a lack of cohesion. It has reflected neither an integrating idea nor a structuring objective. Rather, it has consisted of specific responses to specific problems. As Richard Whish has put it, '. . . much of UK law has developed without any overall conception of the function either of competition or competition law, and . . . this has produced many of the difficulties that exist'.[141] In this, it reflects British parliamentary traditions. In a style reminiscent of common law response patterns, the legislature has tended to eschew well-planned legislative initiatives in favor of repeatedly changing the details of the system and simply adding new statutory material and even new institutions as new problems have arisen.

The bifurcation of the British system in 1956 exemplifies this pattern. The legislature chose to deal with a specific aspect of the problem of competitive

[139] Morgan, *Monopolies*, 32–33.
[140] For further discussion, see Whish & Sufrin, *Competition Law*, 112–20.   [141] Ibid., 16.

restraints—restrictive agreements—by creating a specific normative and procedural regime to treat that problem. This regime has continued to function
virtually independently of other components of the system. Similarly, the
Competition Act of 1980 was enacted to remedy a specific deficiency in the
existing system, but little attention was paid to how well it 'fit' with the treatment of other aspects of the problem. It was merely 'added on'.

The *ad hoc* character of the system is reflected in its discourse. The language
of competition law tends to be specific and fact-intensive rather than abstract
and structured. The concepts used in British competition law generally do not
refer to an ordered conceptual structure such as one finds, for example, in
German competition law, but to the facts of specific cases. In the restrictive
practices component of the system, the formal precedential value of prior
cases and the judicial trappings of the procedure and its institutions further
underline this tendency.

Changes in the competition law system have, however, had a consistent
direction—toward 'juridification'. The legislature has added juridical components and characteristics to a system that was originally based exclusively on
administrative and political discretion and negotiation. Articulated norms,
judicial institutions, and juridical procedures have become increasingly
important and prominent. Each of the regimes within the system reflects a different mixture of administrative and juridical elements, with the restrictive
practices regime the most juridical, the monopolies and mergers regime the
least juridical and the anticompetitive practices regime somewhere in
between.

Yet, despite these efforts and 'improvements', competition law in the UK
has remained a relatively marginal phenomenon. The sanctioning tools available to administrators remain limited; its impact on business decision-making
continues to be spotty; and it plays only a minor role in legal education. There
are differences in impact and importance among the system's regimes, and
they largely correspond to the degree of 'juridification' of the regime. The
restrictive practices regime has achieved, for example, a relatively high status
within the business and legal communities and tends to be taken seriously in
business decision-making, while the mergers and monopolies regime is seldom considered to be a major factor in the shaping of such decisions.

I. ITALY AND IBERIA: COMPETITION LAW AS COMMERCIAL LAW

To round out our picture of European competition law systems during the
four decades after the end of the Second World War, we need to mention
briefly the pattern of experience in Italy and on the Iberian peninsula. While
legislatures in much of the rest of Western Europe were introducing legislation against restraints on competition law, such efforts were unsuccessful in

Italy for decades, and on the Iberian peninsula such legislation either did not exist or was virtually ignored. In both areas there was some coverage of competition law issues in commercial law and in unfair competition law regimes based on the French model.[142]

In Italy there were legislative initiatives to introduce competition laws along northern European lines, but such efforts were not successful until 1990. Many reasons have been adduced for this lack of success, but most center on the unwillingness of legislators and industry to give additional authority to administrators in whom they had little confidence or whose authority they might consider to threaten their own interests. Few in Italy seem to have believed that administrators would enforce competition law in a way acceptable to them—those in major industries were concerned that such administrators might interfere too much with their conduct of business (or require compensation for not doing so), while others, including smaller businesses, feared that such administrators might unduly serve the interests of large firms.

J. ADMINISTRATIVE CONTROL AND THE COMPETITION LAW TRADITION

The pervasiveness of the administrative control model in the development of European competition law systems is striking, and its influence remains profound. It is the only form of national competition law with which most Europeans have had much experience. It has provided concepts, shaped and coded perceptions, configured decisional options and created expectations about what competition law should be and what it should do. Unfortunately, narrow national perspectives on competition law have obscured its trans-European influence.

1. Images of competition law

This experience has provided the dominant images of national competition law in Europe—its identity. As we shall see in Chapter X, there have been potentially significant changes in national competition laws since the mid-1980s, but so far they have not altered the basic characteristics of that identity. In this section, therefore, I will often use the present tense in offering generalizations about national (other than German) competition law experience since the Second World War.

---

[142] For discussion of the 1963 Spanish legislation, which remained virtually unused, see Santiago Martinez Lage, 'Significant Developments in Spanish Anti-Trust Law', 16 *Eur. Comp. L. Rev.* 194–200 (1996). For the situation of competition law in Italy toward the end of the period covered in this chapter, see, e.g., Francesco Galgano, *Trattato di Diritto Commerciale e di Diritto Pubblico Dell'Economia*: Vol. IV, *La Concorrenza e i Consorzi* (Padua, 1981). For an English language treatment of the subject, see in Richard J. Torre, 'Italian Antitrust Law', *14 Am. J. Comp. L.* 489 (1965).

The central feature of this experience has been administrative. The competition law systems we have encountered operate exclusively or primarily as components of administrative regimes. Most important decisions are made by administrators; the procedures are largely administrative; and the institutions typically are located within the economic regulatory bureaucracy or subject to a high degree of control by it. These systems sometimes contain elements such as special courts that are alien to this administrative territory, but their main features have been within the administrative domain.

This location has meant that competition law has been generally understood as a form of economic regulatory activity, often barely distinguishable from other economic regulatory activity such as price controls or industrial policy. This, in turn, has often inhibited the development of clearly recognizable features: 'Competition law is just another form of administrative regulation' is an often heard comment about competition law in Europe. The perception of competition law as a form of administrative regulation has left little basis for attaching 'constitutional' or other 'priority' values to competition law and its 'messages'.

These systems have tended to operate more as economic policy than as 'law'. Their norms have often represented little more than authorization for officials to seek economic policy objectives. Their language and procedures have frequently been those of discretionary policy implementation rather than of juridical decision-making. Those who write about them—their 'experts'—have been more likely to be administrators or economists than lawyers or legal scholars.

Both the mission and the messages of national competition law systems have tended to be vague. They have sought to protect competition, but they have been used for other objectives at the same time, often leaving confusion and uncertainty as to their goals. Powerful guiding principles have been rare. Vague notions of the 'public interest' or 'abuse of economic power' have typically been at the center of these systems rather than enforceable norms defining unacceptable conduct, establishing rights to be protected or delineating social harms to be combated. The general lack of significant sanctions in competition law systems has underscored the weakness of the messages those systems have sought to send. Legislatures have seldom been willing to bear the political costs of providing competition law institutions with powerful tools for coercing compliance with competition law norms.

2. Competition law's role

If we turn from images of what competition law is to what it does, the picture remains murky. We find that administrative control systems have generally been a marginal component of public life. Rarely, if ever, have they achieved important roles in economic, political or legal life, and in some countries there is little general awareness of their existence and roles, even among legal professionals.

With often dubious political and public support and unclear intellectual guidance, administrative decision-makers have generally been reluctant to use even the limited sanctioning authority available to them. In seeking compliance, they have relied primarily or even exclusively on the 'safer' roads provided by publicity and administrative suasion. Their role generally has been to cajole, to pressure, and to persuade. As a consequence, business decision-makers have had little incentive to pay careful attention to the messages being sent by these systems.

'Marginal' also describes the role of national competition laws in their respective legal communities. University law faculties have paid little attention to them in their course offerings and examinations, and they have been the subject of relatively little legal scholarship in most countries. This, in turn, has meant limited theoretical development of the subject. The literature has generally been thin, and much of it has been written by economists for whom legal issues have been less important than economic and policy issues.

There have, of course, been specific areas in which the impact of specific competition law systems has been more than 'marginal'. Consistent with the objective of eliminating obstacles to the improvement of market structures (and, sometimes, in order to protect smaller firms) some systems have imposed, for example, significant sanctions on specific vertical restraints such as price discrimination and refusals to deal. Others have focused their attention on cartels because of the obvious economic harm they can cause, and they have often created major disincentives for cartelization. They generally have not (until recently) prohibited cartels, taking the position instead that those harms can be outweighed by societal benefits and, therefore, that competition laws should merely prevent cartels from abusing their power.

3. Developmental patterns

European national competition law systems have also tended to develop along broadly similar lines. Although gains have been modest, they have generally become more influential and 'stronger'. The scope of application of competition law has expanded; institutions have acquired more resources as well as increased stability and status, and they have increased the intensity with which they have used the compliance-inducement mechanisms at their disposal.

Most, if not all, such systems have become gradually more juridical. As we have seen, the process of juridification took various forms in various countries and for various reasons, but all systems have moved in the direction of increasing the role of juridical elements in their operations. They have, for example, increasingly protected decision-makers from external political and economic influences, relied on juridical methods such as the conceptual development of articulated norms, emphasized consistent treatment of similar fact patterns, made the decision-making process more transparent and less subject to extrinsic influences and enhanced the capacity of competition law institutions to investigate and impose sanctions on individual firms. In some cases juridical elements were added by the legislature, while in others they were developed by competition law institutions themselves.

This process has been driven by a growing perception of the need to protect competitive processes from harm. Initial legislation often established goals for competition law systems before there was sufficient political support to move decisively toward those goals. As communities and interest groups perceived the value of combating restraints on competition, the systems were gradually modified to improve their capacity to attain the original goals.

The growing strength and juridical character of these systems has seldom received much attention. In part, this is because the changes have virtually always been gradual and incremental. It also reflects, however, the extent to which politicians and administrators have been reluctant (again, until recently) to exacerbate fears in national business communities that competition law might be becoming too 'strong'.

Two comparisons have increased awareness of the potential benefits of competition law. One has been German experience with competition law. Germany, as we shall see in the next two chapters, embraced a stronger and far more juridical conception of competition law in the mid-1950s, and as Germany's economic successes multiplied, her neighbors recognized the possibility that those successes might in some measure be attributable to Germany's protection of the competitive process.

Probably more important has been the growing stability and force of European Community competition law, which has called for at least a degree of emulation among its Member States. In some cases, Member States have sought improved enforcement and co-operation by co-ordinating their national competition law systems with Community law, while in others, moving national systems toward the Community model was intended to counteract claims that Brussels should acquire more extensive jurisdiction in the competition law area. Although this 'model' function of Community competition law was to become far stronger from the mid-1980s on, it led to some modifications in many national competition law systems even before that.

Yet the influence of Community competition law on national competition law systems prior to the mid-1980s did not always involve emulation. In some cases it may have reduced the incentives of national legislators to change. Some believed, for example, that Community competition law would take over the function of protecting competition in Europe, and to the extent they did, national politicians had little incentive to incur the political costs of strengthening their own systems. It was easier and safer to maintain relatively non-transparent administrative control systems. Moreover, with the growing importance of the EU, some national politicians and administrators were keen on maintaining control of particular domains of economic life, and from this perspective a system based on administrative discretion is likely to seem more attractive than more juridical systems.

I have emphasized the points of similarity among European national competition law systems, but we have also seen significant variations on the basic themes. The specifics of each country's experience have been scripted by external circumstances such as country size, geography, industrialization patterns, and political affiliations such as membership in the EU. They have also been shaped by internal factors such as legal culture, administrative traditions, the contours and status of economic thought and of the economics profession and the like. The variety of these factors makes the degree of similarity in the basic structures and operations of such systems even more remarkable.

Administrative control systems were first and firmly established, and other conceptions of competition law have been defined by their relationship to that model and coded as proposals for modifying it. This 'model' has also established a set of expectations of what competition law is and should be that has been widely shared throughout Europe, and it has reflected a particular conception of the role of government in economic affairs and of the dynamics of a modern market economy. By the mid-1980s that conception was increasingly being called into question by economic changes, rival conceptions of competition law and the process of European integration. We will return to these issues in Chapter X.

VII

Ordoliberalism: A New Intellectual Framework for Competition Law

One of the ironies of European history in this century is that the intellectual impulses for the extraordinary reversal of direction in social and political development that occurred in the decades after the Second World War came not from a traditional liberal bastion such as England, but from the territory of a recent enemy of liberalism – Germany. As we shall see, competition law was a critical part of this change of direction – as both cause and effect.[1]

More specifically, the geographical source of this impetus can be located in Freiburg – a small university town in the southwestern corner of Germany. Close to the French and Swiss borders, home to liberal traditions, and far from the centers of German political and economic power, Freiburg provided a haven for a small group of intellectuals who rejected both Nazi totalitarianism and state socialism. The ideas of the so-called 'Freiburg School' were the matrix of a new brand of liberal thought that has much influenced the evolution of social and economic policy in Europe since the war and has played a central role in the development of competition law.

The Freiburg School thinkers agreed with earlier conceptions of liberalism in considering a competitive economic system to be necessary for a prosperous, free, and equitable society. They were convinced, however, that such a society could develop only where the market was imbedded in a 'constitutional' framework. This framework was necessary to protect the process of competition from distortion, to assure that the benefits of the market were equitably distributed throughout society and to minimize governmental intervention in the economy. This interpenetration of legal and economic ideas was the essence of the Freiburg School and of the 'ordoliberal' school of thought into which it developed.

Despite its enormous importance, ordoliberal thought—and German neo-liberal thought generally—has received little attention in the English-speaking world.[2] Moreover, except in Germany, awareness of these ideas has

---

[1] As Wolfgang Fikentscher has put it, 'The traditional way of viewing economic policy assumes a thesis-antithesis process and arrives at three types: there are the models of complete liberalism and of the totally-planned economy, and the practice of most states lies somewhere between them. The decisive importance of the Freiburg School was to break this tripartite scheme'. Wolfgang Fikentscher, II *Wirtschaftsrecht* 42 (Munich, 1983).

[2] Walter Eucken's principal theoretical work, *Grundlagen der Nationalökonomie*, was translated into English in 1950 as *Foundations of Economics* (London, 1950), and his more popular

been confined almost exclusively to economists, while lawyers and political scientists seldom have been exposed to them. Finally, there has been little study of the impact of these ideas outside Germany.

This gap in our understanding of European thought and institutions has obscured the dynamics of the European competition law story, and it is in order to close that gap that we explore ordoliberalism in some depth in this chapter. I seek to illuminate ordoliberal thought, the factors that have influenced its development and the roles that ordoliberals and their ideas have played in the evolution of German and European competition law.

A. THE FREIBURG SCHOOL AND ITS CONTEXTS

German neo-liberal ideas took shape in response to the political and social crises of the Weimar Republic and of Nazi Germany. The failings of the 1920s led to the conquest of political power by the Nazis, and neo-liberal thinkers were dedicated to understanding—and avoiding—a recurrence of that fateful process. For them, the core of that process was the accumulation and misuse of power. Law had been degraded to a tool of political power, which, in turn, had been degraded to a tool of economic power.

1. Appointment in Freiburg

In 1933—just as the National Socialists were taking power—one economist (Walter Eucken) and two lawyers (Franz Böhm and Hans Grossmann-Doerth) met in Freiburg and discovered that they had similar readings of the failings of Weimar and similar views of what to do about it.[3] The fortuitous

Unser Zeitalter der Misserfolge was translated the following year as *This Unsuccessful Age* (W. Hodge tr., London, 1951). They seem to have had little circulation since the early 1950s.

There has been a modest revival of interest during the last decade. Two collections of translations of seminal articles in the development of thought regarding the German social market economy, including many by members of the Freiburg School, have been published during the last decade. In 1989, the German economist Hans Willgerodt and the British economist and public policy scholar Alan T. Peacock edited an anthology entitled *Germany's Social Market Economy: Origins and Evolution*. An accompanying volume contains articles on the same topic. See *German Neo-Liberals and the Social Market Economy* (Alan T. Peacock & Hans Willgerodt, eds., New York, 1989). The Ludwig-Erhard Stiftung published a similar anthology in 1982, entitled *Standard Texts on the Social Market Economy* (W. Stützel et al eds., Stuttgart, 1982). See also Manfred E. Streit, 'Economic Order, Private Law and Public Policy: The Freiburg School of Law and Economics', 148 *J. of Institutional and Theoretical Econ.* 675 (1992) and Heinz Rieter & Matthias Schmolz, 'The Ideas of German Ordoliberalism 1938–45: Pointing the Way to a New Economic Order', 1 *Eur. J. of Hist. of Econ. Thought* 87 (1993). I have discussed the ordoliberals and their influence in somewhat greater detail in David J. Gerber, 'Constitutionalizing the Economy: German Neo-Liberalism, Competition Law and the "New" Europe', 42 *Am. J. Comp. L.* 25 (1994).

[3] See generally Andreas Heinemann, *Die Freiburger Schule und ihre geistigen Wurzeln* (Munich, 1989).

occurrence that these three were able to work together for a sustained period of time under conditions that were (for the time) highly favorable made possible the genesis of the 'Freiburg School'.

The interplay of interests and backgrounds of these scholars shaped Freiburg School ideas. Walter Eucken, Professor of Economics in Freiburg since 1927,[4] had been focusing on the theoretical foundations of economic thought.[5] Hans Grossmann-Doerth arrived in Freiburg in 1933 to assume a chair in law. Concentrating on the problems created by private economic power, he had published a major study in 1931 of the use by large corporations and cartels of standard contracts to create their own law and thus avoid societal obligations.[6] The third member of the group, Franz Böhm, also arrived in Freiburg in 1933 to teach law. From 1925 to 1931 he had worked in the cartel section of the German Ministry of Economics, where he had participated in enforcing the German Cartel Law.[7] His pioneering study of the ineffectiveness of legal control over cartels was published in 1933.[8]

The interaction of these three scholars seems to have led to spontaneous intellectual combustion.[9] According to Böhm, '... each had arrived at a point in his own thinking where the spark was ready to jump'.[10] They began to work closely together, offering joint seminars, participating in joint scholarly projects, and discussing the interplay of their respective ideas. Böhm considered this close association critical to the development of their thought, pointing, in particular, to the intense cross-fertilization between the disciplines of law and economics.

    [4] For a brief but fascinating portrait of early influences on Eucken's thought, see Walter A. Jöhr, 'Walter Euckens Lebenswerk', 4 *Kyklos* 257 (1950). See also Francois Bilger, *La Pensée Économique Libérale dans L'Allemagne Contemporaine* 46–48 (Paris, 1964).
    [5] See, e.g., Walter Eucken, *Kapitaltheoretische Untersuchungen* (Leipzig, 1934).
    [6] Hans Grossmann-Doerth, *Selbstgeschaffenes Recht der Wirtschaft und staatliches Recht* (Freiburg i.B., 1933).
    [7] See Heinrich Kronstein, 'Franz Böhm', in *Wirtschaftsordnung und Rechtsordnung: Festschrift für Franz Böhm zum 70. Geburtstag*, at i, ii (Helmut Coing et al eds., Karlsruhe, 1965).
    [8] Franz Böhm, *Wettbewerb und Monopolkampf: Eine Untersuchung zur Frage des wirtschaftlichen Kampfrechts und zur Frage der rechtlichen Struktur der geltenden Wirtschaftsordnung* (Berlin, 1933).
    [9] Another influential figure in both the early development of Freiburg thinking and its propagation after the Second World War was Heinrich Kronstein, a close friend of Franz Böhm and later Professor of Law at Georgetown University Law School, who in 1931 published a book that dealt with the use of subsidiaries by large corporations to avoid legal constraints. See Heinrich Kronstein, *Die abhängige juristische Person* (Munich, 1931). According to Wolfgang Fikentscher, this book provided 'the starting-point for the neo-liberal way of looking at law'. Wolfgang Fikentscher, III *Methoden des Rechts: Mitteleuropäischer Rechtskreis* 418 (Tübingen, 1975). For a discussion of some aspects of Kronstein's life and work, see David J. Gerber, 'Heinrich Kronstein and the Development of United States Antitrust Law', in *Der Einfluss deutscher Emigranten auf die Rechtsentwicklung in den USA und in Deutschland* 155–69 (Marcus Lutter et al eds., Tübingen, 1993).
    [10] Franz Böhm, 'Die Forschungs- und Lehrgemeinschaft zwischen Juristen und Volkswirten an der Universität Freiburg in den dreissiger und vierziger Jahren des 20. Jahrhunderts', in *Franz Böhm—Reden und Schriften* 158, 161 (Ernst-Joachim Mestmäcker, ed., Karlsruhe, 1960).

A common theme soon emerged in their discussions. Each had concluded that the lack of an effective, dependable legal framework had led to the economic and political disintegration of Germany. Each believed that the core of the problem had been the inability of the legal system to prevent the creation and misuse of private economic power. According to Böhm, 'The issue on which we focused together was . . . the issue of private power in a free society'.[11]

The initiators were soon joined by other, mainly younger, legal and economic scholars who began to make their own contributions to the central themes being developed by their mentors. By the late 1930s there was a well-defined group that shared a basic set of objectives, methods and attitudes, and many members of this group played leading roles in propagating these ideas after the war. According to one commentator, '. . . what unified all of them was their active temperament, their idealistic philosophy and their unwillingness to witness events with their "arms crossed" '.[12]

The development of a school of thought espousing views inconsistent with the ideology of a totalitarian regime as powerful and ruthless as that of the Nazis probably could not have occurred in any city in Germany other than Freiburg. Supported by a strong liberal and pluralist tradition in the community and favored by Freiburg's distance from the centers of population and its lack of strategic importance, the university was able to minimize national socialist influences until almost the end of the war.[13] Although members of the Freiburg School were arrested, imprisoned and dismissed from their jobs, local government officials tended to avoid drastic action against them.[14]

The special circumstances in Freiburg are reflected in the existence and operation of the so-called 'Freiburg Circles' (*Freiburger Kreise*).[15] These small cells of resistance to Nazism operated with relatively little interference in Freiburg, often drawing resisting intellectuals from other parts of Germany for meetings there. These groups focused on finding a new basis for German society after the war, emphasizing moral and social issues and frequently relying on religious values for support.

Although the Freiburg School of economic and legal thought must be carefully distinguished from these famous resistance groups, Böhm, Eucken, and

---

[11] Böhm, 'Forschungs- und Lehrgemeinschaft', 162.   [12] Bilger, *La Pensée*, 76.

[13] See generally Constantin von Dietze, 'Die Universität Freiburg im Dritten Reich', 3 *Mitteilungen der List-Gesellschaft* 95 (Aug. 9, 1961). Freiburg has been described as 'a kind of nature preserve of liberal economic scholarship'. Günter Schmölders, *Personalistischer Sozialismus* 29 (Cologne, 1969). See also Christine Blumenberg-Lampe, *Das Wirtschafts-programm der 'Freiburger Kreise'* 15 (Berlin, 1973).

[14] According to one commentator, the Freiburg School represented 'the quiet, but bitterly fought war of resistance of German economic scholarship'. Günter Schmölders, 'Freiburger Imperativ', *Frankfurter Allgemeine Zeitung*, Apr. 26, 1990, at 15. For discussion of the situation of economists during the Third Reich, see Wernhard Krause, *Wirtschaftstheorie unter dem Hakenkreuz: Die bürgerliche Ökonomie in Deutschland während der faschistischen Herrschaft* (Berlin, 1969).

[15] For discussion, see Blumenberg-Lampe, *Das Wirtschaftsprogramm.*

other members of the Freiburg School also belonged to one or more of these circles.[16] Thus the directions and attitudes of the Freiburg School were influenced by these personal contacts, and at the very least the Freiburg scholars found support in the culture of resistance these groups provided.

2. Varieties of neo-liberalism

Before looking more closely at the main core of ordoliberal ideas, it is important to identify several thinkers and schools of thought that did not belong to the 'Freiburg School', but were either included within ordoliberalism or related to it.[17] In the years following the end of the Second World War there were several groups that could loosely be called 'neo-liberal',[18] and categorizations of the thinkers and their ideas often vary widely. The Freiburg School was the most influential, however, and other groups either evolved from it or were much influenced by it.

With the end of the war, the isolation of the Freiburg scholars ended, as did the clear identification of their ideas. The term 'ordoliberalism' was soon being applied to a somewhat broader stream of thought that featured the basic ideas of the Freiburg School, but also included members who were not directly associated with Freiburg.[19] In particular, the ideas of Wilhelm Röpke and his followers now were often included as part of ordoliberalism. Forced by the Nazis to flee Germany in 1935, Röpke eventually moved to Switzerland, where he taught economics and pursued an active journalistic career.[20] He was heavily influenced by Walter Eucken and the Freiburg School and shared their basic ideas.

An even broader categorization that was heavily influenced by the ideas of the Freiburg School was that of the social market economy. The economist Alfred Müller-Armack coined the term (in 1946) and was the writer most

---

[16] See Blumenberg-Lampe, *Das Wirtschaftsprogramm*, 15–54.

[17] For an overview of German neo-liberalism, see Alan T. Peacock & Hans Willgerodt, 'Overall View of the German Liberal Movement', in *German Neo-Liberals and the Social Market Economy* 1–15.

[18] The term 'neo-liberal' is not without difficulties. Walter Eucken, for example, did not consider the term applicable to the Freiburg School because it suggested a return to the prior policies of liberalism, whereas he considered ordoliberalism to be something significantly new. See Walter Eucken, *Grundsätze der Wirtschaftspolitik* 374 (6th ed., Tübingen, 1990).

[19] The term 'ordoliberal' apparently was first used in Hero Moeller, 'Liberalismus', 62 *Jahrbücher für Nationalökonomie* 214, 224 (1950). The reference is to the 'Ordo' or 'natural order' of scholastic philosophy. It was used as the title of the *ORDO* journal that was founded in 1948 by Franz Böhm and Walter Eucken and that became the principal journal of the ordoliberal movement as well as one of the most respected scholarly journals in the German-speaking world relating to economic policy.

[20] For discussion of Röpke's thought and activities, see Bilger, *La Pensée*, 93–114, and Daniel Johnson, 'Exiles and Half-Exiles: Wilhelm Röpke, Alexander Rüstow and Walter Eucken', in *German Neo-Liberals and the Social Market Economy* 40–68.

closely associated with it,[21] while Ludwig Erhard, economics minister of the Federal Republic from 1949 through 1964 and its chancellor from 1964 to 1966, was its most famous adherent. Social market economy supporters agreed on most points of economic policy with the ordoliberals, but they placed greater emphasis on assuring that the benefits of the market be distributed equitably throughout society. From many perspectives, ordoliberal and social market economy doctrine are closely related, and the terms are often used almost interchangeably.

A third identifiable direction within neo-liberalism is the 'pure' economic liberalism of Friedrich von Hayek. Hayek agreed with Eucken about the importance of competition, but, particularly in his later work, he argued that there was no need for the state to play a major role in maintaining the conditions of competition. The market would, he claimed, take care of itself. Although Hayek did not consider himself part of the Freiburg School, he maintained close personal and intellectual ties with it.[22]

B. SETTING THE INTELLECTUAL STAGE

Ordoliberals focused not only on the institutional and political failures of the Weimar and Nazi periods, but on the intellectual failures implicated in them. They saw contemporary economic and legal thought as fundamentally flawed, and a major part of their agenda was to expose those flaws and thereby to avoid them in the future.

According to Walter Eucken, a central problem of economic thought was that it had lost touch with social and political reality.[23] Adam Smith and other classical economists had recognized that the economy was imbedded in the legal and political system, but during the nineteenth century economic thought gradually had become isolated, and economists had lost sight of both the political and social contexts of economic issues. One consequence of this isolation was a narrowing of the liberal tradition. 'Liberal' came to be identified with the idea of '*laissez-faire* capitalism'.

By the 1920s, however, this conception of liberalism had been discredited throughout much of Europe. The social disruptions caused by industrialization combined with the disaster of the First World War to identify 'liberalism' with economic chaos, political corruption and the exploitation of the

---

[21] See Reinhard Blum, *Soziale Marktwirtschaft: Wirtschaftspolitik zwischen Neoliberalismus und Ordoliberalismus* 94 (Tübingen, 1969).

[22] Hayek knew Eucken well and showed much respect for his thought. In addition, he was a principal contributor for decades to the *ORDO* journal. For a comparison of their thinking in this area, see Artur Woll, 'Freiheit durch Ordnung: Die gesellschaftspolitische Leitidee im Denken von Walter Eucken und Friedrich A. von Hayek', 40 *ORDO* 87 (1989).

[23] Walter Eucken, *Grundlagen der Nationalökonomie* 24–37 (9th ed., Berlin, 1989).

working class. In 1926 John M. Keynes had little doubt that this 'liberalism' was dead or very close to it.[24]

Rejecting a disfigured liberalism and overwhelmed by the consequences of the First World War, economists and policy-makers during the 1920s began to experiment with many varieties of governmental intervention. Governments felt not only justified in intervening in the economy, but obliged by political and economic pressures to do so. Active countercyclical and employment-enhancing intervention seemed an attractive and politically defensible antidote to the economic chaos of the period. Eucken called this the 'age of experimentation', and he did not like it.[25]

In Germany the problem of uncertainty was exacerbated, Freiburg writers claimed, by the dominance of historicism.[26] Eucken had himself been trained in the historical school, but by the mid-1920s he had committed himself to 'overcoming' historicism.[27] He believed that historicism had destroyed the ability of German economists and policy-makers to perceive the fundamental principles and necessary components of a market economy.

Eucken agreed that attention had to be paid to economic history and to the particular circumstances within which economic conduct took place, but he argued that historical study alone could not lead to an adequate understanding of economic phenomena. Historical analysis had to be interwoven with theory in order to organize and understand economic data. Historicism's 'helplessness' in the face of the economic crises of the Weimar years contributed to Eucken's change of loyalties.[28] The historical school had provided no answers to the economic chaos of the period, and it seemed unable to offer intellectual tools that could penetrate the frustrating complexity of economic developments.

The inability of economics to supply answers was matched, according to Franz Böhm, by the ineffectiveness of legal thought. Here the culprit was legal positivism. For him, the late nineteenth century German focus on the words of the statute as the primary, if not sole, source of law had once operated as a bulwark against discretionary power and as an objective—and, therefore, dependable—framework for social relations. Under the circumstances of the 1920s, however, it no longer played that role.[29] When the political system from which legislation emanated merely represented those private interests that were strongest at a particular time, legal positivism perverted law into a tool of those interests. According to Eucken, the idea that law was

[24] John M. Keynes, *The End of Laissez-Faire?* (London, 1926).
[25] See Eucken, *Grundsätze*, 55–58.
[26] See generally Willi Meyer, 'Geschichte und Nationalökonomie: Historische Einbettung und allgemeine Theorien', 40 *ORDO* 31 (1989). For Franz Böhm, historicism was still a dominant style of thought in economics in the 1930s. Franz Böhm, *Die Ordnung der Wirtschaft als geschichtliche Aufgabe und rechtsschöpferische Leistung* xi–xviii (Stuttgart, 1937).
[27] Walter Eucken, 'Die Überwindung des Historismus', 63 *Schmollers Jahrbuch* 63 (1938).
[28] Bilger, *La Pensée*, 45.   [29] See Böhm, *Ordnung der Wirtschaft*, ix–xii.

whatever the legislature said it was promoted chaos and injustice rather than providing legal security. It had allowed not only courts, but society in general to lose sight of fundamental values and common objectives, and it had helped pave the way for Nazism.

C. ORDOLIBERAL GOALS

Responding both to economic and political developments and to the perceived failings of legal and economic thought, the ordoliberals sought a new way of thinking about society. They turned to the basic values of liberalism for guidance, but they added new elements that transformed the liberal tradition.

A reconstructive imperative dominated the development of ordoliberal thought. Ordoliberal thinkers were not concerned with gradual change within existing institutions, but with laying the foundations for a different kind of society.[30] Many of the central structures of German society had been destroyed or discredited, and the ordoliberals saw their role as one of restructuring that society. As a result, they tended to think in large terms, to paint their vision of the future with broad strokes, and to seek a new vocabulary of thought.

The ordoliberal vision of society was defined by rejection of the past and by the search for a 'third way' between democracy and socialism, between the Soviet 'East' and the American 'West'. As the economist John M. Clark observed in 1948,

The world is in the grip of a mighty struggle. On one side are forces driving toward chaos and anarchy. . . . On the other side are forces of centralized control. Between them stand the forces and men who are trying desperately to salvage a workable basis for a human and ordered community in which some effective degree of freedom and democracy may be kept alive, without wrecking society by their undisciplined exercise and disruptive excesses.[31]

The ordoliberals were at the center of this conflict.

It is important to recognize that the wellsprings of ordoliberal thought were humanist values rather than efficiency or other purely economic concerns.[32] As his student and associate, Leonhard Miksch, wrote of Eucken, 'The battle that he waged with his growing group of supporters for a free order for the economy and the society did not emerge from economic theory. It was a battle for the eternal truths of humanity. For him, the economic theory was only

---

[30] According to Eucken, 'The normal discussion of economic policy [is] full of outdated concepts and polarities'. Eucken, *Grundsätze*, 2.

[31] John M. Clark, *Alternative to Serfdom* 6–7 (Oxford, 1948).

[32] See also Reinhard Behlke, *Der Neoliberalismus und die Gestaltung der Wirtschaftsverfassung in der Bundesrepublik Deutschland* 38 (Berlin, 1961).

a means to develop an '*Ordnung*' that was to liberate those values from their threatened encirclement by chaotic, anarchic, collectivistic and, finally, neo-liberal forces'.[33] Against the backdrop of chaos, devastation and amassed power, the ordoliberals set out to create a tolerant and humane society that would protect human dignity and personal freedom.

Drawing on the central values of classical liberalism, the ordoliberals envisioned a society in which individuals were as free as possible from state interference and in which democratic institutions dispersed political power by maximizing participation in public decision-making. Government institutions had the power to eliminate or curb freedoms, and thus the ordoliberals sought to keep that power in check and thereby protect individual freedoms.

The focus of ordoliberal thought was on the role of the economy in this society. They accepted the two basic classical liberal starting points—that competition is necessary for economic well-being and that economic freedom is an essential accompaniment to political freedom. They believed that private rather than governmental decision-making had to direct the flow of economic resources, because this would yield a productive and reliable economic system and simultaneously reduce the power of government. The two effects together would then prevent a repetition of the totalitarian disasters that had befallen Europe.

Yet the ordoliberals also expanded the lens of liberalism. For them, it was not sufficient to protect the individual from the power of government, because governments were not the only threats to individual freedom. Having witnessed the use of private economic power to destroy political and social institutions during the Weimar period, the ordoliberals emphasized the need to protect society from the misuse of such power.[34] This meant that the state had to be strong enough to resist the influence of private power groups. In order for government officials to be in a position to create the structures of the new society, the government of which they were a part would have to be able to protect them against private influences.

It also led them to demand the dispersion of not only political power, but economic power as well. For most ordoliberals this meant the elimination of monopolies. For others, such as Wilhelm Röpke, the concentration of economic resources was an evil unto itself, and thus they sought an economy composed to the extent possible of small and medium-sized firms and thus a society with a minimum of 'big business'.[35] Both groups tended to view

---

[33] Leonhard Miksch, 'Walter Eucken', 4 *Kyklos* 279 (1950). Note Miksch's use of 'neo-liberal' here to refer to something separate from, and inimical to, ordoliberalism. Presumably he was here referring to the Hayekian 'pure liberal' version of neo-liberalism.

[34] See, e.g., Eucken, *Grundlagen*, 196–204, and Franz Böhm, 'Das Problem der privaten Macht. Ein Beitrag zur Monopolfrage', 3 *Die Justiz* 324 (1928), reprinted in *Franz Böhm—Reden und Schriften* 25 (Ernst-Joachim Mestmäcker ed., Karlsruhe, 1960).

[35] See, e.g., Wilhelm Röpke, *Civitas Humana* 80 (Erlenbach-Zurich, 1946).

economic concentration with suspicion and sought to protect the existence and the economic freedom of small and medium-sized businesses.

Social goals also played a part in this ordoliberal vision of society. 'Social security and social justice', wrote Eucken, 'are the greatest concerns of our time'.[36] Classical liberals had been content to argue that the market, if left to itself, would promote economic growth and thus eventually enhance social welfare. Eucken and Böhm saw justice concerns in a broader context. For them, the economy was the primary means for integrating society around democratic and humane principles, but it could perform this role effectively only if it had certain characteristics. The market had to function in a way that all members of society perceived as fair and that provided equal opportunities for participation to all. Economic power was, therefore, a major obstacle to social justice, because it created the perception that the market was unfair and thus prevented it from operating as an instrument of social integration.[37]

Finally, the ordoliberals acknowledged that their political, humanist and social justice claims all rested on the assumption that economic competition would generate economic development—and rapidly. They relentlessly argued that the *only* way of achieving *sustained* economic performance and stability was through an economic order based on competition. This promise of economic success was critical to the growth of ordoliberal influence. Given the often desperate economic situation in postwar Germany, few would have heeded the ordoliberals if they had not also promised the quick establishment of a sound economy. Although ordoliberal theory is 'growth-neutral' on its face, under the circumstances of that time the creation of a sound economic system meant the same thing.[38]

D. ORDOLIBERAL THOUGHT: FOUNDATIONS AND BASIC PRINCIPLES

The ordoliberal program for achieving these goals centered on a new relationship between law and the economic system. The ordoliberals believed that economic competition would provide the basis for the society they envisioned, but only where law could create and maintain the conditions under which competition could function properly.

---

[36] Eucken, *Grundsätze*, 1. 'For Eucken, "social" was the equivalent of "independent", that is, to live in a world without monopolies and without power'. Otto Schlecht, 'Macht und Ohnmacht der Ordnungspolitik—Eine Bilanz nach 40 Jahren Sozialer Marktwirtschaft', 40 *ORDO* 303, 309 (1989).

[37] See, e.g., Eucken, *Grundsätze*, 185–93. See also generally Helmut Becker, *Die Soziale Frage im Neoliberalismus* (Heidelberg, 1965). Böhm claimed that a liberal program could not work if it did not satisfy this type of 'social need'. Böhm, *Ordnung der Wirtschaft*, 185.

[38] See, e.g., Röpke, *Civitas Humana*, 372–75, and Eucken, ibid., 350–68. In these contexts the ordoliberals tended to refer not to economic growth, but to 'improving economic performance'. See, e.g., Eucken, ibid., 249.

1. Methods and philosophical foundations

An important factor in the success of ordoliberal thought was its depth. Walter Eucken and his associates did not merely argue from existing intellectual paradigms, but also developed the epistemological and other philosophical bases necessary to give their policy prescriptions intellectual strength and appeal. Referring to his main economic policy work *Grundsätze der Wirtschaftspolitik* (Principles of Economic Policy), Eucken claimed that 'More important than all the details in this book is the method—the economic policy thinking that it calls for and from which the formulation and solution of the problems follows'.[39] Eucken was widely considered to be a deep and creative thinker, Friedrich Hayek calling him 'The most serious thinker in the area of social philosophy that Germany had produced in a century',[40] and he was proposing a new way of thinking about the organization of economic activity and its relation to society.[41]

In Eucken's view, the major obstacle to acquiring economic and social knowledge was what he called the 'great antinomy'. Economic knowledge, he said, had two fundamental, but inconsistent characteristics. It was historical in the sense that all data had a specific temporal locus and could not be fully understood outside that locus. On the other hand, such raw data could be meaningfully interpreted and accessible to scientific analysis only to the extent that a process of abstraction was employed to relate that data to other data through the use of 'general' principles. Viewing economic phenomena exclusively from either an historical or a theoretical perspective, Eucken claimed, necessarily distorted reality.

Yet, said Eucken, that is precisely what had happened in economic thought. Theoretical economists had paid little attention to facts, operating almost exclusively within their own intellectual models.[42] This tendency was strongest, he believed, in England, which had been providing much of the leadership in theoretical economics. The historical school that had reigned in Germany had gone to the other extreme, focusing on facts and paying little attention to theory. Both, therefore, were missing the point.

Eucken thus saw the integration of the theoretical and historical perspectives as opening a new era in economic thought and policy. He argued that in order to overcome the great antinomy, theory had to be used to abstract patterns from raw historical data and thus organize it and make it meaningful,

---

[39] Eucken, *Grundsätze*, 369.

[40] Hans O. Lenel et al., 'Vorwort', 40 *ORDO*, at viii (1989). For discussion, see, e.g., Hans O. Lenel, 'Walter Euckens "Grundlagen der Nationalökonomie" ', 40 *ORDO* 3 (1989).

[41] '[The *Grundlagen*] contained the development of a completely new basis for economic knowledge (*eines neuartigen nationalökonomischen Erkenntnisprogramms*)'. Meyer, 'Geschichte und Nationalökonomie', 31. For references to some of the intellectual influences on Eucken's thought, see Gerber, 'Constitutionalizing the Economy', 38–41.

[42] Eucken, *Grundlagen*, 27–37.

but that theory had to be derived from observation of historical fact and continuously tested against it. Many contemporaries felt that Eucken's work in
these areas was of great significance.[43]

The need to integrate theoretical and historical perspectives led Eucken and
his colleagues to call for another form of intellectual integration—between
legal and economic knowledge. Since economic phenomena occurred in an
institutional and normative context, economic knowledge for Eucken could
not be meaningfully dissociated from legal knowledge. The legal system provided the rules for the economic game, and thus one could not understand
economic processes without integrating knowledge of those rules.[44]

Yet, again, this is what had occurred in Western thought. As Eucken saw
it, economists had considered legal knowledge to be irrelevant to their enterprise, while legal scholars had failed to recognize the interaction between the
legal and economic systems. The result was that neither lawyers nor economists understood the economic-legal phenomena they purported to be interpreting.

Eucken's response to the need to integrate facts with theory and economic
with legal thought was a method he called 'thinking in orders' (*Denken in
Ordnungen*). It may have been his most distinctive and important contribution to postwar European thought.[45] As he put it, 'The perception
(*Erkenntnis*) of economic orders (*Ordnungen*) is the first step in understanding
economic reality'.[46] The basic idea was that beneath the complexity of economic data were fundamental ordering patterns (orders) and that only
through the recognition of these patterns could one penetrate this complexity
and understand the dynamics of economic phenomena.[47]

Eucken saw two fundamental 'orders'.[48] One he called the 'transaction
economy' (*Verkehrswirtschaft*) in which economic conduct was organized
through private, transactional decision-making. Here private enterprises generated their own plans on the basis of their evaluation of the incentives and
disincentives created by economic competition. The second was the centrally
administered economy (*Zentralverwaltungswirtschaft*) in which governmental

---

[43] For discussion, see, e.g., Ernst Heuss, ' "Grundlagen der Nationalökonomie" vor 50 Jahren und Heute', 40 *ORDO* 21 (1989).

[44] See generally Böhm, *Ordnung der Wirtschaft*, 107.

[45] See generally Hans-Günter Krüsselberg, 'Zur Interdependenz von Wirtschaftsordnung und Gesellschaftsordnung: Euckens Plädoyer für ein umfassendes Denken in Ordnungen', 40 *ORDO* 223 (1989).

[46] Eucken, *Grundlagen*, 58.

[47] An intellectual forerunner of ordoliberal thought in this area was the so-called '*Marktformenlehre*' (doctrine of market forms) that was developed primarily in the 1920s and 1930s and whose most influential advocate was Heinrich von Stackelberg. See, e.g., Heinrich von Stackelberg, *Marktform und Gleichgewicht* (Vienna, 1934). For discussion, see Fritz Holzwarth, *Ordnung der Wirtschaft durch Wettbewerb: Entstehung der Ideen der Freiburger Schule* 112–34 (Freiburg i.B., 1985).

[48] See Eucken, *Grundlagen*, 58.

commands organized economic activity according to criteria external to the economic system.[49]

Popular versions of this distinction became commonplace during the Cold War, but its contours were far less perceptible before that time. There had long been rather vague talk of differences between capitalism and socialism, but Eucken was the first—at least in Germany and arguably in all of Europe—to analyze systematically and in detail the systemic characteristics of these two *economic orders*.[50]

The impact of Eucken's analysis lay in this systemic focus. His 'orders' were constructs through which he sought to demonstrate that certain characteristics of economic systems were related to each other systemically—that is, they fit together such that the density of those characteristics in an actual economic system necessarily increased the capacity of that system to achieve its goals. For example, private property, the protection of economic freedom, and low barriers to entry into markets were individual characteristics of a transaction economy that tended to reinforce each other and thereby increase the effectiveness of the system as a whole.

A corollary to this analysis was that the intermingling of components from these two fundamentally incompatible 'orders' in an actual economic system *necessarily* impaired the functioning of that system. A transaction economy would be harmed, for example, by each instance of governmental intervention, and vice versa! The power of this insight can hardly be imagined from today's perspective, but at the time it had great impact.

As one observer put it, 'Morphology gave liberalism a new foundation'.[51] The perception of distinct and mutually incompatible 'orders' provided a new interpretation of the failures of the economy in the interwar period and a new basis for confidence in the market economy. For Eucken, the problems of the twentieth century were a consequence of failing to recognize these orders and their incompatibility. The introduction of command elements into the German and other economies in the wake of the First World War had gradually destroyed the market economy, he said, but no one had perceived what was happening.

2. The competitive order

For Eucken and his colleagues, the essence of the transaction economy was economic competition, because it allowed the system to function effectively.

---

[49] For detailed discussion, see Gernot Gutmann, 'Euckens Ansätze zur Theorie der Zentralverwaltungswirtschaft und die Weiterentwicklung durch Hensel', 40 *ORDO* 55 (1989).

[50] Ludwig von Mises was one of a few others who had taken preliminary steps in this direction. See Norbert Kloten, 'Zur Transformation von Wirtschaftsordnungen', 40 *ORDO* 99, 104–05 (1989).

[51] Bilger, *La Pensée*, 58.

Moreover, the higher the level of competition in the economy, the more effectively the system functioned, thus providing the many economic and non-economic benefits which the ordoliberals expected of such an economy.

Again, the sharpness of the concept is central to its impact. Eucken's concern was not with competition in the loose sense found in common usage, but with a specific form of competition, namely, 'complete' competition—that is, in brief, competition in which no firm in a market has power to coerce conduct by other firms in that market.[52] The concept was not new to Eucken, but he gave it a new function. He made it a guide to government policy and developed it as the lodestar of ordoliberal thought.

3. The concept of an economic constitution

The ordoliberals staked out further new territory by imbedding their analysis of economic phenomena in a political-legal context. It was here that the interplay of legal and economic thought had its greatest creative force. Relying on legal discourse, the ordoliberals added a 'constitutional' dimension to their analysis of economic problems. A community's political constitution and its choices in using law to implement that constitution, they said, must ultimately establish the characteristics of its economic system. Economic systems did not just 'happen'; they were 'formed' through political and legal decision-making. These fundamental choices determined a nation's 'economic constitution' (*Wirtschaftsverfassung*).

This concept of an economic constitution was the means by which the ordoliberals integrated legal and economic thought. As a perceptive French analyst of the Freiburg School has observed, 'With the concept of an economic constitution, the circle had the '*idée-force*' that catalyzed all their individual reflections, oriented all their work and made of them a truly new and original school'.[53]

The Freiburg School did not invent the term 'economic constitution'. It had been used during the 1920s,[54] generally referring loosely to the basic characteristics of an economic system. There was discussion during the Weimar

---

[52] The German term '*vollständiger Wettbewerb*' is often translated as 'perfect competition', but I here use the term 'complete competition' because, as Wernhard Möschel has pointed out, 'What counts for him [Eucken] is the absence of coercive power'. Wernhard Möschel, 'Competition Policy from an Ordo Point of View', in *German Neo-Liberals and the Social Market Economy* 157 n.16 (Alan T. Peacock & Hans Willgerodt, eds., New York, 1989). This reflects the difference in emphasis between the 'perfect competition' of neo-classical price theory and ordoliberal thought. For further discussion, see Fikentscher, II *Wirtschaftsrecht* 186–95.

[53] Bilger, *La Pensée*, 78–79.

[54] The earliest sustained use I have found is in Siegfried Tschierschky, *Wirtschaftsverfassung* (1924). Its underpinnings derive, however, from the Weimar Constitution. See Knut W. Nörr, 'Auf dem Wege zur Kategorie der Wirtschaftsverfassung: Wirtschaftliche Ordnungsvorstellungen im Juristischen Denken vor und nach dem Ersten Weltkrieg', in *Geisteswissenschaften zwischen Kaiserreich und Republik* 423–452 (Knut W. Nörr et al eds., Stuttgart, 1994).

period, for example, of the relative merits of 'capitalist' and 'socialist' economic constitutions. As they did with other key terms, however, the ordoliberals imbued this one with a new analytical precision and a new interpretive framework.

According to the ordoliberals, and here Franz Böhm's contributions were particularly influential,[55] an economic constitution is 'a comprehensive decision concerning the nature and form of the process of socio-economic cooperation'.[56] It is a political decision about the kind of economy a community wants in the same way as the political constitution represents basic decisions about the kind of political system a community wants. According to Böhm, 'Only a focus on this idea makes it possible to achieve truly dependable and cogent principles for the interpretation of parts of private and public law'.[57]

This concept of an economic constitution intertwined legal and economic perspectives and discourses. It turned the core idea of classical liberalism—that the economy should be divorced from law and politics—on its head by arguing that the characteristics and the effectiveness of the economy *depended* on its relationship to the political and legal systems. The ordoliberals recognized that fundamental political choices created the basic structures of an economic system.

4. *Ordnungspolitik*: the untranslatable soul of ordoliberalism

The choice of an economic constitution could only be effective, the ordoliberals said, where the legal system was structured to implement that constitutional choice. Where a political unit chose a transaction economy in its economic constitution, for example, that choice required that governmental policies be designed to create and maintain that system. This the ordoliberals called '*Ordnungspolitik*' (order-based policy),[58] and it was the soul of their program.

According to the ordoliberal conception of *Ordnungspolitik*, individual governmental decisions should flow from the principles embodied in the economic constitution and be constrained by those same principles. Where the economic constitution calls for a transaction economy, for example,

[55] For an analysis of Böhm's contributions to competition law thinking, see Christina Dümchen, *Zur Kartellrechtlichen Konzeption Franz Böhms* (Frankfurt a.M., 1980).

[56] Böhm, *Wettbewerb und Monopolkampf*, 107. Bohm relied here on ideas developed in the late 1920s by Carl Schmitt, a public law theorist who was extremely influential during the Weimar period (but who later employed his theoretical talents in the service of the Nazis). Schmitt defined constitution as a 'comprehensive decision (*Gesamtentscheidung*) concerning the nature and form of the political unit'. Carl Schmitt, *Verfassungslehre*, 20 (Munich, 1928).

[57] Böhm, *Ordnung der Wirtschaft*, at xix.

[58] This term is exceptionally difficult to render into English and other languages, because it depends so much on the ordoliberal thinking with which it is associated. The 'order' in 'order-based policy' is not 'order' merely for the sake of any form of ordering, but 'order' in the sense of Eucken's economic orders. That referent is not, however, apparent in English translation.

Ordnungspolitik demands that the legal system be configured so as to create and maintain the conditions of complete competition which would allow that type of economic system to function most effectively.

For the ordoliberals, this meant that economic knowledge had to be translated into normative language. In order to establish policy based on the economic constitution, Böhm wrote, 'The body of doctrine of classical economic philosophy had to be translated from the language of economics into the language of legal science'.[59] The idea was that economic science would describe the conditions of complete competition, and this information would provide the standards for legal decision-making.

This was the substantive dimension of *Ordnungspolitik*, but there was also a process dimension. In order for a transaction economy to achieve its goals, the governmental involvement must itself have certain characteristics and play certain roles. Above all, government could act only to implement the general norms or laws that derived from the economic constitution. Law would provide basic principles of economic conduct, and government officials would not have discretion to intervene in the economy except for the purpose of enforcing those principles.

This conception of the role of law is critical to the entire ordoliberal program. The ordoliberals emphasized that *Ordnungspolitik* did not permit discretionary governmental intervention in the economy, but required its opposite—legal principles that directed but also *constrained* government conduct! The constitutional dimension of their thought allowed them to call for law to create and maintain the basic structures of the economic system *without* authorizing governmental 'intervention' in the economy.

From a non-ordo perspective, this distinction between governmental 'intervention' and constitutional implementation seems suspect, because governmental action necessarily interferes with the economic system to the extent that it creates incentives and disincentives for economic conduct external to those produced by the market itself. One might assume, therefore, that the ordoliberal scheme inevitably creates a highly regulated economy with all the problems of discretion and uncertainty associated with high levels of regulation.

For the ordoliberals, however, there was no reason why constitutional discourse could not be applied to governmental conduct in the area of economic regulation just as it was to governmental conduct generally. If it is legitimate to ask whether particular governmental conduct conforms to the political constitution, it ought to be similarly legitimate to ask whether such conduct conforms to the economic constitution. Decisions about the legal environment of the market thus would be bound by the economic constitution in the same way as political decisions were subject to the political constitution. They

---

[59] Böhm, *Wettbewerb und Monopolkampf*, ix. See also Böhm, *Ordnung der Wirtschaft*, 54.

could not 'interfere' with the operations of the competitive system, because, by definition, they were consistent with that system.

Ordnungspolitik represented a transfer and adaptation of ideas from liberal political theory to economic policy. Its roots are in the theory of the *Rechtsstaat* or 'law-based state'.[60] Developed in the nineteenth century, this conception of the state focused on the dependability and certainty of the law as a bulwark against abuses of power. It was a means of establishing control over the discretionary power of the sovereign.

Central to this image of law is its neutrality and objectivity: the law has to be outside the discretionary power of those wielding governmental power. The state has to provide a basic level of 'legal security' by assuring that law is knowable, dependable and not subject to manipulation. The ordoliberals used these ideas as the basis for their concept of *Ordnungspolitik*.

5. The principle of indirect regulation

The ordoliberals referred to their conception of *Ordnungspolitik* as 'indirect regulation'. Government did not 'direct' the 'processes' of the economy. It merely established the 'forms' or structural conditions within which those processes could function effectively.[61] This distinction between process and form was fundamental to the ordoliberal conception of economic policy. Where governmental activity relating to the economy was not subject to the ordering function of an economic constitution, they said, it typically was beset by the problems of inconsistency and self-contradiction. The consequences of any individual action were likely to be counteracted by some other actions, and the result was likely to be inefficiency, confusion and, ultimately, economic chaos.[62] *Ordnungspolitik* combated these problems by requiring the organization of governmental action around the principles of the economic constitution.

The concept of indirect regulation was supported by both 'constitutive' and 'regulative' principles.[63] Constitutive principles were the fundamental principles of economic policy for a transaction economy. Their function was to establish the basic 'form' of the economy. For Eucken, they included the principles of monetary stability (the need to maintain a stable monetary unit), open markets, private property, contractual freedom, liability (legal responsibility for one's acts), and policy consistency (the need to avoid frequent

---

[60] See, e.g., Eucken, *Grundsätze*, 48–53. For a detailed discussion of the development of *Rechtsstaat* theory through the early period of ordoliberal thought, see Friedrich Darmstaedter, *Die Grenzen der Wirksamkeit des Rechtsstaates* (Heidelberg, 1930).

[61] See Böhm, *Ordnung der Wirtschaft*, 7–9.

[62] The ordoliberals often referred to this problem as '*Punktualismus*', which means, in effect, that the actions affected particular points (*Punkte*) in the economy without being organized into any coherent whole. See Eucken, *Grundsätze*, 251.

[63] Ibid., 253.

changes in economic policy).[64] Regulatory principles flowed from constitutive principles and were bound by them, but they were more specific and served to maintain the effectiveness of the constitutive principles. For example, the all-important principles of competition law were regulative principles that flowed primarily from the constitutive postulates of open markets and contractual freedom.

The ordoliberal program required a comprehensive view of a community's legal, political and economic systems. Ordoliberals repeatedly emphasized the need for an 'integrated policy perspective in which each individual decision had to be understood as part of a greater whole from which it received its meaning and effect'.[65] According to Eucken, 'All principles—the constitutive as well as the regulative—belong together. To the extent that economic policy is consistently based on them, a competitive order will be created and made operational. Every principle receives its meaning only in the context of the general blueprint of the competitive order'. Only thus could the program function effectively. Monetary, social, labor, and trade policy, for example, all had to flow from the same basic principles and support each other.

This conception of the roles of law in relation to the economy reflected the ordoliberals' deep distrust of the executive branch of government and their confidence in the legislative and judicial branches. In it, the legislature would make the fundamental decisions about the content of the economic constitution and translate the economic model into normative language. The judiciary then had the responsibility for assuring that specific governmental acts were consistent with these basic norms. The executive branch had little power in this scheme. Administrators were to follow the dictates of the legislature, and, in principle at least, there was minimal room for discretion.

The ordoliberal conception of *Ordnungspolitik* also envisioned a community with particular characteristics. The ordoliberals recognized that *Ordnungspolitik* could be effective only where the members of that community willingly supported it and actively co-operated in implementing it. In their view, economic freedom had its correlate in duty, and community members would have to voluntarily implement the principles they chose in their economic constitution if they wanted to reap the benefits that the ordoliberal program promised.[66]

6. The problem of the strong state

In order to accomplish their goals, the ordoliberals called for a strong state, and many have criticized this aspect of their program as an inevitable threat

---

[64] Ibid., 254–89.
[65] Ibid., 304. Eucken believed that US antitrust policy had been ineffective precisely because it had not been integrated in a broader policy framework. Ibid., 305.
[66] See, e.g., Eucken, *Grundsätze*, 350–54.

to economic freedom. For Eucken, Böhm and their colleagues, however, the experience of the Weimar period left no doubt that such a state was necessary. A weak state could be co-opted—as the Weimar state had been—by private economic interests and thus would be unable to create and maintain the conditions of competition. The ordoliberals were convinced that the economy needed the state to protect it, and they placed their full—perhaps inordinate—confidence in the capacity of the legal process to constrain the power of the state.

<h3 style="text-align:center">E. COMPETITION LAW AND ITS ROLES</h3>

The keystone of the ordoliberal program was a new type of law called 'competition law'. While all law relating to the economy should represent *Ordnungspolitik*, the ordoliberals assigned competition law the direct responsibility for creating and protecting the conditions of competition. According to a postwar German commentator, 'Ordoliberalism moved anti-monopoly policy to the center of an entire economic system'.[67] Monetary and other policies designed to foster competition would have little effect, ordoliberals argued, if firms could act in concert in setting prices or determining output, or if firms with economic power could use that power to foreclose opportunities for competition.

1. The ordoliberal conception of competition law

The ordoliberals rejected the administrative control measures that had been in vogue in the late 1920s as fundamentally flawed.[68] The idea of merely granting authority to the executive branch to combat cartels was doomed, they urged, because those being regulated were powerful enough to subvert the objectives of the regulators in favor of their own interests. Moreover, lacking a reliable conceptual framework and support from other similarly oriented policies, the regulators would have little chance of success.

The story that informed ordoliberal thought relating to competition law was the recurring self-destruction of economic freedom, particularly during the 1920s. For Eucken and his colleagues, history—particularly Weimar history—had demonstrated that competition tended to collapse, because enterprises preferred private (that is, contractual) regulation of business activities rather than competition, and because they were frequently able to acquire such high levels of economic power that they could eliminate competition.

The ordoliberals conceived competition law as a means of preventing this degeneration of the competitive process. Competition law would 'enforce'

---

[67] Moeller, 'Liberalismus', 225.
[68] See, e.g., Böhm, *Wettbewerb und Monopolkampf*, 363–70.

competition by creating and maintaining the conditions under which it would flourish! The model of complete competition would establish the general principles, and an independent monopoly office would enforce those principles. This was a fundamentally new conception that flowed from the conceptual framework of ordoliberalism. It was a particular application of *Ordnungspolitik* and rested on its theoretical underpinnings.

The model of complete competition provided the substantive standards for competition law, as it did for all *Ordnungspolitik*. In the competition law context, the complete competition standard demanded that law be used to prevent the creation of monopolistic power, abolish existing monopoly positions where possible and, where this was not possible, control the conduct of monopolies.

This conception of competition law focused attention on one core problem—private economic power.[69] From the ordoliberal perspective, such power necessarily threatened the competitive process, and the primary function of competition law was to eliminate it or at least prevent its harmful effects. The use of a broad conception of economic power as the primary structuring device is one of the features of German and European competition law thinking that most clearly distinguishes it from its analogues in US antitrust law.

2. Prohibiting monopoly

One component of competition law was directed at the structures of monopoly power. Monopoly should be prohibited, they argued, because its very existence distorted the competitive order. A firm or group of firms that had power over price or the power to hinder the performance of its rivals was structurally inconsistent with the complete competition standard. This prohibition was directed primarily at cartels and other agreements between competitors. Such agreements *created* the very power that threatened the competitive process and, therefore, had to be prohibited. The ordoliberals had witnessed the destructive influence of cartels on the German economy, polity and society during the Weimar period, and they considered a prohibition of cartel agreements to be necessary for the maintenance of a competitive economy.

Where a monopoly position was not based on agreement between competitors, the task of competition law was more complicated. Single firms could also acquire monopoly power, even where government policy maintained the basic conditions of competition. This could occur, for example, in cases of natural monopoly, such as utilities, where the market could not sustain more than one enterprise. It could also occur where one firm had won the

---

[69] Franz Böhm's pathbreaking article on this subject was published in 1928. See Böhm, 'Das Problem der privaten Macht'.

competitive battle and had acquired sufficient power to block or discourage attempts by rivals and potential rivals to compete with it.

Ordoliberals generally agreed that where single firms held monopoly power, this should also be eliminated where possible.[70] Competition law thus had to provide a means of requiring that firms divest themselves of components of their operations or otherwise eliminate their monopoly positions. This concept was a far more significant interference with private property than firms in Europe had experienced, except in wartime, and thus it was highly controversial. Moreover, its proponents tended to be vague about how it would work, in part because of the controversy and in part because they assumed that it would seldom be necessary to use the procedure.

3. Conduct control

Such divestiture would not be required, however, in cases of natural monopoly or where the monopoly position was based on a legally protected right (for example, a patent or copyright) or where divestiture would otherwise be impractical or entail economic waste. In such cases competition law was to provide a standard of conduct for such firms. It required that economically powerful firms act *as if* they were subject to competition—that is, as if they did not have such power.[71]

The idea was appealing. It promised—through a single objective legal mechanism—to limit the harms associated with *both* private economic power and state intervention. Application of the 'as-if' standard required that firms not engage in conduct that would not be available to them if they did not have monopoly power. They were to be limited, therefore, to conduct that was consistent with complete competition. They would not be allowed to use their power in ways harmful to competitors or to society in general.

According to the ordoliberals, the as-if standard would not create the danger of governmental intervention. It was conceived as an objectively applicable measure that in most cases would provide clear answers. The monopoly office would be authorized merely to apply this standard, and thus the law would not give discretionary power to regulators to intervene in the economy. The idea promised, therefore, to deal simultaneously with the dual evils of uncontrolled political power and of unrestrained economic power.

This standard found support in a legal distinction that was developed in the 1920s and continues to be central to German competition law. In applying the

---

[70] For Böhm's views, see Dümchen, *Zur Kartellrechtlichen Konzeption*, 80–84.

[71] Leonhard Miksch, a leading student of Walter Eucken, was chiefly responsible for elaborating and refining this idea. See, e.g., Leonhard Miksch, *Wettbewerb als Aufgabe: Grundsätze einer Wettbewerbsordnung* (2d. ed., Godesberg, 1947) and 'Die Wirtschaftspolitik des Als Ob', 105 *Zeitschrift für die gesamte Staatswissenschaft* 310 (1949). Not all ordoliberals were enthusiastic about the 'as-if' standard.

German statute against unfair competition (UWG) a leading scholar named
H. C. Nipperdey had perceived a distinction between 'performance competition' (*Leistungswettbewerb*) and 'impediment competition' (*Behinderungs-
wettbewerb*).[72] The former included conduct that made a firm's products
more attractive to consumers, typically by improving their characteristics or
lowering their prices, while the latter referred to conduct designed to impede
a rival's capacity to perform.

Franz Böhm and other ordoliberals borrowed this distinction and placed it
at the center of their new conception of competition law.[73] Performance competition was consistent with the competitive model, they said, because under
competitive conditions, performance improvement was the sole means by
which a firm could improve its profits. Where, however, a firm used its power
to impede the performance of a rival—for example, by excluding the rival
from the market—it was interfering with the competitive process and thus the
state should prevent such conduct. In effect, the as-if standard of conduct
prohibited impediment competition. Böhm's early work had focused on analyzing the characteristics of competition by economically powerful firms, and
he had identified a catalogue of types of conduct that represented 'impediment' or 'non-performance' competition.[74] These included, for example,
predatory pricing, boycotts and loyalty rebates. In each case, he considered
the conduct inconsistent with the as-if standard, because a firm would not be
able to engage in such practices unless it had monopolistic power.

4. The problem of oligopoly

There was little agreement among ordoliberals with regard to oligopoly situations in which a small number of firms dominated a market and, as a result,
could exercise power over rivals through consciously parallel conduct.
Leonhard Miksch argued that in this situation the government's only means
of opening the market and eliminating the oligopoly was to regulate the market, particularly through controls on prices.[75] This, he believed, would prevent large firms from using their collective dominance of the market to
eliminate competition from smaller firms.

This solution was, however, criticized by some ordoliberals as impracticable. Eucken considered it unnecessary, provided that the controls on monopolies were sufficiently strict. He believed that firms would not be likely to
engage in impediment competition if this would give them monopoly power
and thereby subject them to the highly restrictive as-if conduct standard.[76]

---

[72] H. C. Nipperdey, 'Wettbewerb und Existenzvernichtung', 28 *Kartell-Rundschau* 127 (1930).
[73] See, e.g., Böhm, *Wettbewerb und Monopolkampf*, 178.
[74] Böhm, ibid., 250–56 & 291–317.   [75] See Miksch, *Wettbewerb als Aufgabe*, 91.
[76] Eucken, *Grundsätze*, 298–99.

5. Application and enforcement

The procedural aspects of the ordoliberal conception of competition law often were as distinctive and original as their substantive counterparts. The ordoliberal vision required a specific institutional framework for creating, applying, and enforcing its substantive provisions. The legislature would enact a competition law based on the economic constitution, an independent monopoly office would assure compliance with that law, and the judiciary would supervise interpretation of the principles by the cartel office. The executive branch of government was to play virtually no role in this scheme.

The ordoliberals assigned an important, but comparatively simple, role to the legislature. It was to translate the economic principles embodied in the model of complete competition into normative terms. This meant drafting a statute that identified deviations from the competitive model as violations of legal norms. It thus implemented the 'economic constitution' by imbedding its principles in the legal system. In this role, the legislature had little discretion in fashioning a competition law, because once the constitutional decision in favor of the competitive 'order' had been made, the complete competition model itself generally dictated the provisions of the statute. This would also reduce the legislature's vulnerability to lobbying efforts.

An autonomous monopoly office was to have sole responsibility for enforcing competition law norms. It would investigate alleged violations of the statute, and it would have authority to take enforcement actions. This included, for example, invalidating cartel contracts and ordering that particular conduct be terminated, in some cases with the threat of fines for failure to comply. The actions of the office were to be subject to review by the regular courts for their conformity to the economic constitution. According to Eucken, 'In the situation of the modern industrial state this great, central figure of the monopoly office had to appear. Without it the competitive order and with it the modern *Rechtsstaat* is threatened. The monopoly office is as indispensable as the highest court'.[77]

Eucken did not expect the monopoly office to handle large numbers of cases, because he believed that a consistent and comprehensive *Ordnungspolitik* would keep markets open and reduce instances of monopoly creation to a minimum. He did, however, believe that the office would have to send a clear message to firms that it would enforce these regulative principles strictly.

The most important—and most controversial—characteristic of this office was its autonomy. It was not intended merely to be a part of the state bureaucracy and hence subject to political influence. The ordoliberals had witnessed during the Weimar period the capacity of cartels and large corporations to eviscerate attempts at control by putting political pressure on the executive

[77] Eucken, *Grundsätze*, 294.

branch, and they were convinced that this new office had to be autonomous in order to exclude such influences. They envisioned it as a quasi-judicial office and as such guided not by political considerations, but by the application of judicial methods to authoritative texts.

For the same reasons, the monopoly office would also have to be made into a strong institution. It would have to have significant enforcement authority, so that it could effectively demand compliance, and it would have to have the resources necessary to operate quickly and decisively and to attract and maintain personnel of the highest caliber. This issue was particularly important from the ordoliberal perspective, because in that view the function of the monopoly office was to apply objective criteria. It thus needed career specialists with a high level of economic and legal training, and they had to be largely protected from outside political or pecuniary influences.

The role envisioned for the judiciary in this scheme was limited, but important. The courts were to be available to assure that decisions of the monopoly office correctly interpreted the competition statute and conformed to the economic constitution ('the comprehensive constitutional choice').[78] Actions of the monopoly office were, therefore, made reviewable by the regular courts.

This element of reviewability by the regular courts was a means of emphasizing the autonomous role of law in the ordoliberal program. The actions of the monopoly office did not represent ordinary administrative action that administrative courts could review to determine whether discretion had been abused. The monopoly office was applying legal principles according to objective standards; there was not supposed to be any discretion. Consequently, the regular courts were the appropriate instances for reviewing the conformity of its acts with the economic constitution. Here again the image of the *Rechtsstaat* plays an important role in informing the contents of the ordoliberal program.

F. THE INTEGRITY OF THE ORDOLIBERAL PROGRAM

The ordoliberal program thus represented a well-developed and highly integrated whole. The theoretical and methodological premises generated a set of interpretive principles about the economic system, and these, in turn, were tied directly to the specific substantive and procedural proposals. It integrated sophisticated analytical contributions with practical policy initiatives.

The intellectual dimension of the program focused on what the ordoliberals considered a new method of understanding economic reality, and this methodological and philosophical component of the program broadened and deepened its impact and established a fundament on which to build an

---

[78] Ibid., 307.

integrated policy framework. Eucken's concept of '*Ordnung*' provided a construct that served to organize data about the economy and to elucidate the inter-relationships among the components of an actual economic system, and it promised new levels of certainty and dependability in dealing with the economy.

The introduction of legal-constitutional discourse added a critical dimension to these insights by recoding them as a framework for the articulation of policy. Laws determined the conditions and structures within which market processes operated, and thus economic knowledge had to be translated into the language of law. At the core of the ordoliberal program is the symbiotic character of the relationship between legal and economic processes.

The program's policy dimension was thus directly integrated with its intellectual foundations, and the concept of an 'economic constitution' was the primary integrative tool. Its implementation required a combination of careful 'scientific' analysis of the economy, community participation in the choices based on this knowledge, and the translation of those choices into legal norms and institutional structures.

Competition law was the institutional anchor for this program, and it was also tightly interwoven with the theoretical component of the system and with the overall constitutional framework. Its role was to assure that firms did not create monopoly power or use it to distort the competitive system, and thus its substantive principles were emanations of ordoliberal economic insights. Competition law's roles were tightly circumscribed by the principles of the economic constitution, however, so that the legal regime did not generate opportunities for government to interfere in the economy. According to the ordoliberals, competition law could only be effective where it was part of the larger framework of '*Ordnungspolitik*'. While emphasizing that competition law was necessary as part of an overall framework of economic policy, Eucken continually warned that it could not stand alone and that by itself it would be of little or no value.

The exceptional degree of integration in the ordoliberal program between intellectual and policy dimensions, and between legal and economic processes, is impressive by any measure. It was facilitated, and perhaps made possible, by the unique situation in which a small band of intellectuals managed to operate for years without the need to make political or doctrinal compromises or even to consider fitting their ideas into the existing political and economic framework. This situation allowed them to develop a remarkably comprehensive and tightly integrated theoretical perspective and concomitant policy language, and this high level of integration may have played a role in the postwar success of the program. The ordoliberals did not offer an assortment of recipes from which a postwar regime could pick and choose a few elements. They argued that such a regime would have to take the entire program—from intellectual perspective to policy prescriptions.

G. ORDOLIBERALISM AND THE SHAPING OF MODERN GERMANY

When the war did end, there seemed little likelihood that ordoliberal ideas would become influential. Throughout Europe, liberalism had been so thoroughly discredited that few wished to be associated with it. Socialist solutions had captured the public imagination and/or the fancy of intellectuals. Rage at the governments whose conduct had caused such havoc during the preceding decades and the desire for increased access to political and economic power fueled this enthusiasm. In Germany, in addition, the importance of the '*Volk*' and the excoriation of individualist values that had dominated thought for more than a decade generated a predisposition for collective solutions in many social groups.

Some form of socialism thus seemed all but inevitable in Germany.[79] The Marxist socialism of the Social Democratic Party had a solid base of support in the working class in many areas, and many of its leaders from the pre-Nazi period had returned from exile to provide leadership.[80] Christian socialism also had strong support. The church as an institution seemed to promise not only material support, but also moral strength during a period when both were in great need, and socialism based on Christian values became popular, particularly in Roman Catholic areas.

In this context, members of the Freiburg School emerged from the shadows in which they had operated for over a decade and quickly found themselves at center stage. The US military government sought to develop an economic policy that would both minimize government economic planning and eliminate cartels, and members of the Freiburg School presented a coherent plan for achieving these goals. In addition, they were among the few qualified Germans who were not tainted by ties to Nazism, and thus they met the rigorous US denazification standards. As a result, many members of the group soon assumed leadership positions in German self-government. Leonhard Miksch, for example, was a director of economic policy planning in the bizonal administration,[81] and ordoliberals are reported to have constituted more than 50 per cent of the members of the Academic Advisory Council (*Wissenschaftlicher Beirat*) that was formed in 1947 to give advice to the government and that had great influence on the development of policy.[82]

The ordoliberals began to campaign for their program almost immediately after the end of the war. They poured out an extraordinary spate of books,

---

[79] See generally Edgar Salin, 'Wirtschaft und Wirtschaftslehre nach zwei Weltkriegen', 1 *Kyklos* 26 (1947) and Blum, *Soziale Marktwirtschaft*, 13–38.

[80] See, e.g., Dieter Klink, *Vom Antikapitalismus zur Sozialistischen Marktwirtschaft: Die Entwicklung der Ordnungspolitischen Konzeption der SPD von Erfurt (1891) bis Bad Godesberg (1959)* at 65–134 (Hanover, 1965).

[81] See Gerold Ambrosius, *Die Durchsetzung der sozialen Marktwirtschaft in Westdeutschland 1945–1949* at 114 (Stuttgart, 1977).

[82] See Bilger, *La Pensée*, 211.

pamphlets, and articles directed primarily at German intellectual and political leaders and intended to demonstrate the need for their program.[83] In 1948, for example, Eucken and Böhm together founded the *ORDO* journal, which became highly influential as a forum for debate about economics and economic policy.

Many ordoliberals also pursued their goals on the popular level. For example, perhaps the leading national newspaper of the period, the *Frankfurter Allgemeine Zeitung*, was controlled by ordoliberals, and it effectively disseminated ordoliberal principles.[84] Members of the group also spoke widely to numerous groups on behalf of their program, propagating their ideas to whomever would listen. Fortunately, many of them knew how to present their message in a form that made it accessible to the general population. Franz Böhm, for example, also played the role of politician as a member of the *Bundestag* for two terms (1953–61).

1. Occupation dynamics

The special circumstances of the postwar period provided the ordoliberals with exceptional opportunities to propagate their ideas and put them into practice. The Nazi regime had been crushed, and there was widespread recognition of the need for fundamental changes. Reconstruction was called for, and the ordoliberals were among the few in Germany in a position to provide a well-developed program for such reconstruction. According to Hayek, 'How fortunate and valuable [Eucken's] quiet impact had been even during the National Socialist period became clear only after its collapse, as the circle of his friends and students in Germany emerged as the most important support for economic reason'.[85] Moreover, by 1947, economic policy authority for the British and American zones of occupation had been unified under US leadership, and the strong market-orientation of United States officials led them to provide institutional backing for ordoliberal ideas.[86]

The rupture of co-operation between the Soviet Union and the other occupation authorities that led to the 'Cold War' further intensified United States support for ordoliberal proposals, as economic structure and policy quickly became part of the East-West conflict. The United States sought to demonstrate the superiority of its free-market-based social system through the success of such a system in Germany.[87] This dynamic also impelled efforts to make the German test case as 'pure' an example as possible of a capitalist

[83] For a review of this literature, see Ernst-Wolfram Dürr, *Ordoliberalismus und Sozialpolitik* 13–15 (Winterthur, 1954).
[84] Bilger, *La Pensée*, 269.
[85] Friedrich A. von Hayek, 'Die Überlieferung der Ideale der Wirtschaftsfreiheit', 31 *Schweizer Monatshefte* 333, 337 (1951).
[86] See generally Blum, *Soziale Marktwirtschaft*, 184–215.   [87] See ibid., 182–84.

economy, on the theory that the 'purer' it was, the stronger the proof that the market economy was superior to its socialist competitor.

These efforts of the ordoliberals soon achieved success on the intellectual level. Within a few years after the end of the war, ordoliberal methods, ideas, and values had become the starting point for most serious thinking about economic policy. High-ranking government officials and academics in these areas (the overlap between these two groups was significant) generally had accepted the central notions of ordoliberalism.

2. The road to political success

In the longer term, however, the issue was whether these ideas would find broad-based support within the German population and, in particular, within the emerging political parties. In the western zones of occupation, political activity was allowed to resume soon after war's end. Parties emerged or re-emerged in 1946 in most areas, and elected assemblies with limited rights were formed there by 1947. It was in these parties that the future of Germany would be shaped.

Many of the central elements of the ordoliberal program were eventually successful on this level as well, and many of them achieved enormous influence on the evolution of modern Germany as part of a broader program known as the 'social market economy'. This program, as originally developed by Alfred Müller-Armack,[88] included central components of the ordoliberal program such as the concepts of 'economic constitution' and *Ordnungspolitik*, and it emphasized the need for a law to protect the process of competition.[89] He imbedded these ideas, however, in an idiom that placed greater emphasis on social values and concerns. For him, the economic benefits of *Ordnungspolitik* were valuable in themselves, even necessary, but his focus was on their roles in unifying and integrating German society.

The social market economy became a political program in the context of the evolution of the Christian Democratic party (CDU).[90] This party emerged during the postwar period as the primary representative of the middle class and of Catholic workers. Immediately after the war, Christian socialism was the prevailing credo within the party, and during 1946 and 1947 a

[88] For discussion of Müller-Armack and his roles and ideas, see Christian Watrin, 'Alfred Müller-Armack: 1901–1978', in *Kölner Volkswirte und soziale Wissenschaftler* 39 (Christian Watrin, ed., Cologne, 1988). For description and analysis of the development of social market economy ideas, see Alfred Müller-Armack, *Genealogie der sozialen Marktwirtschaft* (Bern, 1974) and A. J. Nicholls, *Freedom with Responsibility: The Social Market Economy in Germany 1918–1963* (Oxford, 1994).

[89] See, e.g., Müller-Armack, ibid., 29.

[90] See generally Geoffrey Pridham, *Christian Democracy in Western Germany* (New York, 1977) and Arnold J. Heidenheimer, *Adenauer and the CDU* (The Hague, 1960).

struggle ensued within the party to define a platform that appealed to both the middle and working classes.[91]

Under these circumstances, the concept of the social market economy appealed to many leaders of the CDU. At the very least, it was a promising political symbol that in three words appealed to those interested in the market economy, those concerned about receiving a fair share of the social product, and all who sought to unite and integrate the nation. Moreover, the substantive elements of the program promised the prosperity that all considered essential, while emphasizing the politically attractive message that this had to be done in the context of social improvement for all members of society.

The decisive event in the success of the social market economy occurred in 1948. In the midst of the severe economic difficulties of the reconstruction period, Ludwig Erhard—the highest official in German self-government, a member of the CDU and an ardent and vocal supporter of ordoliberal and social market economy ideas[92]—took an extraordinary step. Without the required formal approval of the US authorities (though with tacit support from the US commander General Lucius Clay) he eliminated virtually overnight most rationing and price controls in Germany.[93]

At first, many observers saw this bold move as unlikely to succeed and probably foolhardy. Erhard was, for example, heavily criticized for the inflation that followed his termination of price controls. For several months it seemed that Erhard's critics might be right.

But Erhard's gamble did work.[94] By the end of the first year the economic situation had changed dramatically. Prices had stabilized, and employment, profits, and investment had shown impressive advances. This began a period of continued growth and improvement that has lasted with few interruptions until very recently. The so-called 'German miracle' had begun.

The success of Erhard's action soon generated widespread support for his party and enthusiasm for his social market economy ideas. In 1949 the CDU adopted many of the central principles of the social market economy in its 'Düsseldorf platform' (*Düsseldorfer Leitsätze*),[95] and some version of those ideas has been part of the CDU program ever since. This was particularly important, because the CDU was the governing party in western Germany from then until 1966, and thus those principles were the primary economic

[91] See, e.g., Bilger, *La Pensée*, 248–63, and Rolf Wenzel, *Adenauer und die Gestaltung der Wirtschafts- und Sozialordnung im Nachkriegsdeutschland* 38–108 (Flensburg, 1983).

[92] Erhard had spent the Nazi years as an economics professor in Nürnberg, where he became a supporter of the ideas of the Freiburg School. For discussion of Erhard's thought and the formative influences on it, see Christoph Heusgen, *Ludwig Erhards Lehre von der Sozialen Marktwirtschaft* (Bern, 1981).

[93] See generally, e.g., Henry C. Wallich, *Mainsprings of the German Revival* 113–52 (New Haven, 1955).

[94] For discussion, see generally 'Symposium: Currency and Economic Reform—West Germany After World War II', 135 *Zeitschrift für die gesamte Staatswissenschaft* 301–404 (1979).

[95] Blum, *Soziale Marktwirtschaft*, 280.

policy guidelines in Germany for almost two decades. When the Federal Republic of Germany (FRG) was established in 1949, Konrad Adenauer of the CDU was named its first chancellor, and Ludwig Erhard became its minister of economics, a post he held until 1963, when he replaced Adenauer as chancellor.

Erhard interpreted Germany's economic successes during this period as a direct result of applying social market economy ideas, especially those most closely associated with ordoliberalism.[96] He repeatedly and forcefully propagated this interpretation, and his personal popularity and influence over the development of German economic policy gave that interpretation massive impact. He ascribed particular importance to the concept of the economic constitution as a means of structuring the relationship between government and the economy, and he viewed competition law as vital to the success of the social market economy.[97]

H. FREIBURG AND EUROPE

Scholars generally have paid little attention to ordoliberalism's influence outside Germany. In the early postwar period, in particular, this was tied to ordoliberalism's German origins. Although ordoliberal thought was antithetical to Nazism and although the ordoliberals themselves often were victims of the Nazi regime, they were still German in a world in which there was much resentment toward 'things German'. In recent years the disincentive to studying these ordoliberal influences has been the political dynamic of the process of European unification, which impedes recognition of national influences on this process. The identification of ideas or programs with particular Member States is generally regarded as likely both to increase resistance to such ideas and to interfere with Europeanization, and this creates a powerful incentive to avoid such identification. As a result, I can do little more than sketch the outlines of ordoliberal influence outside of Germany. Intellectual and political factors were intertwined in spreading and deepening this influence, but it is useful to separate the two strands of the process for analytical purposes.

1. Intellectual reception

Neo-liberals living outside Germany during the war prepared the way for the rapid spread of these ideas outside Germany after the war. The ideas spread

---

[96] See, e.g., Ludwig Erhard, *Prosperity through Competition* (New York, 1958). '. . . the economic policy shaped into the mid-1960s by Ludwig Erhard, was quite consciously pursued as *Ordnungspolitik*'. Heuss, ' "Grundlagen der Nationalökonomie" ', 23.

[97] For discussion, see Heusgen, *Ludwig Erhards Lehre*, 144–238.

principally along networks established by Röpke, Hayek and others. Röpke had actively promoted his brand of ordoliberal thought from his base in Switzerland, and his extensive journalistic activities achieved a wide following on both the popular and intellectual levels in many areas of Europe. In particular, he had a coterie of friends and supporters in the media and in government in England, France and Italy.[98] Beginning early in the 1930s, Friedrich von Hayek had preached his neo-liberal message from the London School of Economics. He had there become an important figure in the social sciences,[99] publishing widely in English, and helping to establish that institution as a major center for neo-liberal thought.

During the immediate postwar period, Röpke and Hayek, in particular, continued to use their respective bases to influence European thought. For example, in 1947 Hayek gathered a group of leading economists and politicians from many European countries to a conference on Mont Pelerin, Switzerland. From this meeting developed the Mont Pelerin Society, which has been an influential force in maintaining neo-liberal and particularly Hayekian ideas. As soon as postwar conditions in Germany permitted them to travel, Eucken, Böhm and other ordoliberals joined this proselytizing activity, lecturing and participating in seminars throughout Europe and the United States. Walter Eucken died on a lecture tour in England in 1950.

These activities not only disseminated neo-liberal influence after the war, but also helped to create the conditions for their acceptance. In particular, they highlighted the contrast between neo-liberal ideas and the ideas of the Nazi regime. In a sense, they helped 'cleanse' these ideas of potential associations with the Nazi regime, fostering the perception that they represented a common European front against totalitarianism and the recent past.

By the early 1950s, German neo-liberal ideas were being discussed in academic (economic) circles in several European countries. In France, for example, numerous scholarly analyses of German neo-liberalism were written by influential economists in the 1950s.[100] Raymond Barre, later to become a leading economics professor in France and still later Prime Minister, wrote one of the earliest scholarly articles on ordoliberalism in 1952.[101] In Italy, the

---

[98] Bilger, *La Pensée*, 96–97.

[99] See generally Kurt R. Leube, 'Friedrich A. von Hayek zum 90. Geburtstag', 40 *ORDO* xxi (1989).

[100] See, e.g., Jacques Bertrand, 'La Notion d'Ordre Économique et ses Possibilités d'Utilisation', 31 *Revue D'Histoire Économique et Sociale* 152 (1953); Jean Meynaud, 'Pouvoir Politique et Pouvoir Économique', *Revue Économique* 925 (1958); and Jacques Cros, *Le Néo-Libéralisme: Étude Positive et Critique* (Paris, 1951). Note that the discussion in France tended to focus more on the work of Wilhelm Röpke than on that of the Freiburg School. See Bilger, *La Pensée*, 6.

[101] Raymond Barre, 'L'Analyse économique au service de la Science et de la Politique Économique', 8 *Critique* 331 (1952) (a review essay on the English translation of Eucken's *Grundlagen der Nationalökonomie*). As Prime Minister in 1977, Barre was the impetus behind a significant strengthening of French competition law.

economist Luigi Einaudi maintained an important neo-liberal school in Turin that had ties to Wilhelm Röpke. These economists' channels carried German neo-liberal ideas throughout Europe, often intermingling them with the neo-liberal ideas of the American Walter Lippman in the process.[102]

2. Ordoliberals and European unification

The main vehicle for disseminating the ordoliberal version of neo-liberalism outside of Germany has been, however, the process of European unification. Through their influence on thought and institutions in the European Communities, these ideas have acquired a degree of dispersion and a level of force that they are unlikely to have acquired in any other way.

Ordoliberal ideas suffused the process of European unification at its earliest stages and its highest levels. The leading German representatives in the founding of the European Communities generally were closely associated with ordoliberalism, or at least shared an appreciation of it. Walter Hallstein, for example, was one of the founders of the European Communities and the first president of the European Commission. He had been a law professor in Germany and a friend of Franz Böhm and Heinrich Kronstein. He became associated with the ordoliberals during the 1940s, acquiring a high regard for the ideas of Walter Eucken.[103] Many of his views on the role of law in shaping the future of European institutions clearly reflect ordoliberal ideas, and he actively propagated and pursued these ideas during the formative period of the European Community. Another key figure with strong ties to ordoliberalism was Hans von der Groeben, one of the two principal drafters of the so-called 'Spaak Report', the document on which the Rome treaty was based.[104] Finally, Müller-Armack, the creator and a chief proponent of social market economy ideas, was himself responsible as an official of the German government for influencing the development of European Community economic policy during its formative years.[105]

The primary political impetus for establishing a European common market did not come from the ordoliberals, but ordoliberal thought provided a

[102] For discussion of this intermingling in France, see Cros, *Le Néo-Libéralisme*, 167–222.

[103] For discussion of Hallstein and his roles in European integration, see *Walter Hallstein: Der Vergessene Europäer?* (Wilfried Loth et al eds., Bonn, 1995) and Theo M. Loch, 'Einleitung und biographische Skizze', in *Wege nach Europa: Walter Hallstein und die junge Generation* 7–47 (Theo M. Loch, ed., Andernach am Rhein, 1967). Hallstein's speeches and writings in relation to the Community are replete with ordoliberal concepts and references. See, e.g., Walter Hallstein, *Europe in the Making* 28 (Charles Roetter, tr., New York, 1972) ('What the Community is integrating is the role of the state in establishing the framework within which economic activity takes place'.)

[104] See generally Hans-Jürgen Küsters, *Die Gründung der Europäischen Wirtschaftsgemeinschaft* 135–60 (Baden-Baden, 1982).

[105] For his own discussion of his roles in the development of Community thought and institutions, see Alfred Müller-Armack, *Auf dem Weg nach Europa* (Tübingen, 1971).

comprehensive and theoretically-grounded set of ideas that helped give legal and institutional form to general political goals. It supplied a framework for the process of European integration that has been highly influential among most Germans involved in European unification and has influenced other leaders as well.

Ordoliberal ideas were well suited to the goal of pursuing European integration through creation of a common market. This task called for establishing a new community centered on the operation of a market economy, for example, and this corresponded to the central objective of ordoliberal thought. This community was to be based on a voluntary agreement, and that agreement could play a role something like the one played in ordoliberal thought by the concept of an economic constitution.[106] Thus the body of ordoliberal thought could be seen as directly applicable to the problems of this new European community, and the German representatives in the creation and early structuring of the European Community tended to see the process in that light.[107]

Ordoliberal influence has been particularly important in relation to competition law. As we shall see, Germans were major supporters of the inclusion of competition law provisions in the Rome Treaty. The structure of the two main competition law provisions of the Rome Treaty (Articles 85 and 86) also closely tracked ordoliberal thought and bore little resemblance to anything to be found in other European competition laws at the time. While the prohibition of cartel agreements had analogues in US antitrust law, the concept of prohibiting abuse of a market-dominating position was an important new development that was particularly closely associated with ordoliberal and German competition law thought and very different from the discourse of US law.

Many ordoliberals also emerged as leaders in the competition law area. The ordoliberal Hans von der Groeben was, for example, appointed the first Commissioner for Competition Policy of the European Commission, and the Director General of the competition directorate has customarily been German and thus necessarily imbued, at least in the early years of the Community, with ordoliberal thought.

* * *

[106] The interpretation of the treaty as a 'constitution' has channeled the evolution of the Community, and this interpretation undoubtedly owes much to ordoliberal thought. See, e.g., Hans von der Groeben, 'Der gemeinsame Markt als Kern und Motor der Europäischen Gemeinschaft', in *Europa Ringt um seine Wirtschaftsverfassung* (Festschrift für Karl-Heinz Narjes) 19, 30 (Ernst-Joachim Mestmäcker, ed., Bonn, 1984) and Manfred Zuleeg, 'Die Wirtschaftsverfassung der Europäischen Gemeinschaften', in *Wirtschaftspolitische und Gesellschaftspolitische Ordnungsprobleme der Europäischen Gemeinschaft* 73 (Schriftenreihe des Arbeitskreises Europäische Integration e.V., Würzburg, 1978).

[107] See, e.g., Ernst-Joachim Mestmäcker, 'Auf dem Wege zu einer *Ordnungspolitik* für Europa', in *Eine Ordnungspolitik für Europa* (Festschrift für Hans von der Groeben) 9 (Ernst-Joachim Mestmäcker, et al eds., Baden-Baden, 1987).

Ordoliberals and their ideas have played an important role in shaping German and European thought and institutions during the last half century. Without an appreciation of ordoliberal concepts and the architecture of ordoliberal thought, much of the discourse about economic policy in Germany—and to some extent in the European Community—cannot be understood and is likely to be misunderstood.

The ordoliberals redefined the tradition of economic liberalism and in so doing helped to resuscitate it. They articulated a new version of liberalism in which law was a necessary companion of the market that transformed the market from a source of social divisiveness into a tool for social integration. In this version of liberalism, the market was necessary, but not sufficient. The economy needed to be imbedded in a constitutional-legal framework that would both protect it and help integrate society around it. Competition law was at the center of this project.

VIII

Competition Law and Germany's Social Market Economy

While most European countries reacted to postwar conditions by creating competition law systems that were, at least initially, little more than minor components of economic policy, Germany moved in a new direction that would fundamentally alter the path of competition law in Europe. In 1957 the Federal Republic created a competition law system that was to play a new role and operate on a different set of principles. Its role was 'constitutional'—to promote basic values and protect fundamental rights, and it was to operate at least as much on juridical as on administrative principles.

A. POSTWAR GERMANY: THE CONTEXT OF A NEW DIRECTION

Germany's radical change of course occurred under the influence of defeat and military occupation and is difficult to imagine without those circumstances. The destruction of the war combined with military occupation to force change, but for many, these factors also provided an opportunity for change. For them, prewar economic policies had contributed to the disaster of the Second World War, and they sought a new legal framework for economic conduct in order to avoid the mistakes of the past.

The economic devastation at the end of the Second World War was far greater than that caused by World War I. Most major German cities lay in ruins, productive capacity had been heavily damaged, and for years there were severe shortages of raw materials, housing and food that made Germans dependent on foreign support for their survival. The country's economic infrastructure had to be rebuilt, and this process of rebuilding lasted for about a decade.[1] The destruction of cities and plants did not destroy the economic system or the values and expectations on which it was based, but uncertainty combined with the interruption of existing patterns to provide a window of opportunity to alter its mode of operation.

The window would not long remain open. At least in the Western zones of occupation (and we will only be referring to these) German industry recon-

---

[1] For discussion of the economic situation in the postwar period, see Herbert Giersch, Karl-Heinz Paqué & Holger Schmieding, *The Fading Miracle: Four Decades of Market Economy in Germany* 16–44 (Cambridge, 1994).

stituted itself quickly, and by the end of the decade industrial production had exceeded prewar levels. Moreover, the same firms owned or managed by many of the same people were soon producing many of the same types of goods as they had during the Weimar period and the Second World War, and they naturally sought to continue operating according to the same basic principles.

The question was whether political decisions would intervene to change those patterns of operation. The occupation of Germany represented another 'window of opportunity'. With the unconditional surrender of Germany in 1945, the allies became the 'supreme authority' on German soil, and they thus effectively controlled major national-level political and legal decisions and were in a position to alter the legal framework of business.[2] Although the occupation authorities began returning authority to the reconstituted organs of indigenous government in the late 1940s, Germany did not regain full sovereignty until 1955, and then only as a divided country, having been separated into a Soviet-controlled German Democratic Republic and a western-oriented Federal Republic of Germany.

The opportunities for the allies to institute fundamental change were, however, limited by political realities. Occupation authorities did not seek to eliminate domestic political organizations and initiatives, but to assure that they did not take authoritarian forms. Parties were allowed to reconstitute themselves soon after the end of the war, and by 1946 there were elections for posts in institutions that gradually acquired more extensive political roles.[3] The occupation authorities recognized that the ultimate success of their efforts would depend on what happened when the Germans again controlled their own destiny, and from about 1947 they generally sought to play constructive roles—to fashion Germany as a future ally. With the development of the Cold War and the beginning of the Korean war, this 'constructive' emphasis increased.

A key factor in introducing major changes in the way economic life was organized and conducted in the new Federal Republic was the continuity of leadership in the economic policy area. As we have seen, from the time that the Republic was created in 1949 until 1966 it was governed by the liberal-conservative Christian Democratic Union (CDU) and its sister party from the state of Bavaria, the Christian Social Union (CSU).[4] Not only did the same coalition govern for seventeen years, but there was extraordinary continuity in the political leadership, particularly in regard to economic policy. Konrad Adenauer of the CDU was chancellor until 1963, and during this period

[2] For discussion, see John Gimbel, *The American Occupation of Germany 1945–1949* (Stanford, 1968).
[3] Hans Fenske, *Deutsche Parteiengeschichte: Von den Anfängen bis zur Gegenwart* 220–54 (Paderborn, 1994).
[4] For discussion of this period, see, e.g., Kurt Sontheimer, *Die Adenauer-Ära* (Munich, 1991).

economic policy was in the hands of his economics minister, Ludwig Erhard. When Adenauer left office in 1963 Erhard became his successor. This meant that Erhard was in charge of economic policy for almost twenty years (from 1947 until 1966, when he resigned as chancellor).

B. ALLIED DECARTELIZATION LAWS AND THEIR INFLUENCE

In the shadow of the occupation, the Germans drafted a new competition law, and we will examine how the occupation affected the gestation of that law. First, however, we need to look briefly at the so-called decartelization laws that the allies enacted during the occupation. Here our goal is to identify their roles in the evolution of competition law in Germany and correct some misperceptions about those roles.

As the allies considered postwar policies at Potsdam in 1945, a central theme was the destruction of German war potential. This meant, at the very least, breaking up industrial 'giants' such as IG Farben. Some occupation officials, such as the United States' Hans Morgenthau, wanted completely and permanently to 'de-industrialize' Germany, but it soon became clear that the idea of turning Germany into an agrarian country was impracticable, at best. As tensions with the Soviet Union increased in the late 1940s and the potential value of Germany as an ally increased, the allies rejected radical deindustrialization solutions in favor of laws designed with the more limited objective of preventing the reconcentration of economic power.[5]

These laws reflected the view widely held by occupation officials (in particular US officials) that Hitler's easy access to heavily concentrated and cartelized industries had aided his consolidation of power and encouraged his military aggression. By combating concentration and cartelization, the allies hoped to eliminate these threats without actually preventing or retarding German reconstruction.[6] In addition, US officials believed that an effective antitrust law based on the US model would be a powerful support for democratization efforts in Germany. By enacting such laws during the occupation period they hoped to demonstrate their value.

The US and British decartelization laws that went into effect in 1947 were virtually identical.[7] The title of the US law (Law No. 56 of the military government) was 'Prohibition of Excessive Concentration of German Economic

---

[5] See generally Heinrich-Karl Bock & Heinz Korsch, 'Decartellization and Deconcentration in the West German Economy Since 1945', in *Antitrust Laws: A Comparative Symposium* 138–53 (Wolfgang Friedmann, ed., Toronto, 1956).

[6] For discussion of the circumstances, see generally Rüdiger Robert, *Konzentrationspolitik in der Bundesrepublik—Das Beispiel der Entstehung des Gesetzes gegen Wettbewerbsbeschränkungen* 97–102 (Berlin, 1976).

[7] See *Law No. 56: Prohibition of Excessive Economic Concentration of Economic Power, Text und Erläuterung* (Wilhelm Remmert, ed., Frankfurt a.M., 1947).

Power'. It provided that 'Excessive concentrations of German economic power, whether within or without Germany and whatever their form or character . . . are prohibited, their activities are declared illegal and they shall be eliminated [except in cases of special approval by the military government]. . .'. 'Excessive concentrations of power' included,

Cartels, combines, syndicates, trusts, associations or any other form of understanding or concerted undertaking between persons, which have the purpose or effect of restraining, or of fostering monopolistic control of, domestic or international trade or other economic activity, or of restricting access to domestic or international markets. . . .

This was the basic substantive provision of the text, which also contained guidelines for its application by the military government's implementing agency. The decartelization laws were in effect, first as occupation laws and later on a transitional basis as laws of the Federal Republic, until they were replaced by the new German competition law on January 1, 1958.[8]

The special circumstances of the occupation make it difficult to assess the role and impact of such laws. German firms did not revert to the extensive cartelization practices of the previous decades, and one might be tempted to suppose (as many have) that the decartelization laws played a key role in changing patterns of conduct. These laws were, however, only one of several factors that hindered such a development. Far more important was the political fact that occupation officials would not accept the continued existence of the kinds of cartels that had existed before the war. They had made and announced that political decision, and they had the power and authority to enforce it—whether by formal legislation or otherwise. At the very least, the decartelization laws operated against the backdrop of the extensive power and authority of the occupation officials.

These laws did influence conduct. Large firms and their advisors did have to learn about them and pay attention to them. Through them, therefore, a small group of German lawyers and business leaders gained experience with a US-style competition law, and that experience was undoubtedly important in the development of thought about a German competition law statute.

The role of these decartelization laws in the shaping of German competition law should not, however, be overestimated. Some have assumed that they were the model for the German competition statute that was enacted in 1957 or even that they 'evolved into' that statute. These assumptions are highly misleading for understanding the development of competition law in Germany.

The decartelization laws clearly did not 'become' the new German competition law in the sense that the laws were identical or even similar, as even a

---

[8] See Alfred Gleiss & Wolfgang Fikentscher, 'Weitergeltung des Dekartellierungsrechts', 1955 *Wirtschaft und Wettbewerb* 525 (1955).

cursory look at the texts reveals. The decartelization laws were little more than a general normative provision (albeit with subsequent regulations), whereas, as we shall see, German competition law was a conceptually much more sophisticated text rooted in German conceptions of the role and form of legislation.

Moreover, in the long battle over the shape of the German competition law, the decartelization laws did not play a central role. They were not referred to as a model for the new law, and, at least in the legislative debates, they were seldom used as a reference point for discussion. Although experience with these laws undoubtedly influenced some of the participants in those debates, the influence of these laws on the political and drafting decisions regarding the new statute appears to have been limited.

In addition, the laws were often not strictly enforced, and, therefore, few lawyers or businessmen knew much about them or had occasion to consult them. Nor did they become part of German legal culture, retaining for many 'the odor of an imposed system'?[9] Finally, they did not introduce German decision-makers to the idea of a strong, prohibition-based competition law; as we have seen, this had been done by the ordoliberals, whose ideas were already at the center of discussions of competition law.

C. THE GESTATION OF THE GWB

The impetus for enacting competition law came from two sources. On the formal level, US occupation officials required such a law as part of their agreement to return full sovereignty to the new German state. On another level, however, this requirement was hardly necessary, because all major political parties recognized the need for such legislation and supported the enactment of a competition statute.

The issue was not whether there would be a competition law, but what kind of law it would be. The political and intellectual battle over the shape of the legislation lasted almost a decade, during which it was often a major source of controversy and public interest. Erhard presented competition law as an essential part of his 'Social Market Economy', and thus it took on 'constitutional' dimensions and became a major issue in the formation of the new republic.

---

[9] For discussion of German attitudes toward these laws, see Volker Berghahn, *The Americanisation of West German Industry 1945–1973* 84–110 (Cambridge, 1986). German lawyers and administrators who encountered these laws often found them 'strange'. Reinhard Blum, *Soziale Marktwirtschaft: Wirtschaftspolitik zwischen Neoliberalismus und Ordoliberalismus* 196 (Tübingen, 1969).

1. Teams and conflicts

The battle lines were drawn early and changed little during the long conflict. Two models of competition law (and two corresponding conceptions of the relationship between the state and the economy) were pitted against each other. One was the now familiar administrative control model of competition law in which administrative officials were authorized to control the conduct of economically powerful firms, as they had in the Weimar cartel regulation and in other contemporary European legislation. The other was, in essence, the ordoliberal model, in which competition law operated as a fundamental protection of the competitive process and of the economic freedom of individual firms.

The most prominent issue in the conflict was whether the new competition law should prohibit cartels. A German 'team' heavily influenced by ordoliberal ideas, which I will refer to as the Social Market Economy or SME group, said 'Yes', as did the US occupation authorities. Much of German industry, particularly the traditionally influential heavy industry representatives, and conservative politicians, said 'No', preferring an administrative system in which they could expect to have the same type of influence they had during the Weimar period. The issues were considerably more complex, of course, but this was the basic configuration.

Erhard's SME group sought a competition statute along the lines called for by Böhm and Eucken. He wanted to prohibit cartels, control the abuse of economic power and prevent excessive economic concentration. Above all, he sought a system that would operate according to 'juridical'—even constitutional—principles rather than administrative discretion. The SME group's arguments were largely drawn from ordoliberal discourse.

Another line of argument—one that was not part of the ordoliberal repertoire—referred to US experience. Works describing and analyzing US antitrust became increasingly common.[10] Groups of practicing lawyers, bureaucrats, and academics and influential writers visited the US, and many were impressed by how US antitrust laws operated.[11] These generally positive experiences were then sometimes used to support the theoretical positions staked out by Eucken, Böhm, and their colleagues.

Ludwig Erhard led the SME group throughout the battle for a competition law. As we have noted, he was the most important economic policy figure in the Western zones of occupation, and, after the founding of the Federal

---

[10] For discussion and citations to the literature, see Wolfgang Fikentscher, 'Die Deutsche Kartellrechtswissenschaft 1945–1954: Eine kritische Übersicht', 1955 *Wirtschaft und Wettbewerb* 205–29 (1955), reprinted in II Wolfgang Fikentscher, *Recht und Wirtschaftliche Freiheit* 360, 363 (Tübingen, 1993).

[11] See, e.g., Ernst-Joachim Mestmäcker, 'Diskriminierungen, Dirigismus und Wettbewerb', 1957 *Wirtschaft und Wettbewerb* 21 (1957).

Republic in 1949, he remained basically in charge of economic policy. He was supported by the many ordoliberals who had acquired leading positions in the zonal administrations and then in the new government's bureaucracy. More generally, he was supported by those who were oriented toward fundamental change that would 'rehabilitate' the German political and economic systems. Many of his supporters were young and well-educated, and they tended to be members of the CDU or the FDP (*Freie Demokratische Partei*). But Erhard could also count on support from many SPD leaders, who again, as they had during the Weimar period, saw competition law as a means of benefiting workers as consumers.[12] They did not necessarily share Erhard's justifications for a competition law, but they often supported his objective. Finally, he enjoyed support from those segments of industry that saw cartels as a threat. These were primarily the smaller and medium-sized firms in the processing industries.

Erhard's major opponent on the cartel issue was the powerful BDI (*Bundesverband der deutschen Industrie*), with its forceful president, Fritz Berg. The goal of the BDI and its political allies (primarily in the CDU and CSU) was to enact a competition law based on the abuse model and similar to the Weimar Cartel Regulation (which they had so frequently criticized). They argued that prohibiting cartels was unnecessary and potentially harmful to German industry. An abuse statute, they said, was consistent with German traditions, and cartels had long shown themselves to be valuable means of stabilizing economic development.[13] Their arsenal of arguments was basically the same that had been used against cartel legislation since the late 1890s.

The BDI position received support from two other sources that are worthy of note. First, some unions wanted a mild competition law on the ground that concentration was a step on the desired road to socialism. Labor was, therefore, split on the issue. The other source was an influential group of intellectual property rights lawyers, who saw in the proposed law a source of restrictions on intellectual property rights such as patents and trademarks.[14] This group was important because their expertise was seen as closely related to competition law, and thus its members were often turned to as experts.

US occupation authorities represented the third major player in the conflict. They also sought the inclusion of a cartel prohibition, and thus they were

[12] For discussion, see, Knut W. Nörr, *Die Leiden des Privatrechts: Kartelle in Deutschland von der Holzstoffkartellentscheidung zum Gesetz gegen Wettbewerbsbeschränkungen* 161–62 (Tübingen, 1994), and Robert, *Konzentrationspolitik*, 196–202. For the intellectual background, see Karl Schiller, 'Sozialismus und Wettbewerb', in Karl Schiller, *Der Ökonom und die Gesellschaft: Das freiheitliche und das soziale Element in der modernen Wirtschaftspolitik* 15–47 (Stuttgart, 1964).

[13] For discussion of industry's views, see Lioba Kramny, 'Das Wirken des BDI in der Wettbewerbspolitik', in *10 Jahre Kartellgesetz 1958–1968: Eine Würdigung aus der Sicht der deutschen Industrie* 59, 59–64 (Arbeitskreis Kartellgesetz, ed., Bergisch Gladbach, 1968).

[14] See generally, Fikentscher, 'Die Deutsche Kartellrechtswissenschaft', 218–22.

allied with the SME group in the sense that both were seeking a cartel prohibition. The alliance did not, however, include a close coordination of efforts to achieve that goal. The US authorities generally remained on the sidelines, using their influence on specific occasions to support the goals of the SME group.

2. The ordoliberal (Josten) Draft

The first full draft of a German competition law was presented to Erhard in 1949 by a committee chaired by Paul Josten, who was at the time head of the section on 'economic policy and order' in the German economic policy administration (*Verwaltung für Wirtschaft*) and who had been the head of the cartel section of the economics ministry before Hitler's accession to power.[15] This committee included among its members Franz Böhm, and, according to Knut Nörr, 'Böhm was able to exercise the greatest influence on this draft'.[16] As Nörr points out, the draft closely followed the ordoliberal ideas that Böhm had been developing in his writings since the late 1920s.

This so-called 'Josten Draft' carried the title 'Draft of An Act to Protect Competition Based on Performance and an Act Concerning the Monopoly Office'. It called for the creation of an independent monopoly office that would strictly enforce a set of norms designed to combat harmful uses of economic power and protect 'performance competition'. Most of the substantive provisions defined the conditions under which firms would be deemed to have such power and thus be subject to control by the monopoly office. Cartels were, for example, irrebuttably presumed to have such power when they engaged in price-fixing, agreed on bidding prices, or used a common purchase or sales organization. A similar set of presumptions applied to single firms.

Where a firm possessed economic power within the terms of the draft, it imposed reporting obligations and gave the monopoly office the authority to take steps, including the imposition of fines. The draft also provided private procedural rights on behalf of those harmed by such conduct. Finally, the monopoly office was authorized to prohibit mergers that threatened to create excessive economic power. The Josten Draft thus represented the elaboration of ordoliberal competition law ideas in the form of a detailed legislative proposal.

But the Josten Draft was not warmly received.[17] Representatives of industry objected that enacting it would hamper economic recovery by interfering with decision-making and artificially requiring 'excessive' competition. Given the still perilous economic situation in Germany, any proposal that was

---

[15] *Entwurf zu einem Gesetz zur Sicherung des Leistungswettbewerbs und zu einem Gesetz über das Monopolamt* (Bundeswirtschaftsminister publication, Bonn, 1949). For discussion, see Berghahn, *Americanisation*, 155–62; and Nörr, *Die Leiden des Privatrechts*, 163–84.

[16] Nörr, ibid., 163.   [17] Robert, *Konzentrationspolitik*, 102–06.

suspected of having such an effect had little chance of success. Opponents also denigrated the draft as a product of dogmatic idealism—both unrealistic in its assumptions and unworkable.

Industry was not, however, the only source of criticism of the draft. Eberhard Günther, then a leading official in the bizonal government and later the first president of the Federal Cartel Office, claimed, for example, that despite the apparent conceptual clarity of the as-if standard, the system envisioned by the Josten Draft would give too much discretion to the administrators.[18] There is evidence, as Volker Berghahn has pointed out,[19] that others among Erhard's advisers may also have been opposed to the Josten Draft on the grounds, *inter alia*, that it would generate a level of administrative interference in the economy that was inconsistent with the basic goals of ordoliberalism.

With such criticisms, it is not surprising that Erhard decided against supporting the Josten Draft as the basis for a German competition law. His political position in 1949 was uncertain, and the successes of his social market economy were still in the future. He could ill afford further strains on his relationships with industry or interference with his program of economic resuscitation. Moreover, the draft had to be seen as experimental and risky; it was based on ordoliberal theory and had no experiential backing, and this was hardly the time for Erhard to engage in such potentially dangerous experiments. An additional factor was a decision by the occupation authorities to bifurcate responsibilities for competition issues. Prior to 1949 the allies had maintained full responsibility for all aspects of competition policy, but in March of that year the Allied High Commission directed the German government to draft legislation dealing with only one component of competition law—the standards of competitive conduct—while the allies retained responsibility for all issues relating to deconcentration.[20] This undermined the conceptual and theoretical integrity of the Josten Draft and would in any event have required significant revisions.

3. The long tug-of-war

The Josten Draft was the first step in a long tug-of-war over the shape of German competition law that would last until 1957. During that period well over twenty additional drafts were considered. The details of this story have been told elsewhere, and there would be little point in retelling them.[21] Our

---

[18] See Eberhard Günther, 'Entwurf eines deutschen Gesetzes gegen Wettbewerbsbeschränkungen', 1951 *Wirtschaft und Wettbewerb* 26 (1951).

[19] Berghahn, *Americanisation*, 156–58.

[20] Memorandum of the BiPartite Control Office (49)30, March 29, 1949, cited in Robert, *Konzentrationspolitik*, 111.

[21] For detailed discussion of the long conflict, see Berghahn, *Americanisation* 155–81; Robert, *Konzentrationspolitik*; Viola Gräfin von Bethusy-Huc, *Demoktratie und Interessenpolitik*

concern here is with the basic shape and dynamics of the story. It was an open and dramatic conflict that achieved virtually mythic status. In it, power (that of Germany's industrial leaders) stood opposed to the values that sought to control it.

After Erhard's decision not to introduce the Josten Draft in the legislature, the economics ministry took the lead in seeking to negotiate a draft that would be politically acceptable. In this process the ministry acted as a mediator, repeatedly meeting with representatives of the SME group and of industry, and at least occasionally discussing its plans with US officials.[22] During this phase of the negotiations US pressure to include a ban on cartels was apparently an important factor in maintaining such a ban in the proposals.[23]

In 1952, the government finally submitted a new draft (the so-called 'Government draft' (*Regierungsentwurf*) that had apparently been agreed to by all relevant parties, including the US occupation officials. The basic conception of this draft was heavily influenced by ordoliberal ideas, but it was less consistently ordoliberal than the Josten Draft had been. It still contained a cartel prohibition and merger control provisions, and it expressly stated that the aim of a competition law should be to achieve as nearly as possible 'complete competition'.[24] On the other hand, industry representatives had achieved a number of important exemptions that significantly weakened the draft.

Despite its compromise character and its approval by the occupation authorities, the BDI in 1953 began to attack the draft, renewing their claims that a cartel prohibition would harm German industry and reasserting the value of co-operative and self-regulatory business arrangements. The maneuvering during this period was complex, but the BDI had good reasons for delaying legislative action relating to competition law. US officials were, after all, powerful allies of the SME group, and the occupation period was coming to a close. Soon US officials would be out of the picture. True, the US officials had stated that they would not relinquish the final vestiges of sovereignty until Germany had enacted a competition law, but during 1953 and 1954 they were weakening their demands for what would have to be in the bill. Under these circumstances, opponents of a cartel prohibition had every incentive to delay legislative action until US pressure had been removed.

For the next two years, industry and the SME group sought to outmaneuver each other. There were temporary compromises that were then

---

(Wiesbaden, 1962); and Peter Hüttenberger, 'Wirtschaftsordnung und Interessenpolitik in der Kartellgesetzgebung der Bundesrepublik 1949–1957', 24 *Vierteljahresschrift für Zeitgeschichte* 287 (1976).

[22] For discussion of the various positions in this negotiation see Robert, *Konzentrationspolitik,* 111–96.

[23] Berghahn, *Americanisation,* 172–73.

[24] See 'Begründung zu dem Entwurf eines Gesetzes gegen Wettbewerbsbeschränkungen', 1/2 *Wirtschaft und Wettbewerb* 460 (1951/1952).

abandoned by one or the other side. In 1954, however, a small group of important industrialists 'broke ranks' with Fritz Berg and the BDI and criticized Berg's uncompromising insistence on abuse-type legislation. Perhaps fearing further erosion of its support, the BDI soon thereafter accepted the basic idea of a cartel prohibition, and Erhard, in return, agreed to accept additional exemptions from such an prohibition.[25] It thus appeared in 1954 that a compromise had been reached that could serve as a basis for a competition law statute.

But it was too early. Many participants in the battle rejected the compromise, leading to new confrontations and new drafts that often represented earlier, 'purer' versions of the two positions. Negotiations continued for two more years, during which merger control provisions were, for example, eliminated and additional exemptions to the cartel prohibition were added. Finally, in 1957, a modified version of the 1952 draft was presented to the legislature as a compromise and enacted into law.[26]

The battle (though not the war) was over. It had been highly visible and often dramatic, and one positive result of this long and public gestation period was that it educated the public—and particularly business leaders— about the content of the new competition law and its intended role in the social market economy. On the other hand, it had shown that the power of big industry in the new republic had not been broken. Much as during the Weimar period (though more openly) political leaders continued to accord industrial interest groups a high level of influence over the content of legislation. Under the special circumstances of the occupation, Ludwig Erhard's political power and popularity, rapid improvements in Germany's economic situation, and the attractiveness of elements of the ordoliberal program, finally overcame the opposition of industry, but few could be confident that opposition would not continue to grow in strength.

D. THE GERMAN COMPETITION LAW SYSTEM

The statute that finally emerged from this process and became law on January 1, 1958, contained many key ideas from the ordoliberal competition law program, but it bore little resemblance to the Josten Draft. It was a hybrid that

---

[25] Erhard and his supporters had preferred a 'rule of reason' clause that would have allowed consideration of the extent of anticompetitive harms, but industry had fought hard instead for exemptions in order to weaken the statute. Their cause was aided by harsh criticism within the legal community of a number of Supreme Court (BGH) decisions in the early and mid-1950s that dealt with 'rule of reason' interpretations of allied decartelization law. For discussion of the exemptions, see Bethusy-Huc, *Demokratie*, 44.

[26] There had, of course, also been battles over other issues, most prominently resale price maintenance, merger control provisions, and controls on the discretionary authority of the FCO, but the focus of attention throughout was on the cartel prohibition.

reflected, in addition to ordoliberal ideas, contacts with US antitrust law and residual influences from prior German experience. This hybrid was very different from anything that had preceded it, and in those differences lay its extraordinary importance for the development of competition law in Europe.

The main components of the system have changed little since its inception, and thus I will use the present tense in discussing the basic outlines of the system, noting, as necessary, where changes have been made. I will then discuss additions to the system as part of the narrative of its development.

Before looking at the competition law system, it should be noted that the German legal system contains a highly developed and much used area of law called 'unfair trade law' that has conditioned the development of the competition law system.[27] This system preceded the GWB (the current law was enacted in 1909), and prior to enactment of the GWB, the term 'competition law' (*Wettbewerbsrecht*) was used to refer to it. Today, that term is used generally to refer to both areas of law, with the term '*Kartellrecht*' (cartel law) designating the area of law that we treat in this book.

The unfair trade law system is designed to protect the quality rather than the extent or intensity of competition. It is a specialized part of private law that authorizes economic actors harmed by certain conduct of their competitors to bring suit against them to stop the harmful conduct and/or to recover damages for the harm caused. The existence of this body of law has relieved pressures that otherwise might have required the competition law system to treat some conduct of this type.

The competition law system itself is designed to be 'constitutional' in scope. Its coverage is not limited to a specific phenomenon such as cartels, but covers, in principle, all restrictions on competition (merger control provisions were omitted from the original GWB, but introduced in 1973). As we have seen, Erhard viewed competition law as a pillar of the social market economy and repeatedly presented it in such terms. The influence of this 'constitutional' ideal in the development of German competition law can hardly be overestimated. In Europe, its only analogue is in the competition law of the European Union.

The statute was initially also constitutional in style. The original substantive provisions tended to be general rather than detailed, designed to be more or less permanent and to allow interpretation and flexibility. As we shall see, subsequent amendments have moved away from that style in important areas such as abuse control and merger control.

---

[27] For useful overviews of this area of law, see II Wolfgang Fikentscher, *Wirtschaftsrecht* 226–35 (Munich, 1983) and Fritz Rittner, *Wettbewerbs- und Kartellrecht* 13–126 (4th ed., Heidelberg, 1993).

1. Institutions and roles

The system is an administrative-juridical mix. It is administrative in the sense that the statute relies primarily on the Federal Cartel Office (FCO) for application of its substantive norms. This is consistent with prior German practice and with the administrative model followed elsewhere in Europe. The FCO's roles and modes of operation are, however, highly juridical, and this element was very different from existing precedents.

The FCO's basic role is not to execute political decisions or exercise discretionary authority in the name of 'the public welfare', but to interpret and apply legal norms—'the law'.[28] This is reflected, for example, in the FCO's internal procedures. Decisions are made by 'decision sections' whose procedures largely follow judicial models. They must be carefully justified in writing by reference to the GWB and existing case law. In practice, if not in theory, the FCO enjoys a large measure of independence from the ministerial bureaucracy and thus from political pressures.[29]

In order to emphasize the juridical nature of the FCO's operations as well as its special status outside the regular administrative hierarchy, the statute makes its decisions reviewable by the regular courts (rather than the administrative court system that normally reviews administrative acts). The standard of review is whether the FCO has appropriately interpreted and applied the statute and not (as often in administrative controls systems) whether it has abused its discretion. In general, the FCO's actions are appealable to the federal appeals court in Berlin—the 'Berlin Appeals Court' (*Kammergericht*)—whose decisions may be appealed to the Federal Supreme Court (*Bundesgerichtshof—BGH*) which has a special 'competition law chamber' (*Kartellsenat*). These two courts play important roles in the system, and their judges dealing with competition law are often important members of the competition law community.

The system does include a role for political influence. This is the so-called 'ministerial permission' (*Ministererlaubnis*) which authorizes the minister of economics, if requested, to permit conduct that the FCO had prohibited where he considers this necessary for 'overriding social or economic reasons'. This provision is highly circumscribed, and it has been seldom used.

The GWB authorizes private suits for damages or for injunctions to be brought in the regular courts, but only for violation of a relatively small num-

---

[28] For discussion, see, e.g., Fritz Rittner, 'Das Ermessen der Kartellbehörde', in *Festschrift für Heinz Kaufmann* 307 (Cologne Marienberg, 1972). For a valuable study in English of the legal and policy aspects of the FCO's decision-making, see James Maxeiner, *Policy and Methods in German and American Antitrust Law: A Comparative Study* (New York, 1986).

[29] For discussion of the FCO's operating procedures, see André Fiebig, ' The German Federal Cartel Office and the Application of Competition Law in Reunified Germany', 14 *U. of Penn. J. of Bus. L.* 373 (1993).

ber of provisions that are considered to provide 'individual protection' (*Individualschutz*) (§35). The idea is that certain provisions such as those dealing with price discrimination and boycott are intended to protect private economic actors as well as the process of competition, and thus it is appropriate to allow those harmed to sue for damages resulting from the violation. Private legal actions have become very important in the application of some of those provisions, but in general their role in enforcing the GWB is secondary.

2. The substantive norms

The original GWB contained three groups of substantive norms—those dealing with horizontal restraints, vertical restraints, and abuse of a market-dominating position. A fourth, merger control provisions, was added later (in 1973). The substantive provisions are generally drafted as legal norms rather than as administrative authorizations, and thus their application requires the characterization of conduct and the subsumation of fact patterns rather than discretionary administrative judgments about the 'welfare' of society.

The treatment of cartels as a specific form of horizontal agreement was, as we have seen, the main issue in the battle over the shape of the GWB, and §1 of the statute contains a general prohibition of such agreements. This prohibition is then followed by a series of exemptions for specific types of cartels, such as, for example, those designed to 'rationalize' an industry or to establish shapes and standards for particular types of goods. We will examine more carefully the use and interpretation of these provisions.

A second set of norms treats 'other agreements' that may restrict competition. This category basically includes vertical agreements—that is, those not between competitors—such as tying arrangements, licensing contracts, and exclusive dealing provisions. For this group of agreements there is no general prohibition. The drafters realized that the impact of such agreements on competition depended too much on the specific circumstances of their use to justify a prohibition, and thus they provided a differentiated set of tools to deal with different types of agreements. In general, the statute calls for the FCO to review such agreements to determine whether they have an anticompetitive impact and authorizes it to take steps if it finds such anticompetitive impacts. Some of these provisions are important in specific contexts, but for the most part they have played a secondary role in the development of the system. We will mention some of those specific cases, but we will not investigate the category in depth.

A third group of provisions seeks to prevent the 'abuse' of economic power by powerful firms. The statute does not prohibit specific types of conduct, but authorizes the FCO to take action to prevent powerful firms from engaging in conduct that is deemed to harm the competitive process. It can order a firm not to engage in particular conduct and fine it for failure to desist. There are also several provisions dealing with specific conduct that is considered abusive, such as price discrimination and boycotts.

The GWB originally was not applicable to important sectors of the economy such as, for example, transportation, agriculture, and insurance, although each of these areas is subject to other regulatory regimes. This was an area in which Erhard was forced to make concessions in his negotiations with industry leaders, and it was an important part of his disappointment with the statute's final form. Inroads have been made into these exclusions, and in the 1990s, pressures have increased to reduce or eliminate them.

This system thus reflects ordoliberal ideas in many respects. It contains a cartel prohibition. Its abuse control provisions are generally based on the notion of as-if competition originally developed by Leonard Miksch and others. The FCO is largely independent of political control and operates according to juridical principles in the service of broad 'constitutional' objectives. But how would this new form of competition law work? Many, not only in Germany, were very interested in the answer.

E. ESTABLISHING THE FORCE AND AUTHORITY OF COMPETITION LAW

In contrast to the situation in other European countries, competition law in Germany quickly became an important part of economic, political, and legal life—despite the determined opposition of many industry representatives. In a world full of competition law statutes that have little effect, it is important to ask how this occurred. A systemic analysis again provides useful insights: viewing the interplay of texts, institutions, and modes of thought as a system helps not only to identify factors that play a role in the system's operations and effectiveness, but also to analyze the relationships among these factors.

1. The text

The text of the statute is a starting point for analysis, provided that it is seen in relationship to other components of the system. For our purposes, the characteristics of the text are significant only in so far as they influence decisions and are used by decision-makers.

In this context, four characteristics of the GWB were particularly important in establishing the authority of the system. First, its language provided relatively high levels of information, at least as compared to the vague 'public welfare' language in the Cartel Regulation and in the administrative control systems of other European countries. Although there was room for interpretation, the language provided far more information about the conduct against which decision-makers were likely to take action. It was abstract enough to provide generalized guidelines for conduct, but seldom so abstract as to lose recognizable contact with economic reality.

Second, the key concept was 'restraint of competition' rather than 'cartel', 'agreement' or some other term that referred to the formal legal characteristics of the conduct involved. Such formal terms had been used in the Cartel Regulation, and they continue to be used in other European competition law systems (for example, the UK Restrictive Practices System). The statute thus keyed on the economic effects of conduct rather than its formal characteristics. By using an economic concept and providing an authoritative means for giving it legal structure and content, the statute minimized formalism in analysis and reduced incentives for firms to seek to evade the application of the law through legal maneuvering.

Third, the individual provisions were organized within a structure that aided the process of interpretation and thus provided additional information. The GWB is not a highly technical statute, but it is systematically structured, so that the location of a provision within that structure helps to clarify its meaning. This structuring also distinguished it from other European competition law statutes.[30]

And, fourth, the language reflected patterns of thought that were well-established among those who would apply the law and well enough known to those to whom the law would be applied (or at least their legal advisors). At the outset, all realized that ordoliberal thought would provide the framework within which the language was to be used. This reference framework not only provided information, but also strengthened the community of those committed to the 'social market economy', which included many (probably most) FCO decision-makers, many in the economics ministry, some judges and an important group of academics in the fields of law and economics.

2. The Federal Cartel Office

The key to establishing the authority and force of competition law was, however, the FCO.[31] This institution had primary responsibility for making the system work, and, in order to do so, it had to sculpt internal dynamics and external relations that would produce the requisite respect for the institution and for the field of competition law itself. The obstacles were impressive. The new law sought to subject powerful institutions to controls on conduct that had previously been considered not only legal, but desirable (except under the imposed allied decartelization laws). Above all, it prohibited the form of economic organization (cartels) that had prevailed in Germany for decades.

[30] For discussion, see Ulrich Immenga & Ernst-Joachim Mestäcker, *Kommentar zum GWB*, 45–8 (2d. ed., Munich, 1992).
[31] For discussion of the organization and operation of the FCO during its first decade, see Klaus Weber, 'Geschichte und Aufbau des Bundeskartellamtes', in *Zehn Jahre Bundeskartellamt* 263–70 (Cologne, 1968).

The FCO did not begin its work in a vacuum: the German administrative tradition strengthened its starting position by providing it with at least a presumptive claim to respect and authority. As we have seen, German administrative officials had long been accorded a relatively high level of respect. This was further enhanced during the occupation by the initial absence of an elected legislature and the subsequent relative lack of power of elected officials. During this period, appointed officials had far more power than did elected ones. Postwar privations also enhanced the social position of career 'officials', whose compensation and job security made their positions highly attractive. The accents within the tradition also supported the FCO's mission. As we have seen, German administrative tradition and culture have long been highly 'juridical'—in contrast, for example, to countries such as France in which legal training and juridical methodology have played minor roles in the administrative tradition. This tradition helped in establishing the FCO's authority by enhancing the perceived value of the officials' tasks and thus the expectations they and others had of their conduct.

While this tradition provided a valuable base, the success of the FCO depended on how its officials treated their tasks—on what the officials did and how they did it. By all accounts, the early officials of the FCO often saw their work as a critically important 'mission' that deserved the highest levels of commitment—even 'passion'.[32] Böhm, Eucken, Erhard, and others who were associated with the drive to assure a democratic society and a market-based economy portrayed competition law as the key to the social market economy and the social market economy as the key to a new future for Germany. The GWB was not just another law, and the FCO was not just another administrative office. Together, they symbolized rejection of a failed regime and belief in a democratic alternative. The continuing conflict between the FCO and Fritz Berg's BDI coalition probably intensified this sense of mission, because the latter group often justified their opposition to the FCO by reference to German '(cartel) traditions'—precisely what many in the SME group were rejecting.

One function of ordoliberalism was to articulate this mission. The basic claims of the ordoliberals were that a competitive economic 'order' was fundamentally different from a command-based order, that to choose such an order was the best (only) means of achieving economic stability and democratic freedom, and that competition law was the key to such an order. This was a discourse born of the kind of passion that humiliation, persecution, and devastation can engender; it was also a discourse that could inspire.

---

[32] One BDI observer referred to them as often 'passionate exponents of a certain set of economic and political ideas'. Werner Benisch, '10 Jahre Praxis des Bundeskartellamts', in *10 Jahre Kartellgesetz 1958–1968: Eine Würdigung aus der Sicht der deutschen Industrie* 12 (Arbeitskreis Kartellgesetz, ed., Bergisch Gladbach, 1968).

The leadership of the FCO was another key factor in its early successes, and here the dominant figure was that of its first president, Eberhard Günther, who served as president until 1976.[33] Günther's style and personal background fit the mission well. He apparently had been threatened with the death penalty by the Nazis for his activities during the war,[34] and thus his presence at the head of the new organization symbolized the rejection of the Nazi past. He was well-acquainted with ordoliberal thought, and he was an intense and enthusiastic supporter of social market economy ideas who apparently often inspired similar intensity in officials of the office, particularly during its early years.

He was trained as a lawyer, and, according to his own account, greatly enjoyed the 'scientific' aspects of competition law.[35] He wrote numerous academic articles on the subject and thereby also established leadership credentials on the intellectual level. Yet he had begun his legal career working for a cartel (the nitrogen syndicate)! He thus had an understanding of the workings of business, in general, and cartels, in particular, and this experience not only gave him insight into the analytical problems involved, but also prevented business leaders who were skeptical of the new office from dismissing him as a bureaucrat with little knowledge of practical life.

Despite the zeal of Günther and many of his co-workers, they approached their mission cautiously. Education and negotiation were a major part of their strategy, and they apparently spent much time explaining the GWB and their own positions regarding it and seeking to persuade business leaders to accept those positions. In part, this was because the GWB did not initially provide the office with powerful enforcement tools.[36] It was given authority to levy fines in some cases, but the office could not expect to achieve its goals through pure coercion, and, particularly in the early years, it imposed fines very sparingly. This caution also reflected a belief that the success of competition law was tied to the process of re-education and that, therefore, coercion might be counterproductive.

Günther's belief (shared by Erhard and other social market economy leaders) that Germans had to be re-educated to accept a new model of economic conduct also led the FCO to emphasize the importance of publicity and public education. In newspapers, legal and economic journals, and meetings

---

[33] For a biographical sketch of Günther, see Heinz Ewald, 'Eberhard Günther', in *Wettbewerb im Wandel: Eberhard Günther zum 65. Geburtstag* 11–24 (Helmut Gutzler et al eds., Baden-Baden, 1976).

[34] This claim is based in his own statement in an interview with the author in May, 1991, Königstein im Taunus. I have no independent corroboration of it.

[35] Ibid.

[36] Until the 1965 revisions, the FCO could not itself impose fines; it was merely authorized to request the imposition of fines by the Berlin Court of Appeals. For discussion of the changes, see *Novelle 1965 zum Gesetz gegen Wettbewerbsbeschränkungen* 200–06 (Hans Müller-Hennenberg & Gustav Schwartz, eds., Cologne, 1966).

with business groups, FCO officials explained the GWB and championed its goals. Some critics argued that this mixture of activities was inappropriate: FCO officials were supposed to apply the law rather than engage in apologetics.[37] How, after all, were businesses supposed to react to 'preaching' rather than traditional administrative conduct? Such attacks from business interest groups are perhaps the best indication that these re-education efforts were reducing resistance to the FCO within the business community.

Another factor in the business community's grudging but gradual acceptance of the role of the FCO and of competition law in general was the constraints on the FCO's discretion. Viewing FCO officials as 'opponents' (an inevitable consequence of a decade of conflict over the shape of the competition law statute), business spokesmen such as Berg were highly sensitive to the issue of the FCO's discretionary power. They feared, in essence, that their 'opponents' were likely to pay little attention to their problems and concerns. Some also sought to increase such fears among other businessmen, presumably in order to increase pressure on the FCO to apply the statute leniently.

Yet these attempts foundered on the structure of the system. The FCO's power and authority were circumscribed by juridical methods and procedures and subject to approval by the courts. This provided the business community with a means of knowing the approximate range within which the FCO could make decisions. If one knew the methods being applied and the legal material on which the FCO had to rely, one could assess the constraints on the FCO's conduct. This juridical framework reduced uncertainty as well as fears that the FCO might become overly aggressive in using the authority that had been conferred on it.

3. Support for the mission

External factors also supported the FCO's mission. The flourishing German economy, the German 'economic miracle' as it was now being called, undoubtedly helped. Some German firms complained about the FCO, but most were prospering to a degree that few would have thought possible in the first years after the war, and all were aware that they were participating in an extraordinary economic recovery. Under such circumstances, concerns about the FCO could hardly be taken too seriously. Moreover, these economic successes were widely attributed to Erhard's policies, and competition law was acknowledged as a key component of his policy package. Opposition to competition law and resistance to the FCO ran the risk, therefore, of being counterproductive, of harming the very process that was providing such benefits.

More generally, prosperity undergirded political support for competition law. The economic successes of Erhard's policies secured his party's power

[37] See Werner Benisch, '10 Jahre Praxis', 12–13.

until the mid-1960s, and this continuity of high-level support for competition law gave the FCO credibility and a secure political base. This continuity also meant that competition law was supported by other elements of ordoliberal *Ordnungspolitik* for most of its first decade. Walter Eucken had urged that competition law could only be successful where it was part of a consistent policy package that contained other elements such as monetary stability, and the CDU's continuous control of the political machinery during most of the first decade of the FCO's operations made this possible. As a consequence, the FCO and the economics ministry were operating according to the same codes, and the same basic ideas and goals guided their decision-making. Political and economic pressures prevented this package from being as ordoliberal as Eucken and Böhm might have wished, but it may have been as close to this ideal as is possible in a modern society.

The courts also supported the FCO's mission of developing the authority of competition law. During the early years of the FCO's existence, the Berlin Appeals Court and the Supreme Court tended to agree with FCO decisions, and when they did overturn such decisions they generally applied the same basic analytical framework and differed only on specifics of interpretation or application.[38] The FCO and the two courts that reviewed their actions spoke the same language, and this consistency undoubtedly not only reduced incentives for opponents to resist the FCO's position, but strengthened the FCO's confidence in its ability to achieve its goals.

Finally, the role of the academic community in developing and applying this common language can hardly be overestimated. Ordoliberalism provided a kind of orthodoxy among academic writers dealing with economic policy and competition law, and this orthodoxy was only gradually to lose its hold during the following decades[39]. It anchored a competition law 'community' that included bureaucrats, lawyers, and economists, and thus it provided a unifying discourse, and the legal and economic literature during this period generally used that discourse in explaining, justifying, and criticizing decisions by the FCO and the courts. This unified discourse would begin to disintegrate in the late 1960s, but its integrative, community-forming role during the early years of the system was extraordinary.

One aspect of this discourse that deserves special note was its private law orientation. As we have noted, many of the legal scholars in the area were

---

[38] Moreover, in its early decisions the BGH (Federal Supreme Court) tended to write broad 'basic principles' decisions in an effort to 'eliminate as quickly as possible through clear decisions an initial uncertainty regarding the application of the statute'. Siegfried Klaue, 'Die bisherige Rechtsprechung zum Gesetz gegen Wettbewerbsbeschränkungen,' in *Zehn Jahre Bundeskartellamt* 249, 254 (Cologne, 1968). For discussion of the FCO's efforts to convince the courts of its position, see the comments of former BGH judge Otto Löscher, 'Zehn Jahre Kartellsenat' in *Ehrengabe für Bruno Heusinger* 289, 299–300 (Munich, 1968).

[39] The role of this discourse is frequently overlooked when historians pay inadequate attention to the legal literature.

young, and often they had been strongly influenced by ordoliberal thought. This group viewed competition law as a matter of rights and individual freedoms. Their conceptual world was that of precision (or at least the search for it), systematic analysis and rights. It was this conception of competition law as private law rather than merely a matter of public policy that was so influential in shaping thought and expectations in the area of competition law.[40]

4. Protection from outside influences

In order to establish the authority of competition law, the FCO also needed protection from outside influences. As we have seen, industry, especially big industry, had doggedly opposed enactment of a prohibition-based statute, and after its enactment representatives of big industry did not conceal their desire to weaken and marginalize it. Given the influence of industrial organizations within the political machinery of the Federal Republic, the likelihood of success had to be considered high. Two basic paths were open to such groups, but, fortunately for those who supported the development of competition law along ordoliberal lines, neither of these paths led to significant successes.

One path led through the regular political apparatus—the government, especially the economics ministry. Formally, the FCO is part of the economics ministry, which has the authority to issue directions (*Weisungen*) to it.[41] If industry had been able to convince the ministry to make use of this authority, it could have greatly altered the stature and effectiveness of the FCO. Erhard and the ideas he represented blocked this path. From the beginning, Erhard took the position that such 'directions' should only be issued under the most extraordinary circumstances, and this precedent came to define the position of the office. Since then, no economics ministry has been willing to expose itself to the criticism that a change in this policy could be expected to elicit.[42] In practice, therefore, the FCO is far more independent than it looks on paper, and this is difficult to explain without reference to the force of ordoliberal thought within the relevant communities.

[40] For discussion and historical background, see Fikentscher, *Wettbewerb und Gewerblicher Rechtsschutz* 163–206. The claim that competition law is not only in essence private law, but also establishes individual private rights ('subjective rights') has also been an important part of legal scholarship relating to competition law. It was initially developed in the writings of Wolfgang Fikentscher and Rudolf Lukes. See, e.g., Fikentscher, ibid., 207–231, and Lukes, *Kartellvertrag*, 180–91 and 244–9.

[41] There is no doubt that the economics ministry is authorized to issue so-called 'general directions' to the FCO—i.e., directions relating to general principles. There is, however, considerable controversy as to whether it is authorized to issue directions in individual cases. For discussion of the various contexts of this issue, see Immenga & Mestmäcker, *Kommentar zum GWB* 1780–1.

[42] In the controversy in the mid-1990s between the FCO and the economics ministry over adapting the GWB to more closely resemble the competition law of the EU, the possibility of issuing directions was used as a threat against the FCO. See, e.g., Marc Biese, 'Kartellamt drohen Weisungen', *Handelsblatt* 4 (July 16, 1996).

A second path was more direct—influencing individual FCO decision-makers by making available the many benefits that the resources of big industry had at their disposal (such as high-paying positions in industry or private law firms). Here the internal organization of the office and the procedures it employed generally protected it from such influences. Decisions were, and still are, made according to juridical principles and procedures by 'decision sections', allowing individuals little opportunity to give special attention to particular defendants. Moreover, the personnel of the FCO are largely protected from such temptations by the *Beamten* tradition, according to which such officials generally cannot be removed from office and normally remain in government service throughout their careers.

The FCO's efforts to establish its own authority and that of competition law thus benefited from a combination of favorable factors that allowed the FCO to establish basic patterns of conduct and ways of thinking within the system and to create expectations within the business community that would long channel business conduct. Some of these factors would remain unchanged, but others would soon cease to be so favorable.

F. INTERPRETING AND APPLYING THE GWB: THE CARTEL FOCUS

This system was also shaped and tested by the specific tasks that confronted it, and during its first decade the focus of attention was on interpreting and applying the cartel prohibition. The long legislative fight over the inclusion of such a prohibition had been well-publicized and had come to symbolize the conflict between industry and the social market economy group. With the enactment of the GWB, the struggle moved to another arena. The SME group had achieved the cartel prohibition that it had sought, albeit with important exemptions, and now the question was how that prohibition would be applied and whether it would become the pillar of the economy that many hoped it would be.

1. Process and tasks

The SME group sought to interpret the prohibition broadly and the exemptions—which they had generally opposed—narrowly, thereby moving closer to their original goal of a strong cartel prohibition. Their opponents in industry sought the opposite—a narrow cartel prohibition and broad exemptions. To the extent they were successful, they could achieve a system similar to the abuse statute for which they had fought. As the FCO commented in its first annual report, 'Despite broad agreement on basic issues, segments of German industry continue now as before to reject the prohibition principle and to seek abuse legislation. It is this effort that explains attempts to so weaken the statute through interpretation that it has to be treated like an abuse statute'.[43]

The competition law system thus faced two interrelated tasks. It had to give meaning and substance to the cartel provisions, and it had to achieve an acceptable level of compliance from industry. At issue was the very process of interpreting and applying the statute, and the success and effectiveness of the FCO would depend on perceptions of that process. In this context the capacity of the system to generate useful information about the standards that would be applied to conduct and the reactions that could be expected from the system was critical. Other things being equal, the more reliable the information and the sooner it could be provided, the less resistance the FCO was likely to face from business. In this situation the FCO adopted an active posture, seeking to provide reliable information relatively quickly. Had its stance been more passive, the system might have developed very differently.

While it was aggressive in this sense, the FCO was also cautious. Günther emphasized the need to explore the economic realities faced by business rather than merely operating on the basis of its own theories and assumptions. Consistent with this objective, it focused on the adjudication of cases rather than on legislative pronouncements. Regarding its first year of operation, the FCO commented,

In this situation the FCO entered with caution the new territory that the legislature had referred to it to explore and penetrate. It seems appropriate and natural that the main efforts in the first year must be to grasp the factual situations involved and sort out the substantive and formal problems. The office is at the end of this period not yet in a position to give a response to most of the competition issues, which to a large degree are also structural and sociological.[44]

Caution, case-orientation, willingness to listen—these were the characteristics that the FCO repeatedly emphasized during its early years.

In part, this was influenced by the recognition that the legislation was new and that caution was likely to be necessary to avoid unanticipated problems. From a tactical perspective, the emphasis on caution and case-law adjudication also demonstrated the FCO's practical orientation, and this helped to counter accusations that it was overly dogmatic or theoretical. By the mid-1960s its opponents were readily acknowledging, welcoming and encouraging this approach.

The courts also played an important role in this informational process, because they had the final word regarding the information that the system produced. They would ultimately decide the extent to which firms could rely on the information provided by the FCO. Here the critical factor was that the

---

[43] FCO, *Tätigkeitsbericht des Bundeskartellamtes 1959* at 101 (Berlin, 1960).
[44] FCO, *Tätigkeitsbericht 1958*, in *Berichte des Bundeskartellamtes 1958/59/60* at 91 (Düsseldorf, 1961).

methodology employed by the FCO and the courts is essentially the same. The German system requires the courts to ask—and to answer—the same questions about the cartel prohibition that the FCO asks. In this sense, they act as regular courts of appeal. This is a major difference between the German system and most competition law systems, where any courts that might be involved are likely to be administrative courts, whose role is normally limited to determining whether an administrative agency has abused its discretion, or special courts not subject to normal judicial procedures.

No less important in interpreting the cartel prohibition was the academic community. The long period of controversy over the shape of the GWB and its political and economic significance encouraged numerous academics, primarily those in early stages of their careers, to specialize in the area of competition law, and they produced a large amount of literature about the cartel prohibition. These writers tended to be heavily influenced by ordoliberal ideas, and thus they tended to consider the cartel prohibition a central issue. While there were many 'scientific' disputes about the interpretation of the cartel prohibition, as a whole the community used the same basic values and discourse to produce the same basic kinds of answers.

2. The cartel prohibition

The text of the cartel prohibition left much room for conflict. It read (and still reads): 'Contracts which enterprises or groups of enterprises conclude for a common purpose are invalid, to the extent that they are capable (*geeignet*) of influencing trade in goods or commercial services by restricting competition'.[45] This language was clearly aimed at the classic cartel form that had been so common in Germany—that is, formal agreements among competitors to control prices, production or distribution, but what it included beyond that was less clear, and opponents of the prohibition sought at each turn to narrow its coverage.

Giving meaning to this provision presented the FCO and the courts with two basic problems. One was to give content to concepts such as 'restraints on competition' that had been primarily understood as economic concepts. German legal tradition explicitly requires what is less explicitly dealt with in many other legal systems, namely, that 'non-legal' concepts be 'introduced' into the system so that they can be interpreted. The second basic problem was, in a sense, the reverse—how to deal with the 'baggage' that some of the concepts of the cartel prohibition carried from their use in other contexts such as the civil code or the Cartel Regulation.

Several examples illustrate how the system responded to these problems and shaped the content of the cartel prohibition. The objective here is not to

---

[45] The translation of '*geeignet*' is problematic. The German term is actually located somewhere between 'capable of' and 'appropriate for'.

290 Competition Law in Germany

provide a full discussion of the development of the case law and literature regarding the cartel prohibition, but to provide insights into the key issues and the role played by the cartel prohibition in the evolution of the system.

The cartel prohibition refers only to 'contracts' (*Verträge*) and thus the scope of that concept was a key battleground. If opponents of a strong cartel prohibition could narrow the interpretation of the concept of 'contract', they could restrict the scope and effectiveness of the prohibition. Their chances of doing so were aided by prior and contemporary usages of the concept. It had been the subject of private law controversy for centuries, and it had acquired a technical meaning in the context of the German civil code. There a contract is an 'agreement of wills' for the purpose of achieving a 'juridical' effect, that is, altering rights or obligations of the parties. If, as many feared, the FCO or, more likely, the courts were to apply these private law doctrines in interpreting the GWB, the cartel prohibition might have been very narrow, excluding not only 'gentlemen's agreements' that were enforced by nonlegal sanctions, but also co-ordinated activities that were not based on obligations.

The FCO and many academic writers quickly took the position that the GWB had to be interpreted according to its own standards and in light of its own objectives rather than according to principles developed in other areas of law. If this were done, they argued, the cartel prohibition would apply not only to formal contracts, but to any agreement between the parties, even if it did not involve legally enforceable obligations. This specific issue was thus tied to the project of establishing a fundamental principle of interpretation. Establishing this principle was a critical conceptual move that would eventually allow the competition law system to develop according to its own needs, but there were obstacles.

After more than a decade of wrangling in the lower courts and in the literature about the scope of the provision, the BGH was faced with the issue of whether §1 applied to '*abgestimmte Verhaltensweisen*' (roughly, concerted actions)—that is, tacit understandings that leading firms would essentially follow each other's lead in pricing or other similar decisions. The Court decided that it did not, stating that 'contract' for purposes of the GWB meant 'contract' under private law.[46] This left a 'gap' in the statute, and, as a result, the FCO and the economics ministry appealed to the legislature to override the Supreme Court's decision. In 1973, the statute was amended specifically to prohibit such conduct.

Interpreting the 'common purpose' requirement presented a similar problem. Here there were conceptual ties not only to the civil code (§705), but also to the Cartel Regulation of the Weimar period. The language requiring that a contract be entered into for a common purpose seemed to envisage the clas-

---

[46] BGH, Dec. of Dec. 17, 1970, *WuW/E*, BGH 1147, 52–55 (*Teerfarben*). For discussion, see Otto Sandrock, 'Gentlemen's Agreements, aufeinanderabgestimmte Verhaltensweisen und gleichförmiges Verhalten nach dem GWB', 1971 *Wirtschaft und Wettbewerb* 858 (1971).

sic cartel form in which the cartel was organized as a corporation or at least an association, which would necessarily have a common purpose. If the cartel prohibition had been applied only to such organizations, however, its role would have been severely restricted.

In the early cases, it appeared that this might happen. At first, the Supreme Court interpreted this provision according to principles of the civil code.[47] The legal literature reacted, however, by strongly attacking this interpretation, and early experience also led the FCO to urge the courts to change direction. In response to this pressure, in 1976 the Supreme Court moved away from this interpretation and affirmed that the requirement was met if the participants had a '*gleichgerichtetes Interesse*'—that is, if they had interests that tended in the same direction.[48]

A third major issue was the relationship between the contract and the restraint of competition with which it was associated. Early interpretations of §1 often concluded that a cartel agreement fell within the provision only if the competitive restraint was the 'object' (*Gegenstand*) of the agreement, that is, that it actually formed part of the agreement (the 'object' theory). This interpretation would again have restricted significantly the application of the provision.

Some who sought a broader application of §1 claimed, on the other hand, that it applied wherever the restraint 'resulted' from the contract, regardless of whether it actually formed part of the contract (the '*Folge*' or result theory).[49] This would have expanded the scope of the provision by including fact patterns in which a contract merely had anticompetitive consequences. The theoretical controversy over this issue produced a voluminous literature in which writers explored a wide variety of hermeneutic approaches. It was also seen by many, especially in industry, as having major practical importance.

At first, proponents of the 'object' theory appeared to have succeeded in establishing its validity. In 1968, for example, a prominent representative of industry suggested that acceptance of that theory represented a major victory for industry.[50] The problem was that there seemed to be only two choices— object theory or result theory, and since the majority of commentators and courts concluded that the result theory strayed too far from the language of the provision, this temporarily left only the object theory.

---

[47] See, e.g., BGH, Dec. of Oct. 26, 1959, 31 BGHZ 105, 110–13 (*Gasglühkörper*).

[48] See BGH, Dec. of Oct. 14, 1976, 68 BGHZ 6,10 (*Transportbeton*). For discussion, see Wernhard Möschel, *Recht der Wettbewerbsbeschränkungen* 108–10 (Cologne, 1983).

[49] There are 'pure' forms of the '*Folgetheorie*' as well as modified forms. For description, see, e.g., II Fikentscher, *Wirtschaftsrecht*, 257–62.

[50] Paul Riffel, '10 Jahre deutsche Wettbewerbspolitik', in *10 Jahre Kartellgesetz 1958–1968: Eine Würdigung aus der Sicht der deutschen Industrie* 3, 6 (Arbeitskreis Kartellgesetz, ed., Bergisch Gladbach, 1968).

But the conceptual development did not stop here. As the legal community continued to debate the issue, a young professor named Wolfgang Fikentscher proposed a third theory, which came to be known as the 'intent' (*Zweck*) theory.[51] His claim was that in those cases in which the restraint did not form part of the contract, the proper test for the relationship between the contract and the restraint was whether the contracting parties at least *intended* to achieve the restraint. This theory was positioned between the 'result' and 'object' theories, and by the mid-1970s it had achieved strong support from the courts and the FCO. It has since come to be considered the 'dominant opinion' of the legal community and thus, in practice, 'the law'.[52]

As these examples demonstrate, the task of interpreting the cartel prohibition involved the FCO, the courts and the academic community in an intense process of developing and applying a methodology and a conceptual framework for competition law. In several key areas, early interpretations of the provision remained under the influence of pre-existing methodologies and interpretations from other areas of law, thus temporarily restricting the scope of the provision. Gradually, however, the guiding principle that the GWB had to be interpreted according to its own objectives generated a broad conception of the cartel prohibition.

3. Applying the cartel exemptions

Yet opponents of the cartel prohibition had another potential avenue for weakening it: expansive interpretation and application of the exemptions. As we have seen, they secured broad exemptions as part of the final legislative compromise over the GWB, and Erhard and many others feared that these would be used to undermine the prohibition itself. If the exemptions were interpreted broadly, the system would, in the end, operate very much like an abuse system rather than a prohibition system.

The exemptions involve several different levels of intervention by the FCO, roughly reflecting the legislature's assessment of the degree of harm they pose for the competitive process.[53] Some relatively harmless special cartel types are valid either without notification to the FCO or by virtue of such notification. Others are only valid where they have been reported to the FCO and the FCO has taken no action within a specified period of time (usually three months). This category includes important cartel forms such as standardization cartels (in which the cartel members agree to apply the same standard sales or purchase terms) and cartels regulating the use of rebates by cartel members. Yet other types of cartels require specific approval from the FCO in order to be

---

[51] Wolfgang Fikentscher, 'Nachfragemacht und Wettbewerbsbeschränkung', 1960 *Wirtschaft und Wettbewerb* 680 (1960).

[52] See, e.g., Volker Emmerich, *Kartellrecht* 72 (7th ed., Munich, 1994).

[53] For discussion and analysis, see Möschel, *Recht der Wettbewerbsbeschränkungen*, 155–86.

deemed valid. These were considered the most dangerous cartel forms and include, for example, cartels for the purpose of 'rationalizing' a branch of industry (§5(2) and (3)), cartels to be used in cases of 'structural crisis' in an industry (§4) and cartels approved by the minister of economics on the basis of their overriding social importance ('minister cartels', §8). For all forms of exempted cartels, the FCO has general authority to assure that the exemption is not 'abused' (§11/12).

Applying the exemptions presented the FCO with a different kind of challenge from that of interpreting the cartel prohibition itself. These provisions are much more specific than §1, leaving less room for interpretation and entailing a narrower range of conflicts and interpretational issues. As a result, although some exemptions received attention in the legal literature, in general there was less scholarly (scientific) development of the issues. For these reasons as well as the impracticality of waiting several years for a decision regarding the acceptability of a cartel arrangement, there were also relatively few court decisions. Here the focus was on the FCO's enforcement policies.

I will not attempt to trace the treatment of specific exemptions, but to give a general sense of their various roles in the development of the system. This is made easier by the fact that some potentially important categories of exemption have been very seldom used. These include export and import cartels, and, particularly, the so-called 'minister cartels'. Many in the SME group were concerned that this latter provision would provide a gateway through which political power could influence the system, and argued that it was fundamentally incompatible with the goals of the system. As it turned out, the long reign of Ludwig Erhard precluded that from happening. Erhard early announced that in principle he would not seek such exemptions, and industry soon all but gave up attempts to use it.[54]

With regard to most other exempted cartel forms—for example, rebate cartels, the FCO tended at the outset to take a strict, ordoliberal-based position.[55] This did not prevent industry from forming such cartels, but it often did make their use difficult, uncertain and sometimes costly, leading many firms to live without them.[56] The FCO thus demonstrated the will to stand for the basic objectives and principles of the system, and to treat the exemptions as inimical to those objectives. The academic community tended to support this position, as did the economics ministry, while representatives of industry naturally complained about it.

By the early 1960s, however, industry was increasingly commenting on the degree to which the FCO had become more 'realistic' in its enforcement

---

[54] According to Werner Benisch of the BDI, the economics ministry treated requests for such an exemption as if approval 'would be a sin against the holy ghost of the market economy'. Benisch, '10 Jahre Praxis', 25.

[55] For discussion, see Benisch, ibid., 24–26.

[56] Riffel, '10 Jahre deutsche Wettbewerbspolitik', 4.

policy, more willing to recognize the economic benefits of certain cartel forms. A leading BDI lawyer claimed in 1968 that 'This realistic, understanding-based approach has become increasingly apparent over the years. Its consequence has been that many firms now trust the office, willingly discuss their problems with it, and seek co-operative solutions'.[57] There were reports that as FCO officials gained experience, they acquired a greater appreciation of the practical realities faced by business and thus a willingness to permit conduct that might not have been tolerated earlier.

There were exceptions to this general pattern of gradual loosening of requirements for approval of exempted cartel forms. With regard to 'rationalization' cartels, for example, the economics ministry in 1961 criticized the FCO for applying the exemption too broadly, and, apparently in response to this pressure, the FCO shortly thereafter developed a 'new interpretation' that led to a narrowing of the scope of the exemption.[58]

Although perhaps not directly related to the general pattern of loosening of the FCO's enforcement policy with regard to exempted cartel forms, a shift in the policy discourse relating to the cartel prohibition became evident in the early 1960s. Economic concentration became an increasing concern in academic and economic policy circles, and the economics ministry increasingly warned of the threats that it posed for small and medium-sized business. This created a problem, however, because ordoliberal principles and the need to establish the authority of competition law precluded overtly weakening the cartel prohibition.

As a result, the ministry, apparently in co-operation with sections of industry, began to encourage a reconceptualization of the issues that centered on the idea of 'co-operation'. In 1963, for example, it published the first edition of its '*Kooperationsfibel*' (co-operation guide).[59] The objective of the guide was to encourage small and medium-sized industries to cooperate by describing the many possibilities open to them. In reality, of course, a co-operation agreement may often be the same thing as a cartel, and it may have the same effects, regardless of how it is labelled, but industry and the economics ministry were explicitly seeking to change the way people thought about certain kinds of agreements. Accordingly, the FCO in the following years began to apply the cartel prohibition and its exemptions in the spirit of this modified discourse.[60]

[57] Benisch, '10 Jahre Praxis', 28.

[58] For discussion, see Riffel, '10 Jahre deutsche Wirtschaftspolitik', 3–4, and FCO, *Tätigkeitsbericht 1961*, BT-Drucksache IV/378, at 9–10 and 13–16.

[59] Bundesminister für Wirtschaft, *Zwischenbetriebliche Zusammenarbeit im Rahmen des Gesetzes gegen Wettbewerbsbeschränkungen* (Bonn, Oct. 29, 1963). The BDI republished this guide, together with a commentary and examples by Werner Benisch. Werner Benisch, *Kooperationsfibel des Bundesministers für Wirtschaft* (Bergisch Gladbach, 1964). The guide in this form has gone through numerous subsequent editions.

[60] See *Stellungnahme des Bundesregierung zum Tätigkeitsbericht des Bundeskartellamtes 1967*, BT-Drucksache V/2841, at 2.

A review of the first decade of enforcement policy relating to exemptions thus reveals that the exemptions did not significantly undermine the cartel prohibition, as some had feared they might. The FCO, supported by the academic community, the economics ministry, and the courts, simply did not allow that to happen. The FCO was a distinctly pro-Erhard organization, and thus it generally applied the exemptions narrowly, as Erhard had hoped it would. On the other hand, after the FCO had largely established its own authority and a firm ordoliberal orientation in its decision-making, it showed flexibility in responding to economic developments.

4. Other issues

We have focused our attention here on the cartel prohibition and the exemptions from it because this was the main arena of conflict during the system's first decade and played the central role in the development of the system. The treatment of two other provisions of the statute also deserves brief mention.

The abuse control provisions played in most respects a marginal role during this period. They were invoked in a large number of proceedings (as of 1966, there were 1871),[61] but few of these proceedings led to final decisions, and still fewer were reviewed by the courts. The FCO, contemporary commentators, and industry generally attributed relatively little importance to them. The FCO could use them as a tool to deter dominant enterprises from engaging in conduct that it considered harmful to the competitive process, but the reach of this tool was little tested. At least some FCO decision-makers considered the provisions generally inconsistent with the ordoliberal spirit of the GWB because they involved too high a level of uncertainty and thus excessive administrative discretion.[62] The contemporary literature suggests, however, that no one quite knew what to do with the abuse provisions. Conceptual guidelines for applying it had to be worked out, and this took far longer than with those areas of the statute that dealt with more familiar problems and problems that appeared to be of greater practical importance and, perhaps, ideological comfort.

In general, vertical restraints also played a marginal role—with one exception, the issue of resale price maintenance. The original statute permitted resale price maintenance for trademarked goods, but required such agreements to be notified to the FCO, which could take action against abuse of this prerogative. This treatment was a major source of controversy. Many saw resale price maintenance as a serious competitive restraint and called for its prohibition. Again, however, industry's political power prevented such reforms—for a while.

[61] FCO, *Tätigkeitsbericht 1966*, BT-Drucksache V/1950, at 188.
[62] President Günther of the FCO referred, for example, to the use of §22 as 'interventionistic interference with business management'. Eberhard Günther, '10 Jahre Bundeskartellamt: Rückblick und Ausblick', in *Zehn Jahre Bundeskartellamt* 11, 25 (Cologne, 1968).

5. Results

During the first decade of its operation the competition law system developed modes of operation and created expectations whose basic structures remain in place. The system was a success in the sense that it became an important component of the legal and political apparatus of the new republic and achieved many of the main goals that its supporters had set for it.

Above all, a system was created that operated reasonably effectively. It established a framework of information for business about the conduct and organizational forms that would be legally acceptable. It also developed a methodology for interpreting and applying competition law norms that gave business decision-makers a means of assessing with some degree of confidence what was expected of them in specific situations and what responses they could expect from the competition law system.

The system also achieved a large measure of compliance. The industrial circles that had opposed enactment of the cartel prohibition and sought to marginalize it did not welcome the development of the competition law system, but they generally co-operated and complied with it. Their opposition became increasingly symbolic, contained in a protest discourse rather than part of a concerted effort to eliminate the system. In part at least, this was because it was increasingly obvious that businesses could not only live with the system, but also prosper with it.

During this period the judicial characteristics of the system were emphasized and opportunities for political influence on decision-making were minimized. The discourse of competition law became predominantly juridical, as judicial decisions, legal methodology, and principles of interpretation played the central roles. At its center were courts and the court-like decisional organs of the FCO. In this context, the basic conceptual framework of ordoliberalism played a unifying role. It assured that most officials shared a basic sense of objectives and methods among themselves and with the country's political leaders.

G. SHIFTING THE FOCUS: ECONOMIC CONCENTRATION AND DYNAMIC COMPETITION

The late 1960s marked a turning point in the development of German competition law. Calls for a change of direction became common. The system that had so frequently been praised for its contribution to the extraordinary recovery of the German economy was increasingly criticized. Few seriously argued that the system should be fundamentally changed; instead, the calls were for changes in accent, in emphasis, and in theory. These calls would continue to grow in intensity until 1973, when the first major reform of the GWB was enacted.

1. Toward a new competition law model?

Why the calls for change? One factor was that calls for change had become fashionable in Germany. In many areas of German life there was a sense that a new page had to be turned after so many years of the same leadership and the same ideas.[63] For many younger Germans and those coming into positions of influence the patterns that had been established after the war had acquired a somewhat 'stale' odor reminiscent of 'occupation', the pain of postwar reconstruction and the repression of Nazi-era criminality. For them it was 'time for a change'.

A new political scenery both profited from and contributed to this ethos. In 1966 the basic political situation changed for the first time since the founding of the republic. Ludwig Erhard was replaced as chancellor, and his party's control of government ended. For the next three years the CDU was part of a 'grand coalition' that also included its major opponent, the SPD. The guiding idea was that the two largest parties would have to co-operate to change the country's political direction and deal with the social and economic challenges facing it.[64]

The economic policy of this coalition was more aggressive than its predecessors' had been. The dip in economic fortunes that had precipitated Erhard's fall was, in retrospect, a brief and minor 'hiccup' in Germany's economic advance,[65] but the economy that had been growing at an average rate of some 8 per cent per year for almost two decades suddenly seemed vulnerable. The recession of the mid-1960s seemed more menacing than the facts justified, in part because most Germans had recent recollections of at least some level of privation and were highly sensitive to the possibility of its recurrence, and also because many believed that German social and political stability depended on continued economic advance.

In response to this situation, the new regime promised to take bold action. The emphasis was on the active role of government in achieving and maintaining economic growth. In 1968 the government delivered on its promise by enacting the so-called Statute on Stability and Growth (*Stabilitäts- und Wachstums Gesetz*), which created obligations on the part of the federal government to use economic policy to promote 'stable' growth of the economy.[66] Economic growth as such had not been part of the ordoliberal program, nor had growth been a problem in Germany since the installation of the social market economy, but the recession coupled with the spread of Keynesian economic ideas made 'growth' a new watchword in economic policy circles.

[63] For discussion, see Thomas Ellwein, *Krisen und Reformen: Die Bundesrepublik seit den Sechziger Jahren* 11–20 (2d. ed., Munich, 1993).
[64] See generally Franz Schneider, *Grosse Koalition—Ende oder Neubeginn?* (Munich, 1969).
[65] Giersch et al., *The Fading Miracle*, 125–84.
[66] *Gesetz zur Förderung der Stabilität und des Wachstums der Wirtschaft*, BGBl. I 582 (June 13, 1967).

This landscape encouraged new thinking in all areas of economic policy, including competition policy. The new economics minister was Karl Schiller, a social democrat and former economics professor who had generally supported the competition law system as a means of benefiting consumers, particularly workers as consumers.[67] He expressed his ideal of economic policy as a combination of the 'Freiburg imperative' and the 'Keynesian message'.[68] Schiller announced that the government would review the competition law system from two perspectives: its impact on economic growth and its capacity to deal with the problem of economic concentration.

In 1966, Schiller established a working group within the economics ministry to look into these and other issues surrounding the operation of the competition law system, and in the context of its deliberations the idea of a new 'model' (*Leitbild*) of competition policy was increasingly discussed. This group was chaired by Wolfgang Kartte, a senior official in the economics ministry and later the second president of the FCO. His 1969 book even bore the title *A New Model for Competition Policy*.[69] In it he argued that changed economic circumstances demanded a new and more flexible conception of competition law and that this model should be based on new concepts of 'dynamic competition'.

Many found the idea of a new model attractive, though not necessarily for the same reasons. Representatives of industry had long been arguing that the ordoliberal model of complete competition was outdated and 'unrealistic'. They emphasized that German businesses were subject to increasingly stiff international competition and that a competition law based on the concept of 'complete competition' hindered their capacity to create enterprises of sufficient size to meet this competition. For them a 'new model' promised increased flexibility in competition law and less concern with stability, and it represented a means of breaking the hold of ordoliberal thinking and thus weakening the FCO's firm enforcement policy.

Government policy-makers tended to share industry's concerns about its international competitiveness, but they also tended to see these new policy directions as a response to the increasingly obvious structural challenges facing German industry.[70] Industrial concentration had been a growing concern since the early 1960s, and many viewed this new discourse as a tool for more effectively responding to this phenomenon. The ordoliberal ideal of markets

---

[67] For discussion of Schiller's policies and perspectives during this period, see Jörg Hahn, *Ökonomie, Politik und Krise: Diskutiert am Beispiel der ökonomischen Konzeption Karl Schillers* (Würzburg, 1984).

[68] See, for example, Karl Schiller, 'Wirtschaftspolitik', in Schiller, *Der Ökonom und die Gesellschaft* 69.

[69] Wolfgang Kartte, *Ein neues Leitbild für die Wettbewerbspolitik* (Cologne, 1969).

[70] See, e.g., Arbeitsgruppe Wettbewerbspolitik, Memorandum of Jan. 1, 1968, appendix 1 in Kartte, ibid., 93–100.

in which no firm had economic power seemed to many to have little to do with contemporary reality.

Intellectual movements also contributed to the impetus for change. The ordoliberal emphasis on stability, equilibrium, and minimal governmental intervention had long been out of fashion in England and the United States. There the Keynesian ideal of an active government economic policy had gained favor among economists. As German economists re-entered the international economic community they were exposed to these influences, and many sought a discourse that was more in keeping with economic doctrine elsewhere. For them, Walter Eucken's economic model of complete competition began to seem outmoded.

In the specific area of competition policy, the ideas of 'workable competition' and 'competition as a dynamic process' as formulated by the American economist, John M. Clark, had gained prominence, particularly in the United States.[71] Clark argued that the equilibrium models that had so long governed economic policy were unrealistic and that policies designed to approximate perfect competition might harm rather than foster competition. He advocated competition policy that allowed the creation of economic power positions, but sought to assure that they did not become 'monopolistic'.

Since the US provided the main external reference point for German economists and competition law specialists, these ideas began infiltrating the German economics and policy circles in the 1960s. In 1966 a young German economist named Erhard Kantzenbach published a book on competition policy that applied and modified some of Clark's ideas. The book was entitled *The Functional Capacity of Competition*.[72] It corresponded to the perceived need for new directions, and it became highly influential, making Kantzenbach a key figure in German competition policy.

In Kantzenbach's view, the key issue of competition policy was how to increase the 'intensity' of competition, and his book focused on the theoretical conditions under which 'intensity' could be increased. For him, a 'broad oligopoly' was likely to produce a maximum of competitive intensity, because in this structure the pressure to innovate and to compete is relatively high, while the likelihood that the many members of such an oligopoly would enter into competitive restraints is relatively low. One reason that this conception became attractive was that 'in contrast to American workability ideas, it gave competition policy-makers a straightforward, simple-to-use criterion: competition policy should support broad oligopolies'.[73]

[71] See, e.g., John M. Clark, *Competition as a Dynamic Process* (Washington, D.C., 1961).
[72] Erhard Kantzenbach, *Die Funktionsfähigkeit des Wettbewerbs* (Göttingen, 1966).
[73] *Der Staat in der Wirtschaft der Bundesrepublik* 89 (Dieter Grosser, ed., Opladen, 1985).

2. The contours and impacts of the new model

The new model of competition law that captured the imagination of many during this period was vague, and discussion of it was often dominated by the idea of change itself. Its proponents often focused more on the outdatedness of the ordoliberal ideal of competition law than on the contours of this 'new' image. For many, the discussions represented a message to the competition law community that a change of accent was necessary. The language of the discussion reflects this role. Proponents emphasized attractive terms like 'dynamic' and 'growth-oriented', claiming that this new model would be more 'pragmatic' than ordoliberal ideas and 'closer to economic reality'. This image was repeatedly contrasted with an ordoliberal image of 'atomistic' competition that was portrayed as its opposite—doctrinaire, idealistic, and unrealistic.

The content of the model was largely drawn from Clark and Kantzenbach, and its central notion was that concentration could often 'intensify' competition. This was 'dynamic' competition, which recognized the ebb and flow of market power. It was portrayed as a more effective basis for competition policy than earlier ideals of competition which sought markets with large numbers of powerless suppliers. Here competition policy's role was not to try to eliminate all aggregations of economic power, but to control harmful conduct and to prohibit concentrations that threatened to become monopolistic.

This image of 'dynamic competition' quickly found a lasting place in the discourse of competition policy, and it is still referred to in the competition law literature. In general, however, it has been used loosely, primarily as a symbolic acknowledgment of a vague ideal—and perhaps a mark of membership in a particular group within the competition law community. It is important also to emphasize that this 'model' did not represent a rejection of the basic conceptions of the existing competition law system—including the economic and political value of using a 'constitutional' form of law to protect the process of competition, but rather a more flexible economic ideal as the basis for the substantive operation of the system.

One impact of these additions to the competition law vocabulary was, however, to undermine the integrity of competition law discourse. The conceptual framework of the ordoliberal model—with its emphasis on eliminating economic power positions as a means of enforcing an economic 'constitution'—was no longer as exclusive as it had been in the early years of the system. Moreover, these new elements tended to bifurcate the competition law community. Economists and policy-makers increasingly tended to discuss the system in instrumental, often Keynesian terms—a matter of achieving particular economic results, whereas the legal community continued to focus on the juridical protection of economic 'freedoms' and values.[74]

[74] See, e.g., Ulrich Immenga, *Die Politische Instrumentalisierung des Kartellrechts* (Tübingen, 1976).

The degree to which these changes affected decision-making within the FCO cannot be assessed with any degree of accuracy, but observers tend to view the long-term impact as limited.[75] The FCO itself acknowledged this new conceptualization, but portrayed it as merely an articulation of the practicality and flexibility that it had been developing in its own practice—a gradual change of emphasis and accent toward a more flexible approach to competition policy in which general economic policy considerations had a more explicit and perhaps greater role.[76]

Here timing was the key. By the time these ideas became fashionable the FCO had already established its basic patterns of operation and ways of thinking, and, as we have seen, these had acquired a high degree of authority. This prevented the new 'model' from developing greater influence. Moreover, by the early 1970s criticisms of much of its substance were gaining force.[77]

H. 'IMPROVING' THE SYSTEM—1973: THE LEGISLATURE RE-ENTERS THE PICTURE

In 1969, the SPD finally became—for the first time since the war—the dominant party in a governing coalition, and for the next thirteen years it governed together with the small (generally around 10 per cent or less of the national vote) Free Democratic Party. In his inaugural address, the new Chancellor, Willy Brandt, announced that he would significantly strengthen the competition law statute as part of an economic policy designed to benefit consumers and workers,[78] and in 1973 the legislature enacted the first major amendments to the GWB.[79] These revisions did not fundamentally alter the system, but they inserted important new substantive elements into it.

---

[75] See, e.g., Wernhard Möschel, 'Wettbewerbspolitik vor neuen Herausforderungen', in *Ordnung und Freiheit* 61, 67 (Walter Eucken Institut, ed., Freiburg i.B., 1992).

[76] See, e.g., FCO, *Tätigkeitsbericht 1965*, BT-Drucksache V/530 at 8.

[77] See, e.g., comments and citations in Wolfgang Kartte & Rainer Holtschneider, 'Konzeptionelle Ansätze und Anwendungsprinzipien im Gesetz gegen Wettbewerbsbeschränkungen—Zur Geschichte des GWB', in *Handbuch des Wettbewerbs* 193, 213 (Helmut Cox et al eds., Munich, 1981).

[78] 'The [GWB] will be modernized. Business concentration is necessary in many areas, but it should not lead to elimination of effective competition. For this reason preventive merger controls are necessary. These should apply to all areas of the economy. The creation of an independent monopoly commission can be an important instrument for this purpose. The control of abuse by enterprises who are either in a market-dominant or market-power (*marktstark*) position must be expanded. On the other hand, the performance-improving co-operation among small and medium-sized firms, also in artisanry and retail trade, should be made easier (*erleichtert*)'. Stenographischer Bericht über die 5. Sitzung des Deutschen Bundestages am 28.10.1969, p. 23B, cited in Werner Jäckering, *Die Politischen Auseinandersetzungen um die Novellierung des Gesetzes gegen Wettbewerbsbeschränkungen (GWB)* 71–2 (Berlin, 1977).

[79] *Zweites Gesetz zur Änderung des Gesetzes gegen Wettbewerbsbeschränkungen*, BGBl I 917 (Aug. 3, 1973). Several minor revisions had been made in 1965, including easing the requirements for co-operation among firms, especially among small and medium-sized firms, and introducing a general abuse clause to replace the original provisions which included only enumerated forms of abuse.

The stimulus for change came from two quite different directions. The governing coalition, the FCO, and much of the relevant academic community sought changes that would remedy weaknesses in the GWB. For them, change meant 'reform'. Important segments of industry and their political allies in the CDU, CSU, and FDP, on the other hand, were interested in a more business-friendly statute. They generally sought changes that would permit greater co-operation among firms, especially small and medium-sized firms. The stage was thus set for a second major battle over the shape of German competition law.

1. Reform pressures

The political pressure to 'improve' the GWB by making it more effective came primarily from the SPD. Karl Schiller, the SPD economics minister since 1966, and both economics minister and finance minister in 1971–2, had long been a supporter of competition law, and he saw changes in the GWB as an important aspect of his party's general reform package. In particular, he saw it as a tool for generating economic growth—a companion or 'big brother' of the 'Stability and Growth Statute'.[80] In addition to its role as a tool of economic growth, competition law reform appealed to important constituencies of the SPD: for consumers, it promised lower prices; for workers, it was an additional control over the power of large businesses, and for small business it was the hope of protection from the power of large business. The SPD's coalition partner, the FDP, was the 'liberal' party and thus could hardly oppose the basic thrust of the reforms.

Mergers controls were the central component of the reform package that the government presented in 1970.[81] As we have seen, such provisions had been excluded from the original GWB near the end of the legislative deliberations. The official reason then given was that many German firms had not yet reached their optimal size, and merger controls might have inhibited their doing so. Exclusion of these provisions was also understood, however, as a political sacrifice that had been necessary to ensure enactment of the statute. From the beginning, therefore, the lack of merger control provisions was seen as an imbalance in the system, a lacuna that sooner or later would have to be filled.

Efforts to fill this gap were not new. The FCO had begun to urge the change soon after it began operations,[82] and the SPD had introduced merger control

---

[80] See Karl Schiller, Rede auf der Tagung der Studienvereinigung Kartellrecht in Bonn am 11.1.1968, in 3 *Reden zur Wirtschaftspolitik* 108 (Pressestelle des Wirtschaftsministeriums, no date).

[81] For detailed discussion of the political controversies surrounding the legislation and the legislative process itself, see Jäckering, *Auseinandersetzungen.*

[82] See, for example, the first annual report (*Tätigkeitsbericht*) of the Federal Cartel Office. Bundeskartellamt, Bericht des Bundeskartellamtes über seine Tätigkeit im Jahre 1958 sowie über

legislation as early as 1964.[83] These efforts were initially unsuccessful, largely because the CDU/CSU majority was too closely associated with industry to seek them, and because the economics ministry saw little need for them. The ministry continued to support the idea that German firms needed to be free to merge, so that they could achieve the size appropriate for international competition.[84]

During the late 1960s, however, economic events underscored the need to include merger controls in the GWB. A wave of mergers sharply increased concentration levels in some industries, focusing the attention of officials in the economics ministry on the need for some form of control on the concentration process and moving public opinion increasingly to demand such controls. The ministry's initial response was that the growing problem should be handled by the European Commission, but by 1969 it was welcoming domestic merger control legislation.[85]

Concerns over concentration were also behind a second component of the government's proposal—sharpening the abuse control provisions. As noted, these provisions had played a secondary role in the FCO's practice during its first decade, and the FCO sought legislative changes that would make it easier to enforce them. It concentrated its efforts on finding tools for applying abuse controls to firms that were not necessarily free of significant competition, but possessed economic power by virtue of their position *vis-à-vis* their competitors.

The third major element in the package was the proposal to allow small and medium-sized firms to 'co-operate' without having to fear that they might violate the cartel prohibition. This proposal was obviously supported by industry. More important, however, the economics ministry perceived it as an application of the new 'model' of 'dynamic competition', a means of allowing German firms to achieve co-operative efficiency advantages that would make them better able to compete on foreign markets.

The government's plans for 'improving' the GWB enjoyed widespread support. The governmental bureaucracy, most importantly the economics ministry, had been calling for several of these changes for years.[86] It supported

die Lage und Entwicklung auf seinem Aufgabengebiet, in *Berichte des Bundeskartellamtes 1958/1959/1960* at 85–86 (Düsseldorf, 1961).

[83] See Jäckering, *Auseinandersetzungen*, 38–40.

[84] See, e.g., Stellungnahme der Bundesregierung zum Tätigkeitsbericht des Bundeskartellamtes für 1967. BT-Drucksache V/2841, at 2. According to the government, 'Competition policy must be . . . continually adapted to changing economic circumstances. The Common Market and the international economic integration have created new requirements for competition. Larger markets often require larger, more economically effective business units'.

[85] For discussion, see Jäckering, *Auseinandersetzungen*, 51–52 and for details of this concentration process, see ibid., 52–66.

[86] For discussion of the controversy over merger control during this period, with extensive excerpts from contemporary materials, see *Fusionskontrolle: Für und Wider* (Peter Raisch et al eds., Stuttgart, 1970).

merger control provisions as a means of preventing excessive concentration, and it also supported co-operation as a means of improving the position of small and medium-sized industries. The FCO and much of the competition law community may have been less enthusiastic about the co-operation ideas, but they strongly supported merger control provisions and a strengthening of the abuse control provisions. Consumer groups, who were beginning to play a more important role in the political process, also welcomed the government's proposals. Industry supported those portions of the proposal that sought to improve the opportunities for co-operation between smaller and medium-sized industries, although most industrial groups opposed the merger control proposals and the proposed tightening of the abuse control provisions.[87]

2. The legislative dynamics

The dynamics of this first major revision of the GWB were far different than those that had shaped the original GWB. The SPD/FDP coalition had the political power to enact the legislation it sought. The SPD did not seek to alienate industrial interest groups, but it did not depend on industry for political support, and thus the coalition was in a better position to resist their pressures than had been its CDU/CSU predecessor. Moreover, the economic situation obviously called for some type of response to the problem of concentration. The government saw these changes as an important contribution to price moderation and thus economic and even political stability, and there was widespread political support for this view.[88]

Another reason that the dynamics of this 'reform' process were so different from the original conflicts over the structure of the GWB was an emerging emphasis on protecting the interests of small and medium-sized firms. For both the government and industry, *Mittelstandspolitik*—protecting the interests of small and medium-sized firms—was an important part of this package, and it would continue to grow in importance in the rhetoric of competition law.[89] Each of the main elements of the package could be seen as serving the interests of small and medium-sized firms. On one level, the protection of these interests has powerful roots in German history and society: the somewhat (or very) romanticized image of the entrepreneur who was part of the community, had learned his trade well, and provided high quality products or service was and remains remarkably powerful. At another level, these values and the rhetoric that surrounded them appealed to large groups of voters for

---

[87] For the industry position opposing merger controls, see Arno Sölter, 'Wider die nationale Fusionskontrolle', in *Fusionskontrolle* 45–86 (Peter Raisch et al eds., Stuttgart, 1970).

[88] For discussion, see, e.g., Jäckering, *Auseinandersetzungen*, 217–18.

[89] For general discussion of *Mittelstandspolitik* in Germany, see, e.g., Mathias Schmidt, *Ziele und Intrumente der Mittelstandspolitik in der Bundesrepublik Deutschland* (Cologne, 1988).

which each of the main parties was competing. Finally, the image of protecting these interests symbolized social unity amid the growing political and social conflicts of the late 1960s and early 1970s.[90]

The locus of the conflict was thus in details rather than in fundamental conceptions of the nature and role of competition law, as it had been at the 'birth' of the GWB. Industrial groups were not in a position to block the legislation completely (nor did they want to) and thus their objectives were to weaken certain of the proposals and strengthen others. The legislative process consisted of trying to find textual formulations that were within the basic outlines of Brandt's reform package and that would be generally acceptable to most members of the community.

In the end, the legislative process changed numerous details from the original proposals, but the basic components of the package remained.[91] Moreover, as the process continued, the general sense that the circumstances were favorable to change led to additional 'reforms' that had been politically unacceptable only a few years earlier, and that had therefore not even been part of the original government package.[92] The most notable of these was the prohibition of resale price maintenance. Industry had been powerful enough during the 'grand coalition' to block plans to revise the GWB because those plans contained such a prohibition, but the reform forces now recognized that this could be included in the bill, and it was. The first major revision of the GWB became effective on August 5, 1973.

3. Consequences

The 1973 amendments to the GWB represented a new chapter in the development of German competition law. With regard to the substantive scope of the system, the introduction of merger control provisions added a component to the system that would within a few years become its central focus. It was, as Wolfgang Kartte put it, 'Even more than the cartel prohibition was in its time, something completely new for our legal thinking'.[93] In addition, because Germany was gaining experience with merger control during the decade and a half of discussions of the issue on the European level, this experience had a major impact not only on the European merger statute, but also on its implementation.

The influence of these amendments on the dynamics of the competition law system itself was no less significant. With these amendments, the legislature

---

[90] The late 1960s were years of increased social tension in Germany, as in much of the rest of Western Europe and the United States. For discussion of the situation in Germany, see Dietrich Thränhardt, *Geschichte der Bundesrepublik Deutschland 1949–1990* 167–85 (Frankfurt a.M., 1996).
[91] For discussion, see Jäckering, *Auseinandersetzungen,* 67–88.
[92] For discussion, see ibid. 207–19.
[93] Wolfgang Kartte, 'Fusionskontrolle—aber wie?' 1970 *Wirtschaftsdienst* 121–22 (1970).

became a major part of that system, and since then a central part of the discourse of competition law has been whether the legislature would make particular types of changes and, if so, when. Moreover, significant amendments to the GWB have become frequent, a 'normal' part of the system's operations. In 1976, amendments included special provisions relating to media mergers.[94] In 1980, amendments centered on strengthening the merger control provisions.[95] And in 1990, significant changes were made in the merger control, abuse control and cartel provisions—all basically for the purpose of increasing protection for small and medium-sized industries.[96] A system in which the legislature plays this type of role was diverging—at least arguably—from the ordoliberal image of a competition law system based on 'constitutional' principles.

I. THE ABUSE PROVISIONS: HOPES AND FRUSTRATIONS

As the task of dealing with economic concentration and its consequences replaced the cartel problem at the center of competition law thought and practice, attention shifted to the two main strategies available for the task. The provisions concerning abuse of a market-dominating position seemed to be a means of at least reducing the harms that powerful firms could inflict on the competitive process, while merger control provisions promised to control the process itself. In this section we will deal with the first of these areas.

The battle over the role of the abuse concept was waged primarily during the 1970s, a period marked in Germany as elsewhere by the 'oil shocks' and their consequences. The most important of these consequences in Germany was the extraordinary and rapid increase in the price of oil, which made inflation a major economic policy issue for the first time since the currency reform of 1948. This combined with the collapse of the Bretton Woods international monetary system and the end of fixed exchange rates to usher in a new phase in German economic development. In it, economic growth slowed considerably. Unemployment became increasingly persistent and structural rather than cyclical, as the high cost of German products on international markets led firms to move production to countries with lower costs and intensified efforts to reduce the costs of domestic production.

The economic problems of the period should not, however, be overstated. Germany had become the most powerful economy in Europe, and, although growth slowed markedly in the 1970s, it remained respectable by Western

---

[94] *Drittes Gesetz zur Änderung des Gesetzes gegen Wettbewerbsbeschränkungen*, BGBl.I, p.1697 (June 28, 1976).

[95] *Viertes Gesetz zur Änderung des Gesetzes gegen Wettbewerbsbeschränkungen*, BGBl.I, p.458 (April 26, 1980).

[96] *Fünftes Gesetz zur Änderung des Gesetzes gegen Wettbewerbsbeschränkungen*, BGBl.I, p.2486 (December 22, 1989).

standards. The German economy also remained stable—suffering few of the labor problems encountered during the period in countries such as France, England and Italy.

The coalition government in which the Social Democratic Party shared power with the liberal party (FDP) remained in power until 1982. This meant an enhanced sensitivity in policy-making to the impact of inflation, particularly on workers. The social democrats no longer used the rhetoric of 'exploitation' that had been so much a part of their earlier ideology, but the basic sentiments of protecting workers against 'big business' had not disappeared. When Helmut Schmidt replaced Willy Brandt as chancellor in 1974, these sentiments were somewhat muted, but the political climate required attention to traditional social democratic concerns.

1. The background of the abuse concept

When in the late 1960s and the 1970s the FCO and the academic community began to pay closer attention to the abuse concept as a tool for dealing with inflation and economic concentration, they were confronted with its history. As we have seen, that concept played important roles in ordoliberal thought, where one of the central notions was that in situations where competition was weak or non-existent, the state should require enterprises to conduct themselves *as if* they were faced with 'complete competition'. This meant that they were to be required to compete 'on the merits' rather than 'abuse' their power to gain an unfair advantage over rivals. It was assumed that in enforcing the as-if standard, the state would be assuring that success in the marketplace was the result of better performance rather than of the use of economic power.

Although the concept of abuse had been included in the original GWB, little attention had been paid to it in the long debates over the contents of the legislation. The concept was not defined in the GWB, apparently because it was assumed that the as-if standard would provide adequate guidance for giving content to it.[97] Economic science would determine for a given market what forms of competition would be consistent with full competition on the market, and the FCO and the courts could apply the statute by determining whether particular conduct fit within those parameters. At least in theory, the abuse standard could be consistently and objectively applied.

In order to assure that the abuse concept would not be interpreted too broadly, however, the legislation placed limitations on its scope. According to §22 of the GWB, as originally enacted, the FCO was authorized to take action against the abuse of power by market-dominating enterprises only in conjunction with (1) the establishment of prices, (2) the formulation of terms or conditions of sale, and (3) tying arrangements.

[97] See Fritz Rittner, '§ 22 GWB im Spannungsfeld wirtschaftswissenschaftlicher Theorien und rechtsstaatlicher Postulate', in *Festschrift für Günther Hartmann* 251, 259–62 (Cologne, 1976).

For well over a decade after enactment of the GWB, §22 was little used.[98] In part this was due to the FCO's desire to avoid potentially controversial issues, especially where, as here, there were likely to be significant conflicts with powerful interests. Segments of German industry were strongly opposed to the potential government 'interference' with business activity that the abuse concept represented.[99] In addition, the international competitiveness of German industry was a dominant political concern of the period, and there was little support for any government activity that might hamper the activities of the major corporations which were viewed as the engine of economic recovery.

The concept's vagueness was a major source of concern. In German law, a court must generally refuse to apply a statutory provision which is so vague that accepted methods of legal reasoning cannot be used to interpret it—that is, where the judge must 'legislate' rather than interpret. There was, therefore, a significant risk that the courts would overturn enforcement actions based on the abuse principle, and this increased the FCO's reluctance to enforce the concept.

Finally, developments in economic thought were undermining confidence in the applicability of the abuse concept. The assumption that the concept of as-if competition would provide clear guidelines for applying the abuse concept had been based on the proposition that economic science could effectively use 'perfect competition' as a model against which to measure actual economic behavior. As the influence of Keynesian thought and 'workable competition' models increased in Germany during the 1960s, however, this assumption became less tenable, weakening confidence in the reference framework that had been assumed to be the source of content for the abuse concept.

Nevertheless, in 1965, the legislature expanded the scope of application of the abuse concept in order to make §22 more effective.[100] It eliminated reference to specific types of abuse and authorized the FCO to take action against any conduct which represented abuse of a market-dominating position.[101] The substantive scope of the abuse concept has remained basically unchanged since then.

Expansion of the scope of the concept generated often intense scholarly controversy beginning during the later half of the 1960s,[102] and as this activ-

[98] See Wernhard Möschel, *Der Oligopolmissbrauch im Recht der Wettbewerbsbeschänkungen* 134–37 (Tübingen, 1974).
[99] For a discussion of the view of industry, see Benisch, '10 Jahre Praxis', 26–28. The FCO's reluctance to use the concept also meant that there was little opportunity for the courts to develop the law, because private suits cannot be brought under § 22.
[100] *Zweites Gesetz zur Änderung des Gesetzes gegen Wettbewerbsbeschränkungen*, BGBl. I 1963 (Sept. 15, 1965).
[101] See Jäckering, *Auseinandersetzungen*, 38–42.
[102] For a description, see Jürgen Baur, *Der Missbrauch im deutschen Kartellrecht* 43–54 (Tübingen, 1972).

ity began to generate a degree of clarity concerning basic principles to be used in interpreting §22, the FCO increased its application of the abuse concept. Another reason for the increased activity was growing popular and hence political concern about the power of large enterprises.[103] Legislators repeatedly urged the FCO to increase its use of §22, and they expanded the concept of a market-dominating position in order to increase its opportunities to do so.

By the mid-1970s, case law and legal scholarship had produced a general consensus regarding basic contours of the abuse concept. First, the concept was to be used only to protect the process of economic competition. It was not to be used to protect the 'public interest'.[104] The central values were, therefore, freedom of enterprise and maximum access to markets. Second, neither motive nor intent to harm were to be relevant to the application of the concept; it was to be applied solely with reference to the objective characteristics of the conduct involved.[105] Third, the concept of abuse did not involve moral or ethical values; its interpretation was to be based solely on political and economic values.[106] Fourth, in order to be abusive within the meaning of the statute, conduct had to be related to the firm's economic power. Either the firm's economic power had to make the conduct possible or it had to cause its harmful effects.[107]

Before looking at how the FCO and the courts built on these basic principles in developing the abuse concept, we need to describe briefly the scope of application of the concept. We have seen that the concept initially applied to firms that actually dominated markets (that is, did not face 'significant competition') and that in 1973 this was extended to apply to firms with a 'superior market position'. The statute does not define the latter concept, but the case law has defined it as a situation in which a firm has available to it 'a range of conduct that is not adequately limited by competition'.[108] The statute mentions as factors in assessing whether such a situation exists 'in addition to

[103] See Jäckering, *Auseinandersetzungen*, 127–65. Moreover, especially during the 1970s, the comparative strength of the German economy reduced political opposition to efforts to control large enterprises.

[104] See, e.g. Möschel, *Recht der Wettbewerbsbeschränkungen*, 294.

[105] See Immenga & Mestmäcker, *Kommentar zum GWB*, 736.

[106] See, e.g., Eugen Langen et al., *Kommentar zum Kartellgesetz* 680–81 (6th ed., Neuwied, 1982).

[107] Ibid.

[108] The courts have based their analysis on the official government explanation. 'The market position of an enterprise corresponds to the range of conduct that the enterprise has in employing its means of competition. The competitive ranges of enterprises vary according to their temporal, geographic, technical and personal advantages. Such advantages can create a degree of independence with regard to the use of competitive strategies and thus a degree of influence on the market process'. *Regierungsbegründung zum Entwurf eines Zweiten Gesetzes zur Änderung des Gesetzes gegen Wettbewerbsbeschränkung*, BT-Drucksache VI/2520, at 21 (Aug. 18, 1971). See, e.g., Bundesgerichtshof (BGH), Dec. of July 3, 1976, *WuW/E* BGH 1435, 1439 (Vitamin B-12).

market share, financial power, access to acquisition and sales markets, intra-corporate ties to other firms, and other legal or actual barriers to the entry of other firms' (§22(1)2). The introduction of this concept greatly increased the number of situations to which the abuse concept could be applied.

2. Applying the abuse concept: exploitation

In developing the abuse concept, German scholarship and practice distinguished between two basic forms of abuse. One is 'exploitation abuse' (*Ausbeutungsmissbrauch*) and refers to harm to those who either buy from or sell to dominant enterprises. The other is 'impediment abuse' (*Behinderungsmissbrauch*) which refers primarily to harm to competitors of the dominant enterprise. In both cases, the ultimate concern is with protection of the process of competition.

The concept of exploitation abuse is used to prevent dominant enterprises from 'exploiting' those dealing with them, as, for example, where they raise prices beyond those which a competitive market would allow or force suppliers or purchasers to grant terms more favorable than those that would exist under competitive conditions.[109] Such conduct is seen as inconsistent with a competitive economy, for it allows powerful firms to use their power to 'distort' the competitive process.

This form of abuse was viewed by many as a potentially important tool in combating the new inflationary pressures of the 1970s. In order to apply §22 in such cases, however, German law had to resolve a fundamental issue concerning the relationship between the substantive concept of abuse and the FCO's enforcement power. If the FCO could merely levy a fine against an enterprise for having charged a price above the 'competitive' price, its ability to prevent such pricing abuses might be quite limited. On the other hand, if the FCO could order enterprises not to raise prices above a level which it determined to be 'competitive', this might be viewed as economic *'dirigisme'* and thus inconsistent with the GWB's basic goal of protecting economic freedom.

Legal commentators lined up on both sides of this issue in the early 1970s. Those concerned about the economic freedom of enterprises and the possibility that this interpretation of the abuse concept might lead the FCO to engage in unacceptable interventionism were often associated with the Freiburg economist Erich Hoppmann,[110] while those more concerned with the need to make the abuse concept an effective tool for combating inflation were frequently associated with Erhard Kantzenbach.

[109] For discussion, see Monopolkommission, *Anwendung und Möglichkeiten der Missbrauchsaufsicht über marktbeherrschende Unternehmen seit Inkrafttreten der Kartellgesetznovelle* 31–35 and 41–45 (Sondergutachten l, Baden-Baden 1977).
[110] See, e.g., Erich Hoppmann, *Marktmacht und Wettbewerb* (Tübingen, 1977).

The Supreme Court resolved what appeared to be the key issue in 1976 in the famous *Vitamin B12* case.[111] The case involved the sale of vitamins in Germany at prices significantly above those in neighboring countries.[112] The FCO found German prices to be above those which could have been charged in a competitive market, and ordered the seller to reduce its prices by a specific percentage so as to bring them within the range of competitive prices.[113] The Berlin Appeals Court confirmed the FCO's authority to take such action, while changing the percentage reduction required.[114] The Supreme Court agreed that the FCO could order the defendant to reduce its prices.[115] According to the Court, such an order did not represent administrative interference with the defendants' economic freedom. It merely established a limit beyond which prices would be considered abusive. The defendant could then determine how to respond to that specific order. The Court emphasized that §22 was not to be understood to justify ongoing control by the FCO of business activity; it could merely be used to determine whether specific conduct— such as setting prices above a specified level—was abusive. In terms of substantive law, the *Vitamin B12* decision clarified and strengthened the FCO's position in applying §22.

On another key issue, however, the Supreme Court created a major obstacle to use of the exploitation abuse concept. In order to apply §22 in exploitation cases, it is necessary to posit a hypothetical 'competitive' price range and then ask whether the prices at issue fall within that range. Thus the question of how one establishes that standard is fundamental to application of the concept. This issue came before the Supreme Court in late 1976 in the *Valium* case.[116] The FCO there ordered the manufacturer of the pharmaceuticals Valium and Librium to reduce the prices of those drugs in Germany. In order to establish that the prices were abusive, the FCO compared the prices on the German market with prices in a neighboring country (the Netherlands) where the market was more competitive.[117] The Berlin Appeals Court upheld the FCO's determination of abuse.[118]

The Supreme Court approved the comparison market method of establishing abuse, but made it difficult to use. It held that the FCO had not established the comparability of the markets. It analyzed the various adjustments that had been made by the FCO in order to take account of the structural differences between the two markets and concluded that the FCO had

[111] Bundesgerichtshof [BGH], Dec. of July 3, 1976, *Wirtschaft und Wettbewerb Entscheidungssammlung [WuWlE]* BGH 1435 (*Vitamin B-12*).

[112] For discussion, see Kurt Markert, 'Recent Developments in German Antitrust Law', 43 *Fordham L. Rev.* 697, 711–14 (1975).

[113] FCO, Dec. of March 21, 1974, *WuWlE* BKartA 1482 (*Vitamin B-12*).

[114] KG (Berlin Appeals Court), Dec. of March 19, 1975, *WuWlE* OLG 1599 (*Vitamin B-12*).

[115] BGH, Dec. of July 3, 1976, *WuWlE* BGH 1435, 1437 (*Vitamin B-12*).

[116] BGH, Dec. of Dec. 16, 1976, *WuWlE* BGH 1445 (*Valium*).

[117] FCO, Dec. of Oct. 16, 1974, *WuWlE* BKartA 1526 (*Valium/Librium*).

[118] KG, Dec. of Jan. 5, 1976, *WuWlE* OLG 1645 (*Valium/Librium*).

not adequately established their comparability. The case thus required that in order to establish abuse by means of market comparison, the FCO must provide a detailed factual and theoretical analysis of every significant structural difference between the two markets. In addition, the Court held that prices in the dominated market would be considered abusive only where they exceeded the comparison market price by a 'substantial margin', and that the FCO would also have to provide a detailed analysis of the reasons for its standard of substantiality in each case.[119]

The *Valium* decision demonstrated the difficulty of applying the concept of exploitation abuse in a manner that satisfied judicial standards. The Supreme Court was unwilling to allow the application of a hypothetical standard of conduct without adequate proof of each of the elements on which the derivation of the standard was based. The result was to make this form of abuse difficult to prove.

In an attempt to facilitate application of the exploitation abuse concept, the legislature in 1980 amended §22 to provide that abuse exists where an enterprise demands terms or prices which deviate from those 'which with a high degree of probability would exist if there were effective competition in the market'.[120] This change has been interpreted to eliminate the requirement that prices exceed comparison market prices by a 'substantial margin', but it does not significantly alter the general requirements established by the *Valium* case.[121]

The FCO has continued to apply §22 to exploitation cases, but the problems of proof have reduced its effectiveness. Officials still use the abuse provisions as a threat to induce compliance, but the business community is aware that the FCO faces significant burdens in litigating such cases, and this undermines its negotiating position. As a result, relatively few of these cases have reached the courts or even public hearings since the late 1970s, and there is a widespread belief that the concept of exploitation abuse is ill-adapted to judicial application.[122]

3. Impediment abuse

As application of the exploitation abuse concept foundered on high proof standards, interest and enforcement activity involving the abuse section turned to the other form of abuse, impediment abuse.[123] The main objective

---

[119] BGH, Dec. of Dec. 16, 1976, *WuW/E* BGH 1445,1452 (*Valium*).

[120] *Viertes Gesetz zur Änderung des Gesetzes gegen Wettbewerbsbeschränkungen* BGBl. I 458 (April 26, 1980).

[121] Ernst Niederleithinger, 'Probleme der Missbrauchsaufsicht aus der Sicht des Bundeskartellamtes', in *Die Missbrauchsaufsicht vor dem Hintergrund der Entwicklungen der neueren Wettbewerbstheorie* 65, 72–73 (Burkhardt Röper, ed., Berlin, 1982).

[122] See, e.g., Baur, 'Missbrauchsaufsicht', 132.

[123] For discussion, see, e.g., Kurt Markert, *Die Wettbewerberbehinderung im GWB nach der vierten Kartellnovelle* (Heidelberg, 1982) and Olaf Tyllack, *Wettbewerb und Behinderung* (Munich, 1984).

here is to protect the process of competition by preventing dominant firms from using their power to harm competitors, but there is much controversy concerning the analysis to be applied in impediment cases.[124] The central problem is how to distinguish 'abusive' from competitive conduct. Competition assumes, by definition, that enterprises attempt to 'win' the battle of the marketplace—that is, to cause economic harm to competitors. The fact that conduct is intended to cause such harm and that such harm results cannot, therefore, be the criterion for abusive conduct; that criterion must be sought in the characteristics of the conduct or in its other effects.

The early impediment abuse cases struggled to find an effective analysis. They applied the basic idea of 'performance competition' as called for by ordoliberal theory, but they did so loosely and in conjunction with broader ideas of fairness and the balancing of harms. In a 1969 case, for example, the Berlin Appeals Court found that tying arrangements violated §22 'because they cement a market-dominating position other than by better performance and strangle future competition'.[125] The Court also included, however, a balancing element in its opinion. If the tie-in had been necessary to the defendant's operations, the Court indicated that the arrangement might have been approved on fairness grounds.

As a potentially greater role for the abuse concept was being explored in the 1970s, Professor Peter Ulmer provided a theoretical basis for applying the abuse section,[126] and it was quickly adopted by the Berlin Appeals Court.[127] According to this test, the conduct of a dominant firm constitutes 'abuse' where two conditions are met: the conduct must constitute 'non-performance competition'—that is, it must represent competition which is not 'on the merits'—and it must restrict competition remaining in the dominated market.[128] In order to further define the conceptual contours of the idea of performance competition, Ulmer related its use in the abuse context to German unfair trade law, where it had been introduced by scholars in the 1930s in order to help determine whether conduct was unfair for purposes of that statute.[129] Conduct which represents improved performance in the marketplace generally cannot violate the unfair trade law, whereas non-performance competition may. According to Ulmer, §22 of the GWB requires a higher standard of conduct for dominant firms than is required for other firms. Accordingly,

---

[124] For an overview of the controversy, see Peter Ulmer, 'Kartellrechtswidrige Konkurrentenbehinderung durch Leistungsfremdes Verhalten marktbeherrschender Unternehmen', in *Recht und Wirtschaft Heute: Festschrift für Max Kummer* 565–96 (Bern, 1980).

[125] KG, Dec. of Feb. 2, 1969, *WuW/E* OLG 995, 1000 (*Handpreisauszeichner*).

[126] See, e.g., Ulmer, 'Kartellrechtswidrige Konkurrentenbehinderung', and Peter Ulmer, *Schranken zulässigen Wettbewerbs marktbeherrschender Unternehmen* (Baden-Baden, 1977).

[127] KG, Dec. of Jan. 26, 1977, *WuW/E* OLG 1767, 1773 (*Kombinationstarif*).

[128] For discussion of the performance competition standard in the context of § 22, see Rüdiger Hahn, *Behinderungsmissbräuche marktbeherrschender Unternehmen* 53–81 (Frankfurt a.M., 1984).

[129] See Tyllack, *Wettbewerb und Behinderung*, 188–213.

non-performance competition that does not violate the unfair competition statute may be abusive under §22, provided it also restricts competition in the dominated market.

The Berlin Appeals Court first applied this standard in the *Combination Price Schedule* case in 1977.[130] The Court emphasized that dominant enterprises should be subject to a standard of conduct higher than that of non-dominant firms, because such conduct necessarily distorted competition and increased barriers to entry. The Court went on, however, to require that abuse be found only where the conduct led to the destruction or serious impairment of the competition remaining in the dominated market.[131] For the Court, this meant a deleterious change in the *structure* of the market. It said that this limitation on the scope of the non-performance test was necessary in order not to interfere with the dominant enterprises's right to *use* its market power. The Berlin Appeals Court continued to apply this basic analysis, and its requirement of structural impact became a major obstacle for the FCO in developing the concept of impediment abuse.[132]

There was much criticism of this approach.[133] Although it admittedly identified some conduct that is potentially harmful, its critics claimed that with regard to many important fact situations it did not effectively distinguish between conduct which was economically justified and that which was not.[134] In addition, under this analysis, economic power renders conduct illegal which would otherwise be legal, and critics claimed that it was unclear how much power made what kinds of conduct illegal. Finally, the performance competition concept did not deal directly with certain harms to which §22 was thought to be addressed. For example, if a dominant firm intentionally injures competitors in an overt attempt to monopolize a market, this would not necessarily be abusive under the performance competition analysis.

Such criticism of the performance competition analysis led to substantial support in the legal literature for an alternative analysis of impediment abuse based on interest balancing.[135] According to this view, the conduct of a dominant firm is considered abusive where it impedes the competitive opportunities of another firm and cannot be justified by resulting improvements either in consumer welfare or in the structure or intensity of competition on the market. The courts must, therefore, weigh the harm to competitors against expected economic benefits to society. Proponents of this approach argue that the abuse concept is so vague that it can be given content only through case-by-case analysis of the economic consequences of the dominant firm's

[130] KG, Dec. of Jan. 26, 1977, *WuW/E* OLG 1767.
[131] KG, Dec. of Jan. 26, 1977, *WuW/E* OLG 1767, 1772.
[132] See generally Hahn, *Behinderungsmissbräuche*, 33–38.
[133] See, e.g., Immenga & Mestmäcker, *Kommentar zum GWB*, 806–8.
[134] Möschel, *Recht der Wettbewerbsbeschränkungen*, 328–31.
[135] For references and discussion, see Immenga & Mestmäcker, *Kommentar zum GWB*, 739–40.

behavior. Moreover, they claim, conduct by dominant firms should lead to state interference only where harm to competitors clearly outweighs any resulting economic benefits to society.[136]

In 1980, the legislature sought to override the judicially-imposed restraints on application of the abuse concept by adding a provision to §22 that found abuse where a market-dominating enterprise 'impedes, without a factually justified reason, the competitive opportunities of other enterprises in a way which is significant for competition in the market'.[137] Accordingly, conduct can violate §22 if it has a significant competitive impact and is not 'factually justified', thus relaxing the requirement of an 'extensive effect' on competition that the Berlin Appeals Court had imposed.

The legislature's efforts to support greater use of the abuse concept did not, however, resolve the core analytical issue of how to distinguish impeding conduct from acceptable competitive conduct. The legislation did not refer to the concept of performance competition, although that concept had been included in earlier drafts;[138] nor is there direct reference to its alternative, the balancing test. Moreover, the amendments created a new level of complexity, because the language 'without a factually justified reason' also had to be interpreted and applied.

4. Controlling abuse through private litigation

As the FCO, legal scholars, the courts, and the legislature were trying to 'improve' §22 in various ways—without great success—another provision of the GWB was being expanded to handle important categories of cases that originally had been expected to be treated under §22.[139] The GWB (§26) prohibited certain categories of 'powerful' enterprises from unfairly impeding another enterprise or 'in the absence of facts justifying such differentiation, treat such enterprise, directly or indirectly, in a manner different from the treatment it accords to similar enterprises'. This section was designed to provide a specific prohibition for certain forms of conduct by 'powerful' firms that were necessarily 'abusive'. It was also designated a 'protective provision', and this allowed enterprises suffering harm from the conduct to file private suits to terminate it, and to recover compensation for damages sustained.

In 1973, an additional provision was added to this section in order to make it applicable to firms on which other firms were 'dependent'. Dependency was deemed to exist where a supplier did not have 'sufficient and reasonable possibilities' to shift to another purchaser. This was the concept of 'relative

---

[136] Möschel, *Recht der Wettbewerbsbeschränkungen*, 332.

[137] *Viertes Gesetz zur Änderung des Gesetzes gegen Wettbewerbsbeschränkungen*, BGBl. I 458 (April 26, 1980).

[138] Niederleithinger, 'Probleme der Missbrauchsaufsicht', 74.

[139] For discussion, see, e.g., David J. Gerber, 'The German Approach to Price Discrimination and Other Forms of Business Discrimination', 27 *Antitrust Bull.* 241 (1982).

market power', and its use was to be expanded considerably in the following years. It was developed primarily by the economist Helmut Arndt, who demonstrated that economic power was a problem even where there was no dominance of a market. If a firm was 'dependent' on another firm, the firm with this 'relative power' was in a position to harm or destroy the dependent, and thus it should be prevented from abusing this power.[140]

This change led to a major increase in private litigation under this section, and such litigation has in practice become more important in many respects than the abuse provisions themselves. We need not delve into the details of these special provisions and their evolution.[141] For our purposes, it is important only to recognize that in the German system, private litigation has been successfully developed to supplement administrative application of the abuse concept with respect to certain specific, well-defined forms of abuse.

The German efforts to utilize the abuse concept to protect the competitive process illuminate the interplay among the components of the competition law system and the difficulties of using the abuse concept in a juridically-oriented system. The abuse concept 'fits' easily into an administrative system, but the courts have repeatedly placed significant evidentiary burdens on its use. As a political symbol, the abuse concept retains much of its force: there is a widespread belief that the abuse concept should be used to accomplish its stated objectives, and this has led the legislature to attempt to strengthen the abuse concept as a tool. Nevertheless, despite these efforts, there remains serious doubt as to whether sufficient analytical content can be ascribed to the concept to allow it to operate effectively under the kind of judicial scrutiny provided by the German courts.

J. THE 1980s AND AFTER: THE PRIMACY OF MERGER CONTROL

By the early 1980s it was apparent that court-imposed restrictions on the FCO's use of the abuse control provisions would blunt its utility as a tool in dealing with the consequences of economic concentration, but even before then, merger controls—the other major tool for responding to the problem of economic concentration—were moving to the center of the competition law stage. As one writer put it in 1991, 'To a large extent competition policy is [now] identical with merger control policy'.[142]

Throughout most of the 1980s, the German economic situation did not change dramatically. Unemployment and inflation were low, while the German Mark remained high and relatively stable. The successes of German

---

[140] See Helmut Arndt, *Markt und Macht* (2d ed., Tübingen, 1973) and id., *Wirtschaftliche Macht* (3d ed., Munich, 1980).

[141] For discussion, see Immenga & Mestmäcker, *Kommentar zum GWB*, 1208–1396.

[142] Volker Emmerich, *Kartellrecht* 334 (6th ed., Munich, 1991).

firms on international markets were an important ingredient in the strength of the economy, but in order to maintain international competitiveness, German firms were increasingly investing outside Germany, and domestic job creation lagged. Moreover, foreign investment in Germany fell off sharply—Germany was becoming too expensive. German re-unification in 1989 temporarily solved certain sectoral employment problems, but it also imposed extraordinary new costs on the German economy and exacerbated pressures on the currency and on labor costs.

The political situation also remained stable. In 1982 the CDU/CSU regained its position as the strongest political organization. It formed a coalition with the liberal Free Democratic Party that governed the country for more than a decade and a half. During this time, the economics ministry was in the hands of the FDP, which had become heavily dependent on industry for economic support and was seen by many as a protector of industry. For both the CDU/CSU and the FDP, the political support of small and medium-sized industries was of much importance.

Developing a merger control regime presented the FCO and the courts with new challenges. Whereas the harms to competition from cartel agreements were obvious (even though cartel supporters often saw counterbalancing benefits from cartelization), assessing the harms caused by mergers involves highly complex economic issues on which experts often have differing opinions.[143] Different types of mergers have different potential consequences for the competitive process: a merger among competitors (that is, a horizontal merger) is likely, for example, to be more harmful than a merger between non-competitors. This means greater discretion and uncertainty for decision-makers. Moreover, this discretion must often be exercised under intense time pressures and the glare of public scrutiny. The economic consequences of many mergers also tend to increase political pressure on the decision-making process. The question was how the system would deal with such challenges.

1. The basic system

The main features of the merger control system that was introduced in 1973 have remained unchanged, so that I can use the present tense in presenting a general overview of it.[144] I will then mention major changes—mainly additions—to the system as we encounter them. This may also be the most effective way to grasp the basics of what has become an exceptionally complex statutory scheme.

---

[143] See Ulrich Immenga, 'Fusionskontrolle: Deutsche Konzeption und Erfahrungen', in *Institutionen und Grundfragen des Wettbewerbsrechts* 125, 126–28 (Uwe Blaurock, ed., Frankfurt a.M., 1988).

[144] For detailed discussion of the merger control provisions, see Rainer Bechtold & Werner Kleinmann, *Kommentar zur Fusionskontrolle* (2d. ed., Heidelberg, 1989).

The only provision of the original GWB that related directly to mergers was §23, which established a reporting duty for mergers meeting certain size criteria. Its sole purpose was to provide the FCO and the government with information about the process of concentration. With the introduction of merger controls, this provision retained its original function, but also served the added function of defining 'merger' for purposes of the new controls. Details of this definition have changed over time, as the legislature has tried to include as many forms of 'economic combination' within it as possible, but for our purposes there is no need to investigate it more carefully.

The central provision in the merger control scheme requires the FCO to prohibit mergers where 'it is to be expected that they would create or strengthen a market-dominating position'(§24). The FCO may not prohibit a merger that meets these requirements, however, if the market itself is considered too small to warrant controls or if each of the merging firms has revenues below specified amounts. In addition, the FCO may not prohibit a merger where the defendant can show that 'improvements in the competitive situation will occur' and that these improvements outweigh the likely harms to competition from the merger.

The basic structure of the provisions authorizes the FCO to prohibit mergers within a certain period of time after it learns of the merger. The statute also contains, however, a 'preventive' component that under specified circumstances requires merging firms to notify the FCO of the planned merger prior to its completion and allows the FCO a relatively short period of time (four months) to decide whether to prohibit the merger. Firms may also voluntarily notify the FCO of a proposed merger.

Finally, the merger control scheme also contains a specific provision—§24(3)—permitting political decisions to override a decision of the FCO. The minister of economics may prevent the FCO from prohibiting a merger in any case in which the 'benefits for the economy as a whole' outweigh the harms of the competitive restraint or the restraint is justified by an overriding public interest.

2. Operating the system: basic principles

The FCO's initial task was to develop basic operating principles for the system, and in doing so it relied on the juridical methodology and procedures that it had developed in applying the original sections of the statute. This methodology thus served to integrate merger control into the system rather than allowing it to become—as it often has in other competition law systems—a separate domain of competition law operating on its own principles and according to its own procedures.

The merger control provisions are based primarily on structural assumptions: changes in market structure are likely to lead to changes in the economic process that are, in turn, likely to produce different economic outcomes. This means that the FCO had to (1) define markets, so that the structural concepts could be applied, and (2) apply the structural concepts in ways that were convincing to the relevant courts and acceptable to the relevant political and economic constituencies. We will here concentrate on the second of these tasks. The first, defining markets, is often important in the outcome of specific cases, but its role in the development of the competition law system has been limited.

More central to the development of the system is the issue of how the structural assumptions are applied to the markets thus defined. As we noted in discussing the concept of market dominance in relation to the abuse-control provisions, that concept originally specified that a firm was market-dominating where it was not subject to 'significant competition' in a specific market. This was broadened in 1973, however, to include the concept of 'superior market position', and this concept has played the dominant role in the context of merger control.[145] In the case of merger control, therefore, the issue typically is whether the merger changes the various relationships on the market so that a 'superior position' is either created or strengthened. This issue leaves room for a great deal of discretion, and the FCO and the courts have sought to give structure to such decisions.

In effect this requires giving structure to a prognosis. The statute requires the FCO to predict the economic impact of a merger in a way that is juridically acceptable. According to the government explanation of the statute,

The market-dominating position need not be created or strengthened at the time of the merger; the merger need only be its cause. The FCO is thus not limited to an assessment of the competitive conditions at the time of the merger. A prognosis regarding the future development is possible and also necessary, if on the basis of concrete circumstances it can be said with a high degree of probability that the existing competitive conditions will either worsen or improve within a limited period of time.[146]

This type of test was new, but within a decade the FCO in conjunction with the Berlin Appeals Court and the BGH had established basic principles for applying it.

One such principle is that this prediction has to be based on a 'total evaluation' of the situation. There has been no significant attempt to overly formalize or simplify the evaluation. Given that the concepts involved are imprecise and the situations complex, the FCO and the courts stress the need

---

[145] See, e.g., Gerd Pfeiffer, 'Von der Autokupplung bis zu Chanel No. 5: Neun Jahre Fusionskontrolle des Kartellsenats des Bundesgerichtshofes', in *Wettbewerbspolitik und Wettbewerbsrecht: Zur Diskussion um die Novellierung des GWB* 209–213 (Herbert Helmrich, ed., Cologne, 1987).

[146] *Regierungsbegründung zu dem Entwurf eines Zweiten Gesetzes zur Änderung des GWB*, BT/Drucksache IV/2564, at 29.

to assess all factors that might be relevant for determining the degree of power that would be created as a result of the merger.[147]

A second general principle is the priority of structural analysis. The system did not eliminate the possibility that conduct evidence could play a role in determining the probable effects of a merger, but the courts made clear that such evidence would play a marginal role. It can be considered 'to the extent that [such conduct] provides information about the competitive conditions on which it is based and the changes that can be expected'.[148]

The central analytical issue in applying these provisions is causality: how do we know that a merger is likely to create or strengthen a market-dominating position? According to the courts, it was necessary to develop guidelines based on prior experience (*Erfahrungsgrundsätze*). In effect, these operate as working assumptions regarding causality, and the courts strove to develop standards for deriving them. In particular, they had to shape a role for economic science in this regard.

The most basic and least controversial of these principles involves market share and states that, in general, the larger the market share, the greater the power of the enterprise.[149] Consequently, where a merger produces an enterprise whose market share indicates that it is no longer subject to significant competition, it is to be prohibited. A merger is also to be prohibited where the market share of the resulting firm is so large in relation to the market shares of its competitors that the firm's conduct is no longer 'sufficiently limited' by their competition, or where the existing competition faced by an already dominant firm is weakened.

The other central criterion for determining whether a merger creates or strengthens a market-dominating position is financial strength—to what extent does the merger lead to an increase of financial strength that puts a firm in a superior position with regard to its competitors? This is also a vague concept, and the FCO and the courts have struggled to give it contours. We will discuss it below in the context of 'deterrence' analysis.

By the late 1970s, the FCO and the courts had established a basic methodology for applying the merger control provisions, and there was general agreement that it functioned satisfactorily when applied to horizontal mergers.[150] Where two or more competitors merged, there was an obvious change in the structure of the market that was likely to harm competition. Moreover, the resources of the merging firms were combined, and this tended to support a finding that the merger actually 'created or strengthened' a market-dominating position. The situation with respect to vertical and conglomerate

---

[147] See, e.g., BGH, Dec. of Dec.20, 1980, *WuW/E* BGH 1749 (*Klöckner Becorit*).

[148] *Immenga & Mestmäcker*, 1065.

[149] For discussion, see Pfeiffer, 'Von der Autokupplung', 213–14.

[150] See, e.g., *Begründung zum Regierungsentwurf*, BT-Drucksache 8/2136, at 12 (Sept. 27, 1978).

mergers was less sanguine. Here there were relatively few successful cases, and in its 1976 annual report the FCO argued that the statute did not provide it with the tools to deal adequately with such mergers.[151]

3. Vertical and conglomerate mergers: the promise of presumptions

The widespread belief that existing provisions were inadequate for dealing with conglomerate and vertical mergers was a major factor in the fourth revision of the GWB in 1980. The government sought to remedy this inadequacy in several ways. It proposed, for example, expanding the category of situations in which prenotification of mergers was required and narrowing the category of mergers that were considered '*de minimis*'. The main thrust of the revision was, however, the introduction of presumptions designed to make it easier for the FCO to prohibit vertical and conglomerate mergers.[152]

The Monopoly Commission initially proposed the idea of using presumptions for this purpose in its 1973/5 report, and the proposal soon attracted attention and support.[153] The objective in proposing the introduction of such presumptions was to overcome the juridical hurdles involved in actually proving that a merger had created a 'market-dominating position'. As we have seen, the concept of 'superior market position' that was the main tool for establishing market dominance is vague, and both the courts and the FCO were reluctant to conclude that such a position had been established. Those who supported more aggressive enforcement against vertical and conglomerate mergers hoped that presumptions would help to overcome this reluctance.

These proposals encountered relatively little political resistance. There was opposition from industry, but the coalition of social democrats and liberals was still in power, and, despite the influence of industry on the junior partner in this coalition (the FDP), industry was not in a position to force significant changes in the bill. Moreover, the presumptions were presented as a tool for protecting the *Mittelstand*, an increasingly popular political cause that generated support from all major political parties.

Before reviewing the basic content of these presumptions, it is important to clarify the meaning of 'presumptions' in this context.[154] In essence, such presumptions establish conditions which, if met, authorize the FCO to assume as

[151] See FCO, *Tätigkeitsbericht* 1976, BT-Drucksache 8/704, at 20. See also *Stellungnahme der Bundesregierung zum Tätigkeitsbericht des Bundeskartellamtes* 1976, BT-Drucksache 8/704, at II.

[152] For a discussion of the issue of presumptions in regard to conglomerate mergers, see Meinrad Dreher, *Konglomerate Zusammenschlüsse, Verbotsvermutungen und Widerlegungsgründe* (Berlin, 1987).

[153] Monopoly Commission, *Hauptgutachen der Monopolkommission I: 1973/1975* at 535–40 (Baden-Baden, 1976).

[154] For discussion, see Bechtold & Kleinmann, *Kommentar zur Fusionskontrolle*, 461–62. The merger control provisions already contained other presumptions, but they were used for other purposes.

the first step in its analysis that a merger violates §24's prohibition. This is, however, only the first step in the process. The FCO is required to continue its analysis by examining all circumstances that might affect the conclusion that the merger actually did create or strengthen a market-dominating position. In other words, the office—and the courts—must determine whether the presumption is rebutted by the actual circumstances.

Several examples illustrate this effort to use presumptions to improve the system's capacity to prohibit vertical and conglomerate mergers.[155] One, we can call it the 'market invasion presumption' (*Eindringungsvermutung*), was designed to protect small and medium-sized firms. Specifically, it was a response to situations in which large firms used mergers to enter markets dominated by small and medium-sized firms. This had become an increasingly common pattern since the late 1960s. The concern—based on FCO experience—was that such mergers would often lead to a rapid succession of similar mergers in which the smaller firms would be more or less forced to merge with larger firms because of fear that they would be unable to compete with such larger firms.[156] The statute thus provided that where a firm with revenues of at least two billion DM merged with a firm in a market in which small and medium-sized firms had a combined market share of at least two-thirds, and the firm resulting from the merger had a specified minimum market share, the merger was presumed to violate §24.

A second presumption, the 'reinforcement' presumption, involves situations in which a firm with at least two billion DM in revenues merges with a firm that is already dominant on a particular market. This presumption was intended to respond to mergers that added financial strength to existing market power. The concept was that such combinations were often harmful, but that it was often difficult to prove the strengthening of a market-dominating position.

Finally, a presumption was included to deal with 'giant mergers'. There had been a growing concern that 'elephant marriages' were likely to be harmful to the economy in general as well as to the interests of unions and workers and that it was thus necessary to strengthen the FCO's tools for dealing with them.[157] This provision presumes violation of §24 in cases where the firms involved have combined revenues of at least twelve billion DM.

The idea that these presumptions could significantly improve the merger control system dominated merger control discussions in the years before and after the 1980 amendments, and many believed and/or hoped that they would have that effect.[158] These hopes were soon disappointed, however, and

---

[155] For further discussion of the presumptions, see ibid., 446–98.

[156] See, e.g., FCO, *Tätigkeitsbericht* 1976, BT-Drucksache 8/704, at 21.

[157] See Ulrich Immenga, 'Zusammenschlüsse zwischen Grossunternehmen als Gegenstand des Rechts der Wettbewerbsbeschränkungen', in *Wettbewerbspolitik und Wettbewerbsrecht: Zur Diskussion um die Novellierung des GWB* 185–98 (Herbert Helmrich, ed., Cologne, 1987).

[158] Volker Emmerich, *Kartellrecht* 388 (7th ed., Munich, 1994).

recently there has even been talk of eliminating them. One reason for their ineffectiveness has been the general reluctance of the FCO to prohibit a merger on the basis of a mere presumption.[159] This reluctance has been strengthened by the experience of seeing a large number of cases in which the presumptions have been rebutted by the facts. Indeed, according to one commentator, the FCO typically assumes that the presumptions will be rebutted.[160]

4. The FCO and the courts: deterrence theory

Although the focus of political attention in recent years has often been on the role of the legislature in improving the system, the FCO and the courts have frequently generated the changes that have had the greatest impact. In particular, since the late 1970s they have been giving contours to what has come to be known as 'deterrence' theory, currently the principal tool for dealing with conglomerate and vertical mergers.[161] The basic notion here is that a firm whose financial resources far exceed those of its competitors will generally prevail in economic competition, regardless of the performance of market participants, and that law should be used to reduce such competitive distortions.

The general idea that resources are an important factor in assessing market power entered the GWB in 1973 in defining the new concept of superior market position. According to that provision, resources were to be a major factor in determining the extent to which one firm (or group of firms) was in a position relative to its competitors that allowed it 'an area of conduct' that was not sufficiently controlled by competition.

The FCO, legal scholars, and the courts then developed this concept in order to make it judicially acceptable. The first major step in this direction was a Supreme Court decision (*GKN/Sachs*) in which the Court established the 'subjective' perspective of the competitors as the critical factor in analyzing the impact of resources on a firm's market position. It clarified that the issue was whether the financial strength created by a merger would deter other firms from entering the market or reduce the competitive intensity of firms already operating there.[162]

From this starting point the Supreme Court has developed a three-part analysis for analyzing the role of resources in deterring competition and thus establishing a market-dominating position.[163] The Court first analyzes financial strength. In some early decisions, revenues were seen as a major element

[159] Ibid., 388.
[160] Ibid., 405.
[161] For discussion, see Manfred J. Dirrheimer, *Ressourcenstärke und Abschreckungswirkung in der Fusionskontrolle* (Cologne, 1988).
[162] BGH, Dec. of Feb. 2, 1978, *WuW/E* BGH 1501, 1505–12 (*Kfz-Kupplungen*).
[163] For discussion, see Pfeiffer, 'Von der Autokupplung', 215–18.

in this determination, but the literature and cases have come to focus on a different issue—the extent to which the resources of the acquiring firm are 'freely available' and thus capable of being used on the market. The amount of freely available resources is not to be measured absolutely, but in relation to the freely available resources of the firm's competitors.

A second component of the analysis involves the degree to which the acquiring firm is likely actually to employ the financial strength available to it to support the activities of the acquired firm. Here the Supreme Court and the FCO operate on the 'principle of experience' that a firm is likely to acquire control of another firm only if it is willing to employ its own resources to support the activities of the acquired firm. This presumption has been much criticized, but it at least provides a degree of analytical clarity.

Finally, the courts test the likely impact of these resources on the actual and potential competitors on the market. They look at evidence that the other competitors are likely to be influenced by this new competitive factor on the market. Here the BGH established the additional principle that the mere possibility that a financially powerful firm will use its financial strength on the market is likely to reduce competition by deterring competitive conduct of existing competitors and reducing the likelihood of new entry into the market.[164]

Although many issues still remain with regard to the deterrence theory and aspects of its application, it represents 'at least the beginnings of an appropriate instrument for deciding these [conglomerate and, implicitly, vertical] cases'.[165] The FCO and the courts have together developed a conceptual structure that can be used to analyze the issue of financial strength and its role in merger control.

5. Protecting the retail trade?

Deterrence theory was a response to the general problem of conglomerate and vertical mergers, but since the mid-1970s a specific problem has often dominated discussions of merger control—protecting the retail trade, particularly the food distribution system. During this period, the battle between large retail chains and smaller, independent retailers has played a major political role, and thus the FCO has sought to use the merger control provisions to protect the retail trade.

The FCO responded to the problem of increasing concentration in the retail trade by developing legal theories specifically directed at it. The courts

---

[164] See, e.g., BGH, Dec. of June 25, 1985, *WuW/E* BGH 2150, 2156–57 (*Edelstahlbestecke*). For detailed discussion of the role of barriers to entry in this context, see Joachim Jickeli, *Marktzutrittsschranken im Recht der Wettbewerbsbeschränkungen* (Baden-Baden, 1990) and Jörg-Martin Schultze, *Marktzutrittsschranken in der Fusionskontrolle* (Cologne, 1988).

[165] Emmerich, *Kartellrecht* (7th ed.) 406.

have been generally unwilling, however, to accept such theories. One such theory focused, for example, on the role of demand-side power.[166] This is the 'indispensability' theory, which the FCO used in the early 1980s to prohibit several mergers involving food and consumer products companies.[167] The idea was that large retail chains often purchased such large quantities that they became indispensable to individual suppliers, particularly smaller suppliers, and thus acquired a form of dominance over them.

This theory was extensively criticized, however, and the courts generally rejected it.[168] In two leading cases, the Berlin Appeals Court essentially claimed that the existence of demand-side power did not, in and of itself, represent market domination. The statute was drafted, the Court said, to protect competition, and the existence of power on one side or another of a market did not necessarily affect the extent or intensity of competition.[169]

In the mid-1980s, political pressure began to mount to revise the GWB in order to treat this problem more effectively. The minister of economics appointed a commission to investigate the situation, but this time the group generally saw little reason to pursue statutory changes. Many experts were not convinced that the so-called 'retail trade problem' was actually a problem, or at least they were not confident that it justified legislative responses. Even the FCO was generally skeptical about the need for changes. Yet the political allies of the *Mittelstand* and those who sought votes based on its protection were powerful enough to demand a reform. Not surprisingly, the changes were by many accounts little more than 'window-dressing'. They may have served a political function, but they were not likely to significantly change the legal situation.

For our purposes, the most important of these legislative innovations was an expansion of the criteria for determining 'superior market position' to include the capacity of an enterprise 'to shift its supply or its demand to other goods or services as well as the opportunities available to its contracting partner to switch to other [purchasers or suppliers]' (§22(1)2). The objective was to use the concept of 'economic dependence' to facilitate a finding of market dominance in typical retail trade situations in which the 'normal' criteria for market dominance were not met. Although the provision was intended for the retail trade, it was not limited to application there, because the drafters consciously sought to avoid 'sector-specific' language in the text.

---

[166] See generally Helmut Bergmann, *Nachfragemacht in der Fusionskontrolle* (Berlin, 1989).

[167] For discussion, see Monopoly Commission, *Marktstruktur und Wettbewerb im Handel: Sondergutachten der Monopolkommission No. 23*, at 158–60.

[168] For criticism, see Monopoly Commission, *Die Konzentration im Lebensmittelhandel: Sondergutachten No. 14*, at 86–89 (Baden-Baden, 1985). For discussion generally, see Monopoly Commission, *Sondergutachten No. 23*, at 158–60.

[169] See KG (Kammergericht), Dec. of Nov. 5, 1986, *WuW/E* OLG 3917, 3934 (*Coop/Wandmaker*) and KG, Dec. of April 24, 1985, *WuW/E* OLG 3577, 3589 (*Hussel/Mara*).

Commentators have generally seen the change as unlikely to improve significantly the capacity of the FCO to prohibit mergers involving the retail trade. According to one, 'in the end the change has only a very limited function'.[170] The FCO must apply these criteria as part of a 'total assessment', and the office has not considered this dependence theory an adequate basis for prohibiting a merger.

The merger control system has thus had little effect in protecting the retail trade. The theories that the FCO has developed for this purpose have been generally unsuccessful in the courts, and the FCO has remained skeptical of the legislative changes. From the mid-1980s through the early 1990s the number of merger cases involving the retail trade diminished significantly.[171] At a more basic level, there are many who doubt that the problem of concentration in retail markets—if there is a problem—is tractable through merger control, because competition within the oligopoly structures remains strong. As the monopoly commission put it in its special report on the issue of retail trade, 'all specific proposals for further development of the GWB that have been considered have caused more harms than benefits'.[172]

6. Political intervention

In reviewing the German merger control system, we need to look at one final element—the issue of political intervention. When the merger control provisions were introduced in 1973, both the economics ministry and industry insisted on the need to authorize the economics ministry to override a decision of the FCO to prohibit a merger under specific types of circumstances where overriding national interests were at stake. There was, however, concern at the time that this would provide a portal through which political influence could interfere with the competition law system.

The economics minister has, however, made little use of this authority, and he has emphasized that such power should only be employed under exceptional circumstances. In 1989, the economics minister did use this authority to override the FCO's prohibition of a highly publicized merger involving Germany's largest industrial corporation (Daimler-Benz AG) and a leading manufacturer of airplanes (Messerschmidt-Bolkow-Blohm), and this led to a major controversy over the issue of political interference.[173] The case was made more poignant because it involved a merger that the economics ministry itself had proposed in the interests of the German economy. The case

[170] Michael Martinek, 'Unruhe an der Kartellfront: Die 5. GWB-Novelle gegen Industriemarktfixierung und Ausnahmebereichsexzess', 43 *Neue Juristische Wochenschrift* 793, 796 (1990).

[171] Monopoly Commission, *Sondergutachten No. 23*, at 147.   [172] Ibid., 174.

[173] For discussion, see Ulrich Immenga, 'Fusionskontrolle auf Konglomeraten und vertikalen Märkten: Erfahrungen aus dem Zusammenschluss Daimler Benz/MBB', 1990 *Aktiengesellschaft* 209 (1990).

thus 'provides in exemplary fashion insights into conflicts between industrial policy and competition policy'.[174]

Although the case has been called a 'major psychological defeat' for the FCO, it did not undermine the restraints against political interference that had become part of the system. It did not lead to increased use of this power, and the minister has since emphasized that the limited experience with such interference has been generally negative, and that he is not interested in increased use of the opportunities that this provision presents to override the FCO.[175]

7. Experience with merger controls

The German merger control system has become arguably the strictest in the world. With regard to horizontal mergers, its stringency is comparable to that of US antitrust law, and it tends to be more restrictive in its treatment of vertical and horizontal mergers. Moreover, whereas the US system has significantly reduced its strictures on such mergers during the last decade and a half, the German system has created conceptual and institutional mechanisms designed to combat them more effectively.

Assessing the actual impact of the system is, of course, difficult. Critics often emphasize, for example, that its impact on the process of concentration has been limited, particularly in relation to the direct and indirect costs of operating the system, pointing, for example, to the relatively small number of actual prohibitions of mergers. Yet as of the end of 1996, there had been 115 prohibitions of mergers by the FCO, and the office reported that 280 mergers had been abandoned or modified after the initiation of proceedings.[176] These numbers suggest at the very least an active and serious mechanism for challenging mergers which has had a significant impact on business planning.

Doubts also remain about the conceptual integrity of the system, and during the last decade such doubts may have increased. In the early 1980s, for example, doubts re-emerged about the structural assumptions on which the merger control system is based.[177] Critics argued that proof of conduct should play a greater role in assessing the issue of whether a merger was likely to have the proscribed negative effects on competition. In part, these doubts derived from critical evaluation of the FCO's experience in applying the

---

[174] Sondervotum des Kommissionsmitglieds Immenga, in Monopolkommission, *Sondergutachten No. 18: Zusammenschlussvorhaben der Daimler-Benz AG mit der Messerschmitt-Bolköw-Blohm GmbH* 133 (Baden-Baden, 1989).

[175] See Erfahrungsbericht des Bundeswirtschaftsministeriums über Ministererlaubnis-Verfahren bei Firmen-Fusionen, 1992 *Wirtschaft und Wettbewerb* 925–32 (1992).

[176] FCO, unpublished statistics.

[177] See, e.g., Kurt Markert, 'Zur Bedeutung von Marktstruktur und -verhalten in der materiellen Fusionskontrolle des GWB', in *Neuorientierung des Wettbewerbsschutzes* 35–60 (Forschungsinstitut für Wirtschaftsverfassung und Wettbewerb e.V., ed., Cologne, 1986).

merger control provisions, but intellectual factors such as the influence of the Chicago School of Law and Economics have also played a role. By the early 1990s, the intensity of the debate had diminished, but doubts remain.

For our purposes another question is important: how has the predominance of merger control effected the competition law system? At the very least, the shift of focus to merger control has changed accents and expectations in the German competition law system. A system whose focus is merger control necessarily operates differently than one whose central objective is to apply a cartel prohibition. For example, since the economic consequences of mergers of different kinds are far more complex than the impact of cartels on competition, the shift of emphasis to merger control has involved a blurring of some of the standards of conceptual precision that had prevailed earlier. The growing centrality of merger controls has also tended to change the language of competition law, making it more detailed, more policy-based and more labile than it had been during its early years. Finally, the shift has influenced expectations about the operation of the competition law system as a whole. Frequent mergers, often involving highly powerful firms, are widely reported in the newspapers, leading to criticisms that the competition law system is not functioning effectively and making the system look increasingly like changeable policy rather than stable 'constitutional' law.

K. GERMAN COMPETITION LAW: SUCCESSES, CHALLENGES, AND ROLES

The German competition law system has been in operation for some forty years, and during that period it has often played key roles in the country's economic, political, and legal life. Its basic characteristics have changed little, and while specific aspects of the system have been criticized, there have been no serious calls for abolishing or drastically changing it.[178] Its story has been one of success—not spectacular, not continuous, not unchallenged, but frequent, moderate and often impressive. One reason we have looked at this story in some detail has been to illuminate the factors that have led to these successes.

But we have probed German competition law experience in some depth for yet another reason—to better understand its pivotal role in the evolution of competition law in Europe. We saw in the last chapter that the core ideas of German competition law had a major influence in shaping thought about competition law in the European Union, particularly during its formative stages, and we can now appreciate how German experience in putting them into practice reinforced and extended that impact. The postwar German story has been the central European narrative of national competition law. It is the

---

[178] Some of the calls in the mid-1990s to amend the GWB to reflect more closely the competition law of the European Community would, however, entail significant changes in the GWB.

national experience of which European decision-makers are most likely to be aware and to which they are most likely to refer.

1. The shape of German competition law experience

Constancy may be the most prominent feature of that story. The German competition law system has changed during four decades, but, in contrast to experience in countries such as France and the United Kingdom, its basic principles, institutions, and characteristics have seen little change. The success of the German economy, particularly during the early stages of development of the system, has contributed to this stability, legitimating the system and providing political 'space' within which it could develop. Many have seen competition law as contributing to the effectiveness of the economic system, and thus the success of the economic system has contributed to the success of the competition law system. Moreover, prospering businesses tend to combat competition law regimes less fiercely than do businesses that are struggling, and their pleas that competition law harms them have less political appeal.

Another key factor has been the matrix of ideas within which the system has developed, and the political force of those ideas. The system has been seen in 'constitutional' terms—as a permanent, stable framework of principles for the distribution of power and the conduct of economically powerful institutions. This conception was one of the core ideas of the ordoliberals and of Ludwig Erhard, and the competition law system was created in that image. This also means that competition law has been closely associated from its inception with the social market economy ideas that have been central to economic policy thinking throughout the history of the Federal Republic, and it has thus been symbolically and operationally anchored in a stable political environment, enjoying political support from all postwar governments.

The competition law system itself is distinguished by its balance. It is a hybrid of juridical and administrative components in which the juridical elements provide stability and long-term general information to business decision-makers, while the administrative elements provide flexibility and short-term specific information.

The system is centered around the operations of the FCO, and to that extent it is an administrative system. Although private suits are allowed in a few specific situations, the FCO is basically responsible for initiatives within the system. Its officials decide what objectives to seek, which linguistic and institutional strategies to pursue, and how resources are to be used. Political support for this administrative function has attracted able administrators, encouraged administrative commitment, and contributed to compliance pressures on business decision-makers. Notwithstanding this political support (or perhaps, in part, because of it) FCO officials have also generally sought to exercise their authority with moderation and due attention to the needs of the business community; they have generally preferred co-operation with industry rather than confrontation.

The German system's juridical elements have, however, been its most striking and 'revolutionary' feature. In contrast to the experience of other European countries, legal methods and legal discourse provide the 'ethos' of the system. Juridical institutions, methods, and principles provide the framework within which administrative authority is exercised! This juridical 'framing' of the system operates at two levels. One involves control by the courts. In the German system, the regular courts ultimately determine which values to support and which arguments to accept. They confer durability and authority on language and ideas and subject administrative decision-making to those standards. The other level is internal. The FCO's own decision-making procedures are modeled along judicial lines, requiring the use of juridical methodologies and discourse *within* the FCO. The two levels are related, because the role of the courts in reviewing FCO decisions leads the FCO to ask the same questions that the courts ask. As a result, they have to speak the same 'language' and utilize the same basic discourse.

This language has been constructed around a basic package of ideas and values associated originally with ordoliberalism and thereafter with the social market economy. Many of the original ideas have been modified in practice; some have been excluded; and new ideas have been added. Yet the basic package has provided a durable conceptual framework for the system. This language has been tied to many of the fundamental intellectual issues around which German society has redefined itself during the second half of the twentieth century, and, as a result, there has been often intense intellectual interest in the language of competition law.

The language of competition law has gained power and influence from its relationship to the 'community' in which it is imbedded, and the characteristics of that community have influenced the shape of the language.[179] The community is large and influential in comparison with competition law communities elsewhere in Europe. It includes the leading officials of the FCO, judges involved with reviewing competition law decisions, professors (of both law and economics) who are active in competition law matters, and many of the practitioners who write in the area. Virtually all decisions of importance in German competition law are made, or heavily influenced, by the members of this group. They generally know each other personally, share many of the same basic goals and consider the impact of new decisions on these goals and on the community itself. Without such a community, it is unlikely that the system could have developed as it has.

---

[179] For further discussion of this community, see David J. Gerber, 'Authority, Community and the Civil Law Commentary: An Example from German Competition Law', 42 *Am. J. Comp. L.* 531, 537–42 (1994).

2. German competition law and Europe

Germany's extraordinary importance for the story of competition law in Europe rests on the fundamentally different conception of competition law that it introduced into European experience. It brought new procedures, values and ways of thinking about competition law, and it infused other values common in Western Europe (for example, economic freedom) with new force and impact. The ordoliberal and neo-liberal ideas that we discussed in the last chapter were only ideas; German experience with those ideas greatly enhanced their influence.

In this experience, competition law is not merely a pragmatic tool for achieving specific policy ends, but an important part of a society's 'constitution'. It is a matter of long-term legal and economic structures rather than of short-term policy expedients. In Germany, legal principles and methods became the central dynamic of the story rather than policy and administrative discretion. The discourse of competition law in Germany has tended to be more rigorous, more 'scientific' and at the same time more laden with values than anything that had been known in Europe before. For Europeans, it was little short of a 'revolutionary' conception of competition law.

The impact of German experience has been extensive. We have already discussed the influence of ordoliberal and neo-liberal ideas on architects of European integration such as Walter Hallstein, but it is important to remember that the influence of these ideas depended to a significant degree on their operation in the German competition law system. German officials are not likely to have had the influence they have had in the European Commission's competition directorate, for example, if German competition law had not been seen as so successful. Moreover, that influence has frequently rested on the fact that Germany has had more extensive experience with the issues involved than could be found in other countries. Merger control is an example. Germany's influence on the development of Community merger law, particularly in its first several years, derived from the fact that at that time the German merger control system was by far the most advanced in Europe.

While the main vehicle for German influence on the evolution of the European competition law tradition has been the EU, during the last two decades its direct influence on the development of competition law in other European countries has increased. Particularly since the 1970s, but earlier as well, it has been common for other countries to turn to Germany for ideas and even advice regarding their own competition law decisions. As we shall see, for example, the drafters of the fundamental revision of the French competition law system in 1986 readily acknowledge their debt to German experience.

Timing has been critical to this influence. It was fortuitous that Germany was developing its competition law legislation at the same time that the plans for European integration were taking concrete form in the 1950s, and that no other European country had significant experience with competition law at the time. This gave German ideas a natural 'headstart' which it has maintained. It has meant that for other European countries, Germany has been the one European source of experience in many competition law matters. US antitrust law experience was even deeper, but the differences in legal culture, economic situation and political experience between Europe and the US have often made it attractive to look within Europe where possible.

This headstart might have made little difference if the German competition law system had not been associated with Germany's impressive economic performance. The 'German miracle'—probably the most impressive economic development of the century in Europe—has given competition law credibility. Seen in the 1950s and 1960s as a virtually unfathomable success, the German economy has remained the most powerful economy in Europe, and, until very recently, it has shown itself to be relatively resistant to crises. A competition law system associated with such a miracle deserved attention—and, perhaps, emulation.

Moreover, the German competition law system was an internal success, and it was referred to by leaders as a success. It became an important part of economic and legal life, acquired respect and strength, and achieved compliance. And it remained remarkably stable, standing the 'test of time'. The combination of Europe's most prominent and rigorous competition law with Europe's most effective system brought attention and respect from other Europeans and influence for the German system.

3. Challenges

The future may be less kind to German competition law than the past has been. In Chapter X we will deal more specifically with issues of European integration that are likely to affect the German system, but patterns within German experience itself are also likely to present important challenges to the system. In Germany, circumstances have been favorable for competition law in the conflict between the force of ideas and values supporting competition law, on the one hand, and the economic and political power of those whose conduct is affected by competition law, on the other hand. Yet some of the factors supporting competition law may be weakening, while opposing forces seem to be favored by recent trends and developments.

Commitment to competition law ideas, institutions, and values may, for example, be more difficult to maintain in the future. The intellectual and emotional force of the ordoliberal and social market economy ideas that have united leading officials of the FCO, leading academics, and even judges and practitioners may be diminishing. Many proponents of these ideas have retired or will retire soon, and it is not clear that their successors will be similarly committed to these goals and values. Moreover, the circumstances that gave the ideas force—such as rejection of totalitarianism and the perceived need for social reconstruction and solidarity—are likely to lose their strength over time.

Opponents of a strong competition law may, in contrast, enjoy more favorable circumstances. A leading member of the FCO stated to me not long ago that he did not believe the GWB in its present form could be enacted today. The reason he gave: 'The economic interests are too strong today'. The growing political strength of such interests is in part a function of the economic situation. Germany's growth has slowed during the last two decades, and it is likely to face a long period during which the policy emphasis will be on maintaining employment and competing in international markets. In particular, the issue of attracting new investment in Germany has become acute, and is likely to remain so. Industry critics argue that under these circumstances the GWB is outdated and its rigor is harmful, because it makes investment in Germany less attractive, especially in relation to former eastern bloc countries and in light of the completion of the single market for Europe. Politicians, writers, and voters are likely to give these arguments greater weight than they have in the recent past.

The issue facing the German competition law system is whether the characteristics that have stood it in good stead in the past are likely to prove as effective under what may be very different circumstances in the future. This may, in turn, depend to a great degree on the relationship between the German competition law system and the process of European integration, and it is to that experience that we now turn.

IX

Competition Law and European Integration: The Competition Law of the European Union

The creation of the European Economic Community in 1957 began a process of integration in which competition law has played a pivotal role, and that process has, in turn, imbued competition law with roles and influence far beyond those it is likely to have achieved otherwise. Not only has Community competition law itself become a major factor in economic decision-making throughout Europe, but Member States (and those that envision EU membership) increasingly have modeled their own competition laws on Community competition law. It is a product of the European tradition of competition law and thus influenced by many of the same intellectual currents, historical experiences, and political and legal concepts that have shaped national competition laws, but it has also been a critical factor in shaping, energizing, and giving force to that tradition.

Community competition law is also 'special', however, and in its specialness resides much of the uncertainty about the future of competition law in Europe. It protects against restraints competition, but, unlike national competition law systems, its primary objective has not been to obtain the generic benefits associated with competition such as lower prices to consumers or technological progress. Rather, it has been understood primarily as part of a program for achieving the specific goal of unifying the European market, and it is unclear how a system designed for that primary purpose will operate when that goal has been achieved.

This chapter examines Community competition law and reviews the basic shape of its development over the last four decades.[1] The focus will be on identifying the core elements and the dynamics of that experience. The fol-

---

[1] Terminology in relation to the institutions of European integration is sometimes troublesome because of the changes in nomenclature over time and because of the very complexity of the arrangements. Until the enactment of the Treaty on European Union (the Maastricht Agreement or TEU) in 1993, the institutions we discuss in this chapter were usually referred to as the 'Community'(for 'European Economic Community' and, later, 'European Community'). The TEU created a broader institutional framework that included the European Community as well as other institutions of integration, and thus, since 1993, it has become common to refer to this institutional framework as the 'EU' or the 'Union'. The competition law provisions of the Rome Treaty remain, however, part of the European Community, and, therefore, we will refer throughout to 'Community competition law'.

lowing chapter then looks at the evolving relationship between Community competition law and the competition laws of the Member States and assesses its importance for the future of competition law in Europe.

A. COMPETITION LAW BECOMES 'EUROPEAN'

We saw in Chapter V that during the late 1920s the development of competition law ideas in Europe had an important transnational dimension. International organizations and conferences such as the League of Nations' World Economic Conference and the Interparliamentary Union's London Conference were spreading competition law ideas and creating an 'image' of what competition law should be and what roles it should play. In many European countries, competition law ideas first acquired status and standing as a result of these international efforts, and the 'model' of competition law they created served as the basis for most postwar European competition law systems.

Although the weight of depression and war crushed the institutional movements that carried this model, they found new life after war's end, albeit in altered forms. Initially, this impetus was channeled into the international efforts to establish an International Trade Organization. Although it ultimately failed to become 'law', the Havana Charter was, as we have noted, influential in encouraging European governments to enact competition laws and in shaping those they created.

1. The European Coal and Steel Community as context

As the grand plans for an international law framework foundered in 1948, the transnational path of competition law development moved onto specifically European terrain. The context was the creation in 1951 of the European Coal and Steel Community (ECSC) by the Treaty of Paris. The six countries that a few years later would become the founding members of the European Economic Community there created the first organization of European integration, and competition law was included as an important part of it.[2] It was in this context that competition law officially acquired a 'trans-European' dimension.

The ECSC was seen by many of its supporters as part of larger plans for European unification that were being seriously discussed at the highest levels

---

[2] Treaty of Paris, Apr. 18, 1951, 261 UNTS 142. The classic and very influential account of the origins and early years of the Schuman Plan is William Diebold, *The Schuman Plan* (New York, 1959). For a recent detailed discussion of the beginnings of the Schuman Plan by a group of scholars with access to the many archives that were not opened until the late 1970s, see *Die Anfänge des Schuman-Plans: 1950/51* (Klaus Schwabe, ed., Baden-Baden, 1988).

of government in the late 1940s and early 1950s. These plans called for creation of both a European Defense Community and a European Political Community, and for almost a decade after 1945 many hoped that Europe could be quickly and more or less completely 'unified'.

The coal and steel issue could not, however, wait for progress toward these broader objectives. Coal and steel production was a key factor in both the immediate reconstruction of Europe and its long-run economic prospects, but the postwar political situation created major conflicts about who was going to own and control that production. The core of the problem was Germany. Its coal and steel industry had been dominant in Europe before the war, and as the allies contemplated returning sovereignty to a new German state at the end of the occupation, they were aware that without political intervention German industry was likely to reacquire such dominance. It would either control or have easy access to the necessary raw materials, and it possessed both technological leadership and extensive managerial experience in the relevant industries. In the late 1940s, however, few in Europe (or anywhere else) relished the idea of such extensive economic power in German hands.

In response to this problem and the perceived need for concrete steps toward European integration, political leaders from France, Germany, Italy, and the Benelux countries created a 'legal community' that subjected most of the European coal and steel industry to, in effect, an additional legal regime.[3] This regime created common control over the activities of firms in those industries and thus placed them in the service of the 'community'. It was also designed to eliminate the possibility that Germany would re-establish its dominance in the area and to terminate the often bitter political conflicts within Europe over the resources and power associated with those industries.

As finally structured, this new legal 'community' included an elaborate institutional framework. According to the treaty, a Council representing the participating governments would enact laws, a European administrative authority (the High Authority) would be responsible for applying those laws to the coal and steel industries, and a European court (the European Court of Justice) would resolve disputes about the operations of the system. The ECSC still exists, and its basic governmental structure was adopted as that of the European Economic Community in 1957.

2. Drafting a competition law for the ECSC

Our concern here is not with the details of ECSC competition law, but with the roles it has played in the development of competition law in Europe, particularly its influence on Community competition law. We will pay particular

---

[3] See Gerhard Bebr, 'The European Coal and Steel Community: A Political and Legal Innovation', 63 *Yale L. Rev.* 1 (1953).

attention to the role of US antitrust law in the creation of ECSC competition law, because it is sometimes assumed that it was here that US antitrust ideas had their most important influence on European competition law developments.

The Treaty of Paris was drafted quickly, primarily during the summer and fall of 1950. For the 'Europeanists' who took part in the drafting and negotiations, speed was necessary in order to avoid protracted debates in the participating states that might ultimately stop the process altogether. Portions of the drafting process, including the early drafts of the competition law provisions, were 'semi-private' in the sense that Jean Monnet and a small number of others basically controlled the process and made decisions about who would draft what and what the basic contents should be. The images of highly formalized drafting procedures often associated with international agreements are, therefore, misleading in the case of the Paris treaty.

The central personality in the creation of the ECSC was Jean Monnet of France.[4] A pragmatist who often operated outside 'official' governmental channels, Monnet seems not to have had a firm conception of how the new organization should be structured. His main concern was quickly to find a structure that would be accepted by all potential Member States. By the end of the negotiations, his original conception had been much changed by the national governments, but this seems not to have concerned him greatly.

Once the final conception and structure of the new community became relatively fixed, and it was clear that the treaty would create a full-scale political, administrative, and judicial structure for controlling the European coal and steel industries, there seems to have been little doubt among those participating in the negotiations that the treaty would have to contain some means of combating restraints on competition. A central goal of the entire project was to 'control' the power of the firms within those industries, and the treaty could hardly have accomplished that objective if it had not included such provisions.

The reasons . . . [for Articles 65 and 66] are to be found only partly in the drafters' adherence to competition as an economic way of life. More important, perhaps, was the concern of the drafters that cartels [and concentrations], if permitted to develop, might become the real political power of the Community and might constitute a challenge to the Community's sovereignty.[5]

The question was what kind of competition law it would be.

Monnet called for a strong competition law on the grounds that it was necessary to achieve the broader integrative goals of the Community.[6] This

---

[4] For background on Monnet, see Francois Duchêne, *Jean Monnet: The First Statesman of Interdependence* (New York, 1994) and Jean Monnet, *Mémoires* (Paris, 1976).

[5] Raymond Vernon, 'The Schuman Plan', 47 *Am. J. Int'l L.* 183, 97 n.43 (1953).

[6] For discussion of Monnet's role in this process, see Frances Lynch, 'The Role of Jean Monnet in Setting Up the European Coal and Steel Community', in *Die Anfänge des Schuman-Plans: 1950/51* 117–30 (Klaus Schwabe, ed., Baden-Baden, 1988).

appeal was also useful politically, because it helped to convince the French, in particular, that German companies would not acquire too much power, or use their power to harm their competitors, and it was attractive to the Americans whose support for the project he considered important. Monnet was not legally trained, however, and his image of competition law seems to have been vague. Although he had enough experience in US business affairs to have some idea of the significance of antitrust law in the US, his main experience in government in France had been as the head of the *Commissariat du Plan*, and he was primarily known for his role in implementing *planification*. Moreover, as we have seen, France had no significant competition law at the time, so that he had only minimal direct experience with such legislation.

This is important for setting the circumstances under which the competition provisions of the treaty were drafted. Monnet wanted someone who could draft such provisions quickly and with little political 'fuss'. As it turned out, Robert Bowie, a professor of antitrust law at Harvard, was at the time working in the office of John J. McCloy, the US High Commissioner for Germany and a long-time friend of Monnet, and thus Monnet arranged to 'borrow' Bowie to draft the competition law provisions. Not only could Bowie draw on US experience, but he was in a very useful position for Monnet. A key incentive for Germany to enter the ECSC was that the US occupation authorities had agreed to relinquish their regulatory competence over the German iron and steel industry in the event the ECSC became a reality, and McCloy's office had been involved in preparing for that transition. Using Bowie as a 'private' drafter had the additional advantage of assuring close, but unobtrusive ties to US officials.

Drafts of the competition provisions were reviewed and commented on in Washington, but the US was not part of the negotiations, and the US role was concealed as much as possible for fear that the project would be seen as controlled by the US and rejected by some participants on those grounds alone.[7] George Ball, a US lawyer working in Paris, apparently also commented on the drafts. He had become a personal friend of Monnet and had close ties in Washington and New York.

The proposals worked out in this process were not submitted to the Europeans as drafted. According to Ball, they were 'rewritten in a European idiom by Maurice Lagrange of the *Conseil d'Etat*, who, as a skilled draftsman, had major responsibility for giving formal legal expression to the ideas of Monnet and his colleagues'.[8] As William Diebold described them, the competition law provisions that emerged from this process 'blend several

[7] George Ball notes how during the negotiations he left through the backdoor of the building where Monnet was masterminding the drafting and negotiating of the treaty—'in case Europeans arrived'. George W. Ball, *The Past has Another Pattern: Memoirs* 89 (New York, 1982).

[8] Ibid., 88.

European approaches to cartel questions with elements drawn from American practice and experience'.[9]

3. The competition law provisions of the Treaty of Paris

The competition law provisions of the ECSC treaty served as a point of reference in drafting the analogous provisions of the Rome Treaty some six years later, and this makes it important for us to have a sense of their content and form.[10] The basic structure included two provisions, one prohibiting anticompetitive agreements (Article 65) and another dealing with 'concentrations' (that is, basically, mergers) and 'misuses' of economic power (Article 66).

The cartel provisions of Article 65 were the most controversial component of the package. That article (paragraph 1) prohibits

all agreements among enterprises, all decisions of associations of enterprises, and all concerted practices which would tend, directly or indirectly, to prevent, restrict or distort the normal operation of competition within the common market, and in particular: (a) to fix or influence prices; (b) to restrict or control production, technical development or investments; (c) to allocate markets, products, customers or sources of supply.

It then provides (paragraph 2) that the High Authority will authorize enterprises 'to agree among themselves to specialize in the production of, or to engage in joint buying or selling of specified products' where certain conditions are met. Basically, the conditions are that an arrangement 'contributes to a substantial improvement in the production or marketing of the products', is 'essential to achieve such effects and does not impose any restriction not necessary for that purpose' and is not 'susceptible of giving the interested enterprises the power to influence prices or to control or limit production of the products in question' or of 'protecting them from effective competition by other enterprises within the common market'.

A general prohibition of agreements between competitors was not part of the conception that most Europeans had of competition law, which, as we have seen, favored 'abuse' type legislation rather than prohibitions. That it should have been accepted has often puzzled commentators, leading some to ascribe its inclusion to the influence of the United States. As we have noted, however, Monnet and his colleagues went to great lengths to conceal any role by the United States in this process, and there is little evidence that the US

---

[9] Diebold, *Schuman Plan*, 352.

[10] For a comprehensive, contemporary commentary on these provisions, see Robert Krawielicki, *Das Monopolverbot im Schuman-Plan* (Tübingen, 1952). For comparison of the competition provisions of the Paris and Rome Treaties, see Fernand Spaak & Jean N. Jaeger, 'The Rules of Competition within the European Common Market', 26 *L. and Contemp. Prob.* 485 (1962).

exerted pressure on the participants in this regard. We need, therefore, to look elsewhere for the dynamics.

For participants other than Germany, there was little reason to resist such a prohibition, because their primary concern was to prevent German industry from controlling coal and steel. The impact of the prohibition would, therefore, fall most directly on the Germans. But why did the Germans accept it? One answer is that the other participants insisted, but there is no evidence that other negotiators were enthusiastic about such a prohibition. Moreover, it seems unlikely that they would have been, because they had no experience with such prohibitions and had reason to be wary of their impact.

Awareness of the role of ordoliberalism in Germany may here provide a key to a more convincing explanation. It has generally been assumed that the German negotiators were representing the interests of German industry, which obviously disliked such a prohibition, and, therefore, that they had to be coerced into accepting a cartel prohibition. George Ball's comment is representative: 'From the earliest days, the Germans, by conditioned reflex, have resisted deconcentration and decartelization'.[11] The picture looks quite different, however, when one recognizes the role of ordoliberalism in this context. As we have seen, the ordoliberal-inspired social market economy group behind Ludwig Erhard was calling for just such a prohibition in the German debates over a new competition law. Moreover, the chief negotiator for Germany was Walter Hallstein, an ardent supporter of ordoliberal ideas and later the first president of the European Commission. Given this background, it seems unlikely that the German negotiators fought hard against a cartel prohibition.

The other competition law article of the treaty (Article 66) contained detailed provisions on merger control and a rudimentary provision on abuse of economic power. The merger control provisions are of relatively little importance for our story, because they had little direct influence on subsequent developments. There were no analogous provisions in the Treaty of Rome, and ECSC experience seems to have played relatively little role in the shaping of subsequent merger controls either at the Community or national levels. We need, therefore, only sketch the contents of these provisions.

The basic framework for merger control was that any transaction creating a 'concentration' within the meaning of the statute would be valid only if it received prior authorization from the High Authority. The HA was directed to issue such authorization, however, if the transaction would not give to the interested parties the power

to influence prices, to control or restrain production or marketing, or to impair the maintenance of effective competition in a substantial part of the market for such products; or to evade the rules of competition [of the treaty], particularly by establishing an

[11] Ball, *The Past*, 88.

artificially privileged position involving a material advantage in access to suppliers or markets.

The object of these provisions was to control the process of concentration in the industry, and here US experience with merger controls was valuable, because there was virtually no European experience in the area.

Article 66 also included a provision that authorized the HA to control power positions where they already existed. It authorized the High Authority

to address to public or private enterprises which, in law or in fact, have or acquire on the market for one of the products [subject to the treaty] . . . a dominant position which protects them from effective competition in a substantial part of the common market, any recommendations required to prevent the use of such position for purposes contrary to those of the present Treaty.

This 'abuse' norm was not further defined, and no examples were provided as to what was to be included. Where firms did not fulfil such recommendations in a timely fashion, the HA could, in consultation with the relevant government, 'fix the prices and conditions of sale' for the enterprise or 'establish manufacturing or delivery programs to be executed by it'.

This provision corresponded to the basic 'abuse' concept that had been developed before the Depression—the idea that economic power should be controlled and that administrators should have the authority to devise responses to it where it was used in a way that created harm for society (here, the 'community' formed by the treaty). Its vagueness reflected, however, the lack of experience with the concept as well as the lack of available conceptual referents for it. The treaty gave the Commission virtually unlimited discretion in this respect, but it also required that any sanctions be taken in consultation with the government involved and thus created a disincentive for the Commission to move aggressively in this area.

In general, the competition law provisions were applied through the same procedural and institutional mechanisms as other norms in the treaty. Because private suits were not allowed, the High Authority had sole responsibility for applying and enforcing these provisions. As with other decisions of the HA, however, competition law decisions were generally appealable to the new European Court of Justice, and thus to this extent the competition law system had a juridical component.

4. The operation and impact of the ECSC competition law provisions

The inclusion of competition law provisions in the ECSC treaty was a step in the development of competition law in Europe, creating a base for subsequent international agreements and national authorities to build on. Perhaps its most important role was to provide a precedent for the inclusion of competition provisions in the Treaty of Rome and something of a model for those provisions.

The actual operations of the ECSC competition law system had a limited impact on the development of competition law in Europe.[12] During the initial five years of its operations, that system was little used, and thus experience under the ECSC played little role in the drafting of the Rome Treaty. During that period the Commission did not prohibit any concentrations, and its enforcement of other provisions was quite limited, concentrating on the German coal sales agencies. The Commission was just beginning to develop politically acceptable methods and procedures. As William Diebold wrote in 1959, 'The High Authority is trying to apply a comprehensive, pioneering, international antitrust law when it is itself pioneering in establishing its status, strength and effectiveness'.[13]

Although in the following decades ECSC competition law developed considerably, its role outside its own area of application has been limited. It is seldom referred to in the general literature of Community competition law, not least because it involves relatively few decision-makers and lawyers. This means that few have had occasion to learn about the system and that the literature on it has generally been specialized and narrow. In general, it has been seen as a special form of competition law for a specific context and of little general relevance to the issues of competition law in Europe.

The story of the early development of competition law in the ECSC belies the assumption that the US strongly influenced the development of competition law in Europe because of its involvement in the drafting of the Paris Treaty. That involvement was clandestine and generally limited to supplying basic ideas, many of which were already known to key drafters. The one area where US experience supplied significant content was the merger control provisions, and that area had little subsequent impact on competition law development in Europe.

B. COMPETITION LAW IN THE ROME TREATY

The ECSC was understood by many as a first step in the process of European integration, but it soon appeared that the anticipated further steps might not follow, or at least that the wait for them might be long. The process seemed to lose what force it had when plans for a European Political Community foundered and especially in 1954 after the French rejected plans to establish a European Defense Community.

At this point, pro-integration leaders such as Jean Monnet and Robert Schuman of France, Paul-Henri Spaak of Belgium, Alcide de Gasperi of Italy, and Konrad Adenauer of Germany saw the economic sphere as the one

---

[12] See generally Stuart Scheingold, *The Rule of Law in European Integration: The Path of the Schuman Plan* (New Haven, 1965).

[13] Diebold, *Schuman Plan*, 400.

avenue left for moving toward European integration, and they turned their energies toward the creation of a common market for Europe.[14] By 1955, this idea had acquired sufficient support that a conference was held in Messina, Italy, to devise a plan for economic integration. As a result of it, the Benelux countries joined with France, Italy, and Germany (the UK participated briefly) in drafting the so-called 'Spaak Report' during the following year.[15] This plan was approved by the 'six', who then drafted the Rome Treaty in a very short time, and it went into effect on January 1, 1958.

The plan had two basic objectives. One was political and derived from the impetus to European unification that had been such an important part of political life in Europe during the preceding decade. By creating a common market, the countries of Europe would be tied together economically in a way that would preclude or at least reduce the possibility of conflicts and wars. The other objective was economic, but it had political overtones. It was to increase prosperity in Europe by reducing the barriers to trade between the Member States. This would not only be a benefit in itself, serving the interests of both business and the consumer, but it would also serve the political goal of stability and avoidance of conflict. The memory of the Weimar period and the Depression remained powerful, and one of the clearest lessons of that period seemed to be that economic failures—poverty, lability and crises— were the wellsprings of political and military disasters.

From the inception of this process, there seems to have been little doubt that the Treaty would have to include provisions aimed at combating restraints on competition. Not only had such provisions been included in the ECSC treaty, but there seems to have been general agreement that the elimi- nation of tariff barriers would not achieve its objectives if private agreements or economically powerful firms were permitted to be used to manipulate the flow of trade.

There were, however, differing views on the kind of competition law that should be included. Official records of the Messina conference and of the drafting of the Rome Treaty have not been made public, but, according to Hanns-Jürgen Küsters, one of the members of the German negotiating group, both the French and the German delegations 'tried to transfer important basic elements of their national economic systems to the Common Market'.[16] The German negotiators were imbued with the ordoliberal orthodoxies so powerful in Germany and sought a strict form of competition law, whereas the French sought provisions that, in effect, viewed competition law more as a matter of administrative policy. According to Küsters, the other delegations

---

[14] For background, see Pierre Gerbet, *La Construction de l'Europe* 181–212 (Paris, 1983).

[15] See Comité Intergouvernemental Crée Par La Conférence de Messine, Rapport des Chefs de Délégation aux Ministres des Affaires Étrangères 16–23 (1956) ('Spaak Report').

[16] Hanns-Jürgen Küsters, *Die Gründung der Europäischen Wirtschaftsgemeinschaft* 364 (Baden-Baden, 1982). For discussion of the conflict, see ibid., 364–69.

ranged between these two positions, with the Netherlands closer to the German position and the Italians closer to the French.[17]

The provisions that were eventually included represented a compromise between these two positions. They reflected in a loose way the general format of Articles 65 and 66 of the ECSC treaty, although they did not contain merger control provisions. Their generally greater precision also reflected the long debates in Germany over competition law. As Otto Schlecht, a leading German economic policy official of the period, has put it, 'Without this battle [for the GWB] there probably never would have been the prohibition of cartels or the abuse supervision in the EC treaty'.[18]

The treaty included as one of its goals 'the institution of a system ensuring that competition in the common market is not distorted' (Article 3(f)). It then included two types of provisions that were primarily designed to accomplish that objective. Articles 85 and 86 related to private restraints on competition,[19] and Article 90 related to governmental restraints. Article 90 remained

[17] Hanns-Jürgen Küsters, *Die Gründung der Europäischen Wirtschaftsgemeinschaft* 364 (Baden-Baden, 1982).

[18] Otto Schlecht, 'Macht und Ohnmacht der Ordnungspolitik—Eine Bilanz nach 40 Jahren Sozialer Marktwirtschaft', 40 *ORDO* 303–11 (1989).

[19] According to Article 85:

1. The following shall be prohibited as incompatible with the common market: all agreements between undertakings, decisions by associations of undertakings and concerted practices which may affect trade between Member States and which have as their object or effect the prevention, restriction or distortion of competition within the common market, and in particular those which:

a) directly or indirectly fix purchase or selling prices or any other trading conditions;

b) limit or control production, markets, technical development, or investment;

c) share markets or sources of supply;

d) apply dissimilar conditions to equivalent transactions with other trading parties, thereby placing them at a competitive disadvantage;

e) make the conclusion of contracts subject to acceptance by the other parties of supplementary obligations which, by their nature or according to commercial usage, have no connection with the subject of such contracts.

2. Any agreements or decisions prohibited pursuant to this Article shall be automatically void.

3. The provisions of paragraph 1 may, however, be declared inapplicable in the case of:

– any agreement or category of agreements between undertakings;

– any decision or category of decisions by associations of undertakings;

– any concerted practice or category of concerted practices which contributes to improving the production or distribution of goods or to promoting technical or economic progress, while allowing consumers a fair share of the resulting benefit, and which does not:

a) impose on the undertakings concerned restrictions which are not indispensable to the attainment of these objectives;

b) afford such undertakings the possibility of eliminating competition in respect of a substantial part of the products in question.

Article 86 provides that:

Any abuse by one or more undertakings of a dominant position within the common market or in a substantial part of it shall be prohibited as incompatible with the common market in so far as it may affect trade between Member States.

Such abuse may, in particular, consist in:

a) directly or indirectly imposing unfair purchase or selling prices or other unfair trading conditions;

of marginal importance until much later, so that we can focus here on Articles 85 and 86.

Article 85 follows the basic structure of Article 65 of the ECSC treaty. Section (1) prohibits and declares void agreements 'which may affect trade between Member States and which have as their object or effect the prevention, restriction or distortion of competition within the common market'. It then provides five examples of agreements which, 'in particular', have that effect, including, for example, the fixing of prices, the sharing of markets, and tie-in arrangements.

This broad prohibition is followed, however, by a declaration in Article 85(3) that agreements which meet certain criteria may be exempted from the provisions of Article 85(1). These criteria are of two kinds: those requiring positive benefits as a result of the restraint on competition and those requiring the absence of certain types of harm. According to 85(3), agreements 'may . . . be declared inapplicable' where they contribute to 'improving the production or distribution of goods or to promoting technical or economic progress, while allowing consumers a fair share of the resulting benefit'. The 'negative' conditions are that the agreement 'not a) impose on the undertakings concerned restrictions which are not indispensable to the attainment of these objectives; and b) afford such undertakings the possibility of eliminating competition in respect of a substantial part of the products in question'.

Article 86 prohibits abuse of a market-dominating position. This article is more fully developed than the analogous provision (Article 66) of the ECSC treaty. In contrast to Article 66, it includes examples of abusive conduct, among which are 'directly or indirectly imposing unfair purchase or selling prices or other unfair trading conditions', 'limiting production, markets or technical development to the prejudice of consumers', engaging in discrimination in price or otherwise, and entering into tying arrangements. The treaty does not provide the possibility of exemption in cases of abusive conduct.

Both articles are brief and broadly conceived. Their function was 'constitutional' in the sense that they would have to be given content in practice. The treaty does not elaborate on how they would be applied, nor does it create a specific institutional or procedural framework for the development of a competition law system.

b) limiting production, markets or technical development to the prejudice of consumers;
c) applying dissimilar conditions to equivalent transactions with other trading parties, thereby placing them at a competitive disadvantage;
d) making the conclusion of contracts subject to acceptance by the other parties of supplementary obligations which, by their nature or according to commercial usage, have no connection with the subject of such contracts.

C. THE FOUNDATIONAL PERIOD[20]

The Member States and the institutions of the Community were thus left with the task of constructing a competition law system. They did so gradually, guided by changing perceptions of the needs of the Community and of individual Member State interests, and reflecting shifting configurations of power among Community institutions and in the relationships between those institutions and the Member States. The basic 'foundational' elements of the Community's competition law system were developed during roughly the first decade and a half of its existence.

1. Competing visions of competition law

Competing visions of competition law provided axes along which these decisions had to be made. One was whether the competition provisions of the treaty were to be understood as 'law' or merely as guidelines for decision-making. Here national experiences provided two quite different images of competition law. German participants tended to see the competition law provisions as fundamentally 'juridical'—legal norms that had to be interpreted and applied according to judicial methods.[21] From their ordoliberal-influenced perspective, the treaty provided the 'economic constitution' from which more specific 'regulative principles' were to be derived. At the very least, the decade-long controversy over the introduction of a German competition law conditioned German participants to think of Community competition as 'law'.

Decision-makers from other Member States were often inclined to view Articles 85 and 86 not as 'enforceable law', but rather as programmatic statements of policy intended to guide the administrative decision-making of the Commission.[22] Thus the French, for example, tended to see competition law in political and policy terms, preferring to base decisions on the evaluation by Community officials of the needs of the Community and its Member States. They were steeped in the values and methods of *dirigisme* and *planification* which tended to view competition law in that light.[23]

---

[20] I have adapted the periodization scheme employed in this chapter as well as related terminology from Joseph Weiler. Joseph H. H. Weiler, 'The Transformation of Europe', 100 *Yale L.J.* 2403 (1991).

[21] See, e.g., Hans Kutscher, 'Über den Gerichtshof der Europäischen Gemeinschaft', 16 *Europarecht* 393 (1981). For a representative statement of German perspectives on this general issue, see Walter Hallstein, *Europe in the Making* 30–55 (Charles Roetter, tr., New York, 1972) and Eberhard Günther, 'Die Ordnungspolitischen Grundlagen des EWG-Vertrages', 1963 *Wirtschaft und Wettbewerb* 191 (1963).

[22] See, e.g., Hans von der Groeben & Hans von Boeckh, I *Kommentar zum EWG-Vertrag* 258–69 (Baden-Baden, 1958).

[23] French observers often tended to perceive European competition law as 'neo-liberalism', sometimes viewing it favorably and other times not. See, e.g., Jacques Houssiaux, *Concurrence et Marché Commun* 7 (Paris, 1960).

The second fundamental issue was how large a role competition law should play. If Articles 85 and 86 were to operate as enforceable rules, should the Commission and the Court of Justice view them as important and enforce them seriously? The Germans tended to say 'Yes', but outside Germany, competition law had always played a marginal role, if any, in European business decision-making, and its role in the ECSC had done little to change that. As a result, it was widely assumed that Community competition law provisions would play a limited role.[24] Many apparently believed, for example, that such provisions should be applied only in cases involving the very largest firms and/or firms that were engaged primarily in transnational business.[25]

These respective conceptions of competition law and visions of its roles would compete for decades. Gradually, a juridical conception of competition law took hold, and it also became increasingly clear that competition law would play a major role in European integration. As we shall see, however, the conflicts have never been fully resolved, and recent iterations of them may make them more portentous now than ever.

2. Integration and the goals of competition law

The goal of a unified market dominated the process of constructing the competition law system, because it was *the* central impetus for the 'new Europe'. As Barry Hawk has put it, 'Single market integration, and the elimination of restrictive practices which interfere with that integration, is the first principle of EEC antitrust law. . .'.[26] This 'unification imperative' has shaped institutional structures and competences within the system, supplied much of its legitimacy, and generated the conceptual framework for the development and application of its substantive norms.

To begin to appreciate the centrality and force of this idea, one need only recall that economic co-operation was the last remaining hope for a cooperative Europe that would banish the specter of that continent's nationalist past. Attempts to move toward political union had been rejected, and the plans for a European Defense Community had been defeated. If there was to be a new Europe, it would have to be built on economic co-operation and integration.

In addition to this political goal of replacing conflict with co-operation, the Common Market was seen as serving a variety of economic goals.[27] Above all, many viewed it as necessary for further economic improvement. European national markets were seen as too small to support significant

---

[24] See, e.g., D. G. Goyder, *EEC Competition Law*, 65 (Oxford, 1988).

[25] See Robert LeCourt, *L'Europe des Juges* 82 (Brussels, 1976).

[26] Barry E. Hawk, 'Antitrust in the EEC—The First Decade', 41 *Fordham L. Rev.* 229, 231 (1972).

[27] For discussion, see, e.g., U. W. Kitzinger, *The Politics and Economics of European Integration* 21–59 (New York, 1963).

economic growth. Moreover, an integrated market would allow European firms to acquire sufficient size to compete effectively on world markets, and consumers would benefit from a Europe-sized market with its concomitant economies of scale.

Many Europeans also saw economic integration as the only means of dealing with the combined economic and political power of the United States.[28] These were the years of the Jean-Jacques Servan-Schreiber's famous *Défi Américain*, the 'American Challenge' to Europe,[29] and an integrated market represented a means of regaining independence, power, and status *vis-à-vis* the country that had assumed world leadership in the wake of two world wars.

This does not mean that there was no interest in obtaining the generic benefits of competition. There was. Both the Commission and the Court referred at times to the potential benefits—lower prices, more rapid technological progress, etc.—anticipated as a result of improved competition.[30] These references were imbedded, however, in a discourse and practice that was focused on economic integration.[31] In particular, it is important to remember that socialist thought was still highly influential in many parts of Europe at this time, and thus there were political disincentives to associating competition law too closely with the protection of the competitive process as such.

Furthermore, there was little reason to distinguish between the two goals. They were related, and they reinforced each other. To the extent that competition law eliminated obstacles to the flow of goods, services, and capital across European borders, for example, it served the cause of unifying the market while simultaneously benefiting consumers by increasing the number of actual and potential competitors on European markets.

3. Politics and the role of the Commission

Given the lack of experience with competition law in the Member States and the common assumption that competition law would play the same marginal role in the Community that it played in the Member States, it is not surprising that Member State governments had little interest in becoming directly

---

[28] See, e.g., Richard Mayne, *The Recovery of Europe: 1945–1973* 203–34 (Garden City, N.J., 1973).

[29] Jean-Jacques Servan-Schreiber, *Le Défi Américain* (Paris, 1967).

[30] See, e.g., the Court's opinion in *Consten and Grundig v. Commission*, Cases 56 and 58/64 [1966] ECR 299, 339–40, and the Commission's Action Programme for the Second Stage of the Community (Nov. 1962), *CCH Comm. Mkt. Reps.* 18–24 (Feb., 1963).

[31] The following quote from the Commission demonstrates the imbeddedness of the idea: 'Although it is evident that the competition policy of the Community must be directed towards the creation and proper operation of the common market, its effectiveness would, nevertheless, be considerably improved if it were carried out in conjunction with more active competition policies at the national level and with the removal of certain obstacles to the free play of the market in various sectors, such as the fixing of prices and the placing of orders by public authorities'. Commission of the European Communities, *First Report on Competition Policy* 12 (1972).

involved in the structuring of that system. The Council, that is, the organ of the Communities that represents the political will of the Member States and has final legislative authority, was willing to allow the Commission to play the major role in shaping the competition law system, and the Commission grasped the opportunity.[32]

The preparation of an institutional framework for implementing Articles 85 and 86 dominated the work of the Commission's competition law officials for roughly half a decade. The process involved extensive and sometimes difficult negotiations among the Council, the Commission, the European Parliament, and Member State governments, culminating in enactment of Regulation 17, the blueprint for the institutional structure of the competition law system.[33] The head of the committee of the European Parliament that drafted Regulation 17 was a German attorney named Arvid Deringer, and the Regulation his committee drafted represented German views of the importance of making competition law both juridical and important.

Regulation 17 created a competition law system in which the enforcement and policy-making prerogatives were centered in the Commission and the role of national legal systems was marginalized.

The Commission's preoccupation [with centralizing enforcement in its own hands] was understandable. The principles embodied in the competition law rules were novel and almost revolutionary. They required fundamental changes in deeply ingrained habits of thought and patterns of economic conduct. The officials of the new competition Directorate-General did not trust businessmen, lawyers and judges to apply the rules correctly (or even, as the case might be, in good faith). . . .[34]

The Treaty of Rome did not dictate such centralization, and prior to the enactment of Regulation 17 national authorities had applied the competition law provisions, sometimes actively.[35] Their marginalization was thus a critical step in constructing the system.

A key component of this centralization move was Article 9(3), which required that when the Commission began an investigation under the competition law sections of the treaty, national authorities had to cease their own enforcement activity under the treaty with regard to that conduct. This

---

[32] The Council has the final legislative authority within the Community. It is an explicitly political body in which the Member States are directly represented and pursue their own national interests. The Council may not, however, initiate legislation. This must be done by the Commission, which is the bureaucracy of the Commission and represents the interests of the Community as a whole.

[33] Regulation 17/62, 1962 OJ 204. For discussion, see, e.g., Arved Deringer, 'The Distribution of Powers in the Enforcement of the Rules of Competition under the Rome Treaty', 1 *Comm. Mkt. L. Rev.* 30 (1963).

[34] Ian Forrester & Christopher Norall, 'The Laicization of Community Law: Self-Help and the Rule of Reason: How Competition Law Is and Could be Applied', 21 *Comm. Mkt. L. Rev.* 11, 13 (1984).

[35] See Grant W. Kelleher, 'The Common Market Antitrust Laws: The First Ten Years', 12 *Antitrust Bull.* 1219, 1221 (1967).

provision thus stripped the Member States of incentives to begin investigations, because such investigations would have to be discontinued if the Commission began its own investigation. Behind it was the perceived need to centralize the operations of the competition law system. The fear was that Member States would conceive competition law in the same terms that they saw national competition law systems and that this would create a very different type of system than was necessary for integration. The Commission's monopoly on the right to grant exemptions has been a key element in the relationship between Community and national competition law systems, and it has become increasingly important in recent years as the focus has shifted to decentralizing competition law.

A second central element was Article 9(1), which provided that only the Commission could issue exemptions under Article 85(3). This eliminated incentives to bring suit in national courts, because such courts could only treat one of the two issues relevant to the application of Article 85. The combined effect of these provisions was to eliminate any significant role for national legal systems in the enforcement of Community competition law.

The centrality of the Commission's role was enhanced by the introduction of the notification procedure that was to become a pivotal feature of the Community system. According to Article 4(1) of Regulation 17, agreements that might violate Article 85 were to be notified to the Commission, and exemption from Article 85(1) was made contingent on the filing of such a notification, thus assuring that relevant agreements generally would be notified. This procedure gave significant power to the Commission, for the most important practical question came to be what the Commission would do about notified agreements. Businesses and their representatives had to go to the Commission for the information they needed, and it was there that they could seek to influence decisions.

In addition to greatly expanding the Commission's role, Regulation 17 also secured for the competition directorate (General Directorate IV or DG IV) a high degree of autonomy in decision-making. France had sought to require that DG IV obtain the approval of a majority of the members of a newly established advisory committee on competition law before sending its recommendations to the full Commission for final decision.[36] This committee was to consist of representatives from each Member State, and thus the requirement of approval would have subjected the Commission's decision-making power to a high degree of political influence. Competition law would have developed primarily as a reflection of political decisions by the Member States rather than through juridical processes. This requirement was, however, rejected in Article 10(3). An advisory committee was established, but DG IV was merely required to consult with it before sending decisions to the Commission.

---

[36] For discussion, see Goyder, *EEC Competition Law*, 41.

Finally, Regulation 17 gave the Commission extensive investigatory and enforcement powers. For example, Article 14 vested the Commission with authority to enter into any premises relevant to an investigation for violation of the competition law provisions, to examine the books and records of the firms involved, to make relevant copies and to interview personnel at the site of the investigation. These powers made the Commission a formidable enforcement agency.

In 1965, the Council further buttressed the autonomy of the Commission in competition law matters by granting it broad powers to 'legislate' without approval of the Council. Regulation 17's notification procedure had caused a flood of notifications to the Commission and had placed an enormous burden on a small office. As a consequence, the Council granted the Commission the authority to issue group exemptions under 85(3) in certain situations without its approval.[37] Moreover, the Council included language in the Regulation indicating that it favored such delegation, and it has since expanded the categories of cases in which the Commission may so legislate.

DG IV is the only directorate to have such power, and some consider it unlikely that the Council would initiate such a practice today. Nevertheless, what began as a response to a specific and temporary need (to deal with a flood of notifications) has come to play an important role in the system, because it further shields DG IV's decision-making authority from political interference.

The Community's political institutions thus constructed an institutional framework for competition law that relied heavily on the initiatives and decisions of the Commission. It centralized authority in the Commission and minimized the role of national competition officials and national courts, and on the Community level it helped to protect DG IV from political influences.

4. The Court defines its role

The one institution in the system whose role was not subject to definition by the political process was the Court of Justice. The Court had to mold its own role, and it chose to put itself in a leadership position. Viewing itself as the principal 'motor of integration', the Court took advantage of the special circumstances offered by competition law and made that system an important 'vehicle' of integration whose strength would, in turn, further amplify the Court's power.

The Court's definition of its role in the competition law system was part of the broader process of defining its role within the Community, and here timing was a critical factor. The first significant competition law cases came to

---

[37] Regulation 19/65, 1965 OJ 533.

the Court in the mid-1960s, just as General De Gaulle's resistance to Europeanization threatened to stop the process of integration and destroy the Community. De Gaulle was able to change the 'constitution' of the Community by demanding a unanimity requirement for virtually all Council decisions, thus hobbling the Community's political organs.[38] As a consequence, the Court was the only institution capable of maintaining the momentum of integration.[39] Moreover, these events created a crisis of confidence that encouraged the Court to assert a bold leadership role.

The Court thus developed competition law as a central tool in these efforts to promote integration, structuring the competition law system to achieve that goal. According to Ulrich Everling, a former judge of the European Court of Justice, 'In evaluating the case law of the Court it is necessary to recognize that the competition rules of the Community are placed in the service of the central objective of the Community, namely the opening of the markets of the Member States'.[40] It articulated a broad conception of competition law as central to the process of integration, and its decisions in the competition law area sought to make that conception viable and convincing.

The role the Court sculpted for itself in this competition law system centered on intellectual leadership.[41] The Court frequently enunciated broad principles and values rather than limiting itself to ruling on the facts of individual cases. It looked to the future and aimed at guiding the Commission in its development of competition policy.[42] This role had no precedents in European national competition law systems. To the extent that there had been judicial involvement at all in European competition law systems, the courts had functioned primarily as administrative courts, whose primary role was to develop and apply a principled set of controls on the discretionary action of administrative bodies, or, as in Germany, to restrain the initiatives of administrative decision-makers.

The Court established, for example, a practice of providing the Commission with what one commentator has referred to as 'windows of opportunity'.[43] According to this practice, the Court would go beyond the facts of the case at bar to indicate its willingness to support particular lines of development of competition law doctrine.

[38] See generally, e.g., Kitzinger, *Politics and Economics,* 90–6 and 220–42.
[39] See Kutscher, 'Über den Gerichtshof', 402.
[40] See Ulrich Everling, 'Zur Wettbewerbskonzeption in der neueren Rechtsprechung des Gerichtshofs der Europäischen Gemeinschaften', 1990 *Wirtschaft und Wettbewerb* 995, 1000 (1990).
[41] For discussion of the Court's intellectual role, see, e.g., Giuseppe F. Mancini, 'The Making of a Constitution for Europe', *26 Comm. Mkt. L. Rev.* 595 (1989).
[42] The point here relates not to the source of ideas, but to the role played within the system by authoritative pronouncements of those ideas. As Eric Stein and others have pointed out, the Commission often is the source of new ideas that are then given authoritative force through inclusion in the decisions of the Court. See Eric Stein, 'Lawyers, Judges and the Making of a Transnational Constitution', 75 *Am. J. Int'l. L.* 1, 25 (1981).
[43] Goyder, *EEC Competition Law*, 413.

Reflecting the centrality of the goal of integration, the Court made teleology the cornerstone of its interpretive strategy. As in its constitutional case law, the Court interpreted the treaty's competition law provisions according to its own conception of what was necessary to achieve the integrationist goals of the treaty. It conveyed a clear message that this goal-energized methodology was not merely to be one of a number of principles to be used in interpreting the treaty. It was to be the dominant interpretive method.

The Court's teleological discourse carried centralist values. The Court saw a strong Commission as necessary for achieving integration, and it molded competition law doctrine so as to increase the power of the Commission in relation to national authorities. A prominent and critically important part of this pattern was the Court's consistent expansion of the geographical scope of Article 85. According to Article 85(1), agreements can violate the treaty only where they 'may affect trade between Member States', but the treaty provided little indication of what that phrase meant. The Court consistently expanded this concept of 'effect on trade', and it relied on integrationist goals in justifying this expansion.[44] The effect was to increase the jurisdictional prerogatives of the Commission and to reduce those of the Member States.[45]

5. The Commission and the birth pangs of competition policy

The centrality of the Court's role was also tied to the enormity of the task faced by the Commission. In effect, DG IV had to create an entire substantive and procedural system and explain it, frequently to governmental and business leaders unfamiliar with such norms, and/or dubious of their legitimacy. Moreover, the lack of experience with competition law in most Member States meant that decision-makers in DG IV did not have a broad base of knowledge on which to draw in determining what those norms should be. Finally, the unanimity requirement in the Council meant that the Commission could not depend for political support on a majority of the Council and, as a result, had to avoid taking action that might unduly offend individual Member States.

The Commission thus moved very carefully during the foundational period. It had to establish an experiential base to guide its judgments and a political foundation for confidence in its procedures that would support effective enforcement in the future. For much of the period it focused its efforts on jurisdictional and procedural issues, most notably the creation of Regulation 17. Enforcement was approached delicately, as shown, for example, by the Commission's unwillingness to levy fines until late in the period.

Under these circumstances, the Commission had little choice but to seek a co-operative relationship with the Court. Both recognized the need for such

---

[44] See Hawk, 'Antitrust in the EEC', 247.
[45] See, e.g., Goyder, *EEC Competition Law*, 96–105.

co-operation, because neither could achieve its goals independently. Except where national courts request specific interpretations from the Court, it can only pursue its own goals when the Commission takes enforcement action. Similarly, the Commission cannot accomplish its mission without the Court's support of its interpretations and applications of the Treaty.

In the co-operative relationship that evolved, the Commission tended to follow the lead of the Court, thereby taking advantage of the Court's symbolic status and its relative immunity from political pressure. The Court's decisions were largely shielded from such pressure because they were understood as applications by a neutral, non-political body of juridically-determined principles, and thus the Commission could achieve a degree of political security by operating in the Court's 'tow'.

This is not to suggest that the Commission did not produce its own initiatives. The Commission did create competition policy, and by the end of the period it had begun to enforce the competition rules with a degree of vigor. Nevertheless, it remained dependent on the Court, which was at the time the more secure institution.

In this interplay between Court and Commission, the integration imperative was pivotal, because it represented a common goal for the two institutions. Each saw an expansive reading of the competition provisions as critical to its own role in moving the Community toward integration. As a consequence, they developed the Community's substantive law in the service of this goal.

6. Molding the substance of competition law

The overriding importance of economic integration as a goal for both Court and Commission configured not only the institutional arrangements of competition law, but its substantive content as well. In contrast to national competition law systems, whose primary objective typically is to secure generic benefits associated with competition, Community competition law was shaped to eliminate private restraints on trade across national borders.

a. Article 85: the vertical emphasis

The emphasis in Community competition law on vertical relationships (for example, manufacturer-retailer) between firms may be the most important example of this.[46] While national legal systems frequently focus on horizontal agreements because they represent the most obvious distortions of the market, Community competition law has focused on vertical restraints, largely because these represent the most obvious obstacles to transborder trade.[47]

---

[46] See, e.g., Barry E. Hawk, II *United States, Common Market and International Antitrust: A Comparative Guide* 403–573 (2d. ed., Englewood Cliffs, N.J., 1993).

[47] This focus on vertical relationships sharply distinguished Community competition law from, for example, US antitrust law. See, e.g., Spencer Weber Waller, 'Understanding and

This concern led the Commission to attack a variety of agreements that manufacturers and distributors were using to separate and protect national markets. Where manufacturers could use exclusive distributorships to protect them from parallel imports, for example, they could effectively re-erect through private means the barriers to trade that the Community was designed to eliminate. The Commission thus aggressively attacked such agreements, and the Court supported its attacks in broad language signaling that the Court would strike down any agreements used for these general purposes.[48]

A related problem involved the use of industrial property rights to achieve such market segregation objectives. Manufacturers used both patents and trademarks to prevent parallel importation and protect specific territories for themselves and their distributors. The Commission gave these tactics priority attention, and the Court followed the Commission's lead in concluding that such uses of industrial property rights were inconsistent with the treaty.[49]

The central decision in this line of cases came in 1966 in the *Grundig-Consten* litigation.[50] There the Court signaled the centrality of market integration values and condemned both of the above strategies for market separation. The case involved an arrangement whereby Grundig, a German manufacturer of televisions and other electronic equipment, appointed Consten, a French firm, to be its exclusive distributor in certain designated territories (mainly, France). Consten agreed to sell only in its designated territories, and Grundig agreed to prohibit its other distributors from selling in Consten's territories. To buttress this exclusivity Grundig permitted Consten to register in its designated territories a Grundig trademark that appeared on the products Consten sold.

In 1964, the Commission attacked this arrangement, declaring that by preventing parallel imports into France it 'affected trade' within the meaning of Article 85(1) and must, therefore, be prohibited. Although there were differences between the Court and the Commission on other aspects of the case, the Court agreed with the Commission on this fundamental point. The Court interpreted Article 85(1) to invalidate the agreement because it impaired the free flow of goods within the Community. The language of the opinion made clear that the Commission and the Court viewed Article 85 not merely as a programmatic guide to policy, but as 'law' to be interpreted according to the needs of the Community created by the treaty.

Together, the cases from the foundational period established the basic principle that vertical agreements used to restrict or distort the flow of goods

Appreciating EC Competition Law', 61 *Antitrust L. J.* 55, 66–67 (1992) and Tim Frazer, 'Competition Policy after 1992: The Next Step', 53 *Mod. L. Rev.* 609, 618–20 (1990).

[48] See, e.g., Case 56/65, *Societé Technique Minière v. Machinenbau Ulm GmbH* [1966] ECR 235.

[49] For patents, see Case 24/67, *Parke-Davis v. Probel* [1968] ECR 55. For trademarks, see Case 40/70, *Sirena v. Eda* [1971] ECR 69.

[50] *Commission v. Consten & Grundig*, Cases 58/64 and 56 [1966] ECR 299.

across national borders were incompatible with the treaty. The Commission's enforcement efforts were directed primarily at such agreements, and the Court consistently articulated broad principles designed to support those efforts and, in effect, to urge the Commission further in that direction.

The Commission paid noticeably less attention to horizontal agreements during this period. In part this was because such agreements were less obviously and directly related to the paramount goal of integration. In addition, enforcement action that might inhibit co-operation risked conflict with other policy goals. The Commission was concerned, for example, with assuring that European firms be able to compete with their US rivals, and it thus sought to promote co-operative arrangements among such firms, particularly the small and medium-sized enterprises whose survival appeared to be threatened by international competition.[51]

The result was cautious enforcement of Article 85(1) to horizontal agreements. There was no question that cartels were generally forbidden by that Article, and thus the Court and the Commission concentrated on balancing the competition-distorting effects of competitor agreements against the need to protect other Community interests such as economic progress. They focused, for example, on distinguishing between 'hard' agreements, which were 'basically' anticompetitive, and 'soft' agreements, which were 'basically' designed to improve competitiveness. Moreover, the Commission tended to allow co-operative agreements between small and medium-sized industries, and to concentrate enforcement efforts on agreements involving larger firms.[52]

b. *Article 86*

During the EEC's first decade, Article 86 was little used. The concept of abuse was vague, and the civil law-trained officials of the Commission and judges of the European Court were reluctant to apply vague legal concepts. Moreover, the Commission did not wish to risk losing cases because of the Court's probable reluctance in this regard, and the lack of any well-accepted sense of how the provision should be applied made enforcement by a politically weak Commission highly risky. In addition, Commission policy was focused on the creation of business enterprises of sufficient size to compete with American corporations, and thus it had little incentive to apply legal provisions that might hamper the growth of European firms or reduce their ability to compete internationally. The lack of enforcement under Article 86 led to concern in the early 1960s that it would simply remain a 'dead letter'.[53]

During this period, however, the Commission was attempting to establish a theoretical framework for interpreting the abuse concept. It created an advi-

---

[51] See, e.g., Hawk, 'Antitrust in the EEC', 231 and 234–35.   [52] Ibid., 249–65.
[53] See, e.g., I. Samkaladen & I. E. Druker, 'Legal Problems Relating to Article 86 of the Rome Treaty', in 1965–66 *Comm. Mkt. L. Rev.* 158, 162 (1966).

sory group composed primarily of law professors, and charged this group with working out basic principles. The conclusions of the group were then published in 1966 as the core of the Commission's first major statement concerning interpretation of the abuse concept, its Memorandum on Concentration.[54]

The Memorandum contained two basic principles relating to the interpretation of the abuse concept. The first was that abuse occurs where a dominant firm utilizes the possibilities which flow from its position of dominance in order to obtain benefits which it could not obtain if it were exposed to 'effective competition'.[55] Accordingly, a direct causal link was required between the enterprise's power and its results in the market. This was not intended as a definition of abuse, for it obviously would be overbroad and would label as abusive virtually any conduct by a dominant firm. It represented merely a starting point for interpreting the abuse concept.

The second principle of interpretation utilized a different conceptual reference point. It claimed that abuse is found where a dominant firm's conduct is 'wrong (*fautif*) in regard to the fixed objectives of the treaty'.[56] In defining abuse in relation to the objectives of the treaty, the Memorandum merely was applying the teleological method of interpretation to the abuse concept, but the decision was crucial, for it established the framework within which subsequent development was to take place.

The ECJ's first opportunities to interpret Article 86 came in the late 1960s and early 1970s in a series of three cases which were referred to the Court by national courts.[57] In each of these cases the Court was asked for an advisory opinion as to whether a dominant firm possessing industrial property rights could violate Article 86 by using those rights to increase its prices. The Court took the position that 'The price level of a product is not in itself necessarily indicative of an abuse of a dominant position within the meaning of Article 86, but it can be a decisive indication where it is particularly high and is not justified by the facts'.[58] The Court did not elaborate on what it meant by justification, nor did it discuss in detail any interpretative issues relating to Article 86, but it indicated its willingness to support attempts by the Commission to find abuse in cases of high prices by dominant firms.

In contrast to its efforts to shape a substantive framework for applying Articles 85 and 86, the Commission chose not to enforce vigorously the treaty provisions relating to state aids, governmental monopolies, or government facilitation of private anti-competitive conduct. The Commission recognized

---

[54] EEC Commission, Memorandum sur le Probleme de la Concentration dans le Marché Commun (Dec. 1, 1965), reprinted in *Revue Trimestrielle de Droit Européen* 651–677 (1966).

[55] Memorandum on Concentration, 670.   [56] Ibid., 676.

[57] Case 24/67, *Parke, Davis & Co. v. Probel* [1968] ECR 55; Case 40/70, *Sirena Srl v. Eda GmbH* [1971] ECR 69; Case 78/70, *Deutsche Grammophon GmbH v. Metro-SB-Grossmärkte* [1971] ECR 487.

[58] Case 40/70, *Sirena Srl v. Eda GmbH* [1971] ECR 69, 84.

the potential threat posed by governmental interference with competition, but was apparently leery of the potential political repercussions of seriously activating these provisions.

7. The role of national legal systems

As we have seen, Regulation 17 sharply curtailed incentives to use national legal systems to vindicate rights provided by Community competition law. During the foundational period, the major issue regarding the role of national legal systems was the relationship between Community competition law and national competition laws. Here the basic principle developed by the Court was that national competition authorities could apply their own laws independently of the Commission, provided that their activities did not interfere with the application of Community law.[59] Given that most national competition laws were still weak during this period, this issue remained of secondary importance in most Member States.

8. Conclusions

As the institutions of the Community shaped the competition law system, their primary concern was for the agenda of economic integration. Competition law was politically acceptable precisely because it was a necessary tool of economic integration. Yet the Community was new, and, recognizing this fragility, its institutions sought to construct a competition law system that minimized the political influence of Member States, while avoiding significant threats to the economic interests of those states. This structuring of the competition law system corresponded, therefore, to the political exigencies of the period, as the integration imperative both defined the competition law system and provided it with legitimacy.

The system that emerged from these circumstances had three dominant traits. First, enforcement was centralized in Community institutions, and the role of the national legal systems was minimized. Second, the system was conceived primarily in juridical terms. Decisions that were understood as based on generally applicable principles emanating from the Treaty of Rome were more unifying and stabilizing than political decisions. And, finally, the system's substantive focus was on those practices that were most likely to be harmful to the integration process (for example, vertical restrictions) while potential anti-competitive harms that were likely to engender political resistance from Member States were generally avoided.

---

[59] See Case 14/68, *Walt Wilhelm v. Bundeskartellamt* [1969] ECR 1.

D. 1973 TO THE MID-1980s: FROM OIL SHOCKS TO EUROSCLEROSIS

The 'oil shock' that rolled over Europe in the mid-1970s profoundly changed the economic and political context of Community competition law. The economic pie that had been steadily growing since the late 1940s suddenly threatened to shrink. As unemployment increased, the same democratic mechanisms that during the 1960s had dispensed the fruits of economic advancement throughout society now demanded that governments act to protect their nationals (firms as well as individuals) from economic harm. Member States that were supposed to be co-operating to achieve common goals now found it more attractive to take from each other in what increasingly looked like a zero-sum game. Governments became hesitant to support Community initiatives that might be seen as sacrificing their own national interests on the Community 'altar'.

This external jolt to intra-Community relations occurred just as the first expansion of the Community further increased internal obstacles to co-operation. The United Kingdom, Ireland, and Denmark joined the Community in 1973, bringing with them new cultural, political, and legal traditions. Membership was no longer limited, for example, to countries from the continental legal tradition, but included two common law countries (the UK and Ireland) and a Scandinavian country (Denmark). Moreover, particularly in the case of the UK, they also brought with them attitudes of suspicion and sometimes even hostility toward the Community.[60] With the accession of Greece in 1981, the disparities in levels of economic development among Member States also increased significantly.

This combination of additional external challenges and internal co-ordination burdens led to a period of 'Eurosclerosis'. In the early 1980s there was little positive news from or relating to Brussels. In most substantive areas there was little apparent movement toward Community goals. Confidence in the future of the Community ebbed, as failure to achieve significant progress led to repeated disappointments.

1. The court as 'savior'

These economic and political stresses placed new demands on the competition law system that would eventually alter it in fundamental ways. In the short-run, however, they appeared to reinforce existing arrangements, particularly with regard to the role of the Court.

Despite serious threats to the Community's future and perhaps to its very existence, both Council and Commission remained hobbled by political

---

[60] For the situation in Britain, see Anthony King, *Britain Says Yes* 20–31 (Washington, DC, 1977) and Simon Bulmer, 'Britain and European Integration', in *Britain and the European Community* 5–6 (Stephen George, ed., Oxford, 1991).

conflict and the 'shadow of the veto',[61] thus increasing pressure on the Court to maintain the momentum of integration. As a consequence, the Court remained the principal 'motor of integration' throughout the 1970s and into the 1980s.[62]

In playing this role, the Court relied heavily on the competition law system that had been constructed during the foundational period. That system had come to be perceived as critical to the integration effort and thus enjoyed a large measure of political support. This enabled the Court to use competition law in developing a symbolic discourse of Community progress, even as political events hindered more tangible forms of progress.

The Court continued to provide intellectual leadership by enunciating broad, future-oriented principles in several areas of competition law.[63] Moreover, it continued to expand the scope and enhance the intensity of competition law, relying on the integration imperative for both interpretive guidance and political support.

The force of the integration imperative, and the widespread political support for the Court's use of competition policy in pursuing integration led, however, to decisions that would later undermine the Court's role in the competition law system. By the early 1970s the Court was paying less attention to the constraints of traditional legal methodology in reaching its decisions, and in so doing it began to erode the 'juridical' conception of Community competition law.

The famous *Continental Can* decision revealed how far the Court was prepared to go in this direction.[64] The Commission there sought for the first time in a litigated case to use Article 86 to attack an acquisition, contending that the acquisition represented a change in the structure of the market that increased the dominance of the acquiring firm and thus constituted an abuse of that firm's dominant position within the meaning of Article 86.

Traditional legal analysis provided little support for this use of Article 86. The text of the treaty did not indicate that Article 86 was applicable to acquisitions. On the contrary, it seemed to indicate that that article was not applicable to such cases. Article 86 referred to the 'abuse' of economic dominance,

---

[61] I have borrowed this evocative term from Joseph Weiler, and his insights here are particularly apt. The veto affected *all* decision-making within the Community, not just Council decisions. See Weiler, 'Transformation', 2461–74.

[62] See, e.g., Ulrich Everling, 'Zur neueren EuGH-Rechtsprechung zum Wettbewerbsrecht', 17 *Europarecht* 301, 302 (1982).

[63] The intellectual leadership of the Court in the system is also evidenced by the fact that the Member States' courts paid great attention to the Court's decisions and rather less attention to the decisions of the Commission. See Ernst Steindorff, 'Europäisches Kartellrecht vor staatlichen Gerichten 1971–78: Zur Entwicklung des Europäischen Kartellrechts, Teil III', 146 *ZHR* 140, 142 and 162 (1982) [hereinafter Steindorff, 'Entwicklung III'].

[64] Case 6/72, *Europemballage Corporation v. Commission* [1973] ECR 215 (*Continental Can*).

and power could not be 'abused' unless it was 'used'.[65] Yet in *Continental Can* there was merely a change of ownership of shares. At most, one could say that power was being 'acquired'.

Historical analysis also revealed a clear legislative intent not to provide the Commission with authority to control mergers. Such a provision had been included in the ECSC Treaty of which the framers of the Rome Treaty were well aware, and yet they omitted any such reference. Thus, both textual and historical analyses opposed the application of Article 86 to mergers.

Nevertheless, the Court disregarded these modes of analysis and held that Article 86 could be applied to mergers. Its justification was teleological. It held that the Commission could not accomplish its pro-integration goals without a tool to combat excessive economic concentration and that Article 86 would, therefore, have to be interpreted to provide such a tool. In effect, the Court held that the teleological method could provide the basis for a decision even when the text of the Treaty and the clear intention of the drafters dictated the opposite result. The Court's message seemed to be that its own judgment of the needs of economic integration would dominate its decision-making, regardless of the dictates of more traditional 'juridical' methodology.

2. Relations with the Commission

In some respects the Court's relations with the Commission remained as they had been during the foundational period. The Court continued generally to guide and support the Commission, providing 'windows of opportunity' for the Commission to pursue and sustaining the Commission's attempts to expand the impact and substantive scope of the competition law provisions.[66]

Particularly after the mid-1970s, however, a subtle change occurred in the relationship between the Court and the Commission.[67] The Court began to demand more from the Commission, requiring that it present increasingly detailed evidence concerning the actual economic impact of alleged violations of competition law provisions rather than relying on formalistic criteria of anticompetitiveness.[68] The Court began regularly to annul Commission actions under Articles 85 and 86 on the grounds that there was insufficient

[65] See L. Focsaneau, 'La Notion d'Abus dans le Système de l'Article 86 du Traité Instituant la Communauté Economique Européene', in *Regulating the Behaviour of Monopolies and Dominant Undertakings in Community Law*, 324, 336–40 (J. A. van Damme, ed., Bruges, 1977).

[66] See, e.g., Gordon Slynn, 'E.E.C. Competition Law From the Perspective of the Court of Justice', in 1984 *Fordham Corp. L. Inst.* 383 (New York, 1985).

[67] Others have noted the evolution of this pattern. See generally Ernst Steindorff, 'Europäisches Kartellrecht und Staatenpraxis: Zur Entwicklung des Europäischen Kartellrechts, Teil II', 142 *ZHR* 525, 526 (1978) [hereinafter, Steindorff, 'Entwicklung II'].

[68] See also generally Jean-Francois Verstrynge, 'Current Antitrust Policy Issues in the EEC: Some Reflections on the Second Generation of Competition Policy', 1984 *Fordham Corp L. Inst.* 673, 681 (Barry Hawk, ed., New York, 1985).

evidence to support the claim that a particular restriction on a firm's freedom of action actually would have the effects attributed to it.[69]

One reason for the Court's increased rigor may have been a concern that the Commission might go too far, too fast in the competition law area, thereby spawning resistance to competition law enforcement and impairing the effectiveness of what had become a critically important tool of integration. The Commission's enforcement efforts had begun to intensify during the early 1970s, and the Court may have perceived a risk of political 'backlash'.

At another level, the Court's move appears to reflect a new dynamic within the competition law system created by the political and economic situation of the 1970s. On the one hand, the internal politics of the Community demanded at least the appearance of progress toward integration. On the other hand, however, the economic situation increased resistance to Community action that might impair the capacity of European firms to compete—both internationally and with each other. The Court's response was to supply political 'progress' on a conceptual and symbolic level by strengthening competition law doctrine, but to minimize the economic consequences of these substantive law moves by imposing more stringent evidentiary and procedural requirements on the Commission.[70]

3. The Commission expands its roles

The evolution of the Commission's role in the competition law system reflects a similar dynamic. The Commission co-operated with the Court in aggressively developing competition law norms, but it was not in a position vigorously to pursue the enforcement of those norms.

The combined force of competition law's 'special' status and the integration imperative shaped the dynamics of the situation. While political circumstances reduced the Commission's role in many areas to that of a 'secretariat', competition law offered something of an exception. Here the Commission had more autonomy than elsewhere, allowing it to pursue its goals with less political interference. Moreover, because competition law had come to be viewed as essential to the process of integration, the Commission could also count on general support for its pro-integration activities in this area.

Yet the new political and economic situation made the development of competition policy more complicated than it had been during the foundational period. During the earlier period the goals of economic integration and economic growth had appeared generally to call for the same policy

---

[69] See, e.g., Case 27/76, *United Brands Co. v. Commission* [1978] ECR 207, and Case 86/82, *Hasselblad (GB) Ltd. v. Commission* [1984] ECR 883.

[70] For discussion of procedural reforms, see Harald Kreis, 'Commission Procedures in Competition Proceedings—Recent Reforms in Practice and Law', in 1983 *Fordham Corp. L. Inst.* 147 (Barry E. Hawk, ed., New York, 1984).

measures, because integration was seen as the primary path to prosperity. If the Commission focused on creating and administering the 'neutral' rules needed to achieve integration, growth would follow of itself.

That image was exploded in the 1970s. The economic reversal shattered confidence in the steady improvement of economic conditions and ignited the fear of even more serious disintegration in the future.[71] Progress toward integration no longer seemed an adequate response to the situation. While integration remained an important part of Community economic policy, it was recast as *a* 'long-run' answer rather than *the* answer. There was political pressure on the Commission to take active measures in the short-run to protect European national economies and to strengthen the competitiveness of European firms.

Thus, while competition law remained an important, even necessary, tool for achieving integration, DG IV officials increasingly were impelled to take into account the immediate economic situation of both the Community as a whole and the Member States. The result was to begin to shift the focus of policy-making away from concern with 'general' and 'neutral' principles and toward more immediate and more particularistic policy objectives.

The new situation made not only policy formulation more difficult, but enforcement as well, presenting DG IV with a dilemma. There was pressure on the Commission to enforce the competition laws more vigorously than it had in the past in order to maintain the (faltering) momentum of integration.[72] Whereas during the foundational period the Commission's primary role was to participate with the Court in 'making law'—that is, establishing competition law principles, by the 1970s it had to pay greater attention to securing compliance with the norms that had been established. There was little point to having a sophisticated competition law if its dictates could be ignored with impunity.[73] Moreover, the new economic pressures increased the incentives for firms to do just that—that is, engage in anticompetitive conduct. As a result, the Commission had to become more vigorous in seeking acceptance, and it began, for example, to levy significant fines for violations of Articles 85 and 86.[74]

This intensified enforcement effort came at a time, however, when the obstacles to its success had significantly increased. The expansion of the Community meant a significant increase in the numbers of firms, markets, and transactions subject to the application of the competition laws, and this

---

[71] See, e.g., Thomas Sharpe, 'The Commission's Proposals on Crisis Cartels', 17 *Comm. Mkt. L. Rev.* 75, 76–84 (1980).

[72] See, e.g., Steindorff, 'Entwicklung II', 525.

[73] See, e.g., Ernst Steindorff, 'Zur Entwicklung des europäischen Kartellrechts, Teil I', 137 *ZHR* 203, 209 (1973) [hereinafter, Steindorff, 'Entwicklung I'].

[74] The first fine was levied in the Quinine cartels case [1969] OJ L192/5. For a list of fines levied by the Commission in competition law cases, see *EEC Competition Law* 721–734 (Lennart Ritter et al., Deventer, 1991).

required a major 'educational' effort to assure awareness and understanding of Community norms.[75] Moreover, there was often little experience with competition law in the new Member States, and thus firms had to be convinced of the need to change practices—such as cartel arrangements—that long had been considered not only acceptable, but normal.

In addition, DG IV was not in a position to increase significantly its enforcement activities. Its resources, for example, were augmented only marginally to respond to this situation. Equally important—and not unrelated—was the lack of political support for this aspect of DG IV's responsibility. The new economic pressures on the Member States made it difficult for the Commission to take regulatory action that might harm the competitiveness of European firms, and the Commission's unwillingness to increase funding for DG IV may have reflected concern that it might become too aggressive.

DG IV's enforcement practices were shaped by this dilemma. The introduction of significant fines in a limited number of cases increased incentives for firms to take Community competition law seriously and sent the necessary 'community-building' message that the laws were being used to integrate the market.[76] Yet they caused actual 'harm' to relatively few firms. Moreover, while the level of enforcement activity increased, showing that DG IV was actively pursuing its integrationist activities, the Commission reduced the political risks of this increased activity by focusing disproportionately on non-Member State firms in major cases.

Another Commission response was to seek to improve its own efficiency. For example, it focused during this period on procedural improvements, and by the end of the period DG IV had less backlog and there were fewer delays in their enforcement activities. Moreover, the Commission began to look to legislation as a more efficient means of accomplishing its objectives. Its responses thus tended to reflect a common theme—to seek to establish community-building norms at low economic cost and with minimum political risk.

4. Substantive directions

Throughout this period vertical restraints remained the substantive focus of competition law, reflecting the continuing perception that the system's central goal was integration and that such restraints were the chief obstacles to integration. Both the Court and the Commission continued to expand the

---

[75] The Commission considered publicity exceptionally important in this context. See Frances Graupner, 'Commission Decision-Making on Competition Questions', 10 *Comm. Mkt. L. Rev.* 291, 294 (1973).

[76] By the late 1970s there was a consensus that the vigor of enforcement had increased significantly over the previous ten years. See, e.g., Robert M. Feinberg, 'The Enforcement and Effects of European Competition Policy: Results of a Survey of Legal Opinion', 23 *J. Comm. Mkt. Studies* 373, 376 (1985).

application of Article 85 to vertical restraints, although they increasingly operated within the discourse established by previous Court decisions—that is, they more frequently based their decisions on the application of existing authoritative principles.

While the Commission's enforcement emphasis under Article 85(1) continued to be on vertical restraints, it also paid increasing heed to horizontal restraints during the 1970s.[77] By levying fines in several major and well-publicized cartel cases involving large (and often non-Member State) firms, it sent a message that it was pursuing horizontal enforcement more aggressively. Yet the relatively small number of such cases meant that the actual 'harm' resulting from such fines was not significant enough to generate strong political response.

The Commission was not only not in a political position to increase significantly its enforcement activity in this area, but its policies at the time hardly made such an increase attractive. The Commission was emphasizing the need for co-operation among European firms, particularly small and medium-sized firms, as a means of competing effectively with US corporations, and thus it had to be careful not to allow competition law to become an obstacle to such co-operation.[78]

The potential fragility of DG IV's political position also precluded excessive zeal in enforcement activities against Member State governments. In this area the Commission's action remained primarily 'educational', and state aids issues continued generally to be viewed as distinct from 'competition law'.

The most dramatic development during the period was the activation of Article 86 and its concept of abuse of a market-dominating position. Little used during the foundational period, Article 86 now became a focus of conceptual development and an active area of enforcement.[79] The Court's expansive, teleological reading of Article 86 in *Continental Can* signaled this development, and throughout the period the Commission and the Court together broadened application of the abuse concept.[80] In this, they often drew on developments in applying the similar concepts of abuse in German law.

The new political and economic circumstances of the 1970s encouraged the development of Article 86. The concern during the previous period that

[77] See Paul Sutherland, 'EEC Competition Policy', 54 *Antitrust LJ* 667, 669 (1985).

[78] See, e.g., European Commission, *Ninth Report on Competition Policy* 60 (1979) and Rene Joliet, 'Cartelisation, Dirigism and Crisis in the European Community', 3 *The World Economy* 403 (1981).

[79] For discussion, see, e.g., A. S. Pathak, 'Articles 85–86 and Anticompetitive Exclusion in EC Competition Law', 10 *Eur. Comp. L. Rev.* 74, 84 (1989).

[80] For discussion of these developments, see, e.g., Eleanor Fox, 'Monopolization and Dominance in the United States and the European Community: Efficiency, Opportunity, and Fairness', 61 *Notre Dame L. Rev.* 981 (1986) and David J. Gerber, 'Law and the Abuse of Economic Power in Europe', 62 *Tulane L. Rev.* 57, 86–99 1987.

Article 86 might interfere with the objective of creating enterprises of sufficient size to combat US multinationals was reduced, as technology rather than size came to be seen as the key to international competitiveness.[81] Moreover, the new inflationary pressures that arose during the 1970s generated political support for increased use of legal tools to combat them, and the Commission increasingly used Article 86 in order to discourage dominant firms from adding to these inflationary pressures.[82]

The activation of Article 86 also played another and less obvious role—it provided a vehicle for maintaining the Court's intellectual leadership. It allowed the Court to continue to rely on teleology in its decision-making, and thus many of the leading decisions of the period were decisions under Article 86. These decisions were also supported by the integration imperative, because they focused typically on vertical relationships that did not involve contractual arrangements and thus were not subject to Article 85.

The lack of previous development of Article 86 also provided opportunities for the Commission. It allowed the Commission to work together with the Court in developing this provision and thereby draw on the Court's prestige to bolster its own legitimacy. It also allowed the Commission to maintain the symbolic momentum of integration without subjecting itself to the political risks of significantly increasing enforcement of existing provisions.

The *Continental Can* case that we discussed above set the tone for developing the abuse concept. Its reliance on teleological interpretation turned attention to the goals expressed in the treaty, specifically to Article 3(f), according to which the goals of the Community include 'the institution of a system ensuring that competition in the Common Market is not distorted. . .'.[83] The Court and the Commission used this concept of competitive distortion in creating out of Article 86 a powerful competition law tool.

Having established in *Continental Can* that the actual elimination of a competitor through acquisition could constitute abuse, the Court also labeled conduct as 'abusive' where it destroyed the ability of a significant competitor to compete effectively. For example, in the 1974 *Commercial Solvents* case, the Court applied the idea to refusals to deal.[84] In that case a US corporation, Commercial Solvents (CSC), had a virtual monopoly on world production of certain chemicals which it had been selling in the EEC through a joint venture in Italy. It then decided it would no longer supply the chemicals in Europe, except to the joint venture company for its own manufacturing uses. The effect of this decision was virtually to eliminate a former competitor of CSC

---

[81] For discussion, see generally Ernst-Joachim Mestmäcker, 'Concentration and Competition in the EEC', 6 *J. World Trade L.* 615, 637–47 (1972).

[82] See, e.g., Comm'n of the Eur. Communities, *Second Report on Competition Policy* 25 (1973) and Comm'n of the Eur. Communities, *Third Report on Competition Policy* 26–27 (1974).

[83] Case 6/72, *Europemballage Corporation v. Commission* [1973] ECR 215 (*Continental Can*).

[84] Cases 6 & 7/73, *Istituto Chemioterapico Italiano S.p.A. and Commercial Solvents Corp. v. Commission* [1973] ECR 357.

from the market for certain products manufactured from those chemicals. In finding an abuse of CSC's market-dominating position, the Court reasoned that where a dominant firm's refusal to supply a competitor would effectively eliminate the competitor from the market, this elimination of competition necessarily distorted the competitive structure of the market, at least where the competitor was a major force in the market. The Court's conclusion was based on the conduct's 'effect on the structure of supply of the market'.

Over the next decade the Court developed and refined this reasoning to find a variety of forms of business conduct 'abusive'. In its 1978 opinion in *United Brands*, for example, the Court also applied the abuse concept to resale restrictions, refusals to deal with a former customer and the charging of 'excessive' prices.[85] According to the Court, United Brands Company, a US company with a dominant position in the European banana market (UBC), abused its dominant position by imposing obligations on its European ripener/wholesalers not to sell bananas acquired from UBC to other ripeners, not to sell such bananas when still green, and, in some cases, not to sell such bananas unless they carried UBC brand names. The Court held that these resale restrictions constituted an abuse 'since they limit markets to the prejudice of consumers. . .'.[86] The Court thus used a consumer welfare standard rather than the broader concept of competitive distortion which also would have been applicable.

The Court also applied the abuse concept to UBC's refusal to deal with one of its former distributors. UBC had stopped supplying its former customer, because the latter had co-operated with a major competitor of UBC in certain activities, including, in particular, an advertising campaign. The Court announced as a general rule that a dominant enterprise 'cannot stop supplying a long-standing customer who abides by regular commercial practice if the orders are in no way out of the ordinary. . .', at least where the sale is of a branded product with established goodwill.[87] According to the Court, such a practice constituted abuse because it limited markets to the prejudice of consumers and because it constituted discrimination which might eventually eliminate a firm from the relevant market. Thus, whereas previous refusals to deal had been found abusive where they necessarily eliminated a competitor from the market and thus posed an immediate threat to the structure of competition, UBC's refusal to deal was found abusive because it had the potential, if repeated often enough, to drive firms from the market.

The Court buttressed its conclusions concerning UBC's refusal to deal by referring to its impact on the independence of small and medium-sized enterprises. It held that under the circumstances of the case a refusal to sell 'amounts to a serious interference with the independence of small and medium-sized firms in their commercial relations with the undertaking in a

[85] Case 27/76, *United Brands v. Commission* [1978] 1 ECR 207.   [86] Ibid., 289.
[87] Ibid., 292.

dominant position'.[88] The Court thus introduced a concept of economic coercion into the law of abuse. At least where such coercion would have a 'serious adverse effect on competition . . . by allowing only firms dependent upon the dominant undertaking to stay in business,'[89] a refusal to sell could not be used to coerce purchasers to adhere to a dominant firm's policies.

The Court's reference to the independence of small and medium-sized firms reflected a growing concern throughout Europe about the economic position of smaller firms. This concern was focused on the ability of large firms to extract unfair prices and terms from smaller enterprises. It was also related to conceptual developments in Germany, where, as we have noted, the work of the economist Helmut Arndt had led to the inclusion of a concept of 'relative market power' in the German competition law in 1973. In the *United Brands* case, this concept became part of Community law as well.

In other major cases from this period, the Court extended this type of reasoning to apply where a dominant firm utilized fidelity rebates and exclusive dealing contracts to induce loyalty from its distributors. In the *Hoffman-LaRoche* and *Michelin* cases, it designated conduct as abusive where it placed significant pressure on an enterprise to deal with a dominant enterprise, unless there was economic equivalency in the transactions, the conduct had no significant effect on the structure of competition, or the conduct was normal for non-dominant firms.[90] These examples indicate the Court's boldness in developing the abuse concept.

5. Role of national legal systems

The Community competition law system remained firmly in the hands of the Court and the Commission throughout this period. Community institutions made the important decisions, and national courts and competition officials continued to play a decidedly marginal role. Yet here also new factors entered the picture that eventually would alter the relationship between national and Community institutions.

The critical conceptual move was the Court's declaration in the 1973 *BRT v. Sabam* case that the competition law provisions of the Treaty were directly applicable in the national courts.[91] This decision allowed private firms to seek redress for harms caused by violations of Community competition law by bringing private suits in national courts. The decision opened the way for a shift in the locus of power within the competition law system from Community institutions to national courts, but these implications of the decision would not begin to be felt for more than a decade.

[88] Case 27/76, *United Brands v. Commission* [1978] 1 ECR, 293.   [89] Ibid., 293.
[90] Case 85/76, *Hoffman-La Roche & Co. AG v. Commission* [1979] ECR 461 and Case 322/81, *Nederlandse Banden-Indsutrie Michelin NV v. Commission* [1983] ECR 3461.
[91] Case 127/73, *Belgische Radio en Televise v. SV Sabam* [1974] ECR 51.

6. Tremors of change

From the early 1970s through the mid-1980s the competition law system did not appear to change significantly. Creation of a unified market remained its overriding objective, continuing to structure the relationships between the Council and the Commission and to shape the substantive contours of competition law. The urgency of utilizing competition law in the process of integration may even have increased, because progress seemed so elusive in other areas and because the risk of failure of the enterprise may have seemed even more ominous.

Below the surface, however, new pressures and forces were forming. The respective roles of the Court, the Commission, and the Member States within the competition law system were beginning to change. The full implications of these mutations remained concealed, however, by the critical need to use competition law to maintain psychological momentum toward integration. All institutions had the same vital interest in achieving this goal, and the force of the integration imperative precluded—or obscured—major changes in the competition law system.

E. THE DRIVE TO UNIFY THE EUROPEAN MARKET (MID-1980s TO MID-1990s)

Since the mid-1980s, changes in the contexts in which Community competition law operates as well as in its institutional framework have begun to alter its roles and challenge its identity. The changes often have been kaleidoscopic—numerous small shifts in expectations, roles, and intra-systemic relationships that cumulate to create significant mutations of the system.

1. The scene changes

The most far-reaching change in the context of competition law has been the unification (almost) of the Community's internal market symbolized by the talismanic '1992'. The goal announced in 1985 of achieving a single market by January 1, 1993, may still not have been fully achieved even today, but by the mid-1990s most law-based obstacles to trade had been eliminated.

The process of eliminating these obstacles had been gradual and halting over three decades, failing to ignite major structural changes in the European economy, but the 1992 program engendered widespread confidence that the single market actually would be achieved on or about January 1, 1993, and this confidence translated into rapid economic restructuring, particularly during the late 1980s and early 1990s. A wave of mergers, acquisitions, joint ventures, and 'strategic alliances' has significantly increased industrial concentration, as firms have become less 'national' and more 'European' in both ownership and management structure.[92] This, in turn, has brought with it the development of 'Euro' law firms and the 'Europeanization' of financial, insurance, and other services.

At the same time that the 1992 program was set in motion, the Single European Act of 1986 introduced important changes in the institutional framework of the Community's competition law.[93] That enactment broke the bottleneck of the unanimous voting requirement in the Council that had dominated Community institutional life since the 1960s. While not eliminating the unanimous voting requirement, it significantly increased the range of issues as to which qualified majority voting could be used. It meant that, as Joseph Weiler has put it, *all* decision-making was to be made 'under the shadow of the vote'.[94] It also increased the power and scope of authority of the Commission in several respects and increased the (still marginal) role of the European Parliament in the Community's legislative process.

Buoyed by the psychological success of the 1992 program, Community leaders reached agreement on further unification proposals at the Maastricht Summit in December, 1991, which led to the creation of the European Union through the Treaty on European Union (TEU). There the focus was on eliciting commitments to a common currency by the end of the decade and on maintaining the forward momentum of integration. Although the lukewarm popular political response to Maastricht has slowed progress toward these ambitious goals, it has not called into serious question the prospects for stronger political and monetary integration in the near future. The Maastricht treaty also contained the principle of 'subsidiarity', which was to become an important part of discussions of Community law, including competition law.

The impact of these changes in the context of competition law has been magnified by actual and probable increases in the size of the Community and in the scope of application of Community law. Actual increases occurred in 1986, when the accession of Spain and Portugal increased the population of the Community by more than sixty million, and in 1995, when Sweden, Finland, and Austria added close to twenty million. Community officials, governments, and businesses have also begun planning for probable future members from Eastern Europe, notably Hungary, Poland, and the Czech Republic.

These extensions of the scope of application of Community law take on an additional dimension in the case of competition law. With the exception of

[92] See, e.g., Douglas E. Rosenthal, 'Competition Policy', in *Europe 1992: An American Perspective* 293, 313–15 (Gary C. Hufbauer, ed., Washington, D.C., 1990).
[93] Single European Act, 30 OJ (No. L 169) (1987), reprinted in 25 ILM 506 (1986) [hereinafter SEA]. For commentary and description, see George A. Bermann, 'The Single European Act: A New Constitution for the Community?', 27 *Col. J. Transnat. L.* 529 (1989).
[94] Weiler, 'Transformation', 2403.

Sweden, competition law either has been non-existent or has played a decidedly marginal role in the states to which Community law has been or soon may be extended. This means that businesses are frequently not accustomed to considering competition law issues in making decisions, and, as a result, it enhances the likelihood of competition law violations and increases the educational and enforcement burdens on DG IV.

Finally, the Single European Act and the TEU also changed the context of competition law by formally adding new policy goals and values that compete, at least potentially, with those of competition law. Most important for our purposes is the explicit recognition in the TEU of industrial policy as a Community goal. The new Article 130 of the Treaty authorizes Community institutions to follow policies aimed at improving the 'competitiveness of the Community's industry', including, for example, policies aimed at 'encouraging an environment favorable to co-operation between enterprises'. While Article 130 adds that its provisions 'shall not provide a basis for the introduction by the Community of any measure which could lead to a distortion of competition', the emphasis in the treaty clearly seems to be on increased support for industrial policy measures. The analogous extension of the Commission's authority and responsibility in environmental and social areas may have similar consequences.[95] These objectives and the values they represent compete with the perspectives and values of competition law for the attention of decision-makers.

Taken together, these changes in institutional structures, constitutional relationships and values significantly alter the context in which the Community competition law system operates. Not surprisingly, they are also helping to generate fundamental changes within that system.

2. The changing role of adjudication

One important change in the competition law system involves the role of adjudication. Just as the ECJ molded the role of adjudication in the competition law system during the initial decades of the Community, that court and its new companion court, the Court of First Instance (CFI), have reshaped it during the last decade and a half.

The intellectual leadership of the ECJ that was so important to the development of competition law during its first three decades has, for example, become less apparent. The beginnings of this process can be located in the mid-1980s, when judges and former judges of the ECJ began articulating the notion that the Court should and/or would become less 'activist'. Some have suggested that the Court no longer needs to play as aggressive a role as it has played in the past and that other institutions are now in a position to carry

[95] For extensive discussion of these issues, see R. B. Bouterse, *Competition and Integration—What Goals Count?* (Deventer, 1994).

more of the burden of integrating the Community.[96] Though the depth and ultimate impact of these views remain unclear, any such changes in the Court's self-perception necessarily influence its capacity for intellectual leadership.

Some observers have noted changes in the decisions of the Court that tend to reflect such a change in the Court's conception of its role. In competition law, as in other areas of Community law, 'the Court, which in the first decades issued future-oriented judgments with generalized significance, today prefers to limit itself to the statements required for the decision of the concrete legal controversy'.[97] The Court's opinions tend to focus more narrowly on resolving the issues in the case under litigation through the use of existing concepts, preferably at relatively low levels of abstraction. To the extent that the Court's decisions have become less 'future-oriented', therefore, the Court's intellectual leadership has diminished, for its capacity to 'set the agenda' in competition law matters is necessarily reduced.

There appeared to be some revival of this leadership role during the early 1990s in some areas of Community law other than competition law, although not necessarily in the competition law area. Moreover, the episode of renewed leadership turned out to be brief.[98] Competition law cases in recent years have often involved procedural rather than substantive issues, and the courts have seldom articulated major new conceptual developments or ideals.

This change in the courts' leadership role has been accompanied by the evolution of methods more consistent with such a role. The teleological reasoning that the Court relied on so heavily during earlier periods has become less evident, as the courts turn increasingly to the manipulation of narrower principles drawn largely from their own previous decisions. Teleology is an appropriate tool for an aggressive court, while reasoning that relies primarily on the authority of existing concepts and decisions comports more easily with a more cautionary role.

Reduced reliance on teleology, in turn, undermines the supportive link that the Court had established between teleology and pragmatic style. The predominance of the teleological method allowed the Court to operate without a well-defined conceptual grammar to support its reasoning. Its style could remain relatively imprecise and pragmatic because the primary criterion for interpreting and applying norms was their utility in achieving the single-market goal, and this goal did not require, or even easily permit, conceptual rigor.

---

[96] See, e.g., Thijmen Koopmans, 'The Role of Law in the Next Stage of European Integration', 35 *Int'l & Comp. L.Q.* 925 (1986). For discussion, see Mancini, 'The Making of a Constitution for Europe'.

[97] Ulrich Everling, 'Rechtsvereinheitlichung durch Richterrecht in der Europäischen Gemeinschaft', 50 *Rabels Zeitschrift* 193, 208 (1986).

[98] For discussion, see Giuseppe F. Mancini & David T. Keeling, 'Language, Culture and Politics in the Life of the European Court of Justice', 1 *Col. J. Eur. L.* 397 (1995).

One component of this change in methods has been a shift from the use of relatively formal criteria for evaluating conduct to increasingly 'effects-based' criteria.[99] Whereas during earlier periods the Court often was willing to assess the legal characteristics of conduct by reference to the terms of the relevant agreements, Community courts have increasingly demanded that such assessments be based on the likely consequences of such conduct under the specific circumstances of the case. The idea itself is not new, but 'the tendency [to expand its application] has become obvious in recent years'.[100]

This shift in analysis has important and largely unrecognized implications for the competition law system. Formal criteria are well-suited to judicial application, because they allow decisions to be made on the basis of documentary analysis. They do not require detailed investigation of economic circumstances, nor does their analysis call for sophistication in economic analysis. It is a task for which lawyers are trained and with which judges are comfortable.

In contrast, courts are not well-adapted to evaluating the market effects of conduct. Judges typically have neither the training nor the experience to undertake such evaluations with confidence and expertise. In the case of the Community courts, the problem is exacerbated by the diverse national origins of the judges, each having different economic experiences and different vocabularies for interpreting such conduct. As one former judge of the ECJ describes it,

... The judges come from twelve different Member States with different histories, cultures, economic and social orders, and, above all, legal systems. They bring their varying traditions, methods and values to adjudication. . . . This situation is important for understanding their decisions. The differing historical, economic, and legal experiences of the individual judges are particularly influential in competition law matters that require economic evaluation.[101]

In addition, their procedures—cumbersome in fact-taking and weighted with the need for translations—make detailed factual analysis of economic circumstances particularly difficult and inefficient.

As a result, the shift in methodology toward requiring more such analysis necessarily moves the courts to a more marginal role in the system. Not in a position generally to carry out such analysis themselves, the courts must rely increasingly on the Commission for the evaluation of economic facts and limit themselves to assessing the adequacy of the procedures followed by the Commission in making such evaluations.

[99] For discussion, see, e.g., Valentine Korah, 'From Legal Form Toward Economic Efficiency—Article 85(1) of the EEC Treaty in Contrast to US Antitrust', 35 *Antitrust Bull.* 1009 (1990).
[100] Everling, 'Zur Wettbewerbskonzeption', 995. For a potentially far-reaching manifestation of this tendency, see Case 234/89, *Delimitis v. Henninger Bräu* [1991] 1 ECR 935 (1991).
[101] Everling, 'Zur Wettbewerbskonzeption', 996–97.

The cumulative impact of these mutually reinforcing changes in goals and methods impels the courts toward a role in the competition law system akin to that of an administrative court.[102] According to this conception of their role, the courts' basic function is that of assuring that the Commission as the executive organ of the Community performs its functions correctly and operates within the rules and principles established for it by the Community's political organs.

The Court increasingly articulates its own understanding of its role in such terms. For example, in the *Remia* case, it stated that

Although as a general rule the Court undertakes a comprehensive review of the question whether or not the conditions for the application of Article 85(1) are met, it is clear that in determining the permissible duration of a non-competition clause incorporated in an agreement for the transfer of an undertaking, the Commission has to appraise complex economic matters. The Court must therefore limit its review of such an appraisal to verifying whether the relevant procedural rules have been complied with, whether the statement of the reasons for the decision is adequate, whether the facts have been accurately stated, and whether there has been any manifest error of appraisal or a misuse of powers.[103]

This statement reveals a conception of the courts' role in competition law matters quite different from that of earlier periods. Moreover, it is a conception that is inconsistent with the intellectual leadership that the ECJ had previously exercised.

This narrowing of the courts' role in the competition law system is fueled not only by changes in the courts' general methodology and self-definition, but also by factors internal to the competition law system. The impending evaporation of the single market goal as the keystone of competition law thought undoubtedly plays a role in this context. As we have seen, the Court structured its role in the competition law system around that goal, and political support for the Court's role frequently was associated with the integration imperative. As that goal recedes in importance, it leaves greater intellectual uncertainty in competition law thinking. Moreover, without that imperative, political support for bold steps in competition law is likely to weaken.

The creation of the Court of First Instance in 1989 has added to this uncertainty. The Court of First Instance was created in order to deal primarily with two categories of cases, one of which was cases involving competition law decisions of the Commission, and such cases must generally now be heard by

---

[102] For discussion of the emerging administrative law tradition within the Community, see Ulrich Everling, 'Auf dem Wege zu einem europäischen Verwaltungsrecht', 6 *Neue Zeitschrift für Verwaltungsrecht* 1 (1987). For discussion of the differing conceptions of the role of administrative courts in Europe, see Jürgen Schwarze, *European Administrative Law* 97–203 (1992) and Ulrich Everling, 'The Court of Justice as a Decisionmaking Authority', 82 *Mich. L. Rev.* 1294, 1302–04 (1984).

[103] Case 42/84, *Remia and Nutricia v. Comm'n* [1985] ECR 2545, 75 (*Remia*).

that court. The role of the Court of Justice in the competition law area is thus reduced to deciding appeals from Court of First Instance decisions and responding to questions from Member State courts in Article 177 proceedings. This means that competition law cases have become a less prominent part of the Court's workload, reducing the amount of time the judges spend on such cases, and thus their expertise and familiarity with competition law issues. The creation of the Court of First Instance necessarily reduces the ECJ's control over developments within the system. No longer is there one judicial voice; there are two.

The CFI has, in effect, taken over much of the responsibility for decision-making in the competition law area, but it is not in a position to exercise bold leadership. It is still a court of first instance whose decisions are appealable to the ECJ. As a result, the dynamics of the relationship between the courts provides little room for the CFI to attempt to exercise a leadership function, because it is dependent on the support of the ECJ.

Finally, the sheer growth of case law may tend to reduce the opportunities for the courts to exercise intellectual leadership. The notion here is that where the 'big' issues have already been resolved and the basic conceptual framework has been established, courts have less room to play an aggressive role. There is simply more law in existence, and this tends to restrict the opportunities and incentives for courts to make bold conceptual or doctrinal moves. The extent of this impact is difficult to assess, however, because there is no *a priori* basis for assessing the degree to which existing conceptual structures place constraints on the development of legal doctrine. The rapid changes in economic and political circumstances in recent years might well have justified a high level of aggressiveness on the part of the courts, had they wished to maintain such a posture. They have tended, however, to prefer a more conservative course.

This change in the role of the courts has ramifications for the entire competition law system. As their role narrows, judicial methods and discourse are likely to become less influential in the operation of that system. As the courts play a lesser role in setting the agenda of competition law and shaping its central decisions, there is less reason for the Commission to structure its decision-making by reference to the courts' methods, and there is less incentive for others both inside and outside the system to adhere closely to the language and the methods associated with the courts.

3. The Commission

These changes in the role of the courts are intertwined with changes in the role of the Commission. Growth in the Commission's power, authority, and confidence have both reflected and contributed to the erosion of the leadership role enjoyed by the ECJ in the past.

This evolution can be seen in the changing influences on the Commission's policy-formulation function. In making policy, DG IV looks to a variety of sources for guidance and responds to many forms of influence, and in recent years the relative strength of these sources and influences has changed.

The Commission is, for example, less dependent on the courts today than it was on the ECJ during earlier periods. As long as the Court was articulating broad pro-integration goals and principles for competition law, and enjoyed solid political support for that function, the Commission had to pay careful attention to that Court's agenda in its policy-making. Particularly because of its own somewhat insecure political position during the 1970s and the early 1980s, the Commission could ill afford not to co-operate with the Court. Moreover, the Commission could rely on the Court to approve its policy choices as long as those were pro-integration (which they generally were), and the Court's high status protected the Commission's initiatives from political attack. With the impending loss of the integration imperative and the courts' general reluctance in recent years to engage in broad future-oriented articulations of principle, there is less incentive for the Commission to look to the courts for guidance, and there is less guidance available to it.[104]

Similarly, there is less reason for the Commission to construct policy within the constraints of judicial methodology and discourse. These were central sources of guidance for the Commission when it depended on the ECJ's support for the success of its own initiatives. It was important to look to these sources in order to be in a position to predict the Court's responses. Moreover, by using the Court's own discourse and methods the Commission increased the likelihood of influencing those responses. With the narrowing of the judicial leadership role, these forces are correspondingly diminished, and thus the courts' methods lose some of their force within the competition law system.

The expansion of the Community is also contributing to this erosion, because the newer Member States typically have competition law systems that are based on administrative control models. As a consequence, decision-makers from these states typically have little or no experience with a juridical conception of competition law, and they may be more likely to see competition law in political rather than juridical terms.

This reduction in the force of juridical discourse has occurred as the need to accommodate other goals in the formulation of competition policy has grown. The anchoring of competing values and concerns such as industrial policy, international competitiveness, and environmental protection—first in the SEA and then in the TEU—increases pressure on the Commission to consider these factors in making competition policy decisions. The need for such accommodation provides opportunities for intellectual leadership within the

---

[104] For general discussion, see Koopmans, 'Role of Law', 931.

competition law system, but the courts have contributed little to this accommodation. Instead, to the extent that such accommodations are being made at all, they are being made primarily by the Commission and primarily on the basis of political considerations.[105]

The Commission's enforcement role is also changing in ways that affect the system as a whole, and, because DG IV is responsible for both policy formulation and enforcement, developments that affect one of these functions generally also influence the other. The institutional and economic changes of recent years have further taxed the Commission's capacity to induce compliance with competition law norms, but there has been little increase in the resources of DG IV, forcing the Commission to adopt strategies to compensate for its lack of resources.

One such burden has been the accession of five new Member States since the mid-1980s, which has significantly increased the population and area over which compliance must be induced. Spain and Portugal had virtually no experience with competition law before their accession in 1986, and Sweden, Austria, and Finland had administrative control systems with varying degrees of generally limited effectiveness. Their accession has added to the enforcement burdens of the Commission by increasing the difficulty of adequately informing firms of competition law norms and securing their willingness to respect those norms.

The cross-boundary business consolidations of the late 1980s and early 1990s have also 'upped the ante' in the compliance game. As firms have increased in size, the fines imposed by the Commission have become less significant in relation to their financial resources and to the stakes involved in particular policies or transactions. Their willingness and capacity to resist and/or evade Commission enforcement efforts has grown commensurately. In addition, the elimination of obstacles to the flow of goods and services across national borders increases the incentives for firms to seek private contractual arrangements to shield them from increased transborder competition.

Not only have the obstacles to effective enforcement increased, but support for enforcement of competition policy may also have been compromised. Effective enforcement in the Community context presupposes general acceptance of the goals of enforcement. Yet the combined loss of the integration imperative and the perceived conflict of competition goals with industrial policy, trade, and other goals tends to reduce the moral force behind competition law.

As enforcement obstacles and policy uncertainty have increased, the Commission has turned increasingly from reliance on adjudication as its main tool for accomplishing its objectives to legislation. Rather than depending on

---

[105] See Comm'n of the Eur. Communities, *Community Industrial Policy in an Open and Competitive Environment*, Com (90)56 (Nov. 16, 1990).

individual cases to articulate norms of conduct, it increasingly prescribes such norms itself.

Until the 1980s, the Commission established competition law norms primarily through the process of adjudication. Relying heavily on individual notifications for its information, the Commission evaluated individual fact situations to determine their compliance with the norms of the system—as they had been interpreted by the ECJ—and their relationship to the Commission's own policy objectives. In this process the Court of Justice played a major role, because if the Court failed to support the Commission, it could effectively prevent the Commission from establishing the norms it sought to establish.

In the 1980s, DG IV turned increasingly toward legislation as a means of establishing competition law norms. Since then, it has increasingly promulgated norms directly rather than seeking to establish them through adjudication. From formal and binding group exemptions to relatively informal and non-binding general notices, prescription has become the dominant means of developing conduct norms.

This strategy has numerous attractions for DG IV. It generally operates more quickly than does adjudication and with less cost, thus responding to the growth of DG IV's workload in relation to its resources. It also addresses the increasing demands from both political and business groups for more 'certainty' in competition law,[106] providing companies with clearer information concerning the types of conduct that are likely to lead to Commission action. In addition, whereas adjudication relies on general or at least generalizable principles, legislation allows for differentiation according to economic sectors and geographical regions and thus facilitates the development of industrial policy.[107] And, finally, this type of legislative action tends to increase DG IV's power within the system; legislation is an independent act of the Commission in which the courts have no direct role.

This shift of power within the system from judicial tribunals to the Commission has significant consequences for the operation of the system. Where the Commission legislates, its prescriptions become the authoritative norms of the system, effectively displacing adjudication as a source of such norms. It is then to the Commission and its processes rather than to adjudicative processes that governments, firms, and their legal advisors tend to look for guidance and for opportunities to influence the creation and application of those norms.

This impact is amplified by the characteristics of the Commission's legislation. The most important form of legislation, the block exemption, is highly formalistic.[108] Block exemptions typically provide lists of specific clauses that

---

[106] See, e.g., Verstrynge, 'Reflections on the Second Generation', 685.
[107] See generally ibid., 680.
[108] See, e.g., Valentine Korah & Margot Horspool, 'Competition', 37 *Antitrust Bull.* 337, 356–57 (1992).

are considered, respectively, acceptable, unacceptable, and possibly acceptable. This then tends to induce firms to structure their agreements to conform to these checklists, leading to a relatively inflexible and potentially distortive legal regime. Moreover, such regimes often become virtually mandatory. According to one study, 'Member States and their business communities tend to regard them not as waivers of the law but as compulsory codes of conduct'.[109]

At least in the case of block exemptions, legislative processes also tend to broaden the existing prohibitions beyond levels established by the Court. According to one expert,[110] in group exemptions the Commission

> goes exceptionally far beyond that which the European Court wanted to approve, and then, on the other hand, regulates in a hair-splitting way the very last details. . . . The result is in the end a very broad prohibition . . ., but a large percentage of the contracts affected are exempted under the conditions created by the Commission.

This then further alters the relationship between the courts and the Commission, permitting the Commission to augment its own power and position within the system and undermining the adjudicative role of the courts.

Another factor of significance in altering the role of the Commission within the competition law system is the Merger Regulation (Regulation 4064/89) which was introduced in 1989 and represents the single most important addition to European competition law since its inception.[111] The Commission began to call for merger legislation in the early 1970s, but political opposition prevented enactment of such legislation for almost twenty years until such opposition was overwhelmed by the force of the SEA's pro-integration impulses.[112] While the immediate problems associated with implementation of this new legislation have generated extensive commentary, relatively little attention has been paid to its impact on the system as a whole.[113]

The Merger Regulation provides, in essence, that 'concentrations' (including both mergers and certain joint ventures) that have a 'community dimension' are subject to Community regulation and removed from the jurisdiction of the national competition law authorities.[114] Such mergers must be notified

---

[109] Forrester & Norral, 'Laicization', 15.

[110] Ernst Niederleithinger, 'Comments', in *Wettbewerbsfragen der Europäischen Gemeinschaft* 58 (Helmut Gröner, ed., Berlin, 1990).

[111] Commission Regulation 4064/89, 1990 OJ(L257) 14 [corrected version of 1989 OJ (L395)1].

[112] For discussion of the background of merger control legislation in the Community, see Ritter et al, *EEC Competition Law*, 332–39.

[113] Some observers have paid attention to this set of problems. See, e.g., Ernst-Joachim Mestmäcker, 'Merger Control in the Common Market: Between Competition Policy and Industrial Policy' 1989 *Fordham Corp. L. Inst.*, Ch. 20 (Barry E. Hawk, ed., New York, 1989).

[114] A 'community dimension' is deemed to exist where the concentrating firms have a worldwide turnover of over 5 billion ECU and a minimum of 250 million ECU of sales within the Community, except where more than two-thirds of each firm's sales within the Community are from the same Member State.

to the Commission *prior* to implementation, and the Commission may prohibit the merger where it would 'create or strengthen a dominant position as a result of which effective competition would be impeded in the Common Market or a substantial part of it' (Article 2(2)).

The introduction of this system has 'transformed the landscape' of competition policy in Europe.[115] By centralizing authority to deal with large mergers, it has focused attention on the Commission and greatly enhanced its potential for influencing major business decisions. Whereas prior to the Regulation this authority was scattered among the competition authorities of the Member States (many of which did not, in practice, make significant use of it) efforts to influence decision-making are now directed primarily at DG IV.

The internal impact on the system has been similarly great. Because of its enormous political and economic importance, the Merger Regulation has been a focus of DG IV's attention since its inception, occupying an exceptionally large part of DG IV's time, resources, and interest.[116] Moreover, it has become the most visible component of the competition law system, as governments, firms, and the media have centered their attention on this aspect of the Commission's activity. This has inevitably shifted attention away from the conventional areas of DG IV's activity.

Its also represents a shift of influence from the judicial components of the Commission's activity to its political elements. The courts play a limited role in this area; it is primarily the province of the Commission, and thus political issues are perceived as central to the decision-making process. As a recent French commentary put it, 'With the introduction of these [merger] provisions competition law becomes directly political'.[117]

Early experience with the Regulation demonstrated how far this could go. In 1991, the Commission's first prohibition of a merger—in the *De Havilland* case—underscored that the conflicting conceptions of competition law's role that first appeared in the drafting of the Spaak report were by no means resolved. At the time, the Merger Regulation had been in effect for almost two years, and some sixty-five mergers had been noticed under its provisions without Commission disapproval. This lack of action had led to widespread speculation that the Commission did not have the political courage actually to use the Regulation to prohibit a merger. In October of 1991, however, the Commission issued an order prohibiting a merger involving a Canadian company, De Havilland, and a French/Italian consortium.[118] The result was a

[115] Dumez & Jeunemaitre, *La Concurrence en Europe*, 264.
[116] For discussion, see, e.g., H. Colin Overbury, 'Politics or Policy? The Demystification of EC Merger Control', in 1992 *Fordham Corp. L. Inst.* 557, 564–72 (Barry E. Hawk, ed., New York, 1993).
[117] Dumez & Jeunemaitre, *La Concurrence en Europe*, 264.
[118] For discussion, see, e.g., Andrew Wachtman, 'The European Community Commission de Havilland Decision: Potential Problems in Community Merger Control are Realized', 21 *Capital L. Rev.* 685 (1992).

storm of protest from the French and Italian governments that the Commission had been overly legalistic in applying the statute, and should have paid greater heed to industrial policy factors in applying the Regulation.[119] This campaign was taken so seriously that the French government was said to be threatening to seek the ouster of the entire Commission. After this series of events, the Commission hesitated to prohibit additional mergers for some time. Although it was again issuing prohibitions in the mid-1990s (a total of seven by mid-1997), the belief that political factors can play a role in merger decisions remains widespread.

The Merger Regulation has significantly affected perceptions of competition law and of the forces at play within it.[120] Its enactment underscored the perception that the interesting and important aspects of competition law were moving to Brussels and away from the national competition authorities. Merger control tends to be the most visible and economically and politically significant part of competition law, and its shift to Brussels seemed to signal the rapid approach of a time when important issues would be handled primarily at the Community rather than the Member State level.[121]

During the last few years the Commission has enhanced and expanded its roles in the competition law system. With a new confidence generated by the SEA, the TEU, and the approach of the unified market, it has moved to set the agenda for competition law and provide new momentum for the system. In doing so it has tended to move toward the center of the system as the Community's courts have inched away from it. The impact on the system is likely to be fundamental, for, in essence, it would substitute an administrative institution for a judicial institution as the driving force within the system.

4. Substantive directions

These changes in the dynamics of the competition law system and the forces affecting that system have led to changes in the substantive directions of competition law. In particular, the gradual evaporation of the goal of market unification as the lodestar of the competition law system has begun to have important consequences. As the imperative of market integration loses its force, competition law has to adapt, and the changing accents and directions of the last decade can be seen as responses to this new situation.

---

[119] See, e.g., Boris Johnson, 'Flak for Brittan', *Daily Telegraph*, Oct. 7, 1991, at 21.
[120] See, e.g., Damien Neven et al., *Merger in Daylight* (London, 1993).
[121] Few foresaw, as Joel Davidow did, that the Regulation would encourage more attention by Member States to national merger controls. See Davidow, 'Competition Policy', 38–39.

a. The public turn

Most prominent has been what I have called the 'public turn' of competition law.[122] As the Commission stated in its 1990 report, 'Whilst many barriers to intra-Community trade and competition are created by companies themselves . . . it is felt that at the present stage of economic integration in the Community the barriers are greatest in markets currently subject to state regulation'.[123] During the late 1980s and early 1990s, the Commission shifted the emphasis in competition law away from its traditional concerns with private conduct and toward the problem of government interference with the competitive process, and the courts have supported this shift of focus.

This heightened concern for the role of governments has taken several forms. It includes, for example, the activation and development of treaty provisions that previously had been little used. The focus here has been on Article 90, which applies the competition law provisions of the treaty to 'public' enterprises and enterprises enjoying 'special or exclusive rights'.[124] According to a former Director-General of DG IV, 'Up until the entry into force of the Single European Act, Article 90 was rarely applied, but it has recently become a key treaty provision in connection with the deregulation of certain sectors and in terms of the equal treatment of private and public undertakings'.[125] In the 1985 *Telecommunications Terminals* case, for example,[126] the Court held that British Telecommunications, a state monopoly, was not protected from the application of Article 86 to certain activities that appeared to serve a public purpose. The Court there distinguished sharply between functions that were inherently governmental and those that were essentially commercial. With this decision, the Court signaled that it would construe very narrowly exemptions from the competition provisions for public monopolies. The decision was described by the then director of DG IV as 'One of the most important decisions the Court has ever given in the area of competition law'.[127]

The Commission has also taken several important legislative steps to strengthen the application of the competition provisions to state monopolies. In 1988, for example, it issued a directive under Article 90 which required the elimination of the monopoly rights of state-owned enterprises where they had specified negative impacts on competition.[128] This extended and intensified

[122] David J. Gerber, 'The Transformation of European Community Competition Law', *Harvard Int'l L. J.* 97, 137–41 (1994).
[123] Comm'n of the European Communities, *Twentieth Report on Competition Policy* 50 (1990).
[124] For an extended and insightful discussion, see Andreas Heinemann, *Grenzen staatlicher Monopole im EG-Vertrag* (Munich, 1996).
[125] Claus-Dieter Ehlermann, 'The Contribution of EC Competition Policy to the Single Market', 29 *Comm. Mkt. L. Rev.* 257 (1992). See also Claus-Dieter Ehlermann, 'Neuere Entwicklungen im europäischen Wettbewerbsrecht,' 26 *Europarecht* 307, 319 (1991).
[126] Case 202/88, *France v. Comm'n* [1991] ECR 1223 (1991) (*Telecommunications Terminals*).
[127] Ehlermann, 'Neuere Entwicklungen', 320.
[128] Commission Directive 88/301, OJ L 131/73 (May 27, 1988).

the impact of two prior directives from 1980 and 1985, respectively, requiring greater 'transparency' in regard to state-owned enterprises—that is, disclosure of information regarding the state's financial involvement in such enterprises.[129]

Intensified application of existing rules relating to state aids also reflects the Commission's greater concern with the impact of governments on the competitive process. The potential political cost of vigorous attacks on state aids had tended to constrain enforcement of these principles until the 1980s, but recently the Commission has made state aids a prominent feature of its enforcement activities. Moreover, this entire area of law increasingly has become integrated with competition law rather than being seen as separate and distinct from it, as was often the case in the past.

The Commission and the courts also developed conceptual tools to deal with state support of private restraints on competition. Of primary importance here is the line of cases prohibiting governments from interfering with the effective operation (*effet utile*) of Articles 85 and 86.[130] This obligation to refrain from interference has become an important area only since the ECJ's 1985 decision in *Leclerc v. Au Ble Vert*, where the Court held that

Member states are . . . obliged under the second paragraph of Article 5 of the Treaty not to detract, by means of national legislation, from the full and uniform application of Community law or from the effectiveness of its implementing measures; nor may they introduce or maintain in force measures, even of a legislative nature, which may render ineffective the competition rules applicable to undertakings.[131]

The Court has held that governments may not require compliance with anticompetitive agreements. In the *Flemish Travel Agents* case, for example, the Court ruled that the Belgian government could not prosecute a travel agent for violating a royal decree requiring compliance with trade association rules which prohibited price competition among travel agents.[132] This doctrine of *effet utile* has also been used in cases in which the government has encouraged or otherwise supported anticompetitive private activity.[133]

Even within the traditional competition law areas, this shift toward public rather than private influences on the competitive process has been evident. The Commission has centered its enforcement efforts under Article 86, for example, on abuses of power by firms either owned or controlled by governments or

---

[129] Commission Directive 80/723, OJ L 195/35 (July 29, 1980), amended by Commission Directive 85/413 OJ L 229/20 (August 28, 1985).

[130] For discussion, see Luc Gyselen, 'State Action and the Effectiveness of EC Treaty Competition Provisions', 26 *Comm. Mkt. L. Rev.* 33–60 (1989).

[131] Case 229/83, *Association des Centres Distributeurs Edouard Leclerc and Others v. S.a.r.l. 'Au Blé Vert' and Others* [1985] ECR1.

[132] Case 311/85, *Vereniging van Vlaamse Reisbureaus v. Sociale Dienst* [1987] ECR 3801 (*Flemish Travel Agents*).

[133] See, e.g., Case 66/86, *Ahmed Saeed and Silver Line Reisebüro v. League Against Unfair Competition* [1989] ECR 803.

those whose governmental protection has only recently been eliminated in the process of deregulation. For example, in the *British Telecom* case, the Court held that a British telecommunications monopoly had abused its economic power by refusing to sell advertising time to a potential competitor.[134]

This brief review suggests the degree to which the substantive focus of competition law has shifted since the mid-1980s. For almost three decades the predominant, often almost exclusive, focus of enforcement and intellectual development within Community competition law was private conduct, particularly vertical restraints on competition, but during the last few years concern with the activities of government has tended to shape the development of Community competition law. Yet there has been little analysis of the implications of this change.

b. Towards normalcy

A second major change in the substantive direction of competition law involves greater concern with the 'normal' or generic goals of competition law—that is, the prevention of harm to competition—rather than with market integration. In 1995, DG IV began to evaluate the theoretical foundations for its decision-making in the core areas of private competition law (Articles 85 and 86). Its officials conducted a series of internal reviews of competition policy, and the results of these reviews have led to announcements of new directions and changes of emphasis in Community competition policy. It remains too early to judge their likely impact, but they are consistent with a recognition that in a single market, competition law needs new sources of guidance.

This reorientation of the Commission's policy initiatives can be seen primarily in two areas. First, the Commission has significantly increased its attention to horizontal agreements.[135] It has increased fines in horizontal cases and focused attention on developing conceptual tools for attacking such agreements. In this context the concept of barriers to entry has become a major theme. Second, in 1997 the Commission issued a so-called Green Paper on vertical restraints. In this study, the Commission confronted the issues of whether and how to change its current doctrines.[136] It did not reach policy conclusions, but focused attention on the likelihood that the area of Community competition that was long the centerpiece of Commission efforts may play a different role in the future.

---

[134] Case 41/83, *Italy v. Commission* [1985] ECR 3261 (*British Telecom*). See also Case 311/84, *Centre Belge d'Études de Marché-Télé-Marketing SA v. Compagnie de Télédiffusion SA* [1987] ECR 3261 (*Telemarketing*).

[135] See Karel van Miert, 'La politique européene de concurrence en 1995', 2 *Competition Policy Newsletter* 15–16 (1996).

[136] Competition Directorate—General, *Green Paper: Vertical Restraints in EC Competition Policy* (January 22, 1997) (available on Internet at http://europa.eu.int/en/comm/dg04/dg4-home.htm).

F. COMMUNITY COMPETITION LAW AND ITS ROLES

The political and economic decisions and forces that have shaped the evolution of European integration have also shaped Community competition law. Community institutions have created a competition law system out of the text of the Rome Treaty, and, in turn, the development of that system has helped to shape the process of integration. Competition law has been central to the integration project, and the integration project has been central to competition law.

Competition law's role in European integration has also made it the central reference point in the experience of competition law in Europe. It has operated parallel to and independently of national competition law systems, and in a sense it has overshadowed them. We will explore in the next chapter some of the implications of Community competition law as a model as well as other aspects of its relationships with national competition law systems, but first we need to look back at the story and attempt to identify its basic dynamics, not least because perceptions of the system are themselves factors in the integration process.

1. The system and its dynamics

The sparse competition law provisions of the Rome Treaty did not create the system. It has been sculpted by interactions between that text and political and economic ideas and interests, and changes in those ideas and interests will continue to reshape it. The dominant objective in shaping this system has been to foster the economic integration of the Member States, and this imperative has produced a system directed toward meeting that need.

This dynamic has two prominent features, each of which has important implications. First, the transnational characteristics of the system are basic to its identity. Community competition law experience has been, and is likely to remain for the foreseeable future, the competition law of a transnational organization rather than of a single state. We need not enter into the debate about how to characterize the EU's current legal status, but it is important for our purposes that the Community consists of states, each of which has a significant decree of autonomy, a large sphere of discretion in which it pursues policies designed to maximize its own interests, and a distinct political, economic, and legal tradition. This affects the aims, the methods, and the language of Community competition law.

As the legal regime of a transnational organization, Community competition law is necessarily 'special'. The system is 'competition law'—that is, it is a general normative system that attaches legal sanctions to restraints on competition. Yet the goal of integrating national markets has provided the primary political impetus and legal justification for competition law decisions as well as the central device for perceiving and interpreting substantive law norms. The protection of competition has been ancillary to it.

The second central component of the dynamic is the tension between stability and change. As the process of integration changes the 'constitution' of the Community and the roles its institutions play, tensions between the foundational model and new needs become prominent. That tension is not new, but its form may be changing, and it may be both increasingly important and increasingly opaque.

2. Foundational model

The foundational model centers on administrative decision-making. The lack of private suits for enforcement in Community courts and their rarity in Member State courts means that the Commission makes most decisions regarding objectives to be pursued, conduct to be challenged, resources to be used and the arguments to be employed in justifying decisions. The centrality of administrative decision-making was not, as we have seen, required by the Rome Treaty. It is the result of political decisions taken during the process of integration and in response to the needs of that process (for example, Regulation 17). It has also been impelled and shaped by general expectations of the nature of competition law. In particular, it was consistent with the basic administrative control model of competition law that reigned in Europe during the period when these decisions were taken.

The centrality of administrative decision-making means that most decisions are policy decisions. They are guided by priorities and goals established by Commission officials and by the political leadership of the Union. Juridical processes provide constraints on policy decisions, but they are policy-based nonetheless. These policy decisions are not the economic policy of a single state, but of institutions in which states play a key role. 'Transnational' decisions are developed and implemented by 'transnational' decision-makers within a 'transnational' organization, and they represent 'transnational' policy—that is, they are justified by reference to the welfare of the Community as a whole. The predominant policy goal of that Community has been the unification of the market and the assurance of equal opportunities among states—not competition for the sake of its generic benefits.

The policy decisions of the Commission involve extensive discretion. Commission actions are subject to appeal to the CFI and/or the ECJ, but these courts have relatively few competition law cases, and thus relatively few administrative decisions are likely to be subject to judicial scrutiny. The Commission 'applies' law in making its decisions, and it pays attention to juridical methodology, particularly in cases that it considers likely to be tested judicially, but over a broad range of decisions officials have significant leeway. Given the transnational character of the system, this means, in turn, that the economic policies of states and the influence of large business units can sometimes play a significant role in decision-making.

Constraints on the use of this discretion derive not only from controls by the courts, but also from conceptions of the administrative task. Officials of DG IV have paid close attention to juridical forms and methodology in constructing decisional procedures, and they have generated expectations about the conduct of competition law officials that are now part of the system. These influences can also lose force, however, particularly if competition law begins to lose its special status.

Despite the centrality of administrative decision-making, it operates within a juridical framework. The idea that all decision-making is subject to legal constraints has been a cement of European integration, and this idea has been particularly important to the success of competition law, where the magnitude of economic interests involved calls for 'objective' legal controls. The ECJ has played a central role in shaping and directing the development of competition law. It has set the agenda, identified central values, and established guiding principles and methods of interpreting them. Today the two Community courts symbolize the supremacy of legal process in the Community competition law system.

This judicial function is, however, also conditioned by its transnational characteristics. The judges of the Community courts come from each of the Member States. They have different backgrounds, different training, and often different expectations, and they do not share well-established traditions. Shared perceptions of their roles as Community judges are the primary, if not the exclusive, basis for community within this group. These perceptions are only as strong, however, as the goals and expectations that unite them, and changes in these goals and expectations could change those perceptions.

The leadership of the Community's courts and the political importance of 'neutral' forms of decision-making have made the language of Community competition law primarily legal rather than political. Decisions are understood as either articulations or applications of generally applicable norms derived from interpretation of authoritative texts.

That language is also largely case-based. The treaty language, which is alone 'authoritative', provides little more than a starting point for decision-making. Moreover, the lack of an integrated and influential scholarly community with a shared intellectual tradition has precluded a significant role for theoretical contributions to this language.

The vocabulary of competition law is, however, thin. There are relatively few substantive cases of importance, at least as compared with a country such as Germany, not to mention, of course, the United States. Where, however, there are relatively few cases, the force of case law depends to a greater degree on the clarity and vision of those cases that do exist. In the early years of the system, cases reflecting a broad vision were common in the competition law area. In recent years, they have been rarer. The language is also thin in the sense that the cases are not supported by well-developed methodologies and judicial traditions that can be used to provide consistency in the application of the law, and this has made Community competition law cases notoriously difficult to predict.

This basic framework was established during the first three decades of the Community's existence, and it has come to be seen as the 'model' of Community competition. The assumption is that it will continue to function more or less along the basic patterns thus far established. It may not always be a well-founded assumption.

3. The changing roles of competition law

Since the mid-1980s, the dynamic of this system has been changing along with its goals and methods and the roles of its institutions. A central factor in this changing dynamic is the success of integration itself. Driven and defined throughout its history by the goal of creating a single market for Europe, the competition law system must increasingly operate with a reduced role for its former lodestar. A system constructed and maintained to achieve one primary goal now faces fundamental questions about what it is doing and why. It must redefine its mission. This need for redefinition has already begun to destabilize the system's conceptual framework and suffuse it with uncertainty.

This uncertainty is exacerbated by increasing demands for accommodation between competition law goals and other goals of the Community. Trade policy, social concerns and environmental claims, *inter alia*, demand to be reconciled with the objectives of competition law. Consequently, just as the keystone of the existing goal structure is being removed—and in part because of the imminence of that removal—lateral pressure on that structure from other values and policies is increasing, generating even further uncertainty about the roles of competition law.

One response has been to turn toward more 'generic' competition law goals—that is, generic benefits associated with protecting the process of competition. Such goals have lived in the shadow of the integration imperative since the foundational period, but they have been little explored in their own right, primarily because integrationist and generic goals have been intermingled, and there has been little reason to distinguish between them. This has led to the assumption that 'unbundling' these goals will change little, and to a lack of concern about the potential impact of eliminating integrationist goals. The assumption remains unexamined, however, shielded from examination not only by the natural resistance to changing one's conceptual framework, but also by the political risks of doing so.

Yet removal of the integration imperative necessarily alters competition law goal structures and the discourse associated with them. Without it, there will be increased pressure on DG IV's decision-makers to articulate other goals with far more care than in the past. Should market efficiency be the sole goal? If not, which other values should be served and how should they relate to each other—that is, what should be the new goal structure?

This process of redefining the system's goals will also demand that a language be developed to relate specific decisions to the redefined goal structure. This will give new contours to some competition law issues and focus attention on other issues that have thus far played little or no role in competition law thinking. It is likely to require, for example, that the courts define more carefully the concept of competition that they employ. The ECJ generally was able to skirt this issue in the past, because its primary concern was to reduce barriers to the flow of goods across national borders. That relatively straightforward and 'physical' criterion often did not invite deeper analysis, but a goal structure consisting of generic competition law goals demands a different concept of 'competition' and one that is likely to be more difficult to define. National competition law systems have wrestled with these issues for decades, but the dominance of integrationist goals has obscured such concerns within Community competition law.

Changes in goals and discourse are also likely to redirect policy initiatives and enforcement energies, and this has already begun to happen. The predominant concern with vertical agreements that has been associated with the integration imperative has, for example, diminished. The Green Paper issued by DG IV is the most visible sign of this development.

Removal of the integration imperative as the dominant goal in the competition law system does not mean that integration-related issues will not arise in the future. They will, because the *de jure* integration of the Community does not automatically create a *de facto* integration and because the existence of national cultures and governments will continue to create incentives for firms and groups of firms to evade the full implications of economic integration. The critical point is that the creation of a largely unified market removes such issues from their dominant, identity-defining position within the system.

Another response to the uncertainties facing European competition law is to avoid them and turn to a different set of problems, and this may be contributing to the 'public turn' of competition law. By turning away from the traditional private areas of competition law and focusing attention on the anticompetitive impact of governments, Community decision-makers avoid—at least temporarily—some of the difficulties involved in changing goals and concepts and 'retooling' the system to achieve a set of objectives different from those it has served in the past. If the activities of governments are seen as the primary threat to competition, the courts and the Commission can use this relatively 'clean slate' to maintain the symbolic momentum of integration.

4. Methods: less law, more politics

At this critical juncture in the development of competition law and of European integration, the institutions of the competition law system will make critical choices. Just as the system's goals are changing, so too are the means used to achieve those goals. The 'juridical component' that has been the core of the system since its earliest days may be losing influence relative to its political components. At least in some respects, the competition law system is becoming less juridical and more political.

At one level, this is a natural concomitant of change and uncertainty as to goals. As goals change and/or become less well-defined, concepts and practices developed to achieve those goals may appear less appropriate and reliable.[137] The resulting lack of confidence in generalized principles may, therefore, militate in favor of increasingly *ad hoc*, short-term policy decisions.

A more fundamental and pervasive factor relates to changes in the roles played by the courts and the Commission. As the Commission's role becomes more central and the courts' role becomes less dominant, the relative importance of the methods associated with these institutions changes accordingly. The dominant position of the ECJ in the foundational system assured the centrality of juridical processes. As long as it was supplying intellectual leadership for the system, structuring its thought and guiding its development, the dominant discourse of the system was juridical, because the Court's language is juridical. In that situation the principal decisions within the system were viewed as the result of applying juridical methodology to authoritative texts.

In contrast, the Commission is an explicitly political institution, and the more central its role in the system, the more influence political elements are likely to enjoy. Its decisions reflect a variety of pressures resulting from the perceived interests of Member States and interest groups as well as the institutions of the Community. As the Commission becomes less dependent on the courts for intellectual leadership and political support, its methods and discourse are likely to become more influential, and the influence of juridical discourse may wane.

5. Perspectives on EU competition law

Conventional descriptions of Community competition law tend to paint a different image of its dynamics. In this literature, intimations of fundamental change rarely surface and then only at the margins of discourse. The domi-

---

[137] Some observers have noticed discreet elements of this mutation. See, e.g., Thomas E. Kauper, 'Article 86, Excessive Prices, and Refusals to Deal', 59 *Antitrust L.J.* 441–56 (1991). Yet its sweep and implications have yet to be examined carefully, and it is in uncovering these interdependencies that a systemic perspective holds particular promise.

nant theme is the 'maturation' of Community competition law.[138] The focus tends to be on whether conceptual and doctrinal questions have been 'answered' or 'clarified' and on whether competition law procedures have been made more efficient or fairer. This discourse of 'clarification' and 'continuity' serves valuable functions, but it may also sometimes obscure important changes within that system.

In this chapter we have applied a conceptual lens designed to detect changes in the operation of the competition law system and in the forces affecting it. While Community officials understandably emphasize continuity in the development of competition law rules, and while analysis of doctrinal problems is obviously important, it is also important to examine the system as an operative whole and to ask whether fundamental changes are underway. Our examination here suggests that they are and that even greater change is likely, with potentially profound and as yet largely unrecognized implications for the future of Europe—and beyond.

Viewed from this perspective, the competition law system appears far less stable than it is often assumed to be. The image of a self-confident Commission enforcing an increasingly clear set of well-accepted legal principles under the forward-looking and bold guidance of a court confident in its objectives and methods can no longer be considered persuasive. The system is more convincingly portrayed as featuring an understaffed and somewhat uncertain Commission facing new problems, pressures and demands with diminishing guidance from the courts and increasingly tentative support for its mission.

The defining features of the Community competition law system—integration as the dominant goal and juridical processes as the central source of guidance in decision-making—have mutated. The reduced role of the unification imperative and the weakening of the 'juridical' components of the system in favor of 'political' components are transforming the system. As yet, however, these mutations have been little noticed. In a unified market the goal of unification loses its meaning, but the implications of this loss of meaning remain virtually unexplored.

The Community competition law system now operates differently than it did only a few years ago, but, as is so often true, important changes at the systemic level remain masked by continuities at the levels of formal legal and institutional discourse. The integration of the Community's market has undermined its goal structures at the same time that institutional changes have weakened support for its methods, and the inevitable upshot is a weakening of the system's 'identity'. This becomes particularly poignant in the context of changing relationships between Community competition law and the competition laws of the Member States, and that is our next focus.

---

[138] See, e.g., Jonathan Faull, 'The Enforcement of Competition Policy in the European Community: A Mature System', 15 *Fordham Int'l L. J.* 219 (1991–2) and Verstrynge, 'Reflections on the Second Generation of Competition Policy', 677.

X

1986 and After: Competition Law, the Member States, and the European Union

The rapid intensification of European integration that began with the Single European Act in 1986 also brought changes in the relationship between national competition laws and Community competition law, and gradually moved that relationship to the center of the European competition law story. Since then, decisions regarding the structure and operation of national competition laws have increasingly been made with at least one eye on Community competition law, and the relationship between national and Community competition law has become a focus of attention in Brussels. In this chapter, we look at both this reshaping of national competition laws and the evolving relationship between national competition law and the institutions of the European Union. Although patterns have emerged, it is too early to assess their durability, and thus our concern will not be to describe and analyze developments in detail, but to identify some of the key factors in the dynamics of the new situation and its relationship to the story as a whole.

A. SEPARATE SPHERES: THE FORMAL RELATIONSHIP

We referred briefly to some elements of the relationship between national and Community competition law in the last chapter, but we need to recapitulate briefly in order to set the stage for the developments that began in the mid-1980s. Until then, the relationship between Member State competition laws and Community competition law had been defined largely on a formal basis in which jurisdictional competence was the central and often exclusive issue. By the late 1960s, the ECJ had defined the respective spheres of competence according to the 'two barriers theory', which provided that Community competition law could be applied wherever trade between Member States was effected, but a Member State could also apply its own competition law to conduct affecting its territory, provided that such action did not conflict with the competition law of the Community.

Community competition law and national competition laws thus operated for the most part within their respective areas of competence. There were, in effect, separate spheres of operation for each of the national laws as well as for the law of the Community. This represented the basic architecture of the relationship, and there was little concern either in Brussels or in the Member States to change it.

This architecture provided space for co-ordination among these spheres, but there were few incentives to move in that direction. At least after 1973, there was no doubt that national courts were authorized to apply much of Community competition law, but in order for them to do so, private law suits had to be filed in those courts, and such suits were rare. As we have seen, European competition law systems have relied almost exclusively on administrative agencies to induce compliance, and thus enterprises injured by competitive restraints seldom considered using the courts to seek redress of such harms. It was easier, less expensive and less risky for firms to bring their complaints to the Commission or to their own competition law authorities than to file suits in national courts. Moreover, few Member States provided procedural mechanisms (for example, the availability of damage awards) that would make such suits attractive, and there was much uncertainty about how Community competition law should be applied in national courts.

Limitations on the jurisdictional competence of national courts were also a major obstacle to generating greater use of national courts to apply Community competition law. National courts were only authorized to apply *parts* of Community competition law. Most notably, they were not authorized to issue individual exemptions under Article 85(3) of the Treaty. Under Regulation 17, only the Commission was authorized to issue such exemptions. This virtually eliminated incentives for private litigants to file suits under Article 85 in national courts, because even if a national court found the Article 85(1) prohibition applicable, the defendant might be able to convince the Commission to issue an exemption and thus thwart the objectives of the suit.

Another possibility for increasing co-ordination between national laws and Community laws was for Member State competition authorities to apply Community law, but this was even rarer. National authorities did have authority under Community law to apply most elements of Community competition law, but some had not been granted such authority under their own laws. Moreover, those who did have such authority had little incentive to use it. Above all, they lacked authority to issue Article 85(3) exemptions, so that a national competition authority might expend its resources to pursue a violation of Article 85(1) and then find that the Commission exempted the conduct under Article 85(3).

Until the mid-1980s, these issues were of little concern. Few paid serious attention to altering the formal relationship between national and Community law or increasing co-ordination among the separate European competition law regimes. In particular, Community officials were concerned with establishing the principles of Community competition law, applying them effectively, and protecting their own prerogatives and authority. They were concerned with *centralization* of responsibility for combating restraints on competition.

With the events of the mid-1980s, however, this separate-sphere architecture was increasingly seen as inadequate. The accelerating process of integration put new pressures on the existing distribution of competences and on the very idea that the relationship between Community competition law and national competition laws should be defined primarily by jurisdictional competences. If the states of the Community were moving toward higher levels of integration, would it not be necessary to develop a more co-operative and integrated framework for competition law? These events set in motion two sometimes contradictory processes—a centripetal one that tended to centralize power in Brussels and Luxembourg, and a centrifugal one that called for the devolution of authority to the Member States.

1. Centralization

For many observers, growing confidence in the future of European integration initially seemed to signal even greater centralization of responsibility for competition law matters in Brussels. Their image was that Community competition law and institutions would increasingly come to dominate the competition law scene in Europe, with national competition laws relegated to a marginal status in which they basically dealt only with local competition issues. One expert in the late 1980s said that he advised national competition law officials to 'pack their bags', because soon virtually everything of interest would be happening in Brussels.

The enactment of the Merger Control Regulation in 1989 seemed to confirm this development. Merger control had become the most visible and politically significant component of competition law, and for most purposes that regulation took the largest mergers out of the control of the national authorities and placed them under the exclusive authority of Community institutions. Moreover, the plan was to further reduce the threshold figures for 'Community' mergers within five years, effectively leaving only local mergers for national authorities. Many assumed that what was happening in the merger area was likely to provide the model for the future even in other areas of competition law.

2. Decentralization

But the situation was changing and complex, and its complexity was increasing. The question was asked with increasing frequency, particularly by certain DG IV officials: 'How can DG IV effectively protect the process of competition throughout Europe?' Political and financial factors foreclosed any significant increase in the resources available to the competition directorate. Yet centralization would, by definition, significantly increase its responsibilities. Moreover, the Community was increasing in size, and this would further increase the scope of DG IV's responsibilities. In 1986, Spain and Portugal became members, and countries such as Norway, Sweden, Finland, and Austria seemed likely to become members in the not too distant future. At least some of these new members and potential new members had either no competition law or systems with limited effectiveness. Consequently, enterprises there would have to be 'educated' about competition law norms, and this would increase both the educational and compliance responsibilities of the Commission.

Adding new members was also likely to burden the internal operations of the Community's competition law system, particularly where the new members had little or no experience with competition law. It would mean adding employees to the competition directorate from these states, and this was likely to entail both additional training and additional difficulties in communication. Moreover, those working within DG IV were aware of the degree to which political influence from national governments could affect competition law decisions, and the addition of new Member States would necessarily increase the number of potential sources of such influence.

These developments led the Commission to begin to seek means of decentralizing rather than centralizing responsibility for applying Community competition law. It began in the mid-1980s to talk about the need to involve national courts and authorities in applying Community competition law.[1] Initially, however, the issue was not given much attention. The Commission called for increased use of national institutions, but it did little to foster decentralization.

With the collapse of the Soviet Union in 1989, the Maastricht agreement in 1993, and the impending increase in membership at about the same time, the situation became more pressing. The Maastricht agreement signaled further intensification of the integration process, while the impending accession of Sweden, Finland, and Austria would soon bring the number of Member States to fifteen. Moreover, the changing situation in Eastern Europe meant that the Community would soon have to at least contemplate the possibility of expanding its membership to include Eastern Europe states with little experience of competition, much less of competition law. The need for changes in the relationship between national and Community competition law was becoming increasingly obvious.

The Maastricht agreement also added a new element to the situation by introducing the principle of subsidiarity. Responding to popular concerns

---

[1] See, e.g., John Meade, 'Decentralisation in the Implementation of EEC Competition Law— A Challenge for the Lawyers', 37 *Northern Ireland L.Q.* 101 (1986).

about the centralization of power in Brussels, the Member States there adopted the general principle that the newly renamed 'European Union' should not regulate conduct that the national governments could regulate at least as effectively.[2] While technically the principle of subsidiarity did not require changes in the competition law system, its 'philosophy' quickly became part of the vocabulary of thought about all aspects of the relationship between Brussels and the Member States, and in this form it entered the debate about the decentralization of competition law.

These were some of the factors that led to a new focus on decentralization beginning in the early 1990s. This focus involves, however, a fundamental dilemma. To the extent that decentralization is effective, it reduces the strain on Commission resources, limits or reverses the concentration of political power in Brussels, and improves compliance. On the other hand, it also reduces the capacity of Community institutions to influence the development of competition law and to use it in pursuing their own objectives. Moreover, it amplifies the risk of inconsistencies within the system. This dilemma has precluded rapid progress toward decentralization.

a. The application of Community law by national courts

In the competition law context, decentralization has three basic dimensions, and it is important to examine them separately. One seeks to increase the role of national courts in securing compliance with Community competition law. For the Commission, increasing the use of national courts represents an attractive means of reducing its caseload while increasing awareness of and compliance with Community competition law. It does not require alteration of the formal relationship between national and Community competition law, and it does not require the Commission to relinquish any elements of control over the Community competition law system. From the Commission's perspective, the strategy is also cheap. It costs little more than the publicity and related efforts to encourage litigants to file private suits rather than to take their complaints to Brussels.

In the early 1990s, the Commission intensified the efforts it had begun a few years earlier to encourage complainants to file actions in the national courts rather than to rely on DG IV for redress of their grievances.[3] Lack of significant response to these efforts led the Commission to go a step further, and in 1993 it issued a Notice Concerning Cooperation between the Commission and Courts of the Member States.[4] This notice had several functions. First, it

---

[2] For discussion of the principle of 'subsidiarity' in the context of the decentralization of Community competition law, see, e.g., Wernhard Möschel, 'Subsidiaritätsprinzip und europäisches Kartellrecht', 48 *Neue Juristische Wochenschrift* 281 (1995).

[3] See, e.g., Claus-Dieter Ehlermann, 'The European Community, Its Law and Lawyers', 29 *Comm. Mkt. L. Rev.* 213, 225 (1992).

[4] European Commission, Notice Concerning Cooperation between the Commission and Courts of the Member States in regard to the Application of Articles 85 and 86 of the Treaty,

centered attention on the Commission's attempts to encourage private suits. It signaled the high degree of importance the Commission was now attaching to the issue. Second, it prominently stated the principle that in cases not 'having particular, political, economic or legal significance for the Community . . . complaints should, as a rule, be handled by national courts or authorities'. The idea was not new, but its prominent and clear articulation was designed to give it new force. Issued at virtually the same time that the Maastricht agreement announced the subsidiarity principle, the Notice also suggested to many that the Commission was here applying the principle of subsidiarity to competition law.

Third, the Notice proposed a procedure for national courts to follow in applying Community competition law, specifying the steps that such courts should take and the factors they should consider in making the decisions that were part of it. The objective was to encourage private suits by reducing the procedural uncertainties involved in bringing such suits. In essence, the Notice directs national courts to make decisions on the basis of Community law to the extent they can be reasonably certain as to how Community institutions would decide on the facts presented. In addition to the authoritative force of Community judicial decisions, for example, the Notice recommends that courts take into account as evidence of Community law the informal administrative decisions of the Commission. Where they are not reasonably certain about Community law, they are requested to postpone actions, delay decisions and defer to Community action, and the Notice suggests procedures for doing this.

Finally, the Notice outlines a program by which the Commission agrees to assist the national courts in applying Community law. It agrees, for example, to provide national courts with factual information at its disposal that might be relevant to specific competition law cases, and it agrees to provide advice to the courts on the legal issues involved. Of particular importance here is its emphasis on the potential role of block exemptions in the decentralization process. Since national courts are permitted to issue decisions on the basis of the Commission's block exemptions, the more legal territory these exemptions cover, the less serious an obstacle it is that national courts cannot issue individual exemptions. The Notice indicates that the Commission will actively use this mechanism as a means of fostering decentralization.

Early indications are that the Notice may not generate a significant increase in private suits before national courts. As Claus-Dieter Ehlermann, former director of DG IV, points out, European companies are simply not convinced that the benefits of such suits outweigh the risks, expenses, and uncertainties

Feb. 13, 1993. 1993 OJ C39/6. For discussion, see Rein Wesseling, 'The Commission Notices on Decentralisation of E.C. Antitrust Law: In for a Penny, Not for a Pound', 18 *Eur. Comp. L. Rev.* 94 (1997).

they entail.[5] Neither the Notice itself nor other relevant Commission action have changed the basic calculus and expectations relating to these suits. The Commission has reduced some uncertainties, and it has promised to provide aid, but uncertainties remain, and, more basically, the inability of national courts to issue individual exemptions remains a major obstacle to increased use of national courts for enforcing Community competition law.

b. The application of Community law by national authorities

A second form of decentralization relates to the use of national competition authorities to enforce Community competition law, but until recently there has been relatively little interest in developing it. During the early decades of the Community, it was not realistic, because most national competition authorities had limited resources and experience (Italy did not even have a competition law), and not all were authorized under their own law to apply Community competition law. Moreover, national competition laws often differed significantly from Community competition law.

Even as those obstacles were reduced by new legislation and increased national attention to competition law issues, however, the Commission showed little interest in pursuing this strategy. For the Commission, it is a significantly more complicated and potentially risky form of decentralization than its court-based alternative. It involves co-ordinating the decision-making of at least two sets of officials (the Commission plus one or more national authorities), each of which has a degree of discretion and each of which has to take into account policy considerations and respond to the pressures of its constituents. As a result, orchestrating such a relationship entails high levels of uncertainty and complexity, and these, in turn, may be expected to impose significant additional costs on the Commission as well as interfere with its capacity to control efforts to protect competition in the EU.

National authorities have also perceived little incentive to use Community competition law rather than their own competition laws. In addition to the complexity and uncertainties involved, they remain unable to issue individual exemptions and, therefore, have little incentive to expend their resources for investigations over which they do not have ultimate control. In addition, national competition officials are primarily responsible for the development and enforcement of their own national competition laws, and it is the performance of this task for which they are likely to be primarily evaluated. These laws reflect national values and objectives, and national officials are committed professionally and often personally to those goals and values.

Despite these problems, the paucity of progress in eliciting private suits in the national courts has led the Commission to pay greater attention to this

---

[5] Claus-Dieter Ehlermann, 'Implementation of EC Competition Law by National Anti-Trust Authorities', 17 *Eur. Comp. L. Rev.* 88, 89 (1996).

second alternative. In late 1996, it issued a 'preliminary draft notice' on co-operation between the Commission and national authorities that presented its views on the subject (the 'Draft Notice').[6] The Draft Notice specifically referred to the principle of subsidiarity as justification for increased devolution of responsibility on national competition law authorities. It states that '. . . if, by reason of its scale or effects, the proposed action can best be taken at Community level, it is for the Commission to act. If, on the other hand, the action can be taken satisfactorily at national level, the competition authority of the Member State concerned is better placed to take it'. According to this allocation principle, 'size' and 'effects' determine which authority should apply Community competition law.

The sphere of operation of this principle remains limited, however, primarily because the Commission remains exclusively competent to issue Article 85(3) exemptions. Where conduct might be exempted by the Commission, therefore, the principle would not be applicable. This means that the principle applies only to conduct not subject to exemption (for example, where it has not been notified) and conduct covered by 'enacted law' (such as block exemptions). The Draft Notice does, however, authorize the Commission to reject a complaint and thus send the case to national authorities where notification is made primarily for the purpose of avoiding investigation by a national authority.

For cases subject to this allocation principle, the Commission takes the position that where the main effects of conduct are within one state, that state should normally take the case. Nevertheless, the Commission reserves the right to take a case where it considers that it has important economic or legal significance—if it raises new points of law, for example, or if it involves conduct in which another Member State has a particular interest.

The Draft Notice also proposes closer co-operation between national authorities and the Commission to avoid duplication of efforts. Here the effort is to reduce the likelihood that national authorities will expend effort and resources on cases which the Commission ultimately takes out of their sphere of competence.

In issuing the Draft Notice, DG IV signaled the importance that the Commission now attaches to co-operation with national authorities. It does not, however, significantly alter incentives for Member States to increase their efforts in this direction. The Commission is likely to have to take further steps along this path in order to make this form of decentralization more attractive.

---

[6] Preliminary Draft Commission Notice on Cooperation Between National Authorities and the Commission in Handling Cases Falling within the Scope of Articles 85 and 86 of the EC Treaty, Sept. 10, 1996. 1996 OJ C 262/5.

c. *National authorities applying their own laws*

A third form of decentralization is to increase reliance on the use by Member State authorities of their own competition laws.[7] Discussions of decentralization typically have not included this alternative, using the term to refer only to the decentralized application of *Community* competition law rather than to decentralized application of competition law generally. One reason for this limitation on the scope of the concept of decentralization is that the Commission—and most Community competition law experts—wish it so. Commission policy is to increase the role and effectiveness of Community competition law, and increased reliance on national laws represents a move in the opposite direction.

Yet the principle of subsidiarity would seem to call for increased reliance on national competition law authorities to combat restraints of competition through the use of their own laws wherever they can do so at least as effectively as the Commission can. This would also respond to the values and concerns to which the principle of subsidiarity was addressed, because it would reduce the centralization of power in Brussels and increase the authority of Member States to direct their own affairs.

Moreover, to the extent that national competition authorities can effectively protect competition through the use of their own laws, the Commission would accomplish its objectives without using its own resources. Increased reliance on national competition laws in such cases may also avoid many of the complex problems that arise where two or more sets of institutions apply the same laws (that is, Community law).

For the Commission, however, this form of decentralization also has important disadvantages. Above all, it reverses a forty-year-old process of seeking to establish Community competition law as the basis for market integration. Many officials in DG IV have long been committed to this effort and thus reject a reversal of direction. It also would reduce the prominence and power of the Commission, for to the extent that national competition authorities set the relevant norms, provide advice to business, and make critical decisions, the Commission's role—and the power and status of its officials—is reduced.

The central issue, however, is the extent to which national competition laws may be expected to protect competition at least as effectively as Community competition law. Restraints on competition often have effects in more than one state, and thus they might violate the laws of more than one state and thereby create conflicts among states as well as costly duplication of efforts. Moreover, one state will often not be in a position effectively to combat particular restrictions because it has limited access to evidence in other states.

[7] For discussion, see, e.g., Pierre-Vincent Bos, 'Towards a Clear Distribution of Competence between EC and National Competition Authorities', 16 *Eur. Comp. L. Rev.* 410 (1995).

These disadvantages are, however, likely to be reduced to the extent that national competition authorities are enforcing similar substantive rules in similar ways. As we have seen, national competition law systems already share many basic characteristics. They were becoming increasingly similar even prior to 1986, and, as we shall see in the next section, there has been a dramatic escalation in this process of convergence since then. The more similar these systems are, the easier it should be to develop co-operative means of distributing authority in difficult cases and of regulating evidentiary issues.

C. THE CONVERGENCE OF NATIONAL COMPETITION LAWS

The intense efforts in the mid-1980s to rekindle the 'fire' of integration after a decade of sluggish and generally unproductive development created widespread confidence that a unified market would finally be created by the end of 1992 and that even after that magical date the process of integration would continue to become both deeper and broader. The major steps in this direction at Maastricht in 1993 seemed to justify and reinforce that confidence. This growing confidence has since 1986 led several European countries either to introduce new competition law systems along the lines of the Community 'model', or to alter existing systems to make them conform more closely to that model. In one sense, these decisions represent a continuation and consolidation of the process of juridification that had already been in place for decades in most national competition law systems, but whereas the process was essentially national prior to 1986, it has become increasingly 'European' since then.

The renewed confidence of the late 1980s and early 1990s created both pressure and incentives for national legislatures to accommodate national competition laws to the Community model. The pressure was indirect rather than the result of the efforts of Community institutions. At its inception, the 1992 program entailed significant political risks and uncertainties, and thus the national and Community decision-makers favoring it needed support. A government's decision to accommodate its national competition law to the Community model represented a demonstration of such support. It was a means by which a Member State could demonstrate its solidarity with other states who were pursuing further integration, and it could expect that such support would be rewarded by other supporters of these initiatives, particularly Germany and France.

For countries seeking entry into the EU, incentives to send such a message were even greater. Sweden, Austria, and Finland were in various stages of seeking membership, for example, and by enacting competition laws similar to Community law they could demonstrate their support for the integration efforts of existing members and of Community officials. This, in turn, could be expected to be useful in the often difficult negotiations regarding their conditions of accession.

There were also economic incentives. With the growing confidence that membership in the EU was likely to grow, business groups often argued to their national legislatures that they would benefit from operating under basically the same rules within their own borders that they encountered elsewhere in the newly 'unified' market. The intensifying battle for foreign investment among European states also created incentives for states to follow the Community model, because it allowed them to offer potential investors a domestic legal environment that did not deviate significantly from that of the Community and that, in particular, was not more stringent than Community law.

Although the new confidence in the future of European integration was the most dramatic and obvious source of pressure to reshape national competition laws, two other factors played significant roles. One was the increasing willingness of national competition authorities to learn from each other. Instances of such co-operation grew rapidly during the late 1980s and 1990s, as did the intensity of such efforts. This created an increasingly 'European' pool of ideas, practices, and expectations that was often a factor in shaping new legislation.

The other was a growing recognition throughout Europe of the importance of competition. The market was becoming more fashionable, and this both justified and encouraged measures to protect it. To some extent this represented an ideological shift, particularly after 1989. It also reflected, however, a growing awareness that European economies needed reinvigoration and that increased competition was the most likely means of increasing economic vigor. This provided a direct impetus for strengthening competition law systems, but it also had an indirect effect. It led to a wave of denationalization of state-owned enterprises that frequently left newly privatized companies in dominant positions and led to calls to use competition law to prevent them from abusing their power.

The image most often used in Europe to describe the post-1986 evolution of national competition law systems portrays it as a move away from systems based on the 'abuse' principle and toward greater reliance on the 'prohibition' principle. This imaging is important, because it reveals the extent to which Europeans have tended to view these decisions as fundamental changes in the characteristics of their national competition law systems.

The convergence of national systems has occurred on both the substantive and institutional levels.[8] Most discussions of these changes have focused on

---

[8] For a careful description of trends in convergence, see Meinrad Dreher, 'Kartellrechtsvielfalt und Kartellrechtseinheit in Europa?', 38 *Die Aktiengesellschaft* 437 (1993). An early and influential discussion of the issue was Fritz Rittner, 'Konvergenz oder Divergenz der europäischen Wettbewerbsrechte?' in *Integration oder Desintegration der europäischen*

the norms themselves. In addition to more frequently taking the form of prohibitions, these norms tend to provide less room for the exercise of discretion than did previous legislation. Moreover, they have increasingly followed the structure of Articles 85 and 86 of the Rome Treaty. In some cases, new national laws merely follow the basic structure of those articles (for example, France), while others incorporate their language virtually verbatim (for example, Sweden). These new laws also generally include merger control provisions similar to the Community's 1989 Merger Control Regulation, but here there are often significant variations in specific language and in institutional arrangements.

A second level of convergence involves institutions and their roles, but here the Community system as a 'model' is more ambiguous, and the impetus for change may be more appropriately found in the shared experiences that constitute the 'juridification' process that we identified and discussed in Chapter VI. The general pattern of these changes has been to move toward systems that have more 'juridical' characteristics and institutions that perform more 'juridical' roles. Enforcement agencies have often, for example, been given greater autonomy from administrative and political influence, and they have been assigned roles that require the interpretation, application, and enforcement of articulated norms to a greater extent than was common in the administrative control systems that they often either replaced or modified.

In order to illustrate aspects of this process of convergence of national laws, we will look briefly at the new legislation in France, Italy, and Sweden. I have chosen these national experiences because they play important roles in the process of convergence and because they illustrate important aspects of that process. The discussion of competition law developments in France and Sweden has the additional benefit of continuing stories begun in Chapter VI. The treatment will be superficial. My objective is to illustrate aspects of the process of change rather than to describe the changes in any detail.

D. FRANCE: SETTING THE TONE

The first country to respond to the developments of the mid-1980s by changing its competition law system to bring it closer to that of the Community was France, where in 1986 a fundamentally new competition law was enacted.[9] The significance of France's step should not be underestimated. France has been (along with Germany) a central pillar in the process of integration since

---

Wettbewerbsordnung: Referate des XVI. FIW-Symposiums 31–84 (Cologne, 1983). For a valuable analysis of both aspects of this chapter from the perspective of 'harmonisation', see Hans Ullrich, 'Harmonisation within the European Union', 17 *Eur. Comp. L. Rev.* 178 (1996).

[9] For discussion of the French reform, see, e.g., Frédéric Jenny, 'French Competition Policy in Perspective', in 1987 *Fordham Corp. L. Inst.* 301 (Barry E. Hawk, ed., New York, 1988).

its inception, but ever since the beginnings of that process its representatives have tended to resist and oppose the strengthening of Community competition law, apparently preferring dirigistic models of economic policy to juridical decision-making. Moreover, France's refusal to develop a comprehensive competition law system of its own may have encouraged similar resistance in other countries such as Belgium and, to a lesser extent, Italy, Spain, and Portugal. France's new competition law thus had major symbolic importance for the role of competition law in Europe generally and for the process of convergence of national competition laws, in particular.

The 1986 legislation can be seen as the culmination of a process that had begun in 1977. As we saw in Chapter VI, France had begun in that year to move toward a more juridical system, but the initial steps had been small and tentative, and experience in the five or so years after that reform had done little to generate confidence that there would soon be additional steps in that direction.

By 1984, however, the Mitterrand government had moved away from traditional socialist economic policies such as the nationalization of industry to an intermediate policy position that emphasized the immediate needs of the French economy rather than traditional socialist aims. In this posture, it focused on policies designed to create jobs, improve the competitiveness of French industry and reduce regulatory interference with the economy. One official has called 1984 'the year of competition' in France, because a political consensus developed during that year that the economy required more competition and that price controls should be eliminated or curtailed.[10]

In this situation, the liberal minister of the economy (and later Prime Minister) Eduard Balladur appointed a committee of experts to draft a new and more 'liberal' competition law. This group of experts sought guidance from numerous sources, including German experts. According to Jean Donnedieu de Vabres, chair of the drafting group and former head of the Competition Commission,

. . . the example of the German legislation inspired us [in drafting the legislation]. As president of the earlier Competition Commission, I had many—and always productive—contacts with the Federal Cartel Office. . . . Many factors led to the similarity between [French and German] legislation—common membership in the European Community, the very extensive economic contact between the two countries, and [Germany's] headstart in relation to us concerning the practice of economic liberalism.[11]

---

[10] Dominique Brault, *L'État et L'Esprit de Concurrence en France* 64–8 (Paris, 1987).
[11] Jean Donnedieu de Vabres, 'Die mit der Durchsetzung des Wettbewerbsrechtes beauftragten Institutionen: Das Bundeskartellamt und der Wettbewerbsrat', in *Institutionen und Grundfragen des Wettbewerbsrechts: Referate des 6. deutsch-französischen Juristentreffens* 23, 24 (Uwe Blaurock, ed., Neuwied, 1988).

resist what they consider the maddeningly uncontrollable regime of competition.[20] Moreover, particularly in the years immediately after its enactment, entrenched interventionist expectations and political turf battles hampered the effectiveness of the new system. As a consequence, those who seek a relationship between government and the economy based on competition and economic freedom sometimes find little support for their goals.

Nevertheless, the French move was seen by many in Europe as a major step toward convergence of national competition law systems around the basic model of Community competition law, and the psychological momentum it created has undoubtedly been important not only for the decisions of other Member States to move their competition laws in that direction, but also for the process of integration of itself.

E. ITALY'S FIRST COMPETITION LAW

The renewed *élan* of European integration was powerful enough to lead in 1990 to the enactment of Italy's first competition statute.[21] Italy had long been the only one of the original Member States not to have enacted a competition statute, and there had been numerous attempts since the end of the Second World War to introduce such legislation,[22] but the lack of confidence in the efficacy of such legislation, and the political power of big industry had hitherto been sufficient to block all such efforts. The integration events of the late 1980s overcame that resistance.

In addition to the general pressure not to be the only Member State without a competition law and the general awareness of a need for more competition, two specific factors were important in enacting a competition law in Italy.[23] One was the denationalization of large, state-owned companies. Here the concern was that these newly privatized firms would often be left in

---

[20] For example, Philippe Seguin, President of the French Parliament, has sometimes conducted a virtual campaign against neo-liberalism and its associated Community influences in France, preferring instead a return to more protection of French industry. See, e.g., Jacques Michel Tondre, 'Les clivages apparus lors du référendum de Maastricht rythment toujours la vie politique francaise', Agence France Presse, Sept. 17, 1993 (available in LEXIS, Presse Library, AFP File).

[21] Act of September 27, 1990, Law No. 287/1990, Provisions for the Protection of Competition and the Market, Norme par la tutela della concorrenza e del mercato OJ No. 240 of 13 Oct., 1990. For commentary in English, see David C. Donald, 'Comments on the Italian Antitrust Law of October 10, 1990', 26 *Int'l Law.* 201 (1992).

[22] The various projects are listed in Vincenzo Donativi, *Introduzione della Disciplina Antitrust nel Sistema Legislativo Italiano* 2 n.3 (Milan, 1990).

[23] For discussion, see Mario Siragusa & Giuseppi Scasselati-Sforzolini, 'Italian and EC Competition Law: A New Relationship—Reciprocal Exclusivity and Common Principles', 29 *Comm. Mkt. L. Rev.* 93 (1992) and Guido Rossi, 'Control of Concentrations: The Wake of the EEC Regulation and the Debate in Italy', 1988 *Fordham Corp. L. Inst.* 28-1-21 (Barry E. Hawk, ed., New York, 1989).

regulations]'. This exemption provides a means by which the legislature can assure that its decisions will take precedence over competition law. The second exemption is broader and involves practices whose participants

can justify that [the practices] have the effect of assuring economic progress and that they reserve to consumers an equitable portion of the profits that result, provided that they does not give to the 'interested' enterprises the possibility of eliminating competition for a substantial part of the products involved. These practices may not impose restrictions on competition except to the extent they are indispensable for achieving the objective of progress.

This is similar to the language of Article 85(3), but there are important differences. For example, it also applies to cases of 'abuse' rather than as in the Rome Treaty only to restrictive agreements. It also refers only to the goal of economic progress, excluding reference to technical process or to the goal of improving the production or distribution of goods.

More major differences between the Statute and Community law were in a series of provisions relating to what are called 'restrictive practices' (Title IV). These included, in particular, refusals to deal and discriminatory practices, which had been in practice the most important provisions of prior law. These specific provisions interfered with the conceptual integrity and cohesion that had been one of the goals of the statute's drafters, and some of the provisions have since been eliminated.

The new statute also included merger controls. Here Community law could not function as a model for the simple reason that at the time there were no merger controls on the Community level (other than through application of Articles 85 and 86). Including merger controls in the legislation served the primary function of integrating all aspects of competition law within one statute and subjecting them to one set of procedures. Substantively, however, they did not represent a fundamental change in the intensity of controls over mergers.

A central objective of this reform of the French competition law system was to establish a new procedural and institutional framework for the system. Here the key was to refashion the main enforcement institution, now called the *Conseil de la Concurrence* ('*Conseil*').[15] Drafters of the legislation were aware that it could achieve its aims only if those making decisions within it were in a position to withstand the deeply-rooted influence of *dirigisme*. This meant increased independence for the body administering the law, and they thus renamed it to reflect the image of increased independence. It is now

---

[15] The specific functions of the *Conseil* were actually established by Title I of Décret no. 86-1309, which regulates the application of the Competition Statute. Décret no. 86-1309 du 29 Décembre 1986 fixant les conditions d'application de l'ordonnance no. 86-1243 du 1er Décembre 1986 relative a la liberté des prix et de la concurrence, 1989 OJ 15775, 1987 DSL 42 (Fr.). For discussion, see Antoine Winckler, 'Conseil de la concurrence et concurrence des autorités', 52 *Le Débat* 76–86 (1988) and Gilles de Margerie, 'Un nouveau type d'autorités', 52 *Le Débat* 87–97 (1988).

called a '*conseil*' rather than merely a '*commission*', as its predecessors had been called. Since there are no private suits under the Statute, the system's efficacy depends on the role played by the *Conseil*.

In contrast to its predecessors, the *Conseil* is an independent authority rather than an advisory body.[16] The *Conseil* may hear cases initiated by others, and it may itself initiate proceedings against firms engaged in potentially anticompetitive conduct. Once proceedings are instituted, the *Conseil* has full investigative powers, and it is authorized to grant injunctions, to impose fines, and even to award prison terms.

In addition to its adjudicative and enforcement roles, the *Conseil* also serves a consultative function. In certain situations involving economic intervention, consultation with the *Conseil* is mandatory—when, for example, the *Conseil d'Etat* seeks to impose price controls, or the government seeks to enact legislation which may affect competition, or the minister of the economy wishes to take regulatory action involving mergers.

Nevertheless, despite the relative autonomy that the *Conseil* enjoys, it remains dependent on the administration for its funding and for other forms of support. Moreover, the administration—specifically, the DGCCRF (*Direction Generale de la Concurrence, de la Consommation, et de la Repression des Fraudes*—Directorate General of Competition, Consumer Policy and the Repression of Fraud)—continues to have concurrent authority to investigate anticompetitive activity.[17] This concurrent authority has been a major factor in conflicts between the *Conseil* and the central bureaucracy.

The *Conseil* has become an active and increasingly respected office, but whether it will achieve a status even approaching that of the German Federal Cartel Office remains to be seen.[18] Creation of the new competition law system could not and did not end the conflict between *dirigisme* and competition law in France.[19] Long-standing traditions do not disappear easily or quickly, and there are still many in France who are more comfortable with greater administrative controls over the economy and their concomitant promise of order and national government control of economic developments. They

[16] The Minister of Justice defined the *Conseil* as 'an independent authority of the government entrusted with the control of anti-trust practices, which was previously the domain of the minister of the economy'. 1987 OJ 4923, *Assemblée Nationale*, No. 27448 (daily ed., Aug. 31, 1987).

[17] The DGCCRF is one of the directorates of the Ministry of the Economy. It is responsible for the effective functioning of markets, and it is to ensure 'respect for the rules protecting consumers . . . as well as for the rules of competition. On the basis of a complaint or on its own initiative, the DGCCRF launches investigations aimed at disclosing and establishing the existence of anticompetitve practices'. Jacques Azema, *Le Droit Francais de la Concurrence* 32–33 (2d ed., Paris, 1989).

[18] For discussion of recent developments, see Frédéric Jenny, 'French Competition Law Update: 1987–1994' 1995 *Fordham Corp. L. Inst.* 203 (Barry E. Hawk, ed., New York, 1996).

[19] Richard Azarnia and I have discussed aspects of this conflict in David J. Gerber & Richard Azarnia, 'Dirigisme and the Challenge of Competition Law in France', 3 *Cardozo J. of Int'l L. & Pol.* 9 (1995) (formerly, *New Europe L. J.*).

resist what they consider the maddeningly uncontrollable regime of competition.[20] Moreover, particularly in the years immediately after its enactment, entrenched interventionist expectations and political turf battles hampered the effectiveness of the new system. As a consequence, those who seek a relationship between government and the economy based on competition and economic freedom sometimes find little support for their goals.

Nevertheless, the French move was seen by many in Europe as a major step toward convergence of national competition law systems around the basic model of Community competition law, and the psychological momentum it created has undoubtedly been important not only for the decisions of other Member States to move their competition laws in that direction, but also for the process of integration of itself.

E. ITALY'S FIRST COMPETITION LAW

The renewed *élan* of European integration was powerful enough to lead in 1990 to the enactment of Italy's first competition statute.[21] Italy had long been the only one of the original Member States not to have enacted a competition statute, and there had been numerous attempts since the end of the Second World War to introduce such legislation,[22] but the lack of confidence in the efficacy of such legislation, and the political power of big industry had hitherto been sufficient to block all such efforts. The integration events of the late 1980s overcame that resistance.

In addition to the general pressure not to be the only Member State without a competition law and the general awareness of a need for more competition, two specific factors were important in enacting a competition law in Italy.[23] One was the denationalization of large, state-owned companies. Here the concern was that these newly privatized firms would often be left in

[20] For example, Philippe Seguin, President of the French Parliament, has sometimes conducted a virtual campaign against neo-liberalism and its associated Community influences in France, preferring instead a return to more protection of French industry. See, e.g., Jacques Michel Tondre, 'Les clivages apparus lors du référendum de Maastricht rythment toujours la vie politique francaise', Agence France Presse, Sept. 17, 1993 (available in LEXIS, Presse Library, AFP File).

[21] Act of September 27, 1990, Law No. 287/1990, Provisions for the Protection of Competition and the Market, Norme par la tutela della concorrenza e del mercato OJ No. 240 of 13 Oct., 1990. For commentary in English, see David C. Donald, 'Comments on the Italian Antitrust Law of October 10, 1990', 26 *Int'l Law*. 201 (1992).

[22] The various projects are listed in Vincenzo Donativi, *Introduzione della Disciplina Antitrust nel Sistema Legislativo Italiano* 2 n.3 (Milan, 1990).

[23] For discussion, see Mario Siragusa & Giuseppi Scasselati-Sforzolini, 'Italian and EC Competition Law: A New Relationship—Reciprocal Exclusivity and Common Principles', 29 *Comm. Mkt. L. Rev.* 93 (1992) and Guido Rossi, 'Control of Concentrations: The Wake of the EEC Regulation and the Debate in Italy', 1988 *Fordham Corp. L. Inst.* 28-1-21 (Barry E. Hawk, ed., New York, 1989).

market-dominating positions, and if there were no controls on the uses they made of their power, they might be tempted to exploit it to the disadvantage of consumers, potential rivals, and suppliers and purchasers.

A second such factor was the introduction of merger controls in the European Community in 1989. If Italy remained without merger controls, there was a risk that Community officials might exercise more control over mergers in Italy than if there were an Italian merger control authority, and this prospect was attractive neither to the Italian government nor to Italian industry.

The Italian statute follows Community law more closely than did its French analogue. In its §§2 and 3, for example, it basically adopts, respectively, the language of Articles 85(1) and 86 of the Rome Treaty. The objective was to create basic uniformity of substantive principles between Italian and Community law. To some extent, this uniformity may be more appearance than reality, because those provisions are general, and the real question is how they will be interpreted, but they represent at least a basic level of convergence.

Potentially significant differences appear in defining the conditions under which the new competition office could authorize exemptions from the prohibition of restrictive agreements (§4). The statute provides such authority where, for example, agreements

have the effect of improving the conditions of supply in the market, leading to substantial benefits for consumers. Such improvements shall be identified taking also into account the need to guarantee the undertaking the necessary level of international competitiveness and shall be related, in particular, with increases of production, improvements in the quality of production or distribution, or with technical and technological progress. The exemption may not permit restrictions that are not strictly necessary for the purposes of this subsection, and may not permit competition to be eliminated in a substantial part of the market.

Although this deviates from the language of Article 85(3), it basically incorporates either ideas that had appeared in the case law under that section or values that had been introduced in the Single European Act (for example, protection of international competitiveness).

The Italian legislation was being drafted at approximately the same time that the Community's Merger Control Regulation was being enacted, and this allowed the drafters to follow the basic structure of the Community regulation in their merger control provisions. They did, however, tailor the provisions to better fit the Italian context.

The institutional system created by the Act resembled the Community competition law framework, but here also there were significant modifications. Perhaps most important among them is the relative independence of the new office from political influences. A five-person 'Authority' (*Autorità*) composed of members appointed for fixed terms (seven years) is the final decision-making authority within the system. In contrast to the situation in France, for example, they may not 'exercise any professional or consultancy activities'. At least formally, therefore, they are largely protected from influence from other governmental bodies.

The Italian government quickly sought to underscore the importance of the new legislation.[24] It created the Authority and provided significant resources for its operations. One of the potential problems of establishing such an office was revealed when the government sought to make appointments to leading positions in the Authority. Because competition issues had been a relatively unimportant part of commercial law prior to enactment of the statute, few knew much about it. A small number of lawyers, who often also taught on Italian law faculties, had acquired a degree of expertise in European and international aspects of competition law, but they typically were not prepared to abandon private practice. This meant that in filling key posts, the government often had to turn to economists, even for posts that primarily involved legal issues.

Further indication of support for the new Authority was the appointment of a former Prime Minister of Italy (Giuliano Amato) as president of the Authority. He has energetically sought to make Italian companies aware of the new law and used his political popularity to underscore the importance of the new office. In its first years of operation, the Authority has focused on this informational function, and it has been cautious about the use of its powers of coercion. Whether this pattern continues remains to be seen.

F. SWEDEN IMPORTS COMMUNITY COMPETITION LAW

Sweden in 1993 went further than any other European country has gone in adapting its national competition law to that of the Community.[25] It imported virtually the entire Community competition law system. Here the texture of the interplay between the development of competition law and the process of European integration is particularly intricate.

The initial impetus for a new revision of Sweden's competition law had very little to do with what was happening in the rest of Europe.[26] Sweden was not yet even a member of the Community when the process began in 1990. The initial impetus for reform came from a desire within political circles to

[24] Much of the information on the practical problems of establishing the new Authority was provided in interviews with various officials during April, 1995, in Rome.
[25] For discussion of the new law and its background, see Ulf Bernitz, *Den Nya Konkurrenslagan* (Stockholm, 1996).
[26] I rely heavily in this section on discussions held in Stockholm in April of 1997 with Ulf Bernitz, professor of European Integration Law at the University of Stockholm, and other scholars of competition law in Sweden as well as with various members of the Swedish Competition Authority (*Konkurrensverket*).

enhance the effectiveness of Sweden's competition law and thereby strengthen competition in Sweden. Many felt that the existing system based primarily on negotiations with business leaders was not always strong enough to achieve appropriate levels of compliance.

This led to the appointment in 1990 of a parliamentary commission to study the possibility of strengthening Swedish competition law. The commission issued a report the following year in which it recommended a sharpening of the system. It proposed legislation that would prohibit additional categories of conduct rather than judge them under an 'abuse' standard and that would provide the Competition Ombudsman with additional sanctions. Under normal conditions, these proposals would probably have been enacted into legislation, perhaps with some modifications. Roughly parallel legislative processes in Norway and Finland at about the same time did lead to new legislation similar to that proposed in Sweden.

But the conditions were not 'normal' in Sweden. The 1980s had brought increasingly difficult times for Swedish industry, as the high cost of Sweden's social welfare system had burdened them with taxes that threatened their international competitiveness. By the early 1990s, the situation appeared critical. The Swedish currency had been significantly devalued, and there was a growing realization that Sweden had long lived above its means and would no longer be able to do so. The election of a Conservative government in 1991 symbolized a major change of direction in Swedish politics. The report on competition law was issued in the midst of this change of direction and the controversy it caused. For Sweden's largely export-based industries, additional 'interference' from competition law officials and additional restrictions on their capacity to 'co-operate' with each other represented a major threat to their international competitiveness, and thus Swedish industry vigorously attacked the proposed new law as a threat to its international position and thus to Sweden's effort to re-establish the prosperity to which it had become accustomed.

Yet Swedish industry had another and far more prominent objective at the time—membership in the European Union. Swedish industrial leaders were convinced that entry into the EU was critical for their success, because it would eliminate barriers to continental markets, and they were pressing hard for membership. At this point, representatives of the Conservative government saw an opportunity to play the 'EU-card' in order to accomplish the competition law reform that they were seeking. Their proposal to industrial leaders was that if industry liked 'Europe' so much, they should be willing to take the European competition law system.

This put industry leaders in a difficult situation. Their primary concern was to achieve Sweden's membership in the EU, but public support for Sweden's entry was far from solid, and during 1993 and 1994 there was a major public opinion battle over the issue. If industry refused the proposal to adopt

Community competition law, they ran the risk that this might undermine support for Sweden's entry into the Union. In the end, therefore, they supported the proposal, even though the provisions of Community law are arguably far more restrictive than those contained in the initial domestic proposals that they had rejected.

From the government's perspective, the importation of Community competition law had practical benefits. Politically, it supported the government's efforts to secure political backing for membership in the EU. There was significant resistance to membership in the Union within Sweden, and the acceptance of Community competition law signaled that the government was committed to membership. It also signaled to Community decision-makers that Sweden intended to be a committed supporter of integration.

Economic considerations were also central. Sweden's international firms wanted access to the European market, and they considered it important to have the same rules on competition in Sweden as under Community law. It was thought that by having the same rules in Swedish law, Swedish firms would have the advantage of operating under the same rules both domestically and in their European operations.

The new Swedish competition law basically incorporates substantive Community competition law into Swedish law. Not only are the two central operative provisions of the Swedish law virtually identical to Articles 85 and 86 of the Rome Treaty, but the new law contains most of the block exemptions of Community law, with only minor adaptations to adjust to the size of the Swedish market. In addition, the preparatory materials of the Swedish Act direct that interpretations of the European Court of Justice be considered authoritative in interpreting Swedish law.

The Swedish system was also restructured to conform closely to the system of Community law. The office of the Competition Ombudsman and the Price and Cartel Authority were abolished and replaced by a Competition Office (*Konkurrensverket*), which has virtually the same authority and operational principles as does the Competition Directorate of the European Commission. Appeals can be taken from action of the office to the Stockholm District Court, and further appeals can be taken to the Market Court, whose roles are now somewhat altered from those under the prior system (discussed in Chapter VI).

In one important respect, Swedish law goes beyond Community competition law (as well as other European competition laws). It established (§33) that a firm could bring an action in the regular courts for damages sustained as a result of a restraint of competition. This was apparently intended to signal the importance that the government attached to effective enforcement of the competition laws.

The system is too new to assess its general impact, but, in contrast to the situation in Italy—and to some extent in France—Sweden has a developed tradition of competition law on which it can build. The new competition office brought together some former employees of the office of the Competition Ombudsman and the Price and Cartel Authority, but, according to employees of the office, an important difference in the new authority is greater attention to juridical issues and procedures than had existed under the previous system. Above all, there is clearly both political and popular support in Sweden for increased competition.

G. RESISTING ACCOMMODATION: GERMANY AND THE UK

In the United Kingdom and Germany, efforts to move in the same direction have also acquired force during the 1990s, but the resistance to accommodation has been stronger. Many Germans have seen little reason to change what they consider to be the most effective competition law system in Europe. Such a move, they fear, would weaken competition in Germany and thereby harm the newly vulnerable German economy. The Monopoly Commission, the Federal Cartel Office, and much of the academic community have, therefore, opposed such changes.[27] Representatives of German industry have, however, mounted a major attack on the current system, arguing that the severity of German competition law puts them at a competitive disadvantage. As of this writing (summer, 1997) the government has announced that it will seek significant amendments to the GWB that will bring it somewhat closer to Community competition law.[28]

In the UK, resistance to competition law has been more political. The longstanding theme in British politics that Britain should not relinquish too much of its sovereignty to the 'continentals' has found new strength in the 1990s. To adopt a Brussels-style competition law would be seen by many as doing just that, however, and, as a result, Britain's politicians have not pursued that objective with energy. Even in Britain, however, many informed observers expect progress in that direction.[29]

---

[27] See, e.g., 'Wissenschaftler lehnen Kartellnovelle ab', *Frankfurter Allgemeine Zeitung*, Sept. 19, 1996, at 17.

[28] See 'Das Wettbewerbsgesetz wird europäischer', *Frankfurter Allegemeine Zeitung*, Mar. 21, 1997, at 18. For discussion of reform plans and their relationship to European integration, see Meinrad Dreher, 'Das deutsche Kartellrecht vor der Europäisierung', 1995 *Wirtschaft und Wettbewerb* 881 (1995).

[29] The Department of Trade and Industry in 1996 proposed, for example, a major overhaul of the system. See Department of Trade and Industry, *Tackling Cartels and the Abuse of Market Power: A Draft Bill* (London, August, 1996).

H. TOWARD A 'EUROPEAN' SYSTEM OF COMPETITION LAW?

These developments follow similar patterns of convergence toward Community competition law. The reasons vary, the deviations are sometimes significant, and there has been too little experience to assess the operations of the new systems, but the direction is obvious. In particular, it is toward a more juridical form of competition law. As we have seen, it is a process that has been operating in Europe for several decades.

The interaction of these two processes—the convergence of national competition laws and the efforts to co-ordinate national and Community competition law systems—is likely to play a central role in shaping the future of competition law in Europe. Further integration within Europe calls for an increasingly integrated system of competition law, but how will it be configured and what will its dynamics be? Will the system consist primarily of separate systems—national and Community—tied together by formal jurisdictional rules? Or will its components operate on a more closely integrated basis?

We can begin to identify some of the dimensions of the evolving set of relationships. The system's basic shape will necessarily be 'Community-centered'—that is, Community competition law will provide a center to which Member State systems are primarily related. Community competition law will be in the foreground of the development of competition law in Europe, and decisions within it and with respect to it will for that reason alone be of central importance for the operation of the system.

The distribution of jurisdictional competences will continue to constitute a key dimension of the system. 'Who has authority to do what?' will remain a prominent question. Because political decisions within EU institutions can expand and contract the Commission's jurisdictional prerogatives and the uses made of those prerogatives, political conflicts will be located along that decisional axis. Decision-makers in the Commission and in the Member States will have varying and sometimes inconsistent policy and personal objectives, and political power will be an important factor in resolving the resulting conflicts.

The Commission's power in this context will depend to a large extent on the support it receives from other EU institutions such as the courts and the Parliament and from important national constituencies (for example, segments of industry). The power of national states will derive from factors such as the degree of co-operation between Member States, the importance that national political leaders attach to competition law issues, perceptions of competition law's roles and consequences, and the objectives of a growing number of competent and often influential national competition law officials, who often believe that they can protect competition as well or better than the authorities in Brussels, and prefer expansion rather than contraction of their own roles.

The relationships between Brussels and the Member States will have another dimension that we can call 'vertical co-operation'. Its importance and shape will be defined by factors such as the extent to which decision-makers in the competition directorate and in national competition authorities perceive common interests and create institutional means for pursuing such interests. At one level, they share the common goal of protecting the process of competition from restraints, but the extent to which they will perceive common interests with regard to more specific goals and values is less clear. Forging a common intellectual and communicative base for achieving common goals will remain a major task.

'Co-operation' within this system also includes a horizontal dimension. To what extent will competition law authorities from different Member States develop co-operative relationships among themselves? This will again depend on shared perceptions of common interests and on the will and capacity of those perceiving such interests to pursue them in co-operation with each other and outside of—or even in opposition to—the vertical relationship with Brussels. A major challenge for DG IV is likely to be whether it can manage its relationships with Member State competition officials in such a way as to avoid creating incentives for Member States to define their own interests in opposition to Brussels. Put another way, the effectiveness of its 'vertical' relationships is likely to be a key factor in shaping incentives for horizontal co-operation.

The relative importance of these dimensions of a 'European' system and the degree to which the components of this system are integrated with each other will be influenced by factors that are extrinsic to competition law. Changes in membership in the EU are likely, for example, to be important in this regard—will there be new members, which ones, when will they accede to membership, and what kinds of economic and legal traditions will they bring with them?

Factors intrinsic to the system will also be important. One will be the relative success of individual components of this system. To the extent that the Community's competition law system is perceived as effective and successful, for example, it is likely to gain political support and force. Should one or another national system appear to influential decision-makers to be more effective in responding to the challenges of a particular situation, however, power within the system is likely to shift accordingly.

In assessing these issues of relative effectiveness, perceptions of comparability will play an important role. To the extent that Community competition law is perceived by Member State decision-makers as appropriate for their own circumstances, this will create incentives for them to move their own systems closer to Community law. If, however, national decision-makers pay more attention to its 'special' characteristics as the law of a transnational organization, they may be less likely to make such moves. The issue of comparability has seldom been addressed systematically or comprehensively, but if perceptions of comparability are not based on informed analysis, they will be based on haphazard and perhaps politically-motivated assumptions that are likely to lead to suboptimal policy decisions.

The relationship between national and EU competition laws is central to the process of European integration. To the extent that a co-ordinated system of Community and national competition laws is developed and is seen as effective in preventing national distortions within the 'unified' market, and in protecting against restraints of competition, this will be a major support for the process of integration. If, on the other hand, efforts to create such a system fail or should such a system not be seen as effective, the negative repercussions for the process of integration may be severe.

XI

Law, Regulation, and Competition: Europe and the Market

The idea of using law to combat restraints on competition has played important roles in Europe for more than a century. Institutions, norms, and expectations have developed around it, increasing in importance and in geographical scope until they have become a central component of European economic and legal life and a crucial factor in European integration. This process has created a legal tradition to which many countries have contributed and in which virtually all European countries now participate. More broadly, the story represents the evolution of a new field of social endeavor in Europe, a new component in the relationship between government and society.

A. THE PATH OF COMPETITION LAW IN EUROPE

The development of this tradition has been at the center of the story. A set of basic ideas has been transmitted over time and through an expanding community of political, legal, and economic actors and, sometimes, thinkers. Patterns of thought, perception, and institutional action have become increasingly cohesive, stable, and powerful. The main ideas have acquired new applications and increased political and institutional support, while often being modified in response to new ideas and pressures.

1. The mission

The perception of competition law's potential value has driven this process. Since its articulation in 1894, the idea that government *should* create norms and institutions for the purpose of protecting competition has gained favor and force in an increasing number of countries and communities and on both intellectual and institutional levels.

But why protect competition? The perception of a need to do so rests on two claims—one normative, the other economic. The first is that particular forms or levels of competition are valuable for society. This is a normative judgment and depends on the values a community applies in assessing the impact of competition. The other claim is economic—that the desired levels of competition are unlikely to be achieved unless the legal system is used to protect the competitive process. Failure to distinguish between these two claims and the justifications supporting them has often created confusion and misunderstanding in talking about competition law.

Four sets of objectives have shaped these claims in Europe. One focuses on the freedom of economic actors: protecting competition is intertwined—sometimes even equated—with protecting economic freedom, which is posited as a societal good in its own right. Part of the legacy of nineteenth century liberalism, this goal has seldom been in the foreground of European competition law discourse, but it has been part of the background of thought for both public and private decision-making. In Western Europe in the twentieth century, it has not often been fashionable to talk about economic freedom, but few have failed to recognize its significance.

At a turning point in the story, this objective also played a more prominent role. The new form of liberalism that emerged after the Second World War, most prominently in Germany, sought to reconstruct society on the basis of liberal principles and to use legal and constitutional means to protect economic freedom from disintegration and attack, and the force of those ideas was a key factor in enacting and structuring German competition law. Moreover, an important strand of German thought and scholarship has continued to emphasize the goal of economic freedom as a value in competition law decisions, and that message has often resonated with legislators and judicial decision-makers.

A second, and related, category of objectives sees competition law as a tool for achieving societal ideals. Here the question is 'What kind of society do we want and how can competition law help to achieve it?' The question and the discourse surrounding it are political and often symbolically charged. The images that have guided responses to it have typically been structural—protecting competition in order to create and maintain structures of power that are valued by the society or by communities within it.

This type of objective has not generally played a prominent role in the evolution of competition law systems in Europe, but there have been at least three notable exceptions. One relates to merger controls. Decisions to enact or strengthen merger control provisions have often been justified by reference to the need to prevent excessive concentration of economic resources and its concomitant threats to the operation of democratic political systems.

Another part of the story where this objective has been key is German competition law experience. There the element of social construction—or reconstruction—was central in creating a competition law regime after the Second World War and continuing to provide it with status and impetus. Particularly during the first two decades after that war, the need to restrain private economic power in order to achieve and preserve a democratic polity was prominent in thought relating to competition law, and this theme has continued to sound since then, albeit with decreasing urgency.

Social construction of a somewhat different sort has been an important goal of European Community competition law. Here, competition law has been seen as a tool for combating the use of private power and public authority to maintain barriers between national markets. It has been employed by the Member States to construct an economic community with particular features and structures that transcends national borders.

Justice concerns represent a third set of objectives. Particularly in the early development of the tradition, calls for the enactment of competition laws were often justified by reference to concepts of 'fairness' and 'justice'. In the turn-of-the-century debates about cartel law in Germany, for example, parties seeking political support within the new industrial proletariat portrayed competition law as a tool for assuring fairness to the 'common man', while others have sought fairness for small and medium-sized enterprises. During the 1920s, socialist and social democratic parties often called for competition law as a means of achieving fairness for organized labor. And in the major expansion of competition law after the Second World War, such social justice concerns were often heard and sometimes played important roles.

Explicit reference to these traditional 'social justice' concerns has become weaker during recent decades, but the issues remain. In some countries, for example, the political rhetoric surrounding competition law decisions often still refers to the need to provide equitable treatment to small and medium-sized enterprises, who are seen as unfairly disadvantaged in their efforts to compete with larger firms and thus to survive. Justice concerns also refer to purchasers, but here the referent has subtly shifted during the last quarter century. Whereas it traditionally tended to be seen in 'class' terms (for example, the class of 'workers') it now increasingly refers to individuals in their roles as *consumers*. This often barely perceptible shift has been important because it has provided a locus for the interpenetration of traditional 'leftist' discourse with a more economics-oriented discourse appealing to the center and the right of the political spectrum.

Economic policy objectives constitute the fourth, and most broadly influential, category. Politicians and bureaucrats have frequently made competition law decisions in pursuit of specific economic policy objectives. Particularly in parliamentary systems of government, legislative and administrative elites have created systems which they have themselves managed or controlled, and which they have fashioned in light of their own political and policy objectives.

The most prominent economic policy aim has been to counter inflation. Governments have often enacted, strengthened and shaped competition law with the express intent of thereby counteracting inflationary pressures. In some cases (for example, France, Norway, and Denmark) competition law was until recently understood as ancillary to price control objectives, and in virtually all countries those objectives have played a significant role. The prominence of price reduction objectives has often, therefore, shaped the thought and institutions of European competition law.

Competition law has also been used as a tool for achieving 'economic progress'. It has frequently been understood as a means of eliminating or reducing barriers to economic change and development. The notion has been that the inflexibility of existing economic relationships—both vertical and horizontal—has impeded economic improvement and that competition law can be used to reduce those impediments. This goal has perhaps been most clearly articulated in Sweden, but it has also been part of the discourse in countries such as France and in the European Union.

An associated theme relates to international competitiveness. Politicians and bureaucrats have used competition law to foster the capacity of domestic firms to compete internationally. The basic image has been that competition spurs rationalization and efficiency among domestic firms and, therefore, that combating restraints on domestic competition is likely to increase the capacity of firms to succeed in international competition. In both Germany and Sweden, for example, this has often been a key element in justifying competition law decisions. The persistent motif in European economic policy discourse that European firms are not strong enough to meet foreign competition has nurtured this theme.

Notably marginal has been the goal of economic efficiency that has come to be widely accepted as the central—even exclusive—goal of US antitrust law during the last two decades. That language adopts the abstract vocabulary of micro-economic theory and sees antitrust as a tool for directing resources to their 'highest and best use' and thus benefiting society in general and the consumer in particular. Europeans have not generally received it well. Decision-makers have shown little inclination to view the goals of competition law in these terms. In part, this is because more concrete price-restraint aims have obviated the need for such abstract and indirect approaches to the problem. Perhaps more importantly, the abstract economic language of wealth-maximization does not comport easily with other goals or with administrative discretion, and a multiplicity of goals pursued by informed officials has been considered an essential feature of European competition law systems.

2. Substantive scope

If we look to the substantive scope of these systems—the range of conduct subject to competition law norms—the pattern has been one of expansion. They have dealt with an ever broader range of restraints and problems. Before the 1970s, for example, controls on mergers were rare, but since then most systems have expanded to include them. Such expansion has sometimes been a result of legislative decisions, but competition law institutions have also expanded the scope of competition law by applying existing principles to additional forms of conduct. Abuse of a dominant position, for example, was typically interpreted narrowly and used little in the early years of national competition law systems, but the range of conduct to which it applies has been significantly expanded.

Although this pattern of expansion is found in all systems, starting points have varied. In Germany, the initial focus of the GWB was, for example, to combat the harms associated with cartels, and it expanded from there to include vertical restraints and mergers. In contrast, the countries that created administrative control systems during the decade and a half after the Second World War usually began with an emphasis on vertical restraints, and then gradually turned more attention to horizontal agreements and mergers.

This mixture of objectives and substantive concerns has yielded competition law systems that are multivalent and a discourse of competition law that is multilayered, with a relatively high tolerance of ambiguity. There has been little attempt to pursue the narrowing and winnowing of goals that has been pursued in the United States. US critics of European competition law systems have often complained of the problems caused by this complexity, but it has been an integral component of the development of competition law in Europe.

3. The tools of competition law

The basic European conception of how to combat restraints of competition has changed little in almost a century. Its core idea is that an informed bureaucracy should be given authority to take particular kinds of action against harmful or 'abusive' conduct, and a degree of guidance about the standards to apply in exercising that authority. The bureaucracy is at the center of virtually all European competition law systems, with private suits for enforcement either excluded or available only under highly restricted circumstances.

This choice of means rests on the epistemological assumption that knowledge of the likely consequences of particular forms of conduct is insufficient to justify either vigorous enforcement of specific prohibitions or the application of abstract substantive norms by ordinary courts. Accordingly, administrators are given significant discretion to evaluate harm in the circumstances of a specific case. They typically have the authority to negotiate, to compromise, and to fashion responses appropriate to the varied aims of the law and the economic policy framework in which it operates. This conception of competition law is legitimized, in part, by governmental and bureaucratic traditions that carry expectations about how government officials will exercise such discretion.

Choices relating to institutional tools are intertwined with claims concerning conceptual tools. The institutional framework tends to call for relatively broad concepts that relate to the effects of conduct rather than their characterization and that give administrators significant discretion in applying them. This helps explain the central role of the concept of abuse in European competition law systems. It fits the controlling epistemological assumptions and institutional arrangements because it tends not to label broad abstract categories of conduct as violations. The focus tends to be contextual, constraining conduct by economically powerful firms where such conduct has particular consequences.

This focus is also consistent with the emphasis in such systems on flexibility and on 'constructive' and 'co-operative' responses to the problems created by restraints on competition. The claim is that such a system allows administrators to adapt their responses to the broader policy needs of the situation. This, in turn, permits administrators to secure a measure of co-operation from the business community that they would not receive if their 'enforcement' activity were perceived as repressive rather than creative and constructive.

Another important component of this image of the tools of competition law is that competition law is 'special' and that it requires institutional arrangements that conform to its special role and reflect its special circumstances. In contrast to the US, for example, which has relied on pre-existing concepts and institutional forms—such as, for example, ordinary courts—to protect the competitive process, European legislators have typically designed institutions and procedures specifically for competition law. The most prominent examples here are the many specialized courts that include industry and consumer representatives and operate according to specialized procedures.

Despite the centrality of administrative decision-making in European competition law systems, the tendency in virtually all such systems has been to increase their juridical characteristics—to 'juridify' them. Legislatures have increased the independence of at least some decision-makers from political and economic influence; competition law institutions have acquired and developed methods and procedures increasingly akin to those of courts; and emphasis on the transparency and predictability of decisional outcomes has grown.

The impetus for these developments has varied. Germany embraced a more juridical form of competition law in response to the perceived need to construct a more democratic society, whereas in the United Kingdom, juridification has often been spurred by the perceived need to reduce the political element in administrative decision-making. The process also reflects a perception that juridical elements tend to make competition law systems more 'effective' or at least less susceptible to popular criticism.

The evolution of competition law in the European Community has followed a somewhat different pattern. There, as we have seen, the competition law system was infused with juridical elements early in its development, and the European Court of Justice boldly developed the opportunities that they provided. In recent years, however, political and policy elements in the system have tended to become stronger, arguably at the expense of juridical ones.

As juridical elements have been introduced into competition law systems and they have faced increasingly complex economic problems, the systems themselves have become broader and more complex. Whereas at their inception such systems often represented little more than the decisions of a single bureaucratic institution, with little involvement from other communities or institutions, they have tended to become multi-faceted systems in which not only administrators play important roles, but courts, scholars, and legislators as well.

4. Discourse

The language of these systems has been predominantly pragmatic. In general, it has developed not as a result of scholarly exploration of the subject, but in the course of meeting the practical needs of legislators, administrators and, to some extent, private legal practitioners. With administrators and often lay persons in key decision-making positions, language itself has been accorded less weight in the operation of these systems than it typically would have in more juridical settings.

Little influenced by theoretical considerations and with minimal influence from academics, the language of competition law has generally followed what I call a high/low abstraction pattern. One level utilizes general, vague terms such as 'abuse' and 'public interest', while a second level is highly particularistic and fact specific. Except in Germany, there has been little use of intermediate concepts that structure and organize relations between higher and lower levels of abstraction. The development of such structuring concepts generally occurs only where an academic community invests significant resources into such a process. In Europe, this has often occurred in private law, but seldom in competition law.

Germany again presents an important exception. There a sizeable and high-status community of legal scholars has invested heavily in developing a conceptual apparatus for representing and analyzing competition law issues. As a result, the language of German competition law is more structured and theoretical than elsewhere in Europe. This tends to increase analytical capacities within the competition law community, but it can also impede communication between those who use the language and those who do not, and some view its very elaborateness as an impediment to effectiveness.

5. The scope and cohesion of the tradition

This set of ideas, expectations, and images regarding competition law has become increasingly well-defined during the second half of the twentieth century. Driven by common political and policy concerns and structured by common intellectual and political perspectives, it has become an identifiable 'model' of competition law in which objectives, assumptions, institutional arrangements and language are integrally related.

The tradition that has grown around this model and nurtured its development has also become increasingly cohesive. Primarily as a consequence of the development of Community competition law and its impact on Member States, competition law systems have become increasingly similar. Many differences in detail remain, but as European systems adopt features of Community law and borrow from each other in other ways, the similarities become more pronounced. Even the patterns of change within these systems—for example, toward the inclusion of juridical elements—have the same basic shape.

Finally, the geographical scope of the tradition has expanded impressively. The initial core ideas spread from Austria and Germany, and in the 1920s they became part of a common European conception of competition law which was then enacted into law in the decades after the Second World War. These ideas informed the creation and development of the competition law of the European Community, and Community competition law has, in turn, expanded its influence through an ever wider group of states. Even the states of Eastern Europe have drawn on that model as they have included competition law in their efforts to create market economies and liberal polities.

B. SHAPING THE STORY

What kinds of factors have shaped this story? Which conflicts have sculpted its features? What have been the impulses for development and change? We can hazard some generalizations about its dynamics, again focusing on decisions as the basic 'stuff' of analysis and asking how the interaction of texts, patterns of thought, institutions and communities—the system of competition law—influences those decisions.

Our concern here is with the dynamics of competition law systems, but it is important to note the 'givens'—or external circumstances—that have influenced decision-making. 'Big events' such as war and depression have, for example, played conspicuous roles in the competition law story. World War I created the conditions for enacting the first competition law in the sense used here; the depression of the 1930s crushed the movement toward competition law that had been gathering force in the late 1920s; and the Second World War brought in its wake a wave of competition legislation. The disruptions of war and depression have often undermined political and intellectual resistance to normative controls on economically powerful firms and changed perceptions of the proper relationship between the state and the economy.

Other external factors such as country size, economic prosperity, political stability, and the structures of international trade have played less dramatic, but no less influential roles. An example illustrates some of the issues. In a small, politically stable economy whose borders are open to international competition, competition law is likely to have very different political and economic ramifications and face very different problems than it would in a large, politically unstable country whose economy is protected by high tariffs. The diversities among EU countries in regard to these factors make the similarities among competition law systems particularly striking.

These similarities suggest the influence of a common set of ideas, ideals, and experiences on the development of competition law. As we seek patterns in the data, we focus on the perceived interests of institutions, individuals, and communities, but we use a broad concept of 'interests' that recognizes the role of factors such as ideas, images, and the social location of knowledge in shaping the perception of interests.

1. Enacting and strengthening competition laws

In Europe, decisions about whether to enact or strengthen competition laws (including the specific targets of competition law) have frequently been driven by political organizations—more so than has been the case in the United States since the early years of antitrust law. Political parties have enacted and strengthened competition laws in order to win votes, sometimes by appealing directly to the interests of particular constituencies, sometimes by following policies expected to be viewed as beneficial for the society as a whole.

Support for the competition law project has come from two basic sources. One includes parties seeking to represent the interests of workers and/or consumers. The most politically powerful of these have been socialist and social democratic parties, with occasional assistance from parties with religious affiliations such as the German Center party in the early decades of the century. While leftist parties have generally represented more voters than other parties supporting competition law, their support has seldom been intense and committed. Particularly in the early years of competition law development, for example, their support was weakened by the allegiance of some party leaders to the notion that concentration should be encouraged because it represented a step in the direction of an 'organized' and, therefore, potentially socialist economy. As the ideology of socialist parties abandoned that notion (some beginning in the 1920s, others in the 1950s or later) their support for competition law became somewhat more focused, but competition as a value does not fit easily with the rhetoric of left-oriented parties, and, as a result, they have generally contributed little to articulating arguments in support of competition law.

The other major category of parties that has supported competition law includes 'liberal' parties and 'liberal wings' of conservative parties. Typically representing the professions, the upper middle classes, and small and medium-sized businesses, they have generally been far smaller than leftist parties, but their support has tended to be more focused and committed. Competition law symbolizes liberal ideology, and in some cases it has been a major concern of key constituencies such as small and medium-sized industries. Since at least the end of the Second World War, therefore, liberals have provided most of the literature on competition law, and liberal economists, lawyers and bureaucrats as 'experts' have strongly influenced competition law thinking.

This combination of political support from left-oriented parties with the articulation of competition law goals and values by liberals—that is, from a very different part of the political spectrum—explains much about the shape of European competition law systems. It has contributed to both the multi-layered discourse of competition law and the multiplicity of its aims. In addition, it has favored an administrative conception of competition law in which language is required to bear less weight than it must bear in more juridical systems, and, therefore, ambiguities and value conflicts create fewer or at least less obvious problems.

Predictably, opposition to competition law has typically come from parties associated with big business and/or organized business. For them, the issue has been to avoid constraints on the decisional prerogatives of their constituencies. The political weight of that interest has, however, varied. The greater a country's reliance on the international competitiveness of its industries, for example, and the closer the ties between business and political elites, the more weight the industry position has tended to have. In some cases (for example, Sweden), however, close ties between industry and administrators have led to voluntary co-operation between the two communities that appears to have constrained anticompetitive conduct.

In Germany, the pattern has been different, and the differences may help to explain the force of competition law there. A key factor during the early development of German competition law was the committed support and institutional power of one wing of the ruling conservative party (the Christian Democratic Union). Drawing on the moral capital associated with the rhetoric of the social market economy and on the political capital associated with its success, this group provided a powerful impetus for competition law, and its location within a party that also represents big business interests may have blunted the opposition of organized business. Moreover, the concept of the social market economy created ties to many leaders in the Social Democratic Party who recognized the potential political force of these ideas with their constituencies and began early to support the competition law project.

Government bureaucrats have generally had little impact on decisions regarding the enactment of competition laws. The general tendency (for example, in France in the decades after World War II and in turn-of-the-century Germany) has been for the central administration to see in competition law a threat to its *dirigiste* prerogatives, and this has often led them not to welcome competition laws or to seek competition law systems in which this loss of control is minimized.

Bureaucrats have played a more significant role with regard to decisions concerning the strength of competition law systems. With the creation of administrative control systems, administrators have tended to become the chief 'experts' on competition. They have been viewed, at least within government, as the primary repositories of judgment and information on the operation of such systems, and thus they have generally headed the committees and commissions that have written the reports on which subsequent legislation has been based. Not surprisingly, they have tended to favor the strengthening of such systems. In recent years, the growing influence of Community competition law has created additional incentives for national bureaucrats to strengthen their own systems in order to protect their prerogatives, influence, and jobs against incursions from Brussels' 'Eurocrats'.

Economists have also influenced this category of decisions. The orthodoxies of economists have fashioned views of the economic process, in general, and competition, in particular, and these have often shaped competition law decisions. To the extent that economists have demonstrated, for example, the benefits of competition and the probability that firms will restrain competition, they have fostered the competition law project.

The impact of economics communities has depended, in part, on their social status and cohesion as well as on their relationships with political, legal, and bureaucratic decision-makers. For example, the relatively high status of economists in Sweden, particularly during the middle decades of the century, assured awareness of competition issues within a political discourse that might otherwise have paid little heed to such issues. The ties between economists and lawyers have been particularly important. In general, the closer the relationships between these two communities, the greater has been the influence of economists on competition law development. The role of close ties between economists and lawyers in the development of ordoliberal thought and influence provides a prime example.

2. Fashioning the tools

A different mix of forces has influenced decisions about the tools to be used in combating restraints of competition. In contrast to decisions about enacting and strengthening competition laws, such 'how' or 'modality' decisions have seldom had symbolic value for political parties, and thus they have had little incentive to pay attention to them. These decisions have generally been made by 'experts'—bureaucrats, professors, designated party functionaries, and business representatives. During the shaping of the German competition statute, 'how' issues had a higher symbolic value because of the prominence of the cartel issue and its association with the tragedy of Nazism, but such high profile situations have been rare.

The characteristics of these 'expert' groups have varied greatly, but bureaucrats have generally played the central roles within them. Perceiving little political benefit (and potential harm) in concerning themselves with such issues, political decision-makers generally have been willing to rely on the bureaucrats operating such systems to evaluate their effectiveness, assess the need for change, and propose solutions to perceived problems.

If we look at the concerns expressed by these groups and the explanations they have given for their decisions, two themes are prominent. One is the need to protect domestic (or, in the case of Community competition law, European) industry and thus to develop competition law tools that deter competitive restraints without significantly restraining business decision-making. The other is the conflict between the need to provide certainty and guidance for business decision-making, which tends to favor juridical components in the system, and the need for flexibility and co-operation between government and business, which tends to favor administrative solutions.

Several basic images of competition law have influenced these decisions about the modalities of competition law. Most prominent has been the image that competition law is a policy instrument to be wielded by administrative decision-makers with high levels of discretion. This was the initial conception of competition law in Europe, and it has only gradually surrendered its dominant influence. Its hold on competition law thought and practice derives not only from its temporal primacy, but also on the benefits it provides for politicians, bureaucrats, and business communities.

A second image that has influenced 'how' decisions is the administrative-juridical hybrid often associated with German competition law. The process of juridification to which we have often referred reflects the growing strength of a more juridical conception of competition law in which articulated norms are interpreted and applied according to juridical methods by institutions with substantial protection from political and economic influence. In Europe, the German competition law system has represented this type of system, and the successes of the German economy and its competition law system during the 1960s, 1970s, and 1980s drew much attention to this model.

During the 1980s European Community competition law also became an important model for these decisions. As we have seen, Member States (and others) have enacted competition laws or modified existing laws in order to bring them closer to Community law. The influence of this model has been primarily in the context of decisions about substantive norms, the issue most commonly discussed being emulation of the conceptual structure of Article 85. Here the force of the model rests primarily on the political and economic advantages of being similar to Community competition law rather than on the intrinsic merits of the model itself.

Finally, the US model of antitrust law has influenced such decisions—sometimes in a positive sense, sometimes as a foil or counterimage. Particularly in the early development of thinking about competition law in Europe, US antitrust law was primarily a negative image. It was often portrayed as a haphazard, ineffective means of reaching competition law goals, and arguments favoring an administrative control model were often supported by reference to the 'folly' of US antitrust. After the Second World War, the image of US antitrust law changed for the better. Since then, the image of antitrust has been generally positive, and it has undoubtedly encouraged the general tendency toward more juridical systems. There has, however, been little positive reference to the specific techniques or modalities of US antitrust law, which have generally been viewed as inappropriate for European circumstances.

The evolution of ideas about how competition law should operate can be seen in the relative status of these respective 'models'. In the early development of the tradition, for example, the negative image of US antitrust helped make the administrative control model more attractive, because it was seen as avoiding the mistakes of the US antitrust law. During the last decade, the European competition law model has led to its emulation by Member States.

3. Achieving compliance

How have the tools worked? One lesson of the story is that in talking about compliance issues in Europe it is important to use a wide-angle lens. To limit the inquiry to the narrower issue of 'enforcement' would distort the narrative, precisely because those systems have been premised in varying degrees on the assumption that co-operation and persuasion rather than coercion and confrontation should be the primary tools for inducing compliance. As a practical matter, generally weak enforcement tools and cautious political backing have required that competition law officials emphasize persuasion and compromise rather than confrontation with business decision-makers.

Because most European competition law systems rely almost exclusively on bureaucrats for achieving compliance—rather than, for example, private suits—the degree of commitment of such administrators to the objectives of competition law has been critical to compliance efforts. Here factors such as administrative traditions, the status and training of upper level bureaucrats, their values and ideals, and their economic, political and sometimes social ties to business elites have played key roles.

The degree of commitment and effectiveness of competition law administrators has often, perhaps always, been conditioned by relationships between competition law and economic policy traditions and institutions. Bureaucrats are unlikely to develop commitment to competition law objectives where the bureaucracy in which they are located provides little support for competition law and pursues inconsistent goals such as economic interventionism. In most situations (other than postwar Germany) administrative traditions and economic policy pressures have tended to impede such commitment. In France, for example, bureaucratic traditions, structures, and incentives have tended to favor industrial policy controls over the economy rather than reliance on competition law tools, but such resistance has noticeably weakened over the last two decades. The strength of interventionist traditions in many European countries undoubtedly has been a factor inhibiting the development of commitment to competition law objectives.

Relationships between administrators and business leaders have also been a key to the success of compliance efforts. In many countries, close relations between higher level bureaucrats and leading business decision-makers have generated a degree of co-operation which has led to at least a modicum of voluntary compliance with competition law objectives. Such relationships tend to be based on mutual understanding and trust as well as on shared backgrounds, values, and interests (including, often, a degree of nationalism). This type of 'community interest' between administrators and business leaders has tended to be more prominent in smaller countries such as Sweden and the Netherlands than in larger ones. It also represents an important difference between Community and national competition laws, because EU administrators cannot have this type of co-operative, trust-based relationship with the many business communities of the EU.

The impact of these factors is ultimately conditioned by the discourse of competition law. The capacity to influence business decision-makers as well as the commitment of bureaucrats to that task are enhanced where that discourse contains clear articulations of the goals, principles and means of competition law that acquire symbolic force, and where that discourse is technically sophisticated enough to relate these larger ideas to specific interests and to facilitate communication about them. The impact of ordoliberalism in Germany has been tied, for example, to its capacity to provide and structure such a discourse.

C. THE STORY AND ITS USES

My central aim in this book has been to tell the 'story' (one version of it, to be sure) of competition law in Europe and to contribute insights into how and why it has taken the shape it has. This story calls for a fundamental re-thinking of existing images of European competition law experience. Those images evolved on the basis of facile and sometimes politically motivated assumptions and against the background of national and ideological rivalries, and they often contain serious and potentially dangerous distortions.

First, and perhaps most important, we have seen that there IS a competition law story in Europe! In the prevailing image of European experience with competition law, there is no narrative that relates the experiences of individual European states to each other and to the competition law experience of the European Community. These experiences are assumed to be basically separate and unrelated. Jealousies, suspicion, and resentment have created a perspective on competition law in which it has been uncommon both to look beyond the borders of one's own system and to acknowledge continuities with earlier decisions and institutions. These experiences have, however, been increasingly intertwined throughout the twentieth century, and, as we have seen, viewing them as part of that story is a valuable means of interpreting and understanding them.

Second, there IS a competition law tradition. In current images, there is little awareness of the extent to which European competition law systems share fundamental characteristics and participate in a common 'European' experience. Our traversal of this experience reveals, however, that there is a set of core ideas, perceptions, and expectations that is common to virtually all European competition law systems and that can be seen as a European 'model' of competition law. This model has been transmitted over time, being gradually modified in the process, and its transmission has generated a tradition that has become increasingly cohesive and inclusive, especially during the last two decades.

Third, the story reveals that competition law in Europe is fundamentally *European*. The widespread assumption that competition law in Europe is a US import, a weak form of US antitrust law that was imported from—or, worse yet, imposed by—the US after the Second World War may be understandable, but it radically misrepresents European experience. Competition law in Europe is based primarily on ideas developed by European thinkers and decision-makers in response to European conditions, and it has spread through Europe along indigenous channels rather than through emulation of US antitrust law. US experience has sometimes provided specific ideas for European experts, and for some two decades after the Second World War it encouraged European efforts to enact and strengthen competition laws, but US experience has not provided the central impetus for the major developments that have structured European competition law, nor have European competition law systems been modeled to any significant degree on it.

Another misconception is that European competition law systems represent 'pure' bureaucratic regulation, created for and by bureaucrats for the purpose of controlling economic conduct and with little, if any, popular support. The predominance of administrative elements in European competition law systems has fostered such assumptions, but the dynamic is far more complex. The impetus for major decisions regarding competition law has often been popular pressure, frequently deriving from concerns about fairness to workers, consumers, and small and medium-sized enterprises. Such pressures have often been encouraged, channeled and carried by popular political parties using the rhetoric of fairness and exploitation to frame the issue in ways likely to provide political benefits.

The failure to recognize this aspect of the European competition law history is explained, at least in part, by intellectual, social, and political divisions and animosities between 'bourgeois' parties and traditions (whether liberal or conservative) on the one hand, and socialist and social democratic parties, on the other. These animosities have often obscured the extent to which in this context the values, interests, and objectives of the two groups have been interrelated. Lawyers, economists, and publicists from the 'bourgeois' group have provided most of the literature about competition law in Europe, and they have naturally tended to pay little heed to the roles played by their ideological rivals. It is a potentially serious distortion, however, because that intermingling of values and that interplay of political forces explains much about competition law in Europe.

1. Policy implications

Reducing distortions in existing images of European competition law experience may have potentially important policy implications, because policy decisions are based on assumptions contained in those images. If it is assumed, for example, that competition law in Europe is not 'rooted' in Europe, but was imposed from the outside, or that competition law represents little more than *ad hoc* bureaucratic 'policy' decisions, this may reduce political support for such systems and the decisions taken within them. If it is recognized, however, that competition law in Europe has often been imbedded in the democratic movements that have created modern European states, the likelihood of political support for that project can be expected to increase.

Another example involves assumptions about the dynamics of development of the various European systems and their role in current debates about the relationship between Community competition law and national competition laws. If it is assumed that European competition law systems do not share basic characteristics and patterns of development, for example, this may tend to strengthen the argument that competition law should be centralized in Brussels because the differences would render ineffective a more decentralized system. If, however, European competition law systems are recognized as sharing fundamental characteristics, values, and experiences, that argument loses some of its force. Moreover, to the extent that national decision-makers recognize that they have similar perspectives and often similar experiences regarding competition law, they are likely to be more willing to operate within a decentralized system, because they will have more confidence in their capacity to understand the factors that are driving decisions in other parts of the system.

Awareness of structural affinities between European competition law systems and of shared developmental patterns also has implications for the political legitimacy of the process of European integration. For many, the lack of direct political influence on Community institutions (other than the European Parliament) is a major obstacle to increasing the authority of Community institutions. If competition law is perceived as an imposed or imported legal regime that has had little popular backing, it is not likely to contribute to the political legitimacy of the integration project. When it is realized, however, that there is a competition law tradition in Europe that has often reflected political support from many points in the political spectrum, and that it can be seen as the product of a long struggle to protect consumers from 'exploitation' and society from harms caused by economically powerful firms and arrangements among firms, competition law helps to 'legitimize' the integration project.

2. Beyond Europe

This story should also have particular relevance for two groups outside Europe. One includes those who are evaluating the potential benefits and harms of using competition law for their own purposes and deciding how to shape their own competition law systems. For them, this story greatly enriches the narrative basis for studying and assessing competition law decisions. The assumption that European competition law systems are disparate, dissimilar, and unrelated has tended to deter analysis of those experiences.

This has left US experience as the central optic through which others have viewed the phenomenon of competition law. Particularly because of the depth, breadth, and linguistic accessibility of its literature, and its practical importance for large numbers of foreign lawyers, business people, and government decision-makers, it is the competition law experience that is most commonly known and referred to. Yet the uniqueness of US experience may also make it a poor basis for generalizing about competition law. It is only one story, and assessment of competition law as a social project requires at least two stories from which to view the phenomenon. At the very least, our story suggests that the tapestry of competition law experience has been far denser and richer than some who focus entirely on US experience might believe.

The group whose perspective is most constrained by the centrality of US experience may, however, consist of those imbedded within it. US lawyers, policy-makers, and academics tend to pay little attention to European experience with competition law, but our story reveals that to do so is to disregard much that can be of value in decision-making in the United States. Operating on the basis of many of the same values underlying US antitrust law and responding to many of the same problems, Europeans have developed quite different strategies for protecting interests often thought to deserve protection in the US.

D. PROSPECTS FOR COMPETITION LAW IN EUROPE

Competition law in twentieth century Europe has been a success in the sense that competition law systems have gained increasing recognition, force, and status, but as we near the end of the century its future is clouded. The project of using law to protect the process of competition is firmly enough established: it has become part of the identity of the polity in Europe—part of what European governments do. The uncertainty relates instead to the issues of how much to 'protect' that process, with what tools, and who should decide.

In one scenario, European competition law continues on the path that it has generally followed in this century—a path of gains in importance, status, and sophistication. Yet it is not difficult to imagine a rather different future. Perhaps competition law's trajectory is at or near its apogee. The future may see its gains eroded, and competition law systems may remain—or revert to being—marginal factors on the economic and political landscape.

Much is likely to depend on the relationship of competition law to the projects that have propelled its development. Where those projects continue to have appeal and to support competition law's aims, competition law systems are likely to fare well. To the extent that they lose force or their relationship to competition law changes, the trajectory of competition law may be less favorable.

The liberal project that emblazoned the ideal of freedom under law on European consciousness in the nineteenth century has nurtured and shaped the development of competition law, but its shape may be changing, and its vitality may not be reliable. In recent years, the traditional symbiosis of law and economic freedom has begun to fray at the edges, as some have focused solely on freedom from governmental interference and disregarded the integrative capacity of law. To the extent that the focus of the liberal tradition changes, its relationship to competition law will also change.

No less important for competition law has been the regulatory project of European national governments. Encouraged by wars and crises, and nurtured by administrative traditions, European governments in the twentieth century have sought to 'control', and bureaucrats have been given broad authority to guide social development. Yet confidence in the capacity of government officials to perform this task effectively has waned in recent decades, and on a continent in which bureaucrats are faced with the enormous task of creating an architecture of political integration, this may be a portentous development.

The relationship between competition law and the project of European integration is central in other ways as well. Competition law has been a motor of integration, and that role has given it status and recognition. As we have seen, however, the role of competition law in the EU may also be changing. Its utility in overcoming obstacles to integration may no longer be as great as it has been, and to the extent that it is perceived as less important to the integration project, political commitment to it may wane. In addition, conflicts over decentralization and the extension of membership in the EU to additional countries with little experience of competition law may weaken its force.

The competition law project also faces new challenges, most prominently the growing globalization of economic activity, which some see as undermining the role of competition law. If markets are international, they claim, individual firms will seldom have monopoly power, and cartels will be difficult to arrange and enforce. International competition will, therefore, obviate the need for competition law. In its strong form, this claim is difficult to support, because it disregards the harms that can be wrought on the extensive and innumerable markets that are not subject to international competition and underestimates the growing capacity of firms to achieve economic power *on* international markets and thus restrict competition on such markets. Nevertheless, globalization undoubtedly reduces the role of national boundaries in shaping markets and confronts national and regional competition law decision-makers with new analytical issues and jurisdictional problems.

This process is also likely to strengthen the political force of business opponents of competition law, who have frequently argued that any government 'interference' with the scope of decisional authority of national firms will harm their capacity to compete internationally. As globalization continues and unemployment concerns in Europe grow, that argument may gain strength and become attractive in an increasing number of situations. Moreover, as firms grow ever larger in order to compete in the international arena, their capacity to influence national and Community decision-makers is likely to increase.

This globalization of economic activity may also challenge competition law in Europe by shifting the focus of response to competition problems from the national and regional levels to the international level. If restraints on the competitive process are created by conduct that stretches beyond the borders of existing national and regional competences, the responses may increasingly have to be international. The probable future shape of any such development remains unclear, but to the extent that it does occur, it may divert attention and energy from national and regional competition law projects.

The impact of these changing economic and political circumstances on the force and form of competition law will be determined, in the end, by how competition and competition law are perceived. To the extent that competition law is viewed as a constructive social process that provides value for society or for those in society who have either the political power to secure protection or whose protection is deemed worthy of protection, it is likely to enjoy continued support. To the extent, on the other hand, that it is viewed as 'regulation'—unnecessary and possibly harmful bureaucratic interference with business decisions—resistance to its role is likely to increase.

The European competition law tradition took shape in the midst of profound ambivalence toward the process of competition, and uncertainty about the social roles of competition has been its frequent companion. The idea of protecting competition has gained stature and prominence amidst social values and economic and political forces that have often been cautious about the process to be protected. As a result, the protection of competition in Europe has been and is likely to remain multi-layered and often ambivalent, and therein may lie an important reason for better understanding it. Europeans have long recognized the importance of competition, and they have developed strategies for protecting it—in light of the traditions and ideals that have created modern Europe and according to emerging concepts of what it means to be European.

Bibliography

Abraham, David, *The Collapse of the Weimar Republic: Political Economy and Crisis* (2d. ed., New York, 1986)

Adams, William J., *Restructuring the French Economy: Government and the Rise of Market Competition since World War II* (Washington, D.C., 1989)

Adams, William J. & Christian Stoffaës, eds., *French Industrial Policy* (Washington, D.C., 1986)

Af Trolle, Ulf, *Studier i Konkurrensfilosofi och Konkurrenslagstiftning* (Gothenburg, 1963)

Aldcroft, Derek H., *From Versailles to Wall Street: 1919–1929* (Berkeley, 1977)

Allen, G. C., *Monopoly and Restrictive Practices* (London, 1968)

Alsmoeller, Horst, *Wettbewerbspolitische Ziele und Kooperationstheoretische Hypothesen im Wander der Zeit* (Tübingen, 1982)

Ambrosius, Gerold, *Die Durchsetzung der sozialen Marktwirtschaft in Westdeutschland 1945–1949* (Stuttgart, 1977)

Ambrosius, Gerold & William H. Hubbard, *A Social and Economic History of Twentieth-Century Europe* (Keith Tribe & William H. Hubbard, trs., Cambridge, Mass., 1989)

Andersen, Kristen, *Rettens Stilling til Konkurranseregulerende sammenslutninger og avtaler: En oversikt over Norsk og Fremmed Rett* (Oslo, 1937)

Arndt, Helmut, *Markt und Macht* (2d. ed., Tübingen, 1973)

—— *Wirtschaftliche Macht* (3d. ed., Munich, 1980)

Anderson, Eugene N. & Pauline R., *Political Institutions and Social Change in Continental Europe in the Nineteenth Century* (Berkeley, 1967)

Arbeitskreis Kartellgesetz, ed., *10 Jahre Kartellgesetz 1958–1968: Eine Würdigung aus der Sicht der deutschen Industrie* (Bergisch Gladbach, 1968)

Azema, Jacques, *Le Droit Francais de La Concurrence* (2d. ed., Paris, 1989)

Ball, George W., *The Past Has Another Pattern: Memoirs* (New York, 1982)

Baltl, Hermann, *Österreichische Rechtsgeschichte* (6th ed., Graz, 1986)

Baltzarek, Franz, 'Franz Klein als Wirtschafts- und Sozialpolitiker', in *Franz Klein: Leben und Wirken* 173–81 (Herbert Hofmeister, ed., Vienna, 1988)

Barkin, Kenneth D., *The Controversy over German Industrialization 1890–1902* (Chicago, 1970)

Barnikel, Hans-Heinrich, ed., *Theorie und Praxis der Kartelle* (Darmstadt, 1972)

Barnikel, Hans-Heinrich, 'Kartelle in Deutschland. Entwicklung, theoretische Ansätze und rechtliche Regelungen', in *Theorie und Praxis der Kartelle* (Hans-Heinrich Barnikel, ed., Darmstadt, 1972)

Barre, Raymond, 'L'Analyse économique au service de la Science et de la Politique Économique', 8 *Critique* 331–46 (1952)

—— 'Quelques Aspects de la Regulation du Pouvoir Économique', *Revue Économique* 912–24 (1958)

Barzun, Jacques, *Darwin, Marx und Wagner: Critique of a Heritage* (2d. ed., New York, 1958)

Baum, Warren C., *The French Economy and the State* (Princeton, 1958)

Baums, Theodor, *Kartellrecht in Preussen: Von der Reformära zur Gründerkrise* (Tübingen, 1990)

Baur, Jürgen, *Der Missbrauch im deutschen Kartellrecht* (Tübingen, 1972)

Bebr, Gerhard, 'The European Coal and Steel Community: A Political and Legal Innovation', 63 *Yale L. Rev.* 1–43 (1953)

Bechtold, Rainer & Werner Kleinmann, *Kommentar zur Fusionskontrolle* (2d. ed., Heidelberg, 1989)

Becker, Helmut, *Die Soziale Frage im Neoliberalismus* (Heidelberg, 1965)

Becker, Julius, *Das deutsche Manchestertum* (Karlsruhe, 1907)

Behlke, Reinhard, *Der Neoliberalismus und die Gestaltung der Wirtschaftsverfassung in der Bundesrepublik Deutschland* (Berlin, 1961)

Bellamy, Christopher & Graham D. Child, *Common Market Law of Competition* (3d. ed., London, 1987)

Benedikt, Heinrich, *Die wirtschaftliche Entwicklung in der Franz Josephs Zeit* (Vienna, 1958)

Benisch, Werner, *Kooperationsfibel des Bundesministers für Wirtschaft* (Bergisch Gladbach, 1964)

—— '10 Jahre Praxis des Bundeskartellamts', in *10 Jahre Kartellgesetz 1958–1968: Eine Würdigung aus der Sicht der deutschen Industrie* 11–28 (Arbeitskreis Kartellgesetz, ed., Bergisch Gladbach, 1968)

Berend, Ivan T. & Gyorgy Ranki, *Economic Development in East-Central Europe in the 19th and 20th Centuries* (New York, 1974).

Berghahn, Volker, *The Americanisation of West German Industry 1945–1973* (Cambridge, 1986)

—— 'Corporatism in Germany in Historical Perspective', in *The Corporate State: Corporatism and the State Tradition in Western Europe* 104–22 (Andrew Cox & Noel O'Sullivan, eds., Hants, England, 1988)

Bergmann, Helmut, *Nachfragemacht in der Fusionskontrolle* (Berlin, 1989)

Bermann, George A., 'The Single European Act: A New Constitution for the Community?', 27 *Col. J. Transnat. L.* 529–587 (1989)

Bernitz, Ulf, *Marknadsrätt* (Stockholm, 1969)

—— *Konkurrens och Priser i Norden* (Stockholm, 1971)

—— *Svensk Marknadsrätt* (Stockholm, 1983)

—— *Den Nya Konkurrenslagen* (Stockholm, 1996)

Bertrand, Jacques, 'La Notion d'Ordre Économique et ses Possibilités d'Utilisation', 31 *Revue D'Histoire Économique et Sociale* 152–188 (1953)

Bessel, Richard, 'State and Society in Germany in the Aftermath of the First World War', in *The State and Social Change in Germany, 1880–1980* 200–27 (W. R. Lee & Eve Rosenhaft, eds., Oxford, 1989)

—— *Germany After the First World War* (Oxford, 1993)

Bethusy-Huc, Viola Gräfin (von), *Demoktratie und Interessenpolitik* (Wiesbaden, 1962)

Beveridge, J., *Beveridge and his Plan* (London, 1954)

Beveridge, William (Sir), *Social Insurance and Allied Services* (1942, Cmd. 6404)

Bilger, Francois, *La Pensée Économique Libérale dans L'Allemagne Contemporaine* (Paris, 1964)

Black, Antony, *Guilds and Civil Society in European Political Thought from the Twelfth Century to the Present* (Ithaca, N.Y., 1984)

Black, R. D. Collison et al eds., *The Marginal Revolution in Economics* (Durham, N.C., 1973)

Blackaby, F. T., ed., *British Economic Policy: 1960–74* (Cambridge, 1978)

Blackbourn, David, 'The *Mittelstand* in German Society and Politics 1871–1914', 4 *Social History* 409–33 (1977)

—— 'The Problem of Democratization: German Catholics and the Role of the Centre Party', in *Society and Politics in Wilhelmine Germany* 160–85 (Richard J. Evans, ed., London, 1978)

Blaich, Fritz, 'Der "Standard-Oil-Fall" vor dem Reichstag. Ein Beitrag zur deutschen Monopolpolitik vor 1914', 126 *Zeitschrift für die gesamte Staatswissenschaft* 663–682(1970)

—— 'Die Anfänge der deutschen Antikartellpolitik zwischen 1897 und 1914', 21 *Jahrbuch für Sozialwissenschaft* 127–50 (1970)

—— 'Die Rolle der Amerikanischen Antitrustgesetzgebung in der wirtschaftswissenschaftlichen Diskussion Deutschlands Zwischen 1890 und 1914', 22 *ORDO* 229–54 (1971)

—— *Kartell- und Monopolpolitik im kaiserlichen Deutschland: Das Problem der Marktmacht im deutschen Reichstag zwischen 1879 und 1914* (Düsseldorf, 1973)

—— *Der Trustkampf (1901–1915): Ein Beitrag zum Verhalten der Ministerialbürokratie gegenüber Verbandsinteressen im wilhelminischen Deutschland* (Berlin, 1975)

Blaise, Jean-Bernard, *Ententes et Concentrations Économiques* (Paris, 1983)

Blaurock, Uwe, ed., *Institutionen und Grundfragen des Wettbewerbsrechts* (Neuwied, 1988)

Bleek, Wilhelm, *Von der Kameralausbildung zum Juristenprivileg* (Berlin, 1972)

Bloding, Hermann, *Der Wucher und seine Gesetzgebung: eine socialpolitische Studie* (Vienna, 1893)

Blum, Reinhard, *Soziale Marktwirtschaft: Wirtschaftspolitik zwischen Neoliberalismus und Ordoliberalismus* (Tübingen, 1969)

Blumenberg-Lampe, Christine, *Das Wirtschaftsprogramm der 'Freiburger Kreise'* (Berlin, 1973)

Bock, Heinrich-Karl & Heinz Korsch, 'Decartellization and Deconcentration in the West German Economy Since 1945', in *Antitrust Laws: A Comparative Symposium* 138–53 (Wolfgang Friedmann, ed., Toronto, 1956)

Boese, Franz, *Geschichte des Vereins für Sozialpolitik 1872–1932* (Berlin, 1939)

Böhm, Franz, 'Das Problem der privaten Macht. Ein Beitrag zur Monopolfrage', 3 *Die Justiz* (1928)

—— *Wettbewerb und Monopolkampf: Eine Untersuchung zur Frage des wirtschaftlichen Kampfrechts und zur Frage der rechtlichen Struktur der geltenden Wirtschaftsordnung* (Berlin, 1933)

—— *Die Ordnung der Wirtschaft als geschichtliche Aufgabe und rechtsschöpferische Leistung* (Stuttgart, 1937)

—— 'Das Reichsgericht und die Kartelle', 1 *ORDO* 197–213 (1948)

—— 'Die Forschungs- und Lehrgemeinschaft zwischen Juristen und Volkswirten an der Universität Freiburg in den dreißiger und vierziger Jahren des 20.

Jahrhunderts', in *Franz Böhm—Reden und Schriften* (Ernst-Joachim Mestmäcker, ed., Karlsruhe, 1960)

Böhm-Bawerk, Eugen (von), 'The Austrian Economists', 1 *Annals of Am. Acad. of Pol. and Soc. Sci.* 361–84 (1891)

—— 'The Historical vs. The Deductive Method in Political Economy', 1 *Annals of the Amer. Acad. of Pol. and Soc. Sci.* 244–71 (1891)

Böhme, Helmut, *Deutschlands Weg zur Grossmacht* (Cologne, 1967)

Bolle, Fritz, 'Darwinismus und Zeitgeist', in *Das Wilhelminische Zeitalter* 235–87 (Hans-Joachim Schoeps, ed., Stuttgart, 1967)

Boltho, Andrea, *The European Economy: Growth and Crisis* (Oxford, 1982)

Bolze, Christian, Note on Judgment of January 28, 1988, Cour d'appel de Paris, 1989 *Dalloz-Sirey Jurisprudence [D.S.L.]* 505–507

Borchardt, Knut, *Die Industrielle Revolution in Deutschland* (Munich, 1972)

Borchardt, Knut & Wolfgang Fikentscher, *Wettbewerb, Wettbewerbsbeschränkung, Marktbeherrschung* (Stuttgart, 1957)

Born, Karl Erich, 'Der soziale und wirtschaftliche Strukturwandel Deutschlands am Ende des 19. Jahrhunderts', 50 *Vierteljahreschrift für Sozial- und Wirtschaftsgeschichte* 361–73 (1963)

—— *Wirtschafts- und Sozialgeschichte des deutschen Kaiserreichs (1867/71–1914)* (Stuttgart, 1985)

Borrie, Gordon, 'Competition Policy in Britain: Retrospect and Prospect', 2 *Intl Rev. of L. & Econ.* 139–49 (1982)

Bos, Pierre-Vincent, 'Towards a Clear Distribution of Competence between EC and National Competition Authorities', 16 *Eur. Comp. L. Rev.* 410–16 (1995)

Boserup, William & Uffe Schlichtkrull, 'Alternative Approaches to the Control of Competition: An Outline of European Cartel Legislation and its Administration', in *Competition, Cartels and Their Regulation* (John Perry Miller, ed., Amsterdam, 1962)

Bouterse, R. B., *Competition and Integration—What Goals Count?* (Deventer, 1994)

Bowen, Ralph H., *German Theories of the Corporate State: with special reference to the period 1870–1919* (New York, 1947)

Bracher, Karl D., *The Age of Ideologies* (Ewald Osers, tr., New York, 1984)

Brady, Robert A., *The Rationalization in German Industry. A Study in the Evolution of Planning* (2d. ed., New York, 1974)

Brault, Dominique, *L'État et L'Esprit de Concurrence en France* (Paris, 1987)

Brentano, Lujo, *Mein Leben im Kampf um die soziale Entwicklung Deutschlands* (Jena, 1931)

Brown, L. & F. Jacobs, *The Court of Justice of the European Communities* (2d. ed., 1983)

Brown, William A., *The United States and the Restoration of World Trade* (Washington, D.C., 1950)

Brüggemeier, Gert, *Entwicklung des Rechts im Organisierten Kapitalismus: Materialien zum Wirtschaftsrecht, Vol.1: Von der Gründerzeit bis zur Weimarer Republik* (Frankfurt a.M., 1977)

Bücher, Karl, 'Die wirtschaftlichen Kartelle', 61 *Schriften des Vereins für Sozialpolitik* 138–238 (1895)

Bulmer, Simon, 'Britain and European Integration', in *Britain and the European Community* (Stephen George, ed., Oxford, 1991)

Burst, Jean-Jaques & Robert Kovar, *Droit de la Concurrence* (Paris, 1982)

Bury, J. B., *The Idea of Progress* (New York, 1932)

Buschmann, Arno et al eds., *Festschrift für Rudolf Gmür* (Bielefeld, 1983)

Buxbaum, Richard M., 'Antitrust Regulation within the European Economic Community', 61 *Col. L. Rev.* 402–29 (1961)

Cairncross, Alec, *Years of Recovery: British Economic Policy 1945–1951* (London, 1985)

Caplan, Jane, ' "The Imaginary Universality of Particular Interests": the "tradition of the civil service in German history",' 4 *Social History* 299–317 (1979)

Caro, Leopold, *Der Wucher* (Leipzig, 1893)

Caron, Francois, *An Economic History of Modern France* (Barbara Bray, tr., New York, 1979)

Castel, J. G., 'France', in Antitrust Laws: A Comparative Symposium 91–137 (Wolfgang Friedmann, ed., Toronto, 1956)

Chamberlin, Edward H., *Theory of Monopolistic Competition* (Cambridge, Mass., 1933)

Chandler, Alfred A. Jr. & Herman Deams, eds., *Managerial Hierarchies: Comparative Perspectives on the Rise of the Modern Industrial Enterprise* (Cambridge, Mass., 1980)

Cipolla, Carlo, ed., *The Emergence of Industrial Socities* (Brighton, 1976)

Clapham, J. H., *The Economic Development of France and Germany 1815–1914* (4th ed., Cambridge, 1951)

Clark, John M., *Alternative to Serfdom* (Oxford, 1948)

—— *Competition as a Dynamic Process* (Washington, D.C., 1961)

Cocks, Geoffrey & Konrad H. Jarausch, eds., *German Professionals, 1800–1950* (New York, 1990)

Coing, Helmut, ed., 3/III *Handbuch der Quellen und Literatur der neueren Europäischen Privatrechtsgeschichte: Das 19. Jahrhundert/Gesetzgebung en zu den privatrechtlichen Sondergebieten* (Munich, 1982/6)

—— ed., III *Handbuch der Quellen und Literatur der neueren Europäischen Privatrechtsgeschichte, Das 19. Jahrhundert* (Munich, 1986)

Coing, Helmut & Walter Wilhelm, eds., *Wissenschaft und Kodifikation des Privatrechts im 19. Jahrhundert* 4 Vols. (Frankfurt a.M., 1977/9)

Coing, Helmut, et al eds., *Wirtschaftsordnung und Rechtsordnung: Festschrift für Franz Böhm zum 70. Geburtstag* (Karlsruhe, 1965)

—— *Staat und Unternehmen aus der Sicht des Rechts* (Tübingen, 1994)

Coing, Helmut, 'Allgemeine Züge der privatrechtlichen Gesetzgebung im 19. Jahrhundert', in 3/I *Handbuch der Quellen und Literatur der neueren europäischen Privatrechtsgeschichte: Das 19. Jahrhundert* 3–16 (Helmut Coing, ed., Munich, 1982)

Cole, Charles W., *French Mercantilist Doctrines Before Colbert* (New York, 1931)

Cornish, William R., 'Legal Control over Cartels and Monopolization 1880–1914. A Comparison', in *Law and the Formation of Big Enterprises in the 19th and Early 20th Centuries* 280–305 (Norbert Horn & Jürgen Kocka, eds., Göttingen, 1979)

Cox, Andrew & Noel O'Sullivan, eds., *The Corporate State: Corporatism and the State Tradition in Western Europe* (Hants, England, 1988)

Cox, Helmut et al eds., *Handbuch des Wettbewerbs* (Munich, 1981)

Cros, Jacques, *Le Néo-Libéralisme: Étude Positive et Critique* (Paris, 1951)

Crouzet, F. et al eds., *Essays in European Economic History 1789–1914* (London, 1969)

Dahl, Hans Fredrik, *Norge mellom Krigene: Det Norske Samfunn i Krise og Konflikt 1918–1940* (Oslo, 1971)

Dahrendorf, Ralf, *Europe's Economy in Crisis* (New York, 1982)

Darmstaedter, Friedrich, *Die Grenzen der Wirksamkeit des Rechtsstaates* (Heidelberg, 1930)

Davidow, Joel, 'Competition Policy, Merger Control and the European Community's 1992 Program', 29 *Col. J. Trans. L.* 11–40 (1991)

Dawson, John P., *The Oracles of the Law* (Ann Arbor, 1968)

de Margerie, Gilles, 'Un nouveau type d'autorités', 52 *Le Débat* 87–97 (1988)

de Vabres, Jean Donnedieu, 'Die mit der Durchsetzung des Wettbewerbsrechtes beauftragen Institutionen: Das Bundeskartellamt und der Wettbewerbsrat', in *Institutionen und Grundfragen des Wettbewerbsrechts: Referate des 6. deutschfranzösischen Juristentreffens, Paris 1987* 23–36 (Uwe Blaurock, ed., Neuwied, 1988)

de Wilmars, J. Merten, 'Reflexions sur les methodes d'interpretation de la Cour de Justice des Communautés Européennes', 22 *Cahiers de droit Européen* 5–20 (1986)

Deak, Francis, 'Contracts and Combinations in Restraint of Trade under French Law: A Comparative Study', 21 *Iowa L. Rev.* 397–454 (1936)

Derenberg, Walter J.,'The Influence of the French Code Civil on the Modern Law of Unfair Competition', 4 *Am. J. Comp. L.* 1–34 (1955)

Deringer, Arved, 'The Distribution of Powers in the Enforcement of the Rules of Competition under the Rome Treaty', 1 *Comm. Mkt. L. Rev.* 30–40 (1963)

Dessauer, Friedrich, *Recht, Richtertum und Ministerialbürokratie: Eine Studie über den Einfluss von Machtverschiebungen auf die Gestaltung des Privatrechts* (Mannheim, 1928)

Diebold, William, *The Schuman Plan* (New York, 1959)

Diemer, Alwin, ed., *Beiträge zur Entwicklung der Wissenschaftstheorie im 19. Jahrhundert* (Meisenheim am Glahn, 1968)

Dietze, Constantin (von), 'Die Universität Freiburg im Dritten Reich', 3 *Mitteilungen der List-Gesellschaft* (Aug. 9, 1961)

Dilcher, Gerhard, 'Das Gesellschaftsbild der Rechtswissenschaft und die soziale Frage', in Klaus Vondung, *Das wilhelminische Bildungsbürgertum: Zur Sozialgeschichte seiner Ideen* 53–66 (Göttingen, 1976)

Direction de la Documentation (France), *Les Ententes Professionelles Devant la Loi* (Paris, 1953)

Dirrheimer, Manfred J., *Ressourcenstärke und Abschreckungswirkung in der Fusionskontrolle* (Cologne, 1988)

Donald, David C., 'Comments on the Italian Antitrust Law of October 10, 1990', 26 *Int'l Law.* 201–13 (1992)

Donativi, Vincenzo, *Introduzione della Disciplina Antitrust nel Sistema Legislativo Italiano* (Milan, 1990)

Dreher, Meinrad, *Konglomerate Zusammenschlüsse, Verbotsvermutungen und Widerlegungsgründe* (Berlin, 1987)

—— 'Kartellrechtsvielfalt und Kartellrechtseinheit in Europa?', 38 *Die Aktiengesellschaft* 437–48 (1993)

—— 'Gemeinsamer Markt—einheitliche Wettbewerbsordnung', in *Umbruch der Wettbewerbsordnung in Europa* 1–22 (Forschungs Inst. für Wirtschaftsverfassung, Cologne, 1995)

—— 'Das deutsche Kartellrecht vor der Europäisierung', 1995 *Wirtschaft und Wettbewerb* 881–907 (1995)

Duchêne, Francois, *Jean Monnet: The First Statesman of Interdependence* (New York, 1994)

Dümchen, Christina, *Zur Kartellrechtlichen Konzeption Franz Böhms* (Frankfurt a.M., 1980)

Dumez, Hervé & Alain Jeunemaitre, *Diriger L'Économie: L'État et les Prix en France: 1936–1986* (Paris, 1989)

—— *La Concurrence en Europe* (Paris, 1991)

Durand, Paul, 'L'Evolution Contemporaine du Droit de la Concurrence', in *Mélanges en l'honneur de Paul Roubier* 439–52 (Paris, 1961)

Dürr, Ernst-Wolfram, *Ordoliberalismus und Sozialpolitik* (Winterthur, 1954); also published as *Wesen und Ziele des Ordoliberalismus* (Winterthur, 1954)

Earle, Edward M., ed., *Modern France: Problems of the Third and Fourth Republics* (Princeton, 1951)

Edinger, Lewis J., *Kurt Schumacher: A Study in Personality and Political Behavior* (Stanford, 1965)

Edwards, Corwin D., *Trade Regulation Overseas: The National Laws* (Dobbs Ferry, N.Y., 1966)

—— *Control of Cartels and Monopoly: An International Comparison* (Dobbs Ferry, N.Y., 1967)

Eger, Otto, 'Das Reichsgericht und die Kartelle', in IV *Die Reichsgerichtspraxis im deutschen Rechtsleben: Festgabe der juristischen Fakultäten zum 50 jährigen Bestehen des Reichsgerichts* 231–51 (Berlin, 1929)

Ehlermann, Claus-Dieter, 'Das schwierige Geschäft der Kommission', in *Europäische Gemeinschaft: Verfassung nach drei Jahrzehnten* 335–65 (Gert Nicolaysen & Hans-Jürgen Rabe, eds., Baden-Baden, 1982)

—— 'Neuere Entwicklungen im europäischen Wettbewerbsrecht', 26 *Europarecht* 307–28 (1991)

—— 'The European Community, Its Law and Lawyers', 29 *Comm. Mkt. L. Rev.* 213–27 (1992)

—— 'The Contribution of EC Competition Policy to the Single Market', 29 *Comm. Mkt. L. Rev.* 257–82 (1992)

—— 'Zur Wettbewerbspolitik und zum Wettbewerbsrecht der Europäischen Union', 39 *Hamburger Jahrbuch für Wirtschafts- und Gesellschaftspolitik* 255–79 (1994)

—— 'Implementation of EC Competition Law by National Anti-Trust Authorities', 17 *Eur. Comp. L. Rev.* 88–95 (1996)

Eley, Geoff, 'The Wilhelmine Right', in *Society and Politics in Wilhelmine Germany* 112–35 (Richard J. Evans, ed., London, 1978)

Ellwein, Thomas, *Krisen und Reformen: Die Bundesrepublik seit den Sechziger Jahren* (2d. ed., Munich, 1993)

Emmerich, Volker, *Kartellrecht* (6th ed., Munich, 1991)

Emmerich, Volker, *Kartellrecht* (7th ed., Munich, 1994)

Erhard, Ludwig, *Prosperity through Competition* (New York, 1958)

Eucken, Walter, *Kapitaltheoretische Untersuchungen* (Leipzig, 1934)

—— 'Die Überwindung des Historismus', 63 *Schmollers Jahrbuch* 63–86 (Berlin, 1938)

—— *Foundations of Economics* (London, 1950)

—— *This Unsuccessful Age* (W. Hodge tr., London, 1951)

—— *Unser Zeitalter der Misserfolge* (New York, 1952)

—— *Grundlagen der Nationalökonomie* (9th ed., Berlin, 1989)

—— *Grundsätze der Wirtschaftspolitik* (6th ed., Tübingen, 1990)

European Commission, Industrial Policy in an Open and Competitive Environment, COM(90)556 Final (Nov. 18, 1990)

Evans, Richard J., ed., *Society and Politics in Wilhelmine Germany* (London, 1978)

Everling, Ulrich, 'Zur neueren EuGH-Rechtsprechung zum Wettbewerbsrecht', 17 *Europarecht* 301–14 (1982)

—— 'The Court of Justice as a Decisionmaking Authority', 82 *Mich. L. Rev.* 1294–1310 (1984)

—— 'Rechtsvereinheitlichung durch Richterrecht in der Europäischen Gemeinschaft', 50 *Rabels Zeitschrift* 193–211 (1986)

—— 'Auf dem Wege zu einem europäischen Verwaltungsrecht', 6 *Neue Zeitschrift für Verwaltungsrecht* 1–7 (1987)

—— 'Zur Wettbewerbskonzeption in der neueren Rechtsprechung des Gerichtshofs der Europäischen Gemeinschaften', 1990 *Wirtschaft und Wettbewerb* 995–1009 (1990)

Ewald, Hans, 'Eberhard Günther', in *Wettbewerb im Wandel: Eberhard Günther zum 65. Geburtstag* 11–24 (Helmut Gutzler et al eds., Baden-Baden, 1976)

Eyben, W.E. (von), *Monopoler og Priser* (2 vols., Copenhagen, 1980)

Fairburn, James, 'The Evolution of Merger Policy in Britain', in *Mergers and Merger Policy* (James Fairburn & John Kay, eds., Oxford, 1989)

Fairburn, James & John Kay, eds., *Mergers and Merger Policy* (Oxford, 1989)

Faull, Jonathan, 'The Enforcement of Competition Policy in the European Community: A Mature System', 15 *Fordham Int'l. L. J.* 219–247 (1991–2)

Feinberg, Robert M., 'The Enforcement and Effects of European Competition Policy: Results of a Survey of Legal Opinion', 23 *J. Comm. Mkt. Studies* 373–384 (1985)

Feldman, Gerald D., *Army, Industry and Labor in Germany, 1914–1918* (Princeton, 1966)

—— 'Der deutsche Organisierte Kapitalismus während der Kriegs- und Inflationsjahre 1914–23', in *Organisierter Kapitalismus* 150–71 (Heinrich A. Winkler, ed., Göttingen, 1974)

—— *The Great Disorder: Politics, Economics and Society in the German Inflation, 1914–1924* (New York, 1993)

Felix, David, *Walter Rathenau and the Weimar Republic: The Politics of Reparation* (Baltimore, 1971)

Fenske, Hans, *Deutsche Parteiengeschichte: Von den Anfängen bis zur Gegenwart* (Paderborn, 1994)

Fiebig, André, 'The German Federal Cartel Office and the Application of Competition Law in Reunified Germany', 14 *U. of Penn. J. of Bus. L.* 373–408 (1993)

Fikentscher, Wolfgang, 'Die Deutsche Kartellrechtswissenschaft 1945–1954: Eine kritische Übersicht', 1955 *Wirtschaft und Wettbewerb* 205–29 (1955)

—— *Wettbewerb und Gewerblicher Rechtsschutz* (Munich, 1958)

—— 'Nachfragemacht und Wettbewerbsbeschränkung', 1960 *Wirtschaft und Wettbewerb* 680–85 (1960)

—— III *Methoden des Rechts: Mitteleuropäischer Rechtskreis* (Tübingen, 1975)

—— *Wirtschaftsrecht* (2 vols., Munich, 1983)

—— *Recht und Wirtschaftliche Freiheit* (2 vols., Tübingen, 1993)

Fischel, W. J., 'Der Historismus in der Wirtschaftswissenschaft dargestellt an der Entwicklung von Adam Müller bis Bruno Hildebrand', 47 *Vierteljahresschrift für Sozial- und Wirtschaftsgeschichte* 1–31 (1960)

Fischer, Curt E., 'Die Geschichte der deutschen Versuche zur Lösung des Kartell- und Monopolprobleme', 110 *Zeitschrift für die gesamte Staatswissenschaft* 425–56 (1954)

Fischer, Wolfram, 'Das Verhältnis von Staat und Wirtschaft in Deutschland am Beginn der Industrialisierung', 14 *Kyklos* 337–63 (1961)

—— *Die Wirtschaftspolitik Deutschlands 1918–1945* (Lüneburg, 1961)

Flechtheim, Julius, *Die Rechtliche Organisation der Kartelle* (Mannheim, 1912)

Focsaneau, L., 'La Notion d'Abus dans le Système de l'Article 86 du Traité Instituant la Communauté Économique Européene', in *Regulating the Behaviour of Monopolies and Dominant Undertakings in Community Law* 324–40 (J. A. van Damme, ed., Bruges, 1977)

Forrester, Ian & Christopher Norall, 'The Laicization of Community Law: Self-Help and the Rule of Reason: How Competition Law Is and Could be Applied', 21 *Comm. Mkt. L. Rev.* 11–51 (1984)

Forschungsinstitut für Wirtschaftsverfassung und Wettbewerb e.V., ed., *Neuorientierung des Wettbewerbsschutzes* (Cologne, 1986)

Fourastié, Jean, *Les Trentes Glorieuses: Ou La Révolution Invisible de 1946 à 1975* (Paris, 1979)

Fox, Eleanor, 'Monopolization and Dominance in the United States and the European Community: Efficiency, Opportunity, and Fairness', 61 *Notre Dame L. Rev.* 981–1020 (1986)

Fraenkel, Josef, ed., *The Jews of Austria: Essays on their Life, History and Destruction* (London, 1967)

Francis, Mark, ed., *The Viennese Enlightenment* (New York, 1985)

Franz, Georg, *Liberalismus: Die Deutschliberale Bewegung in der Habsburgischen Monarchie* (Munich, 1955)

Frazer, Tim, 'Competition Policy after 1992: The Next Step', 53 *Mod. L. Rev.* 609–23 (1990)

Freyer, Tony, *Regulating Big Business: Antitrust in Great Britain and America 1880–1990* (Cambridge, 1992)

Friedländer, Heinrich, *Die Rechtspraxis der Kartelle und Konzerne in Europa* (Zürich, 1938)

Friedmann, Wolfgang, ed., *Antitrust Laws: A Comparative Symposium* (Toronto, 1956)

Fuchs, Albert, *Geistige Strömungen in Österreich 1867–1918* (Vienna, 1949)

Fuller, Charles Baden, 'Economic Issues Relating to Property Rights in Trademarks:

Export Bans, Differential Pricing, Restrictions on Resale and Repackaging', 6 *European L. Rev.* 162–79 (1981)

Furre, Berge, *Norsk Historie 1905–1940* (Oslo, 1972)

Galgano, Francesco, *Trattato di Diritto Commerciale e di Diritto Pubblico Dell' Economia:* Vol. IV, *La Concorrenza e i Consorzi* (Padua, 1981)

Gall, Lothar, ed., *Liberalismus* (Cologne, 1976)

Gamm, Otto Friedrich (von), ed., *Festschrift für Gerd Pfeiffer* (Cologne, 1988)

George, Stephen, ed., *Britain and the European Community* (Oxford, 1991)

Gerber, David J., 'The German Approach to Price Discrimination and Other Forms of Business Discrimination', 27 *Antitrust Bull.* 241–73 (1982)

—— 'Antitrust Law and Economic Analysis: The Swedish Approach', 8 *Hastings Int'l & Comp. L. Rev.* 1–39 (1984)

—— 'Law and the Abuse of Economic Power in Europe', 62 *Tulane L. Rev.* 57–107 (1987)

—— 'The Origins of the European Competition Law Tradition in Fin-de-Siècle Austria', 36 *Am. J. Leg. Hist.* 405–440 (1992)

—— 'Heinrich Kronstein and the Development of United States Antitrust Law', in *Der Einfluss deutscher Emigranten auf die Rechtsentwicklung in den USA und in Deutschland* 155–69 (Marcus Lutter et al eds., Tübingen, 1993)

—— 'Authority, Community and the Civil Law Commentary: An Example from German Competition Law', 42 *Am. J. Comp. L.* 531–42 (1994)

—— 'Constitutionalizing the Economy: German Neo-Liberalism, Competition Law and the "New" Europe', 42 *Am. J. Comp. L.* 25–84 (1994)

—— 'Prometheus Born: The High Middle Ages and the Relationship between Law and Economic Conduct', 38 *St. Louis U.L. Rev.* 673–738 (1994)

—— 'The Transformation of European Community Competition Law', *Harvard Int'l L. J.* 97–147 (1994)

Gerber, David J. & Richard Azarnia, 'Dirigisme and the Challenge of Competition Law in France', 3 *Cardozo J. of Int'l L. & Pol.* 9–45 (1995) (formerly, *New Europe L. J.*)

Gerbet, Pierre, *La Construction de l'Europe* (Paris, 1983)

Gerschenkron, Alexander, *Economic Backwardness in Historical Perspective* (Cambridge, 1962)

Giersch, Herbert, Karl-Heinz Paqué & Holger Schmieding, *The Fading Miracle: Four Decades of Market Economy in Germany* (pbk ed., Cambridge, 1994)

Gimbel, John, *The American Occupation of Germany 1945–1949* (Stanford, 1968)

—— *The Origins of the Marshall Plan* (Stanford, 1976)

Glais, Michel, 'L'État de Dépendance Économique au Sens de L'Art. 8 de L'Ordonnance du 1er Décembre 1986: Analyze Économique', *Gazette du Palais* 2–5 (June 14/15, 1989)

Gleiss, A., *Common Market Cartel Law* (3d. ed., Washington, D.C., 1981)

Gleiss, Alfred & Wolfgang Fikentscher, 'Weitergeltung des Dekartellierungsrechts', 1955 *Wirtschaft und Wettbewerb* 525–33 (1955)

Good, David F., *The Economic Rise of the Habsburg Empire: 1750–1914* (Berkeley, 1984)

Gordley, James, *The Philosophical Origins of Modern Contract Doctrine* (Oxford, 1991)

Gotzen, Paul, *Niederländisches Handels- und Wirtschaftsrecht* (Heidelberg, 1979)

Goyder, D. G., *EEC Competition Law* (Oxford, 1988)

Grass, Nikolaus & Werner Ogris, eds., *Festschrift für Hans Lentze* (Innsbruck, 1969)

Graupner, Frances, 'Commission Decision-Making on Competition Questions', 10 *Comm. Mkt. L. Rev.* 291–305 (1973)

Grendell, Timothy J., 'The Antitrust Legislation of the United States, The European Economic Community, Germany and Japan', 29 *Int'l and Comp L.Q.* 64–86 (1980)

Gribben, J.D., *The Post-War Revival of Competition as Industrial Policy* (Government Economic Service Working Paper, No. 19, London, 1978)

Grimm, Dieter, 'Bürgerlichkeit im Recht', in Jürgen Kocka, *Bürger und Bürgerlichkeit im 19. Jahrhundert* 149–88 (Göttingen, 1987)

Gröner, Helmut, ed., *Wettbewerbsfragen der Europäischen Gemeinschaft* (Berlin, 1990)

Gross, N.T., 'The Industrial Revolution in the Habsburg Monarchy', in *The Emergence of Industrial Societies* (Carlo Cipolla, ed., Brighton, 1976)

Grosser, Dieter, ed., *Der Staat in der Wirtschaft der Bundesrepublik* (Opladen, 1985)

Grossfeld, Bernhard, 'Hauptpunkte der Kartellrechtsentwicklung vor dem Ersten Weltkrieg', 141 *Zeitschrift für das gesamte Handelsrecht* 442–56 (1977)

—— 'Zur Kartellrechtsdiskussion vor dem Ersten Weltkrieg', in IV *Wissenschaft und Kodifikation des Privatrechts im 19. Jahrhundert* 255–96 (Helmut Coing & Walter Wilhelm, eds., Frankfurt a.M., 1979).

Grossman, Eugene, *Methods of Economic Rapprochement* (C.E.C.P. 24(I), League of Nations Pub. 1926.II.29, 1927)

Grossmann-Doerth, Hans, *Selbstgeschaffenes Recht der Wirtschaft und staatliches Recht* (Freiburg i.B., 1933)

Grunfeld, C. & B. S. Yamey, 'United Kingdom', in *Anti-Trust Laws: A Comparative Symposium* 340–402 (Wolfgang Friedmann, ed., Toronto, 1956)

Grunzel, Josef, *Über Kartelle* (Leipzig, 1902)

Guénault, Paul H. & J. M. Jackson, *The Control of Monopoly in the United Kingdom* (2d. ed., London, 1960)

Gundersen, Fridtjof F. & Ulf Bernitz, *Norsk og Internasjonal Markedsrett* (Oslo, 1977)

Günther, Eberhard, 'Entwurf eines deutschen Gesetzes gegen Wettbewerbsbeschränkungen', 1951 *Wirtschaft und Wettbewerb* 17–40 (1951)

—— 'Die Ordnungspolitischen Grundlagen des EWG-Vertrages', 1963 *Wirtschaft und Wettbewerb* 191–202 (1963)

—— '10 Jahre Bundeskartellamt: Rückblick und Ausblick', in *Zehn Jahre Bundeskartellamt* 11–37 (Cologne, 1968)

—— 'Die Geistigen Grundlagen des sogenannten Josten-Entwurfs', in *Wirtschaftsordnung und Staatsverfassung. Festschrift für Franz Böhm zum 80. Geburtstag* 183–204 (Heinz Sauermann & Ernst-Joachim Mestmäcker, eds., Tübingen, 1975)

Gutmann, Gernot, 'Euckens Ansätze zur Theorie der Zentralverwaltungswirtschaft und die Weiterentwicklung durch Hensel', 40 *ORDO* 55–69 (1989)

Gutzler, Helmut et al eds., *Wettbewerb im Wandel: Eberhard Günther zum 65. Geburtstag* (Baden-Baden, 1976)

Gyselen, Luc, 'State Action and the Effectiveness of EC Treaty Competition Provisions', 26 *Comm. Mkt. L. Rev.* 33–60 (1989)

Haas, Ernst B., *The Uniting of Europe* (Stanford, 1958)

Hadenius, Stig, *Swedish Politics During the Twentieth Century* (4th ed., Stockholm, 1997)

Hahn, Jörg, *Ökonomie, Politik und Krise: Diskutiert am Beispiel der ökonomischen Konzeption Karl Schillers* (Würzburg, 1984)

Hahn, Rüdiger, *Behinderungsmissbräuche marktbeherrschender Unternehmen* (Frankfurt a.M., 1984)

Hall, Peter A., ed., *The Political Power of Economic Ideas: Keynesianism Across Nations* (Princeton, 1989)

Hall, Peter A., *Governing the Economy: The Politics of State Intervention in Britain and France* (New York, 1986)

Hallstein, Walter, *Europe in the Making* (Charles Roetter, tr., New York, 1972)

Hannah, Leslie, 'Mergers, Cartels and Concentration: Legal Factors in the US and European Experience', in *Law and the Formation of Big Enterprises in the 19th and Early 20th Centuries* 306–17 (Norbert Horn & Jürgen Kocka, eds., Göttingen, 1979)

Hansen, Reginald, 'Der Methodenstreit in den Sozialwissenschaften zwischen Gustav Schmoller und Karl Menger: Seine wissenschaftshistorische und wissenschaftstheoretische Bedeutung', in *Beiträge zur Entwicklung der Wissenschaftstheorie im 19. Jahrhundert* 137–73 (Alwin Diemer, ed., Meisenheim am Glahn, 1968)

Harding, Lars, *Kontroll av Företagsförvärv i Sverige* (Stockholm, 1983)

Harms, Bernhard, *Vom Wirtschaftskrieg zur Weltwirtschaftskonferenz: Weltwirtschaftliche Gestaltungstendenzen im Spiegel gesammelter Vorträge* (Jena, 1927)

Hauser, Karl, 'Das Ende der historischen Schule und die Ambiguität der deutschen Nationalökonomie in den Zwanziger Jahren', in *Geisteswissenschaften zwischen Kaiserreich und Republik* 47–74 (Knut W. Nörr et al eds. Stuttgart, 1994)

Hawk, Barry E., 'Antitrust in the EEC—The First Decade', 41 *Fordham L. Rev.* 229–92 (1972)

—— II *United States, Common Market and International Antitrust: A Comparative Guide* (2d. ed., Englewood Cliffs, N.J., 1993)

Hayek, Friedrich A. (von), 'Die Überlieferung der Ideale der Wirtschaftsfreiheit', 31 *Schweizer Monatshefte* 333–38 (1951)

Hayes, Peter, *Industry and Ideology: IG Farben in the Nazi Era* (Cambridge, 1987)

Hayward, Jack E., *The State and the Market Economy: Industrial Patriotism and Economic Intervention in France* (Brighton, 1985)

Hayward, Jack E., & Michael Watson, eds., *Planning, Politics and Public Policy: The British, French and Italian Experience* (New York, 1975)

Hecht, Wendelin, 'Grundsätzliche Bemerkungen zu den Methoden der deutschen Wirtschafts-Enquete', 67 *Archiv für Sozialwissenschaft und Sozialpolitik* (1932)

Heckscher, Eli, *Mercantilism* (2d. ed., E. Söderlund ed., M. Shapiro tr., London, 1955)

Heffter, Heinrich, *Die Deutsche Selbstverwaltung im 19. Jahrhundert: Geschichte der Ideen und Institutionen* (2d. ed., Stuttgart, 1969)

Heidenheimer, Arnold J., *Adenauer and the CDU* (The Hague, 1960)

Heinemann, Andreas, *Die Freiburger Schule und ihre geistigen Wurzeln* (Munich, 1989)

—— *Grenzen staatlicher Monopole im EG-Vertrag* (Munich, 1996)

Hellmuth, Eckhart, *Naturrechtsphilosophie und Bürokratischer Werthorizont: Studien zur Preussischen Geistes- und Sozialgeschichte des 18. Jahrhunderts* (Göttingen, 1985)

Helmrich, Herbert, ed., *Wettbewerbspolitik und Wettbewerbsrecht: Zur Diskussion um die Novellierung des GWB* (Cologne, 1987)

Hémard, Jean, 'L'évolution contemporaine de la réglementation de la concurrence', in *Études Juridiques offertes à Leon Morandière* 202–22 (Paris, 1964)

Henderson, W. O., *The Rise of German Industrial Power 1834–1914* (London, 1975)

Hennessy, Peter, *Never Again: Britain, 1945–1951* (New York, 1993)

Henning, Hansjoachim, *Die Deutsche Beamtenschaft im 19. Jahrhundert: Zwischen Stand und Beruf* (Stuttgart, 1984)

Hentschel, Volker, *Wirtschaft und Wirtschaftspolitik im Wilhelminischen Deutschland: Organisierter Kapitalismus und Interventionsstaat* (Stuttgart, 1978)

Hermann, Klaus, 'Die Haltung der Nationalökonomie zu den Kartellen bis 1914', in *Kartelle und Kartellgesetzgebung in Praxis und Rechsprechung vom 19. Jahrhundert bis zur Gegenwart* 42–8 (Hans Pohl, ed., Stuttgart, 1985)

Heusgen, Christoph, *Ludwig Erhards Lehre von der Sozialen Marktwirtschaft* (Bern, 1981)

Heuss, Ernst, ' "Grundlagen der Nationalökonomie" vor 50 Jahren und Heute', 40 *ORDO* 21–30 (1989)

—— 'Die Wirtschaftstheorie in Deutschland während der 20er Jahre', in *Geisteswissenschaften zwischen Kaiserreich und Republik* 137–58 (Knut W. Nörr et al eds., Stuttgart, 1994)

Hexner, Ervin, *La Loi Tchecoslovaque sur les Cartels* (Prague, 1935)

Heymann, Annegret, *Der Jurist Julius Flechtheim: Leben und Werk* (Cologne, 1990)

Hirsch, Felix, *Stresemann: Ein Lebensbild* (Göttingen, 1978)

Hitschmann, Max, *Kartelle und Staatsgewalt* (Vienna, 1897)

Hobsbawm, Eric J., *Industry and Empire* (Harmondsworth, England, 1969)

—— *The Age of Capital 1848–1875* (New York, 1975)

—— *The Age of Empire 1875–1914* (New York, 1987)

—— *The Age of Extremes: A History of the World, 1914–1991* (New York, 1994)

Hodne, Fritz, *The Norwegian Economy: 1920–1980* (London, 1983)

Hoffmann, Stanley et al eds., *In Search of France* (Cambridge, Mass., 1963)

Hofmeister, Herbert, ed., *Forschungsband: Franz Klein: 1854–1926—Leben und Wirken* (Vienna, 1988)

Hofmeister, Herbert, 'Die rechtlichen Aspekte der Industrialisierung in der Österreichisch-Ungarischen Monarchie 1873–1918', in 24 *Österreichische Osthefte* 271–90 (1982)

—— 'Franz Klein (1854–1926) zur 130. Wiederkehr seines Geburtstages', 1984 *Österreichische Richterzeitung* 200–3 (1984)

—— 'Die Rolle der Sozialpartnerschaft in der Entwicklung der Sozialversicherung', in *Historische Wurzeln der Sozialpartnerschaft* 278–316 (Gerald Stourzh & Margarete Grandner, eds., Vienna, 1986)

—— 'Franz Klein als Sozialpolitiker auf dem Gebiete des Privatrechts', in *Franz Klein: Leben und Wirken* 203–215 (Herbert Hofmeister, ed., Vienna, 1988)

Holmberg, Stina, *Mot Monopolisering? NO's Verksamhet under 25 År* (Stockholm, 1981)

Holzwarth, Fritz, *Ordnung der Wirtschaft durch Wettbewerb: Entstehung der Ideen der Freiburger Schule* (Freiburg i.B., 1985)

Hoppmann, Erich, 'Zum Schutzobject des GWB', in *Wettbewerb als Aufgabe; nach 10 Jahren Gesetz gegen Wettbewerbsbeschränkungen* 61–104 (Ernst-Joachim Mestmäcker, ed., Bad Homburg, 1968)

Hoppmann, Erich, *Marktmacht und Wettbewerb* (Tübingen, 1977)

Hopt, Klaus J., ed., *European Merger Control* (Berlin, 1982)

Horn, Norbert & Jürgen Kocka, eds., *Law and the Formation of the Big Enterprises in the 19th and Early 20th Centuries* (Göttingen, 1979)

Hornsby, Stephen B., 'Competition Policy in the 80's: More Policy Less Competition?', 12 *Eur. L. Rev.* 79–101 (1987)

Houssiaux, Jacques, *Concurrence et Marché Commun* (Paris, 1960)

Hübinger, Gangolf & Wolfgang J. Mommsen, eds., *Intellektuelle im Deutschen Kaiserreich* (Frankfurt a.M., 1993)

Hutchison, T. W., *A Review of Economic Doctrines 1870–1929* (Oxford, 1953)

Hüttenberger, Peter, 'Wirtschaftsordnung und Interessenpolitik in der Kartellgesetzgebung der Bundesrepublik 1949–1957', 24 *Vierteljahresschrift für Zeitgeschichte* 287–307 (1976)

Immenga, Ulrich, *Die Politische Instrumentalisierung des Kartellrechts* (Tübingen, 1976)

—— 'Fusionskontrolle: Deutsche Konzeption und Erfahrungen', in *Institutionen und Grundfragen des Wettbewerbsrechts* 125–50 (Uwe Blaurock, ed., Frankfurt a.M., 1988)

—— 'Fusionskontrolle auf Konglomeraten und vertikalen Märkten: Erfahrungen aus dem Zusammenschluss Daimler Benz/MBB', 1990 *Aktiengesellschaft* 209–14 (1990)

Immenga, Ulrich & Ernst-Joachim Mestmäcker, *Kommentar zum GWB* (2d. ed., Munich, 1992)

Isay, Rudolf, *Die Geschichte der Kartellgesetzgebungen* (Berlin, 1955)

Isay, Rudolf & Siegfried Tschierschky, *Kartellverordnung* (2d. ed., Mannheim, 1930)

Jäckering, Werner, *Die Politischen Auseinandersetzungen um die Novellierung des Gesetzes gegen Wettbewerbsbeschränkungen* (GWB) (Berlin, 1977)

Jacobs, Francis G., 'Civil Enforcement of EEC Antitrust Law', 82 *Mich. L.R.* 1364–76 (1984)

Jägersköld, Stig, 'The Swedish Ombudsman', 109 *U. Penn. L. Rev.* 1077–99 (1961)

James, Harald, *The German Slump: Politics and Economics 1924–1936* (Oxford, 1986)

Janik, Alan & Stephen Toulmin, *Wittgenstein's Vienna* (New York, 1973)

Jarausch, Konrad, *The Unfree Professions: German Lawyers, Teachers, and Engineers, 1900–1950* (Oxford, 1990)

Jenks, William A., *Austria under the Iron Ring: 1879–1893* (Charlottesville, Va., 1965)

Jenny, Frédéric, 'French Competition Policy in Perspective', in 1987 *Fordham Corp. L. Inst.* 301–22 (Barry E. Hawk, ed., 1988)

—— 'French Competition Law Update: 1987–1994', 1995 *Fordham Corp. L. Inst.* 203–48 (New York, 1996)

Jenny, Frédéric, & André Paul Weber, 'French Antitrust Legislation: An Exercise in Futility', 20 *Antitrust Bull.* 597–639 (1975)

Jickeli, Joachim, *Marktzutrittsschranken im Recht der Wettbewerbsbeschränkungen* (Baden-Baden, 1990)

Joerges, Christian, *The Market Without the State? States Without a Market?* (Eur. Univ. Inst. Working Paper: Law No. 96/2, San Domenico, It., 1996)

John, Michael, *Politics and the Law in Late Nineteenth-Century Germany: The Origins of the Civil Code* (Oxford, 1989)

Johnson, Daniel, 'Exiles and Half-Exiles: Wilhelm Röpke, Alexander Rüstow and Walter Eucken', in *German Neo-Liberals and the Social Market Economy* 40–68 (Alan T. Peacock & Hans Willgerodt, eds., New York, 1989)

Johnston, William M., *The Austrian Mind: An Intellectual and Social History 1848–1938* (Berkeley, 1972)

Jöhr, Walter A., 'Walter Euckens Lebenswerk', 4 *Kyklos* 257–78 (1950)

Joliet, Rene, *The Rule of Reason in Antitrust Law* (The Hague, 1967)

—— 'Cartelisation, Dirigism and Crisis in the European Community', 3 *The World Economy* 403–45 (1981)

Jones, Larry Eugene, *The Dying Middle: German Liberalism and the Dissolution of the Weimar Party System, 1918–1933* (Chapel Hill, 1988)

Jonung, Christina & Ann-Charlotte Ståhlberg, eds., *Ekonomporträtt: Svenska Ekonomer under 300 År* (Stockholm, 1990)

Joye, Pierre, *Les Trusts en Belgique: La Concentration Capitaliste* (4th ed., Brussels, 1964)

Kaelble, Hartmut, *Industrielle Interessenspolitik in der Wilhelminischen Gesellschaft: Zentralverband Deutscher Industrieller 1895–1914* (Berlin, 1967)

Kalinowski, Julian O. (von), ed., *World Law of Competition* (New York, 1985)

Kann, Robert A., *A Study in Austrian Intellectual History* (New York, 1960)

—— *A History of the Habsburg Empire: 1526–1918* (Berkeley, 1974)

Kantzenbach, Erhard, *Die Funktionsfähigkeit des Wettbewerbs* (Göttingen, 1966)

Kartte, Wolfgang, *Ein neues Leitbild für die Wettbewerbspolitik* (Cologne, 1969)

—— 'Fusionskontrolle—aber wie?' 1970 *Wirtschaftsdienst* 121–3 (1970)

—— 'Unternehmensgrösse und internationale Wettbewerbsfähigkeit', in *Wettbewerbspolitik und Wettbewerbsrecht: Zur Diskussion um die Novellierung des GWB* 199–207 (Herbert Helmrich, ed., Cologne, 1987)

Kartte, Wolfgang & Rainer Holtschneider, 'Konzeptionelle Ansätze und Anwendungsprinzipien im Gesetz gegen Wettbewerbsbeschränkungen—Zur Geschichte des GWB', in *Handbuch des Wettbewerbs* 193–224 (Helmut Cox et al eds., Munich, 1981)

Kauper, Thomas E., 'Article 86, Excessive Prices, and Refusals to Deal', 59 *Antitrust L.J.* 441–56 (1991)

Kehr, Eckart, *Schlachtflottenbau und Parteipolitik 1894–1901* (Berlin, 1930)

—— 'The Dictatorship of the Bureaucracy', in Eckart Kehr, *Economic Interest, Militarism, and Foreign Policy* 164–73 (Gordon A. Craig, ed., Grete Heinz, tr., Berkeley, 1977).

—— *Economic Interest, Militarism, and Foreign Policy* (Gordon A. Craig, ed., Grete Heinz, tr., Berkeley, 1977)

—— 'The Social System of Reaction in Prussia under the Puttkamer Ministry', in Eckhart Kehr, *Economic Interest, Militarism, and Foreign Policy* 109–31 (Gordon A. Craig, ed., Grete Heinz, tr., Berkeley, 1977)

Kelleher, Grant W., 'The Common Market Antitrust Laws: The First Ten Years', 12 *Antitrust Bull.* 1219–52 (1967)

Kellenbenz, Hermann, *Deutsche Wirtschaftsgeschichte* (2 vols., Munich, 1977/81)

Kennedy, Paul, *The Rise and Fall of the Great Powers* (New York, 1987)

Kessler, William C., 'German Cartel Regulation under the Decree of 1923', 50 *Quart. J. of Econ.* 680–93 (1936)

Kestner, Fritz, *Der Organisationszwang: Eine Untersuchung über die Kämpfe zwischen Kartellen und Aussenseitern* (Berlin, 1912)

Kestner, Fritz & Oswald Lehnich, *Der Organisationszwang: Eine Untersuchung über die Kämpfe zwischen Kartellen und Aussenseitern* (2d. ed., Berlin, 1927)

Keynes, John M., *The End of Laissez-Faire?* (London, 1926)

Kindleberger, Charles P., *Economic Growth in France and Britain 1851–1950* (Cambridge, Mass., 1964)

—— *The World in Depression 1929–1939* (Berkeley, 1973)

—— *Marshall Plan Days* (London, 1987)

King, Anthony, *Britain Says Yes* (Washington, D.C., 1977)

Kitchen, M., *The Political Economy of Germany 1815–1914* (London, 1978)

Kitzinger, U. W., *The Politics and Economics of European Integration* (New York, 1963)

Klaue, Siegfried, 'Die bisherige Rechtsprechung zum Gesetz gegen Wettbewerbs-beschränkungen', in *Zehn Jahre Bundeskartellamt* 249–62 (Cologne, 1968)

Klein, Franz, *Reden, Vorträge, Aufsätze, Briefe* (2 vols., Vienna, 1927)

Kleinwächter, Friedrich, *Die Kartelle* (Innsbruck, 1883)

Klink, Dieter, *Vom Antikapitalismus zur Sozialistischen Marktwirtschaft: Die Entwicklung der Ordnungspolitischen Konzeption der SPD von Erfurt (1891) bis Bad Godesberg (1959)* (Hanover, 1965)

Kloten, Norbert, 'Zur Transformation von Wirtschaftsordnungen', 40 *ORDO* 99–127 (1989)

Knoph, Ragnar, *Trustloven av 1926 med Kommentar* (Oslo, 1927)

Kocka, Jürgen, *Bürger und Bürgerlichkeit im 19. Jahrhundert* (Göttingen, 1987)

—— 'Bürgertum und Bürgerlichkeit als Probleme der deutschen Geschichte vom späten 18. Jahrhundert zum frühen 20. Jahrhundert', in Jürgen Kocka, *Bürger und Bürgerlichkeit im 19 Jahrhundert* 21–63 (Göttingen, 1987).

—— 'The Rise of the Modern Industrial Enterprise in Germany', in *Managerial Hierarchies: Comparative Perspectives on the Rise of the Modern Industrial Enterprise* 77–116 (Alfred A. Chandler, Jr. & Herman Deams, eds., Cambridge, Mass., 1980)

Köhler, Helmut, *Wettbewerbsbeschränkungen durch Nachfrager* (Munich, 1977)

Komlos, John, ed., *Economic development in the Habsburg Monarchy in the Nineteenth Century* (Boulder, 1983)

Komlos, John, 'Is the Depression in Austria after 1873 a "Myth"?' 31 *Econ. Hist. Rev.* 287–89 (1978)

Koopmans, Thijmen, 'The Role of Law in the Next Stage of European Integration', 35 *Int'l & Comp. L.Q.* 925–31 (1986)

Korah, Valentine, 'The Competition Act 1980', 1980 *J. Bus. L.* 255–59 (1980)

—— 'From Legal Form Toward Economic Efficiency—Article 85(1) of the EEC Treaty in Contrast to US Antitrust', *Antitrust Bull.* 1009–34 (1990)

Korah, Valentine & Margot Horspool, 'Competition', 37 *Antitrust Bull.* 337–85 (1992)

Kramny, Lioba, 'Das Wirken des BDI in der Wettbewerbspolitik', in *10 Jahre Kartellgesetz: 1958–1968: Eine Würdigung aus der Sicht der deutschen Industrie* 59–78 (Arbeitskreis Kartellgesetz, ed., Bergisch Gladbach, 1968)

Krause, Wernhard, *Wirtschaftstheorie unter dem Hakenkreuz: Die bürgerliche Ökonomie in Deutschland während der faschistischen Herrschaft* (Berlin, 1969)

Krawielicki, Robert, *Das Monopolverbot im Schuman-Plan* (Tübingen, 1952)

Kreis, Harold, 'Commission Procedures in Competition Proceedings—Recent Reforms in Practice and Law', in 1983 *Forham Corp. L. Inst.* 147–68 (Barry E. Hawk, ed., New York, 1984)

Krieger, Leonhard, *The German Idea of Freedom: History of a Political Tradition* (Boston, 1957)

Krohn, Claus-Dieter, *Wirtschaftstheorien als Politische Interessen: Die akademische Nationalökonomie in Deutschland 1918–1933* (Frankfurt a.m., 1981)

Kronstein, Heinrich, *Die abhängige juristische Person* (Munich, 1931)

—— 'Franz Böhm', in *Wirtschaftsordnung und Rechtsordnung: Festschrift für Franz Böhm zum 70. Geburtstag* (Helmut Coing et al eds., Karlsruhe, 1965)

Kronstein, Heinrich & Gertrude Leighton, 'Cartel Control: A Record of Failure', 55 *Yale L. J.* 297–335 (1946)

Krüger, Dieter, *Nationalökonomen im wilhelminischen Deutschland* (Göttingen, 1983)

Krüsselberg, Hans-Günter, 'Zur Interdependenz von Wirtschaftsordnung und Gesellschaftsordnung: Euckens Plädoyer für ein umfassendes Denken in Ordnungen', 40 *ORDO* 223–41 (1989)

Kuisel, Richard F., *Ernst Mercier: French Technocrat* (Berkeley, 1967)

—— *Capitalism and the State in Modern France* (Cambridge, 1981)

Kurucz, Jenö, *Struktur und Funktion der Intelligenz Während der Weimarer Republik* (Cologne, 1967)

Küsters, Hanns-Jürgen, *Die Gründung der Europäischen Wirtschaftsgemeinschaft* (Baden-Baden, 1982)

Kutscher, Hans, 'Über den Gerichtshof der Europäischen Gemeinschaft', 16 *Europarecht* 393–413 (1981)

Lage, Santiago Martinez, 'Significant Developments in Spanish Anti-Trust Law', 16 *Eur. Comp. L. Rev.* 194–200 (1996)

Lammel, Siegbert, 'Recht zur Ordnung des Wettbewerbs', in 3/III *Handbuch der Quellen und Literatur der neueren Europäischen Privatrechtsgeschichte: Das 19. Jahrhundert* 3749–3852 (Helmut Coing, ed., Munich, 1986)

Landes, David S., ed., *The Rise of Capitalism* (New York, 1966)

Landes, David S., *The Unbound Prometheus: Technological Change and Industrial Development in Western Europe from 1750 to the Present* (Cambridge, 1972)

Landesberger, Julius, 'Der österreichische Cartellgesetzentwurf', 24 *Zeitschrift für das Privat- und Öffentliche Recht* 575–610 (1897)

—— 'Welche Massregeln empfehlen sich für die rechtliche Behandlung der Industrie-Kartelle?', II *Verhandlungen des 26. Deutschen Juristentages* (Berlin, 1903)

Lange, Hermann et al eds., *Festschrift für Joachim Gernhuber* (Tübingen, 1993)

Langen, Eugen et al., *Kommentar zum Kartellgesetz* (6th ed., Neuwied, 1982)

Langewiesche, Dieter, *Liberalismus in Deutschland* (Frankfurt a.M., 1988)

Larsson, Mats, *En Svensk Ekonomisk Historia: 1850–1985* (Stockholm, 1991)

Lasch, Chrtistopher, *The True and Only Heaven: Progress and Its Critics* (New York, 1991)

LeCourt, Robert, *L'Europe des Juges* (Brussels, 1976)

Lederer, Julius, 'Das Kartellproblem als Verhandlungsgegenstand des Deutschen Juristentages in Salzburg', 26 *Kartell-Rundschau* 537–39 (1928)

Lee, W. R. & Eve Rosenhaft, eds., *The State and Social Change in Germany, 1880–1980* (Oxford, 1989)

Lehnich, Oswald, *Kartelle und Staat* (Berlin, 1928)

—— *Die Wettbewerbsbeschränkung: Eine Grundlegung* (Cologne, 1956)

Lehnich, Oswald & Fritz Kestner, *Der Organisationszwang. Eine Untersuchung über die Kämpfe zwischen Kartellen und Aussenseitern* (2d. ed., Berlin, 1927)

Lenel, Hans O. et al., 'Vorwort', 40 *ORDO* (1989)

—— 'Walter Euckens "Grundlagen der Nationalökonomie" ', 40 *ORDO* 3–20 (1989)

Lenz, Carl Otto, 'Historische Grundlagen des Rechts der Europäischen Gemeinschaften', in *Festschrift für Alfred-Carl Gaedertz* 337–57 (Gisela Wild et al eds., Munich, 1992)

Lepsius, Oliver, *Die gegensatzaufhebende Begriffsbildung: Methodenentwicklungen in der Weimarer Republik und ihr Verhältnis zur Ideologisierung der Rechtswissenschaft im Nationalsozialismus* (Munich, 1994)

Letwin, William, *Law and Economic Policy in America* (Chicago, 1965)

Leube, Kurt R., 'Friedrich A. von Hayek zum 90. Geburtstag', 40 *ORDO* (1989)

Levy, Hermann, *Monopole, Kartelle und Trusts in der Geschichte und Gegenwart der englischen Industrie* (2d. ed., Jena, 1927)

—— *Industrial Germany: A Study of its Monopoly Organizations and their Control by the State* (London, 1966)

Lévy-Leboyer, Maurice, 'The Large Corporation in Modern France', in *Managerial Hierarchies: Comparative Perspectives on the Rise of the Modern Industrial Enterprise* 117–60 (Alfred D. Chandler, Jr. & Herman Daems eds., Cambridge, Mass., 1980)

Liefmann, Robert, *Kartelle, Konzerne und Trusts* (6th ed., Stuttgart, 1924).

—— *Cartels, Concerns and Trusts* (D. H. MacGregor, tr., New York, 1932)

Lindbeck, Assar, *Svensk Ekonomisk Politik* (2d. ed., Stockholm, 1976)

Lindemann, Albert S., *A History of European Socialism* (New Haven, 1983)

Lindenlaub, Dieter, I *Richtungskämpfe im Verein für Sozialpolitik: Wissenschaft und Sozialpolitik im Kaiserreich vornehmlich vom Beginn des 'Neuen Kurses' Bis Zum Ausbruch des Ersten Weltkrieges*, (2 vols., Wiesbaden, 1967)

Loch, Theo M., ed., *Wege nach Europa: Walter Hallstein und die junge Generation* (Andernach am Rhein, 1967)

Loch, Theo M., 'Einleitung und biographische Skizze', in *Wege nach Europa: Walter Hallstein und die junge Generation* (Theo M. Loch, ed., Andernach am Rhein, 1967)

Löscher, Otto, 'Zehn Jahre Kartellsenat', in *Ehrengabe für Bruno Heusinger* 289–307 (Munich, 1968)

Loth, Wilfried et al eds., *Walter Hallstein: Der Vergessene Europäer?* (Bonn, 1995)

Ludwig-Erhard Stiftung, ed., *Ludwig Erhard und seine Politik* (Stuttgart, 1985)

Lukes, Rudolf, *Der Kartellvertrag: Das Kartell als Vertrag mit Auswirkungen* (Munich, 1959)

Lütge, Friedrich, *Deutsche Sozial- und Wirtschaftsgeschichte: Ein Überblick* (2d ed., Berlin, 1960)

Lutter, Marcus, et al eds., *Der Einfluss deutscher Emigranten auf die Rechtsentwicklung in den USA und in Deutschland* (Tübingen, 1993)

Lutz, Friedrich, *Verstehen und Verständigung in der Wirtschaftswissenschaft* (Walter Eucken Institut, ed., Tübingen, 1967)

Lynch, Frances, 'The Role of Jean Monnet in Setting Up the European Coal and Steel Community', in *Die Anfänge des Schuman-Plans: 1950/51* 117–30 (Klaus Schwabe ed., Baden-Baden, 1988)

Maier, Charles S., *Recasting Bourgeois Europe: Stabilization in France, Germany and Italy in the Decade after World War I* (Princeton, 1975)

—— *In Search of Stability: Explorations in Historical Political Economy* (Cambridge, 1987)

—— 'Society as Factory', in Charles S. Maier, *In Search of Stability: Explorations in Historical Political Economy* 19–70 (Cambridge, 1987)

Mancini, Giuseppe F., 'The Making of a Constitution for Europe', 26 *Common Mkt. L. Rev.* 595–614 (1989)

Mancini, Giuseppe F. & David T. Keeling, 'Language, Culture and Politics in the Life of the European Court of Justice', 1 *Col. J. Eur. L.* 397–413 (1995)

Mantoux, Paul, *The Industrial Revolution in the Eighteenth Century: An Outline of the Beginnings of the Modern Factory System in England* (London, 1961)

Markert, Kurt, 'Recent Developments in German Antitrust Law', 43 *Fordham L. Rev.* 697–718 (1975)

—— *Die Wettbewerberbehinderung im GWB nach der vierten Kartellnovelle* (Heidelberg, 1982)

—— 'Zur Bedeutung von Marktstruktur und -verhalten in der materiellen Fusionskontrolle des GWB', in *Neuorientierung des Wettbewerbsschutzes* 35–60 (Forschungsinstitut für Wirtschaftsverfassung und Wettbewerb e.V., ed., Cologne, 1986)

Martenius, Åke, *Lagstiftning om Konkurrensbegränsning* (Stockholm, 1965)

Martinek, Michael, 'Unruhe an der Kartellfront: Die 5. GWB-Novelle gegen Industriemarktfixierung und Ausnahmebereichsexzess', 43 *Neue Juristische Wochenschrift* 793–800 (1990)

März, Eduard, *Österreichische Industrie- und Bankpolitik in der Zeit Franz Josephs I.* (Vienna, 1968)

Maschke, Erich, *Grundzüge der Deutschen Kartellgeschichte bis 1914* (Dortmund, 1964)

—— 'Outline of the History of German Cartels from 1873 to 1914', in *Essays in European Economic History 1789–1914* 227–258 (F. Crouzet, et al eds., London, 1969)

Matis, Herbert, *Österreichs Wirtschaft 1848 bis 1913: Konjunkturelle Dynamik und Gesellschaftlicher Wandel im Zeitalter Franz Josephs I.* (Berlin, 1972)

Maxeiner, James, *Policy and Methods in German and American Antitrust Law: A Comparative Study* (New York, 1986)

May, Arthur J., *The Hapsburg Monarchy: 1867–1914* (Cambridge, Mass., 1965)

Mayne, Richard, *The Recovery of Europe* (New York, 1973)

McArthur, John H. & Bruce R. Scott, *Industrial Planning in France* (Boston, 1969)

Meade, John, 'Decentralisation in the Implementation of EEC Competition Law—A Challenge for the Lawyers', 37 *Northern Ireland L.Q.* 101–25 (1986)

Meadows, P., 'Planning', in *British Economic Policy: 1960–74* 402–17 (F. T. Blackaby, ed., Cambridge, 1978)

Mee, Charles L. Jr., *The Marshall Plan* (New York, 1984)

Menzel, Adolf, 'Referat über die wirtschaftlichen Kartelle und die Rechtsordnung', 61 *Schriften des Vereins für Socialpolitik* 23–47 (1895)

Menzel, Adolf, *Die Kartelle und die Rechtsordnung* (2d. ed., Leipzig, 1902)

Mestmäcker, Ernst-Joachim, ed., *Franz Böhm—Reden und Schriften* (Karlsruhe, 1960)

—— 'Diskriminierungen, Dirigismus und Wettbewerb', 1957 *Wirtschaft und Wettbewerb* 21–34 (1957)

—— 'Dekartellierung und Wettbewerb in der Rechtsprechung der Deutschen Gerichte', 9 *ORDO* 99–130 (1957)

—— *Wettbewerb als Aufgabe; nach 10 Jahren Gesetz gegen Wettbewerbsbeschränkungen* (Bad Homburg, 1968)

—— 'Concentration and Competition in the EEC', 6 *J. World Trade L.* 615–47 (1972) (pt.1) and 7 *J. World Trade L.* 36–63 (1973) (pt.2)

—— *Europäisches Wettbewerbsrecht* (Munich, 1974)

—— *Der Verwaltete Wettbewerb* (Tübingen, 1984)

—— 'Auf dem Wege zu einer Ordnungspolitik für Europa', in *Eine Ordnungspolitik für Europa, Festschrift für Hans von der Groeben* 9–49 (Ernst-Joachim Mestmäcker et al eds., Baden-Baden, 1987)

—— 'Merger Control in the Common Market: Between Competition Policy and Industrial Policy', 1989 *Fordham Corp. L. Inst.* Ch. 20 (Barry E. Hawk, ed., New York, 1989)

Meyer, Willi, 'Geschichte und Nationalökonomie: Historische Einbettung und allgemeine Theorien', 40 *ORDO* 31–54 (1989)

Meynaud, Jean, 'Pouvoir Politique et Pouvoir Économique', *Revue Économique* 925–57 (1958)

Michels, Rudolf K., *Cartels, Combines and Trusts in Post-war Germany* (New York, 1928)

Miksch, Leonhard, *Wettbewerb als Aufgabe: Grundsätze einer Wettbewerbsordnung* (2d. ed., Godesberg, 1947)

—— 'Die Wirtschaftspolitik des Als Ob', 105 *Zeitschrift für die gesamte Staatswissenschaft* 310–338 (1949)

—— 'Walter Eucken', 4 *Kyklos* 279–90 (1950)

Miller, John Perry, ed., *Competition, Cartels and Their Regulation* (Amsterdam, 1962)

Milward, Alan S., *The Reconstruction of Europe, 1945–1951* (Berkeley, 1984)

Milward, Alan S. & S. B. Saul, *The Development of the Economies of Continental Europe 1850–1914* (Cambridge, Mass., 1977)

Mises, Ludwig, 'Soziologie und Geschichte. Epilog zum Methodenstreit in der Nationalökonomie', 61 *Archiv für Sozialwissenschaft und Sozialpolitik* 465–512 (1929)

Moeller, Hero, 'Liberalismus', 62 *Jahrbücher für Nationalökonomie* (1950)

Mokyr, Joel, *The Lever of Riches: Technological Creativity and Economic Progress* (New York, 1990)

Monnet, Jean, *Mémoires* (Paris, 1976)

Morgan, E. Victor, *Monopolies, Mergers and Restrictive Trade Practices: U.K. Competition Policy, 1948–1987* (Edinburgh, 1987)

Möschel, Wernhard, *70 Jahre Deutsche Kartellpolitik* (Tübingen, 1972)

—— *Der Oligopolmissbrauch im Recht der Wettbewerbsbeschränkungen* (Tübingen, 1974)

—— *Recht der Wettbewerbsbeschränkungen* (Cologne, 1983)

—— '30 Jahre Kartellgesetz—erneuter Prüfungs- und Handlungsbedarf?', in *Wettbewerbspolitik und Wettbewerbsrecht: Zur Diskussion um die Novellierung des GWB* 3–18 (Herbert Helmrich, ed., Cologne, 1987)

—— 'Wettbewerbspolitik aus ordoliberaler Sicht', in *Festschrift für Gerd Pfeiffer* 707–25 (Otto Friedrich von Gamm, ed., Cologne, 1988)

—— 'Competition Policy from an Ordo Point of View', in *German Neo- Liberals and the Social Market Economy* 142–59 (Alan T. Peacock & Hans Willgerodt, eds., New York, 1989)

—— 'Untersagung von Zusammenschlüssen aufgrund gesellschaftspolitischer Kriterien?', in *Unternehmenstrukturen im europäischen Binnenmarkt: Referate des XXIII. FIW-Symposions* 93–107 (Cologne 1990)

—— 'The Goals of Antitrust Revisited', 147 *J. Theoretical & Institutional Economics* 7–17 (1991)

—— 'Wettbewerbspolitik vor neuen Herausforderungen,' in *Ordnung und freiheit* 61–78 (Walter Eucken Institut, ed., Freiburg i.B., 1992)

—— 'Subsidiaritätsprinzip und europäisches Kartellrecht', 48 *Neue Juristische Wochenschrift* 281–85 (1995)

Muller, Herbert, J., *Freedom in the Modern World: The 19th and 20th Centuries* (New York, 1966)

Muller, Jerry Z., *Adam Smith in his Time and Ours: Designing the Decent Society* (New York, 1993)

Müller-Armack, Alfred, *Auf dem Weg nach Europa* (Tübingen, 1971)

—— *Genealogie der Sozialen Marktwirtschaft* (Bern, 1974)

Müller-Hennenberg, Hans & Gustav Schwartz eds., *Novelle 1965 zum Gesetz gegen Wettbewerbsbeschränkungen* (Cologne, 1966)

Myhrman, Johan, *Hur Sverige Blev Rikt* (Stockholm, 1994)

Myrdal, Gunnar, *The Political Element in the Development of Political Theory* (Paul Streeten, tr., New Brunswick, N.J., 1990)

Naphthali, Fritz, *Wirtschaftsdemokratie, Ihr Wesen, Weg und Ziel* (Berlin, 1928)

Naumann, Robert, *Theorie und Praxis des Neoliberalismus* (Berlin, 1957)

Nawroth, Egon E., *Die Sozial- und Wirtschaftsphilosophie des Neoliberalismus* (2d. ed., Heidelberg, 1962)

Nelson, Benjamin, *The Idea of Usury* (2d. ed., Chicago, 1969)

Neumann, Franz, 'Gesellschaftliche und staatliche Verwaltung der monopolistischen Unternehmungen', *Die Arbeit* 393–406 (1928)

—— 'Der Salzburger Juristentag', *Die Arbeit* 656–62 (1928)

Neven, Damien, et al., *Merger in Daylight: The Economics and Politics of European Merger Control* (London, 1993)

Nicholls, A. J., *Freedom with Responsibility: The Social Market Economy in Germany 1918–1963* (Oxford, 1994)

Nichols, J. A., *Germany after Bismarck: The Caprivi Era 1890–1894* (Cambridge, Mass., 1958)

Nicolaysen, Gert & Hans Jürgen Rabe, eds., *Europäische Gemeinschaft: Verfassung nach drei Jahrzehnten* (Baden-Baden, 1982)

Niederleithinger, Ernst, 'Probleme der Missbrauchsaufsicht aus der Sicht des Bundeskartellamtes', in *Die Missbrauchsaufsicht vor dem Hintergrund der Entwicklungen der neueren Wettbewerbstheorie* 65–78 (Burkhardt Röper, ed., Berlin, 1982)

Niederleithinger, Ernst, 'Comments', in *Wettbewerbsfragen der Europäischen Gemeinschaft* 58 (Helmut Gröner, ed., Berlin, 1990)

Nipperdey, Hans Carl, 'Wettbewerb und Existenzvernichtung', 28 *Kartell-Rundschau* 127–52 (1930).

Nolan, Mary, *Visions of Modernity: American Business and the Modernization of Germany* (New York, 1994)

Nolte, Paul, *Staatsbildung als Gesellschaftsreform: Politische Reformen in Preussen und den Süddeutschen Staaten 1800–1820* (Frankfurt a.M., 1990)

Nörr, Knut W., *Zwischen den Mühlsteinen: Eine Privatrechtsgeschichte der Weimarer Republik* (Tübingen, 1988)

—— 'Das Reichskaligesetz 1910: Ein Musterstatut der organisierten Wirtschaft', 108 *Zeitschrift der Savigny-Stiftung für Rechtsgeschichte* 347–57 (1991)

—— *Eher Hegel als Kant: Zum Privatrechtsverständnis im 19. Jahrhundert* (Paderborn, 1991)

—— 'Auf dem Wege zur Kategorie der Wirtschaftsverfassung: Wirtschaftliche Ordnungsvorstellungen im Juristischen Denken vor und nach dem Ersten Weltkrieg', in *Geisteswissenschaften zwischen Kaiserreich und Republik* 423–452 (Knut W. Nörr et al, eds., Stuttgart, 1994)

—— *Die Leiden des Privatrechts: Kartelle in Deutschland von der Holzstoffkartellentscheidung zum Gesetz gegen Wettbewerbsbeschränkungen* (Tübingen, 1994).

Nörr, Knut W., et al eds., *Geisteswissenschaften zwischen Kaiserreich und Republik* (Stuttgart, 1994)

North, Douglass C., *Structure and Change in Economic History* (New York, 1981)

Nussbaum, Helga, *Unternehmer gegen Monopole: Über Struktur und Aktionen antimonopolistischer bürgerlicher Gruppen zu Beginn des 20. Jahrhunderts* (Berlin, 1966)

Oesterreich, Ellen, 'Die Entwicklung der Theorie der Wettbewerbspolitik', in *10 Jahre Kartellgesetz 1958–1968: Eine Würdigung aus der Sicht der deutschen Industrie* 87–114 (Arbeitskreis Kartellgesetz, ed., Bergisch Gladbach, 1968)

Ogorek, Regina, *Richterkönig oder Subsumtionsautomat? Zur Justiztheorie im 19. Jahrhundert* (Frankfurt a.M., 1986)

Ogris, Werner, *Der Entwicklungsgang der österreichischen Privatrechtswissenschaft im 19. Jahrhundert* (Berlin, 1968)

—— 'Die Historische Schule der Österreichischen Zivilistik', in *Festschrift für Hans Lentze* 449–96 (Nikolaus Grass & Werner Ogris, eds., Innsbruck, 1969)

Otteryd, Dan, 'Missbruk av Marknadsdominerande Ställning enligt Svensk Rätt', 42 *Tidskrift för Sveriges Advokatsamfundet* 242–254 (1981)

Overbury, H. Colin, 'Politics or Policy? The Demystification of EC Merger Control', in 1992 *Fordham Corp. L. Inst.* 557–89 (Barry E. Hawk, ed., New York, 1993)

Pathak, A. S., 'Articles 85–86 and Anticompetitive Exclusion in EC Competition Law', 10 *Eur. Comp. L. Rev.* 74–104 (1989)

Paulus, Gotthard et al eds., *Festschrift für Karl Larenz* (Munich, 1973)

Peacock, Alan T. & Hans Willgerodt, eds., *German Neo-Liberals and the Social Market Economy* (New York, 1989)

Peacock, Alan T. & Hans Willgerodt, 'Overall View of the German Liberal Movement', in *German Neo-Liberals and the Social Market Economy* 1–15 (Alan T. Peacock & Hans Willgerodt, eds., New York, 1989)

Pegg, Carl H., *The Evolution of the European Idea, 1914–1932* (Chapel Hill, 1983)

Pekkarinen, Jukka, 'Keynesianism and the Scandinavian Models of Economic Policy' in *The Political Power of Economic Ideas: Keynesianism Across Nations* 311–46 (Peter A. Hall, ed., Princeton, 1989)

Peukert, Detlev J., *The Weimar Republic: The Crisis of Classical Modernity* (Richard Deveson, tr., New York, 1992)

Pfeiffer, Gerd, 'Von der Autokupplung bis zu Chanel No. 5: Neun Jahre Fusionskontrolle des Kartellsenats des Bundesgerichtshofes', in *Wettbewerbspolitik und Wettbewerbsrecht: Zur Diskussion um die Novellierung des GWB* 209–20 (Herbert Helmrich, ed., Cologne, 1987)

Piotrowski, Roman, *Cartels and Trusts: Their Origin and Historical Development From the Economic and Legal Aspects* (London, 1933)

Plaisant, René, 'French Legislation Against Restrictive Trade Practices', 10 *Texas Intl L.J.* 26–145 (1975)

Plessen, M.L., *Die Wirksamkeit des Vereins für Socialpolitik 1872–1890* (Berlin, 1975)

Pohl, Hans, ed., *Kartelle und Kartellgesetzgebung in Praxis und Rechsprechung vom 19. Jahrhundert bis zur Gegenwart* (Stuttgart, 1985)

Pohl, Hans, 'Die Entwicklung der Kartelle in Deutschland und die Diskussionen im Verein für Socialpolitik', in IV *Wissenschaft und Kodifikation des Privatrechts im 19. Jahrhundert* 206–35 (Helmut Coing & Walter Wilhelm, eds., Frankfurt a.M., 1977)

—— 'Die Entwicklung der deutschen Volkswirtschaft (1830–1880)', in II *Wissenschaft und Kodifikation des Privatrechts im 19. Jahrhundert* 1–26 (Helmut Coing & Walter Wilhelm, eds., Frankfurt a.M., 1979)

Polanyi, Karl, *The Great Transformation* (Boston, 1957)

Pollard, Sidney, *Peaceful Conquest: The Industrialization of Europe 1760–1970* (Oxford, 1981)

—— *Development of the British Economy: 1914–1990* (4th ed., London, 1992)

Postan, M.M., *An Economic History of Western Europe 1945–1964* (London, 1967)

Pribram, Karl, *Geschichte der österreichischen Gewerbepolitik von 1740 bis 1860* (Leipzig, 1907)

—— *Cartel Problems: An Analysis of Collective Monopolies in Europe with American Application* (Washington, D.C., 1935)

Pridham, Geoffrey, *Christian Democracy in Western Germany* (New York, 1977)

Rahl, James A. ed., *Common Market and American Antitrust* (New York, 1970)

Raisch, Peter et al eds., *Fusionskontrolle: Für und Wider* (Stuttgart, 1970)

Raiser, Thomas, 'Ökonomen im Bundeskartellamt und in den Kartellgerichten', *Betriebs-Berater* 471–75 (1972)

Reimann, Mathias, 'Nineteenth Century German Legal Science', 31 *Boston Coll. L. Rev.* 842–97 (1990)

Remmert, Wilhelm, ed., *Law No. 56: Prohibition of Excessive Economic Concentration of Economic Power, Text und Erläuterung* (Frankfurt a.M., 1947)

Reuffurth, Eduard, *Die Stellung der deutschen Sozialdemokratie zum Problem der staatlichen Kartellpolitik* (Diss. Jena, 1930)

Reuter, Ute K., *Erfahrungen mit staatlicher Kartellpolitik in Deutschland von 1900 bis 1964* (Zurich, 1967)

Riddell, Peter, *The Thatcher Years* (Oxford, 1989)

Riesenfeld, Stefan A., 'The Protection of Competition', in II *American Enterprise in*

Europe: A Legal Profile 197–342 (Eric Stein & Thomas Nicholson, eds., Ann Arbor, 1960)

Rieter, Heinz, and Matthias Schmolz, 'The Ideas of German Ordoliberalism 1938–45: Pointing the Way to a New Economic Order', 1 *Eur. J. of Hist. of Econ. Thought* 87–114 (1993)

Riffel, Paul, '10 Jahre deutsche Wettbewerbspolitik', in *10 Jahre Kartellgesetz: 1958– 1968: Eine Würdigung aus der Sicht der deutschen Industrie* 3–10 (Arbeitskreis Kartellgesetz, ed., Bergisch Gladbach, 1968)

Ringer, Fritz K., ed., *The German Inflation of 1923* (New York, 1969)

Ringer, Fritz K., *The Decline of the German Mandarins: The German Academic Community, 1890–1933* (Cambridge, Mass., 1969)

Ripert, Georges, *Aspects Juridiques du Capitalisme Moderne* (Paris, 1946)

Ritter, Gerhard A., *Social Welfare in Germany and Britain* (Leamington Spa, 1986)

Ritter, Lennart, W. David Braun & Francis Rawlinson, *EEC Competition Law* (Deventer, 1991)

Rittner, Fritz, 'Das Ermessen der Kartellbehörde', in *Festschrift für Heinz Kaufmann* 307– 325 (Cologne Marienberg, 1972)

—— '§22 GWB im Spannungsfeld wirtschaftswissenschaftlicher Theorien und rechtsstaatlicher Postulate', in *Festschrift für Günther Hartmann* 251–71 (Cologne, 1976)

—— 'Konvergenz oder Divergenz der europäischen Wettbewerbsrecht?', in *Integration oder Desintegration der europäischen Wettbewerbsordnung: Referate des XVI. FIW-Symposiums* 31–84 (Cologne, 1983)

—— *Wirtschaftsrecht* (2d. ed., Heidelberg, 1987)

—— *Wettbewerbs- und Kartellrecht* (4th ed., Heidelberg, 1993)

—— 'Über die Privatrechtlichen Grundlagen des Kartellrechts', 160 *Zeitschrift für das gesamte Handelsrecht* 180–201 (1996)

Ritzel, Gerhard, *Schmoller versus Menger: Eine Analyse des Methodenstreits im Hinblick auf den Historismus in der Nationalökonomie* (Diss. Basel, 1951)

Robert, Rüdiger, *Konzentrationspolitik in der Bundesrepublik—Das Beispiel der Entstehung des Gesetzes gegen Wettbewerbsbeschränkungen* (Berlin, 1976)

Robinson, Joan, *The Economics of Imperfect Competition* (London, 1933)

Röper, Burckhardt, 'Der wirtschaftliche Hintergrund der Kartell-Legalisierung durch das Reichsgericht', 3 *ORDO* 239–50 (1950)

Röpke, Wilhelm, *Civitas Humana* (Erlenbach-Zurich, 1946)

—— *The Social Crisis of our Time* (London, 1950)

—— *Die Lehre von der Wirtschaft* (6th ed., Erlenbach-Zurich, 1951)

—— *A Humane Economy: The Social Framework of the Free Market* (Chicago, 1960)

Rosanvallon, Pierre, 'The Development of Keynesianism in France', in *The Political Power of Economic Ideas: Keynesianism Across Nations* 171–94 (Peter A. Hall, ed., Princeton, 1989)

Roscher, Wilhelm, *Geschichte der National-Ökonomie in Deutschland* (Munich, 1874)

Rosenberg, Arthur, *Imperial Germany: The Birth of the German Republic, 1871–1918* (Ian F.D. Morrow, tr., Oxford, 1931)

—— *Democracy and Socialism* (Boston, 1965)

Rosenberg, Hans, 'Political and Social Consequences of the Great Depression of 1873–1896 in Central Europe', 13 *Econ. Hist. Rev.* 58–73 (1943)

—— *Grosse Depression und Bismarckzeit* (Berlin, 1967)

Rosenthal, Douglas E., 'Competition Policy', in *Europe 1992: An American Perspective* 293–343 (Gary C. Hufbauer, ed., Washington, D.C., 1990)

Rossi, Guido, 'Control of Concentrations: The Wake of the EEC Regulation and the Debate in Italy', 1988 *Fordham Corp. L. Inst.* 28-1-21 (Barry E. Hawk, ed., New York, 1989)

Rotthege, Georg, *Die Beurteilung von Kartellen und Genossenschaften durch die Rechtswissenschaft* (Tübingen, 1982)

Rowley, Charles K., *The British Monopolies Commission* (London, 1966)

Rubio de Casas, Maria G., 'The Spanish Law for the Defence of Competition', 11 *Eur. Comp. L. Rev.* 179–89 (1990)

Rudolph, Richard L., *Banking and Industrialization in Austria-Hungary: The Role of Banks in the Industrialization of the Czech Crownlands, 1873–1914* (Cambridge, 1976)

Ruggiero, Guido (de), *The History of European Liberalism* (R.G. Collingwood, tr., Oxford, 1927; reprinted Boston, 1959)

Salin, Edgar, 'Wirtschaft und Wirtschaftslehre nach zwei Weltkriegen', 1 *Kyklos* 26–56 (1947)

Salje, Peter, *Die Mittelständische Kooperation zwischen Wettbewerbspolitik und Kartellrecht* (Tübingen, 1981)

Samkaladen, I. & I. E. Druker, 'Legal Problems Relating to Article 86 of the Rome Treaty', in 1965–66 *Comm. Mkt. L. Rev.* 158–183 (1966)

Sandberg, Lars, 'Antitrust Policy in Sweden', 9 *Antitrust Bull.* 535–58 (1964)

Sandrock, Otto, 'Kritische Bemerkungen zum Entwurf über die Zweiten Kartellgesetz-Novelle', 1969 *Wirtschaft und Wettbewerb* 205–29 (1969)

—— 'Gentlemen's Agreements, aufeinanderabgestimmte Verhaltensweisen und gleichförmiges Verhalten nach dem GWB', 1971 *Wirtschaft und Wettbewerb* 858–68 (1971)

Sandström, Staffan, 'Den Nya Konkurrenslagen', 1 *Pris och Konkurrens* 5–12 (1983)

Sauermann, Heinz & Ernst-Joachim Mestmäcker, eds., *Wirtschaftsordnung und Staatsverfassung. Festschrift für Franz Böhm zum 80. Geburtstag* (Tübingen, 1975)

Saul, S. B., *The Myth of the Great Depression, 1873–1896* (2d. ed., London, 1985)

Sbragia, Alberta, ed., *Europolitics: Institutions and Policymaking in the 'New' European Community* (Washington, D.C., 1992)

Schäffle, Albert, 'Zum Kartellwesen und zur Kartellpolitik', 54 *Zeitschrift für die gesamte Staatswissenschaft* 467–528 (pt.1), 647–719 (pt. 2) (1898)

Scharnweber, Carsten, *Deutsche Kartellpolitik 1926–1929* (Diss. Tübingen, 1970)

Scheingold, Stuart, *The Rule of Law in European Integration: The Path of the Schuman Plan* (New Haven, 1965)

Scheler, Hans-Jürgen, *Kathedersozialismus und Wirtschaftliche Macht* (Diss. Berlin, 1973)

Schiller, Karl, *Der Ökonom und die Gesellschaft: Das freiheitliche und das soziale Element in der modernen Wirtschaftspolitik* (Stuttgart, 1964)

Schlecht, Otto, 'Ein neuer Ordnungsrahmen für dynamischen Wettbewerb?', in *Wettbewerbspolitik und Wettbewerbsrecht: Zur Diskussion um die Novellierung des GWB* 35–48 (Herbert Helmrich, ed., Cologne, 1987)

—— 'Macht und Ohnmacht der Ordnungspolitik—Eine Bilanz nach 40 Jahren Sozialer Marktwirtschaft', 40 *ORDO* 303–20 (1989)

Schlecht, Otto, 'Entscheidungslinien der deutschen Wettbewerbspolitik', 43 *ORDO* 319– 35 (1992)

Schlieder, Willy Christoph, 'European Competition Policy', 50 *Antitrust L.J.* 647–698 (1981)

Schmalenbach, Eugen, 'Theorie der Produktionskosten-Ermittlung' 3 *Zeitschrift für Handelswissenschaftliche Forschung* 41–65 (1908)

Schmidt, Ingo, *Wettbewerbstheorie und -politik* (Stuttgart, 1981)

Schmidt, Mathias, *Ziele und Intrumente der Mittelstandspolitik in der Bundesrepublik Deutschland* (Cologne, 1988)

Schmitt, Carl, *Verfassungslehre* (Munich, 1928)

Schmölders, Günter, *Personalistischer Sozialismus* (Cologne, 1969)

Schmoller, Gustav, 'Das Verhältnis der Kartelle zum Staate', 116 *Schriften des Vereins für Socialpolitik* 237–71 (1906)

Schneider, Franz, *Grosse Koalition—Ende oder Neubeginn?* (Munich, 1969)

Schoenlank, Bruno, 'Die Kartelle: Beiträge zu einer Morphologie der Unternehmer-Verbände', 3 *Archiv für Soziale Gesetzgebung und Statistik* 489–538 (1890)

Schoeps, Hans-Joachim, ed., *Das Wilhelminische Zeitalter* (Stuttgart, 1967)

Schorske, Carl E., *German Social Democracy 1905–1917: The Development of the Great Schism* (Cambridge, Mass., 1955)

—— *Fin-de-Siècle Vienna* (New York, 1980)

Schröder, Rainer, 'Die Richterschaft am Ende des Zweiten Kaiserreiches unter dem Druck Polarer Sozialer und Politischer Anforderungen', in *Festschrift für Rudolf Gmür* 201–53 (Arno Buschmann et al eds., Bielefeld, 1983)

—— *Die Entwicklung des Kartellrechts und des kollectiven Arbeitsrechts durch die Rechtsprechung des Reichsgerichts vor 1914* (Ebelsbach, 1988)

Schulte, Helmut, *Das Österreiche Kartellrecht vor 1938* (Diss. Münster, 1979)

Schultze, Jörg-Martin, *Marktzutrittsschranken in der Fusionskontrolle* (Cologne, 1988)

Schulze, Hagen, 'Die SPD und der Staat von Weimar', in *Die Weimarer Republik* 272–86 (Michael Stürmer, ed., 3d. ed., Frankfurt a.M., 1993)

Schumpeter, Joseph A., *History of Economic Analysis* (New York, 1954)

—— *Capitalism, Socialism and Democracy* (New York, 1970; orig. pub., 1942)

Schwabe, Klause, ed., *Die Anfänge des Schuman-Plans: 1950/51* (Baden-Baden, 1988)

Schwartz, Ivo, 'Antitrust Legislation and Policy in Germany—A Comparative Study', 105 *U. Penn. L. Rev.* 617–90 (1957)

Schwarze, Jürgen, *Europäisches Verwaltungsrecht* (Baden-Baden, 1988)

—— *European Administrative Law* (London, 1992)

Scrapanti, Ernesto & Stefano Zamagni, *An Outline of the History of Economic Thought* (Oxford, 1993)

Seidel, Bruno, 'Zeitgeist und Wirtschaftsgesinnung im Deutschland der Jahrhundertwende', 83 *Schmollers Jahrbuch* 131–52 (1963)

Selinsky, Veronique, *L'Entente Prohibée* (Paris, 1979)

Servan-Schreiber, Jean-Jacques, *Le Defi Américain* (Paris, 1967)

Shackle, G. L. S., *The Years of High Theory: Invention and Tradition in Economic Thought, 1926–1939* (Cambridge, 1967)

Shapiro, Martin, 'The European Court of Justice', in *Europolitics: Institutions and*

Policymaking in the 'New' European Community 123–57 (Alberta Sbragia, ed., Washington, D.C., 1992)

Sharpe, Thomas, 'The Commission's Proposals on Crisis Cartels', 17 *Comm. Mkt. L. Rev.* 75–84 (1980)

Sheahan, John, *Promotion and Control of Industry In Postwar France* (Cambridge, 1963)

Sheehan, James J., *The Career of Lujo Brentano: A Study of Liberalism and Social Reform in Imperial Germany* (Chicago, 1966)

—— *German Liberalism in the Ninteenth Century* (Chicago, 1978)

—— *German History 1770–1866* (Oxford, 1989)

Siragusa, Mario & Giuseppe Scasselati-Sforzolini, 'Italian and EC Competition Law: A New Relationship—Reciprocal Exclusivity and Common Principles', 29 *Comm. Mkt. L. Rev.* 93–131 (1992)

Slynn, Gordon, 'E.E.C. Competition Law From the Perspective of the Court of Justice', in 1984 *Fordham Corp. L. Inst.* 383–408 (New York, 1985)

Small, Albion W., *The Cameralists: The Pioneers of German Social Polity* (Chicago, 1909)

Smith, Adam, *An Inquiry into the Nature and causes of the Wealth of Nations* (R. H. Campbell & A. S. Skinner, eds., Glasgow, 1976; orig. pub., 1776)

Snyder, Francis, *New Directions in European Community Law* (London, 1990)

Sölter, Arno, 'Wider die nationale Fusionskontrolle', in *Fusionskontrolle* 45–86 (Peter Raisch et al eds., Stuttgart, 1970)

Sombart, Werner, *Die Ordnung des Wirtschaftslebens* (2d. ed., Berlin, 1927)

—— *Der Moderne Kapitalismus*, esp. Vol. III: *Das Wirtschaftsleben im Zeitalter des Hochkapitalismus* (Munich, 1927)

—— *Rationalisierung in der Wirtschaft* (Düsseldorf, 1927)

Sonnemann, Rolf & Rudolf Sauerzapf, 'Monopole und Staat in Deutschland 1917–33', in *Monopole und Staat in Deutschland 1917–1945* (Karl Dreschler et al eds., Berlin, 1966)

Sontheimer, Kurt, *Die Adenauer-Ära* (Munich, 1991)

Spaak, Fernand & Jean N. Jaeger, 'The Rules of Competition within the European Common Market,' 26 *L. and Contemp. Prob.* 485–507 (1962)

Spree, Reinhard, *Wachstumstrends und Konjunkturzyklen in der deutschen Wirtschaft von 1820 bis 1913* (Göttingen, 1978)

Stackelberg, Heinrich (von), *Marktform und Gleichgewicht* (Vienna, 1934)

Stegmann, Dirk, *Die Erben Bismarcks: Parteien und Verbände in der Spätphase des wilhelminischen Deutschlands* (Cologne, 1970)

Stein, Eric, 'Lawyers, Judges and the Making of a Transnational Constitution', 75 *Am. J. Int'l L.* 1–27 (1981)

Stein, Eric & Thomas Nicholson, *American Enterprise in Europe: A Legal Profile* (2 vols., Ann Arbor, 1960)

Steinbach, Emil, *Der Staat und die modernen Privatmonopole* (Vienna, 1903)

Steindl, Harald, 'Die Einführung der Gewerbefreiheit', in 3/III *Handbuch der Quellen und Literatur der neueren Europäischen Privatrechtsgeschichte: Das 19. Jahrhundert/ Gesetzgebung zu den privatrechtlichen Sondergebieten* 3527–3633 (Helmut Coing, ed., Munich, 1986)

Steindorff, Ernst, 'Politik des Gesetzes als Auslegungsmassstab im Wirtschaftsrecht', in *Festschrift für Karl Larenz* 217–44 (Gotthard Paulus et al eds., Munich, 1973)

Steindorff, Ernst, 'Zur Entwicklung des europäischen Kartellrechts, Teil I', 137 *Zeitschrift für das gesamte Handelsrecht (ZHR)* 203–36 (1973)

—— 'Europäisches Kartellrecht und Staatenpraxis: Zur Entwicklung des Europäischen Kartellrechts, Teil II', 142 *ZHR* 525–556 (1978)

—— 'Europäisches Kartellrecht vor staatlichen Gerichten 1971–78: Zur Entwicklung des Europäischen Kartellrechts, Teil III', 146 *ZHR* 140–165 (1982)

Stern, Fritz, *Gold and Iron: Bismarck, Bleichröder and the Building of the German Empire* (New York, 1984)

Stevens, R. B. & B. S. Yamey, *The Restrictive Practices Court: A Study of the Judicial Process and Economic Policy* (London, 1965)

Stocking, George & Myron Watkins, *Cartels in Action* (New York, 1947)

Stolleis, Michael & Dieter Simon, eds., *Rechtsgeschichte im Nationalsozialismus: Beiträge zur Geschichte einer Disziplin* (Tübingen, 1989)

Stolleis, Michael, II *Geschichte des öffentlichen Rechts in Deutschland 1800–1914* (Munich, 1992)

Stone, Norman, *Europe Transformed* (Glasgow, 1983)

Stourzh, Gerald & Margarete Grandner, eds., *Historische Wurzeln der Sozialpartnerschaft* (Vienna, 1986)

Strauch, Dieter, 'Unternehmensrecht im 19. Jahrhundert', in *Vom Gewerbe zum Unternehmen: Studien zum Recht der gewerblichen Wirtschaft im 18. und 19. Jahrhundert* 208–49 (Karl Otto Scherner & Dietmar Willoweit, eds., Darmstadt, 1982)

Strauss, Walter, 'Gewerbefreiheit und Vertragsfreiheit: Eine Rechtsgeschichtliche Erinnerung', in *Wirtschaftsordnung und Staatsverfassung (Festschrift für Franz Böhm zum 80. Geburtstag)* 603–14 (Heinz Sauermann & Ernst-Joachim Mestmäcker, eds., Tübingen, 1975)

Streit, Manfred E., 'Economic Order, Private Law and Public Policy: The Freiburg School of Law and Economics', 148 *J. of Institutional and Theoretical Econ.* 675–704 (1992)

Stürmer, Michael, ed., *Die Weimarer Republik* (3d. ed., Frankfurt a.M., 1993)

Stürmer, Michael, 'Koalitionen und Oppositionen: Bedingungen parlamentarischer Instabilität', in *Die Weimarer Republik* 237–53 (Michael Stürmer, ed., 3d. ed., Frankfurt a.M., 1993)

Stützel, W. et al eds., *Standard Texts on the Social Market Economy* (Stuttgart, 1982)

Sutherland, A., *The Monopolies Commission in Action* (Cambridge, 1969)

Sutherland, Paul, 'EEC Competition Policy', 54 *Antitrust L.J.* 667–73 (1985)

Temple Lang, John, 'Monopolization and the Definition of "Abuse" of a Dominant Position under Article 86 EEC Treaty', 16 *Comm. Mkt. L. Rev.* 345–64 (1979)

—— 'Community Antitrust Law—Compliance and Enforcement', 18 *Comm. Mkt. L. Rev.* 335–62 (1981)

Thorelli, Hans B., 'Antitrust in Europe: National Policies after 1945', 29 *U. of Chicago L. Rev.* 222–36 (1959)

Thornton, A. P., *Doctrines of Imperialism* (New York, 1965)

Thränhardt, Dietrich, *Geschichte der Bundesrepublik Deutschland 1949–1990* (Frankfurt a.M., 1996)

Thurow, Lester C., *Head to Head. The Coming Economic Battle between Japan, Europe, and America* (New York, 1992)

Tondre, Jacques Michel, 'Les clivages apparus lors du référendum de Maastricht rythment toujours la vie politique francaise', *Agence France Presse*, Sept. 17, 1993 (available in LEXIS, Presse Library, AFP File)

Tönnies, Ferdinand, *Gemeinschaft und Gesellschaft* (Leipzig, 1887)

Torre, Richard J., 'Italian Antitrust Law', *Am. J. Comp. L.* 489–503 (1965)

Trebilcock, Clive, *The Industrialization of the Continental Powers 1780–1914* (London, 1981)

Tribe, Keith, *Strategies of Economic Order: German Economic Discourse—1750–1950* (Cambridge, 1995)

Tschierschky, Siegfried, *Das Problem der staatlichen Kartellaufsicht* (Mannheim, 1923)

—— *Wirtschaftsverfassung* (Breslau, 1924)

—— 'Der 35. Deutsche Juristentag zur Kartellfrage', 26 *Kartell- Rundschau* 487–504 (1928)

—— 'Die Aufsicht über Trusts und Kartelle in Norwegen', 31 *Kartell- Rundschau* 163–70 (1933)

Turner, Henry Ashby, Jr., *Stresemann and the Politics of the Weimar Republic* (Princeton, 1963)

—— *German Big Business and the Rise of Hitler* (New York, 1985)

Tyllack, Olaf, *Wettbewerb und Behinderung* (Munich, 1984)

Ullrich, Hans, 'Harmonisation within the European Union', 17 *Eur. Comp. L. Rev.* 178– 84 (1996)

Ulmer, Peter, *Schranken zulässigen Wettbewerbs marktbeherrschender Unternehmen* (Baden-Baden, 1977)

—— 'Kartellrechtswidrige Konkurrentenbehinderung durch Leistungsfremdes Verhalten marktbeherrschender Unternehmen', in *Recht und Wirtschaft Heute: Festschrift für Max Kummer* 565–96 (Bern, 1980)

Uth, Dr, 'Die jüngste Kartelldebatte im Reichstag', 6 *Kartell-Rundschau* 250–4 (1908)

van Damme, J. A., ed., *Regulating the Behaviour of Monopolies and Dominant Undertakings in Community Law* (Bruges, 1977)

van Gerven, Walter, 'Twelve Years EEC Competition Law (1962–1973) Revisited', 11 *Comm. Mkt. L. Rev.* 38–61 (1974)

van Miert, Karel, 'Die Wettbewerbspolitik der neuen Kommission', 1995 *Wirtschaft und Wettbewerb* 553–60 (1995)

Varnberg, Viktor, '"Ordnungstheorie" as Constitutional Economics—the German Conception of a "Social Market Economy"', 39 *ORDO* 17–31 (1988)

Venturini, V. G., *Monopolies and Restrictive Trade Practices in France* (Leyden, 1971)

Vernon, Raymond, 'The Schuman Plan', 47 *Am. J. Int'l L.* 183–202 (1953)

Vernon, Raymond, ed., *Big Business and the State* (Cambridge, Mass., 1974)

Verstrynge, Jean-Francois, 'Current Antitrust Policy Issues in the EEC: Some Reflections on the Second Generation of Competition Policy', 1984 *Fordham Corp L. Inst.* 673–98 (Barry Hawk, ed., New York, 1985)

Vogel, Barbara, *Allgemeine Gewerbefreiheit, Die Reformpolitik des Preussischen Staatskanzlers Hardenburg 1810–1820* (Göttingen, 1983)

Vogel, Louis, *Droit de la Concurrence et Concentration Économique: Etude Comparative* (Paris, 1988)

von der Groeben, Hans, *Aufbaujahre der Europaischen Gemeinschaft* (Baden-Baden, 1982) von der Groeben, Hans, 'Der gemeinsame Markt als Kern und Motor der Europäischen Gemeinschaft', in *Europa Ringt um seine Wirtschaftsverfassung (Festschrift für Karl-Heinz Narjes)* (Ernst-Joachim Mestmäcker, ed., Bonn, 1984)

von der Groeben, Hans & Hans von Boeckh, *Kommentar zum EWG-Vertrag* (2 vols., Baden-Baden, 1958)

Vondung, Klaus, *Das wilhelminische Bildungsbürgertum: Zur Sozialgeschichte seiner Ideen* (Göttingen, 1976)

—— 'Zur Lage der Gebildeten in der wilhelminischen Zeit', in Vondung, Klaus, *Das wilhelminische Bildungsbürgertum: Zur Sozialgeschichte seiner Ideen* 20–33 (Göttingen, 1976)

Vopelius, Marie-Elisabeth, *Die altliberalen Ökonomen und die Reformzeit* (Stuttgart, 1968)

Wachtman, Andrew, 'The European Community Commission de Havilland Decision: Potential Problems in Community Merger Control are Realized', 21 *Capital L. Rev.* 685–706 (1992)

Waelbroeck, Michel, 'Competition, Integration and Economic Efficiency in the EEC From the Point of View of the Private Firm', 82 *Mich. L. R.* 1439–46 (1984)

Waentig, Heinrich, 'Welche Massregeln empfehlen sich für die rechtliche Behandlung der Industriekartelle?', I *Verhandlungen des 26. deutschen Juristentages* 63 (Berlin, 1902)

Wagner, Adolph, *Grundlegung der Politischen Ökonomie* (3d. ed., Leipzig, 1892)

Wallace, Helen, et al eds., *Policy-Making in the European Community* (2d. ed., Chichester, 1983)

Wallace, William, *The Dynamics of European Integration* (London, 1990)

Waller, Spencer Weber, 'Understanding and Appreciating EC Competition Law', 61 *Antitrust L. J.* 55–77 (1992)

Wallich, Henry C., *Mainsprings of the German Revival* (New Haven, 1955)

Walter Eucken Institut, ed., *Ordnung und Freiheit* (Freiburg i.B., 1992)

Wandel, Eckhard, *Hans Schäffer: Steuermann in wirtschaftlichen und politischen Krisen* (Stuttgart, 1974)

Wandruszka, A. & P. Urbanitsch, eds., *Die Habsburgermonarchie 1848–1918, Vol.2: Verwaltung und Rechtswesen* (Vienna, 1975)

Watrin, Christian, ed., *Kölner Volkswirte und soziale Wissenschaftler* (Cologne, 1988)

Watrin, Christian, 'Alfred Müller-Armack: 1901–1978', in *Kölner Volkswirte und soziale Wissenschaftler* 39–68 (Christian Watrin, ed., Cologne, 1988)

Watson, Alan, *The Making of the Civil Law* (Cambridge, Mass., 1981)

Weber, Eugen, *The Hollow Years: France in the 1930s* (New York, 1996)

Weber, Klaus, 'Geschichte und Aufbau des Bundeskartellamtes', in *Zehn Jahre Bundeskartellamt* 263–70 (Cologne, 1968)

Weber, W., ed., I *Österreichs Wirtschaftsstruktur: Gestern, Heute, Morgen* (Berlin, 1961)

Wehler, Hans-Ulrich, *Bismarck und der Imperialismus* (Cologne, 1969)

—— 'Sozialdarwinismus im expandierenden Industriestaat', in *Deutschland in der Weltpolitik des 19. und 20. Jahrhunderts* 133–42 (Imanuel Geiss & Bernd Jürgen Wendt, eds., Düsseldorf, 1973)

—— 'Der Aufstieg des Organisierten Kapitalismus und Interventionsstaates in Deutschland', in *Organisierter Kapitalismus*, 36–57 (Heinrich A. Winkler, ed., Göttingen, 1974)

Weidenholzer, Joseph, *Der Sorgende Staat* (Vienna, 1985)

Weiler, Joseph H. H., 'The Transformation of Europe', 100 *Yale L.J.* 2403–83 (1991)

—— *Europe after Maastricht—Do the New Clothes Have an Emperor?* (Harvard Jean Monnet Working Paper 12/95, Cambridge, Mass., 1995)

Weippert, Georg, 'Die wirtschaftstheoretische und wirtschaftspolitische Bedeutung der Kartelldebatte auf der Tagung des Vereins für Socialpolitik im Jahre 1905', 11 *Jahrbuch für Sozialwissenschaft* 125–83 (1960)

Wenzel, Rolf, *Adenauer und die Gestaltung der Wirtschafts- und Sozialordnung im Nachkriegsdeutschland* (Flensburg, 1983)

Wesseling, Rein, 'The Commission Notices on Decentralisation of E.C. Antitrust Law: In for a Penny, Not for a Pound', 18 *Eur. Comp. L. Rev.* 94–97 (1997)

Westerlind, Per, 'Tio Års Praxis i Marknadsdomstolen—Erfarenheter och Värderingar', *Svensk Jurist Tidning* 401–23 (1981)

Whish, Richard & Brenda Sufrin, *Competition Law* (3d. ed., London, 1993)

Wieacker, Franz, *Privatrechtsgeschichte der Neuzeit* (2d. ed., Göttingen, 1967)

—— *Industriegesellschaft und Privatrechtsordnung* (Frankfurt a.M., 1974)

Wilberforce, Lord, et al., *The Law of Restrictive Trade Practices and Monopolies* (2d. ed., London, 1966)

Wilcox, Claire, *A Charter for World Trade* (New York, 1949)

Wild, Gisela et al eds., *Festschrift für Alfred-Carl Gaedertz* (Munich, 1992)

Willgerodt, Hans & Alan T. Peacock, *Germany's Social Market Economy: Origins and Evolution* (New York, 1989)

Winckler, Antoine, 'Conseil de la concurrence et concurrence des autorités', 52 *Le Débat* 76–86 (1988)

Winkel, Harald, *Die Deutsche Nationalökonomie im 19. Jahrhundert* (Darmstadt, 1977)

—— 'Der Umschwung der wirtschaftswissenschaftlichen Auffassungen um die Mitte des 19. Jahrhunderts', in IV *Wissenschaft und Kodifikation des Privatrechts im 19. Jahrhundert* 3–18 (Helmut Coing & Walter Wilhelm, eds., Frankfurt a.M., 1979)

Winkler, Heinrich A., ed., *Organisierter Kapitalismus* (Göttingen, 1974)

Wittelshöfer, Otto, 'Der österreichische Kartellgesetzentwurf', 13 *Archiv für Soziale Gesetzgebung und Statistik* 122–154 (1899)

Wolf, Erik, *Grosse Rechtsdenker der deutschen Geistesgeschichte* (4th ed., Tübingen, 1963)

Wolfers, Arnold, *Das Kartellproblem im Lichte der deutschen Kartell-Literatur* (Munich, 1931)

Woll, Artur, 'Freiheit durch Ordnung: Die gesellschaftspolitische Leitidee im Denken von Walter Eucken und Friedrich A. von Hayek', 40 *ORDO* 87–97 (1989)

Wright, Gordon, *France in Modern Times* (5th ed., New York, 1995)

Zehn Jahre Bundeskartellamt (Cologne, 1968)

Zimmerman, Reinhard, *The Law of Obligations: Roman Foundations of the Civil Law Tradition* (Capetown, 1990)

Zinsmeister, Ute, 'Die Anwendung der Artikel 85 und 86 EG-Vertrag durch die nationalen Behörden', 1997 *Wirtschaft und Wettbewerb* 5–14 (1997)

Zuleeg, Manfred, 'Die Wirtschaftsverfassung der Europäischen Gemeinschaften', in

Wirtschaftspolitische und Gesellschaftspolitische Ordnungsprobleme der Europäis-chen Gemeinschaft 73–100 (Schriftenreihe des Arbeitskreises Europäische Integration e.V., Würzburg, 1978)

Zunkel, Friedrich, *Industrie und Staatssozialismus: Der Kampf um die Wirtschafts-ordnung 1914–18* (Düsseldorf, 1974)

Index

SA

343.
407
21
GER

Printed in the United Kingdom
by Lightning Source UK Ltd.
104195UKS00001B/31